C# 6.0 Cookbook

Jay Hilyard & Stephen Teilhet

Beijing · Boston · Farnham · Sebastopol · Tokyo

C# 6.0 Cookbook

by Jay Hilyard and Stephen Teilhet

Copyright © 2015 Jay Hilyard, Stephen Teilhet. All rights reserved.

Printed in the United States of America.

Published by O'Reilly Media, Inc., 1005 Gravenstein Highway North, Sebastopol, CA 95472.

O'Reilly books may be purchased for educational, business, or sales promotional use. Online editions are also available for most titles (*http://safaribooksonline.com*). For more information, contact our corporate/institutional sales department: 800-998-9938 or *corporate@oreilly.com*.

Editor: Brian MacDonald
Production Editor: Nicholas Adams
Copyeditor: Rachel Monaghan
Proofreader: Kim Cofer

Indexer: Judith McConville
Interior Designer: David Futato
Cover Designer: Ellie Volckhausen
Illustrator: Rebecca Demarest

January 2004:   First Edition
January 2006:   Second Edition
December 2007:   Third Edition
October 2015:   Fourth Edition

Revision History for the Fourth Edition
2015-09-28:   First Release

See *http://oreilly.com/catalog/errata.csp?isbn=9781491921463* for release details.

978-1-4919-2146-3

[LSI]

To Seth, Tom, Katie, and Jenna.
Thank you for your friendship.
Our lives are richer, happier, and more filled with laughter
for having you in them.
—Jay Hilyard

To my dear friend, pastor, and teacher, Damon Thomas.
You and your family have been such a blessing to ours.
—Stephen Teilhet

Table of Contents

Preface

C# is a language targeted at developers for the Microsoft .NET platform. Microsoft portrays C# as a modern and innovative language for .NET development and continues to deliver on that in C# 6.0 with features that help support dynamic programming, parallel programming, and writing less code. C# still allows for both declarative and functional styles of programming, and still includes great object-oriented features as well. In short, C# allows you to use the style of programming that fits your particular problem.

We started writing this book together based on programming problems we ran into when we were first learning C#, and we have continued to expand it based on new challenges and capabilities in the language. In this edition, we have reworked the approach of many solutions to take advantage of the latest innovations in C# like the new expression-level (nameof, string interpolation, null conditional, index initializers), member declaration (auto-property initializers, getter-only auto-properties, expression-bodied function members), and statement-level (exception filters) features. We have also incorporated new uses of dynamic programming (C# 4.0) and asynchronous programming (C# 5.0) into both existing and new recipes to help you understand how to use these language features.

We hope that these additions will help you get past some of the common (and not-so-common) pitfalls and questions everyone has when learning C# for the first time, exploring a new capacity of the language, or working on the slightly off-the-beaten-path items that come up during a development cycle. There are recipes addressing things we found missing from the .NET Framework Class Library (FCL), even though Microsoft has provided tons of functionality to keep folks from reinventing the wheel. Some of these solutions you might immediately use, and some may never darken your door, but we hope this book helps you get the most out of C# and the .NET Framework.

The book is laid out with respect to the types of problems you will solve as you progress through your life as a C# programmer. These solutions are called *recipes*; each recipe consists of a single problem, its solution, a discussion of the solution and other relevant related information, and finally, a list of resources such as where in the FCL you can find more information about the classes used, other books addressing the topic, related articles, and other recipes. The question/answer format provides complete solutions to problems, making the book easy to read and use. Nearly every recipe contains a complete, documented code sample, showing you how to solve the specific problem, as well as a discussion of how the underlying technology works and a list of alternatives, limitations, and other considerations when appropriate.

Who This Book Is For

You don't have to be an experienced C# or .NET developer to use this book—it is designed for users of all levels. This book provides solutions to problems that developers face every day as well as some that may come along less frequently. The recipes are targeted at the real-world developer who needs to solve problems now, not learn lots of theory first. While reference or tutorial books can teach general concepts, they do not generally provide the help you need in solving real-world problems. We choose to teach by example, the natural way for most people to learn.

The majority of the problems addressed in this book are frequently faced by C# developers, but some of the more advanced problems call for more intricate solutions that combine many techniques. Each recipe is designed to help you quickly understand the problem, learn how to solve it, and find out any potential trade-offs or ramifications to help you solve your problems quickly, efficiently, and with minimal effort.

To save you even the effort of typing in the solution, we provide the sample code for the book on the O'Reilly website to facilitate the "editor inheritance" mode of development (copy and paste) as well as to help less experienced developers see good programming practice in action. The sample code provides a running test harness that exercises each of the solutions, but the book includes enough of the code in each solution to allow you to implement the solution without the sample code. The sample code is available from the book's product page (*https://github.com/oreillymedia/ c_sharp_6_cookbook*).

What You Need to Use This Book

To run the samples in this book, you need a computer running Windows 7 or later. A few of the networking and XML solutions require Microsoft Internet Information Server (IIS) version 7.5 or later, and the FTP recipes in Chapter 9 require a locally configured FTP server.

To open and compile the samples in this book, you need Visual Studio 2015. If you are proficient with the downloadable Framework SDK and its command-line compilers, you should not have any trouble following the text of this book and the code samples.

Platform Notes

The solutions in this book were developed using Visual Studio 2015. The differences between C# 6.0 and C# 3.0 are significant, and the sample code has changed from the third edition to reflect that.

It is worth mentioning that although C# is now at version 6.0, the .NET Framework is represented as version 4.6. C# has continued to innovate with each release of the .NET Framework, and now in C# 6.0 there are many capacities in the language to allow you to program in whatever style is best suited to the task at hand.

How This Book Is Organized

This book is organized into 13 chapters, each of which focuses on a particular topic in creating C# solutions. The following paragraphs summarize each chapter to give you an overview of this book's contents:

Chapter 1, Classes and Generics
> This large chapter contains recipes dealing with classes and structure data types as well as the use of generics, which allows you to have code operate uniformly on values of different types. This chapter covers a wide range of recipes, from closures to converting a class to a full-blown command-line argument-processing system to class design topics. There are recipes to enhance your general understanding of generics as well as recipes covering when they are appropriate to use, what support is provided in the Framework for them, and how to create custom implementations of collections.

Chapter 2, Collections, Enumerators, and Iterators
> This chapter examines recipes that make use of collections, enumerators, and iterators. The collection recipes make use of—as well as extend the functionality of—the array (single, multi, and jagged), the List<T>, and many other collection classes. The generic-based collections, and the various ways to create your own strongly typed collections, are also discussed. We explore creating custom enumerators, show how you can implement iterators for generic and nongeneric types and use iterators to implement foreach functionality, and cover custom iterator implementations.

Chapter 3, Data Types
> This chapter covers strings, numbers, and enumerations. These recipes show how to accomplish things like encode/decode strings, perform numeric conversions, and test strings to determine whether they contain a numeric value. We also cover how to display, convert, and test enumeration types and how to use enumerations that consist of bit flags.

Chapter 4, Language Integrated Query (LINQ) and Lambda Expressions

This chapter covers Language Integrated Query (LINQ) and its usage, including an example of parallel LINQ (PLINQ). There are recipes using many of the standard query operators and showing how to use some of the query operators that are not keywords in the language, but are still quite powerful. Lambda expressions are explored, and recipes show their usage in place of old-style delegates.

Chapter 5, Debugging and Exception Handling

This chapter addresses debugging and exception handling. We present recipes that use data types that fall under the System.Diagnostics namespace, like event logs, processes, performance counters, and custom debugger displays for your types. We also focus on the best ways to implement exception handling in your application. Recipes on preventing unhandled exceptions, reading and displaying stack traces, and throwing/rethrowing exceptions are also included. Finally, we provide recipes showing how to overcome some tricky situations, such as exceptions from late-bound called methods and asynchronous exception handling.

Chapter 6, Reflection and Dynamic Programming

This chapter shows ways to use the built-in assembly inspection system provided by the .NET Framework to determine what types, interfaces, and methods are implemented within an assembly and how to access them in a late-bound fashion. It also shows you how to use dynamic, ExpandoObject, and DynamicObject to accomplish dynamic programming in your applications.

Chapter 7, Regular Expressions

This chapter covers a useful set of classes that are employed to run regular expressions against strings. Recipes enumerate regular expression matches, break up strings into tokens, find/replace characters, and verify the syntax of a regular expression. We also include a recipe that contains many common regular expression patterns.

Chapter 8, Filesystem I/O

This chapter deals with filesystem interactions in three distinct ways: first, it looks at typical file interactions; second, it looks at directory- or folder-based interactions; and third, it deals with advanced filesystem I/O topics.

Chapter 9, Networking and Web

This chapter explores the connectivity options provided by the .NET Framework and how to programmatically access network resources and content on the Web. We include recipes for using TCP/IP directly, using named pipes for communication, building your own port scanner, programmatically determining website configuration, and more.

Chapter 10, XML

If you use .NET, it is likely that you will be dealing with XML to one degree or another. In this chapter, we explore some of the uses for XML and how to program against it using LINQ to XML, the XmlReader/XmlWriter, and XmlDocument. We cover examples using both XPath and XSLT, and topics such as validating XML and transforming XML to HTML.

Chapter 11, Security
There are many ways to write insecure code and only a few ways to write secure code. In this chapter, we explore areas such as controlling access to types, encrypting and decrypting, securely storing data, and using programmatic and declarative security.

Chapter 12, Threading, Synchronization, and Concurrency
This chapter addresses the subject of using multiple threads of execution in a .NET program and issues such as implementing threading in your application, protecting resources from and allowing safe concurrent access, storing per-thread data, running tasks in order, and using the synchronization primitives in .NET to write thread-safe code.

Chapter 13, Toolbox
This chapter has recipes for those random sorts of operations that developers run into over and over again, such as determining locations of system resources, sending email, and working with services. It also covers some less frequently accessed but helpful application pieces, such as queuing messages, running code in a separate AppDomain, and finding the versions of assemblies in the Global Assembly Cache (GAC).

Certain recipes are related; in these cases, the See Also section of the recipe as well as some text in the Discussion will note the relationships.

What Was Left Out

This book is not a reference or a primer about C#. Some good primers and reference books, all from O'Reilly, are *C# 6.0 in a Nutshell* by Joseph Albahari and Ben Albahari; *C# 6.0 Pocket Reference*, also by Joseph Albahari and Ben Albahari; and *Concurrency in C# Cookbook* by Stephen Cleary. The MSDN Library is also invaluable. It is included with Visual Studio 2015 and available online at *http://msdn.microsoft.com*.

Conventions Used in This Book

This book uses the following typographic conventions:

Italic
Used for URLs, names of directories and files, options, and occasionally for emphasis.

`Constant width`
Used for program listings and for code items such as commands, options, switches, variables, attributes, keys, functions, types, classes, namespaces, methods, modules,

properties, parameters, values, objects, events, event handlers, XML tags, HTML tags, macros, the contents of files, and the output from commands.

Constant width bold
Used in program listings to highlight an important part of the code.

Constant width italic
Used to indicate replaceable parts of code.

`//...`
Ellipses in C# code indicate text that has been omitted for clarity.

`<!--...-->`
Ellipses in XML schemas and documents' code indicate text that has been omitted for clarity.

This icon indicates a tip, suggestion, or general note.

This icon indicates a warning or caution.

About the Code

Nearly every recipe in this book contains one or more code samples. These samples are included in a single solution and are pieces of code and whole projects that are immediately usable in your application. Most of the code samples are written within a class or structure, making it easier to use within your applications. In addition to this, any `using` directives are included for each recipe so that you will not have to search for which ones to include in your code.

Complete error handling is included only in critical areas, such as input parameters. This allows you to easily see what is correct input and what is not. Many recipes omit error handling. This makes the solution easier to understand by focusing on the key concepts.

Using Code Examples

The sample code for this book can be found at *https://github.com/oreillymedia/ c_sharp_6_cookbook*.

This book is here to help you get your job done. In general, you may use the code in this book in your programs and documentation. You do not need to contact us for permission unless you're reproducing a significant portion of the code. For example, writing a program that uses several chunks of code from this book does not require permission. Selling or distributing a CD-ROM of examples from O'Reilly books does require permission. Answering a question by citing this book and quoting example code does not require permission. Incorporating a significant amount of example code from this book into your product's documentation does require permission.

We appreciate, but do not require, attribution. An attribution usually includes the title, author, publisher, and ISBN. For example: "*C# 6.0 Cookbook*, Fourth Edition, by Jay Hilyard and Stephen Teilhet. Copyright 2015 Jay Hilyard and Stephen Teilhet, 978-1-4919-2146-3."

If you feel your use of code examples falls outside fair use or the preceding permission, feel free to contact us at *permissions@oreilly.com*.

Safari® Books Online

 *Safari Books Online* is an on-demand digital library that delivers expert content in both book and video form from the world's leading authors in technology and business.

Technology professionals, software developers, web designers, and business and creative professionals use Safari Books Online as their primary resource for research, problem solving, learning, and certification training.

Safari Books Online offers a range of plans and pricing for enterprise, government, education, and individuals.

Members have access to thousands of books, training videos, and prepublication manuscripts in one fully searchable database from publishers like O'Reilly Media, Prentice Hall Professional, Addison-Wesley Professional, Microsoft Press, Sams, Que, Peachpit Press, Focal Press, Cisco Press, John Wiley & Sons, Syngress, Morgan Kaufmann, IBM Redbooks, Packt, Adobe Press, FT Press, Apress, Manning, New Riders, McGraw-Hill, Jones & Bartlett, Course Technology, and hundreds more. For more information about Safari Books Online, please visit us online.

How to Contact Us

Please address comments and questions concerning this book to the publisher:

O'Reilly Media, Inc.
1005 Gravenstein Highway North
Sebastopol, CA 95472

800-998-9938 (in the United States or Canada)
707-829-0515 (international or local)
707-829-0104 (fax)

We have a web page for this book, where we list errata, examples, and any additional information. You can access this page at *http://bit.ly/csharp6_cookbook*.

To comment or ask technical questions about this book, send email to *bookquestions@oreilly.com*.

For more information about our books, courses, conferences, and news, see our website at *http://www.oreilly.com*.

Find us on Facebook: *http://facebook.com/oreilly*

Follow us on Twitter: *http://twitter.com/oreillymedia*

Watch us on YouTube: *http://www.youtube.com/oreillymedia*

Acknowledgments

This book began for us as we started exploring C# and has continued to evolve over the years as we have used the language in many new and exciting ways. With the introduction of C# 6.0 as well as all of the new features in C# 4.0 and C# 5.0 since the book's previous edition, we decided it was time to reexamine the first three editions to see how we could improve the existing recipes and learn better ways of accomplishing programming tasks with C#. While we continue to learn an incredible amount about C# and the Framework in general, we've worked hard in this edition to bring you a better understanding of how C# has evolved and how it can help you do your job better.

This book would have been impossible without the following people, and we'd like to acknowledge all of their efforts.

Our appreciation goes out to Brian MacDonald (our editor), Heather Scherer, Rachel Monaghan, Nick Adams, and Sara Peyton, who kept us on schedule and did a great job in getting this book finished and on the shelves. Thank you for all of your efforts.

We extend our gratitude and thanks to our technical review team of Steve Munyan, Lee Coward, and Nick Pinkham. We appreciate all the time you all put into helping us make the book better and your insightful commentary. This book would have been impossible to do without your valuable feedback, and we both thank you for it.

From Jay Hilyard

Thanks to Steve Teilhet for his ideas, sense of humor, and willingness to join me yet again on this journey. I always enjoy working with you, even though most of it was on nights and weekends and mostly virtual.

Thanks to my wife, Brooke. Even knowing full well that it would mean time away from our family, you were still supportive, encouraging, and helpful. As always, this was only possible with your help. Thank you, and I love you!

Thanks to my sons, Owen and Drew, who constantly amaze me with your ability to make me look at things from a different angle and who make me proud with all you have accomplished. To have both of you interested in the field I have spent a lifetime in is gratifying, and I couldn't ask for better sons.

Thanks to Phil and Gail for their support and understanding when I had to work on vacations and for being there to help in ways that only grandparents can, and thanks to my Mom for our monthly dose of sanity.

Thanks to my "flock" of good friends: Seth and Katie Fiermonti, Tom Bebbington, and Jenna Roberts. Friends make everything better, especially when accompanied by good beer. ☺

Thanks to Scott Cronshaw, Bill Bolevic, Melissa Jurkoic, Mike Kennie, Alex Shore, Dave Flanders, Aaron Reddish, Rakshit Jain, Jason Phelps, Josh Clairmont, Bob Blais, Kim Serpa, Stu Savage, Gaurang Patel, Jesse Peters, Ken Jones, Mahesh Unnikrishnan, T Antonio, Mary Ellen Sawyer, Jon Godbout, Atul Kaul, Mark Miller, Rich Labenski, Lance Simpson, Tim Beaulieu, and Lee Horgan for being an awesome team of people to work with. You all work incredibly hard and I appreciate everything you do.

Finally, thanks again to my family and friends for asking about a book they don't understand and for being excited for me.

From Steve Teilhet

I'm proud to count Jay Hilyard as a good friend, excellent coworker, and hardworking coauthor. It's not every day that you find a person who is not only a trusted friend, but whom you also work so well with. Thank you for yet another successful book.

Kandis Teilhet, my wife, was there every step of the way to give me the strength to persevere and finish this work. Words cannot express my love for you.

Patrick and Nicholas Teilhet, my two sons, made the rough patches smooth. I couldn't wish for two better sons. Now that you're entering your next phase of life, I'm excited to see what both of you will accomplish; perhaps you will write a book as well.

Thanks to my mom, dad, and brother, who are always there to listen and support me.

And last but certainly not least, thanks to the IBM team, Larry Rose, Babita Sharma, Jessica Berliner, Jeff Turnham, John Peyton, Kris Duer, Robert Stanzel, Shu Wang, Bingzhou Zheng, Dave Steinberg, Dave Stewart, Jason Todd, Alexei Pivkine, Joshua Clark, William Frontiero, Matthew Murphy, Omer Trip, Marco Pistoia, Enrique Varillas, Guillermo Hurtado, Bao Lu, Mary Santo, Diane Redfearn, Urmi Chatterjee, Joshua Ho, Kenneth Cheung, Andrew Mak, Daniel Nguyen, Jennifer Calder, Tahseen Shabab, Srinivas Sripada, David Marshak, Larry Gerard, Douglas Wilson, Steve Hikida, and so many others. Your hard work and brilliance are inspiring.

CHAPTER 1

Classes and Generics

1.0 Introduction

The recipes in this chapter cover the foundation of the C# language. Topics include classes and structures, how they are used, how they are different, and when you would use one over the other. Building on this, we will construct classes that have inherent functionality such as being sortable, searchable, disposable, and cloneable. In addition, we will dive into topics such as union types, field initialization, lambdas, partial methods, single and multicast delegates, closures, functors, and more. This chapter also contains a recipe on parsing command-line parameters, which is always a favorite.

Before diving into the recipes, let's review some key information about the object-oriented capabilities of classes, structures, and generics. Classes are much more flexible than structures. Like classes, structures can implement interfaces, but unlike classes, they cannot inherit from a class or a structure. This limitation precludes creating structure hierarchies, as you can do with classes. Polymorphism, as implemented through an abstract base class, is also prohibited when you are using a structure, since a structure cannot inherit from another class with the exception of boxing to `Object`, `ValueType`, or `Enum`.

Structures, like any other value type, implicitly inherit from `System.ValueType`. At first glance, a structure is similar to a class, but it is actually very different. Knowing when to use a structure over a class will help you tremendously when you're designing an application. Using a structure incorrectly can result in inefficient and hard-to-modify code.

Structures have two performance advantages over reference types. First, if a structure is allocated on the stack (i.e., it is not contained within a reference type), access to the structure and its data is somewhat faster than access to a reference type on the heap.

Reference-type objects must follow their reference onto the heap in order to get at their data. However, this performance advantage pales in comparison to the second performance advantage of structures—namely, that cleaning up the memory allocated to a structure on the stack requires a simple change of the address to which the stack pointer points, which is done at the return of a method call. This call is extremely fast compared to allowing the garbage collector to automatically clean up reference types for you in the managed heap; however, the cost of the garbage collector is deferred so that it's not immediately noticeable.

The performance of structures falls short in comparison to that of classes when they are passed by value to other methods. Because they reside on the stack, a structure and its data have to be copied to a new local variable (the method's parameter that is used to receive the structure) when it is passed by value to a method. This copying takes more time than passing a method a single reference to an object, unless the structure is the same size as or smaller than the machine's pointer size; thus, a structure with a size of 32 bits is just as cheap to pass as a reference (which happens to be the size of a pointer) on a 32-bit machine. Keep this in mind when choosing between a class and a structure. While creating, accessing, and destroying a class's object may take longer, it also might not balance the performance hit when a structure is passed by value a large number of times to one or more methods. Keeping the size of the structure small minimizes the performance hit of passing it around by value.

Use a class if:

- Its identity is important. Structures get copied implicitly when being passed by value into a method.
- It will have a large memory footprint.
- Its fields need initializers.
- You need to inherit from a base class.
- You need polymorphic behavior; that is, you need to implement an abstract base class from which you will create several similar classes that inherit from this abstract base class. (Note that polymorphism can be implemented via interfaces as well, but it is usually not a good idea to place an interface on a value type, since, if the structure is converted to the interface type, you will incur a performance penalty from the boxing operation.)

Use a structure if:

- It will act like a primitive type (`int`, `long`, `byte`, etc.).
- It must have a small memory footprint.
- You are calling a `P/Invoke` method that requires a structure to be passed in by value. *Platform Invoke*, or P/Invoke for short, allows managed code to call out to

an unmanaged method exposed from within a DLL. Many times, an unmanaged DLL method requires a structure to be passed in to it; using a structure is an efficient method of doing this and is the only way if the structure is being passed by value.

- You need to reduce the impact of garbage collection on application performance.

- Its fields need to be initialized only to their default values. This value would be zero for numeric types, false for Boolean types, and null for reference types. Note that in C# 6.0 structs can have a default constructor that can be used to initialize the struct's fields to nondefault values.

- You do not need to inherit from a base class (other than ValueType, from which all structs inherit).

- You do not need polymorphic behavior.

Structures can also cause degradation in performance when they are passed to methods that require an object, such as any of the nongeneric collection types in the Framework Class Library (FCL). Passing a structure (or any simple type, for that matter) into a method requiring an object causes the structure to be boxed. *Boxing* is wrapping a value type in an object. This operation is time-consuming and may degrade performance.

Finally, adding generics to this mix allows you to write type-safe and efficient collection- and pattern-based code. Generics add quite a bit of programming power, but with that power comes the responsibility to use it correctly. If you are considering converting your ArrayList, Queue, Stack, and Hashtable objects to use their generic counterparts, consider reading Recipes 1.9 and 1.10. As you will read, the conversion is not always simple and easy, and there are reasons why you might not want to do this conversion at all.

1.1 Creating Union-Type Structures

Problem

You need to create a data type that behaves like a union type in C++. A union type is useful mainly in interop scenarios in which the unmanaged code accepts and/or returns a union type; we suggest that you do not use it in other situations.

Solution

Use a structure and mark it with the StructLayout attribute (specifying the LayoutKind.Explicit layout kind in the constructor). In addition, mark each field in the structure with the FieldOffset attribute. The following structure defines a union in which a single signed numeric value can be stored:

```
using System.Runtime.InteropServices;
[StructLayoutAttribute(LayoutKind.Explicit)]
struct SignedNumber
{
    [FieldOffsetAttribute(0)]
    public sbyte Num1;
    [FieldOffsetAttribute(0)]
    public short Num2;
    [FieldOffsetAttribute(0)]
    public int Num3;
    [FieldOffsetAttribute(0)]
    public long Num4;
    [FieldOffsetAttribute(0)]
    public float Num5;
    [FieldOffsetAttribute(0)]
    public double Num6;
}
```

The next structure is similar to the `SignedNumber` structure, except that it can contain a `String` type in addition to the signed numeric value:

```
[StructLayoutAttribute(LayoutKind.Explicit)]
struct SignedNumberWithText
{
    [FieldOffsetAttribute(0)]
    public sbyte Num1;
    [FieldOffsetAttribute(0)]
    public short Num2;
    [FieldOffsetAttribute(0)]
    public int Num3;
    [FieldOffsetAttribute(0)]
    public long Num4;
    [FieldOffsetAttribute(0)]
    public float Num5;
    [FieldOffsetAttribute(0)]
    public double Num6;
    [FieldOffsetAttribute(16)]
    public string Text1;
}
```

Discussion

Unions are structures usually found in C++ code; however, there is a way to duplicate that type of structure using a C# structure data type. A *union* is a structure that accepts more than one type at a specific location in memory for that structure. For example, the `SignedNumber` structure is a union-type structure built using a C# structure. This structure accepts any type of signed numeric type (`sbyte`, `int`, `long`, etc.), but it accepts this numeric type at only one location, or offset, within the structure.

Since `StructLayoutAttribute` can be applied to both structures and classes, you can also use a class when creating a union data type.

Notice the `FieldOffsetAttribute` has the value `0` passed to its constructor. This denotes that this field will be offset by zero bytes from the beginning of the structure. This attribute is used in tandem with the `StructLayoutAttribute` to manually enforce where the fields in this structure will start (that is, the offset from the beginning of this structure in memory where each field will start). The `FieldOffsetAttribute` can be used only with a `StructLayoutAttribute` set to `LayoutKind.Explicit`. In addition, it cannot be used on static members within this structure.

Unions can become problematic, since several types are essentially laid on top of one another. The biggest problem is extracting the correct data type from a union structure. Consider what happens if you choose to store the `long` numeric value `long.Max Value` in the `SignedNumber` structure. Later, you might accidentally attempt to extract a `byte` data type value from this same structure. In doing so, you will get back only the first byte of the long value.

Another problem is starting fields at the correct offset. The `SignedNumberWithText` union overlays numerous signed numeric data types at the zeroth offset. The last field in this structure is laid out at the 16th byte offset from the beginning of this structure in memory. If you accidentally overlay the string field `Text1` on top of any of the other signed numeric data types, you will get an exception at runtime. The basic rule is that you are allowed to overlay a value type on another value type, but you cannot overlay a reference type over a value type. If the `Text1` field is marked with the following attribute:

```
[FieldOffsetAttribute(14)]
```

this exception is thrown at runtime (note that the compiler does not catch this problem):

```
System.TypeLoadException: Could not load type 'SignedNumberWithText' from
assembly 'CSharpRecipes, Version=1.0.0.0, Culture=neutral,
PublicKeyToken=fe85c3941fbcc4c5' because it contains an object field at
offset 14 that is incorrectly aligned or overlapped by a non-object field.
```

It is imperative to get the offsets correct when you're using complex unions in C#.

See Also

The "StructLayoutAttribute Class" topic in the MSDN documentation.

1.2 Making a Type Sortable

Problem

You have a data type that will be stored as an element in a List<T> or a Sorted
List<K,V>. You would like to use the List<T>.Sort method or the internal sorting
mechanism of SortedList<K,V> to allow custom sorting of your data types in the
array. In addition, you may need to use this type in a SortedList collection.

Solution

Example 1-1 demonstrates how to implement the IComparable<T> interface. The
Square class shown in Example 1-1 implements this interface in such a way that the
List<T> and SortedList<K,V> collections can sort and search for these Square
objects.

Example 1-1. Making a type sortable by implementing IComparable<T>

```
public class Square : IComparable<Square>
{
    public Square(){}

    public Square(int height, int width)
    {
        this.Height = height;
        this.Width = width;
    }

    public int Height { get; set; }

    public int Width { get; set; }

    public int CompareTo(object obj)
    {
        Square square = obj as Square;
        if (square != null)
            return CompareTo(square);
        throw
          new ArgumentException(
            "Both objects being compared must be of type Square.");
    }

    public override string ToString()=>
                        ($"Height: {this.Height}     Width: {this.Width}");

    public override bool Equals(object obj)
    {
        if (obj == null)
```

```
        return false;

    Square square = obj as Square;
    if(square != null)
        return this.Height == square.Height;
    return false;
}

public override int GetHashCode()
{
    return this.Height.GetHashCode() | this.Width.GetHashCode();
}

public static bool operator ==(Square x, Square y) => x.Equals(y);
public static bool operator !=(Square x, Square y) => !(x == y);
public static bool operator <(Square x, Square y) => (x.CompareTo(y) < 0);
public static bool operator >(Square x, Square y) => (x.CompareTo(y) > 0);

public int CompareTo(Square other)
{
    long area1 = this.Height * this.Width;
    long area2 = other.Height * other.Width;

    if (area1 == area2)
        return 0;
    else if (area1 > area2)
        return 1;
    else if (area1 < area2)
        return -1;
    else
        return -1;
    }
}
```

Discussion

By implementing the IComparable<T> interface on your class (or structure), you can take advantage of the sorting routines of the List<T> and SortedList<K,V> classes. The algorithms for sorting are built into these classes; all you have to do is tell them how to sort your classes via the code you implement in the IComparable<T>.Compar eTo method.

When you sort a list of Square objects by calling the List<Square>.Sort method, the list is sorted via the IComparable<Square> interface of the Square objects. The Add method of the SortedList<K,V> class uses this interface to sort the objects as they are being added to the SortedList<K,V>.

IComparer<T> is designed to solve the problem of allowing objects to be sorted based on different criteria in different contexts. This interface also allows you to sort types that you did not write. If you also wanted to sort the Square objects by height, you could create a new class called CompareHeight, shown in Example 1-2, which would also implement the IComparer<Square> interface.

Example 1-2. Making a type sortable by implementing IComparer

```
public class CompareHeight : IComparer<Square>
{
    public int Compare(object firstSquare, object secondSquare)
    {
        Square square1 = firstSquare as Square;
        Square square2 = secondSquare as Square;
        if (square1 == null || square2 == null)
            throw (new ArgumentException("Both parameters must be of type Square."));
        else
            return Compare(firstSquare,secondSquare);
    }

    #region IComparer<Square> Members

    public int Compare(Square x, Square y)
    {
        if (x.Height == y.Height)
            return 0;
        else if (x.Height > y.Height)
            return 1;
        else if (x.Height < y.Height)
            return -1;
        else
            return -1;
    }

    #endregion
}
```

This class is then passed in to the IComparer parameter of the Sort routine. Now you can specify different ways to sort your Square objects. The comparison method implemented in the comparer must be consistent and apply a *total ordering* so that when the comparison function declares equality for two items, it is absolutely true and not a result of one item not being greater than another or one item not being less than another.

 For best performance, keep the CompareTo method short and efficient, because it will be called multiple times by the Sort methods. For example, in sorting an array with four items, the Compare method is called 10 times.

The `TestSort` method shown in Example 1-3 demonstrates how to use the `Square` and `CompareHeight` classes with the `List<Square>` and `SortedList<int,Square>` instances.

Example 1-3. TestSort method

```
public static void TestSort()
{
    List<Square> listOfSquares = new List<Square>(){
                           new Square(1,3),
                           new Square(4,3),
                           new Square(2,1),
                           new Square(6,1)};
    // Test a List<String>
    Console.WriteLine("List<String>");
    Console.WriteLine("Original list");
    foreach (Square square in listOfSquares)
    {
        Console.WriteLine(square.ToString());
    }

    Console.WriteLine();
    IComparer<Square> heightCompare = new CompareHeight();
    listOfSquares.Sort(heightCompare);
    Console.WriteLine("Sorted list using IComparer<Square>=heightCompare");
    foreach (Square square in listOfSquares)
    {
        Console.WriteLine(square.ToString());
    }

    Console.WriteLine();
    Console.WriteLine("Sorted list using IComparable<Square>");
    listOfSquares.Sort();
    foreach (Square square in listOfSquares)
    {
        Console.WriteLine(square.ToString());
    }


    // Test a SORTEDLIST
    var sortedListOfSquares = new SortedList<int,Square>(){
                           { 0, new Square(1,3)},
                           { 2, new Square(3,3)},
                           { 1, new Square(2,1)},
                           { 3, new Square(6,1)}};

    Console.WriteLine();
    Console.WriteLine();
    Console.WriteLine("SortedList<Square>");
    foreach (KeyValuePair<int,Square> kvp in sortedListOfSquares)
    {
```

```
            Console.WriteLine ($"{kvp.Key} : {kvp.Value}");
    }
}
```

This code displays the following output:

```
List<String>
Original list
Height:1 Width:3
Height:4 Width:3
Height:2 Width:1
Height:6 Width:1

Sorted list using IComparer<Square>=heightCompare
Height:1 Width:3
Height:2 Width:1
Height:4 Width:3
Height:6 Width:1

Sorted list using IComparable<Square>
Height:2 Width:1
Height:1 Width:3
Height:6 Width:1
Height:4 Width:3

SortedList<Square>
0 : Height:1 Width:3
1 : Height:2 Width:1
2 : Height:3 Width:3
3 : Height:6 Width:1
```

See Also

Recipe 1.3, and the "IComparable<T> Interface" topic in the MSDN documentation.

1.3 Making a Type Searchable

Problem

You have a data type that will be stored as elements in a List<T>. You would like to use the BinarySearch method to allow for custom searching of your data types in the list.

Solution

Use the IComparable<T> and IComparer<T> interfaces. The Square class, from Recipe 1.2, implements the IComparable<T> interface in such a way that the List<T> and SortedList<K,V> collections can sort and search an array or collection of Square objects.

Discussion

By implementing the IComparable<T> interface on your class (or structure), you can take advantage of the search routines of the List<T> and SortedList<K,V> classes. The algorithms for searching are built into these classes; all you have to do is tell them how to search your classes via the code you implement in the IComparable<T>. CompareTo method.

To implement the CompareTo method, see Recipe 1.2.

The List<T> class provides a BinarySearch method to perform a search on the elements in that list. The elements are compared against an object passed to the Binary Search method in the object parameter. The SortedList class does not have a Binary Search method; instead, it has the ContainsKey method, which performs a binary search on the key contained in the list. The ContainsValue method of the Sorted List class performs a linear search when searching for values. This linear search uses the Equals method of the elements in the SortedList collection to do its work. The Compare and CompareTo methods do not have any effect on the operation of the linear search performed in the SortedList class, but they do have an effect on binary searches.

 To perform an accurate search using the BinarySearch methods of the List<T> class, you must first sort the List<T> using its Sort method. In addition, if you pass an IComparer<T> interface to the BinarySearch method, you must also pass the same interface to the Sort method. Otherwise, the BinarySearch method might not be able to find the object you are looking for.

The TestSort method shown in Example 1-4 demonstrates how to use the Square and CompareHeight classes with the List<Square> and SortedList<int,Square> collection instances.

Example 1-4. Making a type searchable

```
public static void TestSearch()
{
    List<Square> listOfSquares = new List<Square> {new Square(1,3),
                                                    new Square(4,3),
                                                    new Square(2,1),
                                                    new Square(6,1)};
    IComparer<Square> heightCompare = new CompareHeight();

    // Test a List<Square>
    Console.WriteLine("List<Square>");
    Console.WriteLine("Original list");
```

```
foreach (Square square in listOfSquares)
{
    Console.WriteLine(square.ToString());
}

Console.WriteLine();
Console.WriteLine("Sorted list using IComparer<Square>=heightCompare");
listOfSquares.Sort(heightCompare);
foreach (Square square in listOfSquares)
{
    Console.WriteLine(square.ToString());
}

Console.WriteLine();
Console.WriteLine("Search using IComparer<Square>=heightCompare");
int found = listOfSquares.BinarySearch(new Square(1,3), heightCompare);
Console.WriteLine($"Found (1,3): {found}");

Console.WriteLine();
Console.WriteLine("Sorted list using IComparable<Square>");
listOfSquares.Sort();
foreach (Square square in listOfSquares)
{
    Console.WriteLine(square.ToString());
}

Console.WriteLine();
Console.WriteLine("Search using IComparable<Square>");
found = listOfSquares.BinarySearch(new Square(6,1)); // Use IComparable
Console.WriteLine($"Found (6,1): {found}");

 // Test a SortedList<Square>
 var sortedListOfSquares = new SortedList<int,Square>(){
                            {0, new Square(1,3)},
                            {2, new Square(4,3)},
                            {1, new Square(2,1)},
                            {4, new Square(6,1)}};
Console.WriteLine();
Console.WriteLine("SortedList<Square>");
foreach (KeyValuePair<int,Square> kvp in sortedListOfSquares)
{
    Console.WriteLine ($"{kvp.Key} : {kvp.Value}");
}

Console.WriteLine();
bool foundItem = sortedListOfSquares.ContainsKey(2);
Console.WriteLine($"sortedListOfSquares.ContainsKey(2): {foundItem}");

// Does not use IComparer or IComparable
// -- uses a linear search along with the Equals method
// which has not been overloaded
Console.WriteLine();
```

```
    Square value = new Square(6,1);
    foundItem = sortedListOfSquares.ContainsValue(value);
    Console.WriteLine("sortedListOfSquares.ContainsValue " +
                      $"(new Square(6,1)): {foundItem}");
}
```

This code displays the following:

```
List"Square>
Original list
Height:1 Width:3
Height:4 Width:3
Height:2 Width:1
Height:6 Width:1

Sorted list using IComparer"Square>=heightCompare
Height:1 Width:3
Height:2 Width:1
Height:4 Width:3
Height:6 Width:1

Search using IComparer"Square>=heightCompare
Found (1,3): 0

Sorted list using IComparable"Square>
Height:2 Width:1
Height:1 Width:3
Height:6 Width:1
Height:4 Width:3

Search using IComparable"Square>
Found (6,1): 2


SortedList"Square>
0 : Height:1 Width:3
1 : Height:2 Width:1
2 : Height:4 Width:3
4 : Height:6 Width:1

sortedListOfSquares.ContainsKey(2): True
sortedListOfSquares.ContainsValue(new Square(6,1)): True
```

See Also

Recipe 1.2, and the "IComparable<T> Interface" and "IComparer<T> Interface" topics in the MSDN documentation.

1.4 Returning Multiple Items from a Method

Problem

In many cases, a single return value for a method is not enough. You need a way to return more than one item from a method.

Solution

Use the out keyword on parameters that will act as return parameters. The following method accepts an `inputShape` parameter and calculates `height`, `width`, and `depth` from that value:

```
public void ReturnDimensions(int inputShape,
                             out int height,
                             out int width,
                             out int depth)
{
    height = 0;
    width = 0;
    depth = 0;

    // Calculate height, width, and depth from the inputShape value.
}
```

This method would be called in the following manner:

```
// Declare output parameters.
int height;
int width;
int depth;

// Call method and return the height, width, and depth.
Obj.ReturnDimensions(1, out height, out width, out depth);
```

Another method is to return a class or structure containing all the return values. The previous method has been modified here to return a structure instead of using out arguments:

```
public Dimensions ReturnDimensions(int inputShape)
{
    // The default ctor automatically defaults this structure's members to 0.
    Dimensions objDim = new Dimensions();

    // Calculate objDim.Height, objDim.Width, objDim.Depth
    //     from the inputShape value...

    return objDim;
}
```

where `Dimensions` is defined as follows:

```
public struct Dimensions
{
    public int Height;
    public int Width;
    public int Depth;
}
```

This method would now be called in this manner:

```
// Call method and return the height, width, and depth.
Dimensions objDim = obj.ReturnDimensions(1);
```

Rather than returning a user-defined class or structure from this method, you can use a `Tuple` object containing all the return values. The previous method has been modified here to return a `Tuple`:

```
public Tuple<int, int, int> ReturnDimensionsAsTuple(int inputShape)
{
    // Calculate objDim.Height, objDim.Width, objDim.Depth from the inputShape
    // value e.g. {5, 10, 15}

    // Create a Tuple with calculated values
    var objDim = Tuple.Create<int, int, int>(5, 10, 15);

    return (objDim);
}
```

This method would now be called in this manner:

```
// Call method and return the height, width, and depth.
Tuple<int, int, int> objDim = obj.ReturnDimensions(1);
```

Discussion

Marking a parameter in a method signature with the out keyword indicates that this parameter will be initialized and returned by this method. This trick is useful when a method is required to return more than one value. A method can, at most, have only one return value, but through the use of the out keyword, you can mark several parameters as a kind of return value.

To set up an out parameter, mark the parameter in the method signature with the out keyword as shown here:

```
public void ReturnDimensions(int inputShape,
                             out int height,
                             out int width,
                             out int depth)
{
    ...
}
```

To call this method, you must also mark the calling method's arguments with the out keyword, shown here:

```
obj.ReturnDimensions(1, out height, out width, out depth);
```

The out arguments in this method call do not have to be initialized; they can simply be declared and passed in to the ReturnDimensions method. Regardless of whether they are initialized before the method call, they must be initialized before they are used within the ReturnDimensions method. Even if they are not used through every path in the ReturnDimensions method, they still must be initialized. That is why this method starts out with the following three lines of code:

```
height = 0;
width = 0;
depth = 0;
```

You may be wondering why you couldn't use a ref parameter instead of the out parameter, as both allow a method to change the value of an argument marked as such. The answer is that an out parameter makes the code somewhat self-documenting. You know that when an out parameter is encountered, it is acting as a return value. In addition, an out parameter does not require the extra work to be initialized before it is passed in to the method, while a ref parameter does.

 An out parameter does not have to be marshaled when the method is called; rather, it is marshaled once when the method returns the data to the caller. Any other type of call (by-value or by-reference using the ref keyword) requires that the value be marshaled in both directions. Using the out keyword in marshaling scenarios improves remoting performance.

An out parameter is great when there are only a few values that need to be returned, but when you start encountering 4, 5, 6, or more values that need to be returned, it can get unwieldy. Another option for returning multiple values is to create and return a user-defined class/structure or to use a Tuple to package up all the values that need to be returned by a method.

The first option, using a class/structure to return the values, is straightforward. Just create the type (in this example it is a structure) like so:

```
public struct Dimensions
{
    public int Height;
    public int Width;
    public int Depth;
}
```

Fill in each field of this structure with the required data and then return it from the method as shown in the Solution section.

The second option, using a `Tuple`, is an even more elegant solution than using a user-defined object. A `Tuple` can be created to hold any number of values of varying types. In addition, the data you store in the `Tuple` is immutable; once you add the data to the `Tuple` through the constructor or the static `Create` method, that data cannot be changed.

`Tuples` can accept up to and including eight separate values. If you need to return more than eight values, you will need to use the special `Tuple` class:

```
Tuple<T1, T2, T3, T4, T5, T6, T7, TRest> Class
```

When creating a `Tuple` with more than eight values, you cannot use the static `Create` method—you must instead use the constructor of the class. This is how you would create a `Tuple` of 10 integer values:

```
var values = new Tuple<int, int, int, int, int, int, int, Tuple<int, int, int>> (
                    1, 2, 3, 4, 5, 6, 7, new Tuple<int, int, int> (8, 9, 10));
```

Of course, you can continue to add more `Tuples` to the end of each embedded `Tuple`, creating any size `Tuple` that you need.

See Also

The "Tuple Class" and "Tuple<T1, T2, T3, T4, T5, T6, T7, TRest> Class" topics in the MSDN documentation.

1.5 Parsing Command-Line Parameters

Problem

You require your applications to accept one or more command-line parameters in a standard format (described in the Discussion section). You need to access and parse the entire command line passed to your application.

Solution

In Example 1-5, use the following classes together to help with parsing command-line parameters: `Argument`, `ArgumentDefinition`, and `ArgumentSemanticAnalyzer`.

Example 1-5. Argument class

```
using System;
using System.Diagnostics;
using System.Linq;
```

```csharp
using System.Collections.ObjectModel;

public sealed class Argument
{
    public string Original { get; }
    public string Switch { get; private set; }
    public ReadOnlyCollection<string> SubArguments { get; }
    private List<string> subArguments;
    public Argument(string original)
    {
        Original = original;
        Switch = string.Empty;
        subArguments = new List<string>();
        SubArguments = new ReadOnlyCollection<string>(subArguments);
        Parse();
    }

    private void Parse()
    {
        if (string.IsNullOrEmpty(Original))
        {
            return;
        }
        char[] switchChars = { '/', '-' };
        if (!switchChars.Contains(Original[0]))

        {
            return;
        }
        string switchString = Original.Substring(1);
        string subArgsString = string.Empty;
        int colon = switchString.IndexOf(':');
        if (colon >= 0)
        {
            subArgsString = switchString.Substring(colon + 1);
            switchString = switchString.Substring(0, colon);
        }
        Switch = switchString;
        if (!string.IsNullOrEmpty(subArgsString))
            subArguments.AddRange(subArgsString.Split(';'));
    }

    // A set of predicates that provide useful information about itself
    //    Implemented using lambdas
    public bool IsSimple => SubArguments.Count == 0;
    public bool IsSimpleSwitch =>
                !string.IsNullOrEmpty(Switch) && SubArguments.Count == 0;
    public bool IsCompoundSwitch =>
                !string.IsNullOrEmpty(Switch) && SubArguments.Count == 1;
    public bool IsComplexSwitch =>
                !string.IsNullOrEmpty(Switch) && SubArguments.Count > 0;
}
```

```csharp
public sealed class ArgumentDefinition
{
    public string ArgumentSwitch { get; }
    public string Syntax { get; }
    public string Description { get; }
    public Func<Argument, bool> Verifier { get; }

    public ArgumentDefinition(string argumentSwitch,
                              string syntax,
                              string description,
                              Func<Argument, bool> verifier)
    {
        ArgumentSwitch = argumentSwitch.ToUpper();
        Syntax = syntax;
        Description = description;
        Verifier = verifier;
    }

    public bool Verify(Argument arg) => Verifier(arg);
}

public sealed class ArgumentSemanticAnalyzer
{

    private List<ArgumentDefinition> argumentDefinitions =
        new List<ArgumentDefinition>();
    private Dictionary<string, Action<Argument>> argumentActions =
        new Dictionary<string, Action<Argument>>();

    public ReadOnlyCollection<Argument> UnrecognizedArguments { get; private set; }
    public ReadOnlyCollection<Argument> MalformedArguments { get; private set; }
    public ReadOnlyCollection<Argument> RepeatedArguments { get; private set; }

    public ReadOnlyCollection<ArgumentDefinition> ArgumentDefinitions =>
         new ReadOnlyCollection<ArgumentDefinition>(argumentDefinitions);

    public IEnumerable<string> DefinedSwitches =>
                       from argumentDefinition in argumentDefinitions
                       select argumentDefinition.ArgumentSwitch;

    public void AddArgumentVerifier(ArgumentDefinition verifier) =>
        argumentDefinitions.Add(verifier);

    public void RemoveArgumentVerifier(ArgumentDefinition verifier)
    {
        var verifiersToRemove = from v in argumentDefinitions
                                where v.ArgumentSwitch == verifier.ArgumentSwitch
                                select v;
        foreach (var v in verifiersToRemove)
            argumentDefinitions.Remove(v);
    }
```

```csharp
public void AddArgumentAction(string argumentSwitch, Action<Argument> action) =>
    argumentActions.Add(argumentSwitch, action);

public void RemoveArgumentAction(string argumentSwitch)
{
    if (argumentActions.Keys.Contains(argumentSwitch))
        argumentActions.Remove(argumentSwitch);
}

public bool VerifyArguments(IEnumerable<Argument> arguments)
{
    // no parameter to verify with, fail.
    if (!argumentDefinitions.Any())

        return false;

    // Identify if any of the arguments are not defined
    this.UnrecognizedArguments =
            ( from argument in arguments
              where !DefinedSwitches.Contains(argument.Switch.ToUpper())
              select argument).ToList().AsReadOnly();

    if (this.UnrecognizedArguments.Any())
        return false;

    //Check for all the arguments where the switch matches a known switch,
    //but our well-formedness predicate is false.
    this.MalformedArguments = ( from argument in arguments
                                join argumentDefinition in argumentDefinitions
                                on argument.Switch.ToUpper() equals
                                    argumentDefinition.ArgumentSwitch
                                where !argumentDefinition.Verify(argument)
                                select argument).ToList().AsReadOnly();

    if (this.MalformedArguments.Any())
        return false;

    //Sort the arguments into "groups" by their switch, count every group,
    //and select any groups that contain more than one element,
    //We then get a read-only list of the items.
    this.RepeatedArguments =
            (from argumentGroup in
                from argument in arguments
                where !argument.IsSimple
                group argument by argument.Switch.ToUpper()
            where argumentGroup.Count() > 1
            select argumentGroup).SelectMany(ag => ag).ToList().AsReadOnly();

    if (this.RepeatedArguments.Any())
    return false;
```

```csharp
            return true;
    }

    public void EvaluateArguments(IEnumerable<Argument> arguments)
    {
        //Now we just apply each action:
        foreach (Argument argument in arguments)
            argumentActions[argument.Switch.ToUpper()](argument);
    }

    public string InvalidArgumentsDisplay()
    {
        StringBuilder builder = new StringBuilder();
        builder.AppendFormat($"Invalid arguments: {Environment.NewLine}");
        // Add the unrecognized arguments

        FormatInvalidArguments(builder, this.UnrecognizedArguments,
            "Unrecognized argument: {0}{1}");

        // Add the malformed arguments
        FormatInvalidArguments(builder, this.MalformedArguments,
            "Malformed argument: {0}{1}");

        // For the repeated arguments, we want to group them for the display,
        // so group by switch and then add it to the string being built.
        var argumentGroups = from argument in this.RepeatedArguments
                             group argument by argument.Switch.ToUpper() into ag
                             select new { Switch = ag.Key, Instances = ag};

        foreach (var argumentGroup in argumentGroups)
        {
            builder.AppendFormat($"Repeated argument:
                            {argumentGroup.Switch}{Environment.NewLine}");
            FormatInvalidArguments(builder, argumentGroup.Instances.ToList(),
                "\t{0}{1}");
        }
        return builder.ToString();
    }

    private void FormatInvalidArguments(StringBuilder builder,
        IEnumerable<Argument> invalidArguments, string errorFormat)
    {
        if (invalidArguments != null)
        {
            foreach (Argument argument in invalidArguments)
            {
                builder.AppendFormat(errorFormat,
                    argument.Original, Environment.NewLine);
            }
        }
    }
}
```

Here is one example of how to use these classes to process the command line for an application:

```csharp
public static void Main(string[] argumentStrings)
{
    var arguments = (from argument in argumentStrings
        select new Argument(argument)).ToArray();

    Console.Write("Command line: ");
    foreach (Argument a in arguments)
    {
        Console.Write($"{a.Original} ");
    }
    Console.WriteLine("");

    ArgumentSemanticAnalyzer analyzer = new ArgumentSemanticAnalyzer();
    analyzer.AddArgumentVerifier(
        new ArgumentDefinition("output",
            "/output:[path to output]",
            "Specifies the location of the output file.",
            x => x.IsCompoundSwitch));
    analyzer.AddArgumentVerifier(
        new ArgumentDefinition("trialMode",
            "/trialmode",
            "If this is specified it places the product into trial mode",
            x => x.IsSimpleSwitch));
    analyzer.AddArgumentVerifier(
        new ArgumentDefinition("DEBUGOUTPUT",
            "/debugoutput:[value1];[value2];[value3]",
            "A listing of the files the debug output " +
            "information will be written to",
            x => x.IsComplexSwitch));
    analyzer.AddArgumentVerifier(
        new ArgumentDefinition("",
            "[literal value]",
            "A literal value",
            x => x.IsSimple));

    if (!analyzer.VerifyArguments(arguments))
    {
        string invalidArguments = analyzer.InvalidArgumentsDisplay();
        Console.WriteLine(invalidArguments);
        ShowUsage(analyzer);
        return;
    }

    // Set up holders for the command line parsing results
    string output = string.Empty;
    bool trialmode = false;
    IEnumerable<string> debugOutput = null;
    List<string> literals = new List<string>();
```

```
//For each parsed argument, we want to apply an action,
// so add them to the analyzer.
analyzer.AddArgumentAction("OUTPUT", x => { output = x.SubArguments[0]; });
analyzer.AddArgumentAction("TRIALMODE", x => { trialmode = true; });
analyzer.AddArgumentAction("DEBUGOUTPUT", x =>
                                    { debugOutput = x.SubArguments;
});

analyzer.AddArgumentAction("", x=>{literals.Add(x.Original);});

// check the arguments and run the actions
analyzer.EvaluateArguments(arguments);

// display the results
Console.WriteLine("");
Console.WriteLine($"OUTPUT: {output}");
Console.WriteLine($"TRIALMODE: {trialmode}");
if (debugOutput != null)
{
    foreach (string item in debugOutput)

    {
        Console.WriteLine($"DEBUGOUTPUT: {item}");
    }
}
foreach (string literal in literals)
{
    Console.WriteLine($"LITERAL: {literal}");
}
}

public static void ShowUsage(ArgumentSemanticAnalyzer analyzer)
{
    Console.WriteLine("Program.exe allows the following arguments:");
    foreach (ArgumentDefinition definition in analyzer.ArgumentDefinitions)
    {
        Console.WriteLine($"\t{definition.ArgumentSwitch}:
                        ({definition.Description}){Environment.NewLine}
                        \tSyntax: {definition.Syntax}");
    }
}
```

Discussion

Before you can parse command-line parameters, you must decide upon a common format. The format for this recipe follows the command-line format for the Visual C# .NET language compiler. The format used is defined as follows:

- All command-line arguments are separated by one or more whitespace characters.

- Each argument may start with either a - or / character, but not both. If it does not, that argument is considered a literal, such as a filename.

- Each argument that starts with either the - or / character may be divided up into a switch followed by a colon followed by one or more arguments separated with the ; character. The command-line parameter -sw:arg1;arg2;arg3 is divided up into a switch (sw) and three arguments (arg1, arg2, and arg3). Note that there should not be any spaces in the full argument; otherwise, the runtime command-line parser will split up the argument into two or more arguments.

- Strings delineated with double quotes, such as "c:\test\file.log", will have their double quotes stripped off. This is a function of the operating system interpreting the arguments passed in to your application.

- Single quotes are not stripped off.

- To preserve double quotes, precede the double quote character with the \ escape sequence character.

- The \ character is handled as an escape sequence character only when followed by a double quote—in which case, only the double quote is displayed.

- The ^ character is handled by the *runtime* command-line parser as a special character.

Fortunately, the runtime command-line parser handles most of this before your application receives the individual parsed arguments.

The runtime command-line parser passes a `string[]` containing each parsed argument to the entry point of your application. The entry point can take one of the following forms:

```
public static void Main()
public static int Main()
public static void Main(string[] args)
public static int Main(string[] args)
```

The first two accept no arguments, but the last two accept the array of parsed command-line arguments. Note that the static `Environment.CommandLine` property will also return a string containing the entire command line, and the static `Environment.GetCommandLineArgs` method will return an array of strings containing the parsed command-line arguments.

The three classes presented in the Solution address the phases of dealing with the command-line arguments:

Argument

Encapsulates a single command-line argument and is responsible for parsing the argument.

`ArgumentDefinition`
> Defines an argument that will be valid for the current command line.

`ArgumentSemanticAnalyzer`
> Performs the verification and retrieval of the arguments based on the `ArgumentDefi` `nitions` that are set up.

Passing in the following command-line arguments to this application:

```
MyApp c:\input\infile.txt -output:d:\outfile.txt -trialmode
```

results in the following parsed switches and arguments:

```
Command line: c:\input\infile.txt -output:d:\outfile.txt -trialmode
OUTPUT: d:\outfile.txt
TRIALMODE: True
LITERAL: c:\input\infile.txt
```

If you input command-line parameters incorrectly, such as forgetting to add arguments to the -output switch, you get the following output:

```
Command line: c:\input\infile.txt -output: -trialmode
Invalid arguments:
Malformed argument: -output

Program.exe allows the following arguments:
        OUTPUT: (Specifies the location of the output file.)
        Syntax: /output:[path to output]
        TRIALMODE: (If this is specified, it places the product into trial mode)
        Syntax: /trialmode
        DEBUGOUTPUT: (A listing of the files the debug output information will be
                     written to)
        Syntax: /debugoutput:[value1];[value2];[value3]
        : (A literal value)
        Syntax: [literal value]
```

There are a few items in the code that are worth pointing out.

Each `Argument` instance needs to be able to determine certain things about itself; accordingly, a set of predicates that tell us useful information about this `Argument` are exposed as properties on the `Argument`. The `ArgumentSemanticAnalyzer` will use these properties to determine the characteristics of the argument:

```
public bool IsSimple => SubArguments.Count == 0;
public bool IsSimpleSwitch =>
        !string.IsNullOrEmpty(Switch) && SubArguments.Count == 0;
public bool IsCompoundSwitch =>
        !string.IsNullOrEmpty(Switch) && SubArguments.Count == 1;
public bool IsComplexSwitch =>
        !string.IsNullOrEmpty(Switch) && SubArguments.Count > 0;
```

For more information on lambda expressions, see the introduction to Chapter 4. Also see Recipe 1.16 for a discussion of using lambda expressions to implement closures.

In a number of places in the code, the `ToArray` or `ToList` methods are called on the result of a LINQ query:

```
var arguments = (from argument in argumentStrings
                 select new Argument(argument)).ToArray();
```

This is because query results use deferred execution, which means that not only are the results calculated in a lazy manner, but they are recalculated every time they are accessed. Using the `ToArray` or `ToList` methods forces the eager evaluation of the results and generates a copy that will not reevaluate during each usage. The query logic does not know if the collection being worked on is changing or not, so it has to reevaluate each time unless you make a "point in time" copy using these methods.

To verify that these arguments are correct, we must create an `ArgumentDefinition` and associate it for each acceptable argument type with the `ArgumentSemanticAnalyzer`:

```
ArgumentSemanticAnalyzer analyzer = new ArgumentSemanticAnalyzer();
analyzer.AddArgumentVerifier(
        new ArgumentDefinition("output",
            "/output:[path to output]",
            "Specifies the location of the output file.",
            x => x.IsCompoundSwitch));
analyzer.AddArgumentVerifier(
        new ArgumentDefinition("trialMode",
            "/trialmode",
            "If this is specified it places the product into trial mode",
            x => x.IsSimpleSwitch));
analyzer.AddArgumentVerifier(
        new ArgumentDefinition("DEBUGOUTPUT",
            "/debugoutput:[value1];[value2];[value3]",
            "A listing of the files the debug output " +
            "information will be written to",
            x => x.IsComplexSwitch));
analyzer.AddArgumentVerifier(
        new ArgumentDefinition("",
            "[literal value]",
            "A literal value",
            x => x.IsSimple));
```

There are four parts to each `ArgumentDefinition`: the argument switch, a string showing the syntax of the argument, a description of the argument, and the verification predicate to verify the argument. This information can be used to verify the argument, as shown here:

```
//Check for all the arguments where the switch matches a known switch,
//but our well-formedness predicate is false.
this.MalformedArguments = ( from argument in arguments
                            join argumentDefinition in argumentDefinitions
                              on argument.Switch.ToUpper() equals
                                argumentDefinition.ArgumentSwitch
                            where !argumentDefinition.Verify(argument)
                            select argument).ToList().AsReadOnly();
```

The `ArgumentDefinitions` also allow you to compose a usage method for the program:

```
public static void ShowUsage(ArgumentSemanticAnalyzer analyzer)
{
    Console.WriteLine("Program.exe allows the following arguments:");
    foreach (ArgumentDefinition definition in analyzer.ArgumentDefinitions)
    {
        Console.WriteLine("\t{0}: ({1}){2}\tSyntax: {3}",
            definition.ArgumentSwitch, definition.Description,
            Environment.NewLine,definition.Syntax);
    }
}
```

To get the values of the arguments so they can be used, we need to extract the information out of the parsed arguments. For the Solution example, we would need the following information:

```
// Set up holders for the command line parsing results
string output = string.Empty;
bool trialmode = false;
IEnumerable<string> debugOutput = null;
List<string> literals = new List<string>();
```

How are these values filled in? Well, we need to associate an action with each `Argu ment` to determine how the value should be retrieved from an `Argument` instance. The action is a predicate, which makes this a very powerful approach, as any predicate can be used here. Here is where those `Argument` actions are defined and associated with the `ArgumentSemanticAnalyzer`:

```
//For each parsed argument, we want to apply an action,
//     so add them to the analyzer.
analyzer.AddArgumentAction("OUTPUT", x => { output = x.SubArguments[0]; });
analyzer.AddArgumentAction("TRIALMODE", x => { trialmode = true; });
analyzer.AddArgumentAction("DEBUGOUTPUT", x =>
                                        { debugOutput = x.SubArguments;});
analyzer.AddArgumentAction("", x=>{literals.Add(x.Original);});
```

Now that all of the actions are set up, we can retrieve the values by using the `Evalua teArguments` method on the `ArgumentSemanticAnalyzer`:

```
// check the arguments and run the actions
analyzer.EvaluateArguments(arguments);
```

Now the arguments have been filled in by the execution of the actions, and the program can run with those values:

```
// Run the program passing in the argument values:
Program program = new Program(output, trialmode, debugOutput, literals);
program.Run();
```

The verification of the arguments uses LINQ to query for unrecognized, malformed, or repeated arguments, any of which will cause the parameters to be invalid:

```
public bool VerifyArguments(IEnumerable<Argument> arguments)
{
    // no parameter to verify with, fail.
    if (!argumentDefinitions.Any())
        return false;

    // Identify if any of the arguments are not defined
    this.UnrecognizedArguments =
            (   from argument in arguments
                where !DefinedSwitches.Contains(argument.Switch.ToUpper())
                select argument).ToList().AsReadOnly();

    if (this.UnrecognizedArguments.Any())
        return false;

    //Check for all the arguments where the switch matches a known switch,
    //but our well-formedness predicate is false.
    this.MalformedArguments = ( from argument in arguments
                                join argumentDefinition in argumentDefinitions
                                on argument.Switch.ToUpper() equals
                                    argumentDefinition.ArgumentSwitch
                                where !argumentDefinition.Verify(argument)
                                select argument).ToList().AsReadOnly();
    if (this.MalformedArguments.Any())
        return false;

    //Sort the arguments into "groups" by their switch, count every group,
    //and select any groups that contain more than one element.
    //We then get a read-only list of the items.
    this.RepeatedArguments =
            (from argumentGroup in
                from argument in arguments
                where !argument.IsSimple
                group argument by argument.Switch.ToUpper()
            where argumentGroup.Count() > 1
            select argumentGroup).SelectMany(ag => ag).ToList().AsReadOnly();

    if (this.RepeatedArguments.Any())
        return false;

    return true;
}
```

Look at how much easier it is to understand each phase of the verification, compared with how it would be done before LINQ—with multiple nested loops, switches, IndexOfs, and other mechanisms. Each query concisely states in the language of the problem domain what task it is attempting to perform.

 LINQ is designed to help with problems where data must be sorted, searched, grouped, filtered, and projected. Use it!

See Also

The "Main" and "Command-Line Arguments" topics in the MSDN documentation.

1.6 Initializing a Constant Field at Runtime

Problem

A field marked as const can be initialized only at compile time. You need to initialize a field to a valid value at runtime, not at compile time. This field must then act as if it were a constant field for the rest of the application's life.

Solution

You have two choices when declaring a constant value in your code. You can use a readonly field or a const field. Each has its own strengths and weaknesses. However, if you need to initialize a constant field at runtime, you must use a readonly field:

```
public class Foo
{
    public readonly int bar;

    public Foo() {}

    public Foo(int constInitValue)
    {
        bar = constInitValue;
    }

    // Rest of class...
}
```

This is not possible using a const field. A const field can be initialized only at compile time:

```
public class Foo
{
```

```
public const int bar;      // This line causes a compile-time error.

public Foo() {}

public Foo(int constInitValue)
{
    bar = constInitValue; // This line also causes a compile-time error.
}
// Rest of class...
}
```

Discussion

A readonly field allows initialization to take place only in the constructor at runtime, whereas a const field must be initialized at compile time. Therefore, implementing a readonly field is the only way to allow a field that must be constant to be initialized at runtime.

There are only two ways to initialize a readonly field. The first is by adding an initializer to the field itself:

```
public readonly int bar = 100;
```

The second way is to initialize the readonly field through a constructor. This approach is demonstrated by the code in the Solution to this recipe. If you look at the following class:

```
public class Foo
{
    public readonly int x;
    public const int y = 1;

    public Foo() {}
    public Foo(int roInitValue)
    {
        x = roInitValue;
    }

    // Rest of class...
}
```

you'll see it is compiled into the following IL (intermediate language):

```
.class auto ansi nested public beforefieldinit Foo
       extends [mscorlib]System.Object        {
.field public static literal int32 y = int32(0x00000001) //<<-- const field
.field public initonly int32 x                    //<<-- readonly field
.method public hidebysig specialname rtspecialname
       instance void  .ctor(int32 roInitValue) cil managed
{
  // Code size       16 (0x10)
  .maxstack  8
```

```
    IL_0000:  ldarg.0
    IL_0001:  call        instance void [mscorlib]System.Object::.ctor()
    IL_0006:  nop
    IL_0007:  nop
    IL_0008:  ldarg.0
    IL_0009:  ldarg.1
    IL_000a:  stfld       int32 CSharpRecipes.ClassesAndGenerics/Foo::x
    IL_000f:  ret
} // end of method Foo::.ctor
.method public hidebysig specialname rtspecialname
        instance void  .ctor() cil managed
{
    // Code size       9 (0x9)
    .maxstack  8
    IL_0000:  ldarg.0
    IL_0001:  call        instance void [mscorlib]System.Object::.ctor()
    IL_0006:  nop
    IL_0007:  nop
    IL_0008:  ret
} // end of method Foo::.ctor
} // End of class Foo
```

Notice that a const field is compiled into a static field, and a readonly field is compiled into an instance field. Therefore, you need only a class name to access a const field.

 A common argument against using const fields is that they do not version as well as readonly fields. If you rebuild a component that defines a const field and the value of that const changes in a later version, any other components that were built against the old version won't pick up the new value. If there is any chance that a field is going to change, don't make it a const field.

The following code shows how to use an instance readonly field:

```
Foo obj1 = new Foo(100);
Console.WriteLine(obj1.bar);
```

See Also

The "const" and "readonly" keywords in the MSDN documentation.

1.7 Building Cloneable Classes

Problem

You need a method of performing a shallow cloning operation, a deep cloning operation, or both on a data type that may also reference other types, but the `ICloneable`
interface should not be used, as it violates the .NET Framework Design Guidelines.

Solution

To resolve the issue with using `ICloneable`, create two other interfaces to establish a
copying pattern, `IShallowCopy<T>` and `IDeepCopy<T>`:

```
public interface IShallowCopy<T>
{
    T ShallowCopy();
}
public interface IDeepCopy<T>
{
    T DeepCopy();
}
```

Shallow copying means that the copied object's fields will reference the same objects as
the original object. To allow shallow copying, implement the `IShallowCopy<T>` interface in the class:

```
using System;
using System.Collections;
using System.Collections.Generic;

public class ShallowClone : IShallowCopy<ShallowClone>
{
    public int Data = 1;
    public List<string> ListData = new List<string>();
    public object ObjData = new object();

    public ShallowClone ShallowCopy() => (ShallowClone)this.MemberwiseClone();
}
```

Deep copying, or cloning, means that the copied object's fields will reference new
copies of the original object's fields. To allow deep copying, implement the `IDeep
Copy<T>` interface in the class:

```
using System;
using System.Collections;
using System.Collections.Generic;
using System.Runtime.Serialization.Formatters.Binary;
using System.IO;

[Serializable]
```

```
public class DeepClone : IDeepCopy<DeepClone>
{
    public int data = 1;
    public List<string> ListData = new List<string>();
    public object objData = new object();

    public DeepClone DeepCopy()
    {
        BinaryFormatter BF = new BinaryFormatter();
        MemoryStream memStream = new MemoryStream();

        BF.Serialize(memStream, this);
        memStream.Flush();
        memStream.Position = 0;

        return (DeepClone)BF.Deserialize(memStream);
    }
}
```

To support both shallow and deep methods of copying, implement both interfaces. The code might appear as follows:

```
using System;
using System.Collections;
using System.Collections.Generic;
using System.Runtime.Serialization.Formatters.Binary;
using System.IO;

[Serializable]
public class MultiClone : IShallowCopy<MultiClone>,
                          IDeepCopy<MultiClone>
{
    public int data = 1;
    public List<string> ListData = new List<string>();
    public object objData = new object();

    public MultiClone ShallowCopy() => (MultiClone)this.MemberwiseClone();

    public MultiClone DeepCopy()
    {
        BinaryFormatter BF = new BinaryFormatter();
        MemoryStream memStream = new MemoryStream();

        BF.Serialize(memStream, this);
        memStream.Flush();
        memStream.Position = 0;

        return (MultiClone)BF.Deserialize(memStream);
    }
}
```

Discussion

The .NET Framework has an interface named `ICloneable`, which was originally designed as the means through which cloning is implemented in .NET. The design recommendation is now that this interface not be used in any public API, because it lends itself to different interpretations. The interface looks like this:

```
public interface ICloneable
{
    object Clone();
}
```

Notice that there is a single method, `Clone`, that returns an object. Is the clone a shallow copy of the object or a deep copy? You can't know from the interface, as the implementation could go either way. This is why it should not be used, and the `IShallowCopy<T>` and `IDeepCopy<T>` interfaces are introduced here.

Cloning is the ability to make an exact copy (a clone) of an instance of a type. Cloning may take one of two forms: a shallow copy or a deep copy. Shallow copying is relatively easy: it involves copying the object on which the `ShallowCopy` method was called.

The reference type fields in the original object are copied over, as are the value type fields. This means that if the original object contains a field of type `StreamWriter`, for instance, the cloned object will point to this same instance of the original object's `StreamWriter`; a new object is not created.

 There is no need to deal with `static` fields when performing a cloning operation. There is only one memory location reserved for each static field per class, per application domain. The cloned object will have access to the same static fields as the original.

Support for shallow copying is implemented by the `MemberwiseClone` method of the `Object` class, which serves as the base class for all .NET classes. So the following code allows a shallow copy to be created and returned by the `Clone` method:

```
public ShallowClone ShallowCopy() => (ShallowClone)this.MemberwiseClone();
```

Making a deep copy is the second way of cloning an object. A deep copy will make a copy of the original object just as the shallow copy does; however, a deep copy will also make separate copies of each reference type field in the original object. Therefore, if the original object contains a `StreamWriter` type field, the cloned object will also contain a `StreamWriter` type field, but the cloned object's `StreamWriter` field will point to a new `StreamWriter` object, not that of the original object.

Support for deep copying is not automatically provided by the .NET Framework, but the following code illustrates an easy way of implementing a deep copy:

```
BinaryFormatter BF = new BinaryFormatter();
MemoryStream memStream = new MemoryStream();

BF.Serialize(memStream, this);
memStream.Flush();
memStream.Position = 0;

return (BF.Deserialize(memStream));
```

Basically, the original object is serialized out to a memory stream via binary serialization, and then it is deserialized into a new object, which is returned to the caller. It is important to reposition the memory stream pointer back to the start of the stream before calling the `Deserialize` method; otherwise, an exception will be thrown indicating that the serialized object contains no data.

Performing a deep copy using object serialization allows you to change the underlying object without having to modify the code that performs the deep copy. If you performed the deep copy by hand, you'd have to make a new instance of all the instance fields of the original object and copy them over to the cloned object. This is a tedious chore in and of itself. If you make a change to the fields of the object being cloned, you must also change the deep copy code to reflect that modification. Using serialization, you rely on the serializer to dynamically find and serialize all fields contained in the object. If the object is modified, the serializer will still make a deep copy without any code modifications.

One reason you might want to do a deep copy by hand is that the serialization technique presented in this recipe works properly only when everything in your object is serializable. Of course, manual cloning doesn't always help there either—some objects are just inherently uncloneable. Suppose you have a network management application in which an object represents a particular printer on your network. What's it supposed to do when you clone it? Fax a purchase order for a new printer?

One problem inherent with deep copying is performing a deep copy on a nested data structure with circular references. This recipe makes it possible to deal with circular references, although it's a tricky problem. So, in fact, you don't need to avoid circular references if you are using this recipe.

See Also

Framework Design Guidelines: Conventions, Idioms, and Patterns for Reusable .NET Libraries by Krzysztof Cwalina and Brad Abrams (Addison-Wesley Professional), and the "Object.MemberwiseClone Method" topic in the MSDN documentation.

1.8 Ensuring an Object's Disposal

Problem

You require a way to always have something happen when an object's work is done or it goes out of scope.

Solution

Use the using statement:

```
using System;
using System.IO;

// ...

using(FileStream FS = new FileStream("Test.txt", FileMode.Create))
{
    FS.WriteByte((byte)1);
    FS.WriteByte((byte)2);
    FS.WriteByte((byte)3);

    using(StreamWriter SW = new StreamWriter(FS))
    {
        SW.WriteLine("some text.");
    }
}
```

Discussion

The using statement is very easy to use and saves you the hassle of writing extra code. If this Solution had not used the using statement, it would look like this:

```
FileStream FS = new FileStream("Test.txt", FileMode.Create);
try
{
    FS.WriteByte((byte)1);
    FS.WriteByte((byte)2);
    FS.WriteByte((byte)3);

    StreamWriter SW = new StreamWriter(FS);

    try
    {
        SW.WriteLine("some text.");
    }
    finally
    {
        if (SW != null)
        {
```

```
        ((IDisposable)SW).Dispose();
        }
    }
}
finally
{
    if (FS != null)
    {
        ((IDisposable)FS).Dispose();
    }
}
```

Several points to note about the using statement:

- There is a using directive, such as:

  ```
  using System.IO;
  ```

  which should be differentiated from the using statement. This is potentially confusing to developers first getting into this language.

- The variable(s) defined in the using statement clause must all be of the same type, and they must have an initializer. However, you are allowed multiple using statements in front of a single code block, so this isn't a significant restriction.

- Any variables defined in the using clause are considered read-only in the body of the using statement. This prevents a developer from inadvertently switching the variable to refer to a different object and causing problems when attempting to dispose of the object that the variable initially referenced.

- The variable should not be declared outside of the using block and then initialized inside of the using clause.

This last point is described by the following code:

```
FileStream FS;
using(FS = new FileStream("Test.txt", FileMode.Create))
{
    FS.WriteByte((byte)1);
    FS.WriteByte((byte)2);
    FS.WriteByte((byte)3);

    using(StreamWriter SW = new StreamWriter(FS))
    {
        SW.WriteLine("some text.");
    }
}
```

For this example code, you will not have a problem. But consider that the variable FS is usable outside of the using block. Essentially, you could revisit this code and modify it as follows:

```
FileStream FS;
using(FS = new FileStream("Test.txt", FileMode.Create))
{
    FS.WriteByte((byte)1);
    FS.WriteByte((byte)2);
    FS.WriteByte((byte)3);

    using(StreamWriter SW = new StreamWriter(FS))
    {
        SW.WriteLine("some text.");
    }
}
FS.WriteByte((byte)4);
```

This code compiles but throws an `ObjectDisposedException` on the last line of this code snippet because the `Dispose` method has already been called on the `FS` object. The object has not yet been collected at this point and still remains in memory in the disposed state.

See Also

The "Cleaning Up Unmanaged Resources," "IDisposable Interface," "Using foreach with Collections," and "Implementing Finalize and Dispose to Clean Up Unmanaged Resources" topics in the MSDN documentation.

1.9 Deciding When and Where to Use Generics

Problem

You want to use generic types in a new project or convert nongeneric types in an existing project to their generic equivalents. However, you do not really know why you would want to do this, and you do not know which nongeneric types should be converted to generic.

Solution

In deciding when and where to use generic types, you need to consider several things:

- Will your type contain or be operating on various unspecified data types (e.g., a collection type)? If so, creating a generic type will offer several benefits over creating a nongeneric type. If your type will operate on only a single specific type, then you may not need to create a generic type.

- If your type will be operating on value types, so that boxing and unboxing operations will occur, you should consider using generics to prevent the performance penalty incurred from boxing and unboxing operations.

- The stronger type checking associated with generics will aid in finding errors sooner (i.e., during compile time as opposed to runtime), thus shortening your bug-fixing cycle.

- Is your code suffering from "code bloat," with you writing multiple classes to handle different data types on which they operate (e.g., a specialized `ArrayList` that stores only `StreamReaders` and another that stores only `StreamWriters`)? It is easier to write the code once and have it just work for each of the data types it operates on.

- Generics allow for greater clarity of code. By eliminating code bloat and forcing stronger type checking on your types, they make your code easier to read and understand.

Discussion

In most cases, your code will benefit from using a generic type. Generics allow for more efficient code reuse, faster performance, stronger type checking, and easier-to-read code.

See Also

The "Generics Overview" and "Benefits of Generics" topics in the MSDN documentation.

1.10 Understanding Generic Types

Problem

You need to understand how the .NET types work for generics and how generic .NET types differ from regular .NET types.

Solution

A couple of quick experiments can show the differences between regular .NET types and generic .NET types. Before we get deep into the code, if you are unfamiliar with generics, jump to the Discussion section in this recipe for a detailed explanation about generics and then come back to this section.

Now, when a regular .NET type is defined, it looks like the `FixedSizeCollection` type defined in Example 1-6.

Example 1-6. FixedSizeCollection: a regular .NET type

```csharp
public class FixedSizeCollection
{
    /// <summary>
    /// Constructor that increments static counter
    /// and sets the maximum number of items
    /// </summary>
    /// <param name="maxItems"></param>
    public FixedSizeCollection(int maxItems)
    {
        FixedSizeCollection.InstanceCount++;
        this.Items = new object[maxItems];
    }
    /// <summary>
    /// Add an item to the class whose type
    /// is unknown as only object can hold any type
    /// </summary>
    /// <param name="item">item to add</param>
    /// <returns>the index of the item added</returns>
    public int AddItem(object item)
    {
        if (this.ItemCount < this.Items.Length)
        {
            this.Items[this.ItemCount] = item;
            return this.ItemCount++;
        }
        else
            throw new Exception("Item queue is full");
    }

    /// <summary>
    /// Get an item from the class
    /// </summary>
    /// <param name="index">the index of the item to get</param>
    /// <returns>an item of type object</returns>
    public object GetItem(int index)
    {
        if (index >= this.Items.Length &&
            index >= 0)
            throw new ArgumentOutOfRangeException(nameof(index));
        return this.Items[index];
    }

    #region Properties
    /// <summary>
    /// Static instance counter hangs off of the Type for
    /// StandardClass
    /// </summary>
    public static int InstanceCount { get; set; }

    /// <summary>
```

```
/// The count of the items the class holds
/// </summary>
public int ItemCount { get; private set; }

/// <summary>
/// The items in the class
/// </summary>
private object[] Items { get; set; }
#endregion // Properties

/// <summary>
/// ToString override to provide class detail
/// </summary>
/// <returns>formatted string with class details</returns>
public override string ToString() =>
            $"There are {FixedSizeCollection.InstanceCount.ToString()}
            instances of {this.GetType().ToString()} and this instance
            contains {this.ItemCount} items...";
}
```

FixedSizeCollection has a static integer property variable, InstanceCount, which is incremented in the instance constructor, and a ToString override that prints out how many instances of FixedSizeCollection exist in this AppDomain.FixedSizeCollec tion. Additionally, this collection class contains an array of objects(Items), the size of which is determined by the item count passed in to the constructor. FixedSizeCol lection also implements methods that add and retrieve items (AddItem, GetItem) and a read-only property to get the number of items currently in the array (Item Count).

FixedSizeCollection<T> is a generic .NET type with the same static property InstanceCount field, the instance constructor that counts the number of instantiations, and the overridden ToString method to tell you how many instances there are of this type. FixedSizeCollection<T> also has an Items array property and methods corresponding to those in FixedSizeCollection, as you can see in Example 1-7.

Example 1-7. FixedSizeCollection<T>: a generic .NET type

```
/// <summary>
/// A generic class to show instance counting
/// </summary>
/// <typeparam name="T">the type parameter used for the array storage</typeparam>
public class FixedSizeCollection<T>
{
    /// <summary>
    /// Constructor that increments static counter and sets up internal storage
    /// </summary>
    /// <param name="items"></param>
    public FixedSizeCollection(int items)
```

```csharp
{
    FixedSizeCollection<T>.InstanceCount++;
    this.Items = new T[items];
}

/// <summary>
/// Add an item to the class whose type
/// is determined by the instantiating type
/// </summary>
/// <param name="item">item to add</param>
/// <returns>the zero-based index of the item added</returns>
public int AddItem(T item)
{
    if (this.ItemCount < this.Items.Length)
    {
        this.Items[this.ItemCount] = item;
        return this.ItemCount++;
    }
    else
        throw new Exception("Item queue is full");
}

/// <summary>
/// Get an item from the class
/// </summary>
/// <param name="index">the zero-based index of the item to get</param>
/// <returns>an item of the instantiating type</returns>
public T GetItem(int index)
{
    if (index >= this.Items.Length &&
        index >= 0)
        throw new ArgumentOutOfRangeException(nameof(index));

    return this.Items[index];
}

#region Properties
/// <summary>
/// Static instance counter hangs off of the
/// instantiated Type for
/// GenericClass
/// </summary>
public static int InstanceCount { get; set; }

/// <summary>
/// The count of the items the class holds
/// </summary>
public int ItemCount { get; private set; }

/// <summary>
/// The items in the class
/// </summary>
```

```
    private T[] Items { get; set; }
    #endregion // Properties

    /// <summary>
    /// ToString override to provide class detail
    /// </summary>
    /// <returns>formatted string with class details</returns>
    public override string ToString() =>
            $"There are {FixedSizeCollection<T>.InstanceCount.ToString()}
            instances of {this.GetType().ToString()} and this instance
            contains {this.ItemCount} items...";
}
```

Things start to differ a little with FixedSizeCollection<T> when you look at the Items array property implementation. The Items array is declared as:

```
    private T[] Items { get; set; }
```

instead of:

```
    private object[] Items { get; set; }
```

The Items array property uses the type parameter of the generic class (<T>) to determine what types of items are allowed. FixedSizeCollection uses object for the Items array property type, which allows any type to be stored in the array of items (since all types are convertible to object), while FixedSizeCollection<T> provides type safety by allowing the type parameter to dictate what types of objects are permitted. Notice also that the properties have no associated private backing field declared for storing the array. This is an example of using the new *automatically implemented properties* feature that was originally introduced in C# 3.0. Under the covers, the C# compiler is creating a storage element of the property's type, but you don't have to write the code for the property storage anymore if you don't have specific code that has to execute when accessing the properties. To make the property read-only, simply mark the set; declaration private.

The next difference is visible in the method declarations of AddItem and GetItem. AddItem now takes a parameter of type T, whereas in FixedSizeCollection, it took a parameter of type object. GetItem now returns a value of type T, whereas in FixedSizeCollection, it returned a value of type object. These changes allow the methods in FixedSizeCollection<T> to use the instantiated type to store and retrieve the items in the array, instead of having to allow any object to be stored as in FixedSize Collection:

```
    /// <summary>
    /// Add an item to the class whose type
    /// is determined by the instantiating type
    /// </summary>
    /// <param name="item">item to add</param>
    /// <returns>the zero-based index of the item added</returns>
```

```
public int AddItem(T item)
{
    if (this.ItemCount < this.Items.Length)
    {
        this.Items[this.ItemCount] = item;
        return this.ItemCount++;
    }
    else
        throw new Exception("Item queue is full");
}

/// <summary>
/// Get an item from the class
/// </summary>
/// <param name="index">the zero-based index of the item to get</param>
/// <returns>an item of the instantiating type</returns>
public T GetItem(int index)
{

    if (index >= this.Items.Length &&
        index >= 0)
        throw new ArgumentOutOfRangeException("index");

    return this.Items[index];
}
```

This provides a few advantages, first and foremost of which is the type safety provided by FixedSizeCollection<T> for items in the array. It was possible to write code like this in FixedSizeCollection:

```
// Regular class
FixedSizeCollection C = new FixedSizeCollection(5);
Console.WriteLine(C);

string s1 = "s1";
string s2 = "s2";
string s3 = "s3";
int i1 = 1;

// Add to the fixed size collection (as object).
C.AddItem(s1);
C.AddItem(s2);
C.AddItem(s3);
// Add an int to the string array, perfectly OK.
C.AddItem(i1);
```

But FixedSizeCollection<T> will give a compiler error if you try the same thing:

```
// Generic class
FixedSizeCollection<string> gC = new FixedSizeCollection<string>(5);
Console.WriteLine(gC);

string s1 = "s1";
```

```
string s2 = "s2";
string s3 = "s3";
int i1 = 1;
// Add to the generic class (as string).
gC.AddItem(s1);
gC.AddItem(s2);
gC.AddItem(s3);
// Try to add an int to the string instance, denied by compiler.
// error CS1503: Argument '1': cannot convert from 'int' to 'string'
//gC.AddItem(i1);
```

Having the compiler prevent this before it can become the source of runtime bugs is a very good idea.

It may not be immediately noticeable, but the integer is actually boxed when it is added to the object array in FixedSizeCollection, as you can see in the IL for the call to GetItem on FixedSizeCollection:

```
IL_0177: ldloc.2
IL_0178: ldloc.s i1
IL_017a: box [mscorlib]System.Int32
IL_017f: callvirt instance int32
        CSharpRecipes.ClassesAndGenerics/FixedSizeCollection::AddItem(object)
```

This boxing turns the int, which is a value type, into a reference type (object) for storage in the array. This requires you to do extra work to store value types in the object array.

You'll encounter another problem when you go to retrieve an item from the class in the FixedSizeCollection implementation. Take a look at how FixedSizeCollection.GetItem retrieves an item:

```
// Hold the retrieved string.
string sHolder;

// Have to cast or get error CS0266:
// Cannot implicitly convert type 'object' to 'string'
sHolder = (string)C.GetItem(1);
```

Since the item returned by FixedSizeCollection.GetItem is of type object, you need to cast it to a string in order to get what you hope is a string for index 1. It may not be a string—all you know for sure is that it's an object—but you have to cast it to a more specific type coming out so you can assign it properly.

These issues are both fixed by the FixedSizeCollection<T> implementation. Unlike with FixedSizeCollection, no unboxing is required in FixedSizeCollection<T>, since the return type of GetItem is the instantiated type, and the compiler enforces this by looking at the value being returned:

```
// Hold the retrieved string.
string sHolder;
```

```
int iHolder;

// No cast necessary
sHolder = gC.GetItem(1);

// Try to get a string into an int.
// error CS0029: Cannot implicitly convert type 'string' to 'int'
//iHolder = gC.GetItem(1);
```

To see one other difference between the two types, instantiate a few instances of each like so:

```
// Regular class
FixedSizeCollection A = new FixedSizeCollection(5);
Console.WriteLine(A);
FixedSizeCollection B = new FixedSizeCollection(5);
Console.WriteLine(B);
FixedSizeCollection C = new FixedSizeCollection(5);
Console.WriteLine(C);

// generic class
FixedSizeCollection<bool> gA = new FixedSizeCollection<bool>(5);
Console.WriteLine(gA);
FixedSizeCollection<int> gB = new FixedSizeCollection<int>(5);
Console.WriteLine(gB);
FixedSizeCollection<string> gC = new FixedSizeCollection<string>(5);
Console.WriteLine(gC);
FixedSizeCollection<string> gD = new FixedSizeCollection<string>(5);
Console.WriteLine(gD);
```

The output from the preceding code shows this:

```
There are 1 instances of CSharpRecipes.ClassesAndGenerics+FixedSizeCollection
    and this instance contains 0 items...
There are 2 instances of CSharpRecipes.ClassesAndGenerics+FixedSizeCollection
    and this instance contains 0 items...
There are 3 instances of CSharpRecipes.ClassesAndGenerics+FixedSizeCollection
    and this instance contains 0 items...
There are 1 instances of CSharpRecipes.ClassesAndGenerics+FixedSizeCollection'1
    [System.Boolean] and this instance contains 0 items...
There are 1 instances of CSharpRecipes.ClassesAndGenerics+FixedSizeCollection'1
    [System.Int32] and this instance contains 0 items...
There are 1 instances of CSharpRecipes.ClassesAndGenerics+FixedSizeCollection'1
    [System.String] and this instance contains 0 items...
There are 2 instances of CSharpRecipes.ClassesAndGenerics+FixedSizeCollection'1
    [System.String] and this instance contains 0 items...
```

Discussion

The type parameters in generics allow you to create type-safe code without knowing the final type you will be working with. In many instances, you want the types to have certain characteristics, in which case you place constraints on the type (see Recipe 1.12). Methods can have generic type parameters whether or not the class itself does.

Notice that while `FixedSizeCollection` has three instances, `FixedSizeCollection<T>` has one instance in which it was declared with `bool` as the type, one instance in which `int` was the type, and two instances in which `string` was the type. This means that, while there is one .NET `Type` object created for each nongeneric class, there is one .NET `Type` object for every constructed type of a generic class.

`FixedSizeCollection` has three instances in the example code because `FixedSizeCollection` has only one type that is maintained by the CLR. With generics, one type is maintained for each combination of the class template and the type arguments passed when a type instance is constructed. In other words, you get one .NET type for `FixedSizeCollection<bool>`, one .NET type for `FixedSizeCollection<int>`, and a third .NET type for `FixedSizeCollection<string>`.

The static `InstanceCount` property helps to illustrate this point, as static properties of a class are actually connected to the type that the CLR hangs on to. The CLR creates any given type only once and then maintains it until the `AppDomain` unloads. This is why the output from the calls to `ToString` on these objects shows that the count is 3 for `FixedSizeCollection` (as there is truly only one of these) and 1 or 2 for the `FixedSizeCollection<T>` types.

See Also

The "Generic Type Parameters" and "Generic Classes" topics in the MSDN documentation.

1.11 Reversing the Contents of a Sorted List

Problem

You want to be able to reverse the contents of a sorted list of items while maintaining the ability to access them in both array and list styles like `SortedList` and the generic `SortedList<T>` classes provide. Neither `SortedList` nor `SortedList<T>` provides a direct way to accomplish this without reloading the list.

Solution

Use *LINQ to Objects* to query the `SortedList<T>` and apply a descending order to the information in the list. After you instantiate a `SortedList<TKey, TValue>`, the key of which is an `int` and the value of which is a `string`, a series of unordered numbers and their text representations are inserted into the list. Those items are then displayed:

```
SortedList<int, string> data = new SortedList<int, string>()
    { [2]="two", [5]="five", [3]="three", [1]="one" };

foreach (KeyValuePair<int, string> kvp in data)
{
    Console.WriteLine($"\t {kvp.Key}\t{kvp.Value}");
}
```

The output for the list is shown sorted in ascending order (the default):

```
1    one
2    two
3    three
5    five
```

Now you reverse the sort order by creating a query using LINQ to Objects and setting the orderby clause to descending. The results are then displayed from the query result set:

```
// query ordering by descending
var query = from d in data
            orderby d.Key descending
            select d;

foreach (KeyValuePair<int, string> kvp in query)
{
    Console.WriteLine($"\t {kvp.Key}\t{kvp.Value}");
}
```

This time the output is in descending order:

```
5    five
3    three
2    two
1    one
```

When you add a new item to the list, it is added in the ascending sort order, but by querying again after adding all of the items, you keep the ordering of the list intact:

```
data.Add(4, "four");

// requery ordering by descending
query = from d in data
        orderby d.Key descending
        select d;

foreach (KeyValuePair<int, string> kvp in query)
{
    Console.WriteLine($"\t {kvp.Key}\t{kvp.Value}");
}
Console.WriteLine("");

// Just go against the original list for ascending
foreach (KeyValuePair<int, string> kvp in data)
```

```
{
    Console.WriteLine($"\t {kvp.Key}\t{kvp.Value}");
}
```

You can see the output in both descending and ascending order with the new item:

```
5    five
4    four
3    three
2    two
1    one

1    one
2    two
3    three
4    four
5    five
```

Discussion

A `SortedList` blends array and list syntax to allow you to access the data in either format, which can be a handy thing to do. The data is accessible as key/value pairs or directly by index and will not allow you to add duplicate keys. In addition, values that are reference or nullable types can be `null`, but keys cannot. You can iterate over the items using a `foreach` loop, with `KeyValuePair` being the type returned. While accessing elements of the `SortedList<T>`, you may only read from them. The usual iterator syntax prohibits you from updating or deleting elements of the list while reading, as it will invalidate the iterator.

The `orderby` clause in the query orders the result set of the query either in `ascending` (the default) or `descending` order. This sorting is accomplished through use of the default comparer for the element type, so you can alter it by overriding the `Equals` method for elements that are custom classes. You can specify multiple keys for the `orderby` clause, which has the effect of nesting the sort order, such as sorting by "last name" and then "first name."

See Also

The "SortedList," "Generic KeyValuePair Structure," and "Generic SortedList" topics in the MSDN documentation.

1.12 Constraining Type Arguments

Problem

Your generic type needs to be created with a type argument that must support the members of a particular interface, such as `IDisposable`.

Solution

Use constraints to force the type arguments of a generic type to be of a type that implements one or more particular interfaces:

```
public class DisposableList<T> : IList<T>
    where T : class, IDisposable
{
    private List<T> _items = new List<T>();

    // Private method that will dispose of items in the list
    private void Delete(T item) => item.Dispose();

    // IList<T> Members
    public int IndexOf(T item) => _items.IndexOf(item);

    public void Insert(int index, T item) => _items.Insert(index, item);

    public T this[int index]
    {
        get    {return (_items[index]);}
        set    {_items[index] = value;}
    }

    public void RemoveAt(int index)
    {
        Delete(this[index]);
        _items.RemoveAt(index);
    }

    // ICollection<T> Members
    public void Add(T item) => _items.Add(item);

    public bool Contains(T item) => _items.Contains(item);

    public void CopyTo(T[] array, int arrayIndex) =>
                    _items.CopyTo(array, arrayIndex);

    public int Count  => _items.Count;

    public bool IsReadOnly  => false;

    // IEnumerable<T> Members
    public IEnumerator<T> GetEnumerator()=> _items.GetEnumerator();

    // IEnumerable Members
    IEnumerator IEnumerable.GetEnumerator()=> _items.GetEnumerator();

    // Other members
    public void Clear()
    {
        for (int index = 0; index < _items.Count; index++)
```

```
        {
            Delete(_items[index]);
        }

        _items.Clear();
    }

    public bool Remove(T item)
    {
        int index = _items.IndexOf(item);

        if (index >= 0)
        {
            Delete(_items[index]);
            _items.RemoveAt(index);

            return (true);
        }
        else
        {
            return (false);
        }
    }
}
```

This `DisposableList` class allows only an object that implements `IDisposable` to be passed in as a type argument to this class. The reason for this is that whenever an object is removed from a `DisposableList` object, the `Dispose` method is always called on that object. This allows you to transparently handle the management of any object stored within this `DisposableList` object.

The following code exercises a `DisposableList` object:

```
public static void TestDisposableListCls()
{
    DisposableList<StreamReader> dl = new DisposableList<StreamReader>();

    // Create a few test objects.
    StreamReader tr1 = new StreamReader("C:\\Windows\\system.ini");
    StreamReader tr2 = new StreamReader("c:\\Windows\\vmgcoinstall.log");
    StreamReader tr3 = new StreamReader("c:\\Windows\\Starter.xml");

    // Add the test object to the DisposableList.
    dl.Add(tr1);
    dl.Insert(0, tr2);
    dl.Add(tr3);

    foreach(StreamReader sr in dl)
    {
        Console.WriteLine($"sr.ReadLine() == {sr.ReadLine()}");
    }
```

```
        // Call Dispose before any of the disposable objects are
        // removed from the DisposableList.
        dl.RemoveAt(0);
        dl.Remove(tr1);
        dl.Clear();
    }
```

Discussion

The `where` keyword is used to constrain a type parameter to accept only arguments that satisfy the given constraint. For example, the `DisposableList` has the constraint that any type argument `T` must implement the `IDisposable` interface:

```
public class DisposableList<T> : IList<T>
        where T : IDisposable
```

This means that the following code will compile successfully:

```
DisposableList<StreamReader> dl = new DisposableList<StreamReader>();
```

but the following code will not:

```
DisposableList<string> dl = new DisposableList<string>();
```

This is because the `string` type does not implement the `IDisposable` interface, and the `StreamReader` type does.

Other constraints on the type argument are allowed, in addition to requiring one or more specific interfaces to be implemented. You can force a type argument to be inherited from a specific base class, such as the `TextReader` class:

```
public class DisposableList<T> : IList<T>
        where T : System.IO.TextReader, IDisposable
```

You can also determine if the type argument is narrowed down to only value types or only reference types. The following class declaration is constrained to using only value types:

```
public class DisposableList<T> : IList<T>
        where T : struct
```

This class declaration is constrained to only reference types:

```
public class DisposableList<T> : IList<T>
        where T : class
```

In addition, you can also require any type argument to implement a public default constructor:

```
public class DisposableList<T> : IList<T>
        where T : IDisposable, new()
```

Using constraints allows you to write generic types that accept a narrower set of available type arguments. If the `IDisposable` constraint is omitted in the Solution for this recipe, a compile-time error will occur. This is because not all of the types that can be used as the type argument for the `DisposableList` class will implement the `IDisposable` interface. If you skip this compile-time check, a `DisposableList` object may contain objects that do not have a public no-argument `Dispose` method. In this case, a runtime exception will occur. Generics and constraints in particular force strict type checking of the class-type arguments and allow you to catch these problems at compile time rather than at runtime.

See Also

The "where Keyword" topic in the MSDN documentation.

1.13 Initializing Generic Variables to Their Default Values

Problem

You have a generic class that contains a variable of the same type as the type parameter defined by the class itself. Upon construction of your generic object, you want that variable to be initialized to its default value.

Solution

Simply use the `default` keyword to initialize that variable to its default value:

```
public class DefaultValueExample<T>
{
    T data = default(T);

    public bool IsDefaultData()
    {
        T temp = default(T);

        if (temp.Equals(data))
        {
            return (true);
        }
        else
        {
            return (false);
        }
    }

    public void SetData(T val) => data = value;
}
```

The code to exercise this class is shown here:

```
public static void ShowSettingFieldsToDefaults()
{
```

```
DefaultValueExample<int> dv = new DefaultValueExample<int>();

// Check if the data is set to its default value; true is returned.
bool isDefault = dv.IsDefaultData();
Console.WriteLine($"Initial data: {isDefault}");
// Set data.
dv.SetData(100);
// Check again, this time a false is returned.
isDefault = dv.IsDefaultData();
Console.WriteLine($"Set data: {isDefault}");
}
```

The first call to `IsDefaultData` returns `true`, while the second returns `false`. The output is shown here:

```
Initial data: True
Set data: False
```

Discussion

When initializing a variable of the same type parameter as the generic class, you cannot just set that variable to `null`. What if the type parameter is a value type such as an `int` or `char`? This will not work because value types cannot be `null`. You may be thinking that a nullable type such as `long?` or `Nullable<long>` can be set to `null` (see "Using Nullable Types (C# Programming Guide)" in the MSDN documentation for more on nullable types). However, the compiler has no way of knowing what type argument the user will use to construct the type.

The `default` keyword allows you to tell the compiler that at compile time the default value of this variable should be used. If the type argument supplied is a numeric value (e.g., `int`, `long`, `decimal`), then the default value is `0`. If the type argument supplied is a reference type, then the default value is `null`. If the type argument supplied is a struct, then you determine the default value by initializing each member field to its default value.

See Also

The "Using Nullable Types (C# Programming Guide)" and "default Keyword in Generic Code" topics in the MSDN documentation.

1.14 Adding Hooks to Generated Entities

Problem

You have a process to generate your partial class business entity definitions, and you want to add a lightweight notification mechanism.

Solution

Use partial methods to add hooks in the generated code for the business entities.

The process to generate the entities may be from UML (Unified Modeling Language), a data set, or some other object-modeling facility, but when the code is generated as partial classes, add partial method hooks into the templates for the properties that call a ChangingProperty partial method, as shown in the GeneratedEntity class:

```
public partial class GeneratedEntity
{
    public GeneratedEntity(string entityName)
    {
        this.EntityName = entityName;
    }

    partial void ChangingProperty(string name, string originalValue,
                                  stringnewValue);

    public string EntityName { get; }
    private string _FirstName;
    public string FirstName
    {
        get { return _FirstName; }
        set
        {
            ChangingProperty("FirstName",_FirstName,value);
            _FirstName = value;
        }
    }
    private string _State;
    public string State
    {
        get { return _State; }
        set
        {
            ChangingProperty("State",_State,value);
            _State = value;
        }
    }
}
```

The GeneratedEntity has two properties, FirstName and State. Notice each of these properties has the same boilerplate code that calls the ChangingProperty method with the name of the property, the original, and the new values. If the generated class is used at this point, the ChangingProperty declaration and method will be removed by the compiler, as there is no implementation for ChangingProperty. If an implementation is supplied to report on property changes as shown here, then all of the partial method code for ChangingProperty will be retained and executed:

```
public partial class GeneratedEntity
{
    partial void ChangingProperty(string name, string originalValue,
                                  string newValue)
    {
        Console.WriteLine($"Changed property ({name}) for entity " +
                          $"{this.EntityName} from " +
                          $"{originalValue} to {newValue}");
    }
}
```

Discussion

When using partial methods, be aware of the following:

- You indicate a partial method with the `partial` modifier.
- Partial methods can be declared only in partial classes.
- Partial methods might have only a declaration and no body.
- From a signature standpoint, a partial method can have arguments, require a void return value, and must not have any access modifier, and `partial` implies that this method is private and can be static, generic, or unsafe.
- For generic partial methods, constraints must be repeated on the declaring and implementing versions.
- A partial method may not implement an interface member since interface members must be public.
- None of the virtual, abstract, override, new, sealed, or extern modifiers may be used.
- Arguments to a partial method cannot use `out`, but they can use `ref`.

Partial methods are similar to conditional methods, except that the method definition is always present in conditional methods, even when the condition is not met. Partial methods do not retain the method definition if there is no matching implementation. The code in the Solution could be used like this:

```
public static void TestPartialMethods()
{
    Console.WriteLine("Start entity work");
    GeneratedEntity entity = new GeneratedEntity("FirstEntity");
    entity.FirstName = "Bob";
    entity.State = "NH";
    GeneratedEntity secondEntity = new GeneratedEntity("SecondEntity");
    entity.FirstName = "Jay";
    secondEntity.FirstName = "Steve";
    secondEntity.State = "MA";
    entity.FirstName = "Barry";
```

```
        secondEntity.State = "WA";
        secondEntity.FirstName = "Matt";
        Console.WriteLine("End entity work");
    }
```

to produce the following output when the ChangingProperty implementation is provided:

```
Start entity work
Changed property (FirstName) for entity FirstEntity from to Bob
Changed property (State) for entity FirstEntity from to NH
Changed property (FirstName) for entity FirstEntity from Bob to Jay
Changed property (FirstName) for entity SecondEntity from to Steve
Changed property (State) for entity SecondEntity from to MA
Changed property (FirstName) for entity FirstEntity from Jay to Barry
Changed property (State) for entity SecondEntity from MA to WA
Changed property (FirstName) for entity SecondEntity from Steve to Matt
End entity work
```

or to produce the following output when the ChangingProperty implementation is *not* provided:

```
Start entity work
End entity work
```

See Also

The "Partial Methods" and "partial (Method)" topics in the MSDN documentation.

1.15 Controlling How a Delegate Fires Within a Multicast Delegate

Problem

You have combined multiple delegates to create a multicast delegate. When this multicast delegate is invoked, each delegate within it is invoked in turn. You need to exert more control over the order in which each delegate is invoked, firing only a subset of delegates, or firing each delegate based on the success or failure of previous delegates. Additionally, you need to be able to handle the return value of each delegate separately.

Solution

Use the GetInvocationList method to obtain an array of Delegate objects. Next, iterate over this array using a for (if enumerating in a nonstandard order) or foreach (for enumerating in a standard order) loop. You can then invoke each Delegate object in the array individually and, optionally, retrieve each delegate's unique return value.

In C#, all delegate types support multicast—that is, any delegate instance can invoke multiple methods each time the instance is invoked if it has been set up to do so. In this recipe, we use the term *multicast* to describe a delegate that has been set up to invoke multiple methods.

The following method creates a multicast delegate called `allInstances` and then uses `GetInvocationList` to allow each delegate to be invoked individually, in reverse order. The `Func<int>` generic delegate is used to create delegate instances that return an `int`:

```
public static void InvokeInReverse()
{
    Func<int> myDelegateInstance1 = TestInvokeIntReturn.Method1;
    Func<int> myDelegateInstance2 = TestInvokeIntReturn.Method2;
    Func<int> myDelegateInstance3 = TestInvokeIntReturn.Method3;

    Func<int> allInstances =
            myDelegateInstance1 +
            myDelegateInstance2 +
            myDelegateInstance3;

    Console.WriteLine("Fire delegates in reverse");
    Delegate[] delegateList = allInstances.GetInvocationList();
    foreach (Func<int> instance in delegateList.Reverse())
    {
        instance();
    }
}
```

Note that to roll over the delegate list retrieved using `GetInvocationList`, we use the `IEnumerable<T>` extension method `Reverse` so that we get the items in the opposite order of how the enumeration would normally produce them.

As the following methods demonstrate by firing every other delegate, you don't have to invoke all of the delegates in the list. `InvokeEveryOtherOperation` uses an extension method created here for `IEnumerable<T>` called `EveryOther` that will return only every other item from the enumeration.

 If a unicast delegate was used and you called `GetInvocationList` on it, you will receive a list of one delegate instance.

```
public static void InvokeEveryOtherOperation()
{
    Func<int> myDelegateInstance1 = TestInvokeIntReturn.Method1;
    Func<int> myDelegateInstance2 = TestInvokeIntReturn.Method2;
    Func<int> myDelegateInstance3 = TestInvokeIntReturn.Method3;
```

```
    Func<int> allInstances = myDelegateInstance1 +
                             myDelegateInstance2 +
                             myDelegateInstance3;

    Delegate[] delegateList = allInstances.GetInvocationList();
    Console.WriteLine("Invoke every other delegate");
    foreach (Func<int> instance in delegateList.EveryOther())
    {
        // invoke the delegate
        int retVal = instance();
        Console.WriteLine($"Delegate returned {retVal}");
    }
}

static IEnumerable<T> EveryOther<T>(this IEnumerable<T> enumerable)
{
    bool retNext = true;
    foreach (T t in enumerable)
    {
        if (retNext) yield return t;
        retNext = !retNext;
    }
}
```

The following class contains each of the methods that will be called by the multicast delegate allInstances:

```
public class TestInvokeIntReturn
{
    public static int Method1()
    {
        Console.WriteLine("Invoked Method1");
        return 1;
    }

    public static int Method2()
    {
        Console.WriteLine("Invoked Method2");
        return 2;
    }

    public static int Method3()
    {
        Console.WriteLine("Invoked Method3");
        return 3;
    }
}
```

You can also specify whether to continue firing delegates in the list based on the return value of the currently firing delegate. The following method fires each delegate, stopping only when a delegate returns a false value:

```
public static void InvokeWithTest()
{
    Func<bool> myDelegateInstanceBool1 = TestInvokeBoolReturn.Method1;
    Func<bool> myDelegateInstanceBool2 = TestInvokeBoolReturn.Method2;
    Func<bool> myDelegateInstanceBool3 = TestInvokeBoolReturn.Method3;

    Func<bool> allInstancesBool =
            myDelegateInstanceBool1 +
            myDelegateInstanceBool2 +
            myDelegateInstanceBool3;

    Console.WriteLine(
        "Invoke individually (Call based on previous return value):");
    foreach (Func<bool> instance in allInstancesBool.GetInvocationList())
    {
        if (!instance())
            break;
    }
}
```

The following class contains each of the methods that will be called by the multicast delegate `allInstancesBool`:

```
public class TestInvokeBoolReturn
{
    public static bool Method1()
    {
        Console.WriteLine("Invoked Method1");
        return true;
    }

    public static bool Method2()
    {
        Console.WriteLine("Invoked Method2");
        return false;
    }

    public static bool Method3()
    {
        Console.WriteLine("Invoked Method3");
        return true;
    }
}
```

Discussion

A delegate, when called, will invoke all delegates stored within its *invocation list*. These delegates are usually invoked sequentially from the first to the last one added. Using the `GetInvocationList` method of the `MulticastDelegate` class, you can obtain each delegate in the invocation list of a multicast delegate. This method accepts no parameters and returns an array of `Delegate` objects that corresponds to the invocation list of the delegate on which this method was called. The returned Del egate array contains the delegates of the invocation list in the order in which they would normally be called; that is, the first element in the Delegate array contains the Delegate object that is normally called first.

This application of the GetInvocationList method enables you to control exactly when and how the delegates in a multicast delegate are invoked, and to prevent the continued invocation of delegates when one delegate fails. This ability is important if each delegate is manipulating data, and one of the delegates fails in its duties but does not throw an exception. If one delegate fails in its duties and the remaining delegates rely on all previous delegates to succeed, you must quit invoking delegates at the point of failure.

This recipe handles a delegate failure more efficiently and also provides more flexibility in dealing with these errors. For example, you can write logic to specify which delegates are to be invoked, based on the return values of previously invoked delegates. The following method creates a multicast delegate called All and then uses GetInvo cationList to fire each delegate individually. After firing each delegate, it captures the return value:

```
public static void TestIndividualInvokesReturnValue()
{
    Func<int> myDelegateInstance1 = TestInvokeIntReturn.Method1;
    Func<int> myDelegateInstance2 = TestInvokeIntReturn.Method2;
    Func<int> myDelegateInstance3 = TestInvokeIntReturn.Method3;

    Func<int> allInstances =
            myDelegateInstance1 +
            myDelegateInstance2 +
            myDelegateInstance3;

    Console.WriteLine("Invoke individually (Obtain each return value):");
    foreach (Func<int> instance in allInstances.GetInvocationList())
    {
        int retVal = instance();
        Console.WriteLine($"\tOutput: {retVal}");
    }
}
```

One quirk of a multicast delegate is that if any or all delegates within its invocation list return a value, only the value of the last invoked delegate is returned; all others are lost. This loss can become annoying—or worse, if your code requires these return values. Consider a case in which the allInstances delegate was invoked normally, as in the following code:

```
retVal = allInstances();
Console.WriteLine(retVal);
```

The value 3 would be displayed because `Method3` was the last method invoked by the `allInstances` delegate. None of the other return values would be captured.

By using the `GetInvocationList` method of the `MulticastDelegate` class, you can get around this limitation. This method returns an array of `Delegate` objects that can each be invoked separately. Note that this method does not invoke each delegate; it simply returns an array of them to the caller. By invoking each delegate separately, you can retrieve each return value from each invoked delegate.

Note that any `out` or `ref` parameters will also be lost when a multicast delegate is invoked. This recipe allows you to obtain the `out` and/or `ref` parameters of each invoked delegate within the multicast delegate.

However, you still need to be aware that any unhandled exceptions emanating from one of these invoked delegates will be bubbled up to the method `TestIndividualIn`
`vokesReturnValue` presented in this recipe. If an exception does occur in a delegate that is invoked from within a multicast delegate and that exception is unhandled, any remaining delegates are not invoked. This is the expected behavior of a multicast delegate. However, in some circumstances, you'd like to be able to handle exceptions thrown from individual delegates and then determine at that point whether to continue invoking the remaining delegates.

An unhandled exception will force the invocation of delegates to cease. Exceptions should be used only for exceptional circumstances, not for control flow.

In the following `TestIndividualInvokesExceptions` method, if an exception is caught it is logged to the event log and displayed, and then the code continues to invoke delegates:

```
public static void TestIndividualInvokesExceptions()
{

    Func<int> myDelegateInstance1 = TestInvokeIntReturn.Method1;
    Func<int> myDelegateInstance2 = TestInvokeIntReturn.Method2;
    Func<int> myDelegateInstance3 = TestInvokeIntReturn.Method3;

    Func<int> allInstances =
            myDelegateInstance1 +
            myDelegateInstance2 +
            myDelegateInstance3;

    Console.WriteLine("Invoke individually (handle exceptions):");

    // Create an instance of a wrapper exception to hold any exceptions
    // encountered during the invocations of the delegate instances
```

```csharp
    List<Exception> invocationExceptions = new List<Exception>();

    foreach (Func<int> instance in allInstances.GetInvocationList())
    {
        try
        {
            int retVal = instance();
            Console.WriteLine($"\tOutput: {retVal}");
        }
        catch (Exception ex)
        {
            // Display and log the exception and continue
            Console.WriteLine(ex.ToString());
            EventLog myLog = new EventLog();
            myLog.Source = "MyApplicationSource";
            myLog.WriteEntry(
                $"Failure invoking {instance.Method.Name} with error " +
                $"{ex.ToString()}",
                EventLogEntryType.Error);
            // add this exception to the list
            invocationExceptions.Add(ex);
        }
    }
    // if we caught any exceptions along the way, throw our
    // wrapper exception with all of them in it.
    if (invocationExceptions.Count > 0)
    {
        throw new MulticastInvocationException(invocationExceptions);
    }
}
```

The MulticastInvocationException class, used in the previous code, can have multiple exceptions added to it. It exposes a ReadOnlyCollection<Exception> through the InvocationExceptions property, as shown here:

```csharp
[Serializable]
public class MulticastInvocationException : Exception
{
    private List<Exception> _invocationExceptions;

    public MulticastInvocationException()
        : base()
    {
    }

    public MulticastInvocationException(
    IEnumerable<Exception> invocationExceptions)
    {
        _invocationExceptions = new List<Exception>(invocationExceptions);
    }

    public MulticastInvocationException(string message)
```

```csharp
        : base(message)
    {
    }

    public MulticastInvocationException(string message, Exception innerException)
        :base(message,innerException)
    {
    }

    protected MulticastInvocationException(SerializationInfo info,
        StreamingContext
            context) :
        base(info, context)
    {
        _invocationExceptions =
            (List<Exception>)info.GetValue("InvocationExceptions",
                typeof(List<Exception>));
    }

    [SecurityPermissionAttribute(SecurityAction.Demand,
        SerializationFormatter = true)]
    public override void GetObjectData(
        SerializationInfo info, StreamingContext context)
    {
        info.AddValue("InvocationExceptions", this.InvocationExceptions);
        base.GetObjectData(info, context);
    }

    public ReadOnlyCollection<Exception> InvocationExceptions =>
            new ReadOnlyCollection<Exception>(_invocationExceptions);
}
```

This strategy allows for as fine-grained handling of exceptions as you need. One option is to store all of the exceptions that occur during delegate processing, and then wrap all of the exceptions encountered during processing in a custom exception. After processing completes, throw the custom exception.

By adding a finally block to this try-catch block, you can be assured that code within this finally block is executed after every delegate returns. This technique is useful if you want to interleave code between calls to delegates, such as code to clean up objects that are not needed or code to verify that each delegate left the data it touched in a stable state.

See Also

The "Delegate Class" and "Delegate.GetInvocationList Method" topics in the MSDN documentation.

1.16 Using Closures in C#

Problem

You want to associate a small amount of state with some behavior without going to the trouble of building a new class.

Solution

Use lambda expressions to implement *closures*, functions that capture the state of the environment that is in scope where they are declared. Put more simply, closures are current state plus some behavior that can read and modify that state. Lambda expressions have the capacity to capture external variables and extend their lifetime, which makes closures possible in C#.

 For more information on lambda expressions, see the introduction to Chapter 4.

As an example, you will build a quick reporting system that tracks sales personnel and their revenue production versus commissions. The closure behavior is that you can build one bit of code that does the commission calculations per quarter and works on every salesperson.

First, you have to define your sales personnel:

```
class SalesPerson
{
    // CTOR's
    public SalesPerson()
    {
    }

    public SalesPerson(string name,
                       decimal annualQuota,
                       decimal commissionRate)
    {
        this.Name = name;
        this.AnnualQuota = annualQuota;
        this.CommissionRate = commissionRate;
    }

    // Private Members
    decimal _commission;

    // Properties
```

```
    public string Name { get; set; }

    public decimal AnnualQuota { get; set; }

    public decimal CommissionRate { get; set; }

    public decimal Commission
    {
        get { return _commission; }
        set
        {
            _commission = value;
            this.TotalCommission += _commission;
        }
    }
    public decimal TotalCommission {get; private set; }
}
```

Sales personnel have a name, an annual quota, a commission rate for sales, and some storage for holding a quarterly commission and a total commission. Now that you have something to work with, let's write a bit of code to do the work of calculating the commissions:

```
delegate void CalculateEarnings(SalesPerson sp);

static CalculateEarnings GetEarningsCalculator(decimal quarterlySales,
                                    decimal bonusRate)
{
    return salesPerson =>
    {
        // Figure out the salesperson's quota for the quarter.
        decimal quarterlyQuota = (salesPerson.AnnualQuota / 4);
        // Did he make quota for the quarter?
        if (quarterlySales < quarterlyQuota)
        {
            // Didn't make quota, no commission
            salesPerson.Commission = 0;
        }
        // Check for bonus-level performance (200% of quota).
        else if (quarterlySales > (quarterlyQuota * 2.0m))
        {
            decimal baseCommission = quarterlyQuota *
            salesPerson.CommissionRate;
            salesPerson.Commission = (baseCommission +
                    ((quarterlySales - quarterlyQuota) *
                    (salesPerson.CommissionRate * (1 + bonusRate))));
        }
        else // Just regular commission
        {
            salesPerson.Commission =
                salesPerson.CommissionRate * quarterlySales;
        }
```

```
        };
    }
```

You've declared the delegate type as `CalculateEarnings`, and it takes a `SalesPerson` type. You have a factory method to construct an instance of this delegate for you, called `GetEarningsCalculator`, which creates a lambda expression to calculate the `SalesPerson`'s commission and returns a `CalculateEarnings` instantiation.

To get started, create your array of salespeople:

```
// set up the salespeople...
SalesPerson[] salesPeople = {
    new SalesPerson { Name="Chas", AnnualQuota=100000m, CommissionRate=0.10m },
    new SalesPerson { Name="Ray", AnnualQuota=200000m, CommissionRate=0.025m },
    new SalesPerson { Name="Biff", AnnualQuota=50000m, CommissionRate=0.001m }};
```

Then set up the earnings calculators based on quarterly earnings:

```
public class QuarterlyEarning
{
    public string Name { get; set; }
    public decimal Earnings { get; set; }
    public decimal Rate { get; set; }
}
QuarterlyEarning[] quarterlyEarnings =
        { new QuarterlyEarning(){ Name="Q1", Earnings = 65000m, Rate = 0.1m },
          new QuarterlyEarning(){ Name="Q2", Earnings = 20000m, Rate = 0.1m },
          new QuarterlyEarning(){ Name="Q3", Earnings = 37000m, Rate = 0.1m },
          new QuarterlyEarning(){ Name="Q4", Earnings = 110000m, Rate = 0.15m}
        };

var calculators = from e in quarterlyEarnings
                select new
                {
                    Calculator =
                        GetEarningsCalculator(e.Earnings, e.Rate),
                    QuarterlyEarning = e
                };
```

Finally, run the numbers for each quarter for all the salespeople, and then you can generate the annual report from this data by calling `WriteCommissionReport`. This will tell the executives which sales personnel are worth keeping:

```
decimal annualEarnings = 0;
foreach (var c in calculators)
{
    WriteQuarterlyReport(c.QuarterlyEarning.Name,
        c.QuarterlyEarning.Earnings, c.Calculator, salesPeople);
    annualEarnings += c.QuarterlyEarning.Earnings;
}

// Let's see who is worth keeping...
WriteCommissionReport(annualEarnings, salesPeople);
```

WriteQuarterlyReport invokes the CalculateEarnings lambda expression implementation (eCalc) for every SalesPerson and modifies the state to assign quarterly commission values based on the commission rates for each one:

```
static void WriteQuarterlyReport(string quarter,
                                 decimal quarterlySales,
                                 CalculateEarnings eCalc,
                                 SalesPerson[] salesPeople)
{
    Console.WriteLine($"{quarter} Sales Earnings on Quarterly Sales of
                      {quarterlySales.ToString("C")}:");
    foreach (SalesPerson salesPerson in salesPeople)
    {
        // Calc commission
        eCalc(salesPerson);
        // Report
        Console.WriteLine($"\tSales person {salesPerson.Name} " +
                          "made a commission of : " +
                          $"{salesPerson.Commission.ToString("C")}");
    }
}
```

WriteCommissionReport checks the revenue earned by the individual salesperson against his commission, and if his commission is more than 20 percent of the revenue he generated, you recommend action be taken:

```
static void WriteCommissionReport(decimal annualEarnings,
                                  SalesPerson[] salesPeople)
{
    decimal revenueProduced = ((annualEarnings) / salesPeople.Length);
    Console.WriteLine("");

    Console.WriteLine($"Annual Earnings were {annualEarnings.ToString("C")}");
    Console.WriteLine("");
    var whoToCan = from salesPerson in salesPeople
                   select new
                   {
                       // if his commission is more than 20%
                       // of what he produced, can him
                       CanThem = (revenueProduced * 0.2m) <
                                 salesPerson.TotalCommission,
                       salesPerson.Name,
                       salesPerson.TotalCommission
                   };

    foreach (var salesPersonInfo in whoToCan)
    {
        Console.WriteLine($"\t\tPaid {salesPersonInfo.Name} " +
                $"{salesPersonInfo.TotalCommission.ToString("C")} to produce" +
                $"{revenueProduced.ToString("C")}");
        if (salesPersonInfo.CanThem)
        {
```

```
                Console.WriteLine($"\t\t\tFIRE {salesPersonInfo.Name}!");
            }
        }
    }
```

The output for your revenue- and commission-tracking program is listed here for your enjoyment:

```
Q1 Sales Earnings on Quarterly Sales of $65,000.00:
        SalesPerson Chas made a commission of : $6,900.00
        SalesPerson Ray made a commission of : $1,625.00
        SalesPerson Biff made a commission of : $70.25
Q2 Sales Earnings on Quarterly Sales of $20,000.00:
        SalesPerson Chas made a commission of : $0.00
        SalesPerson Ray made a commission of : $0.00
        SalesPerson Biff made a commission of : $20.00
Q3 Sales Earnings on Quarterly Sales of $37,000.00:
        SalesPerson Chas made a commission of : $3,700.00
        SalesPerson Ray made a commission of : $0.00
        SalesPerson Biff made a commission of : $39.45
Q4 Sales Earnings on Quarterly Sales of $110,000.00:
        SalesPerson Chas made a commission of : $12,275.00
        SalesPerson Ray made a commission of : $2,975.00
        SalesPerson Biff made a commission of : $124.63

Annual Earnings were $232,000.00

    Paid Chas $22,875.00 to produce $77,333.33
        FIRE Chas!
    Paid Ray $4,600.00 to produce $77,333.33
    Paid Biff $254.33 to produce $77,333.33
```

Discussion

One of the best descriptions of closures in C# is to think of an object as a set of methods associated with data and to think of a closure as a set of data associated with a function. If you need to have several different operations on the same data, an object approach may make more sense. These are two different angles on the same problem, and the type of problem you are solving will help you decide which is the right approach. It just depends on your inclination as to which way to go. There are times when 100% pure object-oriented programming can get tedious and is unnecessary, and closures are a nice way to solve some of those problems. The SalesPerson commission example presented here is a demonstration of what you can do with closures. It could have been done without them, but at the expense of writing more class and method code.

Closures were defined earlier, but there is a stricter definition that essentially implies that the behavior associated with the state should not be able to modify the state in order to be a true closure. We tend to agree more with the first definition, as it expresses what a closure should be, not how it should be implemented, which seems too restrictive. Whether you choose to think of this approach as a neat side feature of lambda expressions or you feel it is worthy of being called a closure, it is another programming trick for your toolbox and should not be dismissed.

See Also

Recipe 1.17 and the "Lambda Expressions" topic in the MSDN documentation.

1.17 Performing Multiple Operations on a List Using Functors

Problem

You want to be able to perform multiple operations on an entire collection of objects at once, while keeping the operations functionally segmented.

Solution

Use a *functor* (or *function object*) as the vehicle for transforming the collection. A functor is any object that can be called as a function. Examples are a delegate, a function, a function pointer, or even an object that defines operator for us C/C++ converts.

Needing to perform multiple operations on a collection is a reasonably common scenario in software. Let's say that you have a stock portfolio with a bunch of stocks in it. Your StockPortfolio class would have a List of Stock objects and would allow you to add stocks:

```
public class StockPortfolio : IEnumerable<Stock>
{
    List<Stock> _stocks;

    public StockPortfolio()
    {
        _stocks = new List<Stock>();
    }

    public void Add(string ticker, double gainLoss)
    {
        _stocks.Add(new Stock() {Ticker=ticker, GainLoss=gainLoss});
    }

    public IEnumerable<Stock> GetWorstPerformers(int topNumber) =>
        _stocks.OrderBy((Stock stock) => stock.GainLoss).Take(topNumber);

    public void SellStocks(IEnumerable<Stock> stocks)
```

```
    {
        foreach(Stock s in stocks)
            _stocks.Remove(s);
    }

    public void PrintPortfolio(string title)
    {
        Console.WriteLine(title);
        _stocks.DisplayStocks();
    }

    #region IEnumerable<Stock> Members
    public IEnumerator<Stock> GetEnumerator() => _stocks.GetEnumerator();
    #endregion

    #region IEnumerable Members
    IEnumerator IEnumerable.GetEnumerator() => this.GetEnumerator();
    #endregion
}
```

The Stock class is rather simple. You just need a ticker symbol for the stock and its percentage of gain or loss:

```
public class Stock
{
    public double GainLoss { get; set; }
    public string Ticker { get; set; }
}
```

To use this StockPortfolio, you add a few stocks to it with gain/loss percentages and print out your starting portfolio. Once you have the portfolio, you want to get a list of the three worst-performing stocks, so you can improve your portfolio by selling them and print out your portfolio again:

```
StockPortfolio tech = new StockPortfolio() {
    {"OU81", -10.5},
    {"C#6VR", 2.0},
    {"PCKD", 12.3},
    {"BTML", 0.5},
    {"NOVB", -35.2},
    {"MGDCD", 15.7},
    {"GNRCS", 4.0},
    {"FNCTR", 9.16},
    {"LMBDA", 9.12},
    {"PCLS", 6.11}};

tech.PrintPortfolio("Starting Portfolio");
// sell the worst 3 performers
var worstPerformers = tech.GetWorstPerformers(3);
Console.WriteLine("Selling the worst performers:");
worstPerformers.DisplayStocks();
```

```
tech.SellStocks(worstPerformers);
tech.PrintPortfolio("After Selling Worst 3 Performers");
```

So far, nothing terribly interesting is happening. Let's take a look at how you figured out what the three worst performers were by looking at the internals of the GetWorst Performers method:

```
public IEnumerable<Stock> GetWorstPerformers(int topNumber) => _stocks.OrderBy(
                  (Stock stock) => stock.GainLoss).Take(topNumber);
```

First you make sure the list is sorted with the worst-performing stocks at the front by calling the OrderBy extension method on IEnumerable<T>. The OrderBy method takes a lambda expression that provides the gain/loss percentage for comparison for the number of stocks indicated by topNumber in the Take extension method.

GetWorstPerformers returns an IEnumerable<Stock> full of the three worst performers. Since they aren't making any money, you should cash in and sell them. For your purposes, selling is simply removing them from the list of stocks in StockPortfolio. To accomplish this, you use yet another functor to iterate over the list of stocks handed to the SellStocks function (the list of worst-performing ones, in your case), and then remove that stock from the internal list that the StockPortfolio class maintains:

```
public void SellStocks(IEnumerable<Stock> stocks)
{
    foreach(Stock s in stocks)
        _stocks.Remove(s);
}
```

Discussion

Functors come in a few different flavors: a *generator* (a function with no parameters), a *unary function* (a function with one parameter), and a *binary function* (a function with two parameters). If the functor happens to return a Boolean value, then it gets an even more special naming convention: a unary function that returns a Boolean is called a *predicate*, and a binary function with a Boolean return is called a *binary predicate*. There are both Predicate<T> and BinaryPredicate<T> delegates defined in the Framework to facilitate these uses of functors.

The List<T> and System.Array classes take predicates (Predicate<T>, BinaryPredicate<T>), actions (Action<T>), comparisons (Comparison<T>), and converters (Converter<T,U>). This allows these collections to be operated on in a much more general way than was previously possible.

Thinking in terms of functors can be challenging at first, but once you put a bit of time into it, you start to see powerful possibilities open up before you. Any code you can write once, debug once, and use many times is valuable, and functors can help you achieve that.

The output for the example is listed here:

```
Starting Portfolio
  (OU81) lost 10.5%
  (C#6VR) gained 2%
  (PCKD) gained 12.3%
  (BTML) gained 0.5%
  (NOVB) lost 35.2%
  (MGDCD) gained 15.7%
  (GNRCS) gained 4%
  (FNCTR) gained 9.16%
  (LMBDA) gained 9.12%
  (PCLS) gained 6.11%
Selling the worst performers:
  (NOVB) lost 35.2%
  (OU81) lost 10.5%
  (BTML) gained 0.5%
After Selling Worst 3 Performers
  (C#6VR) gained 2%
  (PCKD) gained 12.3%
  (MGDCD) gained 15.7%
  (GNRCS) gained 4%
  (FNCTR) gained 9.16%
  (LMBDA) gained 9.12%
  (PCLS) gained 6.11%
```

See Also

The "System.Collections.Generic.List<T>," "System.Linq.Enumerable Class," and "System.Array" topics in the MSDN documentation.

1.18 Controlling Struct Field Initialization

Problem

You need to be able to control the initialization of a struct depending on whether you want the struct to initialize all of its internal fields to their standard default values based on their type (e.g., int is initialized to 0 and string is initialized to an empty string), to a nonstandard set of default values, or to a set of predefined values.

Solution

We can use the various constructors for a struct to accomplish our goals. To initialize all the internal fields in a struct to their standard default values based on their type, we simply use the default initialization of structs, which will be demonstrated later. To initialize the struct's fields to a set of predefined values, we use an overloaded constructor. Finally, to initialize our struct to a set of nonstandard default values, we need to use optional arguments in the struct's constructor. With optional arguments, structs are able to set their internal fields based on the default values placed on the optional arguments in the constructor's parameter list.

The data structure in Example 1-8 uses an overloaded constructor to initialize all the fields of the structure.

Example 1-8. Struct with an overloaded constructor

```
public struct Data
{
    public Data(int intData, float floatData, string strData,
                char charData, bool boolData)
    {
        IntData = intData;
        FloatData = floatData;
        StrData = strData;
        CharData = charData;
        BoolData = boolData;
    }

    public int IntData { get; }
    public float FloatData { get; }
    public string StrData { get; }
    public char CharData { get; }
    public bool BoolData { get; }

    public override string ToString()=> IntData + " :: " + FloatData + " :: " +
                    StrData + " :: " + CharData + " :: " + BoolData;
}
```

This is the typical way to initialize the values of the struct's fields. Note also that an implicit default constructor exists that allows this struct to initialize its fields to their default values. However, you may want to have each field initialized with nondefault values. The data structure in Example 1-9 uses an overloaded constructor with optional arguments to initialize all the fields of the structure with nondefault values.

Example 1-9. Struct with optional arguments in the constructor

```
public struct Data
{
    public Data(int intData, float floatData = 1.1f, string strData = "a",
                char charData = 'a', bool boolData = true) : this()
    {
        IntData = intData;
        FloatData = floatData;
        StrData = strData;
```

```
        CharData = charData;
        BoolData = boolData;
    }

    public int IntData { get; }
    public float FloatData { get; }
    public string StrData { get; }
    public char CharData { get; }
    public bool BoolData { get; }

    public override string ToString()=> IntData + " :: " + FloatData + " :: " +
                        StrData + " :: " + CharData + " :: " + BoolData;
}
```

Of course, a new initialization method could be introduced that makes this even easier. But you need to explicitly call it, as shown in Example 1-10.

Example 1-10. Struct with an explicit initialization method

```
public struct Data
{
    public void Init()
    {
        IntData = 2;
        FloatData = 1.1f;
        StrData = "AA";
        CharData = 'A';
        BoolData = true;
    }

    public int IntData { get; private set; }
    public float FloatData { get; private set; }
    public string StrData { get; private set; }
    public char CharData { get; private set; }
    public bool BoolData { get; private set; }

    public override string ToString()=> IntData + " :: " + FloatData + " :: " +
                        StrData + " :: " + CharData + " :: " + BoolData;
}
```

Note that when using an explicit initialization method such as Init, you'll need to add a private property setter for each property in order for each field to be initialized.

Discussion

We can now create instances of the struct in Example 1-8 using different techniques. Each technique uses a different method of initializing this struct object. The first technique uses the default keyword to create this struct:

```
Data dat = default(Data);
```

The default keyword simply creates an instance of this struct with all of its fields initialized to their default values. Essentially this causes all numeric types to default to 0, bool defaults to false, char defaults to '\0', and string and other reference types default to null.

Now, this is great if you don't mind reference types and char to be set to null values, but say that you need to set these types to something other than null when the struct is created. The second technique for creating an instance of this struct does just this; it uses a default parameterless constructor:

```
Data dat = new Data();
```

This code causes the default parameterless constructor to be invoked. The caveat with using a default parameterless constructor on a struct is that the new keyword must be used to create an instance of this struct. If the new keyword is not used, then this default constructor will not be invoked. Therefore, the following code will not call the default parameterless constructor:

```
Data[] dat = new Data[4];
```

Rather, the system-defined default values for each of the struct's fields will be used.

There are two ways to get around this. You could use the overly lengthy way of creating an array of Data structs:

```
Data[] dat = new Data[4];

dat[0] = new Data();
dat[1] = new Data();
dat[2] = new Data();
dat[3] = new Data();
```

or

```
ArrayList dat = new ArrayList();
dat.Add(new Data());
dat.Add(new Data());
dat.Add(new Data());
dat.Add(new Data());
```

Or you could use the more terse option, which uses LINQ:

```
Data[] dataList = new Data[4];
dataList = (from d in dataList
            select new Data()).ToArray();
```

The LINQ expression iterates over the Data array, explicitly invoking the default parameterless constructor for each Data type struct element.

If neither of the first two options will work for your particular case, you could always create an overloaded constructor that takes arguments for each field that you want to initialize. This third technique requires that the overloaded constructor is used to create a new instance of this struct:

```
public Data(int intData, float floatData, string strData,
            char charData, bool boolData)
{
    IntData = intData;
    FloatData = floatData;
    StrData = strData;
    CharData = charData;
    BoolData = boolData;
}
```

This constructor explicitly initialized each field to a user-supplied value:

```
Data dat = new Data(2, 2.2f, "blank", 'a', false);
```

With C# 6.0 you not only have the option of initializing a struct's fields with the system default values or using an overloaded constructor to initialize its fields to user-defined values, but now you have the additional option of using an overloaded constructor with optional arguments to initialize the struct's fields to nonsystem-default values. This is shown in Example 1-9. The constructor with optional arguments looks like this:

```
public Data(int intData, float floatData = 1.1f, string strData = "a",
            char charData = 'a', bool boolData = true) : this()
{
    ...
}
```

The one issue with using this type of constructor is that you must supply at least one of the parameter values to this constructor. If the intData argument also had an associated optional argument:

```
public Data(int intData = 2, float floatData = 1.1f, string strData = "a",
            char charData = 'a', bool boolData = true) : this()
{
    ...
}
```

then this code:

```
Data dat = new Data();
```

would call the default parameterless constructor for the struct, not the overloaded constructor. This is why at least one of the parameters must be passed into this constructor:

```
Data dat = new Data(3);
```

Now we call the overloaded constructor, setting the first parameter, intData, to 3 and the rest of the parameters to their optional values.

As a final option, you can add an explicit initialization method to the struct to initialize the fields to nondefault values. This technique is shown in Example 1-10.

You add the Init method to the struct, and must call it after the struct is initialized either by using the new or default keyword. The Init method then initializes each field to a nondefault value. The only other code modification that you need to make to the struct's properties is adding a private setter method. This allows the Init method to set the internal fields without having to expose them to the outside world.

See Also

The "Struct" topics in the MSDN documentation.

1.19 Checking for null in a More Concise Way

Problem

You are constantly writing unwieldy if-then statements to determine whether an object is null. You need a more concise and simpler way to write this type of code.

Solution

Use the new null-conditional operator introduced in C# 6.0. In the past you would typically have to check to make sure an object is not null before using it in the following manner:

```
if (val != null)
{
    val.Trim().ToUpper();
    ...
}
```

Now you can simply use the null-conditional operator:

```
val?.Trim().ToUpper();
```

This simplified syntax determines if val is null; if so, the Trim and ToUpper methods will not be invoked and you will not throw that annoying NullReferenceException. If val is not null, the Trim and ToUpper methods will be invoked.

This operator can also be employed to test each object for null when the dot operator is used to chain a series of object member accesses:

```
Person?.Address?.State?.Trim();
```

In this case, if any of the first three objects (Person, Address, or State) is null, the dot operator is not invoked for that null object and execution of this expression ceases.

The `null`-conditional operator works not only on regular objects, but also on arrays and indexes as well as the indexed element that is returned. For example, if `val` is of type `string[]`, this code will check to see if the `val` variable is `null`:

```
val?[0].ToUpper();
```

whereas this code checks to see if the actual string element stored in the zeroth indexed position in the `val` array is `null`:

```
val[0]?.ToUpper();
```

This code is also valid; it determines if both `val` and the zeroth indexed element are not `null`:

```
val?[0]?.ToUpper();
```

Another area where the `null`-conditional operator shines is with invoking delegates and events. For instance, if you have a simple delegate:

```
public delegate bool Approval();
```

and instantiate it using a lambda expression, which for simplicity's sake just returns `true` all the time:

```
Approval approvalDelegate = () => { return true; };
```

then later in the code when you want to invoke this delegate you don't have to write any bulky conditional code to determine whether it is `null`; you simply use the `null`-conditional operator:

```
approvalDelegate?.Invoke()
```

Discussion

Essentially the `null`-conditional operator works similarly to the ternary operator (`?:`). The code:

```
val?.Trim();
```

is shorthand for:

```
(val != null ) ? (string)val.Trim() : null
```

assuming `val` is of type `string`.

Let's take a look at what happens when a value type is returned such as in the following code:

```
val?.Length;
```

The expression is modified to return a nullable value type such as `int?`:

```
(val != null ) ? (int?)val.Length : null
```

This means you can't simply use the `null`-conditional operator and then assign the returned value to just any type—it has to be a nullable type. Therefore, this code will not compile:

```
int len = val?.Length;
```

but this code will:

```
int? len = val?.Length;
```

Notice that we have to make the return type a nullable type only when it is a value type.

Additionally, you cannot attempt to use the `null`-conditional operator where a non-nullable type is expected. For example, the array size expects an `int` value, so you cannot compile this code:

```
byte[] data = new byte[val?.Length];
```

However, you could use the `GetValueOrDefault` method to convert the nullable type's value into a non-nullable-friendly value:

```
byte[] data = new byte[(val?.Length).GetValueOrDefault()];
```

This way if `val` is really `null`, the `byte` array will be initialized to the default value for integer types, which is 0. Just be aware that this method will return the default value for that value type, which is 0 for numeric types and `false` for `bool` types. Your code must take this into account so that your application's behavior is consistent. In this example, the `byte` array is of size 0 if the `val` object is of length 0 or is `null`, so your application logic must account for that.

You also need to take care when using this operator in conditional statements:

```
if (val?.Length > 0)
    Console.WriteLine("val.length > 0");
else
    Console.WriteLine("val.length = 0 or null");
```

In this conditional statement, if the `val` variable is non-null and its length is greater than 0, the true block of the `if` statement is executed and the text `"val.length > 0"` is displayed. If `val` is `null`, the false block is displayed and the text `"val.length = 0 or null"` is displayed. However, you don't know which `val` really is—`null` or 0?

If you need to check for `val` having a length of 0, you could add an extra check to the `if`-`else` statement to take into account all conditions:

```
if (val?.Length > 0)
    Console.WriteLine("val.Length > 0");
else if (val?.Length == 0)
    Console.WriteLine("val.Length = 0");
else
    Console.WriteLine("val.Length = null");
```

The `switch` statement operates in a similar manner:

```
switch (val?.Length)
{
    case 0:
        Console.WriteLine("val.Length = 0");
        break;
    case 1:
        Console.WriteLine("val.Length = 1");
        break;
    default:
        Console.WriteLine("val.Length > 1 or val.Length = null");
        break;
}
```

If `val` is `null`, execution will fall through to the `default` block. You won't know if the length of `val` is greater than 1 or `null` unless you perform more checks.

 Take care when using this operator in conditional statements. This can lead to logic errors in your code if you are not careful.

See Also

The "Null-Conditional Operator" topics in the MSDN documentation.

CHAPTER 2

Collections, Enumerators, and Iterators

2.0 Introduction

Collections are groups of items; in .NET, collections contain objects, and each object contained in a collection is called an *element*. Some collections contain a straightforward list of elements, while others (*dictionaries*) contain a list of key/value pairs. The following collection types consist of a straightforward list of elements:

```
System.Collections.ArrayList
System.Collections.BitArray
System.Collections.Queue
System.Collections.Stack
System.Collections.Generic.LinkedList<T>
System.Collections.Generic.List<T>
System.Collections.Generic.Queue<T>
System.Collections.Generic.Stack<T>
System.Collections.Generic.HashSet<T>
```

The next set of collection types are all dictionaries:

```
System.Collections.Hashtable
System.Collections.SortedList
System.Collections.Generic.Dictionary<T,U>
System.Collections.Generic.SortedList<T,U>
```

This last collection type (HashSet<T>) can be thought of as a list of elements with no duplicates:

```
System.Collections.Generic.HashSet<T>
```

These collection classes are organized under the System.Collections and the Sys tem.Collections.Generic namespaces. In addition to these namespaces, there is a namespace called System.Collections.Specialized, which contains a few more useful collection classes. These classes might not be as well known as the previous classes, so here is a short explanation of them:

ListDictionary

This class operates similarly to the Hashtable. However, this class beats out the Hashtable on performance when it contains 10 or fewer elements.

HybridDictionary

This class consists of two internal collections, the ListDictionary and the Hashtable. Only one of these classes is used at any time. The ListDictionary is used while the collection contains 10 or fewer elements, and then a Hashtable is used once the collection grows beyond 10 elements. This switch is made transparently to the developer. Once the Hashtable is used, the collection cannot revert to using the ListDictionary even if the elements number 10 or fewer. Also note that, when you're using strings as the key, this class supports both case-sensitive (with respect to the invariant culture) and case-insensitive string searches through a Boolean value you set in the constructor.

CollectionsUtil

This class contains two static methods: one to create a case-insensitive Hashtable and another to create a case-insensitive SortedList. When you directly create a Hashtable and SortedList object, you always create a case-sensitive Hashtable or SortedList, unless you use one of the constructors that takes an IComparer and pass CaseInsensitiveComparer.Default to it.

NameValueCollection

This collection consists of key/value pairs in which both the key and the value are of type String. The interesting thing about this collection is that it can store multiple string values with a single key. The multiple string values are comma-delimited. The String.Split method is useful for breaking up multiple strings in a value.

StringCollection

This collection is a simple list containing string elements. This list accepts null elements as well as duplicate strings. This list is case-sensitive.

StringDictionary

This is a Hashtable that stores both the key and value as strings. Keys are converted to all-lowercase letters before being added to the Hashtable, allowing for case-insensitive comparisons. Keys cannot be null, but values may be set to null.

The C# compiler also supports a fixed-size array. You can create arrays of any type using the following syntax:

```
int[] foo = new int[2];
T[] bar = new T[2];
```

Here, `foo` is an integer array containing exactly two elements, and `bar` is an array of unknown type `T`.

Arrays come in several styles as well: single-dimensional, jagged, and even jagged multidimensional. Multidimensional arrays are defined here:

```
int[,] foo = new int[2,3];       // A 2-dimensional array
                                 // containing 6 elements

int[,,] bar = new int[2,3,4];    // A 3-dimensional array
                                 // containing 24 elements
```

A two-dimensional array is usually described as a table with rows and columns. The `foo` array would be described as a table of two rows, each containing three columns of elements. A three-dimensional array can be described as a cube with layers of tables. The `bar` array could be described as four layers of two rows, each containing three columns of elements.

Jagged arrays are arrays of arrays. If you picture a jagged array as a one-dimensional array with each element in that array containing another one-dimensional array, it could have a different number of elements in each row. A jagged array is defined as follows:

```
int[][] baz = new int[2][] {new int[2], new int[3]};
```

The `baz` array consists of a one-dimensional array containing two elements. Each of these elements consists of another array, the first array having two elements and the second array having three.

When dealing with collections, you will likely need to examine all of the values in a collection at some point. To help you accomplish this, C# provides the iterator and enumerator constructs. *Iterators* allow for a block of code to yield an ordered sequence of values, while *enumerators* support the iteration over data sets and can be used to read data in a collection but not modify it.

Iterators are a mechanism for producing data that can be iterated over by the `foreach` loop construct. However, iterators are much more flexible than this. You can easily generate a sequence of data returned by the enumerator (known as *lazy computation*); it does not have to be hardcoded up front (as it does in *eager computation*). For example, you could easily write an enumerator that generates the Fibonacci sequence on demand. Another flexible feature of iterators is that you do not have to set a limit on the number of values returned by the iterator, so in this example, you could choose when to stop producing the Fibonacci sequence. This is an interesting distinction in the LINQ (Language Integrated Query) world. Iterators like the one produced by the `IEnumerable` version of `where` are lazy, but grouping or sorting requires eagerness.

Iterators allow you to hand off the work of writing this class to the C# compiler. Now, you need to add only an iterator to your type. An iterator is a member within your type (e.g., a method, an operator overload, or the get accessor of a property) that returns either a System.Collections.IEnumerator, a System.Collections.Generic.IEnumerator<T>, a System.Collections.IEnumerable, or a System.Collections.Generic.IEnumerable<T> and that contains at least one yield statement. This allows you to write types that can be used by foreach loops.

Iterators play an important role in LINQ, as *LINQ to Objects* is based on being able to work on classes that implement IEnumerable<T>. Iterators allow for the query engine to iterate over collections while performing the various query, projection, ordering, and grouping operations. Without iterator support, LINQ would be much more cumbersome, and the declarative style of programming that it brings would be clumsy, if not lost altogether.

2.1 Looking for Duplicate Items in a List<T>

Problem

You need to be able to either retrieve or count the number of occurrences of an object contained in a List<T> that matches a search criterion.

Solution

Use the four extension methods for List<T>: GetAll, BinarySearchGetAll, CountAll, and BinarySearchCountAll. These methods extend the List<T> class to return either instances of a particular object or the number of times a particular object appears in a sorted and an unsorted List<T>, as shown in Example 2-1.

Example 2-1. Determining the number of times an item appears in a List <T>

```
static class CollectionExtMethods
{
    #region 2.1 Looking for Duplicate Items in a List<T>

    // The method to retrieve all matching objects in a
    // sorted or unsorted List<T>
    public static IEnumerable<T> GetAll<T>(this List<T> myList, T searchValue) =>
        myList.Where(t => t.Equals(searchValue));

    // The method to retrieve all matching objects in a sorted ListEx<T>
    public static T[] BinarySearchGetAll<T>(this List<T> myList, T searchValue)
    {
        List<T> retObjs = new List<T>();

        // Search for first item.
        int center = myList.BinarySearch(searchValue);
        if (center > 0)
```

```
        {
            retObjs.Add(myList[center]);

            int left = center;
            while (left > 0 && myList[left - 1].Equals(searchValue))
            {
                left -= 1;
                retObjs.Add(myList[left]);
            }

            int right = center;
            while (right < (myList.Count - 1) &&
                myList[right + 1].Equals(searchValue))
            {
                right += 1;
                retObjs.Add(myList[right]);
            }
        }

        return (retObjs.ToArray());
    }
    // Count the number of times an item appears in this
    //   unsorted or sorted List<T>
    public static int CountAll<T>(this List<T> myList, T searchValue) =>
        myList.GetAll(searchValue).Count();

    // Count the number of times an item appears in this sorted List<T>
    public static int BinarySearchCountAll<T>(this List<T> myList, T searchValue) =>
        BinarySearchGetAll(myList, searchValue).Count();
    #endregion // 2.1
}
```

Discussion

The GetAll and BinarySearchGetAll methods return the actual items found in a
List<T> object. The CountAll and BinarySearchCountAll methods leverage GetAll
and BinarySearchGetAll to provide the count of the items. The main thing to keep
in mind when choosing between GetAll and BinarySearchGetAll is whether you are
going to be looking at a List<T> that is sorted or unsorted. Choose the GetAll and
CountAll methods to obtain either an array of all found items (GetAll) or the number of found items (CountAll) from an unsorted List<T>, and choose the Binary
SearchGetAll and BinarySearchCountAll methods to work with a sorted List<T>.
GetAll, SearchAll, and BinarySearchAll use the expression-bodied member syntax,
as they are simple functions.

The following code demonstrates these two new extension methods of the List<T>
class:

```
// Retrieval
List<int> listRetrieval =
```

```
                new List<int>() { -1, -1, 1, 2, 2, 2, 2, 3, 100, 4, 5 };

        Console.WriteLine("--GET All--");
        IEnumerable<int> items = listRetrieval.GetAll(2);
        foreach (var item in items)
            Console.WriteLine($"item: {item}");

        Console.WriteLine();
        items = listRetrieval.GetAll(-2);
        foreach (var item in items)
            Console.WriteLine($"item-2: {item}");

        Console.WriteLine();
        items = listRetrieval.GetAll(5);
        foreach (var item in items)
            Console.WriteLine($"item5: {item}");

        Console.WriteLine("\r\n--BINARY SEARCH GET ALL--");
        listRetrieval.Sort();
        int[] listItems = listRetrieval.BinarySearchGetAll(-2);
        foreach (var item in listItems)
            Console.WriteLine($"item-2: {item}");

        Console.WriteLine();
        listItems = listRetrieval.BinarySearchGetAll(2);
        foreach (var item in listItems)
            Console.WriteLine($"item2: {item}");

        Console.WriteLine();
        listItems = listRetrieval.BinarySearchGetAll(5);
        foreach (var item in listItems)
            Console.WriteLine($"item5: {item}");
```

This code outputs the following:

```
--GET All--
item: 2
item: 2
item: 2
item: 2


item5: 5

--BINARY SEARCH GET ALL--

item2: 2
item2: 2
item2: 2
item2: 2

item5: 5
```

The `BinarySearchGetAll` method is faster than the `GetAll` method, especially if the array has already been sorted. If a `BinarySearch` is used on an unsorted `List<T>`, the results returned by the search will be incorrect, as it has been consistently documented as a requirement that `List<T>` be sorted.

The `CountAll` method accepts a search value (`searchValue`) of generic type T. `CountAll` then proceeds to count the number of times the search value appears in the `List<T>` class by using the `GetAll` extension method to get the items and calling `Count` on the result. This method may be used when the `List<T>` is sorted or unsorted. If the `List<T>` is sorted (you sort a `List<T>` by calling the `Sort` method), you can use the `BinarySearchCountAll` method to increase the efficiency of the search. You do so by using the `BinarySearchGetAll` extension method on the `List<T>` class, which is much faster than iterating through the entire `List<T>`. This is especially true as the `List<T>` grows in size.

The following code illustrates these two new methods of the `List<T>` class:

```
List<int> list = new List<int>() {-2,-2,-1,-1,1,2,2,2,2,3,100,4,5};

Console.WriteLine("--CONTAINS TOTAL--");
int count = list.CountAll(2);
Console.WriteLine($"Count2: {count}");

count = list.CountAll(3);
Console.WriteLine($"Count3: {count}");

count = list.CountAll(1);
Console.WriteLine($"Count1: {count}");

Console.WriteLine("\r\n--BINARY SEARCH COUNT ALL--");
list.Sort();
count = list.BinarySearchCountAll(2);
Console.WriteLine($"Count2: {count}");

count = list.BinarySearchCountAll(3);
Console.WriteLine($"Count3: {count}");

count = list.BinarySearchCountAll(1);
Console.WriteLine($"Count1: {count}");
```

This code outputs the following:

```
--CONTAINS TOTAL--
Count2: 4
Count3: 1
Count1: 1

--BINARY SEARCH COUNT ALL--
Count2: 4
```

```
Count3: 1
Count1: 1
```

The `CountAll` and `GetAll` methods use a sequential search that is performed in a `for` loop. A linear search must be used since the `List<T>` is not assumed to be sorted. The `where` statement determines whether each element in the `List<T>` is equal to the search criterion (`searchValue`). The items or count of items are returned by these methods to indicate the number of items matching the search criteria in the `List<T>`.

The `BinarySearchGetAll` method implements a binary search to locate an item matching the search criteria (`searchValue`) in the `List<T>`. If one is found, a `while` loop is used to find the very first matching item in the sorted `List<T>`, and the position of that element is recorded in the `left` variable. A second `while` loop is used to find the very last matching item, and the position of this element is recorded in the `right` variable. The value in the `left` variable is subtracted from the value in the `right` variable, and then 1 is added to this result in order to get the total number of matches. `BinarySearchCountAll` uses `BinarySearchGetAll` to get the items and then just calls `Count` on the resulting set.

See Also

The "List<T> Class" topic in the MSDN documentation.

2.2 Keeping Your List<T> Sorted

Problem

You will be using the `BinarySearch` method of the `List<T>` to periodically search the `List<T>` for specific elements. The addition, modification, and removal of elements will be interleaved with the searches. The `BinarySearch` method, however, presupposes a sorted array; if the `List<T>` is not sorted, the `BinarySearch` method will possibly return incorrect results. You do not want to have to remember to always call the `List<T>.Sort` method before calling the `List<T>.BinarySearch` method, not to mention incurring all the overhead associated with this call. You need a way of keeping the `List<T>` sorted without always having to call the `List<T>.Sort` method.

Solution

The following `SortedList` generic class enhances the addition and modification of elements within a `List<T>`. These methods keep the array sorted when items are added to it and modified. Note that a `DeleteSorted` method is not required because deleting an item does not disturb the sorted order of the remaining items:

```
public class SortedList<T> : List<T>
{
    public new void Add(T item)
    {
        int position = this.BinarySearch(item);
        if (position < 0)
            position = ~position;

        this.Insert(position, item);
    }

    public void ModifySorted(T item, int index)
    {
        this.RemoveAt(index);

        int position = this.BinarySearch(item);
        if (position < 0)
            position = ~position;

        this.Insert(position, item);
    }
}
```

Discussion

Use the Add method to add elements while keeping the List<T> sorted. The Add method accepts a generic type (T) to add to the sorted list.

Instead of using the List<T> indexer directly to modify elements, use the ModifySor ted method to modify elements while keeping the List<T> sorted. Call this method, passing in the generic type T to replace the existing object (item) and the index of the object to modify (index).

The following code demonstrates the SortedList<T> class:

```
// Create a SortedList and populate it with
//     randomly chosen numbers
SortedList<int> sortedList = new SortedList<int>();
sortedList.Add(200);
sortedList.Add(20);
sortedList.Add(2);
sortedList.Add(7);
sortedList.Add(10);
sortedList.Add(0);
sortedList.Add(100);
sortedList.Add(-20);
sortedList.Add(56);
sortedList.Add(55);
sortedList.Add(57);
sortedList.Add(200);
sortedList.Add(-2);
```

```
    sortedList.Add(-20);
    sortedList.Add(55);
    sortedList.Add(55);

    // Display it
    foreach (var i in sortedList)
        Console.WriteLine(i);

    // Now modify a value at a particular index
    sortedList.ModifySorted(0, 5);
    sortedList.ModifySorted(1, 10);
    sortedList.ModifySorted(2, 11);
    sortedList.ModifySorted(3, 7);
    sortedList.ModifySorted(4, 2);
    sortedList.ModifySorted(2, 4);
    sortedList.ModifySorted(15, 0);
    sortedList.ModifySorted(0, 15);
    sortedList.ModifySorted(223, 15);

    // Display it
    Console.WriteLine();
    foreach (var i in sortedList)
        Console.WriteLine(i);
```

This method automatically places the new item in the `List<T>` while keeping its sort order; it does so without your having to explicitly call `List<T>.Sort`. The reason this works is because the `Add` method first calls the `BinarySearch` method and passes it the object to be added to the `ArrayList`. The `BinarySearch` method will either return the index where it found an identical item or a negative number that you can use to determine where the item that you are looking for should be located. If the `Binary Search` method returns a positive number, you can use the `List<T>.Insert` method to insert the new element at that location, keeping the sort order within the `List<T>`. If the `BinarySearch` method returns a negative number, you can use the bitwise complement operator ~ to determine where the item should have been located, had it existed in the sorted list. Using this number, you can use the `List<T>.Insert` method to add the item to the correct location in the sorted list while keeping the correct sort order.

You can remove an element from the sorted list without disturbing the sort order, but modifying an element's value in the `List<T>` most likely will cause the sorted list to become unsorted. The `ModifySorted` method alleviates this problem. This method works similarly to the `Add` method, except that it will initially remove the element from the `List<T>` and then insert the new element into the correct location.

See Also

The "List<T> Class" topic in the MSDN documentation.

2.3 Sorting a Dictionary's Keys and/or Values

Problem

You want to sort the keys and/or values contained in a `Dictionary` in order to display the entire `Dictionary` to the user, sorted in either ascending or descending order.

Solution

Use a LINQ query and the `Keys` and `Values` properties of a `Dictionary<T,U>` object to obtain a sorted `ICollection` of its key and value objects. (See Chapter 4 for more on LINQ). The code shown here displays the keys and values of a `Dictionary<T,U>` sorted in ascending or descending order:

```
// Define a Dictionary<T,U> object
Dictionary<string, string> hash = new Dictionary<string, string>()
{
    ["2"] = "two",
    ["1"] = "one",
    ["5"] = "five",
    ["4"] = "four",
    ["3"] = "three"
};

var x = from k in hash.Keys orderby k ascending select k;
foreach (string s in x)
    Console.WriteLine($"Key: {s}  Value: {hash[s]}");

x = from k in hash.Keys orderby k descending select k;
foreach (string s in x)
    Console.WriteLine($"Key: {s}  Value: {hash[s]}");
```

The code shown here displays the values in a `Dictionary<T,U>` sorted in ascending or descending order:

```
x = from k in hash.Values orderby k ascending select k;
foreach (string s in x)
    Console.WriteLine($"Value: {s}");

Console.WriteLine();

x = from k in hash.Values orderby k descending select k;
foreach (string s in x)
    Console.WriteLine($"Value: {s}");
```

Discussion

The `Dictionary<T,U>` object exposes two useful properties for obtaining a collection of its keys or values. The `Keys` property returns an `ICollection` containing all the keys currently in the Dictionary<T,U>. The Values property returns the same for all values currently contained in the Dictionary<T,U>.

The ICollection object returned from either the Keys or Values property of a Dic tionary<T,U> object contains direct references to the key and value collections within the Dictionary<T,U>. This means that if the keys and/or values change in a Dictionary<T,U>, the key and value collections will be altered accordingly.

Note that you can also use the SortedDictionary<T,U> class, which will automatically keep the keys sorted for you. You can use the constructor overload of SortedDic tionary<T,U> to wrap an existing Dictionary<T,U> as well. The Keys property is in ascending order by default, so if you want descending instead you will need to sort the collection for descending order based on Keys:

```
SortedDictionary<string, string> sortedHash =
    new SortedDictionary<string, string>()
{
    ["2"] = "two",
    ["1"] = "one",
    ["5"] = "five",
    ["4"] = "four",
    ["3"] = "three"
};
foreach (string key in sortedHash.Keys)
    Console.WriteLine($"Key: {key}  Value: {sortedHash[key]}");
foreach (string key in sortedHash.OrderByDescending(item =>
    item.Key).Select(item => item.Key))
    Console.WriteLine($"Key: {key}  Value: {sortedHash[key]}");
```

Why would someone choose the LINQ solution shown versus just using SortedDic tionary<T,U>? It is actually faster to perform the ordering in the LINQ query, and the code is cleaner than the code using the SortedDictionary<T,U>, so that is the recommended approach for all versions of .NET that support LINQ (3.0 and greater). If your solution happens to be on an older version of .NET, you still can use Sorted Dictionary<T,U> to accomplish the result.

See Also

The "Dictionary<T,U> Class," "SortedDictionary<T,U> Class," and "List<T> Class" topics in the MSDN documentation.

2.4 Creating a Dictionary with Min and Max Value Boundaries

Problem

You need to use a generic `Dictionary` object in your project that stores only numeric data in its value (the key can be of any type) between a set, predefined maximum and minimum value.

Solution

Create a class with accessors and methods that enforce these boundaries. The class shown in Example 2-2, `MinMaxValueDictionary`, allows only types to be stored that implement the `IComparable` interface and fall between a maximum and minimum value.

Example 2-2. Creating a dictionary with min and max value boundaries

```
[Serializable]
public class MinMaxValueDictionary<T, U>
    where U : IComparable<U>
{
    protected Dictionary<T, U> internalDictionary = null;

    public MinMaxValueDictionary(U minValue, U maxValue)
    {
        this.MinValue = minValue;
        this.MaxValue = maxValue;
        internalDictionary = new Dictionary<T, U>();
    }

    public U MinValue { get; private set; } = default(U);
    public U MaxValue { get; private set; } = default(U);

    public int Count => (internalDictionary.Count);

    public Dictionary<T, U>.KeyCollection Keys => (internalDictionary.Keys);

    public Dictionary<T, U>.ValueCollection Values => (internalDictionary.Values);

    public U this[T key]
    {
        get { return (internalDictionary[key]); }
        set
        {
            if (value.CompareTo(MinValue) >= 0 &&
                value.CompareTo(MaxValue) <= 0)
                internalDictionary[key] = value;
```

```csharp
            else
                throw new ArgumentOutOfRangeException(nameof(value), value,
                    $"Value must be within the range {MinValue} to {MaxValue}");
        }
    }

    public void Add(T key, U value)
    {
        if (value.CompareTo(MinValue) >= 0 &&
            value.CompareTo(MaxValue) <= 0)
            internalDictionary.Add(key, value);
        else
            throw new ArgumentOutOfRangeException(nameof(value), value,
                $"Value must be within the range {MinValue} to {MaxValue}");
    }

    public bool ContainsKey(T key) => (internalDictionary.ContainsKey(key));

    public bool ContainsValue(U value) => (internalDictionary.ContainsValue(value));

    public override bool Equals(object obj) => (internalDictionary.Equals(obj));

    public IEnumerator GetEnumerator() => (internalDictionary.GetEnumerator());

    public override int GetHashCode() => (internalDictionary.GetHashCode());

    public void GetObjectData(SerializationInfo info, StreamingContext context)
    {
        internalDictionary.GetObjectData(info, context);
    }

    public void OnDeserialization(object sender)
    {
        internalDictionary.OnDeserialization(sender);
    }

    public override string ToString() => (internalDictionary.ToString());

    public bool TryGetValue(T key, out U value) =>
        (internalDictionary.TryGetValue(key, out value));

    public void Remove(T key)
    {
        internalDictionary.Remove(key);
    }

    public void Clear()
    {
        internalDictionary.Clear();
    }
}
```

Discussion

The `MinMaxValueDictionary` class wraps the `Dictionary<T,U>` class, so it can restrict the range of allowed values. Defined here is the overloaded constructor for the `Min MaxValueDictionary` class:

```
public MinMaxValueDictionary(U minValue, U maxValue)
```

This constructor allows the range of values to be set. Its parameters are:

`minValue`
> The smallest value of type `U` that can be added as a value in a key/value pair.

`maxValue`
> The largest value of type `U` that can be added as a value in a key/value pair.

These values are available on the `MinMaxValueDictionary<T,U>` as the properties `Min Value` and `MaxValue`.

The overridden indexer has both `get` and `set`. The `get` accessor returns the value that matches the provided *key*. The `set` accessor checks the *value* parameter to determine whether it is within the boundaries of the `minValue` and `maxValue` fields before it is set.

The `Add` method accepts a type `U` for its *value* parameter and performs the same tests as the `set` accessor on the indexer. If the test passes, the integer is added to the `Min MaxValueDictionary`.

See Also

The "Dictionary<T, U> Class" topics in the MSDN documentation.

2.5 Persisting a Collection Between Application Sessions

Problem

You have a collection such as an `ArrayList`, `List<T>`, `Hashtable`, or `Dictio nary<T,U>` in which you are storing application information. You can use this information to tailor the application's environment to the last known settings (e.g., window size, window placement, and currently displayed toolbars). You can also use it to allow the user to start the application at the same point where it was last shut down. In other words, if the user is editing an invoice and needs to shut down the computer for the night, the application will know exactly which invoice to initially display when it is started again.

Solution

Serialize the object(s) to and from a file:

```
public static void SerializeToFile<T>(T obj, string dataFile)
{
    using (FileStream fileStream = File.Create(dataFile))
    {
        BinaryFormatter binSerializer = new BinaryFormatter();
        binSerializer.Serialize(fileStream, obj);
    }
}

public static T DeserializeFromFile<T>(string dataFile)
{
    T obj = default(T);
    using (FileStream fileStream = File.OpenRead(dataFile))
    {
        BinaryFormatter binSerializer = new BinaryFormatter();
        obj = (T)binSerializer.Deserialize(fileStream);
    }
    return obj;
}
```

Discussion

The `dataFile` parameter accepts a string value to use as a filename. The `SerializeToFile<T>` method accepts an object and attempts to serialize it to a file. Conversely, the `DeserializeFromFile<T>` method removes the serialized object from the file created in the `SaveObj<T>` method.

Example 2-3 shows how to use these methods to serialize an `ArrayList` object (note that this will work for any type that is marked with the `SerializableAttribute`).

Example 2-3. Persisting a collection between application sessions

```
ArrayList HT = new ArrayList() {"Zero","One","Two"};

foreach (object O in HT)
    Console.WriteLine(O.ToString());
SerializeToFile<ArrayList>(HT, "HT.data");

ArrayList HTNew = new ArrayList();
HTNew = DeserializeFromFile<ArrayList>("HT.data");
foreach (object O in HTNew)
    Console.WriteLine(O.ToString());
```

If you serialize your objects to disk at specific points in your application, you can then deserialize them and return to a known state—for instance, in the event of an unintended shutdown.

You could also serialize the object(s) to and from a byte stream for storage in isolated storage or remote storage:

```
public static byte[] Serialize<T>(T obj)
{
    using (MemoryStream memStream = new MemoryStream())
    {
        BinaryFormatter binSerializer = new BinaryFormatter();
        binSerializer.Serialize(memStream, obj);
        return memStream.ToArray();
    }
}

public static T Deserialize<T>(byte[] serializedObj)
{
    T obj = default(T);
    using (MemoryStream memStream = new MemoryStream(serializedObj))
    {
        BinaryFormatter binSerializer = new BinaryFormatter();
        obj = (T)binSerializer.Deserialize(memStream);
    }
    return obj;
}
```

If you rely on serialized objects to store persistent information, you need to figure out what you are going to do when you deploy a new version of the application. You should plan ahead with either a strategy for making sure the types you serialize don't get changed or a technique for dealing with changes. Otherwise, you are going to have big problems when you deploy an update. Check out the "Version Tolerant Serialization" article in MSDN for ideas and best practices on handling this situation.

See Also

The "ArrayList Class," "Hashtable Class," "List<T> Class," "Dictionary<T,U> Class," "File Class," "Version Tolerant Serialization," and "BinaryFormatter Class" topics in the MSDN documentation.

2.6 Testing Every Element in an Array or List<T>

Problem

You need an easy way to test every element in an Array or List<T>. The results of this test should indicate that the test passed for all elements in the collection, or it failed for at least one element in the collection.

Solution

Use the `TrueForAll` method, as shown here:

```
// Create a List of strings
List<string> strings = new List<string>() {"one",null,"three","four"};

// Determine if there are no null values in the List
string str = strings.TrueForAll(delegate(string val)
{
    if (val == null)
        return false;
    else
        return true;
}).ToString();

// Display the results
Console.WriteLine(str);
```

Discussion

The addition of the `TrueForAll` method on the `Array` and `List<T>` classes allows you to easily set up tests for all elements in these collections. The code in the Solution for this recipe tests all elements to determine if any are `null`. You could just as easily set up tests to determine, for example:

- if any numeric elements are above a specified maximum value;
- if any numeric elements are below a specified minimum value;
- if any string elements contain a specified set of characters;
- if any data objects have all of their fields filled in; and
- any others you may come up with.

The `TrueForAll` method accepts a generic delegate `Predicate<T>` called `match` and returns a Boolean value:

```
public bool TrueForAll(Predicate<T> match)
```

The `match` parameter determines whether or not a `true` or `false` should be returned by the `TrueForAll` method.

The `TrueForAll` method basically consists of a loop that iterates over each element in the collection. Within this loop, a call to the `match` delegate is invoked. If this delegate returns `true`, the processing continues on to the next element in the collection. If this delegate returns `false`, processing stops and a `false` is returned by the `TrueForAll` method. When the `TrueForAll` method finishes iterating over all the elements of the collection and the match delegate has not returned a `false` value for any element, the `TrueForAll` method returns a `true`.

There is not a `FalseForAll` method, but you can reverse your logic and use `TrueForAll` to accomplish the same thing:

```
List<string> nulls = new List<string>() { null, null, null, null };

// Determine if there are all null values in the List
string result = nulls.TrueForAll(delegate (string val)
{
    if (val == null)
        return true;
    else
        return false;
}).ToString();

// Display the results
Console.WriteLine(result);
```

One other consideration here is that `TrueForAll` stops the first time the condition is not `true`. This means that not all nodes are checked. If you have an array of, say, file handles or resources that need to be processed or freed, you would need to iterate over all of them even if the action performed during the check fails. In this case you'd want to note if any of them failed, but it would still be important to visit each `Array` or `List<T>` element and perform the action.

See Also

The "Array Class," "List<T> Class," and "TrueForAll Method" topics in the MSDN documentation.

2.7 Creating Custom Enumerators

Problem

You need to add `foreach` support to a class, but the normal way of adding an iterator (i.e., implementing `IEnumerable` on a type and returning a reference to this `IEnumerable` from a member function) is not flexible enough. Instead of simply iterating from the first element to the last, you also need to iterate from the last to the first, and you need to be able to step over, or skip, a predefined number of elements on each iteration. You want to make all of these types of iterators available to your class.

Solution

The `Container<T>` class shown in Example 2-4 acts as a container for a private `List<T>` called `internalList`. `Container` is implemented so you can use it in a `foreach` loop to iterate through the private `internalList`.

Example 2-4. Creating custom iterators

```
public class Container<T> : IEnumerable<T>
{
    public Container() { }

    private List<T> _internalList = new List<T>();

    // This iterator iterates over each element from first to last
    public IEnumerator<T> GetEnumerator() => _internalList.GetEnumerator();

    // This iterator iterates over each element from last to first
    public IEnumerable<T> GetReverseOrderEnumerator()
    {
        foreach (T item in ((IEnumerable<T>)_internalList).Reverse())
            yield return item;
    }

    // This iterator iterates over each element from first to last, stepping
    // over a predefined number of elements
    public IEnumerable<T> GetForwardStepEnumerator(int step)
    {
        foreach (T item in _internalList.EveryNthItem(step))
            yield return item;
    }

    // This iterator iterates over each element from last to first, stepping
    // over a predefined number of elements
    public IEnumerable<T> GetReverseStepEnumerator(int step)
    {
        foreach (T item in (
            (IEnumerable<T>)_internalList).Reverse().EveryNthItem(step))
            yield return item;
    }

    #region IEnumerable Members

    IEnumerator IEnumerable.GetEnumerator() => GetEnumerator();

    #endregion

    public void Clear()
    {
        _internalList.Clear();
    }
```

```
    public void Add(T item)
    {
        _internalList.Add(item);
    }

    public void AddRange(ICollection<T> collection)
    {
        _internalList.AddRange(collection);
    }
}
```

Discussion

Iterators provide an easy method of moving from item to item within an object using the familiar `foreach` loop construct. The object can be an array, a collection, or some other type of container. This is similar to using a `for` loop to manually iterate over each item contained in an array. In fact, an iterator can be set up to use a `for` loop—or any other looping construct, for that matter—as the mechanism for yielding each item in the object. In fact, you do not even have to use a looping construct. The following code is perfectly valid:

```
public static IEnumerable<int> GetValues()
{
    yield return 10;
    yield return 20;
    yield return 30;
    yield return 100;
}
```

With the `foreach` loop, you do not have to worry about watching for the end of the list, since you cannot go beyond the bounds of the list. The best part about the `foreach` loop and iterators is that you do not have to know how to access the list of elements within its container. In fact, you do not even have to have access to the list of elements, as the iterator member(s) implemented on the container handle this for you.

To see what `foreach` is doing here, let's look at code to iterate over the `Container` class:

```
// Iterate over Container object
foreach (int i in container)
    Console.WriteLine(i);
```

`foreach` will take the following actions while this code executes:

1. Get the enumerator from the container using `IEnumerator.GetEnumerator()`.

2. Access the `IEnumerator.Current` property for the current object (`int`) and place it into `i`.

3. Call `IEnumerator.MoveNext()`. If MoveNext returns `true`, go back to step 2, or else end the loop.

The `Container` class contains a private `List` of items called `internalList`. There are four iterator members within this class:

```
GetEnumerator
GetReverseOrderEnumerator
GetForwardStepEnumerator
GetReverseStepEnumerator
```

The `GetEnumerator` method iterates over each element in the `internalList` from the first to the last element. This iterator, similar to the others, uses a `for` loop to yield each element in the `internalList`.

The `GetReverseOrderEnumerator` method implements an iterator in its `get` accessor (set accessors cannot be iterators). This iterator is very similar in design to the `GetEnumerator` method, except that the `foreach` loop works on the `internalList` in the reverse direction by using the `IEnumerable<T>.Reverse` extension method. The last two iterators, `GetForwardStepEnumerator` and `GetReverseStepEnumerator`, are similar in design to `GetEnumerator` and `GetReverseOrderEnumerator`, respectively. The main difference is that the `foreach` loop uses the `EveryNthItem` extension method to skip over the specified number of items in the `internalList`:

```
public static IEnumerable<T> EveryNthItem<T>(this IEnumerable<T> enumerable,
    int step)
{
    int current = 0;
    foreach (T item in enumerable)
    {
        ++current;
        if (current % step == 0)
            yield return item;
    }
}
```

Notice also that only the `GetEnumerator` method must return an `IEnumerator<T>` interface; the other three iterators must return `IEnumerable<T>` interfaces.

To iterate over each element in the `Container` object from first to last, use the following code:

```
Container<int> container = new Container<int>();
    //...Add data to container here ...
foreach (int i in container)
    Console.WriteLine(i);
```

To iterate over each element in the `Container` object from last to first, use the following code:

```
Container<int> container = new Container<int>();
    //...Add data to container here ...
foreach (int i in container.GetReverseOrderEnumerator())
    Console.WriteLine(i);
```

To iterate over each element in the `Container` object from first to last while skipping every other element, use the following code:

```
Container<int> container = new Container<int>();
    //...Add data to container here ...
foreach (int i in container.GetForwardStepEnumerator(2))
    Console.WriteLine(i);
```

To iterate over each element in the `Container` object from last to first while skipping to every third element, use the following code:

```
Container<int> container = new Container<int>();
    //...Add data to container here ...
foreach (int i in container.GetReverseStepEnumerator(3))
    Console.WriteLine(i);
```

In each of the last two examples, the iterator method accepts an integer value, `step`, which determines how many items will be skipped.

One last note on `yield`: while it is technically possible to use `yield` inside of a `lock` statement (see the Discussion in Recipe 9.9 for more on `lock`), you should avoid doing so, as it could cause deadlocks in your application. The code you `yield` to could be taking out `lock`s itself and causing the deadlocking. The code inside the `lock` could then resume on another thread (since when you `yield`, it doesn't have to resume on the same thread), so you would be unlocking from a different thread than the one on which you established the lock.

See Also

The "Iterators," "yield," "IEnumerator Interface," "IEnumerable(T) Interface," and "IEnumerable Interface" topics in the MSDN documentation, and Recipe 9.9.

2.8 Dealing with finally Blocks and Iterators

Problem

You have added a `try-finally` block to your iterator, and you notice that the `finally` block is not being executed when you think it should.

Solution

Wrap a `try` block around the iteration code in the `GetEnumerator` iterator with a `finally` block following this `try` block:

```csharp
public class StringSet : IEnumerable<string>
{
    private List<string> _items = new List<string>();

    public void Add(string value)
    {
        _items.Add(value);
    }

    public IEnumerator<string> GetEnumerator()
    {
        try
        {
            for (int index = 0; index < _items.Count; index++)
            {
                yield return (_items[index]);
            }
        }
        // Cannot use catch blocks in an iterator
        finally
        {
            // Only executed at end of foreach loop (including on yield break)
            Console.WriteLine("In iterator finally block");
        }
    }

    #region IEnumerable Members

    IEnumerator IEnumerable.GetEnumerator() => GetEnumerator();

    #endregion
}
```

The foreach code that calls this iterator looks like this:

```csharp
//Create a StringSet object and fill it with data
StringSet strSet =
    new StringSet()
        {"item1",
            "item2",
            "item3",
            "item4",
            "item5"};

// Use the GetEnumerator iterator.
foreach (string s in strSet)
    Console.WriteLine(s);
```

When this code is run, the following output is displayed:

```
item1
item2
item3
```

```
item4
item5
In iterator finally block
```

Discussion

You may have thought that the output would display the "In iterator finally block" string after displaying each item in the strSet object. However, this is not the way that finally blocks are handled in iterators. All finally blocks associated with try blocks that have yield returns inside the iterator member body are called only after the iterations are complete, code execution leaves the foreach loop (such as when a break, return, or throw statement is encountered), or when a yield break statement is executed, effectively terminating the iterator.

To see how iterators deal with catch and finally blocks (note that there can be no catch blocks inside of a try block that contains a yield), consider the following code:

```
//Create a StringSet object and fill it with data
StringSet strSet =
    new StringSet()
        {"item1",
            "item2",
            "item3",
            "item4",
            "item5"};

// Display all data in StringSet object
try
{
    foreach (string s in strSet)
    {
        try
        {
            Console.WriteLine(s);
            // Force an exception here
            //throw new Exception();
        }
        catch (Exception)
        {
            Console.WriteLine("In foreach catch block");
        }
        finally
        {
            // Executed on each iteration
            Console.WriteLine("In foreach finally block");
        }
    }
}
catch (Exception)
```

```
{
    Console.WriteLine("In outer catch block");
}
finally
{
    // Executed on each iteration
    Console.WriteLine("In outer finally block");
}
```

Assuming that your original `StringSet.GetEnumerator` method is used (i.e., the one that contained the `try-finally` block), you will see the following behaviors.

If no exception occurs, you see this:

```
item1
In foreach finally block
item2
In foreach finally block
item3
In foreach finally block
item4
In foreach finally block
item5
In foreach finally block
In iterator finally block
In outer finally block
```

We see that the `finally` block that is within the `foreach` loop is executed on each iteration. However, the `finally` block within the iterator is executed only after all iterations are finished. Also, notice that the iterator's `finally` block is executed before the `finally` block that wraps the `foreach` loop.

If an exception occurs in the iterator itself, during processing of the second element, the following is displayed:

```
item1
In foreach finally block
    (Exception occurs here...)
In iterator finally block
In outer catch block
In outer finally block
```

Notice that immediately after the exception is thrown, the `finally` block within the iterator is executed. This can be useful if you need to clean up only after an exception occurs. If no exception happens, then the `finally` block is not executed until the iterator completes. After the iterator's `finally` block executes, the exception is caught by the `catch` block outside the `foreach` loop. At this point, the exception could be handled or rethrown. Once this `catch` block is finished processing, the outer `finally` block is executed.

Notice that the `catch` block within the `foreach` loop was never given the opportunity to handle the exception. This is because the corresponding `try` block does not contain a call to the iterator.

If an exception occurs in the `foreach` loop during processing of the second element, the following is displayed:

```
item1
In foreach finally block
    (Exception occurs here...)
In foreach catch block
In foreach finally block
In iterator finally block
In outer finally block
```

Notice in this situation that the `catch` and `finally` blocks within the `foreach` loop are executed first, then the iterator's `finally` block. Lastly, the outer `finally` block is executed.

Understanding the way `catch` and `finally` blocks operate inside iterators will help you add them in the correct location. If you need a `finally` block to execute once immediately after the iterations are finished, add this `finally` block to the iterator method. If, however, you want the `finally` block to execute on each iteration, you need to place it within the `foreach` loop body.

If you need to catch iterator exceptions immediately after they occur, consider wrapping the `foreach` loop in a `try-catch` block. Any `try-catch` block within the `foreach` loop body will miss exceptions thrown from the iterator.

See Also

The "try-catch," "Iterators," "yield," "IEnumerator Interface," and "IEnumerable Interface" topics in the MSDN documentation.

2.9 Implementing Nested foreach Functionality in a Class

Problem

You need a class that contains a list of objects, with each of these objects itself containing a list of objects. You want to use a nested `foreach` loop to iterate through all objects in both the outer and inner lists in the following manner:

```
foreach (Group<Item> subGroup in topLevelGroup)
{
    // do work for groups
    foreach (Item item in subGroup)
    {
        // do work for items
```

```
        }
    }
```

Solution

Implement the `IEnumerable<T>` interface on the class. The `Group` class shown in Example 2-5 contains a `List<T>` that can hold `Group` objects, and each `Group` object contains a `List<Item>`.

Example 2-5. Implementing foreach functionality in a class

```
public class Group<T> : IEnumerable<T>
{
    public Group(string name)
    {
        this.Name = name;
    }

    private List<T> _groupList = new List<T>();

    public string Name { get; set; }

    public int Count => _groupList.Count;

    public void Add(T group)
    {
        _groupList.Add(group);
    }

    IEnumerator IEnumerable.GetEnumerator() => GetEnumerator();

    public IEnumerator<T> GetEnumerator() => _groupList.GetEnumerator();
}


public class Item
{
    public Item(string name, int location)
    {
        this.Name = name;
        this.Location = location;
    }
    public string Name { get; set; }
    public int Location { get; set; }
}
```

Discussion

Building functionality into a class to allow it to be iterated over using the `foreach` loop is much easier using iterators in the C# language. In versions of the .NET

Framework prior to 3.0, you not only had to implement the IEnumerable interface on the type that you wanted to make enumerable, but you also had to implement the IEnumerator interface on a nested class. You then had to write the MoveNext and Reset methods and the Current property by hand in this nested class. Iterators allow you to hand off the work of writing this nested class to the C# compiler. If you wrote an old-style enumerator yourself, it would look like this:

```csharp
public class GroupEnumerator<T> : IEnumerator
{
    public T[] _items;

    int position = -1;

    public GroupEnumerator(T[] list)
    {
        _items = list;
    }

    public bool MoveNext()
    {
        position++;
        return (position < _items.Length);
    }

    public void Reset()
    {
        position = -1;
    }

    public object Current
    {
        get
        {
            try
            {
                return _items[position];
            }
            catch (IndexOutOfRangeException)
            {
                throw new InvalidOperationException();
            }
        }
    }
}
```

The IEnumerator.GetEnumerator method would be modified on the Group<T> class to look like this:

```csharp
IEnumerator IEnumerable.GetEnumerator() =>
    new GroupEnumerator<T>(_groupList.ToArray());
```

and the code to walk over it would look like this:

```
IEnumerator enumerator = ((IEnumerable)hierarchy).GetEnumerator();
while (enumerator.MoveNext())
{
    Console.WriteLine(((Group<Item>)enumerator.Current).Name);
    foreach (Item i in ((Group<Item>)enumerator.Current))
    {
        Console.WriteLine(i.Name);
    }
}
```

Aren't you glad you don't have to do that? Leave it to the compiler; it's quite good at writing this for you.

Enabling a class to be used by the `foreach` loop requires the inclusion of an iterator. An iterator can be a method, an operator overload, or the `get` accessor of a property that returns either a `System.Collections.IEnumerator`, a `System.Collec` `tions.Generic.IEnumerator<T>`, a `System.Collections.IEnumerable`, or a `Sys` `tem.Collections.Generic.IEnumerable<T>` and that contains at least one `yield` statement.

The code for this recipe is divided between two classes. The container class is the `Group` class, which contains a `List` of `Group<Item>` objects. The `Group` object also contains a `List`, but this `List` contains `Item` objects. To enumerate the contained list, the `Group` class implements the `IEnumerable` interface. It therefore contains a `GetE` `numerator` iterator method, which returns an `IEnumerator`. The class structure looks like this:

```
Group (Implements IEnumerable<T>)
  Group (Implements IEnumerable<T>)
      Item
```

By examining the `Group` class, you can see how classes usable by a `foreach` loop are constructed. This class contains:

- A simple `List<T>`, which will be iterated over by the class's enumerator.

- A property, `Count`, which returns the number of elements in the `List<T>`.

- An iterator method, `GetEnumerator`, which is defined by the `IEnumerable<T>` interface. This method yields a specific value on each iteration of the `foreach` loop.

- A method, `Add`, which adds an instance such as `Subgroup` to the `List<T>`.

- A method, `GetGroup`, which returns a typed instance such as `Subgroup` from the `List<T>`.

To create the `Subgroup` class, you follow the same pattern as with the `Group` class—except the `Subgroup` class contains a `List<Item>`.

The final class is `Item`. This class is the lowest level of this structure and contains data. It has been grouped within the `Subgroup` objects, all of which are contained in the `Group` object. There is nothing out of the ordinary with this class; it simply contains data and the means to set and retrieve this data.

Using these classes is quite simple. The following method shows how to create a `Group` object that contains multiple `Subgroup` objects, which in turn contain multiple `Item` objects:

```
public static void CreateNestedObjects()
{
    Group<Group<Item>> hierarchy =
        new Group<Group<Item>>("root") {
            new Group<Item>("subgroup1"){
                new Item("item1",100),
                new Item("item2",200)},
            new Group<Item>("subgroup2"){
                new Item("item3",300),
                new Item("item4",400)}};

    IEnumerator enumerator = ((IEnumerable)hierarchy).GetEnumerator();
    while (enumerator.MoveNext())
    {
        Console.WriteLine(((Group<Item>)enumerator.Current).Name);
        foreach (Item i in ((Group<Item>)enumerator.Current))
        {
            Console.WriteLine(i.Name);
        }
    }

    // Read back the data
    DisplayNestedObjects(hierarchy);
}
```

The `CreateNestedObjects` method first creates a `hierarchy` object of the `Group` class and then creates two subgroups within it named `subgroup1` and `subgroup2`. Each of these subgroup objects, in turn, is filled with two `Item` objects called `item1`, `item2`, `item3`, and `item4`.

The next method shows how to read all of the `Item` objects contained within the `Group` object that was created in the `CreateNestedObjects` method:

```
private static void DisplayNestedObjects(Group<Group<Item>> topLevelGroup)
{
    Console.WriteLine($"topLevelGroup.Count: {topLevelGroup.Count}");
    Console.WriteLine($"topLevelGroupName:  {topLevelGroup.Name}");

    // Outer foreach to iterate over all objects in the
    // topLevelGroup object
    foreach (Group<Item> subGroup in topLevelGroup)
    {
```

```
        Console.WriteLine($"\tsubGroup.SubGroupName:  {subGroup.Name}");
        Console.WriteLine($"\tsubGroup.Count: {subGroup.Count}");

        // Inner foreach to iterate over all Item objects in the
        // current SubGroup object
        foreach (Item item in subGroup)
        {
            Console.WriteLine($"\t\titem.Name:    {item.Name}");
            Console.WriteLine($"\t\titem.Location: {item.Location}");
        }
    }
}
```

This method displays the following:

```
topLevelGroup.Count: 2
topLevelGroupName:  root
        subGroup.SubGroupName:  subgroup1
        subGroup.Count: 2
                item.Name:      item1
                item.Location: 100
                item.Name:      item2
                item.Location: 200
        subGroup.SubGroupName:  subgroup2
        subGroup.Count: 2
                item.Name:      item3
                item.Location: 300
                item.Name:      item4
                item.Location: 400
```

As you see here, the outer foreach loop is used to iterate over all Subgroup objects that are stored in the top-level Group object. The inner foreach loop is used to iterate over all Item objects that are stored in the current Subgroup object.

See Also

The "Iterators," "yield," "IEnumerator Interface," "IEnumerable(T) interface," and "IEnumerable Interface" topics in the MSDN documentation.

2.10 Using a Thread-Safe Dictionary for Concurrent Access Without Manual Locking

Problem

You need to make a collection of key/value pairs accessible from multiple threads for reading and writing concurrently without having to manually use synchronization primitives to protect it.

Solution

Use the `ConcurrentDictionary<TKey, TValue>` to contain the items and access them in a thread-safe manner.

As an example, consider a simulation of fans entering a stadium or field to watch their favorite sporting event (Super Bowl, World Cup, World Series, or the ICC World Cricket League Championship) and there are only a certain number of gates.

First, we will need some `Fans` and we will keep track of their `Names`, when they are `Admitted`, and what `AdmittanceGateNumber` they enter by:

```
public class Fan
{
    public string Name { get; set; }
    public DateTime Admitted { get; set; }
    public int AdmittanceGateNumber { get; set; }
}

// set up a list of fans attending the event
List<Fan> fansAttending = new List<Fan>();
for (int i = 0; i < 100; i++)
    fansAttending.Add(new Fan() { Name = "Fan" + i });
Fan[] fans = fansAttending.ToArray();
```

Each gate can admit only one person at a time and at crowded events such as these, the gates are usually monitored by cameras. We will use a static `ConcurrentDiction ary<int,Fan>` to represent the stadium gates as well as which `Fan` is currently at the gate, and a `static bool` (`monitorGates`) to indicate when the gates should no longer be monitored (i.e., when all fans have entered the event):

```
private static ConcurrentDictionary<int, Fan> stadiumGates =
    new ConcurrentDictionary<int, Fan>();

private static bool monitorGates = true;
```

We will say there are 10 gates (`gateCount`) to the event and launch a `Task` for each gate with the `AdmitFans` method to have each gate admit a certain number of fans. We will also launch a corresponding `Task` for each gate to have the security monitors turned on with the `MonitorGate` method. Once all of the fans have been admitted, we will stop monitoring the gates:

```
int gateCount = 10;
Task[] entryGates = new Task[gateCount];
Task[] securityMonitors = new Task[gateCount];

for (int gateNumber = 0; gateNumber < gateCount; gateNumber++)
{
    //FUN FACT:
    //You might think that as gateNumber changes in the for loop that the
    //creation of the Task admitting the Fan would capture the value (0,1,2,etc.)
```

```
//at the point in time that the Task was created. As it turns out, the Task
//will use the CURRENT value in the gateNumber variable when it runs.
//This means that even though you launched a Task for gate 0, it might get a
//gateNumber variable with 9 in it as the loop has progressed since the Task
//was created.
//To deal with this, we assign the values to a local variable which fixes the
//scope and the value you wanted can be captured by the Task appropriately.
int GateNum = gateNumber;
int GateCount = gateCount;
Action action = delegate () { AdmitFans(fans, GateNum, GateCount); };
entryGates[gateNumber] = Task.Run(action);
}

for (int gateNumber = 0; gateNumber < gateCount; gateNumber++)
{
    int GateNum = gateNumber;
    Action action = delegate () { MonitorGate(GateNum); };
    securityMonitors[gateNumber] = Task.Run(action);
}

await Task.WhenAll(entryGates);

// Shut down monitoring
monitorGates = false;
```

AdmitFans does the work of admitting a section of the fans by using the Concurrent
Dictionary<TKey, TValue>.AddOrUpdate method to show that the Fan is in the gate
and then uses the ConcurrentDictionary<TKey, TValue>.TryRemove method to
show that the Fan was admitted to the event:

```
private static void AdmitFans(Fan[] fans, int gateNumber, int gateCount)
{
    Random rnd = new Random();
    int fansPerGate = fans.Length / gateCount;
    int start = gateNumber * fansPerGate;
    int end = start + fansPerGate - 1;
    for (int f = start; f <= end; f++)
    {
        Console.WriteLine($"Admitting {fans[f].Name} through gate {gateNumber}");
        var fanAtGate =
            stadiumGates.AddOrUpdate(gateNumber, fans[f],
                (key, fanInGate) =>
                {
                    Console.WriteLine($"{fanInGate.Name} was replaced by " +
                        $"{fans[f].Name} in gate {gateNumber}");
                    return fans[f];
                });
        // Perform patdown check and check ticket
        Thread.Sleep(rnd.Next(500, 2000));
        // Let them through the gate
        fans[f].Admitted = DateTime.Now;
        fans[f].AdmittanceGateNumber = gateNumber;
```

```
            Fan fanAdmitted;
            if(stadiumGates.TryRemove(gateNumber, out fanAdmitted))
                Console.WriteLine($"{fanAdmitted.Name} entering event from gate " +
                    $"{fanAdmitted.AdmittanceGateNumber} on " +
                    $"{fanAdmitted.Admitted.ToShortTimeString()}");
            else // if we couldn't admit them, security must have gotten them...
                Console.WriteLine($"{fanAdmitted.Name} held by security " +
                    $"at gate {fanAdmitted.AdmittanceGateNumber}");
        }
    }
```

MonitorGate watches the provided gate number (gateNumber) by inspecting the Con
currentDictionary<TKey, TValue> using the TryGetValue method. MonitorGate
will continue to monitor until the monitorGates flag is set to false (after the Admit
Fan Tasks have completed):

```
    private static void MonitorGate(int gateNumber)
    {
        Random rnd = new Random();
        while (monitorGates)
        {
            Fan currentFanInGate;
            if (stadiumGates.TryGetValue(gateNumber, out currentFanInGate))
                Console.WriteLine($"Monitor: {currentFanInGate.Name} is in Gate " +
                    $"{gateNumber}");
            else
                Console.WriteLine($"Monitor: No fan is in Gate {gateNumber}");

            // Wait and then check gate again
            Thread.Sleep(rnd.Next(500, 5000));
        }
    }
```

Discussion

ConcurrentDictionary<TKey, TValue> is located in the System.Collections.Con
current namespace and is available from .NET 4.0 and up. It is a collection that is
most useful in multiple read and multiple write scenarios. If you are simply doing
multiple reads after an initialization, ImmutableDictionary<TKey,TValue> would be
a better choice. Since the dictionary is immutable once loaded, it is a much faster
readable collection. When you manipulate an immutable dictionary a whole new
copy of the original dictionary is made, which can be very expensive, so keep this in
your back pocket for collections you load up once and read from a lot.

Note that the Immutable classes are not part of the core .NET Framework libraries;
they are in the System.Collections.Immutable assembly in the Micro
soft.Bcl.Immutable NuGet package, which you would need to include in your
application.

There are a number of properties and methods on ConcurrentDictionary<TKey, TValue> that cause the entire collection to lock, as they are operating on all of the items in the collection at once. These properties give you a "point in time" snapshot of the data:

- Count property
- Keys property
- Values property
- ToArray method

A "point in time" representation of the data means that you're not necessarily getting the current data while enumerating. If you need the absolutely current data from the dictionary, use the GetEnumerator method, which provides an enumerator that rolls over the key/value pairs in the dictionary. Since GetEnumerator guarantees that the enumerator is safe for use even in the face of concurrent updates and it doesn't take any locks, you can access the underlying data while it is being changed. Note that this means that your results could change during the enumeration. See the "IEnumerable<T>.GetEnumerator" topic in MSDN for a more detailed description.

LINQ uses GetEnumerator frequently to accomplish its goals, so you can avoid the lock penalty of using the Keys and Values properties by instead using a LINQ Select to get the items:

```
var keys = stadiumGates.Select(gate => gate.Key);
var values = stadiumGates.Select(gate => gate.Value);
```

For counting, LINQ is optimized to use the Count property on collections that support the ICollection interface, which is not what we want in this case. This example demonstrates the logic of the Count method; the Count property is used if the enumerable supports ICollection or ICollection<T>:

```
public static int Count<TSource>(this IEnumerable<TSource> source)
{
    if (source == null)
    {
        throw Error.ArgumentNull("source");
    }
    ICollection<TSource> tSources = source as ICollection<TSource>;
    if (tSources != null)
    {
        return tSources.Count;
    }
    ICollection collections = source as ICollection;
    if (collections != null)
    {
        return collections.Count;
    }
```

```
        int num = 0;
        using (IEnumerator<TSource> enumerator = source.GetEnumerator())
        {
            while (enumerator.MoveNext())
            {
                num++;
            }
        }
        return num;
    }
```

To work around this, get an enumerable collection of the items that doesn't support
ICollection or ICollection<T> and call Count() on it:

```
    var count = stadiumGates.Select(gate => gate).Count();
```

The call to Select returns a System.Linq.Enumerable.WhereSelectEnumerableIter
ator that does not support ICollection or ICollection<T> but does support GetE
numerator.

The main manipulation operations on ConcurrentDictionary<TKey, TValue> are
summed up in Table 2-1.

Table 2-1. ConcurrentDictionary manipulation operations

Method	When to use
TryAdd	Add new item only if key doesn't exist.
TryUpdate	Update an existing key with a new value if the current value is available.
Indexing	Set a key/value in the dictionary unconditionally whether the key exists or not.
AddOrUpdate	Set a key/value in the dictionary with delegates to allow different entries if the key is being added or updated.
GetOrAdd	Get the value for a key or default the value and return it (*lazy initialization*).
TryGetValue	Get the value for the key or return false.
TryRemove	Remove the value for the key or return false.

The beginning output from the example code will look similar to this:

```
    Admitting Fan0 through gate 0
    Admitting Fan10 through gate 1
    Admitting Fan20 through gate 2
    Admitting Fan30 through gate 3
    Admitting Fan40 through gate 4
    Fan0 entering event from gate 0 on 6:00 PM
    Admitting Fan1 through gate 0
    Fan20 entering event from gate 2 on 6:00 PM
    Fan10 entering event from gate 1 on 6:00 PM
    Admitting Fan11 through gate 1
    Fan30 entering event from gate 3 on 6:00 PM
    Admitting Fan31 through gate 3
```

```
Admitting Fan21 through gate 2
Fan40 entering event from gate 4 on 6:00 PM
Admitting Fan41 through gate 4
Admitting Fan50 through gate 5
Fan11 entering event from gate 1 on 6:00 PM
Admitting Fan12 through gate 1
Fan1 entering event from gate 0 on 6:00 PM
```

The output from the monitors in the middle of the example code run will look similar to this:

```
...
Admitting Fan17 through gate 1
Fan6 entering event from gate 0 on 6:00 PM
Admitting Fan7 through gate 0
Fan26 entering event from gate 2 on 6:00 PM
Admitting Fan27 through gate 2
Fan36 entering event from gate 3 on 6:00 PM
Admitting Fan37 through gate 3
Monitor: Fan17 is in Gate 1
Fan83 entering event from gate 8 on 6:00 PM
Admitting Fan55 through gate 5
Fan17 entering event from gate 1 on 6:00 PM
Admitting Fan18 through gate 1
...
```

The output at the end of the example code will look like this:

```
...
Monitor: Fan97 is in Gate 9
Monitor: No fan is in Gate 0
Fan77 entering event from gate 7 on 6:00 PM
Admitting Fan78 through gate 7
Monitor: No fan is in Gate 1
Fan97 entering event from gate 9 on 6:00 PM
Admitting Fan98 through gate 9
Monitor: No fan is in Gate 2
Monitor: No fan is in Gate 3
Monitor: No fan is in Gate 4
Monitor: No fan is in Gate 5
Monitor: No fan is in Gate 6
Monitor: Fan78 is in Gate 7
Monitor: No fan is in Gate 8
Fan78 entering event from gate 7 on 6:00 PM
Admitting Fan79 through gate 7
Monitor: Fan98 is in Gate 9
Monitor: No fan is in Gate 2
Fan98 entering event from gate 9 on 6:00 PM
Admitting Fan99 through gate 9
Monitor: No fan is in Gate 1
Monitor: No fan is in Gate 2
Fan79 entering event from gate 7 on 6:00 PM
Fan99 entering event from gate 9 on 6:00 PM
```

See Also

The "IEnumerable<T>.GetEnumerator" and "ConcurrentDictionary<TKey, TValue>" topics in the MSDN documentation.

CHAPTER 3

Data Types

3.0 Introduction

Simple types are value types that are a subset of the built-in types in C#, although, in fact, the types are defined as part of the .NET Framework Class Library (.NET FCL). Simple types are made up of several numeric types and a bool type. Numeric types consist of a decimal type (decimal), nine integral types (byte, char, int, long, sbyte, short, uint, ulong, and ushort), and two floating-point types (float and double). Table 3-1 lists the simple types and their fully qualified names in the .NET Framework.

Table 3-1. The simple data types

Fully qualified name	Alias	Value range
System.Boolean	bool	true or false
System.Byte	byte	0 to 255
System.SByte	sbyte	-128 to 127
System.Char	char	0 to 65535
System.Decimal	decimal	-79,228,162,514,264,337,593,543,950,335 to 79,228,162,514,264,337,593,543,950,335
System.Double	double	-1.79769313486232e308 to 1.79769313486232e308
System.Single	float	-3.40282347E+38 to 3.40282347E+38
System.Int16	short	-32768 to 32767
System.Uint16	ushort	0 to 65535
System.Int32	int	-2,147,483,648 to 2,147,483,647
System.UInt32	uint	0 to 4,294,967,295
System.Int64	long	-9,223,372,036,854,775,808 to 9,223,372,036,854,775,807

Fully qualified name	Alias	Value range
System.UInt64	ulong	0 to 18,446,744,073,709,551,615

When you are dealing with floating-point data types, precision can be more important than the range of the data values. The precision of the floating-point data types is listed in Table 3-2.

Table 3-2. Floating-point precision

Floating-point type	Precision
System.Single (float)	7 digits
System.Double (double)	15–16 digits
System.Decimal (decimal)	28–29 digits

When trying to decide between using floats and decimals, consider the following:

- Floats were designed for scientists to represent inexact quantities over the entire range of precisions and magnitudes used in physics.
- Decimals were designed for use by ordinary humans who do math in base10 and do not require more than a handful of digits past the decimal point, or who are keeping track of money in situations where every penny counts (such as reconciling a checkbook).

The C#-reserved words for the various data types are simply aliases for the fully qualified type name. Therefore, it does not matter whether you use the type name or the reserved word: the C# compiler will generate identical code.

Note that sbyte, ushort, uint, and ulong are not compliant with the Common Language Specification (CLS), and as a result, they might not be supported by other .NET languages. Enumerations implicitly inherit from System.Enum, which in turn inherits from System.ValueType. Enumerations have a single use: to describe items of a specific group. For example, red, blue, and yellow could be defined by the enumeration ShapeColor; likewise, square, circle, and triangle could be defined by the enumeration Shape. These enumerations would look like the following:

```
enum ShapeColor
{
    Red, Blue, Yellow
}

enum Shape
{
    Square = 2, Circle = 4, Triangle = 6
}
```

Each item in the enumeration receives a numeric value regardless of whether you assign one or not. Since the compiler automatically adds the numbers starting with zero and increments by one for each item in the enumeration, the ShapeColor enumeration previously defined would be exactly the same if it were defined in the following manner:

```
enum ShapeColor
{
    Red = 0,Blue = 1,Yellow = 2
}
```

Enumerations are good code-documenting tools. For example, it is more intuitive to write the following:

```
ShapeColor currentColor = ShapeColor.Red;
```

instead of this:

```
int currentColor = 0;
```

Either mechanism will work, but the first method is easy to read and understand, especially for a new developer taking over someone else's code. It also has the benefit of being type-safe in C#, which the use of raw ints does not provide. The CLR sees enumerations as members of their underlying types, so it is not type-safe for all languages.

3.1 Encoding Binary Data as Base64

Problem

You have a byte[] representing some binary information, such as a bitmap. You need to encode this data into a string so that it can be sent over a binary-unfriendly transport, such as email.

Solution

Using the static method Convert.ToBase64String on the Convert class, you can encode a byte[] to its String equivalent:

```
static class DataTypeExtMethods
{
    public static string Base64EncodeBytes(this byte[] inputBytes) =>
        (Convert.ToBase64String(inputBytes));
}
```

Discussion

Converting a string into its base64 representation has several uses. It allows binary data to be embedded in nonbinary files such as XML and email messages. Base64-

encoded data can also be transmitted via HTTP, GET, and POST requests in a more compact format than hex encoding. It is important to understand that data that is converted to base64 format is only obfuscated, not encrypted. To securely move data from one place to another, you should use the cryptography algorithms available in the FCL. For an example of using the FCL cryptography classes, see Recipe 11.4.

The Convert class makes encoding between a byte[] and a String a simple matter. The parameters for this method are quite flexible, enabling you to start and stop the conversion at any point in the input byte array.

To encode a bitmap file into a string that can be sent to some destination, you can use the EncodeBitmapToString method:

```
public static string EncodeBitmapToString(string bitmapFilePath)
{
    byte[] image = null;
    FileStream fstrm =
        new FileStream(bitmapFilePath,
                            FileMode.Open, FileAccess.Read);
    using (BinaryReader reader = new BinaryReader(fstrm))
    {
        image = new byte[reader.BaseStream.Length];
        for (int i = 0; i < reader.BaseStream.Length; i++)
            image[i] = reader.ReadByte();
    }
    return image.Base64EncodeBytes();
}
```

 The MIME standard requires that each line of the base64-encoded string be 76 characters long. To send the bmpAsString string as an embedded MIME attachment in an email message, you must insert a CRLF on each 76-character boundary.

The code to turn a base64-encoded string into a MIME-ready string is shown in the following MakeBase64EncodedStringForMime method:

```
public static string MakeBase64EncodedStringForMime(string base64Encoded)
{
    StringBuilder originalStr = new StringBuilder(base64Encoded);
    StringBuilder newStr = new StringBuilder();
    const int mimeBoundary = 76;
    int cntr = 1;
    while ((cntr * mimeBoundary) < (originalStr.Length - 1))
    {
        newStr.AppendLine(originalStr.ToString(((cntr - 1) * mimeBoundary),
            mimeBoundary));
        cntr++;
    }
    if (((cntr - 1) * mimeBoundary) < (originalStr.Length - 1))
```

```
    {
        newStr.AppendLine(originalStr.ToString(((cntr - 1) * mimeBoundary),
            ((originalStr.Length) - ((cntr - 1) * mimeBoundary)))));
    }
    return newStr.ToString();
}
```

To decode an encoded string to a `byte[]`, see Recipe 3.2.

See Also

Recipe 3.2, and the "Convert.ToBase64CharArray Method" topic in the MSDN documentation.

3.2 Decoding a Base64-Encoded Binary

Problem

You have a `String` that contains information such as a bitmap encoded as base64. You need to decode this data (which may have been embedded in an email message) from a `String` into a `byte[]` so that you can access the original binary.

Solution

Using the static method `Convert.FromBase64String` on the `Convert` class, you can decode an encoded `String` to its equivalent `byte[]` as follows:

```
static class DataTypeExtMethods
{
    public static byte[] Base64DecodeString(this string inputStr)
    {
        byte[] decodedByteArray =
                Convert.FromBase64String(inputStr);
        return (decodedByteArray);
    }
}
```

Discussion

The static `FromBase64String` method on the `Convert` class makes decoding a base64-encoded string a simple matter. This method returns a `byte[]` that contains the decoded elements of the `String`.

If you receive a file via email, such as an image file (*.bmp*) that has been converted to a string, you can convert it back into its original bitmap file using something like the following:

```
// Use the encoding method from 3.1 to get the encoded byte array
string bmpAsString = EncodeBitmapToString(@"CSCBCover.bmp");
//Get a temp file name and path to write to
string bmpFile = Path.GetTempFileName() + ".bmp";

// decode the image with the extension method
byte[] imageBytes = bmpAsString.Base64DecodeString();
FileStream fstrm = new FileStream(bmpFile,
                    FileMode.CreateNew, FileAccess.Write);
using (BinaryWriter writer = new BinaryWriter(fstrm))
{
    writer.Write(imageBytes);
}
```

In this code, the `bmpAsString` variable was obtained from the code in the Discussion section of Recipe 3.3. The `imageBytes byte[]` is the `bmpAsString String` converted back to a `byte[]`, which can then be written back to disk.

To encode a `byte[]` to a `String`, see Recipe 3.1.

See Also

Recipe 3.1, and the "Convert.FromBase64CharArray Method" topic in the MSDN documentation.

3.3 Converting a String Returned as a Byte[] Back into a String

Problem

Many methods in the FCL return a `byte[]` because they are providing a byte stream service, but some applications need to pass strings over these byte stream services. Some of these methods include:

```
System.Diagnostics.EventLogEntry.Data
System.IO.BinaryReader.Read
System.IO.BinaryReader.ReadBytes
System.IO.FileStream.Read
System.IO.FileStream.BeginRead
System.IO.MemoryStream // Constructor
System.IO.MemoryStream.Read
System.IO.MemoryStream.BeginRead
System.Net.Sockets.Socket.Receive
System.Net.Sockets.Socket.ReceiveFrom
System.Net.Sockets.Socket.BeginReceive
System.Net.Sockets.Socket.BeginReceiveFrom
System.Net.Sockets.NetworkStream.Read
System.Net.Sockets.NetworkStream.BeginRead
```

```
System.Security.Cryptography.CryptoStream.Read
System.Security.Cryptography.CryptoStream.BeginRead
```

In many cases, this byte[] might contain ASCII- or Unicode-encoded characters. You need a way to recombine this byte[] to obtain the original string.

Solution

To convert a byte array of ASCII values to a complete string, use the GetString method on the ASCII Encoding class:

```
byte[] asciiCharacterArray = {128, 83, 111, 117, 114, 99, 101,
                              32, 83, 116, 114, 105, 110, 103, 128};
string asciiCharacters = Encoding.ASCII.GetString(asciiCharacterArray);
```

To convert a byte array of Unicode values to a complete string, use the GetString method on the Unicode Encoding class:

```
byte[] unicodeCharacterArray = {128, 0, 83, 0, 111, 0, 117, 0, 114, 0, 99, 0,
                                101, 0, 32, 0, 83, 0, 116, 0, 114, 0, 105, 0, 110,
                                0, 103, 0, 128, 0};
string unicodeCharacters = Encoding.Unicode.GetString(unicodeCharacterArray);
```

Discussion

The GetString method of the Encoding class (returned by the ASCII property) converts 7-bit ASCII characters contained in a byte array to a string. Any value larger than 127 (0x7F) will be ANDed with the value 127 (0x7F), and the resulting character value will be displayed in the string. For example, if the byte[] contains the value 200 (0xC8), this value will be converted to 72 (0x48), and the character equivalent of 72 (0x48), H, will be displayed. The Encoding class can be found in the System.Text namespace. The GetString method is overloaded to accept additional arguments as well. The overloaded versions of the method convert all or part of a string to ASCII and then store the result in a specified range inside a byte[].

The GetString method returns a string containing the converted byte[] of ASCII characters.

The GetString method of the Encoding class (returned by the Unicode property) converts Unicode characters into 16-bit Unicode values. The Encoding class can be found in the System.Text namespace. The GetString method returns a string containing the converted byte[] of Unicode characters.

See Also

The "ASCIIEncoding Class" and "UnicodeEncoding Class" topics in the MSDN documentation.

3.4 Passing a String to a Method That Accepts Only a Byte[]

Problem

Many methods in the FCL accept a `byte[]` consisting of characters instead of a `string`. Some of these methods include:

```
System.Diagnostics.EventLog.WriteEntry
System.IO.BinaryWriter.Write
System.IO.FileStream.Write
System.IO.FileStream.BeginWrite
System.IO.MemoryStream.Write
System.IO.MemoryStream.BeginWrite
System.Net.Sockets.Socket.Send
System.Net.Sockets.Socket.SendTo
System.Net.Sockets.Socket.BeginSend
System.Net.Sockets.Socket.BeginSendTo
System.Net.Sockets.NetworkStream.Write
System.Net.Sockets.NetworkStream.BeginWrite
System.Security.Cryptography.CryptoStream.Write
System.Security.Cryptography.CryptoStream.BeginWrite
```

In many cases, you might have a `string` that you need to pass into one of these methods or some other method that accepts only a `byte[]`. You need a way to break up this string into a `byte[]`.

Solution

To convert a `string` to a `byte[]` of ASCII values, use the `GetBytes` method on the `ASCII Encoding` class:

```
byte[] asciiCharacterArray = {128, 83, 111, 117, 114, 99, 101,
                             32, 83, 116, 114, 105, 110, 103, 128};
string asciiCharacters = Encoding.ASCII.GetString(asciiCharacterArray);

byte[] asciiBytes = Encoding.ASCII.GetBytes(asciiCharacters);
```

To convert a string to a `byte[]` of Unicode values, use the `GetBytes` method on the `Unicode Encoding` class:

```
byte[] unicodeCharacterArray = {128, 0, 83, 0, 111, 0, 117, 0, 114, 0, 99, 0,
                               101, 0, 32, 0, 83, 0, 116, 0, 114, 0, 105, 0, 110,
                               0, 103, 0, 128, 0};
string unicodeCharacters = Encoding.Unicode.GetString(unicodeCharacterArray);

byte[] unicodeBytes = Encoding.Unicode.GetBytes(unicodeCharacters);
```

Discussion

The `GetBytes` method of the `Encoding` class (returned by the `ASCII` property) converts ASCII characters—contained in either a `char[]` or a `string`—into a `byte[]` of 7-bit ASCII values. Any value larger than 127 (0x7F) is converted to the ? character. The `Encoding` class can be found in the `System.Text` namespace. The `GetBytes` method is overloaded to accept additional arguments as well. The overloaded versions of the method convert all or part of a string to ASCII and then store the result in a specified range inside a `byte[]`, which is returned to the caller.

The `GetBytes` method of the `Encoding` class (returned by the `Unicode` property) converts Unicode characters into 16-bit Unicode values. The `Encoding` class can be found in the `System.Text` namespace. The `GetBytes` method returns a `byte[]`, each element of which contains the Unicode value of a single character of the string.

A single Unicode character in the source `string` or in the source `char[]` corresponds to two elements of the `byte[]`. For example, the following `byte[]` contains the `ASCII` value of the letter *S*:

```
byte[] sourceArray = {83};
```

However, for a `byte[]` to contain a Unicode representation of the letter *S*, it must contain two elements. For example:

```
byte[] sourceArray2 = {83, 0};
```

The Intel architecture uses a little-endian encoding, which means that the first element is the least significant byte, and the second element is the most significant byte. Other architectures may use big-endian encoding, which is the opposite of little-endian encoding. The `UnicodeEncoding` class supports both big-endian and little-endian encodings. Using the `UnicodeEncoding` instance constructor, you can construct an instance that uses either big-endian or little-endian ordering. You do so by using one of the two following constructors:

```
public UnicodeEncoding (bool bigEndian, bool byteOrderMark);
public UnicodeEncoding (bool bigEndian, bool byteOrderMark,
                        bool throwOnInvalidBytes);
```

The first parameter, `bigEndian`, accepts a Boolean argument. Set this argument to `true` to use big-endian or `false` to use little-endian.

In addition, you have the option to indicate whether a byte order mark preamble should be generated so that readers of the file will know which endianness is in use.

See Also

The "ASCIIEncoding Class" and "UnicodeEncoding Class" topics in the MSDN documentation.

3.5 Determining Whether a String Is a Valid Number

Problem

You have a string that possibly contains a numeric value. You need to know whether this string contains a valid number.

Solution

Use the static `TryParse` method of any of the numeric types. For example, to determine whether a string contains a double, use the following method:

```
string str = "12.5";
double result = 0;
if(double.TryParse(str,
        System.Globalization.NumberStyles.Float,
        System.Globalization.NumberFormatInfo.CurrentInfo,
        out result))
{
    // Is a double!
}
```

Discussion

This recipe shows how to determine whether a string contains only a numeric value. The `TryParse` method returns `true` if the string contains a valid number without the exception that you will get if you use the `Parse` method.

See Also

The "Parse" and "TryParse" topics in the MSDN documentation.

3.6 Rounding a Floating-Point Value

Problem

You need to round a number to a whole number or to a specific number of decimal places.

Solution

To round any number to its nearest whole number, use the overloaded static `Math.Round` method, which takes only a single argument:

```
int i = (int)Math.Round(2.5555); // i == 3
```

If you need to round a floating-point value to a specific number of decimal places, use the overloaded static `Math.Round` method, which takes two arguments:

```
double dbl = Math.Round(2.5555, 2); // dbl == 2.56
```

Discussion

The Round method is easy to use; however, you need to be aware of how the rounding operation works. The Round method follows IEEE Standard 754, section 4. This means that if the number being rounded is halfway between two numbers, the Round operation will always round to the even number. This example illustrates the standard:

```
double dbl1 = Math.Round(1.5); // dbl1 == 2
double dbl2 = Math.Round(2.5); // dbl2 == 2
```

Notice that 1.5 is rounded up to the nearest even whole number (2) and 2.5 is rounded down to the nearest even whole number (also 2). Keep this in mind when using the Round method.

This method is known as Banker's Rounding; it was invented because it introduces less bias when you're rounding large sets of numbers that include halves, as sets containing currencies often do.

See Also

The "Math Class" topic in the MSDN documentation.

3.7 Choosing a Rounding Algorithm

Problem

The `Math.Round` method will round the value 1.5 to 2; however, it will also round the value 2.5 to 2. You might prefer to round to the greater number (e.g., round 2.5 to 3 instead of 2). Conversely, you might prefer to round to the lesser number (e.g., round 1.5 to 1).

Solution

Use the static `Math.Floor` method to always round up when a value is halfway between two whole numbers:

```
public static double RoundUp(double valueToRound) =>
    Math.Floor(valueToRound + 0.5);
```

Use the following technique to always round down when a value is halfway between two whole numbers:

```
public static double RoundDown(double valueToRound)
{
    double floorValue = Math.Floor(valueToRound);
    if ((valueToRound - floorValue) > .5)
        return (floorValue + 1);
    else
        return (floorValue);
}
```

Discussion

The static `Math.Round` method rounds to the nearest even number. However, there are times that you do not want to round a number in this manner. The static `Math.Floor` method can be used to allow for different manners of rounding.

 The methods used to round numbers in this recipe do not round to a specific number of decimal points; rather, they round to the nearest whole number.

See Also

The "Math Class" topic in the MSDN documentation.

3.8 Safely Performing a Narrowing Numeric Cast

Problem

You need to cast a value from a larger value to a smaller one, while gracefully handling conditions that result in a loss of information. For example, casting a `long` to an `int` results in a loss of information only if the `long` data type is greater than `int.Max Size`.

Solution

The simplest way to handle this scenario is to use the `checked` keyword. The following extension method accepts two `long` data types and attempts to add them together. The result is stuffed into an `int` data type. If an overflow condition exists, the `Over flowException` is thrown:

```
public static class DataTypeExtMethods
{
    public static int AddNarrowingChecked(this long lhs, long rhs) =>
```

```
            checked((int)(lhs + rhs));
    }

    // Code that uses the extension method
    long lhs = 34000;
    long rhs = long.MaxValue;
    try
    {
        int result = lhs.AddNarrowingChecked(rhs);
    }
    catch(OverflowException)
    {
        // could not be added
    }
```

This is the simplest method. However, if you do not want the overhead of throwing an exception and having to wrap a lot of code in try-catch blocks to handle the overflow condition, you can use the MaxValue and MinValue fields of each type. You can perform a check using these fields prior to the conversion to ensure that no information is lost. If the cast will cause an information loss, the code can inform the application beforehand. You can use the following conditional statement to determine whether sourceValue can be cast to a short without losing any information:

```
    // Our two variables are declared and initialized.
    int sourceValue = 34000;
    short destinationValue = 0;

    // Determine if sourceValue will lose information in a cast to a short.
    if (sourceValue <= short.MaxValue && sourceValue >= short.MinValue)
        destinationValue = (short)sourceValue;
    else
    {
        // Inform the application that a loss of information will occur.
    }
```

Discussion

A *narrowing conversion* occurs when a larger type is cast down to a smaller type. For instance, consider casting a value of type Int32 to a value of type Int16. If the Int32 value is less than or equal to the Int16.MaxValue field and the Int32 value is greater than or equal to the Int16.MinValue field, the cast will occur without error or loss of information. Loss of information occurs when the Int32 value is greater than the Int16.MaxValue field or the Int32 value is less than the Int16.MinValue field. In either case, the most significant bits of the Int32 value are truncated and discarded, changing the value after the cast.

If a loss of information occurs in an unchecked context, it will occur silently without the application noticing. This problem can cause some very insidious bugs that are hard to track down. To prevent this, check the value to be converted to determine whether it is within the lower and upper bounds of the type that it will be cast to. If the value is outside these bounds, then code can be written to handle this situation. This code could prevent the cast from occurring and/or inform the application of the casting problem. This solution can help prevent hard-to-find arithmetic bugs from creeping into your applications.

Both techniques shown in the Solution section are valid. However, the technique you use will depend on whether you expect to hit the overflow case on a regular basis or only occasionally. If you expect to hit the overflow case quite often, you might want to choose the second technique of manually testing the numeric value. Otherwise, it might be easier to use the checked keyword, as in the first technique.

 In C#, code can run in either a *checked* or *unchecked* context; by default, the code runs in an unchecked context. In a checked context, any arithmetic and conversions involving integral types are examined to determine whether an overflow condition exists. If so, an OverflowException is thrown. In an unchecked context, no OverflowException will be thrown when an overflow condition exists.

You can set up a checked context by using the /checked{+} compiler switch to set the Check for Arithmetic Overflow/Underflow project property to true, or by using the checked keyword. You can set up an unchecked context by using the /checked- compiler switch to set the Check for Arithmetic Overflow/Underflow project property to false, or by using the unchecked keyword.

You should be aware of the following when performing a conversion:

- Casting from a float, double, or decimal type to an integral type results in the truncation of the fractional portion of this number. Furthermore, if the integral portion of the number exceeds MaxValue for the target type, the result will be undefined unless the conversion is done in a checked context, in which case it will trigger an OverflowException.

- Casting from a float or double to a decimal results in the float or double being rounded to 28 decimal places.

- Casting from a double to a float results in the double being rounded to the nearest float value.

- Casting from a decimal to a float or double results in the decimal being rounded to the resulting type (float or double).

- Casting from an int, uint, or long to a float could result in the loss of precision, but never magnitude.

- Casting from a `long` to a `double` could result in the loss of precision, but never magnitude.

See Also

The "Checked Keyword" and "Checked and Unchecked" topics in the MSDN documentation.

3.9 Testing for a Valid Enumeration Value

Problem

When you pass a numeric value to a method that accepts an enumeration type, it is possible to pass a value that does not exist in the enumeration. You want to perform a test before using this numeric value to determine if it is indeed one of the ones defined in this enumeration type.

Solution

To prevent this problem, test for the specific enumeration values that you allow for the enumeration-type parameter using a `switch` statement to list the values.

Using the following `Language` enumeration:

```
public enum Language
{
    Other = 0, CSharp = 1, VBNET = 2, VB6 = 3,
    All = (Other | CSharp | VBNET | VB6)
}
```

Suppose you have a method that accepts the `Language` enumeration, such as the following method:

```
public void HandleEnum(Language language)
{
    // Use language here...
}
```

You need a method to define the enumeration values you can accept in `HandleEnum`. The `CheckLanguageEnumValue` method shown here does that:

```
public static bool CheckLanguageEnumValue(Language language)
{
    switch (language)
    {
        // all valid types for the enum listed here
        // this means only the ones we specify are valid
        // not any enum value for this enum
```

```
            case Language.CSharp:
            case Language.Other:
            case Language.VB6:
            case Language.VBNET:
                break;
            default:
                Debug.Assert(false,
                    $"{language} is not a valid enumeration value to pass.");
                return false;
        }
        return true;
    }
```

Discussion

Although the Enum class contains the static IsDefined method, it should not be used. IsDefined uses reflection internally, which incurs a performance penalty. Also, versioning of the enumeration is not handled well. Consider the scenario in which you add the value ManagedCPlusPlus to the Languages enum in the next version of your software. If IsDefined is used to check the argument here, it will allow MgdCpp as a valid value, since it is defined in the enumeration, even though the code for which you are validating the parameter is not designed to handle it. By being specific with the switch statement shown in CheckLanguageEnumValue, you reject the MgdCpp value, and the code does not try to run in an invalid context. This is, after all, what you were after in the first place.

The enumeration check should always be used whenever the method is visible to external objects. An external object can invoke methods with public visibility, so any enumerated value passed in to this method should be screened before it is actually used.

Methods with private visibility may not need this extra level of protection. Use your own judgment on whether to use the CheckLanguageEnumValue method to evaluate enumeration values passed in to private methods.

The HandleEnum method can be called in several different ways, two of which are shown here:

```
HandleEnum(Language.CSharp);
HandleEnum((Language)1); // 1 is CSharp
```

Either of these method calls is valid. Unfortunately, the following method calls are also valid:

```
HandleEnum((Language)100);
int someVar = 42;
HandleEnum((Language)someVar);
```

These method calls will also compile without errors, but odd behavior will result if the code in HandleEnum tries to use the value passed in to it (in this case, the value 100). In many cases, an exception will not even be thrown; HandleEnum just receives the value 100 as an argument, as if it were a legitimate value of the Language enumeration.

The CheckLanguageEnumValue method prevents this from happening by screening the argument for valid Language enumeration values. The following code shows the modified body of the HandleEnum method:

```
public static void HandleEnum(Language language)
{
    if (CheckLanguageEnumValue(language))
    {
        // Use language here
        Console.WriteLine($"{language} is an OK enum value");
    }
    else
    {
        // Deal with the invalid enum value here
        Console.WriteLine($"{language} is not an OK enum value");
    }
}
```

See Also

To test for a valid enumeration within an enumeration marked with the Flags attribute, see Recipe 3.10.

3.10 Using Enumerated Members in a Bit Mask

Problem

You need an enumeration of values to act as bit flags that can be ORed together to create a combination of values (flags) in the enumeration.

Solution

Mark the enumeration with the Flags attribute:

```
[Flags]
public enum RecycleItems
{
    None        = 0x00,
    Glass       = 0x01,
    AluminumCans = 0x02,
    MixedPaper  = 0x04,
```

```
    Newspaper    = 0x08
}
```

Combining elements of this enumeration is a simple matter of using the bitwise OR operator (|). For example:

```
RecycleItems items = RecycleItems.Glass | RecycleItems.Newspaper;
```

Discussion

Adding the Flags attribute to an enumeration marks this enumeration as individual bit flags that can be ORed together. Using an enumeration of flags is no different than using a regular enumeration type. Note that failing to mark an enumeration with the Flags attribute will not generate an exception or a compile-time error, even if the enumeration values are used as bit flags.

The addition of the Flags attribute provides you with two benefits. First, if the Flags attribute is placed on an enumeration, the ToString and ToString("G") methods return a string consisting of the name of the constant(s) separated by commas. Otherwise, these two methods return the numeric representation of the enumeration value. Note that the ToString("F") method returns a string consisting of the name of the constant(s) separated by commas, regardless of whether this enumeration is marked with the Flags attribute. The second benefit is that when you examine the code and encounter an enumeration, you can better determine the developer's intention for this enumeration. If the developer explicitly defined it as containing bit flags (with the Flags attribute), you can use it as such.

An enumeration tagged with the Flags attribute can be viewed as a single value or as one or more values combined into a single enumeration value. If you need to accept multiple languages at a single time, you can write the following code:

```
RecycleItems items = RecycleItems.Glass | RecycleItems.Newspaper;
```

The variable items is now equal to the bit values of the two enumeration values ORed together. These values ORed together will equal 3, as shown here:

```
RecycleItems.Glass          0001
RecycleItems.AluminumCans   0010
ORed bit values             0011
```

The enumeration values were converted to binary and ORed together to get the binary value 0011, or 3 in base10. The compiler views this value both as two individual enumeration values (RecycleItems.Glass and RecycleItems.AluminumCans) ORed together or as a single value (3).

To determine if a single flag has been turned on in an enumeration variable, use the bitwise AND (&) operator, as follows:

```
RecycleItems items = RecycleItems.Glass | RecycleItems.Newspaper;
if((items & RecycleItems.Glass) == RecycleItems.Glass)
    Console.WriteLine("The enum contains the C# enumeration value");
else
    Console.WriteLine("The enum does NOT contain the C# value");
```

This code will display the text The enum contains the C# enumeration value. The
ANDing of these two values will produce 0 if the variable items does not contain the
value RecycleItems.Glass, or produce RecycleItems.Glass if items contains this
enumeration value. Basically, ANDing these two values looks like this in binary:

```
RecycleItems.Glass | RecycleItems.AluminumCans 0011
RecycleItems.Glass                              0001
ANDed bit values                                0001
```

We will deal with this in more detail in Recipe 3.11.

In some cases, the enumeration can grow quite large. You can add many other recyclable items to this enumeration, as shown here:

```
[Flags]
public enum RecycleItems
{
    None        = 0x00,
    Glass       = 0x01,
    AluminumCans = 0x02,
    MixedPaper  = 0x04,
    Newspaper   = 0x08,
    TinCans     = 0x10,
    Cardboard   = 0x20,
    ClearPlastic = 0x40,
}
```

If you needed a RecycleItems enumeration value to represent all recyclable items,
you would have to OR together each value of this enumeration:

```
RecycleItems items = RecycleItems.Glass | RecycleItems.AluminumCans |
                     RecycleItems.MixedPaper;
```

Instead of doing this, you can simply add a new value to this enumeration that
includes all recyclable items:

```
[Flags]
public enum RecycleItems
{
    None         = 0x00,
    Glass        = 0x01,
    AluminumCans  = 0x02,
    MixedPaper   = 0x04,
    Newspaper    = 0x08,
    TinCans      = 0x10,
    Cardboard    = 0x20,
    ClearPlastic = 0x40,
```

```
    All = (None | Glass | AluminumCans | MixedPaper | Newspaper | TinCans |
        Cardboard | ClearPlastic)
}
```

Now there is a single enumeration value, All, that encompasses every value of this enumeration. Notice that there are two methods of creating the All enumeration value. The second method is much easier to read. Regardless of which method you use, if individual language elements of the enumeration are added or deleted, you will have to modify the All value accordingly.

 You should provide a None value for all enums even where "none of the above" does not make sense, because it is always legal to assign literal 0 to an enum, and because enum variables, which begin their lives assigned to their default values, start as 0.

Similarly, you can also add values to capture specific subsets of enumeration values as follows:

```
[Flags]
enum Language
{
    CSharp = 0x0001, VBNET = 0x0002, VB6 = 0x0004, Cpp = 0x0008,
    CobolNET = 0x000F, FortranNET = 0x0010, JSharp = 0x0020,
    MSIL = 0x0080,
    All = (CSharp | VBNET | VB6 | Cpp | FortranNET | JSharp | MSIL),
    VBOnly = (VBNET | VB6),
    NonVB = (CSharp | Cpp | FortranNET | JSharp | MSIL)
}
```

Now you have two extra members in the enumerations—one that encompasses VB-only languages (Languages.VBNET and Languages.VB6) and one that encompasses non-VB languages.

3.11 Determining Whether One or More Enumeration Flags Are Set

Problem

You need to determine if a variable of an enumeration type, consisting of bit flags, contains one or more specific flags. For example, given the following enumeration Language:

```
[Flags]
enum Language
{
    CSharp = 0x0001, VBNET = 0x0002, VB6 = 0x0004, Cpp = 0x0008
}
```

determine, using Boolean logic, if the variable `lang` in the following line of code contains a language such as `Language.CSharp` and/or `Language.Cpp`:

```
Language lang = Language.CSharp | Language.VBNET;
```

Solution

To determine if a variable contains a single bit flag that is set, use the following conditional:

```
if((lang & Language.CSharp) == Language.CSharp)
{
    // Lang contains at least Language.CSharp.
}
```

To determine if a variable exclusively contains a single bit flag that is set, use the following conditional:

```
if(lang == Language.CSharp)
{
    // lang contains only the Language.CSharp
}
```

To determine if a variable contains a set of bit flags that are all set, use the following conditional:

```
if((lang & (Language.CSharp | Language.VBNET)) ==
  (Language.CSharp | Language.VBNET))
{
    // lang contains at least Language.CSharp and Language.VBNET.
}
```

To determine if a variable exclusively contains a set of bit flags that are all set, use the following conditional:

```
if((lang | (Language.CSharp | Language.VBNET)) ==
  (Language.CSharp | Language.VBNET))
{
    // lang contains only the Language.CSharp and Language.VBNET.
}
```

Discussion

When enumerations are used as bit flags and are marked with the `Flags` attribute, they usually will require some kind of conditional testing to be performed. This testing necessitates the use of the bitwise AND (&) and OR (|) operators.

To test for a variable having a specific bit flag set, use the following conditional statement:

```
if((lang & Language.CSharp) == Language.CSharp)
```

where `lang` is of the `Language` enumeration type.

The `&` operator is used with a bit mask to determine if a bit is set to `1`. The result of ANDing two bits is `1` only when both bits are `1`; otherwise, the result is `0`. You can use this operation to determine if a specific bit flag is set to `1` in the number containing the individual bit flags. If you AND the variable `lang` with the specific bit flag you are testing for (in this case, `Language.CSharp`), you can extract that single specific bit flag. The expression (`lang & Language.CSharp`) is solved in the following manner if `lang` is equal to `Language.CSharp`:

```
Language.CSharp   0001
lang              0001
ANDed bit values 0001
```

If `lang` is equal to another value, such as `Language.VBNET`, the expression is solved as follows:

```
Language.CSharp   0001
lang              0010
ANDed bit values 0000
```

Notice that ANDing the bits together returns the value `Language.CSharp` in the first expression and `0x0000` in the second expression. Comparing this result to the value you are looking for (`Language.CSharp`) tells you whether that specific bit was turned on.

This method is great for checking specific bits, but what if you want to know whether only one specific bit is turned on (and all other bits turned off) or off (and all other bits turned on)? To test if only the `Language.CSharp` bit is turned on in the variable `lang`, you can use the following conditional statement:

```
if(lang == Language.CSharp)
```

If the variable `lang` contained only the value `Language.CSharp`, the expression using the OR operator would look like this:

```
lang = Language.CSharp;
if ((lang != 0) &&(Language.CSharp == (lang | Language.CSharp)))
{
    // CSharp is found using OR logic
}

Language.CSharp 0001
lang 0001
ORed bit values 0001
```

Now, add a language value or two to the variable `lang` and perform the same operation on `lang`:

```
lang = Language.CSharp | Language.VB6 | Language.Cpp;
if ((lang != 0) &&(Language.CSharp == (lang | Language.CSharp)))
```

```
{
    // CSharp is found using OR logic
}
```

```
Language.CSharp 0001
lang 1101
ORed bit values 1101
```

The first expression results in the same value as the one you are testing against. The second expression results in a much larger value than `Language.CSharp`. This indicates that the variable `lang` in the first expression contains only the value `Language.CSharp`, whereas the second expression contains other languages besides `Language.CSharp` (and may not contain `Language.CSharp` at all).

Using the OR version of this formula, you can test multiple bits to determine if they are on and all other bits are off, as shown in the following conditional statement:

```
if((lang != 0) && ((lang | (Language.CSharp | Language.VBNET)) ==
    (Language.CSharp | Language.VBNET)))
```

Notice that to test for more than one language, you simply OR the language values together. By switching the first | operator to an & operator, you can determine if at least these bits are turned on, as shown in the following conditional statement:

```
if((lang != 0) && ((lang & (Language.CSharp | Language.VBNET)) ==
    (Language.CSharp | Language.VBNET)))
```

When testing for multiple enumeration values, you may find it beneficial to add a value to your enumeration, which ORs together all the values you want to test for. If you wanted to test for all languages except `Language.CSharp`, your conditional statement(s) would grow quite large and unwieldy. To fix this, you add a value to the `Language` enumeration that ORs together all languages except `Language.CSharp`. The new enumeration looks like this:

```
[Flags]
enum Language
{
    CSharp = 0x0001, VBNET = 0x0002, VB6 = 0x0004, Cpp = 0x0008,
    AllLanguagesExceptCSharp = VBNET | VB6 | Cpp
}
```

and your conditional statement might look similar to the following:

```
if((lang != 0) && (lang | Language.AllLanguagesExceptCSharp) ==
    Language. AllLanguagesExceptCSharp)
```

This is quite a bit smaller, easier to manage, and easier to read.

Use the AND operator when testing if one or more bits are set to 1.
Use the OR operator when testing if one or more bits are set to 0.

CHAPTER 4
Language Integrated Query (LINQ) and Lambda Expressions

4.0 Introduction

Language Integrated Query (LINQ) is a great way to access data from many different sources. LINQ provides a single querying model that can operate against different data domains individually or all together in a single query. LINQ brings the ability to query data to .NET languages, and some of the languages have provided extensions to make its use even more intuitive. One of these languages is C#; there are a number of extensions to the language in C# that help to facilitate querying in a rich and intuitive manner.

Traditional object-oriented programming is based on an imperative style wherein developers describe in detail not only what they want to happen, but also exactly how it should be performed through code. LINQ helps to take coding down a more declarative path that facilitates describing what the developer wants to do instead of detailing how to accomplish the goal. LINQ also enables a more functional style of programming. These changes can dramatically shorten the amount of code it takes to perform some tasks. That said, object-oriented programming is still very much alive and well in C# and .NET, but for the first time the language is offering you the chance to choose the style of programming based on your needs. Note, however, that LINQ will not fit into every scenario and is not a replacement for good design or practice. You can write bad code using LINQ just as you can write bad object-oriented or procedural code. The trick, as it always has been, is to figure out when it is appropriate to use which technique.

The initial version of LINQ encompasses a number of data domains:

- LINQ to Objects
- LINQ to XML
- LINQ to ADO.NET
- LINQ to SQL
- LINQ to DataSet
- LINQ to Entities

As you begin your examination of LINQ, it is easy to think of it as a new object relational mapping layer, or some neat new widget on IEnumerable<T>, or a new XML API, or even just an excuse to not write SQL directly anymore. You can use it as any of these things, but we would encourage you to instead think of LINQ as how your program asks for, calculates, or transforms sets of data from both single and disparate sources. It takes a bit of time and playing with LINQ for its functionality to click, but once it does, you will be surprised at what you can do with it. This chapter begins to show some of what is possible with LINQ and will hopefully get you thinking of which of your scenarios are applicable to this new capability in C#.

To write the LINQ query expressions to specify criteria and select data, we use lambda expressions. They are a convenient way to represent the delegate passed to LINQ queries like System.Func<T, TResult> when the Enumerable.Where method is called as part of narrowing down a result set. *Lambda expressions* are functions with a different syntax that enables them to be used in an expression context instead of the usual object-oriented method of being a member of a class. This means that with a single syntax, we can express a method definition, declaration, and the invocation of delegate to execute it, just as anonymous methods can, but with a more terse syntax. A *projection* is a lambda expression that translates one type into another.

A lambda expression looks like this:

```
j => j * 42
```

This means "using j as the parameter to the function, j goes to the result of j * 42." The => can be read as "goes to" for both this and a projection declared like so:

```
j => new { Number = j*42 };
```

If you think about it, in C# 1.0 you could do the same thing:

```
public delegate int IncreaseByANumber(int j);
public delegate int MultipleIncreaseByANumber(int j, int k, int l);

static public int MultiplyByANumber(int j)
{
    return j * 42;
```

```
    }

    public static void ExecuteCSharp1_0()
    {
        IncreaseByANumber increase =
            new IncreaseByANumber(
                DelegatesEventsLambdaExpressions.MultiplyByANumber);
        Console.WriteLine(increase(10));
    }
```

In C# 2.0 with anonymous methods, the C# 1.0 syntax could be reduced to the following example, as it is no longer necessary to provide the name for the delegate since all we want is the result of the operation:

```
public delegate int IncreaseByANumber(int j);

public static void ExecuteCSharp2_0()
{
    IncreaseByANumber increase =
        new IncreaseByANumber(
        delegate(int j)
        {
            return j * 42;
        });
    Console.WriteLine(increase(10));
}
```

This brings us back to C# today and lambda expressions, where we can now just write:

```
public static void ExecuteCSharp6_0()
{
    // declare the lambda expression
    IncreaseByANumber increase = j => j * 42;
    // invoke the method and print 420 to the console
    Console.WriteLine(increase(10));

    MultipleIncreaseByANumber multiple = (j, k, l) => ((j * 42) / k) % l;
    Console.WriteLine(multiple(10, 11, 12));
}
```

Type inference helps the compiler to infer the type of j from the declaration of the IncreaseByANumber delegate type. If there were multiple arguments, then the lambda expression could look like this:

```
MultipleIncreaseByANumber multiple = (j, k, l) => ((j * 42) / k) % l;
Console.WriteLine(multiple(10, 11, 12));
```

This chapter's recipes make use of delegates, events, and lambda expressions. Among other topics, these recipes cover:

- Handling each method invoked in a multicast delegate separately

- Synchronous delegate invocation versus asynchronous delegate invocation
- Enhancing an existing class with events
- Various uses of lambda expressions, closures, and functors

If you are not familiar with delegates, events, or lambda expressions, you should read the MSDN documentation on these topics. There are also good tutorials and example code showing you how to set them up and use them in a basic fashion.

4.1 Querying a Message Queue

Problem

You want to be able to query for messages with specific criteria from an existing message queue.

Solution

Use the EnumerableMessageQueue class to write a LINQ query to retrieve messages using the System.Messaging.MessageQueue type:

```
string queuePath = @".\private$\LINQMQ";
EnumerableMessageQueue messageQueue = null;
if (!EnumerableMessageQueue.Exists(queuePath))
    messageQueue = EnumerableMessageQueue.Create(queuePath);
else
    messageQueue = new EnumerableMessageQueue(queuePath);

using (messageQueue)
{
    BinaryMessageFormatter messageFormatter = new BinaryMessageFormatter();

    // Query the message queue for specific messages with the following criteria:
    // 1) the label must be less than 5
    // 2) the name of the type in the message body must contain 'CSharpRecipes.D'
    // 3) the results should be in descending order by type name (from the body)

    var query = from Message msg in messageQueue
        // The first assignment to msg.Formatter is so that we can touch the
        // Message object. It assigns the BinaryMessageFormatter to each message
        // instance so that it can be read to determine if it matches the
        // criteria. This is done and then checks that the formatter was
        // correctly assigned by performing an equality check which satisfies the
        // where clause's need for a Boolean result while still executing the
        // assignment of the formatter.
        where ((msg.Formatter = messageFormatter) == messageFormatter) &&
                    int.Parse(msg.Label) < 5 &&
                    msg.Body.ToString().Contains("CSharpRecipes.D")
                orderby msg.Body.ToString() descending
```

```
            select msg;

    // check our results for messages with a label > 5 and containing
    // a 'D' in the name
    foreach (var msg in query)
        Console.WriteLine($"Label: {msg.Label}" +
            $" Body: {msg.Body}");
}
```

The query retrieves the data from the `MessageQueue` by selecting the messages where the `Label` is a number greater than 5 and the message body contains the text "CSharpRecipes.D". These messages are then returned, sorted by the message body in descending order.

Discussion

There are a number of keywords in this LINQ code that were not previously used to access a message queue:

`var`

> `var` instructs the compiler to infer the variable type from the right side of the statement. In essence, the variable type is determined by what is on the right side of the operator, separating the `var` keyword and the expression. This allows for implicitly typed local variables.

`from`

> The `from` keyword sets out the source collection to query against and a range variable to represent a single element from that collection. It is always the first clause in a query operation. This may seem counterintuitive if you are used to SQL and expect `select` to be first, but if you consider that we need to know what to work on before we determine what to return, it makes sense. In fact, if we weren't already used to how SQL works, it would be SQL that seems counterintuitive.

`where`

> The `where` keyword specifies the constraints by which the elements to return are filtered. Each condition must evaluate to a Boolean result, and when all expressions evaluate to `true`, the element of the collection is allowed to be selected.

`orderby`

> `orderby` indicates that the result set should be sorted according to the criteria specified. The default order is ascending, and elements use the default comparer.

`select`

> `select` allows the projection of an entire element from the collection, the construction of a new type with parts of that element and other calculated values, or a subcollection of items into the result.

The messageQueue collection is of type System.Messaging.MessageQueue, which implements the IEnumerable interface. This is important, as the LINQ methods provided need a set or collection to implement at least IEnumerable in order to work with that set or collection. It is possible to implement a set of extension methods that do not need IEnumerable, but most people will not have the need to do so. It is even better when the set or collection implements IEnumerable<T>, as LINQ then knows the type of element in the set or collection with which it is working.

Even though MessageQueue implements the IEnumerable interface (but not IEnumerable<T>), the original implementation of IEnumerable had some problems, so now if you try to use it, it doesn't actually enumerate any results. You will also get a deprecation warning reading This method returns a MessageEnumerator that implements RemoveCurrent family of methods incorrectly. Please use GetMessageEnumerator2 instead. if you try to use GetEnumerator on MessageQueue.

To address this, we have created the EnumerableMessageQueue, which derives from MessageQueue but uses the suggested GetMessageEnumerator2 method to implement both IEnumerable and IEnumerable<Message>. So we can just use the EnumerableMessageQueue instance with LINQ:

```
public class EnumerableMessageQueue : MessageQueue, IEnumerable<Message>
{
    public EnumerableMessageQueue() :
        base() { }
    public EnumerableMessageQueue(string path) : base(path) { }
    public EnumerableMessageQueue(string path, bool sharedModeDenyReceive) :
        base (path, sharedModeDenyReceive) { }
    public EnumerableMessageQueue(string path, QueueAccessMode accessMode) :
        base (path, accessMode) { }
    public EnumerableMessageQueue(string path, bool sharedModeDenyReceive,
        bool enableCache) : base (path, sharedModeDenyReceive, enableCache) { }
    public EnumerableMessageQueue(string path, bool sharedModeDenyReceive,
        bool enableCache, QueueAccessMode accessMode) :
            base (path, sharedModeDenyReceive, enableCache, accessMode) { }

    public static new EnumerableMessageQueue Create(string path) =>
        Create(path, false);

    public static new EnumerableMessageQueue Create(string path,
        bool transactional)
    {
        // Use MessageQueue directly to make sure the queue exists
        if (!MessageQueue.Exists(path))
            MessageQueue.Create(path, transactional);
        // create the enumerable queue once we know it is there
        return new EnumerableMessageQueue(path);
    }

    public new MessageEnumerator GetMessageEnumerator()
```

```
    {
        throw new NotSupportedException("Please use GetEnumerator");
    }

    public new MessageEnumerator GetMessageEnumerator2()
    {
        throw new NotSupportedException("Please use GetEnumerator");
    }

    IEnumerator<Message> IEnumerable<Message>.GetEnumerator()
    {
        //NOTE: In .NET 3.5, you used to be able to call "GetEnumerator" on
        //MessageQueue via normal LINQ semantics and have it work. Now we
        //have to call GetMessageEnumerator2, as GetEnumerator has been
        //deprecated. Now we use EnumerableMessageQueue which deals with
        //this for us...
        MessageEnumerator messageEnumerator = base.GetMessageEnumerator2();
        while (messageEnumerator.MoveNext())
        {
            yield return messageEnumerator.Current;
        }
    }

    IEnumerator IEnumerable.GetEnumerator()
    {
        //NOTE: In .NET 3.5, you used to be able to call "GetEnumerator" on
        //MessageQueue via normal LINQ semantics and have it work. Now we have
        // to call GetMessageEnumerator2, as GetEnumerator has been deprecated.
        //Now we use EnumerableMessageQueue which deals with this for us...
        MessageEnumerator messageEnumerator = base.GetMessageEnumerator2();
        while (messageEnumerator.MoveNext())
        {
            yield return messageEnumerator.Current;
        }
    }
}
```

Now the query provides the element type Message, as shown in the from line in the LINQ query:

```
var query = from Message msg in messageQueue
```

In the Solution, the messages in the queue have been sent with BinaryFormatter. To be able to query against them correctly, the Formatter property must be set on each Message before it is examined as part of the where clause:

```
// The first assignment to msg.Formatter is so that we can touch the
// Message object. It assigns the BinaryMessageFormatter to each message
// instance so that it can be read to determine if it matches the criteria.
// This is done, and then it checks that the formatter was correctly assigned
// by performing an equality check, which satisfies the where clause's need
// for a boolean result, while still executing the assignment of the formatter.
where ((msg.Formatter = messageFormatter) == messageFormatter) &&
```

There are two uses of the var keyword in the Solution code:

```
var query = from Message msg in messageQueue
        ...

foreach (var msg in query)
...
```

The first usage infers that an IEnumerable<Message> will be returned and assigned to the query variable. The second usage infers that the type of msg is Message because the query variable is of type IEnumerable<Message> and the msg variable is an element from that IEnumerable.

It is also worth noting that when performing operations in a query, you can use actual C# code to determine the conditions, and there is more than just the predetermined set of operators. In the where clause of this query, both int.Parse and string. Contains are used to help filter messages:

```
int.Parse(msg.Label) > 5 &&
msg.Body.ToString().Contains('CSharpRecipes.D')
```

Finally, the orderby is used to sort the results in descending order:

```
orderby msg.Body.ToString() descending
```

See Also

Recipe 4.9, and the "MessageQueue class," "Implicitly typed local variable," "from keyword," "where keyword," "orderby keyword," and "select keyword" topics in the MSDN documentation.

4.2 Using Set Semantics with Data

Problem

You would like to work with your collections using set operations for union, intersections, exceptions, and distinct items.

Solution

Use the set operators provided as part of the standard query operators to perform those operations.

Distinct:

```
IEnumerable<string> whoLoggedIn =
    dailySecurityLog.Where(
        logEntry => logEntry.Contains("logged in")).Distinct();
```

Union:

```
// Union
Console.WriteLine("Employees for all projects");
var allProjectEmployees = project1.Union(project2.Union(project3));
```

Intersect:

```
// Intersect
Console.WriteLine("Employees on every project");
var everyProjectEmployees = project1.Intersect(project2.Intersect(project3));
```

Except:

```
Console.WriteLine("Employees on only one project");
var onlyProjectEmployees = allProjectEmployees.Except(unionIntersect);
```

Discussion

The standard query operators are the set of methods that represent the LINQ pattern. This set includes operators to perform many different types of operations, such as filtering, projection, sorting, grouping, and many others, including set operations.

The set operations for the standard query operators are:

- Distinct
- Union
- Intersect
- Except

The Distinct operator extracts all nonduplicate items from the collection or result set being worked with. Say, for example, that we had a set of strings representing today's login and logout behavior for a virtual machine in a common use development environment:

```
string[] dailySecurityLog = {
        "Rakshit logged in",
        "Aaron logged in",
        "Rakshit logged out",
        "Ken logged in",
        "Rakshit logged in",
        "Mahesh logged in",
        "Jesse logged in",
        "Jason logged in",
        "Josh logged in",
        "Melissa logged in",
        "Rakshit logged out",
        "Mary-Ellen logged out",
        "Mahesh logged in",
        "Alex logged in",
```

```
        "Scott logged in",
        "Aaron logged out",
        "Jesse logged out",
        "Scott logged out",
        "Dave logged in",
        "Ken logged out",
        "Alex logged out",
        "Rakshit logged in",
        "Dave logged out",
        "Josh logged out",
        "Jason logged out"};
```

From that collection, we would like to determine the list of people who logged in to the virtual machine today. Since people can log in and log out many times during the course of a day or remain logged in for the whole day, we need to eliminate the duplicate login entries. Distinct is an extension method on the System.Linq.Enumerable class (which implements the standard query operators) that we can call on the string array (which supports IEnumerable) in order to get the distinct set of items from the collection. (For more information on extension methods, see Recipe 4.4.) To get the set, we use another of the standard query operators, where, which takes a lambda expression that determines the filter criteria for the set and examines each string in the IEnumerable<string> to determine if the string has "logged in." Lambda expressions are inline statements (similar to anonymous methods) that can be used in place of a delegate. (See Recipe 4.12 for more on lambda expressions.) If the strings have logged in, then they are selected. Distinct narrows down the set of strings further to eliminate duplicate "logged in" records, leaving only one per user:

```
IEnumerable<string> whoLoggedIn =
    dailySecurityLog.Where(
        logEntry => logEntry.Contains("logged in")).Distinct();
Console.WriteLine("Everyone who logged in today:");
foreach (string who in whoLoggedIn)
    Console.WriteLine(who);
```

To make things a bit more interesting, for the rest of the operators we will work with sets of employees on various projects in a company. An Employee is a pretty simple class with a Name and overrides for ToString, Equals, and GetHashCode, as shown here:

```
public class Employee
{
    public string Name { get; set; }
    public override string ToString() => this.Name;
    public override bool Equals(object obj) =>
        this.GetHashCode().Equals(obj.GetHashCode());
    public override int GetHashCode() => this.Name.GetHashCode();
}
```

You might wonder why `Equals` and `GetHashCode` are overloaded for such a simple class. The reason is that when LINQ compares elements in the sets or collections, it uses the default comparison, which in turn uses `Equals` and `GetHashCode` to determine if one instance of a reference type is the same as another. If you do not include the semantics in the reference type class to provide the same hash code or equals value when the data for two instances of the object is the same, then by default the instances will be different, as two reference types have different hash codes by default. We override that so that if the `Name` is the same for each `Employee`, the hash code and the equals value will both correctly identify the instances as the same. There are also overloads for the set operators that take a custom comparer, which would also allow you to make this determination even for classes for which you can't make the changes to `Equals` and `GetHashCode`.

Having done this, we can now assign `Employees` to projects like so:

```
Employee[] project1 = {
            new Employee(){ Name = "Rakshit" },
            new Employee(){ Name = "Jason" },
            new Employee(){ Name = "Josh" },
            new Employee(){ Name = "Melissa" },
            new Employee(){ Name = "Aaron" },
            new Employee() { Name = "Dave" },
            new Employee() {Name = "Alex" } };
Employee[] project2 = {
            new Employee(){ Name = "Mahesh" },
            new Employee() {Name = "Ken" },
            new Employee() {Name = "Jesse" },
            new Employee(){ Name = "Melissa" },
            new Employee(){ Name = "Aaron" },
            new Employee(){ Name = "Alex" },
            new Employee(){ Name = "Mary-Ellen" } };
Employee[] project3 = {
            new Employee(){ Name = "Mike" },
            new Employee(){ Name = "Scott" },
            new Employee(){ Name = "Melissa" },
            new Employee(){ Name = "Aaron" },
            new Employee(){ Name = "Alex" },
            new Employee(){ Name = "Jon" } };
```

To find all `Employees` on all projects, we can use `Union` to get all nonduplicate `Employees` in all three projects and write them out, as `Union` will give you all distinct `Employees` of all three projects:

```
// Union
Console.WriteLine("Employees for all projects");
var allProjectEmployees = project1.Union(project2.Union(project3));
foreach (Employee employee in allProjectEmployees)
    Console.WriteLine(employee);
```

We can then use `Intersect` to get the `Employees` on every project, as `Intersect` will determine the common `Employees` from each project and return those:

```
// Intersect
Console.WriteLine("Employees on every project");
var everyProjectEmployees = project1.Intersect(project2.Intersect(project3));
foreach (Employee employee in everyProjectEmployees)
    Console.WriteLine(employee);
```

Finally, we can use a combination of `Union` and `Except` to find `Employees` that are on only one project, as `Except` filters out all `Employees` on more than one project:

```
// Except
var intersect1_3 = project1.Intersect(project3);
var intersect1_2 = project1.Intersect(project2);
var intersect2_3 = project2.Intersect(project3);
var unionIntersect = intersect1_2.Union(intersect1_3).Union(intersect2_3);

Console.WriteLine("Employees on only one project");
var onlyProjectEmployees = allProjectEmployees.Except(unionIntersect);
foreach (Employee employee in onlyProjectEmployees)
    Console.WriteLine(employee);
```

Output for the code shown is:

```
Everyone who logged in today:
Rakshit logged in
Aaron logged in
Ken logged in
Mahesh logged in
Jesse logged in
Jason logged in
Josh logged in
Melissa logged in
Alex logged in
Scott logged in
Dave logged in
Employees for all projects
Rakshit
Jason
Josh
Melissa
Aaron
Dave
Alex
Mahesh
Ken
Jesse
Mary-Ellen
Mike
Scott
Jon
Employees on every project
```

```
Melissa
Aaron
Alex
Employees on only one project
Rakshit
Jason
Josh
Dave
Mahesh
Ken
Jesse
Mary-Ellen
Mike
Scott
Jon
```

See Also

The "Standard Query Operators," "Distinct method," "Union method," "Intersect method," and "Except method" topics in the MSDN documentation.

4.3 Reusing Parameterized Queries with LINQ to SQL

Problem

You need to execute the same parameterized query multiple times with different parameter values, but you want to avoid the overhead of parsing the query expression tree to build the parameterized SQL each time the query executes.

Solution

Use the `CompiledQuery.Compile` method to build an expression tree that will not have to be parsed each time the query is executed with new parameters:

```
var GetEmployees =
    CompiledQuery.Compile((NorthwindLinq2Sql.NorthwindLinq2SqlDataContext nwdc,
        string ac, string ttl) =>
            from employee in nwdc.Employees
            where employee.HomePhone.Contains(ac) &&
                    employee.Title == ttl
            select employee);

var northwindDataContext = new NorthwindLinq2Sql.NorthwindLinq2SqlDataContext();
```

The first time the query executes is when it actually compiles (where `GetEmployees` is called the first time in the `foreach` loop). Every other iteration in this loop and in the next loop uses the compiled version, avoiding the expression tree parsing:

```
foreach (var employee in GetEmployees(northwindDataContext, "(206)",
    "Sales Representative"))
    Console.WriteLine($"{employee.FirstName} {employee.LastName}");

foreach (var employee in GetEmployees(northwindDataContext, "(71)",
    "Sales Manager"))
    Console.WriteLine($"{employee.FirstName} {employee.LastName}");
```

Discussion

We used `var` for the query declaration because it was cleaner, but in this case `var` is actually:

```
System.Func<NorthwindLinq2Sql.NorthwindLinq2SqlDataContext, string, string,
System.Linq.IQueryable<NorthwindLinq2Sql.Employee>>
```

which is the delegate signature for the lambda expression we created that contains the query. That's right—all this crazy query stuff, and we just instantiated a delegate. To be fair, the `Func` delegate was brought about in the `System` namespace as part of LINQ, so do not despair: we are still doing cool stuff!

This illustrates that we are not returning an `IEnumerable`- or `IQueryable`-based result set from `Compile`, but rather an expression tree that represents the potential for a query rather than the query itself. Once we have that tree, LINQ to SQL then has to convert it to actual SQL that can run against the database. Interestingly enough, if we had put in a call to `string.Format` as part of detecting the area code in the employee's home phone number, we would get a `NotSupportedException` informing us that `string.Format` can't be translated to SQL:

```
where employee.HomePhone.Contains(string.Format($"({ac})")) &&

System.NotSupportedException:
Method 'System.String Format(System.String,System.Object)'
  has no supported translation to SQL.
```

This is understandable, as SQL has no concept of .NET Framework methods for performing actions, but keep in mind as you design your queries that this is a limitation of using LINQ to SQL.

After the first execution, the query is compiled, and for every iteration after that, we do not pay the transformation cost for turning the expression tree into the parameterized SQL.

Compiling your queries is recommended for parameterized queries that get a lot of traffic, but if a query is infrequently used, it may not be worth the effort. As always, profile your code to see the areas where doing so could be useful.

Note that in the templates for Entity Framework 5 and up, you could not use `Compi ledQuery` with the context that is generated, because those templates were redone to use `DbContext`, not `ObjectContext`, and `CompiledQuery.Compile` requires an `Object Context`. The good news is that if you are using Entity Framework 5 and up, `DbCon text` does precompilation of queries for you! You can still use `CompiledQuery` with the LINQ to SQL data context.

Microsoft recommends using a `DbContext` in new development, but if you have existing code on prior data access mechanisms, `CompiledQuery` can still help!

See Also

The "CompiledQuery.Compile method" and "Expression Trees" topics in the MSDN documentation.

4.4 Sorting Results in a Culture-Sensitive Manner

Problem

You want to ensure that when you sort in a query, the sort order is for an application-specific culture that may not be the same as the thread's current culture.

Solution

Use the overload of the `OrderBy` query operator, which accepts a custom comparer, in order to specify the culture in which to perform comparisons:

```
// Create CultureInfo for Danish in Denmark.
CultureInfo danish = new CultureInfo("da-DK");
// Create CultureInfo for English in the U.S.
CultureInfo american = new CultureInfo("en-US");

CultureStringComparer comparer =
    new CultureStringComparer(danish,CompareOptions.None);
var query = names.OrderBy(n => n, comparer);
```

Discussion

Handling localization issues such as sorting for a specific culture is a relatively trivial task in .NET if the current culture of the thread is the one you want to use. To access the framework classes that assist in handling culture issues in C, you include the `Sys tem.Globalization` namespace. You'd include this namespace in order to make the code in the Solution run. One example of overriding the thread's current culture would be an application that needs to display a sorted list of Danish words on a version of Windows that is set for US English. This functionality might also be useful if you are working with a multitenant web service or website with global clients.

The current thread in the application may have a `CultureInfo` for "en-US" and, by default, the sort order for `OrderBy` will use the current culture's sort settings. To specify that this list should sort according to Danish rules instead, you must do a bit of work in the form of a custom comparer:

```
CultureStringComparer comparer =
    new CultureStringComparer(danish,CompareOptions.None);
```

The comparer variable is an instance of the custom comparer class `CultureString Comparer`, which is defined to implement the `IComparer<T>` interface specialized for strings. This class is used to provide the culture settings for the sort order:

```
public class CultureStringComparer : IComparer<string>
{
    private CultureStringComparer()
    {
    }

    public CultureStringComparer(CultureInfo cultureInfo, CompareOptions options)
    {
        if (cultureInfo == null)
            throw new ArgumentNullException(nameof(cultureInfo));

        CurrentCultureInfo = cultureInfo;
        Options = options;
    }

    public int Compare(string x, string y) =>
        CurrentCultureInfo.CompareInfo.Compare(x, y, Options);

    public CultureInfo CurrentCultureInfo { get; set; }

    public CompareOptions Options { get; set; }
}
```

To demonstrate how this could be used, first we compile a list of words to order by. Since the Danish language treats the character Æ as an individual letter, sorting it after Z in the alphabet, and the English language treats the character Æ as a special symbol, sorting it before the letter A in the alphabet, this example will demonstrate the sort difference:

```
string[] names = { "Jello", "Apple", "Bar", "Æble",
    "Forsooth", "Orange", "Zanzibar" };
```

Now, we can set up the `CultureInfos` for both Danish and US English and call `OrderBy` with the comparer specific to each culture. This query does not use the query expression syntax, but rather uses the functional style of `IEnumera ble<string>.OrderBy()`:

```
// Create CultureInfo for Danish in Denmark.
CultureInfo danish = new CultureInfo("da-DK");
```

```
// Create CultureInfo for English in the U.S.
CultureInfo american = new CultureInfo("en-US");

CultureStringComparer comparer =
    new CultureStringComparer(danish,CompareOptions.None);
var query = names.OrderBy(n => n, comparer);
Console.WriteLine($"Ordered by specific culture : " +
    $"{comparer.CurrentCultureInfo.Name}");
foreach (string name in query)
    Console.WriteLine(name);


comparer.CurrentCultureInfo = american;
query = names.OrderBy(n => n, comparer);
Console.WriteLine($"Ordered by specific culture : " +
    $"{comparer.CurrentCultureInfo.Name}");
foreach (string name in query)
    Console.WriteLine(name);



query = from n in names
        orderby n
        select n;
Console.WriteLine("Ordered by Thread.CurrentThread.CurrentCulture : " +
    $"{ Thread.CurrentThread.CurrentCulture.Name}");
foreach (string name in query)
    Console.WriteLine(name);



// Create CultureInfo for Danish in Denmark.
    CultureInfo danish = new CultureInfo("da-DK");
    // Create CultureInfo for English in the U.S.
    CultureInfo american = new CultureInfo("en-US");

    CultureStringComparer comparer =
        new CultureStringComparer(danish, CompareOptions.None);
    var query = names.OrderBy(n => n, comparer);
    Console.WriteLine("Ordered by specific culture : " +
        comparer.CurrentCultureInfo.Name);
    foreach (string name in query)
    {
        Console.WriteLine(name);
    }
    comparer.CurrentCultureInfo = american;
    query = names.OrderBy(n => n, comparer);
    Console.WriteLine("Ordered by specific culture : " +
        comparer.CurrentCultureInfo.Name);
    foreach (string name in query)
    {
        Console.WriteLine(name);
    }
```

These output results show that the word *Æble* is last in the Danish list and first in the US English list:

```
Ordered by specific culture : da-DK
Apple
Bar
Forsooth
Jello
Orange
Zanzibar
Æble
Ordered by specific culture : en-US
Æble
Apple
Bar
Forsooth
Jello
Orange
Zanzibar
```

See Also

The "OrderBy," "CultureInfo," and "IComparer<T>" topics in the MSDN documentation.

4.5 Adding Functional Extensions for Use with LINQ

Problem

There are operations you perform on collections frequently that currently reside in utility classes. You would like to be able to have these operations be used on collections in a more seamless manner than having to pass the reference to the collection to the utility class.

Solution

Use extension methods to help achieve a more functional style of programming for your collection operations. For example, to add a weighted moving average calculation operation to numeric collections, implement a set of `WeightedMovingAverage` extension methods in a static class and then call them as part of those collections:

```
decimal[] prices = new decimal[10] { 13.5M, 17.8M, 92.3M, 0.1M, 15.7M,
                            19.99M, 9.08M, 6.33M, 2.1M, 14.88M };
Console.WriteLine(prices.WeightedMovingAverage());

double[] dprices = new double[10] { 13.5, 17.8, 92.3, 0.1, 15.7,
                            19.99, 9.08, 6.33, 2.1, 14.88 };
Console.WriteLine(dprices.WeightedMovingAverage());
```

```
    float[] fprices = new float[10] { 13.5F, 17.8F, 92.3F, 0.1F, 15.7F,
                                      19.99F, 9.08F, 6.33F, 2.1F, 14.88F };
    Console.WriteLine(fprices.WeightedMovingAverage());

    int[] iprices = new int[10] { 13, 17, 92, 0, 15,
                                  19, 9, 6, 2, 14 };
    Console.WriteLine(iprices.WeightedMovingAverage());

    long[] lprices = new long[10] { 13, 17, 92, 0, 15,
                                    19, 9, 6, 2, 14 };
    Console.WriteLine(lprices.WeightedMovingAverage());
```

To provide WeightedMovingAverage for the full range of numeric types, methods for both the nullable and non-nullable numeric types are included in the LinqExten
sions class:

```
public static class LinqExtensions
{
    public static decimal? WeightedMovingAverage(
        this IEnumerable<decimal?> source)
    {
        if (source == null)
            throw new ArgumentNullException(nameof(source));

        decimal aggregate = 0.0M;
        decimal weight;
        int item = 1;
        // count how many items are not null and use that
        // as the weighting factor
        int count = source.Count(val => val.HasValue);
        foreach (var nullable in source)
        {
            if (nullable.HasValue)
            {
                weight = item / count;
                aggregate += nullable.GetValueOrDefault() * weight;
                count++;
            }
        }
        if (count > 0)
            return new decimal?(aggregate / count);
        return null;
    }
    // The same method pattern as above is followed for each of the other
    // types and its nullable counterparts (double / double?, int / int?, etc.)
}
```

Discussion

Extension methods allow you to create operations that appear to be part of a collection. They are static methods that can be called as if they were instance methods,

allowing you to extend existing types. Extension methods must also be declared in static classes that are not nested. Once a static class is defined with extension methods, the `using` directive for the namespace of the class makes those extensions available in the source file.

 If an instance method exists with the same signature as the extension method, the extension method will never be called. Conflicting extension method declarations will resolve to the method in the closest enclosing namespace.

You cannot use extension methods to create:

- Properties (get and set methods)
- Operators (+, -, = , etc.)
- Events

To declare an extension method, you specify the `this` keyword in front of the first parameter of a method declaration, and the type of that parameter is the type being extended. For example, in the `Nullable<decimal>` version of the `WeightedMovingA verage` method, collections that support `IEnumerable<decimal?>` (or `IEnumera ble<Nullable<decimal>>`) are supported:

```
public static decimal? WeightedMovingAverage(this IEnumerable<decimal?> source)
{
    if (source == null)
        throw new ArgumentNullException(nameof(source));

    decimal aggregate = 0.0M;
    decimal weight;
    int item = 1;
    // count how many items are not null and use that
    // as the weighting factor
    int count = source.Count(val => val.HasValue);
    foreach (var nullable in source)
    {
        if (nullable.HasValue)
        {
            weight = item / count;
            aggregate += nullable.GetValueOrDefault() * weight;
            count++;
        }
    }
    if (count > 0)
        return new decimal?(aggregate / count);
    return null;
}
```

The extension methods that support much of the LINQ functionality are on the Sys
tem.Linq.Extensions class, including an Average method. The Average method has
most of the numeric types but does not provide an overload for short (Int16). We
can easily rectify that by adding one ourselves for short and Nullable<short>:

```
public static double? Average(this IEnumerable<short?> source)
{
    if (source == null)
        throw new ArgumentNullException(nameof(source));

    double aggregate = 0.0;
    int count = 0;
    foreach (var nullable in source)
    {
        if (nullable.HasValue)
        {
            aggregate += nullable.GetValueOrDefault();
            count++;
        }
    }
    if (count > 0)
        return new double?(aggregate / count);
    return null;
}

public static double Average(this IEnumerable<short> source)
{
    if (source == null)
        throw new ArgumentNullException(nameof(source));

    double aggregate = 0.0;
    // use the count of the items from the source
    int count = source.Count();
    foreach (var value in source)
    {
        aggregate += value;
    }
    if (count > 0)
        return aggregate / count;
    else
        return 0.0;
}

public static double? Average<TSource>(this IEnumerable<TSource> source,
    Func<TSource, short?> selector) =>
        source.Select<TSource, short?>(selector).Average();

public static double Average<TSource>(this IEnumerable<TSource> source,
    Func<TSource, short> selector) =>
        source.Select<TSource, short>(selector).Average();

#endregion // Extend Average
```

We can then call `Average` on short-based collections just like `WeightedMovingAverage`:

```
short[] sprices = new short[10] { 13, 17, 92, 0, 15, 19, 9, 6, 2, 14 };
Console.WriteLine(sprices.WeightedMovingAverage());
// System.Linq.Extensions doesn't implement Average for short but we do for them!
Console.WriteLine(sprices.Average());
```

See Also

The "Extension Methods" topic in the MSDN documentation.

4.6 Querying and Joining Across Data Repositories

Problem

You have two sets of data from different data domains, and you want to be able to combine the data and work with it.

Solution

Use LINQ to bridge across the disparate data domains. LINQ is intended to be used in the same manner across different data domains and supports combining those sets of data with join syntax.

To demonstrate this, we will join an XML file full of categories with the data from a database (Northwind) of products to create a new set of data for product information that holds the product name, the category description, and the category name:

```
Northwind dataContext =
    new Northwind(Settings.Default.NorthwindConnectionString);
ProductsTableAdapter adapter = new ProductsTableAdapter();
Products products = new Products();
adapter.Fill(products._Products);

XElement xmlCategories = XElement.Load("Categories.xml");

var expr = from product in products._Products
           where product.Units_In_Stock > 100
           join xc in xmlCategories.Elements("Category")
           on product.Category_ID equals int.Parse(
               xc.Attribute("CategoryID").Value)
           select new
           {
               ProductName = product.Product_Name,
               Category = xc.Attribute("CategoryName").Value,
               CategoryDescription = xc.Attribute("Description").Value
           };
```

```
foreach (var productInfo in expr)
{
    Console.WriteLine("ProductName: " + productInfo.ProductName +
        " Category: " + productInfo.Category +
        " Category Description: " + productInfo.CategoryDescription);
}
```

The new set of data is printed to the console, but this could easily have been rerouted to another method, transformed in another query, or written out to a third data format:

```
ProductName: Grandma's Boysenberry Spread Category: Condiments Category
Description: Sweet and savory sauces, relishes, spreads, and seasonings
ProductName: Gustaf's Knäckebröd Category: Grains/Cereals Category Description:
Breads, crackers, pasta, and cereal
ProductName: Geitost Category: Dairy Products Category Description:
Cheeses
ProductName: Sasquatch Ale Category: Beverages Category Description: Soft drinks,
coffees, teas, beer, and ale
ProductName: Inlagd Sill Category: Seafood Category Description:
Seaweed and fish
ProductName: Boston Crab Meat Category: Seafood Category Description:
Seaweed and fish
ProductName: Pâté chinois Category: Meat/Poultry Category Description:
Prepared meats
ProductName: Sirop d'érable Category: Condiments Category Description:
Sweet and savory sauces, relishes, spreads, and seasonings
ProductName: Röd Kaviar Category: Seafood Category Description:
Seaweed and fish
ProductName: Rhönbräu Klosterbier Category: Beverages Category Description:
Soft drinks, coffees, teas, beer, and ale
```

Discussion

The Solution combines data from two different data domains: XML and a SQL database. Before LINQ, to do this you would have had to not only create a third data repository by hand to hold the result, but also write the specific code for each domain to query that domain for its part of the data (XPath for XML; SQL for database) and then manually transform the result sets from each domain into the new data repository. LINQ enables you to write the query to combine the two sets of data, automatically constructs a type via projecting a new anonymous type, and places the pertinent data in the new type, all in the same syntax. Not only does this simplify the code, but it also allows you to concentrate more on getting the data you want and less on determining exactly how to read both data domains.

This example uses both LINQ to DataSet and LINQ to XML to access the multiple data domains:

```
var dataContext = new NorthwindLinq2Sql.NorthwindLinq2SqlDataContext();
```

```
ProductsTableAdapter adapter = new ProductsTableAdapter();
Products products = new Products();
adapter.Fill(products._Products);

XElement xmlCategories = XElement.Load("Categories.xml");
```

NorthwindLinq2SqlDataContext is a DataContext class. A DataContext is analogous to an ADO.NET Connection and Command object rolled into one. You use it to establish your connection, execute queries, or access tables directly via entity classes. You can generate a DataContext directly from the database through Visual Studio by adding a new "LINQ to SQL Classes" item. This provides access to the local *Northwind.mdf* database for the query. A Products DataSet is loaded from the Products table in the *Northwind.mdf* database for use in the query.

XElement is one of the main classes in LINQ to XML. It enables the loading of existing XML, creation of new XML, or retrieval of the XML text for the element via ToString. Example 4-1 shows the *Categories.xml* file that will be loaded. For more on XElement and LINQ to XML, see Chapter 10.

Example 4-1. Categories.xml

```
<?xml version="1.0" encoding="utf-8"?>
<Categories>
  <Category Id="1" Name="Beverages"
    Description="Soft drinks, coffees, teas, beers, and ales" />
  <Category Id="2" Name="Condiments"
    Description="Sweet and savory sauces, relishes, spreads, and seasonings" />
  <Category Id="3" Name="Confections"
    Description="Desserts, candies, and sweet breads" />
  <Category Id="4" Name="Dairy Products" Description="Cheeses" />
  <Category Id="5" Name="Grains/Cereals"
    Description="Breads, crackers, pasta, and cereal" />
  <Category Id="6" Name="Meat/Poultry" Description="Prepared meats" />
  <Category Id="7" Name="Produce" Description="Dried fruit and bean curd" />
  <Category Id="8" Name="Seafood" Description="Seaweed and fish" />
</Categories>
```

The two sets of data are joined via LINQ and, in particular, the join keyword. We join the data by matching the category ID in the Products table with the category ID in the XML file to combine the data. In SQL terms, the join keyword represents an inner join:

```
var expr = from product in products._Products
           where product.UnitsInStock > 100
           join xc in xmlCategories.Elements("Category")
           on product.CategoryID equals int.Parse(xc.Attribute("Id").Value)
```

Once the join result is complete, we project a new type using the select keyword:

```
select new
{
    ProductName = product.ProductName,
    Category = xc.Attribute("Name").Value,
    CategoryDescription = xc.Attribute("Description").Value
};
```

This allows us to combine different data elements from the two sets of data to make a third set that can look completely different than either of the original two.

Doing joins on two sets of database data would be a bad idea, as the database can do this much faster for those sets, but when you need to join disparate data sets, LINQ can lend a helping hand.

See Also

The "join keyword," "System.Data.Linq.DataContext," and "XElement" topics in the MSDN documentation.

4.7 Querying Configuration Files with LINQ

Problem

Data sets can be stored in many different locations, such as configuration files. You want to be able to query your configuration files for sets of information.

Solution

Use LINQ to query against the configuration sections. In the following example, we do this by retrieving all chapter titles with even numbers and the word *and* in the title from the custom configuration section containing chapter information:

```
CSharpRecipesConfigurationSection recipeConfig =
    ConfigurationManager.GetSection("CSharpRecipesConfiguration") as
CSharpRecipesConfigurationSection;

var expr = from ChapterConfigurationElement chapter in
    recipeConfig.Chapters.OfType<ChapterConfigurationElement>()
            where (chapter.Title.Contains("and")) &&
             ((int.Parse(chapter.Number) % 2) == 0)
            select new
            {
                ChapterNumber = $"Chapter {chapter.Number}",
                chapter.Title
            };

foreach (var chapterInfo in expr)
    Console.WriteLine($"{chapterInfo.ChapterNumber} : {chapterInfo.Title}");
```

The configuration section being queried looks like this:

```
<CSharpRecipesConfiguration CurrentEdition="4">
  <Chapters>
    <add Number="1" Title="Classes and Generics" />
    <add Number="2" Title="Collections, Enumerators, and Iterators" />
    <add Number="3" Title="Data Types" />
    <add Number="4" Title="LINQ &amp; Lambda Expressions" />
    <add Number="5" Title="Debugging and Exception Handling" />
    <add Number="6" Title="Reflection and Dynamic Programming" />
    <add Number="7" Title="Regular Expressions" />
    <add Number="8" Title="Filesystem I/O" />
    <add Number="9" Title="Networking and Web" />
    <add Number="10" Title="XML" />
    <add Number="11" Title="Security" />
    <add Number="12" Title="Threading, Synchronization, and Concurrency" />
    <add Number="13" Title="Toolbox" />
  </Chapters>
  <Editions>
    <add Number="1" PublicationYear="2004" />
    <add Number="2" PublicationYear="2006" />
    <add Number="3" PublicationYear="2007" />
    <add Number="4" PublicationYear="2015" />
  </Editions>
</CSharpRecipesConfiguration>
```

The output from the query is:

```
Chapter 2 : Collections, Enumerators, and Iterators
Chapter 6 : Reflection and Dynamic Programming
Chapter 12 : Threading, Synchronization, and Concurrency
```

Discussion

Configuration files in .NET play a significant role in achieving manageability and ease of deployment for .NET-based applications. It can be challenging to get all of the various settings right in the hierarchy of configuration files that can affect an application, so understanding how to write utilities to programmatically check configuration file settings is of great use during development, testing, deployment, and ongoing management of an application.

 To access the configuration types, you will need to reference the System.Configuration assembly.

Even though the ConfigurationElementCollection class (the base of data sets in configuration files) supports only IEnumerable and not IEnumerable<T>, we can still use it to get the elements we need by using the OfType<ChapterConfigurationEle

---

ment> method on the collection, which selects elements of that type from the collection:

```
var expr = from ChapterConfigurationElement chapter in
    recipeConfig.Chapters.OfType<ChapterConfigurationElement>()
```

ChapterConfigurationElement is a custom configuration section class that holds the chapter number and title:

```
/// <summary>
/// Holds the information about a chapter in the configuration file
/// </summary>
public class ChapterConfigurationElement : ConfigurationElement
{
    /// <summary>
    /// Default constructor
    /// </summary>
    public ChapterConfigurationElement()
    {
    }

    /// <summary>
    /// The number of the Chapter
    /// </summary>
    [ConfigurationProperty("Number", IsRequired=true)]
    public string Number
    {
        get { return (string)this["Number"]; }
        set { this["Number"] = value; }
    }

    /// <summary>
    /// The title of the Chapter
    /// </summary>
    [ConfigurationProperty("Title", IsRequired=true)]
    public string Title
    {
        get { return (string)this["Title"]; }
        set { this["Title"] = value; }
    }
}
```

This technique can be used on the standard configuration files, such as *machine.config*, as well. This example determines which sections in *machine.config* require access permissions. For this collection, OfType<ConfigurationSection> is used, as this is a standard section:

```
System.Configuration.Configuration machineConfig =
    ConfigurationManager.OpenMachineConfiguration();

var query = from ConfigurationSection section in
machineConfig.Sections.OfType<ConfigurationSection>()
```

```
        where section.SectionInformation.RequirePermission
        select section;

foreach (ConfigurationSection section in query)
    Console.WriteLine(section.SectionInformation.Name);
```

The sections detected will look something like this:

```
configProtectedData
satelliteassemblies
assemblyBinding
system.codedom
system.data.dataset
system.data.odbc
system.data
system.data.oracleclient
system.data.oledb
uri
system.windows.forms
system.runtime.remoting
runtime
system.diagnostics
windows
mscorlib
system.webServer
system.data.sqlclient
startup
```

See Also

The "Enumerable.OfType method," "ConfigurationSectionCollection class" and "ConfigurationElementCollection class" topics in the MSDN documentation.

4.8 Creating XML Straight from a Database

Problem

You want to be able to take a data set from a database and represent it as XML.

Solution

Use LINQ to Entities and LINQ to XML to retrieve and transform the data all in one query. In this case, we will select the top five customers in the Northwind database whose contact is the owner and those owners who placed orders totaling more than $10,000, then create XML containing the company name, contact name, phone number, and total amount of the orders. Finally, the results are written out to the *BigSpenders.xml* file:

```
NorthwindEntities dataContext = new NorthwindEntities();
```

```
// Log the generated SQL to the console
dataContext.Database.Log = Console.WriteLine;

// select the top 5 customers whose contact is the owner and
// those owners placed orders spending more than $10000 this year
var bigSpenders = new XElement("BigSpenders",
    from top5 in
        (
            (from customer in
                (
                    from c in dataContext.Customers
                        // get the customers where the contact is the
                        // owner and they placed orders
                    where c.ContactTitle.Contains("Owner")
                    && c.Orders.Count > 0
                    join orderData in
                        (
                            from c in dataContext.Customers
                                // get the customers where the contact is the
                                // owner and they placed orders
                            where c.ContactTitle.Contains("Owner")
                            && c.Orders.Count > 0
                            from o in c.Orders
                                // get the order details
                            join od in dataContext.Order_Details
                                on o.OrderID equals od.OrderID
                            select new
                            {
                                c.CompanyName,
                                c.CustomerID,
                                o.OrderID,
                                // have to calc order value from orderdetails
                                //(UnitPrice*Quantity as Total)-
                                // (Total*Discount) as NetOrderTotal
                                NetOrderTotal = (
                                    (((double)od.UnitPrice) * od.Quantity) -
                                    ((((double)od.UnitPrice) * od.Quantity) *
                                        od.Discount))
                            }
                        )
                    on c.CustomerID equals orderData.CustomerID
                    into customerOrders
                    select new
                    {
                        c.CompanyName,
                        c.ContactName,
                        c.Phone,
                        // Get the total amount spent by the customer
                        TotalSpend = customerOrders.Sum(order =>
                                    order.NetOrderTotal)
                    }
                )
```

```
                    // only worry about customers that spent > 10000
                where customer.TotalSpend > 10000
                orderby customer.TotalSpend descending
                // only take the top 5 spenders
                select new
                {
                    CompanyName = customer.CompanyName,
                    ContactName = customer.ContactName,
                    Phone = customer.Phone,
                    TotalSpend = customer.TotalSpend
                }).Take(5)
        ).ToList()
    // format the data as XML
    select new XElement("Customer",
            new XAttribute("companyName", top5.CompanyName),
            new XAttribute("contactName", top5.ContactName),
            new XAttribute("phoneNumber", top5.Phone),
            new XAttribute("amountSpent", top5.TotalSpend)));
using (XmlWriter writer = XmlWriter.Create("BigSpenders.xml"))
{
    bigSpenders.WriteTo(writer);
}
```

When building larger queries, you may find it is sometimes easier to use the functional approach (`.Join()`) to build up the query instead of the query expression manner (`join x on y equals z`) if you have done more C# than SQL.

Discussion

LINQ to SQL is the part of LINQ to ADO.NET that facilitates rapid database development. It is targeted at the scenarios where you want to program almost directly against the database schema. Most of these scenarios have one-to-one correlations between strongly typed classes and database tables. If you are in more of an enterprise development scenario with lots of stored procedures and databases that have moved away from "one table equals one entity" scenarios, you would want to look into LINQ to Entities.

You can access the LINQ to SQL visual designer by adding a new or opening an existing "LINQ to SQL Classes" item (*.dbml* file) to the project, which opens the designer. This helps you to build out the `DataContext` and entity classes for your database, which can then be used with LINQ (or other programming constructs if you wish). A `DataContext` is analogous to an ADO.NET `Connection` and `Command` object rolled into one. You use it to establish your connection, execute queries, or access tables directly via entity classes. The `NorthwindLinq2Sql` data context is a strongly typed instance of a `DataContext` and is partially shown here:

```
public partial class NorthwindLinq2SqlDataContext : System.Data.Linq.DataContext
{

    private static System.Data.Linq.Mapping.MappingSource mappingSource = new
AttributeMappingSource();

#region Extensibility Method Definitions
partial void OnCreated();
partial void InsertCategory(Category instance);
partial void UpdateCategory(Category instance);
partial void DeleteCategory(Category instance);
partial void InsertTerritory(Territory instance);
partial void UpdateTerritory(Territory instance);
partial void DeleteTerritory(Territory instance);
partial void InsertCustomerCustomerDemo(CustomerCustomerDemo instance);
partial void UpdateCustomerCustomerDemo(CustomerCustomerDemo instance);
partial void DeleteCustomerCustomerDemo(CustomerCustomerDemo instance);
partial void InsertCustomerDemographic(CustomerDemographic instance);
partial void UpdateCustomerDemographic(CustomerDemographic instance);
partial void DeleteCustomerDemographic(CustomerDemographic instance);
partial void InsertCustomer(Customer instance);
partial void UpdateCustomer(Customer instance);
partial void DeleteCustomer(Customer instance);
partial void InsertEmployee(Employee instance);
partial void UpdateEmployee(Employee instance);
partial void DeleteEmployee(Employee instance);
partial void InsertEmployeeTerritory(EmployeeTerritory instance);
partial void UpdateEmployeeTerritory(EmployeeTerritory instance);
partial void DeleteEmployeeTerritory(EmployeeTerritory instance);
partial void InsertOrder_Detail(Order_Detail instance);
partial void UpdateOrder_Detail(Order_Detail instance);
partial void DeleteOrder_Detail(Order_Detail instance);
partial void InsertOrder(Order instance);
partial void UpdateOrder(Order instance);
partial void DeleteOrder(Order instance);
partial void InsertProduct(Product instance);
partial void UpdateProduct(Product instance);
partial void DeleteProduct(Product instance);
partial void InsertRegion(Region instance);
partial void UpdateRegion(Region instance);
partial void DeleteRegion(Region instance);
partial void InsertShipper(Shipper instance);
partial void UpdateShipper(Shipper instance);
partial void DeleteShipper(Shipper instance);
partial void InsertSupplier(Supplier instance);
partial void UpdateSupplier(Supplier instance);
partial void DeleteSupplier(Supplier instance);
#endregion

    public NorthwindLinq2SqlDataContext() :
    base(
global::NorthwindLinq2Sql.Properties.Settings.Default.NorthwindConnectionString,
```

```csharp
 mappingSource)    {
    OnCreated();
}

public NorthwindLinq2SqlDataContext(string connection) :
        base(connection, mappingSource)
{
    OnCreated();
}

public NorthwindLinq2SqlDataContext(System.Data.IDbConnection connection) :
        base(connection, mappingSource)
{
    OnCreated();
}

public NorthwindLinq2SqlDataContext(string connection,
    System.Data.Linq.Mapping.MappingSource mappingSource) :
        base(connection, mappingSource)
{
    OnCreated();
}

public NorthwindLinq2SqlDataContext(System.Data.IDbConnection connection,
System.Data.Linq.Mapping.MappingSource mappingSource) :
        base(connection, mappingSource)
{
    OnCreated();
}

public System.Data.Linq.Table<Category> Categories
{
    get
    {
        return this.GetTable<Category>();
    }
}

public System.Data.Linq.Table<Territory> Territories
{
    get
    {
        return this.GetTable<Territory>();
    }
}

public System.Data.Linq.Table<CustomerCustomerDemo> CustomerCustomerDemos
{
    get
    {
        return this.GetTable<CustomerCustomerDemo>();
    }
```

```
        }

        public System.Data.Linq.Table<CustomerDemographic> CustomerDemographics
        {
            get
            {
                return this.GetTable<CustomerDemographic>();
            }
        }

        public System.Data.Linq.Table<Customer> Customers
        {
            get
            {
                return this.GetTable<Customer>();
            }
        }

        public System.Data.Linq.Table<Employee> Employees
        {
            get
            {
                return this.GetTable<Employee>();
            }
        }

        public System.Data.Linq.Table<EmployeeTerritory> EmployeeTerritories
        {
            get
            {
                return this.GetTable<EmployeeTerritory>();
            }
        }

        public System.Data.Linq.Table<Order_Detail> Order_Details
        {
            get
            {
                return this.GetTable<Order_Detail>();
            }
        }

        public System.Data.Linq.Table<Order> Orders
        {
            get
            {
                return this.GetTable<Order>();
            }
        }

        public System.Data.Linq.Table<Product> Products
        {
```

```
        get
        {
            return this.GetTable<Product>();
        }
    }

    public System.Data.Linq.Table<Region> Regions
    {
        get
        {
            return this.GetTable<Region>();
        }
    }

    public System.Data.Linq.Table<Shipper> Shippers
    {
        get
        {
            return this.GetTable<Shipper>();
        }
    }

    public System.Data.Linq.Table<Supplier> Suppliers
    {
        get
        {
            return this.GetTable<Supplier>();
        }
    }
}
```

The entity class definitions for the Northwind database are all present in the generated code as well, with each table having an entity class defined for it. The entity classes are indicated by the Table attribute with no parameters. This means that the name of the entity class matches the table name:

```
[global::System.Data.Linq.Mapping.TableAttribute(Name="dbo.Customers")]
public partial class Customer : INotifyPropertyChanging, INotifyPropertyChanged
{

    private static PropertyChangingEventArgs emptyChangingEventArgs = new
PropertyChangingEventArgs(String.Empty);

    private string _CustomerID;

    private string _CompanyName;

    private string _ContactName;

    private string _ContactTitle;

    private string _Address;
```

```
    private string _City;

    private string _Region;

    private string _PostalCode;

    private string _Country;

    private string _Phone;

    private string _Fax;

    private EntitySet<CustomerCustomerDemo> _CustomerCustomerDemos;

    private EntitySet<Order> _Orders;

#region Extensibility Method Definitions
partial void OnLoaded();
partial void OnValidate(System.Data.Linq.ChangeAction action);
partial void OnCreated();
partial void OnCustomerIDChanging(string value);
partial void OnCustomerIDChanged();
partial void OnCompanyNameChanging(string value);
partial void OnCompanyNameChanged();
partial void OnContactNameChanging(string value);
partial void OnContactNameChanged();
partial void OnContactTitleChanging(string value);
partial void OnContactTitleChanged();
partial void OnAddressChanging(string value);
partial void OnAddressChanged();
partial void OnCityChanging(string value);
partial void OnCityChanged();
partial void OnRegionChanging(string value);
partial void OnRegionChanged();
partial void OnPostalCodeChanging(string value);
partial void OnPostalCodeChanged();
partial void OnCountryChanging(string value);
partial void OnCountryChanged();
partial void OnPhoneChanging(string value);
partial void OnPhoneChanged();
partial void OnFaxChanging(string value);
partial void OnFaxChanged();
#endregion

    public Customer()
    {
        this._CustomerCustomerDemos = new EntitySet<CustomerCustomerDemo>(new
Action<CustomerCustomerDemo>(this.attach_CustomerCustomerDemos), new
Action<CustomerCustomerDemo>(this.detach_CustomerCustomerDemos));
        this._Orders = new EntitySet<Order>(
            new Action<Order>(this.attach_Orders), new
```

```
    Action<Order>(this.detach_Orders));
        OnCreated();
    }

    public event PropertyChangingEventHandler PropertyChanging;

    public event PropertyChangedEventHandler PropertyChanged;

    protected virtual void SendPropertyChanging()
    {
        if ((this.PropertyChanging != null))
        {
            this.PropertyChanging(this, emptyChangingEventArgs);
        }
    }

    protected virtual void SendPropertyChanged(String propertyName)
    {
        if ((this.PropertyChanged != null))
        {
            this.PropertyChanged(this,
                new PropertyChangedEventArgs(propertyName));
        }
    }
```

The standard property change notifications are implemented via INotifyProperty
Changing and INotifyPropertyChanged and have PropertyChanging and Property
Changed events for conveying the change to a property. There is also a set of partial
methods that will report when a specific property is modified on this entity class if
they are implemented in another partial class definition for the entity class.

Many of the classes generated by Microsoft .NET are generated as
partial classes. This is so that you can extend them in your own
partial class and add methods and properties to the class without
being in danger of the code generator stomping on your code the
next time it is regenerated.

In this case, if no other partial class definition is found, the compiler will remove those notifications. Partial methods enable the
declaration of a method signature in one file of a partial class declaration and the implementation of the method in another. If the signature is found but the implementation is not, the signature is
removed by the compiler.

The properties in the entity class match up to the columns in the database via the
Column attribute, where the Name value is the database column name and the Storage
value is the internal storage for the class of the data. Events for the property changes
are wired into the setter for the property:

```
[global::System.Data.Linq.Mapping.ColumnAttribute(Storage="_CompanyName",
DbType="NVarChar(40) NOT NULL", CanBeNull=false)]
public string CompanyName
{
    get
    {
        return this._CompanyName;
    }
    set
    {
        if ((this._CompanyName != value))
        {
            this.OnCompanyNameChanging(value);
            this.SendPropertyChanging();
            this._CompanyName = value;
            this.SendPropertyChanged("CompanyName");
            this.OnCompanyNameChanged();
        }
    }
}
```

For a one-to-many child relationship, an `EntitySet<T>` of the child entity class is declared with an `Association` attribute. The `Association` attribute specifies the relationship information between the parent and child entity classes, as shown here for the `Orders` property on `Customer`:

```
[global::System.Data.Linq.Mapping.AssociationAttribute(Name="Customer_Order",
Storage="_Orders", ThisKey="CustomerID", OtherKey="CustomerID")]
public EntitySet<Order> Orders
{
    get
    {
        return this._Orders;
    }
    set
    {
        this._Orders.Assign(value);
    }
}
```

LINQ to SQL covers much more than what has been shown here, and we encourage you to investigate it more. Now, however, let's move on to the other data domain we are dealing with: LINQ to XML.

LINQ to XML is not only how you perform queries against XML, it is also a more developer-friendly way to work with XML. One of the main classes in LINQ to XML is `XElement`, which allows you to create XML in a manner that more closely resembles the structure of the XML itself. This may not seem like a big deal, but when you can see the XML taking shape in your code, it's easier to know where you are. (Ever forget which `XmlWriter.WriteEndElement` you were on? We have!) You can get more details and examples about using XElement in Chapter 10, so we won't go much further into it here, but as you can see, it is very easy to build up XML in a query.

The first part of the query deals with setting up the main XML element, BigSpenders, and getting the initial set of customers where the contact is the owner:

```
var bigSpenders = new XElement("BigSpenders",
            from top5 in
            (
                (from customer in
                    (
                        from c in dataContext.Customers
                        // get the customers where the contact is the owner
                        // and they placed orders
                        where c.ContactTitle.Contains("Owner")
                            && c.Orders.Count > 0
```

The middle of the query deals with joining the order and order detail information with the customer information to get the NetOrderTotal for the order. It also creates order data containing that value, the customer and order IDs, and the company name. We need the NetOrderTotal in the last part of the query, so stay tuned!

```
    join orderData in
        (
            from c in dataContext.Customers
            // get the customers where the contact is the owner
            // and they placed orders
            where c.ContactTitle.Contains("Owner")
                && c.Orders.Count > 0
            from o in c.Orders
            // get the order details
            join od in dataContext.OrderDetails
                on o.OrderID equals od.OrderID
            select new
            {
                c.CompanyName,
                c.CustomerID,
                o.OrderID,
                // have to calc order value from orderdetails
                //(UnitPrice*Quantity as Total)
                  (Total*Discount)
                // as NetOrderTotal
                NetOrderTotal = (
((((double)od.UnitPrice) * od.Quantity) -
(((((double)od.UnitPrice) * od.Quantity) * od.Discount))
            }
        )
    on c.CustomerID equals orderData.CustomerID
    into customerOrders
```

The last part of the query determines the TotalSpend for that customer across all orders using the Sum function on NetOrderTotal for the generated customerOrders collection. Finally, the query selects only the top five customers with a `TotalSpend` value greater than 10,000 by using the `Take` function. (`Take` is the equivalent to `TOP` in SQL.) We then use those records to construct one inner `Customer` element with attributes that nest inside the `BigSpenders` root element we set up in the first part of the query:

```
              select new
              {
                      c.CompanyName,
                      c.ContactName,
                      c.Phone,
                      // Get the total amount spent by the customer
                      TotalSpend = customerOrders.Sum(order => order. NetOrderTotal)
              }
          )
      // only worry about customers that spent > 10000
      where customer.TotalSpend > 10000
      orderby customer.TotalSpend descending
      // only take the top 5 spenders
      select customer).Take(5)
)
// format the data as XML
select new XElement("Customer",
              new XAttribute("companyName", top5.CompanyName),
              new XAttribute("contactName", top5.ContactName),
              new XAttribute("phoneNumber", top5.Phone),
              new XAttribute("amountSpent", top5.TotalSpend)));
```

It is much easier to build large-nested queries as individual queries first and then put them together once you are sure the inner query is working.

At this point, for all of the code here, nothing has happened yet. That's right: until the query is accessed, nothing happens because of the magic of deferred execution. LINQ has constructed a query expression, but nothing has talked to the database; there is no XML in memory, nada. Once the `WriteTo` method is called on the `bigSpenders` query expression, the query is evaluated by LINQ to SQL, and the XML is constructed. The `WriteTo` method writes out the constructed XML to the `XmlWriter` provided, and we are done:

```
using (XmlWriter writer = XmlWriter.Create("BigSpenders.xml"))
{
    bigSpenders.WriteTo(writer);
}
```

If you are interested in what that SQL will look like, connect the `DataContext.Log` property to a `TextWriter` (like the console):

```
// Log the generated SQL to the console
dataContext.Log = Console.Out;
```

This query generates SQL that looks like this:

```
Generated SQL for query - output via DataContext.Log
SELECT [t10].[CompanyName], [t10].[ContactName], [t10].[Phone],
    [t10].[TotalSpend]
FROM (
    SELECT TOP (5) [t0].[Company Name] AS [CompanyName],
        [t0].[Contact Name] AS
[ContactName], [t0].[Phone], [t9].[value] AS [TotalSpend]
    FROM [Customers] AS [t0]
    OUTER APPLY (
        SELECT COUNT(*) AS [value]
        FROM [Orders] AS [t1]
        WHERE [t1].[Customer ID] = [t0].[Customer ID]
        ) AS [t2]
    OUTER APPLY (
        SELECT SUM([t8].[value]) AS [value]
        FROM (
            SELECT [t3].[Customer ID], [t6].[Order ID],
                ([t7].[Unit Price] *
                (CONVERT(Decimal(29,4),[t7].[Quantity]))) -
                    ([t7].[Unit Price] *
                    (CONVERT(Decimal(29,4),[t7].[Quantity])) *
                        (CONVERT(Decimal(29,4),[t7].[Discount]))) AS
                            [value],
                [t7].[Order ID] AS [Order ID2],
                [t3].[Contact Title] AS [ContactTitle],
                [t5].[value] AS [value2],
                [t6].[Customer ID] AS [CustomerID]
            FROM [Customers] AS [t3]
            OUTER APPLY (
                SELECT COUNT(*) AS [value]
                FROM [Orders] AS [t4]
                WHERE [t4].[Customer ID] = [t3].[Customer ID]
                ) AS [t5]
            CROSS JOIN [Orders] AS [t6]
            CROSS JOIN [Order Details] AS [t7]
            ) AS [t8]
        WHERE ([t0].[Customer ID] = [t8].[Customer ID]) AND ([t8].[Order ID] = [
t8].[Order ID2]) AND ([t8].[ContactTitle] LIKE @p0) AND ([t8].[value2] > @p1) AN
D ([t8].[CustomerID] = [t8].[Customer ID])
        ) AS [t9]
    WHERE ([t9].[value] > @p2) AND ([t0].[Contact Title] LIKE @p3) AND
        ([t2].[va
lue] > @p4)
    ORDER BY [t9].[value] DESC
    ) AS [t10]
ORDER BY [t10].[TotalSpend] DESC
-- @p0: Input String (Size = 0; Prec = 0; Scale = 0) [%Owner%]
-- @p1: Input Int32 (Size = 0; Prec = 0; Scale = 0) [0]
```

```
-- @p2: Input Decimal (Size = 0; Prec = 29; Scale = 4) [10000]
-- @p3: Input String (Size = 0; Prec = 0; Scale = 0) [%Owner%]
-- @p4: Input Int32 (Size = 0; Prec = 0; Scale = 0) [0]
-- Context: SqlProvider(SqlCE) Model: AttributedMetaModel Build: 3.5.20706.1
```

Here is the final XML:

```
<BigSpenders>
  <Customer companyName="Folk och fa HB" contactName="Maria Larsson"
            phoneNumber="0695-34 67 21" amountSpent="39805.162472039461" />
  <Customer companyName="White Clover Markets" contactName="Karl Jablonski"
            phoneNumber="(206) 555-4112" amountSpent="35957.604972146451" />
  <Customer companyName="Bon app'" contactName="Laurence Lebihan"
            phoneNumber="91.24.45.40" amountSpent="22311.577472746558" />
  <Customer companyName="LINO-Delicateses" contactName="Felipe Izquierdo"
            phoneNumber="(8) 34-56-12" amountSpent="20458.544984650609" />
  <Customer companyName="Simons bistro" contactName="Jytte Petersen"
            phoneNumber="31 12 34 56" amountSpent="18978.777493602414" />
</BigSpenders>
```

See Also

The "The Three Parts of a LINQ Query," "DataContext.Log, property," "DataContext class," "XElement class," and "LINQ to SQL" topics in the MSDN documentation.

4.9 Being Selective About Your Query Results

Problem

You want to be able to get a dynamic subset of a query result.

Solution

Use the TakeWhile extension method to retrieve all results until the criteria are matched:

```
NorthwindEntities dataContext = new NorthwindEntities();

// find the products for all suppliers
var query =
    dataContext.Suppliers.GroupJoin(dataContext.Products,
        s => s.SupplierID, p => p.SupplierID,
        (s, products) => new
        {
            s.CompanyName,
            s.ContactName,
            s.Phone,
            Products = products
        }).OrderByDescending(supplierData => supplierData.Products.Count());
```

```
var results =
    query.AsEnumerable().TakeWhile(supplierData =>
        supplierData.Products.Count() > 3);
Console.WriteLine($"Suppliers that provide more than three products: " +
    $"{results.Count()}");
foreach (var supplierData in results)
{
    Console.WriteLine($"  Company Name : {supplierData.CompanyName}");
    Console.WriteLine($"  Contact Name : {supplierData.ContactName}");
    Console.WriteLine($"  Contact Phone : {supplierData.Phone}");
    Console.WriteLine($"  Products Supplied : {supplierData.Products.Count()}");
    foreach (var productData in supplierData.Products)
        Console.WriteLine($"        Product: {productData.ProductName}");
}
```

You can also use the SkipWhile extension method to retrieve all results once the criteria are matched:

```
NorthwindEntities dataContext = new NorthwindEntities();

// find the products for all suppliers
var query =
    dataContext.Suppliers.GroupJoin(dataContext.Products,
        s => s.SupplierID, p => p.SupplierID,
        (s, products) => new
        {
            s.CompanyName,
            s.ContactName,
            s.Phone,
            Products = products
        }).OrderByDescending(supplierData => supplierData.Products.Count());

var results =
    query.AsEnumerable().SkipWhile(supplierData =>
    supplierData.Products.Count() > 3);
Console.WriteLine($"Suppliers that provide more than three products: " +
    $"{results.Count()}");
foreach (var supplierData in results)
{
    Console.WriteLine($"    Company Name : {supplierData.CompanyName}");
    Console.WriteLine($"    Contact Name : {supplierData.ContactName}");
    Console.WriteLine($"    Contact Phone : {supplierData.Phone}");
    Console.WriteLine($"    Products Supplied : {supplierData.Products.Count()}");
    foreach (var productData in supplierData.Products)
        Console.WriteLine($"        Product: {productData.ProductName}");
}
```

Discussion

In this example using LINQ to Entities, we determine the number of products each supplier provides, and sort the result set in descending order by product count:

```
var query =
    dataContext.Suppliers.GroupJoin(dataContext.Products,
        s => s.SupplierID, p => p.SupplierID,
        (s, products) => new
        {
            s.CompanyName,
            s.ContactName,
            s.Phone,
            Products = products
        }).OrderByDescending(supplierData => supplierData.Products.Count());
```

From that result, the supplier data is accepted into the final result set only if the supplier provides more than three products and the results are displayed. TakeWhile is used with a lambda expression to determine if the product count is greater than 3, and if so, the supplier is accepted into the result set:

```
var results = query.AsEnumerable().TakeWhile(supplierData =>
    supplierData.Products.Count() > 3);
```

If SkipWhile were used instead, all of the suppliers that provide three or fewer products would be returned:

```
var results = query.AsEnumerable().SkipWhile(supplierData =>
    supplierData.Products.Count() > 3);
```

Being able to write code-based conditions allows for more flexibility than the regular Take and Skip methods, which are based on absolute record count, but keep in mind that once the condition is hit for either TakeWhile or SkipWhile, you get all records after that, which is why it's important to sort the result set before using them.

The query also uses GroupJoin, which is comparable to a SQL LEFT or RIGHT OUTER JOIN, but the result is not flattened. GroupJoin produces a hierarchical result set instead of a tabular one, which is used to get the collection of products by supplier in this example:

```
dataContext.Suppliers.GroupJoin(dataContext.Products,
    s => s.SupplierID, p => p.SupplierID,
```

This is the output for the TakeWhile:

```
Suppliers that provide more than three products: 4
    Company Name : Pavlova, Ltd.
    Contact Name : Ian Devling
    Contact Phone : (03) 444-2343
    Products Supplied : 5
        Product: Pavlova
        Product: Alice Mutton
        Product: Carnarvon Tigers
        Product: Vegie-spread
        Product: Outback Lager
    Company Name : Plutzer Lebensmittelgroßmärkte AG
    Contact Name : Martin Bein
```

```
Contact Phone : (069) 992755
Products Supplied : 5
    Product: Rössle Sauerkraut
    Product: Thüringer Rostbratwurst
    Product: Wimmers gute Semmelknödel
    Product: Rhönbräu Klosterbier
    Product: Original Frankfurter grüne Soße
Company Name : New Orleans Cajun Delights
Contact Name : Shelley Burke
Contact Phone : (100) 555-4822
Products Supplied : 4
    Product: Chef Anton's Cajun Seasoning
    Product: Chef Anton's Gumbo Mix
    Product: Louisiana Fiery Hot Pepper Sauce
    Product: Louisiana Hot Spiced Okra
Company Name : Specialty Biscuits, Ltd.
Contact Name : Peter Wilson
Contact Phone : (161) 555-4448
Products Supplied : 4
    Product: Teatime Chocolate Biscuits
    Product: Sir Rodney's Marmalade
    Product: Sir Rodney's Scones
    Product: Scottish Longbreads
```

See Also

The "Enumerable.TakeWhile method," "Enumerable.SkipWhile method," and "Enumerable.GroupJoin method" topics in the MSDN documentation.

4.10 Using LINQ with Collections That Don't Support IEnumerable<T>

Problem

There are a whole bunch of collections that don't support the generic versions of IEnumerable or ICollection but that do support the original nongeneric versions of the IEnumerable or ICollection interfaces, and you would like to be able to query those collections using LINQ.

Solution

The type cannot be inferred from the original IEnumeration or ICollection interfaces, so you must provide it using either the OfType<T> or Cast<T> extension methods or by specifying the type in the from clause, which inserts a Cast<T> for you. The first example uses Cast<XmlNode> to let LINQ know that the elements in the XmlNodeList returned from XmlDocument.SelectNodes are of type XmlNode. For an example of how to use the OfType<T> extension method, see the Discussion section:

```
// Make some XML with some types that you can use with LINQ
// that don't support IEnumerable<T> directly
XElement xmlFragment = new XElement("NonGenericLinqableTypes",
                    new XElement("IEnumerable",
                        new XElement("System.Collections",
                            new XElement("ArrayList"),
                            new XElement("BitArray"),
                            new XElement("Hashtable"),
                            new XElement("Queue"),
                            new XElement("SortedList"),
                            new XElement("Stack")),
                        new XElement("System.Net",
                            new XElement("CredentialCache")),
                        new XElement("System.Xml",
                            new XElement("XmlNodeList")),
                        new XElement("System.Xml.XPath",
                            new XElement("XPathNodeIterator"))),
                    new XElement("ICollection",
                        new XElement("System.Diagnostics",
                            new XElement("EventLogEntryCollection")),
                        new XElement("System.Net",
                            new XElement("CookieCollection")),
                        new XElement("System.Security.AccessControl",
                            new XElement("GenericAcl")),
                        new XElement("System.Security",
                            new XElement("PermissionSet"))));

XmlDocument doc = new XmlDocument();
doc.LoadXml(xmlFragment.ToString());

// Select the names of the nodes under IEnumerable that have children and are
// named System.Collections and contain a capital S and return that list in
// descending order
var query =
from node in
    doc.SelectNodes("/NonGenericLinqableTypes/IEnumerable/*").Cast<XmlNode>()
    where node.HasChildNodes &&
        node.Name == "System.Collections"
    from XmlNode xmlNode in node.ChildNodes
    where xmlNode.Name.Contains('S')
    orderby xmlNode.Name descending
    select xmlNode.Name;

foreach (string name in query)
    Console.WriteLine(name);
```

The second example works against the application event log and retrieves the errors that occurred in the last six hours. The type of the element in the collection (EventLogEntry) is provided next to the from keyword, which allows LINQ to infer the rest of the information it needs about the collection element type:

```
EventLog log = new EventLog("Application");
query = from EventLogEntry entry in log.Entries
        where entry.EntryType == EventLogEntryType.Error &&
            entry.TimeGenerated > DateTime.Now.Subtract(new TimeSpan(6, 0, 0))
        select entry.Message;

Console.WriteLine($"There were {query.Count<string>()}" +
    " Application Event Log error messages in the last 6 hours!");
foreach (string message in query)
    Console.WriteLine(message);
```

Discussion

Cast<T> will transform the IEnumerable into IEnumerable<T> so that LINQ can access each item in the collection in a strongly typed manner. Before you use Cast<T>, it would behoove you to check that all elements of the collection really are of type T; otherwise, you will get an InvalidCastException if the type of the element is not convertible to the type T specified, because all elements will be cast using that type. Placing the type of the element next to the from keyword acts just like a Cast<T>:

```
ArrayList stuff = new ArrayList();
stuff.Add(DateTime.Now);
stuff.Add(DateTime.Now);
stuff.Add(1);
stuff.Add(DateTime.Now);

var expr = from item in stuff.Cast<DateTime>()
            select item;
foreach (DateTime item in expr)
    Console.WriteLine(item);
```

 Because of the deferred execution semantics, the exception that occurs with Cast<T> or from happens only once that element has been iterated to.

Another way to approach this issue is to use OfType<T>, as it will return only the elements of a specific type and not try to cast elements from one type to another:

```
var expr = from item in stuff.OfType<DateTime>()
            select item;
// only three elements, all DateTime returned. No exceptions
foreach (DateTime item in expr)
    Console.WriteLine(item);
```

See Also

The "OfType<TResult> method" and "Cast<TResult> method" topics in the MSDN documentation.

4.11 Performing an Advanced Interface Search

Problem

You are searching for an interface using the `Type` class. However, complex interface searches are not available through the `GetInterface` and `GetInterfaces` methods of a `Type` object.

Solution

Use LINQ to query the type interface information and perform rich searches. The method shown in Example 4-2 demonstrates one complex search that can be performed with LINQ.

Example 4-2. Performing complex searches of interfaces on a type

```
// set up the interfaces to search for
Type[] interfaces = {
    typeof(System.ICloneable),
    typeof(System.Collections.ICollection),
    typeof(System.IAppDomainSetup) };

// set up the type to examine
Type searchType = typeof(System.Collections.ArrayList);

var matches = from t in searchType.GetInterfaces()
              join s in interfaces on t equals s
              select s;

Console.WriteLine("Matches found:");
foreach (Type match in matches)
    Console.WriteLine(match.ToString());
```

The code in Example 4-2 searches for any of the three interface types contained in the `Names` array that are implemented by the `System.Collections.ArrayList` type. It does this by using LINQ to query if the type is an instance of any of the set of interfaces.

The `GetInterface` method searches for an interface only by name (using a case-sensitive or case-insensitive search), and the `GetInterfaces` method returns an array of all the interfaces implemented on a particular type. To execute a more focused search—for example, searching for interfaces that define a method with a specific signature, or implemented interfaces that are loaded from the Global Assembly Cache (GAC) where common assemblies are stored—you need to use a different mechanism, like LINQ. LINQ gives you a more flexible and more advanced searching capability for interfaces without requiring you to create your own interface search engine. You might use this capability to load assemblies with a specific interface, to generate code from existing assemblies, or even as a reverse-engineering tool!

Discussion

There are many ways to use LINQ to search for interfaces implemented on a type. Here are just a few other searches that can be performed:

- A search for all implemented interfaces that are defined within a particular namespace (in this case, the System.Collections namespace):

    ```
    var collectionsInterfaces = from type in searchType.GetInterfaces()
                                where type.Namespace == "System.Collections"
                                select type;
    ```

- A search for all implemented interfaces that contain a method called Add, which returns an Int32 value:

    ```
    var addInterfaces = from type in searchType.GetInterfaces()
                        from method in type.GetMethods()
                        where (method.Name == "Add") &&
                              (method.ReturnType == typeof(int))
                        select type;
    ```

- A search for all implemented interfaces that are loaded from the GAC:

    ```
    var gacInterfaces = from type in searchType.GetInterfaces()
                        where type.Assembly.GlobalAssemblyCache
                        select type;
    ```

- A search for all implemented interfaces that are defined within an assembly with the version number 4.0.0.0:

    ```
    var versionInterfaces = from type in searchType.GetInterfaces()
                            where type.Assembly.GlobalAssemblyCache &&
                                type.Assembly.GetName().Version.Major == 4 &&
                                type.Assembly.GetName().Version.Minor == 0 &&
                                type.Assembly.GetName().Version.Build == 0 &&
                                type.Assembly.GetName().Version.Revision == 0
                            select type;
    ```

See Also

The "Lambda Expressions (C# Programming Guide)" and "where keyword [LINQ] (C#)" topics in the MSDN documentation.

4.12 Using Lambda Expressions

Problem

C# includes a feature called *lambda expressions*. While you can view lambda expressions as syntactic sugar for making anonymous method definition less difficult, you also want to understand all of the different ways that you can use them to help you in your daily programming chores as well as the ramifications of those uses.

Solution

Lambda expressions can be implemented by the compiler from methods created by the developer. There are two orthogonal characteristics that lambda expressions may have:

- Parameter lists may have explicit or implicit types.
- Bodies may be expressions or statement blocks.

Let's start with the original way to use delegates. First, you would declare a delegate type—DoWork in this case—and then create an instance of it (as shown here in the WorkItOut method). Declaring the instance of the delegate requires that you specify a method to execute when the delegate is invoked, and here the DoWorkMethodImpl method has been connected. The delegate is invoked, and the text is written to the console via the DoWorkMethodImpl method:

```
class OldWay
{
    // declare delegate
    delegate int DoWork(string work);

    // have a method to create an instance of and call the delegate
    public void WorkItOut()
    {
        // declare instance
        DoWork dw = new DoWork(DoWorkMethodImpl);
        // invoke delegate
        int i = dw("Do work the old way");
    }

    // Have a method that the delegate is tied to with a matching signature
    // so that it is invoked when the delegate is called
    public int DoWorkMethodImpl(string s)
    {
        Console.WriteLine(s);
        return s.GetHashCode();
    }
}
```

Lambda expressions allow you to set up code to run when a delegate is invoked, but you do not need to give a named formal method declaration to the delegate. The method thus declared is nameless and closed over the scope of the outer method. For example, you could have written the preceding code using a lambda expression such as this:

```
class LambdaWay
{
    // declare delegate
    delegate int DoWork(string work);

    // have a method to create an instance of and call the delegate
    public void WorkItOut()
    {
        // declare instance
        DoWork dw = s =>
        {
            Console.WriteLine(s);
            return s.GetHashCode();
        };
        // invoke delegate
        int i = dw("Do some inline work");
    }
}
```

Notice that instead of having a method called DoWorkMethodImpl, you use the => operator to directly assign the code from that method inline to the DoWork delegate. The assignment looks like this:

```
DoWork dw = s =>
{
    Console.WriteLine(s);
    return s.GetHashCode();
};
```

You also provide the parameter required by the DoWork delegate (string), and your code returns an int (s.GetHashCode()) as the delegate requires. When you're setting up a lambda expression, the code must match the delegate signature, or you will get a compiler error.

By "match," we mean:

- If explicitly typed, the lambda parameters must exactly match the delegate parameters. If implicitly typed, the lambda parameters get the delegate parameter types.

- The body of the lambda must be a legal expression or statement block given the parameter types.

- The return type of the lambda must be implicitly convertible to the return type of the delegate. It need not match exactly.

There is yet another way you can set up the delegate: through the magic of *delegate inference*. Delegate inference allows you to assign the method name directly to the delegate instance without having to write the code to create a new delegate object. Under the covers, C# actually writes the IL for creating the delegate object, but you don't have to do it explicitly here. Using delegate inference instead of writing out new [*Delegate Type*]([*Method Name*]) everywhere helps to unclutter the code involved in delegate use, as shown here:

```
class DirectAssignmentWay
{
    // declare delegate
    delegate int DoWork(string work);

    // have a method to create an instance of and call the delegate
    public void WorkItOut()
    {
        // declare instance and assign method
        DoWork dw = DoWorkMethodImpl;
        // invoke delegate
        int i = dw("Do some direct assignment work");
    }
    // Have a method that the delegate is tied to with a matching signature
    // so that it is invoked when the delegate is called
    public int DoWorkMethodImpl(string s)
    {
        Console.WriteLine(s);
        return s.GetHashCode();
    }
}
```

Notice that all that is assigned to the DoWork delegate instance dw is the method name DoWorkMethodImpl. There is no new DoWork(DoWorkMethodImpl) call as there was in older C# code.

 Remember, the underlying delegate wrapper does not go away; delegate inference just simplifies the syntax a bit by hiding some of it.

Alternatively, you can also set up lambda expressions that take generic type parameters to enable working with generic delegates, as you see here in the GenericWay class:

```
class GenericWay
{
    // have a method to create two instances of and call the delegates
```

```
public void WorkItOut()
{
    Func<string, string> dwString = s =>
    {
        Console.WriteLine(s);
        return s;
    };

    // invoke string delegate
    string retStr = dwString("Do some generic work");

    Func<int, int> dwInt = i =>
    {
        Console.WriteLine(i);
        return i;
    };

    // invoke int delegate
    int j = dwInt(5);

}
}
```

Discussion

One of the useful things about lambda expressions is the concept of outer variables. The official definition of *outer variable* is any local variable, value parameter, or parameter array with a scope that contains the lambda expression.

This means that, inside the code of the lambda expression, you can touch variables outside the scope of that method. This introduces the concept of "capturing" the variables, which occurs when a lambda expression actually makes reference to one of the outer variables. In the following example, the count variable is captured and incremented by the lambda expression. The count variable is not part of the original scope of the lambda expression but rather part of the outer scope. It is incremented, and then the incremented value is returned and totaled:

```
public void SeeOuterWork()
{
    int count = 0;
    int total = 0;
    Func<int> countUp = () => count++;
    for (int i = 0; i < 10; i++)
        total += countUp();
    Debug.WriteLine($"Total = {total}");
}
```

What capturing actually does is extend the lifetime of the outer variable to coincide with the lifetime of the underlying delegate instance that represents the lambda expression. This should encourage you to be careful about what you touch from inside a lambda expression. You could be causing things to hang around a lot longer than you originally planned. The garbage collector won't get a chance to clean up those outer variables until later, when they are used in the lambda expression. Capturing outer variables has another garbage-collector effect: when locals or value parameters are captured, they are no longer considered to be fixed but are now movable, so any unsafe code must now fix that variable—via the `fixed` keyword—before the variable is used.

Outer variables can affect how the compiler generates the internal IL for the lambda expression. If the lambda expression uses outer variables, the lambda expression is generated as a private method of a nested class. If the lambda expression does not use outer variables, it would be generated as another private method of the class in which it is declared. If the outer method is static, then the lambda expression cannot access instance members via the `this` keyword, as the nested class will also be generated as static.

There are two types of lambda expressions: expression lambdas and statement lambdas. This expression lambda has no parameters and simply increments the `count` variable in an expression:

```
int count = 0;
Func<int> countUp = () => count++;
```

Statement lambdas have the body enclosed in curly braces and can contain any number of statements like this:

```
Func<int, int> dwInt = i =>
{
    Console.WriteLine(i);
    return i;
};
```

A few last things to remember about lambda expressions:

- They can't use `break`, `goto`, or `continue` to jump from the lambda expression to a target outside the lambda expression block.

- No unsafe code can be executed inside a lambda expression.

- Lambda expressions cannot be used on the left side of the `is` operator.

- Since lambda expressions are a superset of anonymous methods, all restrictions that apply to anonymous methods also apply to lambda expressions.

See Also

The "Lambda Expressions (C# Programming Guide)" topic in the MSDN documentation.

4.13 Using Different Parameter Modifiers in Lambda Expressions

Problem

You know you can pass parameters to lambda expressions, but you need to figure out what parameter modifiers are valid with them.

Solution

Lambda expressions can use `out` and `ref` parameter modifiers but not the `params` modifier in their parameter list. However, this does not prevent the creation of delegates with any of these modifiers, as shown here:

```
// declare out delegate
delegate int DoOutWork(out string work);

// declare ref delegate
delegate int DoRefWork(ref string work);

// declare params delegate
delegate int DoParamsWork(params object[] workItems);
```

Even though the `DoParamsWork` delegate is defined with the `params` keyword on the parameter, it can still be used as a type for a lambda expression, as you'll see in a bit. To use the `DoOutWork` delegate, create a lambda expression inline using the `out` keyword and assign it to the `DoOutWork` delegate instance. Inside the lambda expression body, the `out` variable `s` is assigned a value first (as it doesn't have one by definition as an `out` parameter), writes it to the console, and returns the string hash code. Note that in the parameter list, you must provide the type of `s` (i.e., `string`), as type is not inferred for variables marked with the `out` or `ref` keywords. It is not inferred for `out` or `ref` variables to preserve the representation at the call site and the parameter declaration site to help the developer clearly reason about the possible assignment to these variables:

```
// declare instance and assign method
DoOutWork dow = (out string s) =>
{
    s = "WorkFinished";
    Console.WriteLine(s);
    return s.GetHashCode();
};
```

To run the lambda expression code, invoke the delegate with an `out` parameter, and then print out the result to the console:

```
// invoke delegate
string work;
int i = dow(out work);
Console.WriteLine(work);
```

To use the `ref` parameter modifier in a lambda expression, create an inline method to hook up to the `DoRefWork` delegate with a `ref` parameter. In the method, you write the original value out, reassign the value, and get the hash code of the new value. Remember that, as with the `out` keyword, you must provide the type of s (`string`) in the parameter list, as type cannot be inferred for a variable marked with the `ref` keyword:

```
// declare instance and assign method
DoRefWork drw = (ref string s) =>
{
    Console.WriteLine(s);
    s = "WorkFinished";
    return s.GetHashCode();
};
```

To run the lambda expression, assign a value to the string work and then pass it as a `ref` parameter to the `DoRefWork` delegate that is instantiated. Upon the return from the delegate call, write out the new value for the work string:

```
// invoke delegate
work = "WorkStarted";
i = drw(ref work);
Console.WriteLine(work);
```

While it is possible to declare a delegate with the `params` modifier, you cannot hook up the delegate using a lambda expression with the `params` keyword in the parameter list. If you try this, the compiler displays the `CS1670 params is not valid in this context` compiler error on the `DoParamsWork` line:

```
////Done as an lambda expression you also get
////CS1670 "params is not valid in this context"
//DoParamsWork dpwl = (params object[] workItems) =>
//{
//    foreach (object o in workItems)
//    {
//        Console.WriteLine(o.ToString());
//    }
//    return workItems.GetHashCode();
//};
```

Even if you attempt this using an anonymous method instead of a lambda expression, you still cannot hook up this delegate with the `params` keyword in the parameter list.

If you try, the compiler still displays the CS1670 `params is not valid in this con`
`text` compiler error on the `DoParamsWork` line:

```
//Done as an anonymous method you get CS1670
    "params is not valid in this context"
//DoParamsWork dpwa = delegate (params object[] workItems)
//{
//    foreach (object o in workItems)
//    {
//        Console.WriteLine(o.ToString());
//    }
//    return workItems.GetHashCode();
//};
```

You can, however, omit the `params` keyword and still set up the lambda expression for the delegate, as shown here:

```
// All we have to do is omit the params keyword.
DoParamsWork dpw = workItems =>
{
    foreach (object o in workItems)
        Console.WriteLine(o.ToString());
    return workItems.GetHashCode();
};
```

Notice that although you've removed the `params` keyword from the lambda expression, this doesn't stop you from using the same syntax. The `params` keyword is present on the delegate type, so you can invoke it thusly:

```
int i = dpw("Hello", "42", "bar");
```

So this illustrates that you can bind a lambda expression to a delegate declared using `params`, and once you've done that, you can invoke the lambda expression, passing in any number of parameters you like, just as you'd expect.

Discussion

Lambda expressions cannot access the `ref` or `out` parameters of an outer scope. This means any `out` or `ref` variables that were defined as part of the containing method are off-limits for use inside the body of the lambda expression:

```
public void TestOut(out string outStr)
{
    // declare instance
    DoWork dw = s =>
    {
        Console.WriteLine(s);
        // Causes error CS1628:
        // "Cannot use ref or out parameter 'outStr' inside an
        // anonymous method, lambda expression, or query expression"
        outStr = s;
```

```
        return s.GetHashCode();
    };
    // invoke delegate
    int i = dw("DoWorkMethodImpl1");
}

public void TestRef(ref string refStr)
{
    // declare instance
    DoWork dw = s =>
    {
        Console.WriteLine(s);
        // Causes error CS1628:
        // "Cannot use ref or out parameter 'refStr' inside an
        // anonymous method, lambda expression, or query expression"
        refStr = s;
        return s.GetHashCode();
    };
    // invoke delegate
    int i = dw("DoWorkMethodImpl1");
}
```

Interestingly enough, lambda expressions can access outer variables with the `params` modifier:

```
// declare delegate
delegate int DoWork(string work);

public void TestParams(params string[] items)
{
    // declare instance
    DoWork dw = s =>
    {
        Console.WriteLine(s);
        foreach (string item in items)
            Console.WriteLine(item);
        return s.GetHashCode();
    };
    // invoke delegate
    int i = dw("DoWorkMethodImpl1");
}
```

Because the `params` modifier is there for the benefit of the calling site (so the compiler knows to make this a method call that supports variable-length argument lists) and because lambda expressions are never called directly (they're always called via a delegate), it makes no sense for a lambda expression to be decorated with something there for the benefit of the calling site—as there is no calling site. This is why it doesn't matter that you can't use the `params` keyword on a lambda expression. For lambda expressions, the calling site is always calling through the delegate, so what matters is whether that delegate has the `params` keyword or not.

See Also

Recipe 1.17; the "CS1670," "CS1525," "CS1628," "out," "ref," "params," and "System.ParamArrayAttribute" topics in the MSDN documentation.

4.14 Speeding Up LINQ Operations with Parallelism

Problem

You have a LINQ query that performs an expensive operation that slows down the processing, and you would like to speed it up.

Solution

Use PLINQ (Parallel LINQ) to utilize the full capacities of your machine to process the query faster.

To demonstrate this, let's consider the plight of Brooke and Katie. Brooke and Katie are working on a cookbook together and they need to evaluate all of the recipes for all of the chapters. Since there are so many recipes, they want to be able to hand off the rudimentary validation steps for the recipes and then Brooke or Katie gets a final pass at each recipe as the main editor for final fit and finish.

Each `Chapter` has a number of `Recipes` in it, and the `Recipe` validation steps are:

1. Read the text of the recipe for premise.
2. Check the recipe accuracy of ingredients and measurements.
3. Prepare the recipe and taste once for each rank of difficulty for the recipe.
4. Have Brooke or Katie perform the final editing pass.

If any stage of the recipe evaluation fails, that stage needs to be redone unless it is the tasting stage. If a `Recipe` fails the tasting stage, it needs to start over.

To process the collection of `RecipeChapters` (chapters in the example) with regular LINQ, we could use the following statement:

```
chapters.Select(c => TimedEvaluateChapter(c, rnd)).ToList();
```

`TimedEvaluateChapter` is a method that performs the evaluation of the `RecipeChapter` and all of the `Recipes` in the `RecipeChapter` while timing the evaluation. `EvaluateRecipe` is called once for each `Recipe` in the `RecipeChapter` to perform the `Recipe` validation steps:

```
private static RecipeChapter TimedEvaluateChapter(RecipeChapter rc, Random rnd)
{
    Stopwatch watch = new Stopwatch();
```

```
        LogOutput($"Evaluating Chapter {rc}");
        watch.Start();
        foreach (var r in rc.Recipes)
            EvaluateRecipe(r, rnd);
        watch.Stop();
        LogOutput($"Finished Evaluating Chapter {rc}");
        return rc;
    }
```

In order to process the Recipes faster, we add a call to the AsParallel extension method before we call Select to invoke TimedEvaluateChapter for each RecipeChapter:

```
    chapters.AsParallel().Select(c => TimedEvaluateChapter(c, rnd)).ToList();
```

Your results will vary based on your hardware, but the following times were recorded on a run using regular LINQ and then subsequently PLINQ:

```
    Full Chapter Evaluation with LINQ took: 00:01:19.1395258
    Full Chapter Evaluation with PLINQ took: 00:00:25.1708103
```

Discussion

When you're using PLINQ, the main thing to keep in mind is that the unit of work being parallelized must be significant enough to justify the cost of the parallelization. There are additional setup and teardown costs to doing operations in parallel (like partitioning of the data set) and if the data set is too small or the operation on each member of the set is not expensive enough to be helped by using parallel techniques, you could actually perform worse. If PLINQ determines that it cannot effectively parallelize the query, it will process it sequentially. If this happens, there are a number of additional methods you can use to adjust depending upon your particular situation (WithExecutionMode, WithDegreeOfParallelism).

As in all engineering, measuring your results is the key to understanding if you are improving or not, so with that in mind, we created the TimedEvaluateChapter method to call from our Select statement:

```
    chapters.AsParallel().Select(c => TimedEvaluateChapter(c, rnd)).ToList();
```

TimedEvaluateChapter times the process of evaluating every Recipe in the Recipe Chapter and wraps that value in calls to Stopwatch.Start and Stopwatch.Stop for timing. The timing results are then available in Stopwatch.Elapsed. Note that if you restart the Stopwatch without calling Stopwatch.Reset, the timer will add to the value already in the Stopwatch and you may get a bigger value than you expected:

```
    private static RecipeChapter TimedEvaluateChapter(RecipeChapter rc, Random rnd)
    {
        Stopwatch watch = new Stopwatch();
        LogOutput($"Evaluating Chapter {rc}");
        watch.Start();
```

```
        foreach (var r in rc.Recipes)
            EvaluateRecipe(r, rnd);
        watch.Stop();
        LogOutput($"Finished Evaluating Chapter {rc}");
        return rc;
    }
```

EvaluateRecipe performs the validation steps on each recipe recursively until it
passes the final edit from Brooke and Katie. Thread.Sleep is called to simulate work
for each step:

```
    private static Recipe EvaluateRecipe(Recipe r, Random rnd)
    {
        //Recipe Editing steps
        if (!r.TextApproved)
        {
            //Read the recipe to make sure it makes sense
            Thread.Sleep(50);
            int evaluation = rnd.Next(1, 10);
            // 7 means it didn't make sense so don't approve it,
            // send it back for rework
            if (evaluation == 7)
            {
                LogOutput($"{r} failed the readthrough! Reworking...");
            }
            else
                r.TextApproved = true;
            return EvaluateRecipe(r, rnd);
        }
        else if (!r.IngredientsApproved)
        {
            //Check the ingredients and measurements
            Thread.Sleep(100);
            int evaluation = rnd.Next(1, 10);
            // 3 means the ingredients or measurements are incorrect,
            // send it back for rework
            if (evaluation == 3)
            {
                LogOutput($"{r} had incorrect measurements! Reworking...");
            }
            else
                r.IngredientsApproved = true;
            return EvaluateRecipe(r, rnd);
        }
        else if (r.RecipeEvaluated != r.Rank)
        {
            //Prepare recipe and taste
            Thread.Sleep(50 * r.Rank);
            int evaluation = rnd.Next(1, 10);
            // 4 means it didn't taste right, send it back for rework
            if (evaluation == 4)
            {
```

```
                r.TextApproved = false;
                r.IngredientsApproved = false;
                r.RecipeEvaluated = 0;
                LogOutput($"{r} tasted bad!  Reworking...");
            }
            else
                r.RecipeEvaluated++;
            return EvaluateRecipe(r, rnd);
        }
        else
        {
            //Final editing pass(Brooke or Katie)
            Thread.Sleep(50 * r.Rank);
            int evaluation = rnd.Next(1, 10);
            // 1 means it just wasn't quite ready, send it back for rework
            if (evaluation == 1)
            {
                r.TextApproved = false;
                r.IngredientsApproved = false;
                r.RecipeEvaluated = 0;
                LogOutput($"{r} failed final editing!  Reworking...");
                return EvaluateRecipe(r, rnd);
            }
            else
            {
                r.FinalEditingComplete = true;
                LogOutput($"{r} is ready for release!");
            }
        }
    }
    return r;
}
```

Here are the definitions of the `RecipeChapter` and `Recipe` classes used to help Brooke and Katie evaluate all of the recipes:

```
public class RecipeChapter
{
    public int Number { get; set; }
    public string Title { get; set; }
    public List<Recipe> Recipes { get; set; }
    public override string ToString() => $"{Number} - {Title}";
}

public class Recipe
{
    public RecipeChapter Chapter { get; set; }
    public string MainIngredient { get; set; }
    public int Number { get; set; }
    public bool TextApproved { get; set; }
    public bool IngredientsApproved { get; set; }

    /// <summary>
    /// Recipe should be evaluated as many times as the Rank of the recipe
```

```
/// </summary>
public int RecipeEvaluated { get; set; }

public bool FinalEditingComplete { get; set; }

public int Rank { get; set; }

public override string ToString() =>
    $"{Chapter.Number}.{Number} ({Chapter.Title}:{MainIngredient})";
}
```

Sample output from the LINQ run looks like this and processes the collection in sequential order:

```
Running Cookbook Evaluation
Evaluating Chapter 1 - Soups
1.1 (Soups:Sprouts, Mung Bean) is ready for release!
1.2 (Soups:Potato Bread) is ready for release!
1.3 (Soups:Chicken Liver) tasted bad!  Reworking...
1.3 (Soups:Chicken Liver) is ready for release!
1.4 (Soups:Cherimoya) tasted bad!  Reworking...
1.4 (Soups:Cherimoya) had incorrect measurements! Reworking...
1.4 (Soups:Cherimoya) is ready for release!
1.5 (Soups:High-Protein Bread) is ready for release!
1.6 (Soups:Flat Bread) failed the readthrough! Reworking...
1.6 (Soups:Flat Bread) is ready for release!
1.7 (Soups:Pomegranate) is ready for release!
1.8 (Soups:Carissa, Natal Plum) had incorrect measurements! Reworking...
1.8 (Soups:Carissa, Natal Plum) is ready for release!
1.9 (Soups:Ideal Flat Bread) is ready for release!
1.10 (Soups:Banana Bread) tasted bad!  Reworking...
1.10 (Soups:Banana Bread) is ready for release!
Finished Evaluating Chapter 1 - Soups
Evaluating Chapter 2 - Salads
2.1 (Salads:Caraway) tasted bad!  Reworking...
2.1 (Salads:Caraway) tasted bad!  Reworking...
2.1 (Salads:Caraway) had incorrect measurements! Reworking...
2.1 (Salads:Caraway) is ready for release!
2.2 (Salads:Potatoes, Red) had incorrect measurements! Reworking...
2.2 (Salads:Potatoes, Red) tasted bad!  Reworking...
2.2 (Salads:Potatoes, Red) is ready for release!
2.3 (Salads:Lemon) is ready for release!
2.4 (Salads:Cream cheese) is ready for release!
2.5 (Salads:Artichokes, Domestic) is ready for release!
2.6 (Salads:Grapefruit) is ready for release!
2.7 (Salads:Lettuce, Iceberg) is ready for release!
2.8 (Salads:Fenugreek) is ready for release!
2.9 (Salads:Ostrich) is ready for release!
2.10 (Salads:Brazil Nuts) tasted bad!  Reworking...
2.10 (Salads:Brazil Nuts) had incorrect measurements! Reworking...
2.10 (Salads:Brazil Nuts) tasted bad!  Reworking...
2.10 (Salads:Brazil Nuts) is ready for release!
Finished Evaluating Chapter 2 - Salads
```

Evaluating Chapter 3 - Appetizers
3.1 (Appetizers:Loquat) tasted bad! Reworking...
3.1 (Appetizers:Loquat) had incorrect measurements! Reworking...
3.1 (Appetizers:Loquat) tasted bad! Reworking...
3.1 (Appetizers:Loquat) is ready for release!
3.2 (Appetizers:Bergenost) is ready for release!
3.3 (Appetizers:Tomato Red Roma) had incorrect measurements! Reworking...
3.3 (Appetizers:Tomato Red Roma) tasted bad! Reworking...
3.3 (Appetizers:Tomato Red Roma) tasted bad! Reworking...
3.3 (Appetizers:Tomato Red Roma) is ready for release!
3.4 (Appetizers:Guava) failed final editing! Reworking...
3.4 (Appetizers:Guava) is ready for release!
3.5 (Appetizers:Squash Flower) is ready for release!
3.6 (Appetizers:Radishes, Red) is ready for release!
3.7 (Appetizers:Goose Liver) tasted bad! Reworking...
3.7 (Appetizers:Goose Liver) had incorrect measurements! Reworking...
3.7 (Appetizers:Goose Liver) is ready for release!
3.8 (Appetizers:Okra) had incorrect measurements! Reworking...
3.8 (Appetizers:Okra) is ready for release!
3.9 (Appetizers:Borage) is ready for release!
3.10 (Appetizers:Peppers) is ready for release!
Finished Evaluating Chapter 3 - Appetizers
Evaluating Chapter 4 - Entrees
4.1 (Entrees:Plantain) is ready for release!
4.2 (Entrees:Pignola (Pine)) is ready for release!
4.3 (Entrees:Potatoes, Gold) is ready for release!
4.4 (Entrees:Ribeye) failed the readthrough! Reworking...
4.4 (Entrees:Ribeye) is ready for release!
4.5 (Entrees:Sprouts, Mung Bean) failed the readthrough! Reworking...
4.5 (Entrees:Sprouts, Mung Bean) had incorrect measurements! Reworking...
4.5 (Entrees:Sprouts, Mung Bean) failed final editing! Reworking...
4.5 (Entrees:Sprouts, Mung Bean) is ready for release!
4.6 (Entrees:Squash) had incorrect measurements! Reworking...
4.6 (Entrees:Squash) is ready for release!
4.7 (Entrees:Squash, Winter) tasted bad! Reworking...
4.7 (Entrees:Squash, Winter) is ready for release!
4.8 (Entrees:Corn, Blue) is ready for release!
4.9 (Entrees:Snake) had incorrect measurements! Reworking...
4.9 (Entrees:Snake) tasted bad! Reworking...
4.9 (Entrees:Snake) tasted bad! Reworking...
4.9 (Entrees:Snake) is ready for release!
4.10 (Entrees:Prosciutto) is ready for release!
Finished Evaluating Chapter 4 - Entrees
Evaluating Chapter 5 - Desserts
5.1 (Desserts:Mushroom, White, Silver Dollar) tasted bad! Reworking...
5.1 (Desserts:Mushroom, White, Silver Dollar) had incorrect measurements!
Reworking...
5.1 (Desserts:Mushroom, White, Silver Dollar) tasted bad! Reworking...
5.1 (Desserts:Mushroom, White, Silver Dollar) tasted bad! Reworking...
5.1 (Desserts:Mushroom, White, Silver Dollar) had incorrect measurements!
Reworking...
5.1 (Desserts:Mushroom, White, Silver Dollar) is ready for release!

5.2 (Desserts:Eggplant) is ready for release!
5.3 (Desserts:Asparagus Peas) tasted bad! Reworking...
5.3 (Desserts:Asparagus Peas) failed the readthrough! Reworking...
5.3 (Desserts:Asparagus Peas) failed the readthrough! Reworking...
5.3 (Desserts:Asparagus Peas) is ready for release!
5.4 (Desserts:Squash, Kabocha) failed the readthrough! Reworking...
5.4 (Desserts:Squash, Kabocha) tasted bad! Reworking...
5.4 (Desserts:Squash, Kabocha) is ready for release!
5.5 (Desserts:Sprouts, Radish) is ready for release!
5.6 (Desserts:Mushroom, Black Trumpet) is ready for release!
5.7 (Desserts:Tea Cakes) tasted bad! Reworking...
5.7 (Desserts:Tea Cakes) tasted bad! Reworking...
5.7 (Desserts:Tea Cakes) failed the readthrough! Reworking...
5.7 (Desserts:Tea Cakes) is ready for release!
5.8 (Desserts:Blueberries) had incorrect measurements! Reworking...
5.8 (Desserts:Blueberries) tasted bad! Reworking...
5.8 (Desserts:Blueberries) is ready for release!
5.9 (Desserts:Sago Palm) is ready for release!
5.10 (Desserts:Opossum) had incorrect measurements! Reworking...
5.10 (Desserts:Opossum) is ready for release!
Finished Evaluating Chapter 5 - Desserts
Evaluating Chapter 6 - Snacks
6.1 (Snacks:Cheddar) tasted bad! Reworking...
6.1 (Snacks:Cheddar) is ready for release!
6.2 (Snacks:Melon, Bitter) is ready for release!
6.3 (Snacks:Scallion) is ready for release!
6.4 (Snacks:Squash Chayote) failed final editing! Reworking...
6.4 (Snacks:Squash Chayote) is ready for release!
6.5 (Snacks:Roasted Turkey) is ready for release!
6.6 (Snacks:Lime) is ready for release!
6.7 (Snacks:Hazelnut) is ready for release!
6.8 (Snacks:Radishes, Daikon) tasted bad! Reworking...
6.8 (Snacks:Radishes, Daikon) tasted bad! Reworking...
6.8 (Snacks:Radishes, Daikon) failed the readthrough! Reworking...
6.8 (Snacks:Radishes, Daikon) tasted bad! Reworking...
6.8 (Snacks:Radishes, Daikon) is ready for release!
6.9 (Snacks:Salami) failed the readthrough! Reworking...
6.9 (Snacks:Salami) is ready for release!
6.10 (Snacks:Mushroom, Oyster) failed the readthrough! Reworking...
6.10 (Snacks:Mushroom, Oyster) is ready for release!
Finished Evaluating Chapter 6 - Snacks
Evaluating Chapter 7 - Breakfast
7.1 (Breakfast:Daikon Radish) had incorrect measurements! Reworking...
7.1 (Breakfast:Daikon Radish) is ready for release!
7.2 (Breakfast:Lettuce, Red Leaf) failed final editing! Reworking...
7.2 (Breakfast:Lettuce, Red Leaf) is ready for release!
7.3 (Breakfast:Alfalfa Sprouts) is ready for release!
7.4 (Breakfast:Tea Cakes) is ready for release!
7.5 (Breakfast:Chia seed) is ready for release!
7.6 (Breakfast:Tangerine) is ready for release!
7.7 (Breakfast:Spinach) is ready for release!
7.8 (Breakfast:Flank Steak) is ready for release!

```
7.9 (Breakfast:Loganberries) had incorrect measurements! Reworking...
7.9 (Breakfast:Loganberries) had incorrect measurements! Reworking...
7.9 (Breakfast:Loganberries) had incorrect measurements! Reworking...
7.9 (Breakfast:Loganberries) is ready for release!
7.10 (Breakfast:Opossum) is ready for release!
Finished Evaluating Chapter 7 - Breakfast
Evaluating Chapter 8 - Sandwiches
8.1 (Sandwiches:Rhubarb) tasted bad!  Reworking...
8.1 (Sandwiches:Rhubarb) is ready for release!
8.2 (Sandwiches:Pickle, Brine) is ready for release!
8.3 (Sandwiches:Oranges) tasted bad!  Reworking...
8.3 (Sandwiches:Oranges) had incorrect measurements! Reworking...
8.3 (Sandwiches:Oranges) is ready for release!
8.4 (Sandwiches:Chayote, Pipinella, Vegetable Pear) tasted bad!  Reworking...
8.4 (Sandwiches:Chayote, Pipinella, Vegetable Pear) is ready for release!
8.5 (Sandwiches:Bear) is ready for release!
8.6 (Sandwiches:Panela) had incorrect measurements! Reworking...
8.6 (Sandwiches:Panela) is ready for release!
8.7 (Sandwiches:Peppers, Red) had incorrect measurements! Reworking...
8.7 (Sandwiches:Peppers, Red) tasted bad!  Reworking...
8.7 (Sandwiches:Peppers, Red) failed the readthrough! Reworking...
8.7 (Sandwiches:Peppers, Red) failed the readthrough! Reworking...
8.7 (Sandwiches:Peppers, Red) had incorrect measurements! Reworking...
8.7 (Sandwiches:Peppers, Red) tasted bad!  Reworking...
8.7 (Sandwiches:Peppers, Red) is ready for release!
8.8 (Sandwiches:Oat Bread) is ready for release!
8.9 (Sandwiches:Peppers, Green) is ready for release!
8.10 (Sandwiches:Garlic) is ready for release!
Finished Evaluating Chapter 8 - Sandwiches
************************************************
Full Chapter Evaluation with LINQ took: 00:01:19.1395258
************************************************
```

Sample output from the PLINQ run looks like this, processes in parallel (note the evaluation of four `RecipeChapters` at the beginning), and processes items out of sequential order:

```
Evaluating Chapter 5 - Desserts
Evaluating Chapter 3 - Appetizers
Evaluating Chapter 1 - Soups
Evaluating Chapter 7 - Breakfast
7.1 (Breakfast:Daikon Radish) failed the readthrough! Reworking...
1.1 (Soups:Sprouts, Mung Bean) failed the readthrough! Reworking...
3.1 (Appetizers:Loquat) had incorrect measurements! Reworking...
1.1 (Soups:Sprouts, Mung Bean) had incorrect measurements! Reworking...
7.1 (Breakfast:Daikon Radish) tasted bad!  Reworking...
5.1 (Desserts:Mushroom, White, Silver Dollar) tasted bad!  Reworking...
3.1 (Appetizers:Loquat) failed final editing!  Reworking...
7.1 (Breakfast:Daikon Radish) is ready for release!
3.1 (Appetizers:Loquat) tasted bad!  Reworking...
5.1 (Desserts:Mushroom, White, Silver Dollar) tasted bad!  Reworking...
1.1 (Soups:Sprouts, Mung Bean) is ready for release!
```

3.1 (Appetizers:Loquat) is ready for release!
1.2 (Soups:Potato Bread) had incorrect measurements! Reworking...
1.2 (Soups:Potato Bread) is ready for release!
1.3 (Soups:Chicken Liver) failed the readthrough! Reworking...
3.2 (Appetizers:Bergenost) is ready for release!
1.3 (Soups:Chicken Liver) had incorrect measurements! Reworking...
7.2 (Breakfast:Lettuce, Red Leaf) failed final editing! Reworking...
5.1 (Desserts:Mushroom, White, Silver Dollar) is ready for release!
5.2 (Desserts:Eggplant) is ready for release!
7.2 (Breakfast:Lettuce, Red Leaf) tasted bad! Reworking...
3.3 (Appetizers:Tomato Red Roma) is ready for release!
1.3 (Soups:Chicken Liver) is ready for release!
3.4 (Appetizers:Guava) is ready for release!
5.3 (Desserts:Asparagus Peas) is ready for release!
1.4 (Soups:Cherimoya) is ready for release!
5.4 (Desserts:Squash, Kabocha) is ready for release!
1.5 (Soups:High-Protein Bread) had incorrect measurements! Reworking...
7.2 (Breakfast:Lettuce, Red Leaf) failed final editing! Reworking...
1.5 (Soups:High-Protein Bread) failed final editing! Reworking...
5.5 (Desserts:Sprouts, Radish) is ready for release!
3.5 (Appetizers:Squash Flower) is ready for release!
3.6 (Appetizers:Radishes, Red) failed the readthrough! Reworking...
1.5 (Soups:High-Protein Bread) is ready for release!
5.6 (Desserts:Mushroom, Black Trumpet) tasted bad! Reworking...
1.6 (Soups:Flat Bread) is ready for release!
1.7 (Soups:Pomegranate) is ready for release!
3.6 (Appetizers:Radishes, Red) is ready for release!
7.2 (Breakfast:Lettuce, Red Leaf) is ready for release!
5.6 (Desserts:Mushroom, Black Trumpet) failed final editing! Reworking...
1.8 (Soups:Carissa, Natal Plum) is ready for release!
7.3 (Breakfast:Alfalfa Sprouts) is ready for release!
7.4 (Breakfast:Tea Cakes) is ready for release!
5.6 (Desserts:Mushroom, Black Trumpet) is ready for release!
3.7 (Appetizers:Goose Liver) is ready for release!
1.9 (Soups:Ideal Flat Bread) is ready for release!
5.7 (Desserts:Tea Cakes) tasted bad! Reworking...
3.8 (Appetizers:Okra) is ready for release!
3.9 (Appetizers:Borage) tasted bad! Reworking...
3.9 (Appetizers:Borage) failed the readthrough! Reworking...
3.9 (Appetizers:Borage) failed the readthrough! Reworking...
7.5 (Breakfast:Chia seed) is ready for release!
3.9 (Appetizers:Borage) is ready for release!
1.10 (Soups:Banana Bread) is ready for release!
Finished Evaluating Chapter 1 - Soups
Evaluating Chapter 2 - Salads
3.10 (Appetizers:Peppers) is ready for release!
Finished Evaluating Chapter 3 - Appetizers
Evaluating Chapter 4 - Entrees
5.7 (Desserts:Tea Cakes) is ready for release!
7.6 (Breakfast:Tangerine) is ready for release!
4.1 (Entrees:Plantain) is ready for release!
4.2 (Entrees:Pignola (Pine)) failed the readthrough! Reworking...

2.1 (Salads:Caraway) is ready for release!
5.8 (Desserts:Blueberries) is ready for release!
5.9 (Desserts:Sago Palm) failed the readthrough! Reworking...
5.9 (Desserts:Sago Palm) tasted bad! Reworking...
5.9 (Desserts:Sago Palm) is ready for release!
4.2 (Entrees:Pignola (Pine)) is ready for release!
2.2 (Salads:Potatoes, Red) is ready for release!
2.3 (Salads:Lemon) had incorrect measurements! Reworking...
4.3 (Entrees:Potatoes, Gold) is ready for release!
7.7 (Breakfast:Spinach) failed final editing! Reworking...
2.3 (Salads:Lemon) had incorrect measurements! Reworking...
4.4 (Entrees:Ribeye) had incorrect measurements! Reworking...
7.7 (Breakfast:Spinach) tasted bad! Reworking...
4.4 (Entrees:Ribeye) is ready for release!
2.3 (Salads:Lemon) tasted bad! Reworking...
5.10 (Desserts:Opossum) is ready for release!
Finished Evaluating Chapter 5 - Desserts
Evaluating Chapter 6 - Snacks
6.1 (Snacks:Cheddar) is ready for release!
4.5 (Entrees:Sprouts, Mung Bean) is ready for release!
7.7 (Breakfast:Spinach) is ready for release!
6.2 (Snacks:Melon, Bitter) is ready for release!
6.3 (Snacks:Scallion) failed the readthrough! Reworking...
7.8 (Breakfast:Flank Steak) tasted bad! Reworking...
2.3 (Salads:Lemon) failed final editing! Reworking...
7.8 (Breakfast:Flank Steak) is ready for release!
4.6 (Entrees:Squash) is ready for release!
2.3 (Salads:Lemon) tasted bad! Reworking...
4.7 (Entrees:Squash, Winter) failed the readthrough! Reworking...
4.7 (Entrees:Squash, Winter) had incorrect measurements! Reworking...
6.3 (Snacks:Scallion) is ready for release!
6.4 (Snacks:Squash Chayote) is ready for release!
4.7 (Entrees:Squash, Winter) is ready for release!
7.9 (Breakfast:Loganberries) is ready for release!
2.3 (Salads:Lemon) is ready for release!
7.10 (Breakfast:Opossum) is ready for release!
Finished Evaluating Chapter 7 - Breakfast
Evaluating Chapter 8 - Sandwiches
8.1 (Sandwiches:Rhubarb) had incorrect measurements! Reworking...
4.8 (Entrees:Corn, Blue) is ready for release!
2.4 (Salads:Cream cheese) failed final editing! Reworking...
2.4 (Salads:Cream cheese) is ready for release!
6.5 (Snacks:Roasted Turkey) failed final editing! Reworking...
4.9 (Entrees:Snake) is ready for release!
4.10 (Entrees:Prosciutto) failed the readthrough! Reworking...
6.5 (Snacks:Roasted Turkey) had incorrect measurements! Reworking...
2.5 (Salads:Artichokes, Domestic) tasted bad! Reworking...
4.10 (Entrees:Prosciutto) tasted bad! Reworking...
8.1 (Sandwiches:Rhubarb) tasted bad! Reworking...
4.10 (Entrees:Prosciutto) had incorrect measurements! Reworking...
4.10 (Entrees:Prosciutto) is ready for release!
Finished Evaluating Chapter 4 - Entrees

```
6.5 (Snacks:Roasted Turkey) is ready for release!
6.6 (Snacks:Lime) had incorrect measurements! Reworking...
2.5 (Salads:Artichokes, Domestic) failed final editing!  Reworking...
8.1 (Sandwiches:Rhubarb) is ready for release!
6.6 (Snacks:Lime) tasted bad!  Reworking...
6.6 (Snacks:Lime) is ready for release!
2.5 (Salads:Artichokes, Domestic) is ready for release!
6.7 (Snacks:Hazelnut) is ready for release!
8.2 (Sandwiches:Pickle, Brine) is ready for release!
2.6 (Salads:Grapefruit) is ready for release!
2.7 (Salads:Lettuce, Iceberg) failed final editing!  Reworking...
2.7 (Salads:Lettuce, Iceberg) is ready for release!
6.8 (Snacks:Radishes, Daikon) is ready for release!
8.3 (Sandwiches:Oranges) is ready for release!
6.9 (Snacks:Salami) tasted bad!  Reworking...
2.8 (Salads:Fenugreek) is ready for release!
8.4 (Sandwiches:Chayote, Pipinella, Vegetable Pear) tasted bad!  Reworking...
2.9 (Salads:Ostrich) failed the readthrough! Reworking...
6.9 (Snacks:Salami) is ready for release!
6.10 (Snacks:Mushroom, Oyster) is ready for release!
Finished Evaluating Chapter 6 - Snacks
2.9 (Salads:Ostrich) failed final editing!  Reworking...
2.9 (Salads:Ostrich) failed the readthrough! Reworking...
2.9 (Salads:Ostrich) failed the readthrough! Reworking...
8.4 (Sandwiches:Chayote, Pipinella, Vegetable Pear) is ready for release!
8.5 (Sandwiches:Bear) is ready for release!
2.9 (Salads:Ostrich) failed final editing!  Reworking...
8.6 (Sandwiches:Panela) tasted bad!  Reworking...
8.6 (Sandwiches:Panela) failed the readthrough! Reworking...
2.9 (Salads:Ostrich) is ready for release!
8.6 (Sandwiches:Panela) had incorrect measurements! Reworking...
8.6 (Sandwiches:Panela) is ready for release!
2.10 (Salads:Brazil Nuts) is ready for release!
Finished Evaluating Chapter 2 - Salads
8.7 (Sandwiches:Peppers, Red) tasted bad!  Reworking...
8.7 (Sandwiches:Peppers, Red) tasted bad!  Reworking...
8.7 (Sandwiches:Peppers, Red) is ready for release!
8.8 (Sandwiches:Oat Bread) is ready for release!
8.9 (Sandwiches:Peppers, Green) is ready for release!
8.10 (Sandwiches:Garlic) is ready for release!
Finished Evaluating Chapter 8 - Sandwiches
************************************************
Full Chapter Evaluation with PLINQ took: 00:00:25.1708103
************************************************
Cookbook Evaluation Complete
```

If you are running a PLINQ query and the operation invoked throws an exception, it will not stop the set evaluation at that point but will continue to the end, recording any exceptions into an `AggregateException`, which can be caught after the query is evaluated (not declared).

See Also

The "Parallel LINQ" topic in the MSDN documentation.

CHAPTER 5

Debugging and Exception Handling

5.0 Introduction

This chapter contains recipes covering the exception-handling mechanism, including the `try`, `catch`, and `finally` blocks. Along with these recipes are others covering the mechanisms used to throw exceptions manually from within your code. The final recipes deal with the `Exception` classes and their uses, as well as subclassing them to create new types of exceptions.

Often, the design and implementation of exception handling is performed later in the development cycle. But with the power and complexities of C# exception handling, you need to plan and even implement your exception-handling scheme much earlier. Doing so will increase the reliability and robustness of your code while minimizing the impact of adding exception handling after most or all of the application is coded.

Exception handling in C# is very flexible. It allows you to choose a fine- or coarse-grained approach to error handling, or any level between. This means that you can add exception handling around any individual line of code (the fine-grained approach) or around a method that calls many other methods (the coarse-grained approach), or you can use a mix of the two, with mainly a coarse-grained approach and a more fine-grained approach in specific critical areas of the code. When using a fine-grained approach, you can intercept specific exceptions that might be thrown from just a few lines of code. The following method sets an object's property to a numeric value using fine-grained exception handling:

```
protected void SetValue(object value)
{
    try
    {
        myObj.Property1 = value;
    }
```

```
catch (NullReferenceException)
        {
            // Handle potential exceptions arising from this call here.
        }
    }
```

Consequently, this approach can add a lot of extra baggage to your code if used throughout your application. This fine-grained approach to exception handling should be used when you have a single line or just a few lines of code, and you need to handle that exception in a specific manner. If you do not have specific handling for errors at that level, you should let the exception bubble up the stack. For example, using the previous SetValue method, you may have to inform the user that an exception occurred and provide a chance to try the action again. If a method exists on myObj that needs to be called whenever an exception is thrown by one of its methods, you should make sure that this method is called at the appropriate time.

Coarse-grained exception handling is quite the opposite; it uses fewer try-catch or try-catch-finally blocks. One example of a coarse-grained approach would be to place a try-catch block around all of the code in every public method in an application or component. Doing this allows exceptions to be handled at the highest level in your code. If an exception is thrown at any location in your code, it will be bubbled up the call stack until a catch block is found that can handle it. If try-catch blocks are placed on all public methods, then all exceptions will be bubbled up to these methods and handled. This allows you to write much less exception-handling code, but it diminishes your ability to handle specific exceptions that may occur in particular areas of your code. You must determine how best to add exception-handling code to your application. This means applying the right balance of fine- and coarse-grained exception handling in your application.

C# allows you to write catch blocks without any parameters. An example of this is shown here:

```
public void CallCOMMethod()
{
    try
    {
        // Call a method on a COM object.
        myCOMObj.Method1();
    }
    catch
    {
        //Handle potential exceptions arising from this call here.
    }
}
```

The catch with no parameters is a holdover from C++, where exception objects did not have to be derived from the Exception class. Writing a catch clause in this manner in C++ allows any type of object thrown as an exception to be caught. However,

---

in C#, only objects derived from the `Exception` base class may be thrown as an exception. Using the `catch` block with no parameters allows all exceptions to be caught, but you lose the ability to view the exception and its information. A `catch` block written in this manner:

```
catch
{
    // NOT able to write the following line of code
    //Console.WriteLine(e.ToString);
}
```

is equivalent to this:

```
catch (Exception e)
{
    // Able to write the following line of code
    Console.WriteLine(e.ToString);
}
```

except that in the second case, the `Exception` object can be accessed now that the exception parameter is provided.

Avoid writing a `catch` block without any parameters. Doing so will prevent you from accessing the actual `Exception` object that was thrown.

When catching exceptions in a `catch` block, you should determine up front when exceptions need to be rethrown, when exceptions need to be wrapped in an outer exception and thrown, and when exceptions should be handled immediately and not rethrown.

Wrapping an exception in an outer exception is a good practice when the original exception would not make sense to the caller. When wrapping an exception in an outer exception, you need to determine what exception is most appropriate to wrap the caught exception. As a rule of thumb, the wrapping exception should always aid in tracking down the original problem by not obscuring the original exception with an unrelated or vague wrapping exception. One of the rare cases that can justify obscuring exceptions is if the exception is going to cross a trust boundary, and you have to obscure it for security reasons.

Another useful practice when catching exceptions is to provide `catch` blocks to handle specific exceptions in your code. And remember that base class exceptions—when used in a `catch` block—catch not only that type, but also all of its subclasses.

The following code uses specific `catch` blocks to handle different exceptions in the appropriate manner:

```
public void CallCOMMethod()
{
    try
    {
```

```
        // Call a method on a COM object.
        myCOMObj.Method1();
    }
    catch (System.Runtime.InteropServices.ExternalException)
    {
        // Handle potential COM exceptions arising from this call here.
    }
    catch (InvalidOperationException)
    {
        // Handle any potential method calls to the COM object that are
        // not valid in its current state.
    }
}
```

In this code, ExternalException and its derivatives are handled differently than Inva
lidOperationException and its derivatives. If any other types of exceptions are
thrown from the myCOMObj.Method1, they are not handled here, but are bubbled up
until a valid catch block is found. If no valid catch block is found, the exception is
considered unhandled and the application terminates.

At times, cleanup code must be executed regardless of whether an exception is
thrown. Any object must be placed in a stable known state when an exception is
thrown. In these situations, when code must be executed, use a finally block. The
following code has been modified (see boldface lines) to use a finally block:

```
public void CallCOMMethod()
{
    try
    {
        // Call a method on a COM object.
        myCOMObj.Method1();
    }
    catch (System.Runtime.InteropServices.ExternalException)
    {
        // Handle potential COM exceptions arising from this call here.
    }
    finally
    {
        // Clean up and free any resources here.
        // For example, there could be a method on myCOMObj to allow us to clean
        // up after using the Method1 method.
    }
}
```

The finally block will always execute, no matter what happens in
the try and catch blocks. The finally block executes even if a
return, break, or continue statement is executed in the try or
catch blocks or if a goto is used to jump out of the exception handler. This allows for a reliable method of cleaning up after the try
(and possibly catch) block code executes.

The finally block is also very useful for final resource cleanup when no catch blocks are specified. This pattern would be used if the code being written can't handle exceptions from calls it is making but wants to make sure that resources it uses are cleaned up properly before moving up the stack. The following example makes sure that SqlConnection and SqlCommand are cleaned up properly in the finally block through the use of the using keyword, which wraps a try-finally block around the scope of the using statement:

```
public static int GetAuthorCount(string connectionString)
{
    SqlConnection sqlConn = null;
    SqlCommand sqlComm = null;

    using(sqlConn = new SqlConnection(connectionString))
    {
        using (sqlComm = new SqlCommand())
        {
            sqlComm.Connection = sqlConn;
            sqlComm.Parameters.Add("@pubName",
                SqlDbType.NChar).Value = "O''Reilly";
            sqlComm.CommandText = "SELECT COUNT(*) FROM Authors " +
                "WHERE Publisher=@pubName";

            sqlConn.Open();
            object authorCount = sqlComm.ExecuteScalar();
            return (int)authorCount;
        }
    }
}
```

When determining how to structure exception handling in your application or component, consider doing the following:

- Use a single try-catch or try-catch-finally exception handler at locations higher up in your code. These exception handlers can be considered coarse-grained.

- Code farther down the call stack should contain try-finally exception handlers. These exception handlers can be considered fine-grained.

The fine-grained try-finally exception handlers allow for better control over cleanup after an exception occurs. The exception is then bubbled up to the coarser-grained try-catch or try-catch-finally exception handler. This technique allows for a more centralized scheme of exception handling and minimizes the code that you have to write to handle exceptions.

To improve performance, you should handle the case when an exception could be thrown (rather than catch the exception after it is thrown) if you know the code will be run in a single-threaded environment. If the code will run on multiple threads, there is still the potential that the initial check could succeed, but the object value could change (perhaps to `null`) in another thread before the actions following the check can be taken.

For example, in a single-threaded environment, if a method has a good chance of returning a `null` value, you should test the returned value for `null` before that value is used, as opposed to using a `try-catch` block and allowing the `NullReferenceException` to be thrown. If you think a `null` value is possible, check for it. If it shouldn't happen, then it is an exceptional condition when it does, and exception handling should be used. To illustrate this, the following method uses exception-handling code to process the `NullReferenceException`:

```
public void SomeMethod()
{
    try
    {
        Stream s = GetAnyAvailableStream();
        Console.WriteLine("This stream has a length of " + s.Length);
    }
    catch (NullReferenceException)
    {
        // Handle a null stream here.
    }
}
```

Here is the method implemented to use an `if-else` conditional instead:

```
public void SomeMethod()
{
    Stream s = GetAnyAvailableStream();
    if (s != null)
    {
        Console.WriteLine("This stream has a length of " + s.Length);
    }
    else
    {
        // Handle a null stream here.
    }
}
```

Additionally, you should make sure that this stream is closed by using the `finally` block as follows:

```
public void SomeMethod()
{
    Stream s = null;
    using(s = GetAnyAvailableStream())
    {
        if (s != null)
        {
            Console.WriteLine("This stream has a length of " + s.Length);
```

```
        }
        else
        {
            // Handle a null stream here.
        }
    }
}
```

The `finally` block contains the method call that will close the stream, ensuring that there is no data loss.

Consider throwing exceptions instead of returning error codes. With well-placed exception-handling code, you should not have to rely on methods that return error codes, such as a Boolean `true-false`, to correctly handle errors, making for much cleaner code. Another benefit is that you do not have to look up any values for the error codes to understand the code.

 The biggest advantage to exceptions is that when an exceptional situation arises, you cannot just ignore it as you can with error codes. This helps you find and fix bugs.

Throw the most specific possible exception, not general ones. For example, throw an `ArgumentNullException` instead of an `ArgumentException`, which is the base class of `ArgumentNullException`. Throwing an `ArgumentException` just tells you that there was a problem with a parameter value to a method. Throwing an `ArgumentNullExcep tion` tells you more specifically what the problem with the parameter really is. Another potential problem is that a more general exception may not be caught if the catcher of the exception is looking for a more specific type derived from the thrown exception.

The FCL provides several exception types that you will find very useful to throw in your own code. Many of these exceptions are listed here with a definition of where and when they should be thrown:

- Throw an `InvalidOperationException` in a property, indexer, or method when it is called with the object in an inappropriate state (e.g., when an indexer is called on an object that has not yet been initialized or methods are called out of sequence).

- Throw `ArgumentException` if invalid parameters are passed into a method, property, or indexer. The `ArgumentNullException`, `ArgumentOutOfRangeException`, and `InvalidEnumArgumentException` are three subclasses of the `ArgumentExcep tion` class. It is more appropriate to throw one of these subclassed exceptions because they are more indicative of the root cause of the problem. The `Argument`

`NullException` indicates that a parameter was passed in as `null` and that this parameter cannot be `null` under any circumstance. The `ArgumentOutOfRangeEx ception` indicates that an argument was passed in that was outside of a valid acceptable range. This exception is used mainly with numeric values. The `Inva lidEnumArgumentException` indicates that an enumeration value was passed in that does not exist in that enumeration type.

- Throw a `FormatException` when an invalid formatting parameter is passed in to a method. You'd use this technique mainly when overriding/overloading methods such as `ToString` that can accept formatting strings, as well as in the parse methods on the various numeric types.

- Throw `ObjectDisposedException` when a property, indexer, or method is called on an object that has already been disposed.

- Many exceptions that derive from the `SystemException` class, such as `NullRefer enceException`, `ExecutionEngineException`, `StackOverflowException`, `OutOf MemoryException`, and `IndexOutOfRangeException`, are thrown only by the CLR and should not be explicitly thrown with the `throw` keyword in your code.

The .NET Framework Class Library (FCL) also contains many classes to obtain diagnostic information about your application, as well as the environment in which it is running. In fact, there are so many classes that a namespace, `System.Diagnostics`, was created to contain all of them. This chapter includes recipes for instrumenting your application with debug/trace information, obtaining process information, using the built-in event log, and taking advantage of mechanisms like performance counters or Event Tracing for Windows (ETW) and `EventSource`. It should be noted that ETW and `EventSource` are becoming the preferred performance telemetry mechanism for the .NET Framework.

Debugging (via the `Debug` class) is turned on by default in debug builds only, and tracing (via the `Trace` class) is turned on by default in both debug and release builds. These defaults allow you to ship your application instrumented with tracing code using the `Trace` class. You ship your code with tracing compiled in but turned off in the configuration so that the tracing code is not called (for performance reasons) unless it is a server-side application (where the value of the instrumentation may outweigh the performance hit, and in the cloud, nobody can hear you scream without logs!). If a problem occurs on a production machine and you cannot re-create it on your development computer, you can enable tracing and allow the tracing information to be dumped to a file. You can then inspect this file to help you pinpoint the real problem.

Since both the `Debug` and `Trace` classes contain the same members with the same names, you can interchange them in your code by renaming `Debug` to `Trace` and vice versa. Most of the recipes in this chapter use the `Trace` class; to modify them so that they use the `Debug` class instead, simply replace each instance of `Trace` with `Debug` in the code.

5.1 Knowing When to Catch and Rethrow Exceptions

Problem

You want to establish when it is appropriate to catch and rethrow an exception.

Solution

Catching and rethrowing exceptions is appropriate if you have a section of code where you want to perform some action if an exception occurs, but not perform any actions to actually handle the exception. To get the exception so that you can perform the initial action on it, establish a `catch` block to catch the exception. Then, once the action has been performed, rethrow the exception from the `catch` block in which the original exception was handled. Use the `throw` keyword, followed by a semicolon, to rethrow an exception:

```
try
{
    Console.WriteLine("In try");
    int z2 = 9999999;
    checked { z2 *= 999999999; }
}
catch (OverflowException oe)
{
    // Record the fact that the overflow exception occurred.
    EventLog.WriteEntry("MyApplication", oe.Message, EventLogEntryType.Error);
    throw;
}
```

Here, you create an `EventLog` entry that records the occurrence of an overflow exception. Then the exception is propagated up the call stack by the `throw` statement.

Discussion

Establishing a `catch` block for an exception is essentially saying that you want to do something about that exceptional case.

 If you do not rethrow the exception, or create a new exception to wrap the original exception and throw it, the assumption is that you have handled the condition that caused the exception and that the program can continue normal operation.

By choosing to rethrow the exception, you are indicating that there is still an issue to be dealt with and that you are counting on code farther up the stack to handle the condition. If you need to perform an action based on a thrown exception *and* need to allow the exception to continue after your code executes, then rethrowing is the mechanism to handle this. If both of those conditions are not met, don't rethrow the exception; just handle it or remove the catch block.

 Remember that throwing exceptions is expensive. Try not to needlessly throw and rethrow exceptions, because this might bog down your application.

When rethrowing an exception, use throw; instead of throw ex; as the former will preserve the original call stack of the exception. Using throw with the catch parameter will reset the call stack to that location, and information about the error will be lost. There might be some scenarios where you want the call stack changed (to hide details of the internals of a portion of your application that performs sensitive operations, for example) but on the whole, give yourself the best chance to debug things and don't truncate the call stack.

5.2 Handling Exceptions Thrown from Methods Invoked via Reflection

Problem

Using reflection, you invoke a method that generates an exception. You want to obtain the real exception object and its information in order to diagnose and fix the problem.

Solution

The real exception and its information can be obtained through the InnerException property of the TargetInvocationException that is thrown by MethodInfo.Invoke.

Discussion

Example 5-1 handles an exception that occurs within a method invoked via reflection. The Reflect class contains a ReflectionException method that invokes the static TestInvoke method using the reflection classes.

Example 5-1. Obtaining information on an exception invoked by a method accessed through reflection

```
using System;
using System.Reflection;

public static class Reflect
{
    public static void ReflectionException()
    {
        Type reflectedClass = typeof(DebuggingAndExceptionHandling);

        try
        {
            MethodInfo methodToInvoke = reflectedClass.GetMethod("TestInvoke");
            methodToInvoke?.Invoke(null, null);
        }
        catch(Exception e)
        {
            Console.WriteLine(e.ToShortDisplayString());
        }
    }

    public static void TestInvoke()
    {
        throw (new Exception("Thrown from invoked method."));
    }
}
```

This code displays the following text:

```
Message: Exception has been thrown by the target of an invocation.
Type: System.Reflection.TargetInvocationException
Source: mscorlib
TargetSite: System.Object InvokeMethod(System.Object, System.Object[], System.Si
gnature, Boolean)
**** INNEREXCEPTION START ****
Message: Thrown from invoked method.
Type: System.Exception
Source: CSharpRecipes
TargetSite: Void TestInvoke()
**** INNEREXCEPTION END ****
```

When the methodToInvoke?.Invoke method is called, the TestInvoke method is called and throws an exception. The question mark next to methodToInvoke is a null-conditional operator to handle the case where the MethodInfo could not be retrieved and is null. This way, we didn't have to write the check for null around the invocation. The outer exception is the TargetInvocationException; this is the generic exception thrown when a method invoked through reflection throws an exception. The CLR automatically wraps the original exception thrown by the invoked method inside of the TargetInvocationException object's InnerException

property. In this case, the exception thrown by the invoked method is of type Sys
tem.Exception. This exception is shown after the section that begins with the text
**** INNEREXCEPTION START ****.

To display the exception information, we call the ToShortDisplayString method:

```
Console.WriteLine(e.ToShortDisplayString());
```

The ToShortDisplayString extension method for Exception uses a StringBuilder
to create the string of information about the exception and all inner exceptions. The
WriteExceptionShortDetail method populates the StringBuilder with specific
parts of the exception data. To get the inner exceptions, we use the GetNestedExcep
tionList extension method:

```
public static string ToShortDisplayString(this Exception ex)
{
    StringBuilder displayText = new StringBuilder();
    WriteExceptionShortDetail(displayText, ex);
    foreach(Exception inner in ex.GetNestedExceptionList())
    {
        displayText.AppendFormat("**** INNEREXCEPTION START ****{0}",
            Environment.NewLine);
        WriteExceptionShortDetail(displayText, inner);
        displayText.AppendFormat("**** INNEREXCEPTION END ****{0}{0}",
            Environment.NewLine);
    }
    return displayText.ToString();
}

public static IEnumerable<Exception> GetNestedExceptionList(
        this Exception exception)
{
    Exception current = exception;
    do
    {
        current = current.InnerException;
        if (current != null)
            yield return current;
    }
    while (current != null);
}

public static void WriteExceptionShortDetail(StringBuilder builder, Exception ex)
{
    builder.AppendFormat("Message: {0}{1}", ex.Message, Environment.NewLine);
    builder.AppendFormat("Type: {0}{1}";, ex.GetType(), Environment.NewLine);
    builder.AppendFormat("Source: {0}{1}", ex.Source, Environment.NewLine);
    builder.AppendFormat("TargetSite: {0}{1}", ex.TargetSite,
        Environment.NewLine);
}
```

See Also

The "Type Class," "Null-Conditional Operator," and "MethodInfo Class" topics in the MSDN documentation.

5.3 Creating a New Exception Type

Problem

None of the built-in exceptions in the .NET Framework provide the implementation details that you require for an exception that you need to throw. You need to create your own exception class that operates seamlessly with your application, as well as other applications. Whenever an application receives this new exception, it can inform the user that a specific error occurred in a specific component. This report will greatly reduce the time required to debug the problem.

Solution

Create your own exception class. To illustrate, let's create a custom exception class, `RemoteComponentException`, that will inform a client application that an error has occurred in a remote server assembly.

Discussion

The exception hierarchy starts with the `Exception` class; from this are derived two classes: `ApplicationException` and `SystemException`. The `SystemException` class and any classes derived from it are reserved for the developers of the FCL. Most of the common exceptions, such as the `NullReferenceException` or the `OverflowExcep` `tion`, are derived from `SystemException`. The FCL developers created the `Applica` `tionException` class for other developers using the .NET languages to derive their own exceptions from. This partitioning allows for a clear distinction between user-defined exceptions and the built-in system exceptions. However, Microsoft now recommends deriving directly from `Exception`, rather than `ApplicationException`. Nothing actively prevents you from deriving a class from either `SystemException` or `ApplicationException`. But it is better to be consistent and use the convention of always deriving from the `Exception` class for user-defined exceptions.

You should follow the naming convention for exceptions when determining the name of your exception. The convention is very simple: decide on the exception's name, and add the word `Exception` to the end of it (e.g., use `UnknownException` as the exception name instead of just `Unknown`).

Every user-defined exception should include *at least* three constructors, which are described next. This is not a requirement, but it makes your exception classes operate similarly to every other exception class in the FCL and minimizes the learning curve for other developers using your new exception. These three constructors are:

The default constructor
> This constructor takes no arguments and simply calls the base class's default constructor.

A constructor with a parameter that accepts a message string
> This message string overwrites the default contents of the Message field of this exception. Like the default constructor, this constructor also calls the base class's constructor, which also accepts a message string as its only parameter.

A constructor that accepts a message string and an inner exception as parameters
> The object contained in the innerException parameter is added to the InnerException property of this exception object. Like the other two constructors, this constructor calls the base class's constructor of the same signature.

Fields and their accessors should be created to hold data specific to the exception. Since this exception will be thrown as a result of an error that occurs in a remote server assembly, you will add a private field to contain the name of the server or service. In addition, you will add a public read-only property to access this field. Since you're adding this new field, you should add two constructors that accept an extra parameter used to set the value of the serverName field.

If necessary, override any base class members whose behavior is inherited by the custom exception class. For example, since you have added a new field, you need to determine whether it will need to be added to the default contents of the Message field for this exception. If it does, you must override the Message property:

```
public override string Message => $"{base.Message}{Environment.NewLine}" +
        $"The server ({this.ServerName ?? "Unknown"})" +
        "has encountered an error.";
```

Notice that the Message property in the base class is displayed on the first line, and your additional text is displayed on the next line. This organization takes into account that a user might modify the message that will appear in the Message property by using one of the overloaded constructors that takes a message string as a parameter.

Your exception object should be serializable and deserializable. This involves performing the following two additional steps:

1. Add the Serializable attribute to the class definition. This attribute specifies that this class can be serialized and deserialized. A SerializationException is thrown if this attribute does not exist on this class, and an attempt is made to serialize this class.

2. The class should implement the ISerializable interface if you want control over how serialization and deserialization are performed, and it should provide

an implementation for its single member, `GetObjectData`. Here you implement it because the base class implements it, which means that you have no choice but to reimplement it if you want the fields you added (e.g., `serverName`) to get serialized:

```
// Used during serialization to capture information about extra fields
public override void GetObjectData(SerializationInfo exceptionInfo,
                                   StreamingContext exceptionContext)
{
    base.GetObjectData(exceptionInfo, exceptionContext);
    exceptionInfo.AddValue("ServerName", this.ServerName);
}
```

In addition, we need a new overridden constructor that accepts information to deserialize this object:

```
// Serialization ctor
protected RemoteComponentException(SerializationInfo exceptionInfo,
        StreamingContext exceptionContext)
        : base(exceptionInfo, exceptionContext)
{
    this.serverName = exceptionInfo.GetString("ServerName");
}
```

 Even though it is not required, you should make all user-defined exception classes serializable and deserializable. That way, the exceptions can be propagated properly over remoting and application domain boundaries.

For the case where this exception will be caught in unmanaged code, such as a COM object, you can also set the HRESULT value for this exception. An exception caught in unmanaged code becomes an HRESULT value. If the exception does not alter the HRESULT value, it defaults to the HRESULT of the base class exception, which, in the case of a user-defined exception object that inherits from `ApplicationException`, is COR_E_APPLICATION (0x80131600). To change the default HRESULT value, simply set the value of this field in the constructor. The following code demonstrates this technique:

```
public class RemoteComponentException : Exception
{
    public RemoteComponentException() : base()
    {
        HResult = 0x80040321;
    }

    public RemoteComponentException(string message) :
        base(message)
    {
```

```
        HResult = 0x80040321;
    }

    public RemoteComponentException(string message, Exception innerException)
        : base(message, innerException)
    {
        HResult = 0x80040321;
    }
}
```

Now the HResult that the COM object will see is the value 0x80040321.

It is usually a good idea to override the Message property in order to incorporate any new fields into the exception's message text. Always remember to include the base class's message text along with any additional text you add to this property.

At this point, the RemoteComponentException class contains everything you need for a complete user-defined exception class.

As a final note, it is generally a good idea to place all user-defined exceptions in a separate assembly, which allows for easier reuse of these exceptions in other applications and, more importantly, allows other application domains and remotely executing code to both throw and handle these exceptions correctly no matter where they are thrown. The assembly that holds these exceptions should be signed with a strong name and added to the Global Assembly Cache (GAC), so that any code that uses or handles these exceptions can find the assembly that defines them. See Recipe 11.7 for more information on how to do this.

If you are sure that the exceptions being defined won't ever be thrown or handled outside of your assembly, then you can leave the exception definitions there. But if for some reason an exception that you throw finds its way out of your assembly, the code that ultimately catches it will not be able to resolve it.

The complete source code for the RemoteComponentException class is shown in Example 5-2.

Example 5-2. RemoteComponentException class

```
using System;
using System.IO;
using System.Runtime.Serialization;
using System.Runtime.Serialization.Formatters.Binary;
using System.Security.Permissions;

[Serializable]
public class RemoteComponentException : Exception, ISerializable
```

```csharp
{
    #region Constructors
    // Normal exception ctor's
    public RemoteComponentException() : base()
    {
    }

    public RemoteComponentException(string message) : base(message)
    {
    }

    public RemoteComponentException(string message, Exception innerException)
        : base(message, innerException)
    {
    }

    // Exception ctor's that accept the new ServerName parameter
    public RemoteComponentException(string message, string serverName) :
        base(message)
    {
        this.ServerName = serverName;
    }

    public RemoteComponentException(string message,
                Exception innerException, string serverName)
        : base(message, innerException)
    {
        this.ServerName = serverName;
    }

    // Serialization ctor
    protected RemoteComponentException(SerializationInfo exceptionInfo,
        StreamingContext exceptionContext)
        : base(exceptionInfo, exceptionContext)
    {
        this.ServerName = exceptionInfo.GetString("ServerName");
    }
    #endregion // Constructors

    #region Properties
    // Read-only property for server name
    public string ServerName { get; }

    public override string Message => $"{base.Message}{Environment.NewLine}" +
            $"The server ({this.ServerName ?? "Unknown"})" +
            "has encountered an error.";
    #endregion // Properties

    #region Overridden methods
    // ToString method
    public override string ToString() =>
```

```
        "An error has occurred in a server component of this client." +
          $"{Environment.NewLine}Server Name: " +
          $"{this.ServerName}{Environment.NewLine}" +
          $"{this.ToFullDisplayString()}";


    // Used during serialization to capture information about extra fields
    [SecurityPermission(SecurityAction.LinkDemand, Flags =
        SecurityPermissionFlag.SerializationFormatter)]
    public override void GetObjectData(SerializationInfo info,
        StreamingContext context)
    {
        base.GetObjectData(info, context);
        info.AddValue("ServerName", this.ServerName);
    }
    #endregion // Overridden methods

    public string ToBaseString() => (base.ToString());
}
```

The `ToFullDisplayString` call made in the `ToString` override is an extension
method for `Exception`, with the `GetNestedExceptionList` extension method used to
get the list of exceptions and the `WriteExceptionDetail` method to handle each
`Exception`'s details:

```
    public static string ToFullDisplayString(this Exception ex)
    {
        StringBuilder displayText = new StringBuilder();
        WriteExceptionDetail(displayText, ex);
        foreach (Exception inner in ex.GetNestedExceptionList())
        {
            displayText.AppendFormat("**** INNEREXCEPTION START ****{0}",
                Environment.NewLine);
            WriteExceptionDetail(displayText, inner);
            displayText.AppendFormat("**** INNEREXCEPTION END ****{0}{0}",
                Environment.NewLine);
        }
        return displayText.ToString();
    }

    public static IEnumerable<Exception> GetNestedExceptionList(
        this Exception exception)
    {
        Exception current = exception;
        do
        {
            current = current.InnerException;
            if (current != null)
                yield return current;
        }
        while (current != null);
    }
```

```
public static void WriteExceptionDetail(StringBuilder builder, Exception ex)
{
    builder.AppendFormat("Message: {0}{1}", ex.Message, Environment.NewLine);
    builder.AppendFormat("Type: {0}{1}", ex.GetType(), Environment.NewLine);
    builder.AppendFormat("HelpLink: {0}{1}", ex.HelpLink, Environment.NewLine);
    builder.AppendFormat("Source: {0}{1}", ex.Source, Environment.NewLine);
    builder.AppendFormat("TargetSite: {0}{1}", ex.TargetSite,
        Environment.NewLine);
    builder.AppendFormat("Data:{0}", Environment.NewLine);
    foreach (DictionaryEntry de in ex.Data)
    {
        builder.AppendFormat("\t{0} : {1}{2}",
            de.Key, de.Value, Environment.NewLine);
    }
    builder.AppendFormat("StackTrace: {0}{1}", ex.StackTrace,
        Environment.NewLine);
}
```

A partial listing of the code to test the `RemoteComponentException` class is shown in Example 5-3.

Example 5-3. Testing the RemoteComponentException class

```
public void TestSpecializedException()
{
    // Generic inner exception used to test the
    // RemoteComponentException's inner exception.
    Exception inner = new Exception("The inner Exception");

    RemoteComponentException se1 = new RemoteComponentException ();
    RemoteComponentException se2 =
      new RemoteComponentException ("A Test Message for se2");
    RemoteComponentException se3 =
      new RemoteComponentException ("A Test Message for se3", inner);
    RemoteComponentException se4 =
      new RemoteComponentException ("A Test Message for se4",
                                    "MyServer");
    RemoteComponentException se5 =
      new RemoteComponentException ("A Test Message for se5", inner,
                                    "MyServer");

    // Test overridden Message property.
    Console.WriteLine(Environment.NewLine +
      "TEST -OVERRIDDEN- MESSAGE PROPERTY");
    Console.WriteLine("se1.Message == " + se1.Message);
    Console.WriteLine("se2.Message == " + se2.Message);
    Console.WriteLine("se3.Message == " + se3.Message);
    Console.WriteLine("se4.Message == " + se4.Message);
    Console.WriteLine("se5.Message == " + se5.Message);

    // Test -overridden- ToString method.
```

```
    Console.WriteLine(Environment.NewLine +
      "TEST -OVERRIDDEN- TOSTRING METHOD");
    Console.WriteLine("se1.ToString() == " + se1.ToString());
    Console.WriteLine("se2.ToString() == " + se2.ToString());
    Console.WriteLine("se3.ToString() == " + se3.ToString());
    Console.WriteLine("se4.ToString() == " + se4.ToString());
    Console.WriteLine("se5.ToString() == " + se5.ToString());
    Console.WriteLine(Environment.NewLine + "END TEST" + Environment.NewLine);
}
```

The output from Example 5-3 is presented in Example 5-4.

Example 5-4. Output displayed by the RemoteComponentException class

```
TEST -OVERRIDDEN- MESSAGE PROPERTY
se1.Message == Exception of type 'CSharpRecipes.ExceptionHandling+RemoteComponen
tException' was thrown.
A server with an unknown name has encountered an error.
se2.Message == A Test Message for se2
A server with an unknown name has encountered an error.
se3.Message == A Test Message for se3
A server with an unknown name has encountered an error.
se4.Message == A Test Message for se4
The server (MyServer) has encountered an error.
se5.Message == A Test Message for se5
The server (MyServer) has encountered an error.


TEST -OVERRIDDEN- TOSTRING METHOD
se1.ToString() == An error has occurred in a server component of this client.
Server Name:
Message: Exception of type 'CSharpRecipes.ExceptionHandling+RemoteComponentExcep
tion' was thrown.
A server with an unknown name has encountered an error.

Type: CSharpRecipes.ExceptionHandling+RemoteComponentException
HelpLink:
Source:
TargetSite:
Data:
StackTrace:

se2.ToString() == An error has occurred in a server component of this client.
Server Name:
Message: A Test Message for se2
A server with an unknown name has encountered an error.
Type: CSharpRecipes.ExceptionHandling+RemoteComponentException
HelpLink:
Source:
TargetSite:
Data:
StackTrace:
```

```
se3.ToString() == An error has occurred in a server component of this client.
Server Name:
Message: A Test Message for se3
A server with an unknown name has encountered an error.
Type: CSharpRecipes.ExceptionHandling+RemoteComponentException
HelpLink:
Source:
TargetSite:
Data:
StackTrace:
**** INNEREXCEPTION START ****
Message: The Inner Exception
Type: System.Exception
HelpLink:
Source:
TargetSite:
Data:
StackTrace:
**** INNEREXCEPTION END ****

se4.ToString() == An error has occurred in a server component of this client.
Server Name: MyServer
Message: A Test Message for se4
The server (MyServer) has encountered an error.
Type: CSharpRecipes.ExceptionHandling+RemoteComponentException
HelpLink:
Source:
TargetSite:
Data:
StackTrace:

se5.ToString() == An error has occurred in a server component of this client.
Server Name: MyServer

Message: A Test Message for se5
The server (MyServer) has encountered an error.
Type: CSharpRecipes.ExceptionHandling+RemoteComponentException
HelpLink:
Source:
TargetSite:
Data:
StackTrace:
**** INNEREXCEPTION START ****
Message: The Inner Exception
Type: System.Exception
HelpLink:
Source:
TargetSite:
Data:
StackTrace:
**** INNEREXCEPTION END ****
```

See Also

Recipe 11.7, and the "Using User-Defined Exceptions" and "Exception Class" topics in the MSDN documentation.

5.4 Breaking on a First-Chance Exception

Problem

You need to fix a problem with your code that is throwing an exception. Unfortunately, an exception handler is trapping the exception, and you are having a tough time pinpointing where and when the exception is being thrown.

Forcing the application to break on an exception before the application has a chance to handle it is very useful in situations in which you need to step through the code at the point where the exception is first being thrown. If this exception were thrown and not handled by your application, the debugger would intervene and break on the line of code that caused the unhandled exception. In this case, you can see the context in which the exception was thrown. However, if an exception handler is active when the exception is thrown, the exception handler will handle it and continue on, preventing you from being able to see the context at the point where the exception was thrown. This is the default behavior for all exceptions.

Solution

Select Debug→Exceptions or press Ctrl-Alt-E within Visual Studio 2015 to display the Exception Settings tool window (see Figure 5-1). Select the exception from the tree that you want to modify and then click on the checkbox in the tree view. Click OK and then run your application. Any time the application throws a `System.Argu mentOutOfRangeException`, the debugger will break on that line of code before your application has a chance to handle it.

Using the Exception Settings tool window, you can target specific exceptions or sets of exceptions for which you wish to alter the default behavior. This dialog has three main sections. The first is the TreeView control, which contains the list of categorized exceptions. Using this TreeView, you can choose one or more exceptions or groups of exceptions whose behavior you wish to modify.

The next section on this dialog is the column Thrown in the list next to the TreeView. This column contains a checkbox for each exception that will enable the debugger to break when that type of exception is first thrown. At this stage, the exception is considered a *first-chance exception*. Checking the checkbox in the Thrown column forces the debugger to intervene when a first-chance exception of the type chosen in the TreeView control is thrown. Unchecking the checkbox allows the application to attempt to handle the first-chance exception.

Figure 5-1. The Exceptions Settings tool window

You can also click on the Filter icon in the top left of the window in order to narrow down the view of the exceptions to just the ones you have selected to break on a first-chance exception, as shown in Figure 5-2.

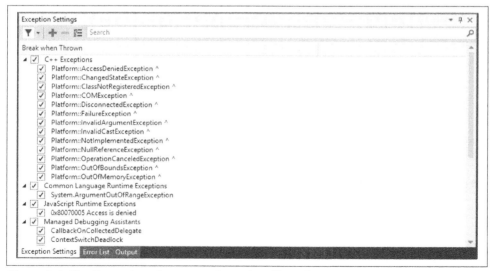

Figure 5-2. The Exceptions Settings tool window filtered

The Exception Settings tool window also provides a Search bar at the top to allow you to search for exceptions in the window. If you type **argumentnullexception** in the window, you will see the selection narrow to just items that match that text, as shown in Figure 5-3.

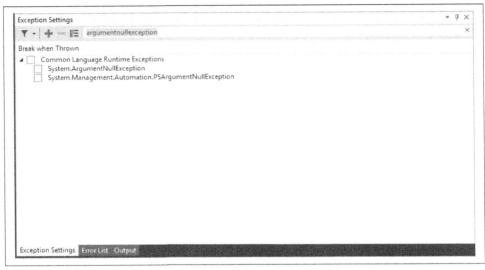

Figure 5-3. The Exceptions Settings tool window search

To add a user-defined exception to the Exception Settings, click the Add button. You'll see the dialog box shown in Figure 5-4.

Figure 5-4. Adding a user-defined exception to the Exception Settings

Press Yes to use the original Exceptions dialog, which is shown in Figure 5-5.

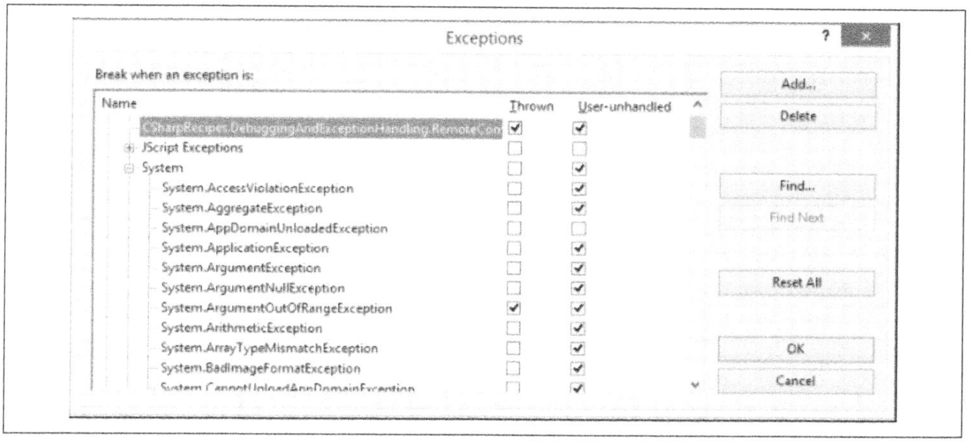

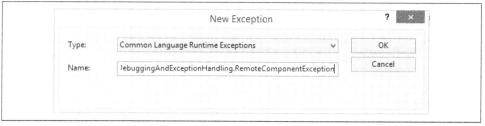

Figure 5-5. *The Exceptions dialog*

This dialog contains two helpful buttons, Find and Find Next, to allow you to search for an exception rather than dig into the TreeView control and search for it on your own. In addition, three other buttons—Reset All, Add, and Delete—allow you to reset to the original state and to add and remove user-defined exceptions, respectively.

For example, you can create your own exception, as you did in Recipe 5.3, and add this exception to the TreeView list. You must add any managed exception such as this to the TreeView node entitled Common Language Runtime Exceptions. This setting tells the debugger that this is a managed exception and should be handled as such. Figure 5-6 shows the addition of the custom exception.

Figure 5-6. *Adding a user-defined exception to the Exceptions dialog*

Type the name of the exception—exactly as its class name is spelled with the full namespace scoping into the `Name` field of this dialog box. Do not append any other information to this name, such as the namespace it resides in or a class name that it is nested within. Doing so will prevent the debugger from seeing this exception when it is thrown. Clicking the OK button places this exception into the TreeView under the Common Language Runtime Exceptions node. The Exceptions dialog box will look something like the one in Figure 5-7 after you add this user-defined exception.

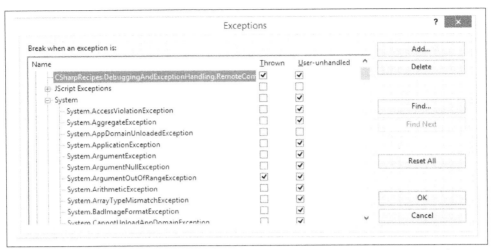

Figure 5-7. The Exceptions dialog box after you add a user-defined exception to the TreeView

The Delete button deletes any selected user-defined exception that you added to the TreeView. The Reset All button deletes any and all user-defined exceptions that have been added to the TreeView. Check the Thrown column to have the debugger stop when that exception type is thrown.

There is one other setting that can affect your exception debugging: Just My Code (Figure 5-8). You should turn this off to get the best picture of what is really happening in your application when debugging; when it is enabled, you cannot see the related actions of the framework code that your code calls. Being able to see where your code calls into the framework and where it goes from there is very educational and can help you understand the issue you are debugging better. The setting is under *Tools\Options\Debugging\General* in Visual Studio 2015.

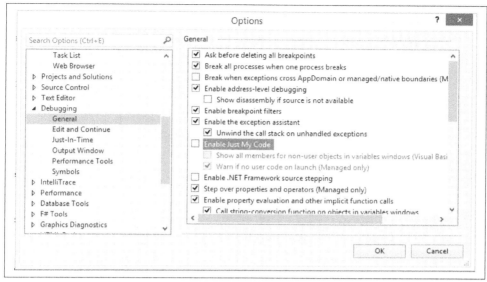

Figure 5-8. The Just My Code setting disabled

See Also

The "Exception Handling (Debugging)" topic in the MSDN documentation.

5.5 Handling Exceptions Thrown from an Asynchronous Delegate

Problem

When using a delegate asynchronously, you want to be notified if the delegate has thrown any exceptions.

Solution

Wrap the EndInvoke method of the delegate in a try-catch block:

```
using System;
using System.Threading;

public class AsyncAction
{
    public void PollAsyncDelegate()
    {
        // Create the async delegate to call Method1 and call its
        // BeginInvokemethod.
        AsyncInvoke MI = new AsyncInvoke(TestAsyncInvoke.Method1);
```

```
        IAsyncResult AR = MI.BeginInvoke(null, null);

        // Poll until the async delegate is finished.
        while (!AR.IsCompleted)
        {
            System.Threading.Thread.Sleep(100);
            Console.Write('.');
        }
        Console.WriteLine("Finished Polling");
        // Call the EndInvoke method of the async delegate.
        try
        {
            int RetVal = MI.EndInvoke(AR);
            Console.WriteLine("RetVal (Polling): " + RetVal);
        }
        catch (Exception e)
        {
            Console.WriteLine(e.ToString());
        }
    }
}
```

The following code defines the `AsyncInvoke` delegate and the asynchronously invoked static method `TestAsyncInvoke.Method1`:

```
public delegate int AsyncInvoke();

public class TestAsyncInvoke
{
    public static int Method1()
    {
        throw (new Exception("Method1")); // Simulate an exception being thrown.
    }
}
```

Discussion

If the code in the `PollAsyncDelegate` method did not contain a call to the delegate's `EndInvoke` method, the exception thrown in `Method1` either would simply be discarded and never caught or, if the application had the top-level exception handlers wired up (Recipes 5.2, 5.7, and 5.8), it would be caught. If `EndInvoke` is called, then this exception would occur when `EndInvoke` is called and could be caught there. This behavior is by design; for all unhandled exceptions that occur within the thread, the thread immediately returns to the thread pool, and the exception is lost.

If a method that was called asynchronously through a delegate throws an exception, the only way to trap that exception is to include a call to the delegate's `EndInvoke` method and wrap this call in an exception handler. You must call the `EndInvoke` method to retrieve the results of the asynchronous delegate; in fact, you must call it

---

even if there are no results. You can obtain these results through a return value or any `ref` or out parameters of the delegate.

See Also

For information about wiring up top-level exception handlers in your application, see Recipes 5.2, 5.7, and 5.8.

5.6 Giving Exceptions the Extra Info They Need with Exception.Data

Problem

You want to send some additional information along with an exception.

Solution

Use the `Data` property on the `System.Exception` object to store key/value pairs of information relevant to the exception.

For example, say there is a `System.ArgumentException` being thrown from a section of code, and you want to include the underlying cause and the length of time it took. You would add two key/value pairs to the `Exception.Data` property by specifying the key in the indexer and then assigning the value.

In the example that follows, the `Data` for the `irritable` exception uses `"Cause"` and `"Length"` for its keys. Once the items have been set in the `Data` collection, the exception can be thrown and caught, and more data can be added in subsequent `catch` blocks for as many levels of exception handling as the exception is allowed to traverse:

```
try
{
    try
    {
        try
        {
            try
            {
                ArgumentException irritable =
                    new ArgumentException("I'm irritable!");
                irritable.Data["Cause"]="Computer crashed";
                irritable.Data["Length"]=10;
                throw irritable;
            }
            catch (Exception e)
            {
```

```
                    // See if I can help...
                    if(e.Data.Contains("Cause"))
                        e.Data["Cause"]="Fixed computer"
                    throw;
                }
            }
            catch (Exception e)
            {
                e.Data["Comment"]="Always grumpy you are";
                throw;
            }
        }
        catch (Exception e)
        {
            e.Data["Reassurance"]="Error Handled";
            throw;
        }
    }
```

The final `catch` block can then iterate over the `Exception.Data` collection and display all of the supporting data that has been gathered in the `Data` collection since the initial exception was thrown:

```
catch (Exception e)
{
    Console.WriteLine("Exception supporting data:");
    foreach(DictionaryEntry de in e.Data)
    {
        Console.WriteLine("\t{0} : {1}",de.Key,de.Value);
    }
}
```

Discussion

`Exception.Data` is an object that supports the `IDictionary` interface. This allows you to:

- Add and remove name/value pairs.
- Clear the contents.
- Search the collection to see if it contains a certain key.
- Get an `IDictionaryEnumerator` for rolling over the collection items.
- Index into the collection using the key.
- Access an `ICollection` of all of the keys and all of the values separately.

Items placed into Exception.Data need to be Serializable or they will throw an ArgumentException on the addition to the collection. If you are adding a class to Exception.Data, mark it as Serializable and make sure it can be serialized.

```
public void TestExceptionDataSerializable()
{
    Exception badMonkey =
        new Exception("You are a bad monkey!");
    try
    {
        badMonkey.Data["Details"] = new Monkey();
    }
    catch (ArgumentException aex)
    {
        Console.WriteLine(aex.Message);
    }
}

//[Serializable]  // Uncomment to make serializable and work
public class Monkey
{
    public string Name { get; } = "George";
}
```

It is very handy to be able to tack on code-specific data to the system exceptions, as it allows you to give a more complete picture of what happened in the code when the error occurred. The more information available to the poor soul (probably yourself) who is trying to figure out why the exception was thrown in the first place, the better the chance of it being fixed. Do yourself and your team a favor and give a little bit of extra information when throwing exceptions; you won't be sorry you did.

See Also

The "Exception.Data Property" topic in the MSDN documentation.

5.7 Dealing with Unhandled Exceptions in WinForms Applications

Problem

You have a WinForms-based application in which you want to catch and log any unhandled exceptions on any thread.

Solution

You need to hook up handlers for both the `System.Windows.Forms.Application.ThreadException` event *and* the `System.Appdomain.UnhandledException` event. Both of these events need to be hooked up, as the WinForms support in the Framework does a lot of exception trapping itself. It exposes the `System.Windows.Forms.Application.ThreadException` event to allow you to get any unhandled exceptions that happen on the UI thread that the WinForms and their events are running on. In spite of its deceptive name, the `System.Windows.Forms.Application.ThreadException` event handler will *not* catch unhandled exceptions on worker threads constructed by the program or from `ThreadPool` threads. In order to catch all of those possible routes for unhandled exceptions in a WinForms application, you need to hook up a handler for the `System.AppDomain.UnhandledException` event (`System.Windows.Forms.Application.ThreadException` will catch UI thread exceptions).

To hook up the necessary event handlers to catch all of your unhandled exceptions in a WinForms application, add the following code to the `Main` function in your application:

```
static void Main()
{
    // Adds the event handler to catch any exceptions that happen
    // in the main UI thread.
    Application.ThreadException +=
        new ThreadExceptionEventHandler(OnThreadException);

    // Add the event handler for all threads in the appdomain except
    // for the main UI thread.
    appdomain.CurrentDomain.UnhandledException +=
        new UnhandledExceptionEventHandler(CurrentDomain_UnhandledException);

    Application.EnableVisualStyles();
    Application.Run(new Form1());
}
```

The `System.AppDomain.UnhandledException` event handler is hooked up to the current `Appdomain` via the `appdomain.CurrentDomain` property, which gives access to the current `Appdomain`. The `ThreadException` handler for the application is accessed through the `Application.ThreadException` property.

The event handler code is established in the `CurrentDomain_UnhandledException` and `OnThreadException` handler methods. See Recipe 5.8 for more information on the `UnhandledExceptionEventHandler`. The `ThreadExceptionEventHandler` is passed the sender object and a `ThreadExceptionEventArgs` object. `ThreadExceptionEventArgs` has an `Exception` property that contains the unhandled exception from the WinForms UI thread:

```
// Handles the exception event for all other threads
static void CurrentDomain_UnhandledException(object sender,
                           UnhandledExceptionEventArgs e)
{
    // Just show the exception details.
    MessageBox.Show("CurrentDomain_UnhandledException: " +
            e.ExceptionObject.ToString());
}

// Handles the exception event from a UI thread
static void OnThreadException(object sender, ThreadExceptionEventArgs t)
{
    // Just show the exception details.
    MessageBox.Show("OnThreadException: " + t.Exception.ToString());
}
```

Discussion

Exceptions are the primary way to convey errors in .NET, so when you build an application, it is imperative that there be a final line of defense against unhandled exceptions. An unhandled exception will crash the program (even if it looks a bit nicer in .NET); this is not the impression you wish to make on your customers. It would have been nice to have one event to hook up to for all unhandled exceptions. The appdomain.UnhandledException event comes pretty close to that, but having to handle one extra event isn't the end of the world, either. In coding event handlers for both appdomain.UnhandledException and Application.ThreadException, you can easily call a single handler that writes the exception information to the event log, the debug stream, or custom trace logs or even sends you an email with the information. The possibilities are limited only by how you want to handle errors that can happen to any program given enough exposure.

See Also

The "ThreadExceptionEventHandler Delegate" and "UnhandledExceptionEventHandler Delegate" topics in the MSDN documentation.

5.8 Dealing with Unhandled Exceptions in WPF Applications

Problem

You have a Windows Presentation Foundation (WPF)–based application in which you want to catch and log any unhandled exceptions on any thread.

Solution

To hook up the necessary event handlers to catch all of your unhandled exceptions in a WPF application, add the following code to the *App.xaml* file in your application:

```
<Application x:Class="UnhandledWPFException.App"
    xmlns="http://schemas.microsoft.com/winfx/2006/xaml/presentation"
    xmlns:x="http://schemas.microsoft.com/winfx/2006/xaml"
    StartupUri="Window1.xaml"
    DispatcherUnhandledException="Application_DispatcherUnhandledException">
    <Application.MainWindow>
        <Window />
    </Application.MainWindow>
    <Application.Resources>
    </Application.Resources>
</Application>
```

Then, in the codebehind file *App.xaml.cs*, add the `Application_DispatcherUnhandle dException` method to handle otherwise unhandled exceptions:

```
private void Application_DispatcherUnhandledException(object sender,
        System.Windows.Threading.DispatcherUnhandledExceptionEventArgs e)
{
    // Log the exception information in the event log
    EventLog.WriteEntry("UnhandledWPFException Application",
        e.Exception.ToString(), EventLogEntryType.Error);
    // Let the user know what happened
    MessageBox.Show("Application_DispatcherUnhandledException: " +
        e.Exception.ToString());
    // indicate we handled it
    e.Handled = true;
    // shut down the application
    this.Shutdown();
}
```

Discussion

Windows Presentation Foundation provides another way to create Windows-based applications for .NET. Protecting users from unsightly unhandled exceptions requires a bit of code in WPF, just as it does in WinForms (see Recipe 5.7 for doing this in WinForms).

The `System.Windows.Application` class is the base class for WPF-based applications, and it is from here that the unhandled exceptions are handled via the `DispatcherUn handledException` event. You set up this event handler by specifying the method to handle the event in the *App.xaml* file shown here:

```
DispatcherUnhandledException="Application_DispatcherUnhandledException">
```

You can also set this up in code directly instead of doing it the XAML way by adding the Startup event handler (which is where Microsoft recommends you put the initialization code for the application in WPF) to the XAML file like this:

```
<Application x:Class="UnhandledWPFException.App"
    xmlns="http://schemas.microsoft.com/winfx/2006/xaml/presentation"
    xmlns:x="http://schemas.microsoft.com/winfx/2006/xaml"
    StartupUri="Window1.xaml"
  Startup="Application_Startup" >
    <Application.MainWindow>
        <Window />
    </Application.MainWindow>
    <Application.Resources>

    </Application.Resources>
</Application>
```

In the Startup event, establish the event handler for the DispatcherUnhandledExcep tion like this:

```
private void Application_Startup(object sender, StartupEventArgs e)
{
    this.DispatcherUnhandledException +=
        new System.Windows.Threading.DispatcherUnhandledExceptionEventHandler(
            Application_DispatcherUnhandledException);
}
```

This is great for handling exceptions for WPF applications: just hook up and get all those unhandled exceptions delivered to your single handler, right? Wrong. Just as was necessary in WinForms applications, if you have any code running on any threads other than the UI thread (which you almost always will), you still have to hook up to the AppDomain for the AppDomain.UnhandledException handler to catch those exceptions on threads other than the UI thread. In order to do that, we update our *App.xaml.cs* file as follows:

```
/// <summary>
/// Interaction logic for App.xaml
/// </summary>
public partial class App : Application
{
    private void Application_DispatcherUnhandledException(object sender,
        System.Windows.Threading.DispatcherUnhandledExceptionEventArgs e)
    {
        // indicate we handled it
        e.Handled = true;
        ReportUnhandledException(e.Exception);
    }

    private void Application_Startup(object sender, StartupEventArgs e)
    {
        // WPF UI exceptions
```

```
this.DispatcherUnhandledException +=
  new System.Windows.Threading.DispatcherUnhandledExceptionEventHandler(
    Application_DispatcherUnhandledException);

// Those dirty thread exceptions
AppDomain.CurrentDomain.UnhandledException +=
    new UnhandledExceptionEventHandler(CurrentDomain_UnhandledException);
}

private void CurrentDomain_UnhandledException(object sender,
                          UnhandledExceptionEventArgs e)
{
    ReportUnhandledException(e.ExceptionObject as Exception);
}

private void ReportUnhandledException(Exception ex)
{
    // Log the exception information in the event log
    EventLog.WriteEntry("UnhandledWPFException Application",
        ex.ToString(), EventLogEntryType.Error);
    // Let the user know what happenned
    MessageBox.Show("Unhandled Exception: " + ex.ToString());
    // shut down the application
    this.Shutdown();
}
}
```

See Also

Recipe 5.7; the "DispatcherUnhandledException event" and "AppDomain. Unhandle-dException handler" topics in the MSDN documentation.

5.9 Determining Whether a Process Has Stopped Responding

Problem

You need to watch one or more processes to determine whether the user interface has stopped responding to the system. This functionality is similar to the column in the Task Manager that displays the text "Responding" or "Not Responding," depending on the state of the application.

Solution

Use the `GetProcessState` method and `ProcessRespondingState` enumeration shown in Example 5-5 to determine whether a process has stopped responding.

Example 5-5. Determining whether a process has stopped responding

```
public enum ProcessRespondingState
{
    Responding,
    NotResponding,
    Unknown
}

public static ProcessRespondingState GetProcessState(Process p)
{
    if (p.MainWindowHandle == IntPtr.Zero)
    {
        Trace.WriteLine($"{p.ProcessName} does not have a MainWindowHandle");
        return ProcessRespondingState.Unknown;
    }
    else
    {
        // This process has a MainWindowHandle
        if (!p.Responding)
            return ProcessRespondingState.NotResponding;
        else
            return ProcessRespondingState.Responding;
    }
}
```

Discussion

The GetProcessState method accepts a single parameter, process, identifying a process. The Responding property is then called on the Process object represented by the process parameter. This property returns a ProcessRespondingState enumeration value to indicate that a process is currently responding (Responding), that it is not currently responding (NotResponding), or that a response cannot be determined for this process as there is no main window handle (Unknown).

The Responding property always returns true if the process in question does not have a MainWindowHandle. Processes such as Idle, spoolsv, Rundll32, and svchost do not have a main window handle, and therefore the Responding property always returns true for them. To weed out these processes, you can use the MainWindowHandle property of the Process class, which returns the handle of the main window for a process. If this property returns 0, the process has no main window.

To determine whether all processes on a machine are responding, you can call the GetProcessState method as follows:

```
var processes = Process.GetProcesses().ToArray();
Array.ForEach(processes, p =>
    {
        var processState = GetProcessState(p);
```

```
    switch (processState)
    {
        case ProcessRespondingState.NotResponding:
            Console.WriteLine($"{p.ProcessName} is not responding.");
            break;
        case ProcessRespondingState.Responding:
            Console.WriteLine($"{p.ProcessName} is responding.");
            break;
        case ProcessRespondingState.Unknown:
            Console.WriteLine(
                $"{p.ProcessName}'s state could not be determined.");
            break;
    }
});
```

This code snippet iterates over all processes currently running on your system. The static `GetProcesses` method of the `Process` class takes no parameters and returns an array of `Process` objects with information for all processes running on your system. Each `Process` object is then passed in to your `GetProcessState` method to determine whether it is responding. Other static methods on the `Process` class that retrieve `Process` objects are `GetProcessById`, `GetCurrentProcess`, and `GetProcessesByName`.

See Also

The "Process Class" topic in the MSDN documentation.

5.10 Using Event Logs in Your Application

Problem

You need to add the ability for your application to log events that occur in your application, such as startup, shutdown, critical errors, and even security breaches. Along with reading and writing to a log, you need the ability to create, clear, close, and remove logs from the event log.

Your application might need to keep track of several logs at one time. For example, your application might use a custom log to track specific events, such as startup and shutdown, as they occur in your application. To supplement the custom log, your application could make use of the security log already built into the event log system to read/write security events that occur in your application.

Support for multiple logs comes in handy when one log needs to be created and maintained on the local computer and another, duplicate log needs to be created and maintained on a remote machine. This remote machine might contain logs of all running instances of your application on each user's machine. An administrator could use these logs to quickly find any problems that occur or discover if security is breached in your application. In fact, an application could be run in the background on the remote administrative machine that watches for specific log entries to be written to this log from any user's machine. Recipe 13.6 uses an event mechanism to watch for entries written to an event log and could easily be used to enhance this recipe.

Solution

Use the event log built into the Microsoft Windows operating system to record specific events that occur infrequently.

 Don't flood the event log with many different entries that you could handle by enabling or disabling tracing. Errors are a must, followed by the very important items, but not everything should be written to the event log. Be judicious when writing to the event log so you don't have to sort through all of it when you are looking for the clues.

The `AppEvents` class shown in Example 5-6 contains all the methods needed to create and use an event log in your application.

Example 5-6. Creating and using an event log

```
using System;
using System.Diagnostics;

public class AppEvents
{
    // If you encounter a SecurityException trying to read the registry
    // (Security log) follow these instructions:
    // 1) Open the Registry Editor (search for regedit or type regedit at the Run
    // prompt) 2) Navigate to the following key:
    // 3) HKEY_LOCAL_MACHINE\SYSTEM\CurrentControlSet\Services\Eventlog\Security
    // 4) Right-click on this entry and select Permissions
    // 5) Add the user you are logged in as and give the user the Read permission

    // If you encounter a SecurityException trying to write to the event log
    // "Requested registry access is not allowed.", then the event source has not
    // been created.  Try re-running the EventLogInstaller for your custom event or
    // for this sample code, run %WINDOWS%\Microsoft.NET\Framework\v4.0.30319\
    // InstallUtil.exe AppEventsEventLogInstallerApp.dll"
    // If you just ran it, you may need to wait a bit until Windows catches up and
    // recognizes the log that was added.

    const string localMachine = ".";
    // Constructors
    public AppEvents(string logName) :
        this(logName, Process.GetCurrentProcess().ProcessName)
    { }
```

```csharp
public AppEvents(string logName, string source) :
    this(logName, source, localMachine)
{ }

public AppEvents(string logName, string source,
    string machineName = localMachine)
{
    this.LogName = logName;
    this.SourceName = source;
    this.MachineName = machineName;

    Log = new EventLog(LogName, MachineName, SourceName);
}


private EventLog Log { get; set; } = null;

public string LogName { get; set; }

public string SourceName { get; set; }

public string MachineName { get; set; } = localMachine;


// Methods
public void WriteToLog(string message, EventLogEntryType type,
    CategoryType category, EventIDType eventID)
{
    if (Log == null)
        throw (new ArgumentNullException(nameof(Log),
            "This Event Log has not been opened or has been closed."));

    EventLogPermission evtPermission =
        new EventLogPermission(EventLogPermissionAccess.Write, MachineName);
    evtPermission.Demand();

    // If you get a SecurityException here, see the notes at the
    // top of the class
    Log.WriteEntry(message, type, (int)eventID, (short)category);
}

public void WriteToLog(string message, EventLogEntryType type,
    CategoryType category, EventIDType eventID, byte[] rawData)
{
    if (Log == null)
        throw (new ArgumentNullException(nameof(Log),
            "This Event Log has not been opened or has been closed."));

    EventLogPermission evtPermission =
        new EventLogPermission(EventLogPermissionAccess.Write, MachineName);
    evtPermission.Demand();
```

```csharp
        // If you get a SecurityException here, see the notes at the
        // top of the class
        Log.WriteEntry(message, type, (int)eventID, (short)category, rawData);
    }

    public IEnumerable<EventLogEntry> GetEntries()
    {
        EventLogPermission evtPermission =
            new EventLogPermission(EventLogPermissionAccess.Administer, MachineName);
        evtPermission.Demand();
        return Log?.Entries.Cast<EventLogEntry>().Where(evt =>
            evt.Source == SourceName);
    }

    public void ClearLog()
    {
        EventLogPermission evtPermission =
            new EventLogPermission(EventLogPermissionAccess.Administer, MachineName);
        evtPermission.Demand();
        if (!IsNonCustomLog())
            Log?.Clear();
    }

    public void CloseLog()
    {
        Log?.Close();
        Log = null;
    }

    public void DeleteLog()
    {
        if (!IsNonCustomLog())
            if (EventLog.Exists(LogName, MachineName))
                EventLog.Delete(LogName, MachineName);

        CloseLog();
    }

    public bool IsNonCustomLog()
    {
        // Because Application, Setup, Security, System, and other non-custom logs
        // can contain crucial information  you can't just delete or clear them
        if (LogName == string.Empty || // same as application
            LogName == "Application" ||
            LogName == "Security" ||
            LogName == "Setup" ||
            LogName == "System")
        {
            return true;
        }
        return false;
```

```
        }
}
```

The `EventIDType` and `CategoryType` enumerations used in this class are defined as follows:

```csharp
public enum EventIDType
{
    NA = 0,
    Read = 1,
    Write = 2,
    ExceptionThrown = 3,
    BufferOverflowCondition = 4,
    SecurityFailure = 5,
    SecurityPotentiallyCompromised = 6
}

public enum CategoryType : short
{
    None = 0,
    WriteToDB = 1,
    ReadFromDB = 2,
    WriteToFile = 3,
    ReadFromFile = 4,
    AppStartUp = 5,
    AppShutDown = 6,
    UserInput =7
}
```

As a last note, the `EventIDType` and `CategoryType` enumerations are designed mainly to log security-type breaches as well as potential attacks on the security of your application. Using these event IDs and categories, the administrator can more easily track down potential security threats and do postmortem analysis after security is breached. You can easily modify or replace these enumerations with your own to track different events that occur as a result of your application running.

Discussion

The `AppEvents` class created for this recipe provides applications with an easy-to-use interface for creating, using, and deleting single or multiple event logs in your application. The methods of the `AppEvents` class are described as follows:

WriteToLog

   This method is overloaded to allow an entry to be written to the event log with or without a byte array containing raw data.

GetEntries

   Returns all the event log entries for this event log and source in an `IEnumerable<EventLogEntry>`.

ClearLog

> Removes all the event log entries from this event log if it is a custom log.

CloseLog

> Closes this event log, preventing further interaction with it.

DeleteLog

> Deletes this event log if it is a custom log.

You can add an AppEvents object to an array or collection containing other AppE
vents objects; each AppEvents object corresponds to a particular event log. The following code creates two AppEvents classes and adds them to a ListDictionary collection:

```
public void CreateMultipleLogs()
{
    AppEvents AppEventLog = new AppEvents("AppLog", "AppLocal");
    AppEvents GlobalEventLog = new AppEvents("AppSystemLog", "AppGlobal");

    ListDictionary LogList = new ListDictionary();
    LogList.Add(AppEventLog.Name, AppEventLog);
    LogList.Add(GlobalEventLog.Name, GlobalEventLog);
```

To write to either of these two logs, obtain the AppEvents object by name from the
ListDictionary object, cast the resultant object type to an AppEvents type, and call
the WriteToLog method:

```
((AppEvents)LogList[AppEventLog.Name]).WriteToLog("App startup",
    EventLogEntryType.Information, CategoryType.AppStartUp,
    EventIDType.ExceptionThrown);

((AppEvents)LogList[GlobalEventLog.Name]).WriteToLog(
    "App startup security check",
    EventLogEntryType.Information, CategoryType.AppStartUp,
    EventIDType.BufferOverflowCondition);
```

Containing all AppEvents objects in a ListDictionary object allows you to easily
iterate over all the AppEvents that your application has instantiated. Using a foreach
loop, you can write a single message to both a local and a remote event log:

```
foreach (DictionaryEntry Log in LogList)
{
    ((AppEvents)Log.Value).WriteToLog("App startup",
        EventLogEntryType.FailureAudit,
        CategoryType.AppStartUp, EventIDType.SecurityFailure);
}
```

To delete each log in the logList object, you can use the following foreach loop:

```
foreach (DictionaryEntry Log in LogList)
{
    ((AppEvents)Log.Value).DeleteLog();
```

```
    }
        LogList.Clear();
```

You should be aware of several key points. The first concerns a small problem with constructing multiple AppEvents classes. If you create two AppEvents objects and pass in the same source string to the AppEvents constructor, an exception will be thrown. Consider the following code, which instantiates two AppEvents objects with the same source string:

```
AppEvents appEventLog = new AppEvents("AppLog", "AppLocal");
AppEvents globalEventLog = new AppEvents("Application", "AppLocal");
```

The objects are instantiated without errors, but when the WriteToLog method is called on the globalEventLog object, the following exception is thrown:

```
An unhandled exception of type 'System.ArgumentException' occurred in system.dll.

Additional information: The source 'AppLocal' is not registered in log
'Application'. (It is registered in log 'AppLog'.) " The Source and Log
properties must be matched, or you may set Log to the empty string, and
it will automatically be matched to the Source property.
```

This exception occurs because the WriteToLog method internally calls the WriteEntry method of the EventLog object. The WriteEntry method internally checks to see whether the specified source is registered to the log you are attempting to write to. In this case, the AppLocal source was registered to the first log it was assigned to—the AppLog log. The second attempt to register this same source to another log, Application, failed silently. You do not know that this attempt failed until you try to use the WriteEntry method of the EventLog object.

Another key point about the AppEvents class is the following code, placed at the beginning of each method (except for the DeleteLog method):

```
if (log == null)
    throw (new ArgumentNullException("log",
        "This Event Log has not been opened or has been closed."));
```

This code checks to see whether the private member variable log is a null reference. If so, an ArgumentException is thrown, informing the user of this class that a problem occurred with the creation of the EventLog object. The DeleteLog method does not check the log variable for null since it deletes the event log source and the event log itself. The EventLog object is not involved in this process except at the end of this method, where the log is closed and set to null, if it is not already null. Regardless of the state of the log variable, the source and event log should be deleted in this method.

The `ClearLog` and `DeleteLog` methods make a critical choice when determining whether to delete a log. The following code prevents the application, security, setup, and system event logs from being deleted from your system:

```
public bool IsNonCustomLog()
{
    // Because Application, Setup, Security, System, and other non-custom logs
    // can contain crucial information  you can't just delete or clear them
    if (LogName == string.Empty || // same as application
        LogName == "Application" ||
        LogName == "Security" ||
        LogName == "Setup" ||
        LogName == "System")
    {
        return true;
    }
    return false;
}
```

If any of these logs is deleted, so are the sources registered with the particular log. Once the log is deleted, it is permanent; believe us, it is not fun to try to re-create the log and its sources without a backup.

In order for the `AppEvents` class to work, however, it first needs an event source created. The event log uses event sources to determine which application logged the event. You can establish an event source only when running in an administrative context, and there are two ways to accomplish this:

- Call the `EventLog.CreateEventSource` method.
- Use an `EventLogInstaller`.

While you could create a console application that calls the `CreateEventSource` method and have a user run it in an administrative context on her machine, the recommended option is to build an `EventLogInstaller` class that can be used with InstallUtil.exe (provided by the .NET Framework) to create your initial event sources and custom logs.

The `AppEventsEventLogInstaller`, shown next, will establish the event logs and sources for us. This installer can be called not only by `InstallUtil` but also by most major installation packages, so you can plug it into your favorite installation software to register your event logs and sources at install time when your users have administrative access (or at least the help of an IT professional with said access):

```
/// <summary>
/// To INSTALL: C:\Windows\Microsoft.NET\Framework\v4.0.30319\InstallUtil.exe
[PathToBinary]\AppEventsEventLogInstallerApp.dll
/// To UNINSTALL: C:\Windows\Microsoft.NET\Framework\v4.0.30319\InstallUtil.exe -u
[PathToBinary]\AppEventsEventLogInstallerApp.dll
```

```
/// </summary>
[RunInstaller(true)]
public class AppEventsEventLogInstaller : Installer
{
    private EventLogInstaller evtLogInstaller;

    public AppEventsEventLogInstaller()
    {
        evtLogInstaller = new EventLogInstaller();
        evtLogInstaller.Source = "APPEVENTSSOURCE";
        evtLogInstaller.Log = ""; // Default to Application
        Installers.Add(evtLogInstaller);

        evtLogInstaller = new EventLogInstaller();
        evtLogInstaller.Source = "AppLocal";
        evtLogInstaller.Log = "AppLog";
        Installers.Add(evtLogInstaller);

        evtLogInstaller = new EventLogInstaller();
        evtLogInstaller.Source = "AppGlobal";
        evtLogInstaller.Log = "AppSystemLog";
        Installers.Add(evtLogInstaller);
    }
    public static void Main()
    {
        AppEventsEventLogInstaller appEventsEventLogInstaller =
            new AppEventsEventLogInstaller();
    }
}
```

If you are using InstallUtil to set this up locally, here is a sample of what you may
see when installing using a proper administrative context ("Run As Administrator"):

```
C:\Windows\Microsoft.NET\Framework\v4.0.30319\InstallUtil.exe
C:\CSCB6\AppEventsEventLogInstallerApp\bin\Debug\
AppEventsEventLogInstallerApp.dll


C:\WINDOWS\system32>C:\Windows\Microsoft.NET\Framework\v4.0.30319\InstallUtil.ex
e C:\CSCB6\AppEventsEventLogInstallerApp\bin\Debug\
AppEventsEventLogInstallerApp.dll
Microsoft (R) .NET Framework Installation utility Version 4.0.30319.33440
Copyright (C) Microsoft Corporation.  All rights reserved.


Running a transacted installation.

Beginning the Install phase of the installation.
See the contents of the log file for the
C:\CSCB6\AppEventsEventLogInstallerApp\bin\Debug\
AppEventsEventLogInstallerApp.dll
assembly's progress.
The file is located at C:\CSCB6\AppEventsEventLogInstallerApp\bin\Debug\
```

```
AppEventsEventLogInstallerApp.InstallLog.
Installing assembly 'C:\CSCB6\AppEventsEventLogInstallerApp\bin\Debug\
AppEventsEventLogInstallerApp.dll'.
Affected parameters are:
   logtoconsole =
   logfile = C:\CSCB6\AppEventsEventLogInstallerApp\bin\Debug\
AppEventsEventLogInstallerApp.InstallLog
   assemblypath =
C:\CSCB6\AppEventsEventLogInstallerApp\bin\Debug\
AppEventsEventLogInstallerApp.dll
Creating EventLog source APPEVENTSSOURCE in log ...
Creating EventLog source AppLocal in log AppLog...
Creating EventLog source AppGlobal in log AppSystemLog...

The Install phase completed successfully, and the Commit phase is beginning.
See the contents of the log file for the
C:\CSCB6\AppEventsEventLogInstallerApp\bin\Debug\
AppEventsEventLogInstallerApp.dll
assembly's progress.
The file is located at C:\CSCB6\AppEventsEventLogInstallerApp\bin\Debug\
AppEventsEventLogInstallerApp.InstallLog.
Committing assembly
'C:\CSCB6\AppEventsEventLogInstallerApp\bin\Debug\
AppEventsEventLogInstallerApp.dll'.
Affected parameters are:
   logtoconsole =
   logfile = C:\CSCB6\AppEventsEventLogInstallerApp\bin\Debug\
AppEventsEventLogInstallerApp.InstallLog
   assemblypath =
C:\CSCB6\AppEventsEventLogInstallerApp\bin\Debug\
AppEventsEventLogInstallerApp.dll

The Commit phase completed successfully.

The transacted install has completed.
```

If you attempt to run InstallUtil in a nonadministrative context, you will see results similar to the following:

```
C:\Windows\Microsoft.NET\Framework\v4.0.30319\InstallUtil.exe
C:\CSCB6\AppEventsEventLogInstallerApp\bin\Debug\
AppEventsEventLogInstallerApp.dll
Microsoft (R) .NET Framework Installation utility Version 4.0.30319.33440
Copyright (C) Microsoft Corporation.  All rights reserved.


Running a transacted installation.

Beginning the Install phase of the installation.
See the contents of the log file for the
C:\CSCB6\AppEventsEventLogInstallerApp\bin\Debug\AppEventsEventLogInstallerApp.dll
assembly's progress.
The file is located at C:\CSCB6\AppEventsEventLogInstallerApp\bin\Debug\
```

```
AppEventsEventLogInstallerApp.InstallLog.
Installing assembly
'C:\CSCB6\AppEventsEventLogInstallerApp\bin\Debug\
AppEventsEventLogInstallerApp.dll'.
Affected parameters are:
   logtoconsole =
   logfile = C:\CSCB6\AppEventsEventLogInstallerApp\bin\Debug\
AppEventsEventLogInstallerApp.InstallLog
   assemblypath =
C:\CSCB6\AppEventsEventLogInstallerApp\bin\Debug\
AppEventsEventLogInstallerApp.dll
Creating EventLog source APPEVENTSSOURCE in log APPEVENTSLOG...

An exception occurred during the Install phase.
System.Security.SecurityException: The source was not found, but some or all
event logs could not be searched. Inaccessible logs: Security.

The Rollback phase of the installation is beginning.
See the contents of the log file for the
C:\CSCB6\AppEventsEventLogInstallerApp\bin\Debug\
AppEventsEventLogInstallerApp.dll
assembly's progress.
The file is located at C:\CSCB6\AppEventsEventLogInstallerApp\bin\Debug\
AppEventsEventLogInstallerApp.InstallLog.
Rolling back assembly
'C:\CSCB6\AppEventsEventLogInstallerApp\bin\Debug\
AppEventsEventLogInstallerApp.dll'.
Affected parameters are:
   logtoconsole =
   logfile = C:\CSCB6\AppEventsEventLogInstallerApp\bin\Debug\
AppEventsEventLogInstallerApp.InstallLog
   assemblypath =
C:\CSCB6\AppEventsEventLogInstallerApp\bin\Debug\
AppEventsEventLogInstallerApp.dll
Restoring event log to previous state for source APPEVENTSSOURCE.
An exception occurred during the Rollback phase of the
System.Diagnostics.EventLogInstaller installer.
System.Security.SecurityException: Requested registry access is not allowed.
An exception occurred during the Rollback phase of the installation. This except
ion will be ignored and the rollback will continue. However, the machine might n
ot fully revert to its initial state after the rollback is complete.

The Rollback phase completed successfully.

The transacted install has completed.
The installation failed, and the rollback has been performed.
```

Not only can `InstallUtil` install your event logs and sources, it can help remove them too using the -u parameter!

```
C:\Windows\Microsoft.NET\Framework\v4.0.30319\InstallUtil.exe -u
C:\CSCB6\AppEventsEventLogInstallerApp\bin\Debug\
AppEventsEventLogInstallerApp.dll
```

```
Microsoft (R) .NET Framework Installation utility Version 4.0.30319.33440
Copyright (C) Microsoft Corporation.  All rights reserved.

The uninstall is beginning.
See the contents of the log file for the
C:\CSCB6\AppEventsEventLogInstallerApp\bin\Debug\
AppEventsEventLogInstallerApp.dll
assembly's progress.
The file is located at C:\CSCB6\AppEventsEventLogInstallerApp\bin\Debug\
AppEventsEventLogInstallerApp.InstallLog.
Uninstalling assembly
'C:\CSCB6\AppEventsEventLogInstallerApp\bin\Debug\
AppEventsEventLogInstallerApp.dll'.
Affected parameters are:
   logtoconsole =
   logfile = C:\CSCB6\AppEventsEventLogInstallerApp\bin\Debug\
AppEventsEventLogInstallerApp.InstallLog
   assemblypath =
C:\CSCB6\AppEventsEventLogInstallerApp\bin\Debug\
AppEventsEventLogInstallerApp.dll
Removing EventLog source AppGlobal.
Deleting event log AppSystemLog.
Removing EventLog source AppLocal.
Deleting event log AppLog.
Removing EventLog source APPEVENTSSOURCE.

The uninstall has completed.
```

You should minimize the number of entries written to the event log from your application, as writing to the event log causes a performance hit and some logs are not set to roll over or clear after a certain number of entries. Writing too much information to the event log can noticeably slow your application or cause the server problems. Choose the entries you write to the event log wisely.

See Also

The "EventLog Class," "InstallUtil.exe," and "EventLogInstaller Class" topics in the MSDN documentation.

5.11 Watching the Event Log for a Specific Entry

Problem

You may have multiple applications that write to a single event log. For each of these applications, you want a monitoring application to watch for one or more specific log entries to be written to the event log. For example, you might want to watch for a log entry that indicates that an application encountered a critical error or shut down unexpectedly. These log entries should be reported in real time.

Solution

Monitoring an event log for a specific entry requires the following steps:

1. Create the following method to set up the event handler to handle event log writes:

```
public void WatchForAppEvent(EventLog log)
{
    log.EnableRaisingEvents = true;
    // Hook up the System.Diagnostics.EntryWrittenEventHandler.
    log.EntryWritten += new EntryWrittenEventHandler(OnEntryWritten);
}
```

2. Create the event handler to examine the log entries and determine whether further action is to be performed. For example:

```
public static void OnEntryWritten(object source,
                                  EntryWrittenEventArgs entryArg)
{
    if (entryArg.Entry.EntryType == EventLogEntryType.Error)
    {
        Console.WriteLine(entryArg.Entry.Message);
        Console.WriteLine(entryArg.Entry.Category);
        Console.WriteLine(entryArg.Entry.EntryType.ToString());
        // Do further actions here as necessary...
    }
}
```

Discussion

This recipe revolves around the `EntryWrittenEventHandler` delegate, which calls back to a method whenever any new entry is written to the event log. The `EntryWrittenEventHandler` delegate accepts two arguments: a source of type `object` and an `entryArg` of type `EntryWrittenEventArgs`. The `entryArg` parameter is the more interesting of the two. It contains a property called `Entry` that returns an `EventLogEntry` object. This `EventLogEntry` object contains all the information you need concerning the entry that was written to the event log.

This event log that you are watching is passed as the `WatchForAppEvent` method's `log` parameter. This method performs two actions. First, it sets `log`'s `EnableRaisingEvents` property to `true`. If this property were set to `false`, no events would be raised for this event log when an entry is written to it. The second action this method performs is to add the `OnEntryWritten` callback method to the list of event handlers for this event log.

To prevent this delegate from calling the `OnEntryWritten` callback method, you can set the `EnableRaisingEvents` property to `false`, effectively turning off the delegate.

Note that the `Entry` object passed to the `entryArg` parameter of the `OnEntryWritten` callback method is read-only, so the entry cannot be modified before it is written to the event log.

See Also

The "EventLog.EntryWritten Event" topic in the MSDN documentation.

5.12 Implementing a Simple Performance Counter

Problem

You need to use a performance counter to track application-specific information. The simpler performance counters find, for example, the change in a counter value between successive samplings or just count the number of times an action occurs. Other, more complex counters exist but are not dealt with in this recipe. For example, you could build a custom counter to keep track of the number of database transactions, the number of failed network connections to a server, or even the number of users connecting to your web service per minute.

Solution

Create a simple performance counter that finds, for example, the change in a counter value between successive samplings or that just counts the number of times an action occurs. Use the following method (`CreateSimpleCounter`) to create a simple custom counter:

```
public static PerformanceCounter CreateSimpleCounter(string counterName,
    string counterHelp, PerformanceCounterType counterType, string categoryName,
    string categoryHelp)
{
    CounterCreationDataCollection counterCollection =
        new CounterCreationDataCollection();

    // Create the custom counter object and add it to the collection of counters
    CounterCreationData counter =
        new CounterCreationData(counterName, counterHelp, counterType);
    counterCollection.Add(counter);

    // Create category
    if (PerformanceCounterCategory.Exists(categoryName))
```

```
        PerformanceCounterCategory.Delete(categoryName);

    PerformanceCounterCategory appCategory =
        PerformanceCounterCategory.Create(categoryName, categoryHelp,
            PerformanceCounterCategoryType.SingleInstance, counterCollection);

    // Create the counter and initialize it
    PerformanceCounter appCounter =
        new PerformanceCounter(categoryName, counterName, false);

    appCounter.RawValue = 0;

    return (appCounter);
}
```

Discussion

The first action this method takes is to create the `CounterCreationDataCollection` object and `CounterCreationData` object. The `CounterCreationData` object is created using the `counterName`, `counterHelp`, and `counterType` parameters passed to the `Cre ateSimpleCounter` method. The `CounterCreationData` object is then added to the `counterCollection`.

The `ASPNET` user account, as well as many other user accounts, by default prevents performance counters from being read for security reasons. You can either increase the permissions allowed for these accounts or use impersonation with an account that has access to enable this functionality. However, this then becomes a deployment requirement of your application.

There is also risk in doing this, as you as the developer are the first line of defense for security matters. If you build it and make choices that loosen security restrictions, you are assuming that responsibility, so please don't do it indiscriminately or without a full understanding of the repercussions.

If `categoryName`—a string containing the name of the category that is passed as a parameter to the method—is not registered on the system, a new category is created from a `PerformanceCounterCategory` object. If one is registered, it is deleted and created anew. Finally, the actual performance counter is created from a `Performance Counter` object. This object is initialized to 0 and returned by the method. `Performan ceCounterCategory` takes a `PerformanceCounterCategoryType` as a parameter. The possible settings are shown in Table 5-1.

Table 5-1. PerformanceCounterCategoryType enumeration values

Name	Description
MultiInstance	There can be multiple instances of the performance counter.
SingleInstance	There can be only one instance of the performance counter.
Unknown	Instance functionality for this performance counter is unknown.

The CreateSimpleCounter method returns a PerformanceCounter object that will be used by an application. The application can perform several actions on a Performan ceCounter object. An application can increment or decrement it using one of these three methods:

```
long value = appCounter.Increment();
long value = appCounter.Decrement();
long value = appCounter.IncrementBy(i);
// Additionally, a negative number may be passed to the
// IncrementBy method to mimic a DecrementBy method
// (which is not included in this class). For example:
long value = appCounter.IncrementBy(-i);
```

The first two methods accept no parameters, while the third accepts a long containing the number by which to increment the counter. All three methods return a long type indicating the new value of the counter.

In addition to incrementing or decrementing this counter, you can also take samples of the counter at various points in the application. A sample is a snapshot of the counter and all of its values at a particular instance in time. You may take a sample using the following line of code:

```
CounterSample counterSampleValue = appCounter.NextSample();
```

The NextSample method accepts no parameters and returns a CounterSample structure.

At another point in the application, a counter can be sampled again, and both samples can be passed in to the static Calculate method on the CounterSample class. These actions may be performed on a single line of code as follows:

```
float calculatedSample = CounterSample.Calculate(counterSampleValue,
                                    appCounter.NextSample());
```

The calculated sample calculatedSample may be stored for future analysis.

The simpler performance counters already available in the .NET Framework are:

CounterDelta32/CounterDelta64
    Determines the difference (or change) in value between two samplings of this counter. The CounterDelta64 counter can hold larger values than CounterDelta32.

CounterTimer

Calculates the percentage of the `CounterTimer` value change over the `CounterTimer` time change. Tracks the average active time for a resource as a percentage of the total sample time.

CounterTimerInverse

Calculates the inverse of the `CounterTimer` counter. Tracks the average inactive time for a resource as a percentage of the total sample time.

CountPerTimeInterval32/CountPerTimeInterval64

Calculates the number of items waiting within a queue to a resource over the time elapsed. These counters give the delta of the queue length for the last two sample intervals divided by the interval duration.

ElapsedTime

Calculates the difference in time between when this counter recorded the start of an event and the current time, measured in seconds.

NumberOfItems32/NumberOfItems64

These counters return their value in decimal format. The `NumberOfItems64` counter can hold larger values than `NumberOfItems32`. This counter does not need to be passed to the static `Calculate` method of the `CounterSample` class; there are no values that must be calculated. Instead, use the `RawValue` property of the `Performance Counter` object (i.e., in this recipe, the `appCounter.RawValue` property would be used).

RateOfCountsPerSecond32/RateOfCountsPerSecond64

Calculates the `RateOfCountsPerSecond*` value change over the `RateOfCountsPerSec ond*` time change, measured in seconds. The `RateOfCountsPerSecond64` counter can hold larger values than the `RateOfCountsPerSecond32` counter.

Timer100Ns

Shows the active component time as a percentage of the total elapsed time of the sample interval measured in 100 nanoseconds (ns) units. Processor\ % User Time is an example of this type of counter.

Timer100nsInverse

Percentage-based counter showing the average active percentage of time tracked during the sample interval. Processor\ % Processor Time is one example of this type of counter.

See Also

The "PerformanceCounter Class," "PerformanceCounterType Enumeration," "PerformanceCounterCategory Class," "ASP.NET Impersonation," and "Monitoring Performance Thresholds" topics in the MSDN documentation.

5.13 Creating Custom Debugging Displays for Your Classes

Problem

You have a set of classes that are used in your application. You would like to see at a glance in the debugger what a particular instance of the class holds. The default debugger display doesn't show any useful information for your class today.

Solution

Add a `DebuggerDisplayAttribute` to your class to make the debugger show you something you consider useful about your class. For example, if you had a `Citizen` class that held the honorific and name information, you could add a `DebuggerDisplayAttribute` like this one:

```
[DebuggerDisplay("Citizen Full Name = {Honorific}{First}{Middle}{Last}")]
public class Citizen
{
    public string Honorific { get; set; }
    public string First { get; set; }
    public string Middle { get; set; }
    public string Last { get; set; }
}
```

Now, when instances of the `Citizen` class are instantiated, the debugger will show the information as directed by the `DebuggerDisplayAttribute` on the class. To see this, instantiate two `Citizen`s, Mrs. Alice G. Jones and Mr. Robert Frederick Jones, like this:

```
Citizen mrsJones = new Citizen()
{
    Honorific = "Mrs.",
    First = "Alice",
    Middle = "G.",
    Last = "Jones"
};
Citizen mrJones = new Citizen()
{
    Honorific = "Mr.",
    First = "Robert",
    Middle = "Frederick",
    Last = "Jones"
};
```

When this code is run under the debugger, the custom display is used, as shown in Figure 5-9.

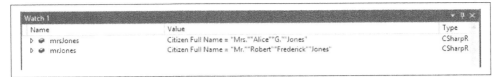

Figure 5-9. Debugger display controlled by DebuggerDisplayAttribute

Discussion

It is nice to be able to quickly see the pertinent information for classes that you are creating, but the more powerful part of this feature is the ability for your team members to quickly understand what this class instance holds. The `this` pointer is accessible from the `DebuggerDisplayAttribute` declaration, but any properties accessed via the `this` pointer will not evaluate the property attributes before processing. Essentially, if you access a property on the current object instance as part of constructing the display string, if that property has attributes, they will not be processed, and therefore you may not get the value you thought you would. If you have custom `ToString()` overrides in place already, the debugger will use these as the `DebuggerDisplayAttribute` without your specifying it, provided the correct option is enabled under *Tools\Options\Debugging*, as shown in Figure 5-10.

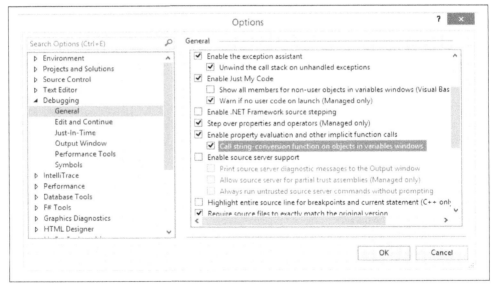

Figure 5-10. Setting the debugger to call ToString() for object display

See Also

The "Using DebuggerDisplayAttribute" and "DebuggerDisplayAttribute" topics in the MSDN documentation.

5.14 Tracking Where Exceptions Come From

Problem

You want to be able to determine what method an exception was caught in or who called the method that caused an exception to be thrown to help debug the issue.

Solution

Use the `CallerMemberName`, `CallerFilePath`, and `CallerLineNumber` attributes (also known as the `Caller Info` attributes) from the `System.Runtime.CompilerServices` namespace to determine the calling method.

For example, if you wanted to record the location of the `catch` block that caught an exception, you could use a method like `RecordCatchBlock`:

```
public void RecordCatchBlock(Exception ex,
    [CallerMemberName] string memberName = "",
    [CallerFilePath] string sourceFilePath = "",
    [CallerLineNumber] int sourceLineNumber = 0)
{
    string catchDetails =
        $"{ex.GetType().Name} caught in member \"{memberName}\" " +
        $"in catch block encompassing line {sourceLineNumber} " +
        $"in file {sourceFilePath} " +
        $"with message \"{ex.Message}\"";
    Console.WriteLine(catchDetails);
}
```

You would then call this method from your `catch` blocks like this:

```
public void TestCallerInfoAttribs()
{
    try
    {
        LibraryMethod();
    }
    catch(Exception ex)
    {
        RecordCatchBlock(ex);
    }
}
```

This would allow you to see the type of the exception caught, the class member name it was caught in, and the source file and line number that is encompassed by the catch block where the exception was caught without having to traverse the call stack:

```
LibraryException caught in member "TestCallerInfoAttribs" in catch block encompa
ssing line 1303 in file C:\CSCB6\CSharpRecipes\
05_DebuggingAndExceptionHandling.cs
with message "Object reference not set to an instance of an object."
```

You could also use this to help determine what method called into a library method, as it can sometimes be difficult to debug which function called the library method:

```
public void LibraryMethod(
            [CallerMemberName] string memberName = "",
            [CallerFilePath] string sourceFilePath = "",
            [CallerLineNumber] int sourceLineNumber = 0)
{
    try
    {
        // Do some library action
        // had a problem
        throw new NullReferenceException();
    }
    catch(Exception ex)
    {
        // Wrap the exception and capture the source of where the
        // library method was called from
        throw new LibraryException(ex)
        {
            CallerMemberName = memberName,
            CallerFilePath = sourceFilePath,
            CallerLineNumber = sourceLineNumber
        };
    }
}
```

Using the LibraryException, you can record at runtime the attributes of the calling method and convey that with the originating exception:

```
[Serializable]
public class LibraryException : Exception
{
    public LibraryException(Exception inner) : base(inner.Message,inner)
    {
    }
    public string CallerMemberName { get; set; }
    public string CallerFilePath { get; set; }
    public int CallerLineNumber { get; set; }

    public override void GetObjectData(SerializationInfo info,
                                       StreamingContext context)
    {
        base.GetObjectData(info, context);
```

```
info.AddValue("CallerMemberName", this.CallerMemberName);
info.AddValue("CallerFilePath", this.CallerFilePath);
info.AddValue("CallerLineNumber", this.CallerLineNumber);
}

public override string ToString() => "LibraryException originated in " +
    $"member \"{CallerMemberName}\" " +
    $"on line {CallerLineNumber} " +
    $"in file {CallerFilePath} " +
    $"with exception details: {Environment.NewLine}" +
    $"{InnerException.ToString()}";
}
```

The `LibraryException.ToString` method will provide a synopsis of the issue:

```
LLibraryException originated in member "TestCallerInfoAttribs" on line 1299 in
file C:\CSCB6\CSharpRecipes\05_DebuggingAndExceptionHandling.cs with exception
details:
System.NullReferenceException: Object reference not set to an instance of an obj
etc.
    at CSharpRecipes.DebuggingAndExceptionHandling.LibraryMethod(String memberNam
e, String sourceFilePath, Int32 sourceLineNumber) in D:\PRJ32\Book_6_0\CS60_Cook
book\CSCB6\CSharpRecipes\05_DebuggingAndExceptionHandling.cs:line 1318
```

Discussion

As the `CallerInfo` attributes are determined at compile time, there is no cost during runtime to retrieve the information about where the previous method on the stack came from. While not as comprehensive as a full stack trace, it is a cheaper and simpler alternative that could give you method, file, and line information with which you can enhance your exception logging. Any time you can have that sort of information handed to you with a defect/bug report/issue ticket (pick your favorite way to be notified that the code is broken), your life will become much easier.

You may notice that the `CallerInfo` attributes require a default value:

```
public void RecordCatchBlock(Exception ex,
    [CallerMemberName] string memberName = "",
    [CallerFilePath] string sourceFilePath = "",
    [CallerLineNumber] int sourceLineNumber = 0)
```

Those parameters need a default value because the `CallerInfo` attributes were implemented using optional parameters, and optional parameters require a default value. Here's how you can still call the method hosting the attributes without providing a value for them:

```
RecordCatchBlock(ex);
```

See Also

See the "CallerMemberNameAttribute," "CallerFilePathAttribute," and "CallerLine-NumberAttribute" topics in the MSDN documentation.

5.15 Handling Exceptions in Asynchronous Scenarios

Problem

You are working with asynchronous methods using `async` and `await` and you need to be able to catch any possible exceptions that may result during the method (or methods) execution.

Solution

When you're handling exceptions from the invocation of a single method, the .NET Framework will handle the return of an exception that occurs between the asynchronous invocation and awaiting of the return. When you're handling exceptions from the simultaneous invocation of multiple methods asynchronously, a bit more work is required to extract all of the exception detail. Finally, when dealing with the result of an exception, you can call an asynchronous method in the `catch` block to handle the work.

To demonstrate this, let's work with the rather common scenario of a software development team manager named Bill who needs to have some work done.

User story 1: Bill needs Steve to implement a new feature in the product

Bill comes to Steve's desk and asks him to implement the new feature in this sprint, then walks away, leaving Steve to implement on his own (asynchronously from Bill's request):

```
try
{
    // Steve, get that project done!
    await SteveCreateSomeCodeAsync();
}
catch (DefectCreatedException dce)
{
    Console.WriteLine($"Steve introduced a Defect: {dce.Message}");
}
```

Steve works hard, as all developers do, but even the best of us can have an off day. Steve happens to generate a defect in the feature he was asked to implement in `Steve CreateSomeCodeAsync`. Luckily, even though Steve was doing this asynchronously, we can still catch the `DefectCreatedException` and handle it normally, as the `async` and `await` support transports the exception back to the `catch` block automatically. (More about how this happens in the Discussion section. Look for `ExceptionDispatch Info`!)

The output we captured from the caught exception lets us know where the issue is so Steve can fix it later:

```
Steve introduced a Defect: A defect was introduced: (Null Reference on line 42)
```

User story 2: Bill has a large set of features to be implemented by Jay, Tom, and Seth

Bill knows Steve is busy, so he approaches the other members of the team (Jay, Tom, and Seth) to get a whole new set of features completed in the sprint. It looks like they are going to have to come in on Saturday! Jay, Tom, and Seth get together, divide up the work, and all start coding at the same time. Even though they may finish at different times, Bill still wants to be on the lookout for any defects they created:

```
// OK Team, make that new thing this weekend! You guys better hurry up with that!
Task jayCode = JayCreateSomeCodeAsync();
Task tomCode = TomCreateSomeCodeAsync();
Task sethCode = SethCreateSomeCodeAsync();

Task teamComplete = Task.WhenAll(new Task[] { jayCode, tomCode, sethCode });
try
{
    await teamComplete;
}
catch
{
    // Get the messages from the exceptions thrown from
    // the set of actions
    var defectMessages =
        teamComplete.Exception?.InnerExceptions.Select(e =>
            e.Message).ToList();
    defectMessages?.ForEach(m =>
        Console.WriteLine($"{m}"));
}
```

First, each unit of work (`JayCreateSomeCodeAsync`, `TomCreateSomeCodeAsync`, `Seth CreateSomeCodeAsync`) is turned into a `Task`. The `Task.WhenAll` method is then called to create an encompassing `Task` (`teamComplete`), which will complete when all of the individual `Task`s are completed.

Once all of the tasks have completed, the `await` will throw an `AggregateException` if any of the `Task`s threw an `Exception` during execution. This `AggregateException` is accessed on the `teamComplete.Exception` property, and it holds a list of `InnerExcep tions`, which is of type `ReadOnlyCollection<Exception>`.

Since the developers introduced this set of exceptions, they are more `DefectCreate dExceptions`!

The resulting logging tells us where the team will need to clean up:

```
A defect was introduced: (Ambiguous Match on line 2)
A defect was introduced: (Quota Exceeded on line 11)
A defect was introduced: (Out Of Memory on line 8)
```

User story 3: Bill wants to record if there are any issues implementing a new feature

Finally, Bill realizes that he needs a better system to determine if there were defects introduced into the code. Bill adds logging to the code that will write the details of the defect to the EventLog when a DefectCreatedException is caught. Since writing to the EventLog can be a hit to performance, he decides to do this asynchronously.

```
try
{
    await SteveCreateSomeCodeAsync();
}
catch (DefectCreatedException dce)
{
    await WriteEventLogEntryAsync("ManagerApplication", dce.Message,
        EventLogEntryType.Error);
    throw;
}
```

Discussion

Running code asynchronously doesn't mean you don't still need to have proper error handling, it just complicates the process a bit. Luckily, the C# and .NET teams at Microsoft have done a lot to make this task as painless as possible.

Awaiting these operations means that they are run in a context, either the current SynchronizationContext or the TaskScheduler. This context is captured when the async method awaits another method, and is restored when work resumes in the async method.

The context captured depends on where your async method code is executing:

- User interface (WinForms/WPF): UI context
- ASP.NET: ASP.NET request context
- Other: ThreadPool context

In user story 1, we mentioned that the implementation of async and await used a class called System.Runtime.ExceptionServices.ExceptionDispatchInfo to handle when an exception is thrown on one thread and needs to be caught on another as the result of an asynchronous operation.

ExceptionDispatchInfo allows the capture of an exception that was thrown in one thread and then allows it to be rethrown—without losing any of the information (exception data and stack trace)—from another thread. This is what happens from an error-handling standpoint when you `await` an `async` method.

One other item of note is the use of `ConfigureAwait`, which allows you to change the behavior of context resumption after the `async` method has completed. If you pass `false` to `ConfigureAwait`, it will not attempt to resume the original context:

```
await MyAsyncMethod().ConfigureAwait(false);
```

 If you use `ConfigureAwait(false)`, then any code after the `await` finishes and the `async` method resumes cannot rely on the original context, as the thread on which the code continues will not have it. If this async method were called from an ASP.NET context, for example, the request context will not be available once it resumes.

The code for the hardworking team is presented in Example 5-7.

Example 5-7. Teamwork in action!

```
public async Task TestHandlingAsyncExceptionsAsync()
{
    // Team producing software
    // Manager sends Steve to create code, exception"DefectCreatedException" thrown
    // Manager sends Jay, Tom, Seth to write code, all throw DefectCreatedExceptions

    // Single async method call
    try
    {
        // Steve, get that project done!
        await SteveCreateSomeCodeAsync();
    }
    catch (DefectCreatedException dce)
    {
        Console.WriteLine($"Steve introduced a Defect: {dce.Message}");
    }

    // Multiple async methods (WaitAll)
    // OK Team, make that new thing this weekend! You guys better hurry up with that!
    Task jayCode = JayCreateSomeCodeAsync();
    Task tomCode = TomCreateSomeCodeAsync();
    Task sethCode = SethCreateSomeCodeAsync();

    Task teamComplete = Task.WhenAll(new Task[] { jayCode, tomCode, sethCode });
    try
    {
        await teamComplete;
    }
    catch
    {
```

```csharp
            // Get the messages from the exceptions thrown from
            // the set of actions
            var defectMessages =
                teamComplete.Exception?.InnerExceptions.Select(e =>
                    e.Message).ToList();
            defectMessages?.ForEach(m =>
                Console.WriteLine($"{m}"));
        }

        // awaiting an action in an exception handler
        // discuss how the original throw location is preserved via
        // System.Runtime.ExceptionServices.ExceptionDispatchInfo
        try
        {
            try
            {
                await SteveCreateSomeCodeAsync();
            }
            catch (DefectCreatedException dce)
            {
                Console.WriteLine(dce.ToString());
                await WriteEventLogEntry("ManagerApplication", dce.Message,
                    EventLogEntryType.Error);
                throw;
            }
        }
        catch(DefectCreatedException dce)
        {
            Console.WriteLine(dce.ToString());
        }
    }
}

public async Task WriteEventLogEntryAsync(string source, string message,
    EventLogEntryType type)
{
    await Task.Factory.StartNew(() => EventLog.WriteEntry(source, message, type));
}

public async Task SteveCreateSomeCodeAsync()
{
    Random rnd = new Random();
    await Task.Delay(rnd.Next(100, 1000));
    throw new DefectCreatedException("Null Reference",42);
}

public async Task JayCreateSomeCodeAsync()
{
    Random rnd = new Random();
    await Task.Delay(rnd.Next(100, 1000));
    throw new DefectCreatedException("Ambiguous Match",2);
}
```

```
public async Task TomCreateSomeCodeAsync()
{
    Random rnd = new Random();
    await Task.Delay(rnd.Next(100, 1000));
    throw new DefectCreatedException("Quota Exceeded",11);
}
public async Task SethCreateSomeCodeAsync()
{
    Random rnd = new Random();
    await Task.Delay(rnd.Next(100, 1000));
    throw new DefectCreatedException("Out Of Memory", 8);
}
```

The custom DefectCreatedException is listed in Example 5-8.

Example 5-8. Defect tracking

```
[Serializable]
public class DefectCreatedException : Exception
{
    #region Constructors
    // Normal exception ctor's
    public DefectCreatedException() : base()
    {
    }

    public DefectCreatedException(string message) : base(message)
    {
    }

    public DefectCreatedException(string message, Exception innerException)
        : base(message, innerException)
    {
    }

    // Exception ctor's that accept the new parameters
    public DefectCreatedException(string defect, int line) : base(string.Empty)
    {
        this.Defect = defect;
        this.Line = line;
    }

    public DefectCreatedException(string defect, int line, Exception innerException)
        : base(string.Empty, innerException)
    {
        this.Defect = defect;
        this.Line = line;
    }


    // Serialization ctor
    protected DefectCreatedException(SerializationInfo exceptionInfo,
```

```
        StreamingContext exceptionContext)
        : base(exceptionInfo, exceptionContext)
    {
    }
    #endregion // Constructors

    #region Properties
    public string Defect { get; }
    public int Line { get; }

    public override string Message =>
        $"A defect was introduced: ({this.Defect ?? "Unknown"} on line {this.Line})";
    #endregion // Properties

    #region Overridden methods
    // ToString method
    public override string ToString() =>
        $"{Environment.NewLine}{this.ToFullDisplayString()}";

    // Used during serialization to capture information about extra fields
    [SecurityPermission(SecurityAction.LinkDemand,
        Flags = SecurityPermissionFlag.SerializationFormatter)]
    public override void GetObjectData(SerializationInfo info,
        StreamingContext context)
    {
        base.GetObjectData(info, context);
        info.AddValue("Defect", this.Defect);
        info.AddValue("Line", this.Line);
    }
    #endregion // Overridden methods

    public string ToBaseString() => (base.ToString());
}
```

See Also

The "async," "await," "AggregateException," "ConfigureAwait," and "System.Runtime.ExceptionServices.ExceptionDispatchInfo" topics in the MSDN documentation.

5.16 Being Selective About Exception Processing

Problem

You want to handle only a particular instance of an exception that is thrown for multiple reasons.

Solution

Use exception filters to catch only exceptions where you want to do something about the condition.

As an example, say you called a database and you wanted to handle timeouts differently. If you were calling from ASP.NET WebApi, you might even want to return a 503 Service Unavailable message to indicate that the service is busy when you start seeing timeout errors from the database.

The ProtectedCallTheDatabase method wraps the CallTheDatabase method in a try-catch block and adds an exception filter (using the when keyword) to check for a DatabaseException where the allotted Number property is set to -2. When the Number property is set to -2 on a DatabaseException, it indicates a timeout (much like a current Microsoft database offering) and we will catch the exception and can handle it from there. If Number is not set to -2, we will not catch the exception and it will propagate up the call stack to the caller of the ProtectedCallTheDatabase method:

```
private void ProtectedCallTheDatabase(string problem)
{
    try
    {
        CallTheDatabase(problem);
        Console.WriteLine("No error on database call");
    }
    catch (DatabaseException dex) when (dex.Number == -2) // watch for timeouts
    {
        Console.WriteLine(
            "DatabaseException catch caught a database exception: " +
            $"{dex.Message}");
    }
}
```

The CallTheDatabase method simulates calling the database and encountering a problem:

```
private void CallTheDatabase(string problem)
{
    switch (problem)
    {
        case "timeout":
            throw new DatabaseException(
                "Timeout expired. The timeout period elapsed prior to " +
                "completion of the operation or the server is not " +
                "responding. (Microsoft SQL Server, Error: -2).")
            {
                Number = -2,
                Class = 11
            };
        case "loginfail":
```

```
            throw new DatabaseException("Login failed for user")
            {
                Number = 18456,
            };
        }
    }
```

We can call the `ProtectedCallTheDatabase` method in the three ways shown in Example 5-9.

Example 5-9. Testing exception filters

```
Console.WriteLine("Simulating database call timeout");
try
{
    ProtectedCallTheDatabase("timeout");
}
catch(Exception ex)
{
    Console.WriteLine($"Exception catch caught a database exception: {ex.Message}");
}
Console.WriteLine("");

Console.WriteLine("Simulating database call login failure");
try
{
    ProtectedCallTheDatabase("loginfail");
}
catch (Exception ex)
{
    Console.WriteLine($"Exception catch caught a database exception: {ex.Message}");
}
Console.WriteLine("");

Console.WriteLine("Simulating successful database call");
try
{
    ProtectedCallTheDatabase("noerror");
}
catch (Exception ex)
{
    Console.WriteLine($"Exception catch caught a database exception: {ex.Message}");
}
Console.WriteLine("");
```

We get the output shown in Example 5-10.

Example 5-10. Exception filter testing output

```
Simulating database call timeout
DatabaseException catch caught a database exception: Timeout expired.
```

The timeout period elapsed prior to completion of the operation or the server
is not responding. (Microsoft SQL Server, Error: -2).

Simulating database call login failure
Exception catch caught a database exception: Login failed for user

Simulating successful database call
No error on database call

Note that the timeout was caught in the catch block in ProtectedCallTheDatabase,
while the login failure was not caught until it returned to the catch block in the testing code.

Discussion

Exception filters allow you to conditionally evaluate if a catch block should catch an
exception, which is quite powerful and allows you to handle only exceptions you can
do something about at a finer-grained level than was previously possible.

Another advantage of using exception filters is that it does not require the constant
catching and rethrowing of exceptions. When this is done improperly it can affect the
call stack of the exception and hide errors (see Recipe 5.1 for more details), whereas
exception filters let you examine and even perform operations with exceptions (like
logging) without interfering with the original flow of the exception. In order to not
interfere, the code executed in the exception filter must return false so that the
exception continues to propagate normally. The code introduced to make the true or
false determination in the exception filter should be kept to a minimum, as you are
in a catch handler and the same rules apply. Don't do things that could cause other
exceptions and mask the original error condition you were trying to trap for in the
first place.

The full listing for the DatabaseException is shown in Example 5-11.

Example 5-11. Exception filter testing output

```
[Serializable]
public class DatabaseException : DbException
{
    public DatabaseException(string message) : base(message) { }
    public byte Class { get; set; }
    public Guid ClientConnectionId { get; set; }
    [DesignerSerializationVisibility(DesignerSerializationVisibility.Content)]
    public SqlErrorCollection Errors { get; set; }
    public int LineNumber { get; set; }
    public int Number { get; set; }
    public string Procedure { get; set; }
    public string Server { get; set; }
    public override string Source => base.Source;
```

```csharp
    public byte State { get; set; }
    public override void GetObjectData(SerializationInfo si,
        StreamingContext context)
    {
        base.GetObjectData(si, context);
    }
}
```

See Also

The "Exception Filters" topic in the MSDN documentation.

CHAPTER 6

Reflection and Dynamic Programming

6.0 Introduction

Reflection is the mechanism provided by the .NET Framework to allow you to inspect how a program is constructed. Using reflection, you can obtain information such as the name of an assembly and what other assemblies a given assembly imports. You can even dynamically call methods on an instance of a type in a given assembly. Reflection also allows you to create code dynamically and compile it to an in-memory assembly or to build a symbol table of type entries in an assembly.

Reflection is a very powerful feature of the Framework and, as such, is guarded by the runtime. The ReflectionPermission must be granted to assemblies that are going to access the protected or private members of a type. If you are going to access only the public members of a public type, you will not need to be granted the ReflectionPermission. Code Access Security (CAS) has only two permission sets that give all reflection access by default: FullTrust and Everything. The LocalIntranet permission set includes the ReflectionEmit privilege, which allows for emitting metadata and creating assemblies, and the MemberAccess privilege, which allows for performing dynamic invocation of methods on types in assemblies.

In this chapter, you will see how you can use reflection to dynamically invoke members on types, figure out all of the assemblies a given assembly is dependent on, and inspect assemblies for different types of information. Reflection is a great way to understand how things are put together in .NET, and this chapter provides a starting point.

This chapter will also cover the dynamic keyword in C#, which is supported by the Dynamic Language Runtime (DLR) in .NET. It is used to help extend C# to identify the type of an object at runtime instead of statically at compile time, and to support dynamic behavior. To use these features, you need to reference the System.Dynamic assembly and namespace.

The DLR was introduced to support the following use cases:

- Porting other languages (like Python and Ruby) to .NET
- Enabling dynamic features in static languages (like C# and Visual Basic)
- Enabling more sharing of libraries between languages
- Caching binding operations (like Reflection) to improve performance instead of determining everything at runtime each time

The DLR provides three main services:

- Expression trees (to represent language semantics such as those used in LINQ)
- Call site caching (caches the characteristics of the operation the first time it is performed)
- Dynamic object interoperability (through the use of IDynamicMetaObjectPro vider, DynamicMetaObject, DynamicObject, and ExpandoObject)

The three main constructs provided to do dynamic programming in C# are the dynamic type (an object that is not bound by compile-time checking), the ExpandoOb ject class (used to construct or deconstruct the members of an object at runtime), and the DynamicObject class (a base class for adding dynamic behavior to your own objects). All three constructs are demonstrated in this chapter.

6.1 Listing Referenced Assemblies

Problem

You need to determine each assembly imported by a particular assembly. This information can show you if this assembly is using one or more of your assemblies or if it is using another specific assembly.

Solution

Use the Assembly.GetReferencedAssemblies method, as shown in Example 6-1, to obtain the imported assemblies of a particular assembly.

Example 6-1. Using the Assembly.GetReferencedAssemblies method

```
public static void BuildDependentAssemblyList(string path,
    StringCollection assemblies)
{
```

```
    // maintain a list of assemblies the original one needs
    if(assemblies == null)
        assemblies = new StringCollection();

    // have we already seen this one?
    if(assemblies.Contains(path)==true)
        return;

    try
    {
        Assembly asm = null;

        // look for common path delimiters in the string
        // to see if it is a name or a path
        if ((path.IndexOf(@"\", 0, path.Length, StringComparison.Ordinal) != -1) ||
            (path.IndexOf("/", 0, path.Length, StringComparison.Ordinal) != -1))
        {
            // load the assembly from a path
            asm = Assembly.LoadFrom(path);
        }
        else
        {
            // try as assembly name
            asm = Assembly.Load(path);
        }

        // add the assembly to the list
        if (asm != null)
            assemblies.Add(path);

        // get the referenced assemblies
        AssemblyName[] imports = asm.GetReferencedAssemblies();

        // iterate
        foreach (AssemblyName asmName in imports)
        {
            // now recursively call this assembly to get the new modules
            // it references
            BuildDependentAssemblyList(asmName.FullName, assemblies);
        }
    }
    catch (FileLoadException fle)
    {
        // just let this one go...
        Console.WriteLine(fle);
    }
}
```

This code returns a `StringCollection` containing the original assembly, all imported assemblies, and the dependent assemblies of the imported assemblies.

If you ran this method against the assembly *C:\CSharpRecipes\bin\Debug\CSharpRecipes.exe*, you'd get the following dependency tree:

```
Assembly C:\CSharpRecipes\bin\Debug\CSharpRecipes.exe has a dependency tree of
these assemblies :

    C:\CSharpRecipes\bin\Debug\CSharpRecipes.exe
    mscorlib, Version=4.0.0.0, Culture=neutral, PublicKeyToken=b77a5c561934e089
    System, Version=4.0.0.0, Culture=neutral, PublicKeyToken=b77a5c561934e089
    System.Configuration, Version=4.0.0.0, Culture=neutral,
PublicKeyToken=b03f5f7f11d50a3a
    System.Xml, Version=4.0.0.0, Culture=neutral, PublicKeyToken=b77a5c561934e089
    System.Data.SqlXml, Version=4.0.0.0, Culture=neutral,
PublicKeyToken=b77a5c561934e089
    System.Security, Version=4.0.0.0, Culture=neutral,
PublicKeyToken=b03f5f7f11d50a3a
    System.Core, Version=4.0.0.0, Culture=neutral,
PublicKeyToken=b77a5c561934e089
    System.Numerics, Version=4.0.0.0, Culture=neutral,
PublicKeyToken=b77a5c561934e089
    System.Messaging, Version=4.0.0.0, Culture=neutral,
PublicKeyToken=b03f5f7f11d50a3a
    System.DirectoryServices, Version=4.0.0.0, Culture=neutral,
PublicKeyToken=b03f5f7f11d50a3a
    System.Transactions, Version=4.0.0.0, Culture=neutral,
PublicKeyToken=b77a5c561934e089
    System.EnterpriseServices, Version=4.0.0.0, Culture=neutral,
PublicKeyToken=b03f5f7f11d50a3a
    System.Runtime.Remoting, Version=4.0.0.0, Culture=neutral,
PublicKeyToken=b77a5c561934e089
    System.Web, Version=4.0.0.0, Culture=neutral, PublicKeyToken=b03f5f7f11d50a3a
    System.Drawing, Version=4.0.0.0, Culture=neutral,
PublicKeyToken=b03f5f7f11d50a3a
    System.Data, Version=4.0.0.0, Culture=neutral,
PublicKeyToken=b77a5c561934e089
    System.Web.RegularExpressions, Version=4.0.0.0, Culture=neutral,
PublicKeyToken=b03f5f7f11d50a3a
    System.Design, Version=4.0.0.0, Culture=neutral,
PublicKeyToken=b03f5f7f11d50a3a
    System.Windows.Forms, Version=4.0.0.0, Culture=neutral,
PublicKeyToken=b77a5c561934e089
    Accessibility, Version=4.0.0.0, Culture=neutral,
PublicKeyToken=b03f5f7f11d50a3a
    System.Runtime.Serialization.Formatters.Soap, Version=4.0.0.0,
    Culture=neutral,
PublicKeyToken=b03f5f7f11d50a3a
    System.Deployment, Version=4.0.0.0, Culture=neutral,
PublicKeyToken=b03f5f7f11d50a3a
    System.Data.OracleClient, Version=4.0.0.0, Culture=neutral,
PublicKeyToken=b77a5c561934e089
    System.Drawing.Design, Version=4.0.0.0, Culture=neutral,
PublicKeyToken=b03f5f7f11d50a3a
```

```
    System.Web.ApplicationServices, Version=4.0.0.0, Culture=neutral,
PublicKeyToken=31bf3856ad364e35
    System.ComponentModel.DataAnnotations, Version=4.0.0.0, Culture=neutral,
PublicKeyToken=31bf3856ad364e35
    System.DirectoryServices.Protocols, Version=4.0.0.0, Culture=neutral,
PublicKeyToken=b03f5f7f11d50a3a
    System.Runtime.Caching, Version=4.0.0.0, Culture=neutral,
PublicKeyToken=b03f5f7f11d50a3a
    System.ServiceProcess, Version=4.0.0.0, Culture=neutral,
PublicKeyToken=b03f5f7f11d50a3a
    System.Configuration.Install, Version=4.0.0.0, Culture=neutral,
PublicKeyToken=b03f5f7f11d50a3a
    System.Runtime.Serialization, Version=4.0.0.0, Culture=neutral,
PublicKeyToken=b77a5c561934e089
    System.ServiceModel.Internals, Version=4.0.0.0, Culture=neutral,
PublicKeyToken=31bf3856ad364e35
    SMDiagnostics, Version=4.0.0.0, Culture=neutral,
    PublicKeyToken=b77a5c561934e089
    System.Web.Services, Version=4.0.0.0, Culture=neutral,
PublicKeyToken=b03f5f7f11d50a3a
    Microsoft.Build.Utilities.v4.0, Version=4.0.0.0, Culture=neutral,
PublicKeyToken=b03f5f7f11d50a3a
    Microsoft.Build.Framework, Version=4.0.0.0, Culture=neutral,
PublicKeyToken=b03f5f7f11d50a3a
    System.Xaml, Version=4.0.0.0, Culture=neutral,
    PublicKeyToken=b77a5c561934e089
    Microsoft.Build.Tasks.v4.0, Version=4.0.0.0, Culture=neutral,
PublicKeyToken=b03f5f7f11d50a3a
    NorthwindLinq2Sql, Version=1.0.0.0, Culture=neutral,
PublicKeyToken=fe85c3941fbcc4c5
    System.Data.Linq, Version=4.0.0.0, Culture=neutral,
PublicKeyToken=b77a5c561934e089
    System.Xml.Linq, Version=4.0.0.0, Culture=neutral,
PublicKeyToken=b77a5c561934e089
    EntityFramework, Version=6.0.0.0, Culture=neutral,
PublicKeyToken=b77a5c561934e089
    Microsoft.CSharp, Version=4.0.0.0, Culture=neutral,
PublicKeyToken=b03f5f7f11d50a3a
    System.Dynamic, Version=4.0.0.0, Culture=neutral,
    PublicKeyToken=b03f5f7f11d50a3a
    System.Data.DataSetExtensions, Version=4.0.0.0, Culture=neutral,
PublicKeyToken=b77a5c561934e089
```

Discussion

Obtaining the imported types in an assembly is useful in determining what assemblies another assembly is using. This knowledge can greatly aid you in learning to use a new assembly. This method can also help you determine dependencies between assemblies for shipping purposes or to perform compliance management if you are restricted from using or exporting certain types of assemblies.

The `GetReferencedAssemblies` method of the `System.Reflection.Assembly` class obtains a list of all the imported assemblies. This method accepts no parameters and returns an array of `AssemblyName` objects instead of an array of `Types`. The `Assembly Name` type is made up of members that allow access to the information about an assembly, such as the name, version, culture information, public/private key pairs, and other data.

To call the `BuildDependentAssemblyList` method on the current executable, run this example code:

```
string file = GetProcessPath();

StringCollection assemblies = new StringCollection();

ReflectionAndDynamicProgramming.BuildDependentAssemblyList(file,assemblies);

Console.WriteLine($"Assembly {file} has a dependency tree of these
assemblies:{Environment.NewLine}");
foreach(string name in assemblies)
{
    Console.WriteLine($"\t{name}{Environment.NewLine}");
}
```

`GetProcessPath`, shown here, returns the current path to the process executable:

```
private static string GetProcessPath()
{
    // fix the path so that if running under the debugger we get the original
    // file
    string processName = Process.GetCurrentProcess().MainModule.FileName;
    int index = processName.IndexOf("vshost", StringComparison.Ordinal);
    if (index != -1)
    {
        string first = processName.Substring(0, index);
        int numChars = processName.Length - (index + 7);
        string second = processName.Substring(index + 7, numChars);

        processName = first + second;
    }
    return processName;
}
```

Note that this method does not account for assemblies loaded via `Assembly. Reflec tionOnlyLoad*` methods, as it is inspecting for only compile-time references.

When loading assemblies for inspection using reflection, you should use the `ReflectionOnlyLoad*` methods. These methods do not allow you to execute code from the loaded assembly. The reasoning is that you may not know if you are loading assemblies containing hostile code or not. These methods prevent any hostile code from executing.

See Also

The "Assembly Class" topic in the MSDN documentation.

6.2 Determining Type Characteristics in Assemblies

Problem

You need to find types with certain characteristics in an assembly, such as:

- By method name
- Types available outside the assembly
- Serializable types
- Subclasses of a given type
- Nested types

Solution

Use reflection to enumerate the types that match the characteristics you are looking for. For the characteristics we have outlined, you would use the methods listed in Table 6-1.

Table 6-1. Finding types by characteristics

Characteristic	Reflection method
Method name	`Type.GetMember`
Exported types	`Assembly.GetExportedTypes()`
Serializable types	`Type.IsSerializeable`
Subclasses of a type	`Type.IsSubclassOf`
Nested types	`Type.GetNestedTypes`

To find methods by name in an assembly, use the extension method `GetMembersInAssembly`:

```
public static IEnumerable<MemberInfo> GetMembersInAssembly(this Assembly asm,
    string memberName) =>
    from type in asm.GetTypes()
        from ms in type.GetMember(memberName, MemberTypes.All,
            BindingFlags.Public | BindingFlags.NonPublic |
            BindingFlags.Static | BindingFlags.Instance)
        select ms;
```

GetMembersInAssembly uses Type.GetMember to search for all members that have a matching name and returns the set of MethodInfos for those:

```
var members = asm.GetMembersInAssembly(memberSearchName);
```

For types available outside an assembly, use Assembly.GetExportedTypes to obtain the exported types of an assembly:

```
var types = asm.GetExportedTypes();
```

To determine the Serializable types in an assembly, use the extension method Get SerializableTypes:

```
public static IEnumerable<Type> GetSerializableTypes(this Assembly asm) =>
    from type in asm.GetTypes()
    where type.IsSerializable &&
        !type.IsNestedPrivate // filters out anonymous types
    select type;
```

GetSerializableType uses the Type.IsSerializable property to determine if the type supports serialization and returns a set of serializable types. Instead of testing the implemented interfaces and attributes on every type, you can query the Type.IsSeri alized property to determine whether it is marked as serializable:

```
var serializeableTypes = asm.GetSerializableTypes();
```

To get the set of types in an assembly that subclass a particular type, use the extension method GetSubclassesForType:

```
public static IEnumerable<Type> GetSubclassesForType(this Assembly asm,
                                                      Type baseClassType) =>
    from type in asm.GetTypes()
    where type.IsSubclassOf(baseClassType)
    select type;
```

GetSubclassesForType uses the Type.IsSubclassOf method to determine which types in the assembly subclass the given type and accepts an assembly path string and a type to represent the base class. This method returns an IEnumerable<Type> representing the subclasses of the type passed to the baseClassType parameter. In the example, first you get the assembly path from the current process, and then you set up use of CSharpRecipes.ReflectionUtils+BaseOverrides as the type to test for subclasses. You call GetSubClassesForType, and it returns an IEnumerable<Type>:

```
Type type = Type.GetType(
    "CSharpRecipes.ReflectionAndDynamicProgramming+BaseOverrides");
var subClasses = asm.GetSubclassesForType(type);
```

Finally, to determine the nested types in an assembly, use the extension method Get
NestedTypes:

```
public static IEnumerable<Type> GetNestedTypes(this Assembly asm) =>
    from t in asm.GetTypes()
        from t2 in t.GetNestedTypes(BindingFlags.Instance |
                    BindingFlags.Static |
                    BindingFlags.Public |
                    BindingFlags.NonPublic)
        where !t2.IsEnum && !t2.IsInterface &&
            !t2.IsNestedPrivate // filters out anonymous types
        select t2;
```

GetNestedTypes uses the Type.GetNestedTypes method and inspects each type in
the assembly to determine if it has nested types:

```
var nestedTypes = asm.GetNestedTypes();
```

Discussion

Why should you care about these random facts about types in assemblies? Because
they help you figure out how you are constructing your code and discover coding
practices you may or may not want to allow. Let's look at each one individually so you
can see why you might want to know about it.

Method name

The memberName argument can contain the wildcard character * to indicate any character or characters. So, to find all methods starting with the string "Test", pass the
string "Test*" to the memberName parameter. Note that the memberName argument is
case-sensitive, but the asmPath argument is not. If you'd like to do a case-insensitive
search for members, add the BindingFlags.IgnoreCase flag to the other Binding
Flags in the call to Type.GetMember.

The GetMember method of the System.Type class is useful for finding one or more
methods within a type. This method returns an array of MemberInfo objects that
describe any members that match the given parameters.

> The * character may be used as a wildcard character only at the end
> of the *name* parameter string. If placed anywhere else in the string,
> it will not be treated as a wildcard character. In addition, it must be
> the only character in the *name* parameter to ensure that all mem-
> bers are returned. No other wildcard characters, such as ?, are sup-
> ported.

Once you obtain an array of `MemberInfo` objects, you need to examine what kind of members they are. The `MemberInfo` class contains a `MemberType` property that returns a `System.Reflection.MemberTypes` enumeration value, which can be any of the values defined in Table 6-2 except `All`.

Table 6-2. MemberTypes enumeration values

Enumeration value	Definition
All	All member types
Constructor	A constructor member
Custom	A custom member type
Event	An event member
Field	A field member
Method	A method member
NestedType	A nested type
Property	A property member
TypeInfo	A type member that represents a `TypeInfo` member

Exported types

Obtaining the exported types in an assembly is useful when you are trying to determine the public interface to that assembly. This ability can greatly aid someone learning to use a new assembly or can aid the assembly developer in determining all the assembly's access points to verify that they are adequately secure from malicious code. To get these exported types, use the `GetExportedTypes` method on the `System.Reflection.Assembly` type. The exported types consist of all of the types that are publicly accessible from outside of the assembly. A type may be publicly accessible but not be accessible from outside of the assembly. Take, for example, the following code:

```
public class Outer
{
    public class Inner {}
    private class SecretInner {}
}
```

The exported types are `Outer` and `Outer.Inner`; the type `SecretInner` is not exposed to the world outside of this assembly. If you change the `Outer` accessibility from `public` to `private`, you now have no types accessible to the outside world—the `Inner` class access level is downgraded because of the `private` on the `Outer` class.

Serializable types

A type may be marked as serializable with the `SerializableAttribute` attribute. Testing for `SerializableAttribute` on a type can turn into a fair amount of work. This is because `SerializableAttribute` is a magic attribute that the C# compiler actually strips off your code at compile time. Using `ildasm` (the .NET platform decompiler), you will see that this custom attribute just isn't there—normally you see a `.custom` entry for each custom attribute, but not with `SerializableAttribute`. The C# compiler removes it and instead sets a flag in the metadata of the class. In source code, it looks like a custom attribute, but it compiles into one of a small set of attributes that gets a special representation in metadata. That's why it gets special treatment in the reflection APIs. Fortunately, you do not have to do all of this work. The `IsSerializable` property on the `Type` class returns `true` if the current type is marked as serializable with the `SerializableAttribute`; otherwise, this property returns `false`.

Subclasses of a type

The `IsSubclassOf` method on the `Type` class allows you to determine whether the current type is a subclass of the type passed in to this method. Knowing if a type has been subclassed allows you to explore the type hierarchy that your team or company has created and can lead to opportunities for code reuse, refactoring, or developing a better understanding of the dependencies in the code base.

Nested types

Determining the nested types allows you to programmatically examine various aspects of some design patterns. Various design patterns may specify that a type will contain another type; for example, the Decorator and State design patterns make use of object containment.

The `GetNestedTypes` extension method uses a LINQ query to query all types in the assembly specified by the `asmPath` parameter. The LINQ query also queries for the nested types with the assembly by using the `Type.GetNestedTypes` method of the `Type` class.

Usually the dot operator is used to delimit namespaces and types; however, nested types are somewhat special. You set nested types apart from other types by using the + operator in their fully qualified name when dealing with them in the reflection APIs. By passing this fully qualified name in to the static `GetType` methods, you can acquire the actual type that it represents.

These methods return a `Type` object that represents the type identified by the `type Name` parameter.

Calling `Type.GetType` to retrieve a type defined in a dynamic assembly (one that is created using the types defined in the `System.Reflection.Emit` namespace) returns a `null` if that assembly has not already been persisted to disk. Typically, you would use the static `Assembly.GetType` method on the dynamic assembly's `Assembly` object.

See Also

The "Assembly Class," "Type Class," "TypeAttributes Enumeration," "Determining and Obtaining Nested Types Within an Assembly," "BindingFlags Enumeration," "MemberInfo Class," and "Finding Members in an Assembly" topics in the MSDN documentation.

6.3 Determining Inheritance Characteristics

Problem

You need to determine the inheritance characteristics of types such as:

- The inheritance hierarchy
- Base class methods that are overridden

Solution

Use reflection to enumerate the inheritance chains and base class method overrides, as shown in Table 6-3.

Table 6-3. Finding types by characteristics

Characteristic	Reflection method
Inheritance hierarchy	`Type.BaseType`
Base class methods	`MethodInfo.GetBaseDefinition`

Use the extension method `GetInheritanceChain` to retrieve the entire inheritance hierarchy for a single type. `GetInheritanceChain` uses the `GetBaseTypes` method to enumerate the types and then reverses the default order to present the enumerated list sorted from base type to derived type. In other words, when `GetBaseTypes` traverses the `BaseType` property of each type it encounters, the resulting list of types is ordered from most derived to least derived, so we call `Reverse` to order the list with the least derived type (`Object`) first:

```
public static IEnumerable<Type> GetInheritanceChain(this Type derivedType) =>
    (from t in derivedType.GetBaseTypes()
    select t).Reverse();

private static IEnumerable<Type> GetBaseTypes(this Type type)
{
    Type current = type;
    while (current != null)
    {
        yield return current;
        current = current.BaseType;
    }
}
```

If you wanted to do this for all types in an assembly, you could use the extension method GetTypeHierarchies, which uses the custom TypeHierarchy class to represent the derived type and its inheritance chain:

```
public class TypeHierarchy
{
    public Type DerivedType { get; set; }
    public IEnumerable<Type> InheritanceChain { get; set; }
}

public static IEnumerable<TypeHierarchy> GetTypeHierarchies(this Assembly asm) =>
    from Type type in asm.GetTypes()
    select new TypeHierarchy
    {
        DerivedType = type,
        InheritanceChain = GetInheritanceChain(type)
    };
```

GetTypeHierarchies projects each type as the DerivedType and uses GetInheritanceChain to determine the InheritanceChain for the type.

To determine if base class methods are being overridden, use the MethodInfo.GetBaseDefinition method to determine which method is overridden in what base class. The extension method GetMethodOverrides shown in Example 6-1 examines all of the public instance methods in a class and displays which methods override their respective base class methods. This method also determines which base class the overridden method is in. This extension method is based on Type and uses the type to find overriding methods.

Example 6-2. The GetMethodOverrides methods

```
public class ReflectionUtils
{
    public static IEnumerable<MemberInfo> GetMethodOverrides(this Type type) =>
        from ms in type.GetMethods(BindingFlags.Instance |
                            BindingFlags.NonPublic | BindingFlags.Public |
```

```
                         BindingFlags.Static | BindingFlags.DeclaredOnly)
            where ms != ms.GetBaseDefinition()
            select ms.GetBaseDefinition;
```

The next extension method, GetBaseMethodOverridden, allows you to determine whether a particular method overrides a method in its base class and to get the Meth odInfo for that overridden method back. It also extends Type, the full method name, and an array of Type objects representing its parameter types:

```
public class ReflectionUtils
{
    public static MethodInfo GetBaseMethodOverridden(this Type type,
                                    string methodName, Type[] paramTypes)
    {
        MethodInfo method = type.GetMethod(methodName, paramTypes);
        MethodInfo baseDef = method?.GetBaseDefinition();
        if (baseDef != method)
        {
            bool foundMatch = (from p in baseDef.GetParameters()
                        join op in paramTypes
                            on p.ParameterType.UnderlyingSystemType
                                equals op.UnderlyingSystemType
                        select p).Any();

            if (foundMatch)
                return baseDef;
        }
        return null;
    }
}
```

Discussion

Inheritance hierarchy

Unfortunately, no property of the Type class exists to obtain the inheritance hierarchy of a type. The DisplayInheritanceChain methods in this recipe, however, allow you to do so. All that is required is the assembly path and the name of the type with the inheritance hierarchy you wish to obtain. The DisplayInheritanceChain method requires only an assembly path since it displays the inheritance hierarchy for all types within that assembly.

The core code of this recipe exists in the GetBaseTypes method. This is a recursive method that walks each inherited type until it finds the ultimate base class—which is always the object class. Once it arrives at this ultimate base class, it returns to its caller. Each time the method returns to its caller, the next base class in the inheritance hierarchy is added to the list until the final GetBaseTypes method returns the completed inheritance chain.

To display the inheritance chain of a type, use the `DisplayInheritanceChain` method call.

```
private static void DisplayInheritanceChain(IEnumerable<Type> chain)
{
    StringBuilder builder = new StringBuilder();
    foreach (var type in chain)
    {
        if (builder.Length == 0)
            builder.Append(type.Name);
        else
            builder.AppendFormat($"<-{type.Name}");
    }
    Console.WriteLine($"Base Type List: {builder.ToString()}");
}
```

To display the inheritance hierarchy of all types in an assembly, use `GetTypeHierar chies` in conjunction with `DisplayInheritanceChain`:

```
// all types in the assembly
var typeHierarchies = asm.GetTypeHierarchies();
foreach (var th in typeHierarchies)
{
    // Recurse over all base types
    Console.WriteLine($"Derived Type: {th.DerivedType.FullName}");
    DisplayInheritanceChain(th.InheritanceChain);
    Console.WriteLine();
}
```

These methods result in output like the following:

```
Derived Type: CSharpRecipes.Reflection
Base Type List: Object<-Reflection
Derived Type: CSharpRecipes.ReflectionUtils+BaseOverrides
Base Type List: Object<-BaseOverrides

Derived Type: CSharpRecipes.ReflectionUtils+DerivedOverrides
Base Type List: Object<-BaseOverrides <-DerivedOverrides
```

This output shows that the base type list (or inheritance hierarchy) of the `Reflection` class in the `CSharpRecipes` namespace starts with `Object` (like all class and struct types in .NET). The nested class `BaseOverrides` also shows a base type list starting with `Object`. The nested class `DerivedOverrides` shows a more interesting base type list, where `DerivedOverrides` derives from `BaseOverrides`, which derives from `Object`.

Base class methods that are overridden

Determining which methods override their base class methods would be a tedious chore if it were not for the `GetBaseDefinition` method of the `System.Reflec tion.MethodInfo` type. This method takes no parameters and returns a `MethodInfo` object that corresponds to the overridden method in the base class. If this method is used on a `MethodInfo` object representing a method that is not being overridden—as is the case with a virtual or abstract method—`GetBaseDefinition` returns the original `MethodInfo` object.

The `Type` object's `GetMethod` method is called when both the method name and its parameter array are passed in to `GetBaseMethodOverridden`; otherwise, `GetMethods` is used for `GetMethodOverrides`. If the method is correctly located and its `Method Info` object obtained, the `GetBaseDefinition` method is called on that `MethodInfo` object to get the first overridden method in the nearest base class in the inheritance hierarchy. This `MethodInfo` type is compared to the `MethodInfo` type on which the `GetBaseDefinition` method was called. If these two objects are the same, it means that there were no overridden methods in any base classes; therefore, nothing is returned. This code will return only the overridden method; if no methods are overridden, then `null` is returned.

The following code shows how to use each of these overloaded methods:

```
Type derivedType =
  asm.GetType("CSharpRecipes.ReflectionAndDynamicProgramming+DerivedOverrides",
    true, true);

var methodOverrides = derivedType.GetMethodOverrides();
foreach (MethodInfo mi in methodOverrides)
{
    Console.WriteLine();
    Console.WriteLine($"Current Method: {mi.ToString()}");
    Console.WriteLine($"Base Type FullName:  {mi.DeclaringType.FullName}");
    Console.WriteLine($"Base Method:  {mi.ToString()}");
    // list the types of this method
    foreach (ParameterInfo pi in mi.GetParameters())
    {
        Console.WriteLine($"\tParam {pi.Name} : {pi.ParameterType.ToString()}");
    }
}

// try the signature findmethodoverrides
string methodName = "Foo";
var baseTypeMethodInfo = derivedType.GetBaseMethodOverridden(methodName,
    new Type[3] { typeof(long), typeof(double), typeof(byte[]) });
Console.WriteLine(
    $"{Environment.NewLine}For [Type] Method: [{derivedType.Name}]" +
    $" {methodName}");
Console.WriteLine(
    $"Base Type FullName: {baseTypeMethodInfo.ReflectedType.FullName}");
Console.WriteLine($"Base Method: {baseTypeMethodInfo}");
foreach (ParameterInfo pi in baseTypeMethodInfo.GetParameters())
{
    // list the params so we can see which one we got
```

```
        Console.WriteLine($"\tParam {pi.Name} : {pi.ParameterType.ToString()}");
    }
```

In the usage code, you get the path to the test code assembly (*CSharpRecipes.exe*) via
the Process class. You then use that to find a class that has been defined in the Reflec
tionUtils class, called DerivedOverrides, which derives from BaseOverrides. Deri
vedOverrides and BaseOverrides are both shown here:

```
public abstract class BaseOverrides
{
    public abstract void Foo(string str, int i);

    public abstract void Foo(long l, double d, byte[] bytes);
}

public class DerivedOverrides : BaseOverrides
{
    public override void Foo(string str, int i)
    {
    }

    public override void Foo(long l, double d, byte[] bytes)
    {
    }
}
```

GetMethodOverrides returns every overridden method for each method it finds in
the Reflection.DerivedOverrides type. If you want to display all overriding methods and their corresponding overridden methods, you can remove the Binding
Flags.DeclaredOnly binding enumeration from the GetMethods method call:

```
return from ms in type.GetMethods(BindingFlags.Instance |
        BindingFlags.NonPublic | BindingFlags.Public)
    where ms != ms.GetBaseDefinition()
    select ms.GetBaseDefinition();
```

GetBaseMethodOverridden passes a method name, and the parameters for this
method, to find the override that specifically matches the signature based on the
parameters. In this case, the parameter types of method Foo are long, double, and
byte[]. This method displays the method that DerivedOverrides.Foo overrides.

See Also

The "Assembly Class," "Type.BaseType Method," "Finding Members in an Assembly,"
"MethodInfo Class," and "ParameterInfo Class" topics in the MSDN documentation.

6.4 Invoking Members Using Reflection

Problem

You have a list of method names that you wish to invoke dynamically within your application. As your code executes, it will pull names off this list and attempt to invoke these methods. This technique might be useful to create a test harness for components that reads in the methods to execute from an XML (or JSON) file and executes them with the given arguments.

Solution

The `TestReflectionInvocation` method shown in Example 6-3 calls the `ReflectionInvoke` method, which opens the XML configuration file, reads out the test information using LINQ, and executes each test method.

Example 6-3. Invoking members via reflection

```
public static void TestReflectionInvocation()
{
    XDocument xdoc =
        XDocument.Load(@"..\..\SampleClassLibrary\SampleClassLibraryTests.xml");
    ReflectionInvoke(xdoc, @"SampleClassLibrary.dll");
}
```

This is the XML document in which the test method information is contained:

```
<?xml version="1.0" encoding="utf-8" ?>
<Tests>
    <Test className='SampleClassLibrary.SampleClass'
    methodName='TestMethod1'>
        <Argument>Running TestMethod1</Argument>
    </Test>
    <Test className='SampleClassLibrary.SampleClass'
    methodName='TestMethod2'>
        <Parameter>Running TestMethod2</Parameter>
        <Parameter>27</Parameter>
    </Test>
</Tests>
```

`ReflectionInvoke`, as shown in Example 6-4, dynamically invokes the method that is passed to it using the information contained in the `XDocument`. This code determines each parameter's type by examining the `ParameterInfo` items on the `MethodInfo`, and then converts the values to the actual type from a string via the `Convert.Change Type` method. Finally, the return value of the invoked method is returned by the `Meth odBase.Invoke` method.

Example 6-4. ReflectionInvoke method

```
public static void ReflectionInvoke(XDocument xdoc, string asmPath)
{
    var test = from t in xdoc.Root.Elements("Test")
               select new
               {
                   typeName = (string)t.Attribute("className").Value,
                   methodName = (string)t.Attribute("methodName").Value,
                   parameter = from p in t.Elements("Parameter")
                               select new { arg = p.Value }
               };

    // Load the assembly
    Assembly asm = Assembly.LoadFrom(asmPath);

    foreach (var elem in test)
    {
        // create the actual type
        Type reflClassType = asm.GetType(elem.typeName, true, false);

        // Create an instance of this type and verify that it exists
        object reflObj = Activator.CreateInstance(reflClassType);
        if (reflObj != null)
        {
            // Verify that the method exists and get its MethodInfo obj
            MethodInfo invokedMethod = reflClassType.GetMethod(elem.methodName);
            if (invokedMethod != null)
            {
                // Create the argument list for the dynamically invoked methods
                object[] arguments = new object[elem.parameter.Count()];
                int index = 0;

                // for each parameter, add it to the list
                foreach (var arg in elem.parameter)
                {
                    // get the type of the parameter
                    Type paramType =
                        invokedMethod.GetParameters()[index].ParameterType;

                    // change the value to that type and assign it
                    arguments[index] =
                        Convert.ChangeType(arg.arg, paramType);
                    index++;
                }

                // Invoke the method with the parameters
                object retObj = invokedMethod.Invoke(reflObj, arguments);

                Console.WriteLine($"\tReturned object: {retObj}");
                Console.WriteLine($"\tReturned object: {retObj.GetType().FullName}");
            }
```

```
            }
        }
    }
```

These are the dynamically invoked methods located on the `SampleClass` type in the `SampleClassLibrary` assembly:

```
public bool TestMethod1(string text)
{
    Console.WriteLine(text);
    return (true);
}

public bool TestMethod2(string text, int n)
{
    Console.WriteLine(text + " invoked with {0}",n);
    return (true);
}
```

And here is the output from these methods:

```
Running TestMethod1
        Returned object: True
        Returned object: System.Boolean
Running TestMethod2 invoked with 27
        Returned object: True
        Returned object: System.Boolean
```

Discussion

Reflection enables you to dynamically invoke both static and instance methods within a type in either the same assembly or in a different one. This can be a very powerful tool to allow your code to determine at runtime which method to call. This determination can be based on an assembly name, a type name, or a method name, though the assembly name is not required if the method exists in the same assembly as the invoking code, if you already have the `Assembly` object, or if you have a `Type` object for the class the method is on.

 As always, with great power comes great responsibility. Dynamically loading an assembly without knowing the origin (or even invoking a legit one in an elevated context) can cause unwanted consequences, so use this technique wisely and securely!

This technique may seem similar to delegates since both can dynamically determine at runtime which method is to be called. Delegates, on the whole, require you to know signatures of methods you might call at runtime, whereas with reflection, you can invoke methods when you have no idea of the signature, providing a much looser binding. However, you will still have to pass in reasonable arguments. More dynamic invocation can be achieved with `Delegate.DynamicInvoke`, but this is more of a reflection-based method than the traditional delegate invocation.

The `DynamicInvoke` method shown in the Solution contains all the code required to dynamically invoke a method. This code first loads the assembly using its assembly name (passed in through the `asmPath` parameter). Next, it gets the `Type` object for the class containing the method to invoke (it obtains the class name from the `Test` element's `className` attribute using LINQ). It then retrieves the method name from the `Test` element's `methodName` attribute using LINQ. Once you have all of the information from the `Test` element, an instance of the `Type` object is created, and you then invoke the specified method on this created instance:

- First, the static `Activator.CreateInstance` method is called to actually create an instance of the `Type` object contained in the local variable `dynClassType`. The method returns an object reference to the instance of `type` that was created or throws an exception if the object cannot be created.

- Once you have successfully obtained the instance of this class, the `MethodInfo` object of the method to be invoked is acquired through a call to `GetMethod` on the `Type` object.

The instance of the object created with the `CreateInstance` method is then passed as the first parameter to the `MethodInfo.Invoke` method. This method returns an object containing the return value of the invoked method. This object is then returned by `InvokeMethod`. The second parameter to `MethodInfo.Invoke` is an object array containing any parameters to be passed to this method. This array is constructed based on the number of `Parameter` elements under each `Test` element in the XML. You then look at the `ParameterInfo` of each parameter (obtained from `MethodInfo. Get Parameters`) and use the `Convert.ChangeType` method to coerce the string value from the XML to the proper type.

The `DynamicInvoke` method finally displays each returned object value and its type. Note that there is no extra logic required to return different return values from the invoked methods since they are all returned as an object, unlike when you pass differing arguments to the invoked methods.

See Also

The "Activator Class," "MethodInfo Class," "Convert.ChangeType Method," and "ParameterInfo Class" topics in the MSDN documentation.

6.5 Accessing Local Variable Information

Problem

You are building a tool that examines code, and you need to get access to the local variables within a method.

Solution

Use the `LocalVariables` property on the `MethodBody` class to return an `IList` of `LocalVariableInfo` objects, each of which describes a local variable within the method:

```
public static ReadOnlyCollection<LocalVariableInfo>
GetLocalVars(string asmPath, string typeName, string methodName)
{
    Assembly asm = Assembly.LoadFrom(asmPath);
    Type asmType = asm.GetType(typeName);
    MethodInfo mi = asmType.GetMethod(methodName);
    MethodBody mb = mi.GetMethodBody();

    System.Collections.ObjectModel.ReadOnlyCollection<LocalVariableInfo> vars =
        (System.Collections.ObjectModel.ReadOnlyCollection<LocalVariableInfo>)
            mb.LocalVariables;

    // Display information about each local variable
    foreach (LocalVariableInfo lvi in vars)
    {
        Console.WriteLine($"IsPinned: {lvi.IsPinned}");
        Console.WriteLine($"LocalIndex: {lvi.LocalIndex}");
        Console.WriteLine($"LocalType.Module: {lvi.LocalType.Module}");
        Console.WriteLine($"LocalType.FullName: {lvi.LocalType.FullName}");
        Console.WriteLine($"ToString(): {lvi.ToString()}");
    }

    return (vars);
}
```

You can call the `GetLocalVars` method using the following code:

```
public static void TestGetLocalVars()
{
    string file = GetProcessPath();

    // Get all local var info for the
    // CSharpRecipes.Reflection.GetLocalVars method
    System.Collections.ObjectModel.ReadOnlyCollection<LocalVariableInfo> vars =
        GetLocalVars(file, "CSharpRecipes.ReflectionAndDynamicProgramming",
            "GetLocalVars");
}
```

GetProcessPath, shown here, returns the current path to the process executable:

```
private static string GetProcessPath()
{
    // fix the path so that if running under the debugger we get the
    // original file
    string processName = Process.GetCurrentProcess().MainModule.FileName;
    int index = processName.IndexOf("vshost", StringComparison.Ordinal);
    if (index != -1)
    {
        string first = processName.Substring(0, index);
        int numChars = processName.Length - (index + 7);
        string second = processName.Substring(index + 7, numChars);

        processName = first + second;
    }
    return processName;
}
```

Here is the output of this method:

```
IsPinned: False
LocalIndex: 0
LocalType.Module: CommonLanguageRuntimeLibrary
LocalType.FullName: System.Reflection.Assembly
ToString(): System.Reflection.Assembly (0)
IsPinned: False
LocalIndex: 1
LocalType.Module: CommonLanguageRuntimeLibrary
LocalType.FullName: System.Type
ToString(): System.Type (1)
IsPinned: False
LocalIndex: 2
LocalType.Module: CommonLanguageRuntimeLibrary
LocalType.FullName: System.Reflection.MethodInfo
ToString(): System.Reflection.MethodInfo (2)
IsPinned: False
LocalIndex: 3
LocalType.Module: CommonLanguageRuntimeLibrary
LocalType.FullName: System.Reflection.MethodBody
ToString(): System.Reflection.MethodBody (3)
IsPinned: False
LocalIndex: 4
LocalType.Module: CommonLanguageRuntimeLibrary
LocalType.FullName: System.Collections.ObjectModel.ReadOnlyCollection`1[[System.
Reflection.LocalVariableInfo, mscorlib, Version=4.0.0.0, Culture=neutral, Public
KeyToken=b77a5c561934e089]]
ToString(): System.Collections.ObjectModel.ReadOnlyCollection`1[System.Reflectio
n.LocalVariableInfo] (4)
IsPinned: False
LocalIndex: 5
LocalType.Module: CommonLanguageRuntimeLibrary
LocalType.FullName: System.Collections.Generic.IEnumerator`1[[System.Reflection.
```

```
LocalVariableInfo, mscorlib, Version=4.0.0.0, Culture=neutral, PublicKeyToken=b7
7a5c561934e089]]
ToString(): System.Collections.Generic.IEnumerator`1[System.Reflection.LocalVari
ableInfo] (5)
IsPinned: False
LocalIndex: 6
LocalType.Module: CommonLanguageRuntimeLibrary
LocalType.FullName: System.Reflection.LocalVariableInfo
ToString(): System.Reflection.LocalVariableInfo (6)
IsPinned: False
LocalIndex: 7
LocalType.Module: CommonLanguageRuntimeLibrary
LocalType.FullName: System.Collections.ObjectModel.ReadOnlyCollection`1[[System.
Reflection.LocalVariableInfo, mscorlib, Version=4.0.0.0, Culture=neutral, Public
KeyToken=b77a5c561934e089]]
ToString(): System.Collections.ObjectModel.ReadOnlyCollection`1[System.Reflectio
n.LocalVariableInfo] (7)
```

The `LocalVariableInfo` objects for each local variable found in the `CSharpRe
cipes.Reflection.GetLocalVars` method will be returned in the `vars` `IList` collec-
tion.

Discussion

The `LocalVariables` property can give you a good amount of information about
variables within a method. It returns an `IList<LocalVariableInfo>` collection. Each
`LocalVariableInfo` object contains the information described in Table 6-4.

Table 6-4. LocalVariableInfo information

Member	Definition
`IsPinned`	Returns a `bool` indicating if the object that this variable refers to is pinned in memory (`true`) or not (`false`). In unmanaged code, an object must be pinned before it can be referred to by an unmanaged pointer. While it is pinned, it cannot be moved by garbage collection.
`LocalIndex`	Returns the index of this variable within this method's body.
`LocalType`	Returns a `Type` object that describes the type of this variable.
`ToString`	Returns the `LocalType.FullName`, a space, and then the `LocalIndex` value surrounded by parentheses.

See Also

The "MethodInfo Class," "MethodBody Class," "ReadOnlyCollection<T> Class," and
"LocalVariableInfo Class" topics in the MSDN documentation.

6.6 Creating a Generic Type

Problem

You want to create a generic type using only the reflection APIs.

Solution

You create a generic type similarly to how you create a nongeneric type; however, there is an extra step to create the type arguments you want to use and to bind these type arguments to the generic type's type parameters at construction. You will use a new method added to the Type class called BindGenericParameters:

```
public static void CreateDictionary()
{
    // Get the type we want to construct
    Type typeToConstruct = typeof(Dictionary<,>);
    // Get the type arguments we want to construct our type with
    Type[] typeArguments = {typeof(int), typeof(string)};
    // Bind these type arguments to our generic type
    Type newType = typeToConstruct.MakeGenericType(typeArguments);

    // Construct our type
    Dictionary<int, string> dict =
        (Dictionary<int, string>)Activator.CreateInstance(newType);

    // Test our newly constructed type
    Console.WriteLine($"Count == {dict.Count}");
    dict.Add(1, "test1");
    Console.WriteLine($"Count == {dict.Count}");
}
```

This is the code to test the CreateDictionary method:

```
public static void TestCreateMultiMap()
{
    Assembly asm = Assembly.LoadFrom("C:\\CSCB6 " +
            "\\Code\\CSharpRecipes\\bin\\Debug\\CSharpRecipes.exe");
    CreateDictionary(asm);
}
```

And here is the output of this method:

```
Count == 0
Count == 1
```

Discussion

Type parameters are defined on a class and indicate that any type that can be converted to an Object can be substituted for this type parameter (unless, of course, there are constraints placed on this type parameter via the `where` keyword). For example, the following class has two type parameters, T and U:

```
public class Foo<T, U> {...}
```

 Of course, you do not have to use T and U; you can instead use another letter or even a full name, such as `TypeParam1` and `TypeParam2`.

A type argument is defined as the actual type that will be substituted for the type parameter. In the previously defined class Foo, you can replace type parameter T with the type argument `int`, and type parameter U with the type argument `string`.

The `BindGenericParameters` method allows you to substitute type parameters with actual type arguments. This method accepts a single `Type` array parameter. This `Type` array consists of each type argument that will be substituted for each type parameter of the generic type. These type arguments must be added to this `Type` array in the same order as they are defined on the class. For example, the Foo class defines type parameters T and U, in that order. The `Type` array that you define contains an `int` type and a `string` type, in that order. This means that the type parameter T will be substituted for the type argument `int`, and U will be replaced with a `string` type. The `BindGenericParameters` method returns a `Type` object of the type you specified along with the type arguments.

See Also

The "Type.BindGenericParameters method" topic in the MSDN documentation.

6.7 Using dynamic Versus object

Problem

You want to know the differences between using `dynamic` and `object` as the type specification.

Solution

To demonstrate the primary difference between `dynamic` and `object`, we will revisit the sample class we used in Recipe 6.4. That code dynamically loaded an instance of the `SampleClass` type and then, using an XML file and reflection, ran certain operations on the instance. That instance was of type `object`. If we created the type and made it `dynamic`, we could actually write the code to call the methods right in the code (giving up the flexibility of the first example but making the code much neater) even though our dynamic object instance is not of type SampleClass:

```
// Load the assembly
Assembly asm = Assembly.LoadFrom(@"SampleClassLibrary.dll");

// Get the SampleClass type
Type reflClassType = asm?.GetType("SampleClassLibrary.SampleClass", true, false);

if (reflClassType != null)
{
    // Create our sample class instance
    dynamic sampleClass = Activator.CreateInstance(reflClassType);
    Console.WriteLine($"LastMessage: {sampleClass.LastMessage}");
    Console.WriteLine("Calling TestMethod1");
    sampleClass.TestMethod1("Running TestMethod1");
    Console.WriteLine($"LastMessage: {sampleClass.LastMessage}");
    Console.WriteLine("Calling TestMethod2");
    sampleClass.TestMethod2("Running TestMethod2", 27);
    Console.WriteLine($"LastMessage: {sampleClass.LastMessage}");
}
```

Notice that we can call the methods directly without error even though the type of the object instance is dynamic. This is because the compiler knows to defer type checking of these calls (LastMessage, TestMethod1, TestMethod2) until runtime. Although dynamic is treated like object and even ultimately compiles to object, it tells the compiler, "Hey relax, I know what I'm doing!" and allows you to invoke methods and properties that the compiler can't resolve.

The output of this example is shown here:

```
LastMessage: Not set yet
Calling TestMethod1
Running TestMethod1
LastMessage: Running TestMethod1
Calling TestMethod2
Running TestMethod2 invoked with 27
LastMessage: Running TestMethod2
```

Discussion

The dynamic type allows you to bypass compile-time type checking and binds the operations to call sites at runtime.

 Just remember, if you aren't finding out until runtime, you might see exceptions you weren't expecting if you access things on a dynamic object that are not present.

Most of the time, dynamic acts just like object, with the main difference being the deferred checking. Once the operation for a dynamic type is invoked, the results of the binding are cached to help with performance the next time the operation is called. If you look at the IL for a dynamic method, you will see that the sampleClass local variable actually compiles down to the type object:

```
.locals init ([0] class [mscorlib]System.Reflection.Assembly asm,
        [1] class [mscorlib]System.Type reflClassType,
        [2] bool V_2,
        [3] object sampleClass)
```

If we tried to do the same operations on our SampleClass instance using object instead of dynamic, like this:

```
object objSampleClass = Activator.CreateInstance(reflClassType);
Console.WriteLine($"LastMessage: {objSampleClass.LastMessage}");
Console.WriteLine("Calling TestMethod1");
objSampleClass.TestMethod1("Running TestMethod1");
Console.WriteLine($"LastMessage: {objSampleClass.LastMessage}");
Console.WriteLine("Calling TestMethod2");
objSampleClass.TestMethod2("Running TestMethod2", 27);
Console.WriteLine($"LastMessage: {objSampleClass.LastMessage}");
```

We would get the following compiler errors:

```
Error CS1061  'object' does not contain a definition for 'LastMessage' and no
extension method 'LastMessage' accepting a first argument of type 'object' could
be found(are you missing a using directive or an assembly reference ?)
06_ReflectionAndDynamicProgramming.cs  482

Error CS1061  'object' does not contain a definition for 'TestMethod1' and no
extension method 'TestMethod1' accepting a first argument of type 'object' could
be found(are you missing a using directive or an assembly reference ?)
06_ReflectionAndDynamicProgramming.cs  484

Error CS1061  'object' does not contain a definition for 'LastMessage' and no
extension method 'LastMessage' accepting a first argument of type 'object' could
be found(are you missing a using directive or an assembly reference ?)
06_ReflectionAndDynamicProgramming.cs  485

Error CS1061  'object' does not contain a definition for 'TestMethod2' and no
extension method 'TestMethod2' accepting a first argument of type 'object' could
be found(are you missing a using directive or an assembly reference ?)
06_ReflectionAndDynamicProgramming.cs  487

Error CS1061  'object' does not contain a definition for 'LastMessage' and no
extension method 'LastMessage' accepting a first argument of type 'object' could
be found(are you missing a using directive or an assembly reference ?)
06_ReflectionAndDynamicProgramming.cs  488
```

See Also

The "dynamic" topic in the MSDN documentation.

6.8 Building Objects Dynamically

Problem

You want to be able to build up an object to work with on the fly at runtime.

Solution

Use ExpandoObject to create an object that you can add properties, methods, and events to and be able to bind data to in a user interface.

We can use ExpandoObject to create an initial object to hold someone's Name and current Country:

```
dynamic expando = new ExpandoObject();
expando.Name = "Brian";
expando.Country = "USA";
```

Once we have added properties directly, we can also add properties to our object in a more dynamic fashion using the AddProperty method we have provided for you. One example of why you might do this is to add properties to your object from another source of data. We will add the Language property:

```
// Add properties dynamically to expando
AddProperty(expando, "Language", "English");
```

The AddProperty method takes advantage of ExpandoObject's support for IDiction ary<string, object> and allows us to add properties using values we determine at runtime:

```
public static void AddProperty(ExpandoObject expando, string propertyName,
    object propertyValue)
{
    // ExpandoObject supports IDictionary so we can extend it like this
    var expandoDict = expando as IDictionary<string, object>;
    if (expandoDict.ContainsKey(propertyName))
        expandoDict[propertyName] = propertyValue;
    else
        expandoDict.Add(propertyName, propertyValue);
}
```

We can also add methods to the ExpandoObject by using the Func<> generic type, which represents a method call. In our example, we will add a validation method for our object:

```
// Add method to expando
expando.IsValid = (Func<bool>)(() =>
{
    // Check that they supplied a name
    if(string.IsNullOrWhiteSpace(expando.Name))
        return false;
    return true;
});

if(!expando.IsValid())
{
    // Don't allow continuation...
}
```

Now we can also define and add events to the ExpandoObject using the Action<>
generic type. We will add two events, LanguageChanged and CountryChanged. We'll
add LanguageChanged after defining the eventHandler variable to hold the
Action<object,EventArgs>, and we'll add CountryChanged directly as an inline
anonymous method. CountryChanged looks at the Country that changed and invokes
the LanguageChanged event with the proper Language for the Country. (Note that Lan
guageChanged is also an anonymous method, but sometimes it can make for cleaner
code to have a variable for these.)

```
// You can also add event handlers to expando objects
var eventHandler =
    new Action<object, EventArgs>((sender, eventArgs) =>
    {
        dynamic exp = sender as ExpandoObject;
        var langArgs = eventArgs as LanguageChangedEventArgs;
        Console.WriteLine($"Setting Language to : {langArgs?.Language}");
        exp.Language = langArgs?.Language;
    });

// Add a LanguageChanged event and predefined event handler
AddEvent(expando, "LanguageChanged", eventHandler);

// Add a CountryChanged event and an inline event handler
AddEvent(expando, "CountryChanged",
    new Action<object, EventArgs>((sender, eventArgs) =>
{
    dynamic exp = sender as ExpandoObject;
    var ctryArgs = eventArgs as CountryChangedEventArgs;
    string newLanguage = string.Empty;
    switch (ctryArgs?.Country)
    {
        case "France":
            newLanguage = "French";
            break;
        case "China":
            newLanguage = "Mandarin";
            break;
```

```
            case "Spain":
                newLanguage = "Spanish";
                break;
        }
        Console.WriteLine($"Country changed to {ctryArgs?.Country}, " +
            $"changing Language to {newLanguage}");
        exp?.LanguageChanged(sender,
            new LanguageChangedEventArgs() { Language = newLanguage });
    }));
```

We have provided the AddEvent method for you to encapsulate the details of adding the event to the ExpandoObject. This again takes advantage of ExpandoObject's support of IDictionary<string,object>:

```
public static void AddEvent(ExpandoObject expando, string eventName,
Action<object, EventArgs> handler)
{
    var expandoDict = expando as IDictionary<string, object>;
    if (expandoDict.ContainsKey(eventName))
        expandoDict[eventName] = handler;
    else
        expandoDict.Add(eventName, handler);
}
```

Finally, ExpandoObject supports INotifyPropertyChanged, which is the foundation of binding data to properties in .NET. We hook up the event handler, and when the Country property is changed we fire the CountryChanged event:

```
((INotifyPropertyChanged)expando).PropertyChanged +=
    new PropertyChangedEventHandler((sender, ea) =>
{
    dynamic exp = sender as dynamic;
    var pcea = ea as PropertyChangedEventArgs;
    if(pcea?.PropertyName == "Country")
        exp.CountryChanged(exp, new CountryChangedEventArgs()
            { Country = exp.Country });
});
```

Now that we've finished constructing our object, we can invoke it like this to simulate our friend travelling around the world:

```
Console.WriteLine($"expando contains: {expando.Name}, {expando.Country}, " +
    $"{expando.Language}");
Console.WriteLine();

Console.WriteLine("Changing Country to France...");
expando.Country = "France";
Console.WriteLine($"expando contains: {expando.Name}, {expando.Country},  " +
    $"{expando.Language}");
Console.WriteLine();

Console.WriteLine("Changing Country to China...");
expando.Country = "China";
```

```
Console.WriteLine($"expando contains: {expando.Name}, {expando.Country},  " +
    $"{expando.Language}");
Console.WriteLine();

Console.WriteLine("Changing Country to Spain...");
expando.Country = "Spain";
Console.WriteLine($"expando contains: {expando.Name}, {expando.Country},  " +
    $"{expando.Language}");
Console.WriteLine();
```

The output of this example is shown here:

```
expando contains: Brian, USA, English

Changing Country to France...
Country changed to France, changing Language to French
Setting Language to: French
expando contains: Brian, France, French

Changing Country to China...
Country changed to China, changing Language to Mandarin
Setting Language to: Mandarin
expando contains: Brian, China, Mandarin

Changing Country to Spain...
Country changed to Spain, changing Language to Spanish
Setting Language to: Spanish
expando contains: Brian, Spain, Spanish
```

Discussion

ExpandoObject allows you to write code that is more readable than typical reflection code with GetProperty("Field") syntax. When you're dealing with XML or JSON, ExpandoObject can be useful for quickly setting up a type to program against instead of always having to create data transfer objects. ExpandoObject's support for data binding through INotifyPropertyChanged is a huge win for anyone using WPF, MVC, or any other binding framework in .NET, as it allows you to use these objects, as well as other statically typed classes, "on the fly."

Since ExpandoObject can take delegates as members, you can attach methods and events to these dynamic types while the code looks like you are addressing a static type:

```
public static void AddEvent(ExpandoObject expando, string eventName,
Action<object, EventArgs> handler)
{
    var expandoDict = expando as IDictionary<string, object>;
    if (expandoDict.ContainsKey(eventName))
        expandoDict[eventName] = handler;
    else
```

```
        expandoDict.Add(eventName, handler);
    }
```

You might be wondering why we didn't use extension methods for `AddProperty` and `AddEvent`. They both could hang off of `ExpandoObject` and make the syntax even cleaner, right? Unfortunately, no. The way extension methods work is that the compiler does a search on all classes that might be a match for the extended class. This means that the DLR would have to know all of this information at runtime as well (since `ExpandoObject` is handled by the DLR), and currently not all of that information is encoded into the call site for the class and methods.

The event argument classes for the `LanguageChanged` and `CountryChanged` events are listed here:

```
public class LanguageChangedEventArgs : EventArgs
{
    public string Language { get; set; }
}

public class CountryChangedEventArgs : EventArgs
{
    public string Country { get; set; }
}
```

See Also

The "ExpandoObject class," "Func<> delegate," "Action<> delegate," and "INotifyPropertyChanged interface" topics in the MSDN documentation.

6.9 Make Your Objects Extensible

Problem

You want to have a base class for objects that will allow you to extend the objects at runtime so that you can derive your models from it and avoid duplicated code.

Solution

Use the `DynamicBase<T>` class derived from `DynamicObject` to create a new class or encapsulate an existing class:

```
public class DynamicBase<T> : DynamicObject
    where T : new()
{
    private T _containedObject = default(T);

    [JsonExtensionData] //JSON.NET 5.0 and above
    private Dictionary<string, object> _dynamicMembers =
        new Dictionary<string, object>();
```

```csharp
    private List<PropertyInfo> _propertyInfos =
        new List<PropertyInfo>(typeof(T).GetProperties());

    public DynamicBase()
    {
    }
    public DynamicBase(T containedObject)
    {
        _containedObject = containedObject;
    }

    public override bool TryInvokeMember(InvokeMemberBinder binder,
        object[] args, out object result)
    {
        if (_dynamicMembers.ContainsKey(binder.Name)
        && _dynamicMembers[binder.Name] is Delegate)
        {
            result = (_dynamicMembers[binder.Name] as Delegate).DynamicInvoke(
                args);
            return true;
        }

        return base.TryInvokeMember(binder, args, out result);
    }

    public override IEnumerable<string> GetDynamicMemberNames() =>
        _dynamicMembers.Keys;

    public override bool TryGetMember(GetMemberBinder binder, out object result)
    {
        result = null;
        var propertyInfo = _propertyInfos.Where(pi =>
            pi.Name == binder.Name).FirstOrDefault();
        // Make sure this member isn't a property on the object yet
        if (propertyInfo == null)
        {
            // look in the additional items collection for it
            if (_dynamicMembers.Keys.Contains(binder.Name))
            {
                // return the dynamic item
                result = _dynamicMembers[binder.Name];
                return true;
            }
        }
        else
        {
            // get it from the contained object
            if (_containedObject != null)
            {
                result = propertyInfo.GetValue(_containedObject);
                return true;
            }
        }
```

```
            }
        }
        return base.TryGetMember(binder, out result);
    }

    public override bool TrySetMember(SetMemberBinder binder, object value)
    {
        var propertyInfo = _propertyInfos.Where(pi =>
            pi.Name == binder.Name).FirstOrDefault();
        // Make sure this member isn't a property on the object yet
        if (propertyInfo == null)
        {
            // look in the additional items collection for it
            if (_dynamicMembers.Keys.Contains(binder.Name))
            {
                // set the dynamic item
                _dynamicMembers[binder.Name] = value;
                return true;
            }
            else
            {
                _dynamicMembers.Add(binder.Name, value);
                return true;
            }
        }
        else
        {
            // put it in the contained object
            if (_containedObject != null)
            {
                propertyInfo.SetValue(_containedObject, value);
                return true;
            }
        }
        return base.TrySetMember(binder, value);
    }

    public override string ToString()
    {
        StringBuilder builder = new StringBuilder();
        foreach (var propInfo in _propertyInfos)
        {
            if(_containedObject != null)
                builder.AppendFormat("{0}:{1}{2}", propInfo.Name,
                    propInfo.GetValue(_containedObject), Environment.NewLine);
            else
                builder.AppendFormat("{0}:{1}{2}", propInfo.Name,
                    propInfo.GetValue(this), Environment.NewLine);
        }
        foreach (var addlItem in _dynamicMembers)
        {
            // exclude methods that are added from the description
```

```
                Type itemType = addlItem.Value.GetType();
                Type genericType =
                    itemType.IsGenericType ?
                        itemType.GetGenericTypeDefinition() : null;
                if (genericType != null)
                {
                    if (genericType != typeof(Func<>) &&
                        genericType != typeof(Action<>))
                        builder.AppendFormat("{0}:{1}{2}", addlItem.Key,
                            addlItem.Value, Environment.NewLine);
                }
                else
                    builder.AppendFormat("{0}:{1}{2}", addlItem.Key, addlItem.Value,
                        Environment.NewLine);
            }
        return builder.ToString();
    }
}
```

To understand how DynamicBase<T> is used, consider a scenario where we have a web service that is receiving a serialized JSON payload of athlete information. Currently we have defined the DynamicAthlete class with properties for both a Name and a Sport:

```
public class DynamicAthlete : DynamicBase<DynamicAthlete>
{
    public string Name { get; set; }
    public string Sport { get; set; }
}
```

In the payload being sent to us, the supplier has started to send additional information about the Position the athlete plays. This can happen at times when legacy system integrations change and all systems cannot update at the same time. For our receiving system, we don't want to lose the new data being sent from some systems. We simulate the construction of the JSON payload using dynamic and the JSON.NET serializer available via NuGet (thank you, James Newton-King—this thing rocks!):

```
// Create a set of information on athletes
// Note that the service receiving these doesn't have Position as a
// property on the Athlete object
dynamic initialAthletes = new[]
{
    new
    {
        Name = "Tom Brady",
        Sport = "Football",
        Position = "Quarterback"
    },
    new
    {
        Name = "Derek Jeter",
```

```
                Sport = "Baseball",
                Position = "Shortstop"
        },
        new
        {
                Name = "Michael Jordan",
                Sport = "Basketball",
                Position = "Small Forward"
        },
        new
        {
                Name = "Lionel Messi",
                Sport = "Soccer",
                Position = "Forward"
        }
    };

    // serialize the JSON to send to a web service about athletes...
    string serializedAthletes = JsonNetSerialize(initialAthletes);
```

Assume the JSON payload for the athletes comes in to your service and is deserialized (once again, props to JSON.NET) and we deserialize it as an array of DynamicAth letes:

```
    // deserialize the JSON we were sent
    var athletes = JsonNetDeserialize<DynamicAthlete[]>(serializedAthletes);
```

Now, everyone who has done any kind of web service development (or any serialization development, for that matter) knows that if you don't have a place to put things while deserializing, they get lost or cause errors. So what happens to the Position property value that was passed in since that property is not declared on DynamicAth lete? If you look back at the declaration of DynamicBase<T> (from which DynamicAth lete derives), you will see an internal private Dictionary<string,object> that is marked with the JsonExtensionData attribute. This attribute tells the serializer where to put property values that do not have a place in the derived object. How cool is that?! So our Position value is stored in this internal dictionary, which is great, but how do we access it?

```
    [JsonExtensionData] //JSON.NET 5.0 and above
    private Dictionary<string, object> _dynamicMembers =
        new Dictionary<string, object>();
```

Since our DynamicAthlete is derived from DynamicBase<T>, which in turn derives from DynamicObject, we can assign the first athlete we received into the dynamic variable da. Once it is in a dynamic variable, we can access Position just as if it were one of the defined properties of DynamicAthlete:

```
    dynamic da = athletes[0];
    Console.WriteLine($"Position of first athlete: {da.Position}");
```

So we can preserve the value of the properties sent to us even if we don't know about them directly when we deploy the service, which is a nice robustness feature. We could also add a new method to each `DynamicAthlete` to get the `Name` in uppercase while printing out the contents we received:

```
// Inspect the athletes and see that we not only got the Position
// information, but we can also add an operation to work on the
// entity and invoke that as part of the dynamic entity
foreach(var athlete in athletes)
{
    dynamic dynamicAthlete = (dynamic)athlete;
    dynamicAthlete.GetUppercaseName =
        (Func<string>)(() =>
        {
            return ((string)dynamicAthlete.Name).ToUpper();
        });
    Console.WriteLine($"Athlete:");
    Console.WriteLine(athlete);
    Console.WriteLine($"Uppercase Name: {dynamicAthlete.GetUppercaseName()}");
    Console.WriteLine();
    Console.WriteLine();
}
```

`GetUppercaseName` is added to the object and then called to return the uppercase version of the `Name`. Here is the output:

```
Athlete:
Name:Tom Brady
Sport:Football
Position:Quarterback

Uppercase Name: TOM BRADY


Athlete:
Name:Derek Jeter
Sport:Baseball
Position:Shortstop

Uppercase Name: DEREK JETER


Athlete:
Name:Michael Jordan
Sport:Basketball
Position:Small Forward

Uppercase Name: MICHAEL JORDAN


Athlete:
Name:Lionel Messi
```

```
Sport:Soccer
Position:Forward

Uppercase Name: LIONEL MESSI
```

What about the case where we already have our objects defined? How can we get in on this extension goodness? Let's look at the StaticAthlete class as an example:

```
public class StaticAthlete
{
    public string Name { get; set; }
    public string Sport { get; set; }
}
```

StaticAthlete looks almost the same as DynamicAthlete, but it is not derived from anything.

If we create an instance of StaticAthlete, we can still use DynamicBase<T> to wrap it and get the same extension behavior as we did when DynamicAthlete was inheriting from DynamicBase<T>. DynamicBase<T> is no Super Bass-O-Matic '76, but it slices and dices classes pretty well too!

```
//Wrap an existing athlete
StaticAthlete staticAthlete = new StaticAthlete()
{
    Sport = "Hockey"
};

dynamic extendedAthlete = new DynamicBase<StaticAthlete>(staticAthlete);
extendedAthlete.Name = "Bobby Orr";
extendedAthlete.Position = "Defenseman";
extendedAthlete.GetUppercaseName =
        (Func<string>)(() =>
        {
            return ((string)extendedAthlete.Name).ToUpper();
        });
Console.WriteLine($"Static Athlete (extended):");
Console.WriteLine(extendedAthlete);
Console.WriteLine($"Uppercase Name: {extendedAthlete.GetUppercaseName()}");
Console.WriteLine();
Console.WriteLine();
```

You can see that the output for StaticAthlete is exactly the same as it was for the DynamicAthletes:

```
Static Athlete (extended):
Name:Bobby Orr
Sport:Hockey
Position:Defenseman

Uppercase Name: BOBBY ORR
```

Discussion

DynamicObject acts as a base class to help you add dynamic behaviors to your classes. Unlike ExpandoObject it cannot be instantiated, but it can be derived from. With DynamicObject, you can override many different types of operations, such as property or method access or any binary, unary, or type conversion operations, which allows you the flexibility to determine how the class will react at runtime.

We do some of these things in DynamicBase<T> by overriding the following methods on DynamicObject:

- TryInvokeMember
- GetDynamicMemberNames
- TryGetMember
- TrySetMember

TryInvokeMember allows us to determine what should happen when a member is invoked on the object. We use it in DynamicBase<T> to look at the internal collection and if we have a matching item, we invoke it dynamically as a delegate:

```
    public override bool TryInvokeMember(InvokeMemberBinder binder,
        object[] args,
out object result)
    {
        if (_dynamicMembers.ContainsKey(binder.Name) &&
            _dynamicMembers[binder.Name] is Delegate)
        {
            result = (_dynamicMembers[binder.Name] as Delegate).DynamicInvoke(
                args);
            return true;
        }

        return base.TryInvokeMember(binder, args, out result);
    }
```

GetDynamicMemberNames gets the set of all members that were added dynamically:

```
    public override IEnumerable<string> GetDynamicMemberNames()
    {
        return _dynamicMembers.Keys;
    }
```

TryGetMember is overridden to allow the caller to get property values for the items that have been added dynamically. If we don't find it in the main property information for the class, we look in the internal dictionary of dynamic members and return it from there:

```
public override bool TryGetMember(GetMemberBinder binder, out object result)
{
    result = null;
    var propertyInfo = _propertyInfos.Where(pi =>
        pi.Name == binder.Name).FirstOrDefault();
    // Make sure this member isn't a property on the object yet
    if (propertyInfo == null)
    {
        // look in the additional items collection for it
        if (_dynamicMembers.Keys.Contains(binder.Name))
        {
            // return the dynamic item
            result = _dynamicMembers[binder.Name];
            return true;
        }
    }
    else
    {
        // get it from the contained object
        if (_containedObject != null)
        {
            result = propertyInfo.GetValue(_containedObject);
            return true;
        }
    }
    return base.TryGetMember(binder, out result);
}
```

The override for `TrySetMember` handles when a property value is being set. Once again, we look at the typed object first and then look to the dynamic dictionary for where to store the value:

```
public override bool TrySetMember(SetMemberBinder binder, object value)
{
    var propertyInfo = _propertyInfos.Where(pi =>
        pi.Name == binder.Name).FirstOrDefault();
    // Make sure this member isn't a property on the object yet
    if (propertyInfo == null)
    {
        // look in the additional items collection for it
        if (_dynamicMembers.Keys.Contains(binder.Name))
        {
            // set the dynamic item
            _dynamicMembers[binder.Name] = value;
            return true;
        }
        else
        {
            _dynamicMembers.Add(binder.Name, value);
            return true;
        }
    }
}
```

```
    else
    {
        // put it in the contained object
        if (_containedObject != null)
        {
            propertyInfo.SetValue(_containedObject, value);
            return true;
        }
    }
    return base.TrySetMember(binder, value);
}
```

We have also overridden ToString so that we can get all of the properties (static and dynamic) on the class to be represented in the string:

```
public override string ToString()
{
    StringBuilder builder = new StringBuilder();
    foreach (var propInfo in _propertyInfos)
    {
        if(_containedObject != null)
            builder.AppendFormat("{0}:{1}{2}", propInfo.Name,
                propInfo.GetValue(_containedObject), Environment.NewLine);
        else
            builder.AppendFormat("{0}:{1}{2}", propInfo.Name,
                propInfo.GetValue(this), Environment.NewLine);
    }
    foreach (var addlItem in _dynamicMembers)
    {
        // exclude methods that are added from the description
        Type itemType = addlItem.Value.GetType();
        Type genericType =
            itemType.IsGenericType ? itemType.GetGenericTypeDefinition() : null;
        if (genericType != null)
        {
            if (genericType != typeof(Func<>) &&
                genericType != typeof(Action<>))
                builder.AppendFormat("{0}:{1}{2}", addlItem.Key, addlItem.Value,
                    Environment.NewLine);
        }
        else
            builder.AppendFormat("{0}:{1}{2}", addlItem.Key, addlItem.Value,
                Environment.NewLine);
    }
    return builder.ToString();
}
```

We do a bit of filtering to handle the cases where dynamic methods or events are added and when the member or method is on the contained object. This allows us to get the representation of all properties like this:

```
Name:Bobby Orr
Sport:Hockey
Position:Defenseman
```

As you can see, `DynamicObject` gives you all the power you need to extend your objects as far as you want to take them.

See Also

The "DynamicObject Class" topic in the MSDN documentation.

CHAPTER 7

Regular Expressions

7.0 Introduction

The .NET Framework Class Library (FCL) includes the `System.Text.RegularExpres` `sions` namespace, which is devoted to creating, executing, and obtaining results from regular expressions executed against a string.

Regular expressions take the form of a pattern that matches zero or more characters within a string. The simplest of these patterns, such as `.*` (which matches anything except newline characters) and `[A-Za-z]` (which matches any letter) are easy to learn, but more advanced patterns can be difficult to learn and even more difficult to implement correctly. Learning and understanding regular expressions can take considerable time and effort, but the work will pay off.

 Two books that will help you learn and expand your understanding of regular expressions are Michael Fitzgerald's *Introducing Regular Expressions* and Jan Goyvaerts and Steven Levithan's *Regular Expressions Cookbook*, both from O'Reilly.

Regular expression patterns can take a simple form—such as a single word or character—or a much more complex pattern. The more complex patterns can recognize and match such items as the year portion of a date, all of the `<SCRIPT>` tags in an ASP page, or a phrase in a sentence that varies with each use. The .NET regular expression classes provide a very flexible and powerful way to perform tasks such as recognizing text, replacing text within a string, and splitting up text into individual sections based on one or more complex delimiters.

Despite the complexity of regular expression patterns, the regular expression classes in the FCL are easy to use in your applications. Executing a regular expression consists of the following steps:

1. Create an instance of a `Regex` object that contains the regular expression pattern along with any options for executing that pattern.

2. Retrieve a reference to an instance of a `Match` object by calling the `Match` instance method if you want only the first match found. Or, retrieve a reference to an instance of the `MatchesCollection` object by calling the `Matches` instance method if you want more than just the first match found. If, however, you want to know only whether the input string was a match and do not need the extra details on the nature of the match, you can use the `Regex.IsMatch` method.

3. If you've called the `Matches` method to retrieve a `MatchCollection` object, iterate over the `MatchCollection` using a `foreach` loop. Each iteration will allow access to every `Match` object that the regular expression produced.

7.1 Extracting Groups from a MatchCollection

Problem

You have a regular expression that contains one or more named groups (also known as *named capture groups*), such as the following:

```
\\\\(?<TheServer>\w*)\\(?<TheService>\w*)\\
```

where the named group `TheServer` will match any server name within a UNC string, and `TheService` will match any service name within a UNC string.

 This pattern does not match the UNCW format.

You need to store the groups that are returned by this regular expression in a keyed collection (such as a `Dictionary<string, Group>`) in which the key is the group name.

Solution

The `ExtractGroupings` method shown in Example 7-1 obtains a set of `Group` objects keyed by their matching group name.

Example 7-1. ExtractGroupings method

```
using System;
using System.Collections;
using System.Collections.Generics;
using System.Text.RegularExpressions;

public static List<Dictionary<string, Group>> ExtractGroupings(string source
                                                    string matchPattern,
                                                    bool wantInitialMatch)
{
    List<Dictionary<string, Group>> keyedMatches =
        new List<Dictionary<string, Group>>();
    int startingElement = 1;
    if (wantInitialMatch)
    {
        startingElement = 0;
    }

    Regex RE = new Regex(matchPattern, RegexOptions.Multiline);
    MatchCollection theMatches = RE.Matches(source);

    foreach(Match m in theMatches)
    {
        Dictionary<string, Group> groupings = new Dictionary<string, Group>();

        for (int counter = startingElement; counter < m.Groups.Count; counter++)
        {
            // If we had just returned the MatchCollection directly, the
            // GroupNameFromNumber method would not be available to use.
            groupings.Add(RE.GroupNameFromNumber(counter), m.Groups[counter]);
        }
        keyedMatches.Add(groupings);
    }
    return (keyedMatches);
}
```

The ExtractGroupings method can be used in the following manner to extract named groups and organize them by name:

```
public static void TestExtractGroupings()
{
    string source = @"Path = ""\\MyServer\MyService\MyPath;
                    \\MyServer2\MyService2\MyPath2\""";
    string matchPattern = @"\\\\(?<TheServer>\w*)\\(?<TheService>\w*)\\";

    foreach (Dictionary<string, Group> grouping in
            ExtractGroupings(source, matchPattern, true))
    {
        foreach (KeyValuePair<string, Group> kvp in grouping)
            Console.WriteLine($"Key/Value = {kvp.Key} / {kvp.Value}");
        Console.WriteLine("");
    }
}
```

```
        }
    }
```

This test method creates a `source` string and a regular expression pattern in the `Match Pattern` variable. The two groupings in this regular expression are highlighted here:

```
string matchPattern = @"\\\\(?<TheServer>\w*)\\(?<TheService>\w*)\\";
```

The names for these two groups are `TheServer` and `TheService`. Text that matches either of these groupings can be accessed through these group names.

The `source` and `matchPattern` variables are passed in to the `ExtractGroupings` method, along with a Boolean value, which is discussed shortly. This method returns a `List<T>` containing `Dictionary<string,Group>` objects. These `Dictionary<string,Group>` objects contain the matches for each of the named groups in the regular expression, keyed by their group name.

This test method, `TestExtractGroupings`, returns the following:

```
Key / Value = 0 / \\MyServer\MyService\
Key / Value = TheService / MyService
Key / Value = TheServer / MyServer

Key / Value = 0 / \\MyServer2\MyService2\
Key / Value = TheService / MyService2
Key / Value = TheServer / MyServer2
```

If the last parameter to the `ExtractGroupings` method were to be changed to `false`, the following output would result:

```
Key / Value = TheService / MyService
Key / Value = TheServer / MyServer

Key / Value = TheService / MyService2
Key / Value = TheServer / MyServer2
```

The only difference between these two outputs is that the first grouping is not displayed when the last parameter to `ExtractGroupings` is changed to `false`. The first grouping is always the complete match of the regular expression.

Discussion

Groups within a regular expression can be defined in one of two ways. The first way is to add parentheses around the subpattern that you wish to define as a grouping. This type of grouping is sometimes labeled as *unnamed*. Later you can easily extract this grouping from the final text in each returned `Match` object by running the regular expression. The regular expression for this recipe could be modified, as follows, to use a simple unnamed group:

```
string matchPattern = @"\\\\(\w*)\\(\w*)\\";
```

After running the regular expression, you can access these groups using a numeric integer value starting with 1.

The second way to define a group within a regular expression is to use one or more *named groups*. You define a named group by adding parentheses around the subpattern that you wish to define as a grouping *and* adding a name to each grouping, using the following syntax:

```
(?<Name>\w*)
```

The *Name* portion of this syntax is the name you specify for this group. After executing this regular expression, you can access this group by the name *Name*.

To access each group, you must first use a loop to iterate each `Match` object in the `MatchCollection`. For each `Match` object, you access the `GroupCollection`'s indexer, using the following unnamed syntax:

```
string group1 = m.Groups[1].Value;
string group2 = m.Groups[2].Value;
```

or the following named syntax, where m is the `Match` object:

```
string group1 = m.Groups["Group1_Name"].Value;
string group2 = m.Groups["Group2_Name"].Value;
```

If the `Match` method was used to return a single `Match` object instead of the `MatchCollection`, use the following syntax to access each group:

```
// Unnamed syntax
string group1 = theMatch.Groups[1].Value;
string group2 = theMatch.Groups[2].Value;

// Named syntax
string group1 = theMatch.Groups["Group1_Name"].Value;
string group2 = theMatch.Groups["Group2_Name"].Value;
```

where `theMatch` is the `Match` object returned by the `Match` method.

See Also

The ".NET Framework Regular Expressions" and "Dictionary Class" topics in the MSDN documentation.

7.2 Verifying the Syntax of a Regular Expression

Problem

You have constructed a regular expression dynamically, either from your code or based on user input. You need to test the validity of this regular expression's syntax before you actually use it.

Solution

Use the `VerifyRegEx` method shown in Example 7-2 to test the validity of a regular expression's syntax.

Example 7-2. VerifyRegEx method

```
using System;
using System.Text.RegularExpressions;

public static bool VerifyRegEx(string testPattern)
{
    bool isValid = true;
    if ((testPattern?.Length ?? 0) > 0)
    {
        try
        {
            Regex.Match("", testPattern);
        }
        catch (ArgumentException)
        {
            // BAD PATTERN: syntax error
            isValid = false;
        }
    }
    else
    {
        //BAD PATTERN: pattern is null or empty
        isValid = false;
    }

    return (isValid);
}
```

To use this method, pass it the regular expression that you wish to verify:

```
public static void TestUserInputRegEx(string regEx)
{
    if (VerifyRegEx(regEx))
        Console.WriteLine("This is a valid regular expression.");
    else
        Console.WriteLine("This is not a valid regular expression.");
}
```

Discussion

The `VerifyRegEx` method calls the static `Regex.Match` method, which is useful for running regular expressions on the fly against a string. The static `Regex.Match` method returns a single `Match` object. By using this static method to run a regular expression against a string (in this case, an empty string), you can determine whether

---

the regular expression is invalid by watching for a thrown exception. The Regex.Match method will throw an ArgumentException if the regular expression is not syntactically correct. The Message property of this exception contains the reason the regular expression failed to run, and the ParamName property contains the regular expression passed to the Match method. Both of these properties are read-only.

Before testing the regular expression with the static Match method, VerifyRegEx tests the regular expression to see if it is null or blank. A null regular expression string returns an ArgumentNullException when passed in to the Match method. On the other hand, if a blank regular expression is passed in to the Match method, no exception is thrown (as long as a valid string is also passed to the first parameter of the Match method).

While this recipe validates whether or not the regular expression syntax is correct, it does not look for poorly written expressions. One common case of poorly written regular expressions is when the expressions rely on *backtracking*. Backtracking can cause the regular expression to take an exponentially long time to complete, making it appear as if the code executing the regular expression has frozen.

 For a thorough explanation of backtracking in regular expressions, read the MSDN topic "Backtracking" under the ".NET Framework Regular Expressions" parent topic.

In cases where regular expressions use backtracking, it is recommended that you use a timeout value to limit the time a regular expression has to complete. Use the following RegEx constructor:

```
Regex (String, RegexOptions, TimeSpan)
```

where TimeSpan is the length of time within which the regular expression is allowed to execute:

```
Regex regex = new RegEx(bkTrkPattern, RegexOptions.None,
                        TimeSpan.FromMilliseconds(1000));
```

You can then execute the regular expression within a try-catch block, using the RegexMatchTimeoutException to catch a poorly written regular expression that takes an unusually long time to execute.

7.3 Augmenting the Basic String Replacement Function

Problem

You need to replace character patterns within the target string with a new string. However, in this case, each replacement operation has a unique set of conditions that must be satisfied in order to allow the replacement to occur.

Solution

Use the overloaded instance `Replace` method shown in Example 7-3, which accepts a `MatchEvaluator` delegate along with its other parameters. The `MatchEvaluator` delegate is a callback method that overrides the default behavior of the `Replace` method.

Example 7-3. Overloaded Replace method that accepts a MatchEvaluator delegate

```
using System;
using System.Text.RegularExpressions;

public static string MatchHandler(Match theMatch)
{
    // Handle all ControlID_ entries.
    if (theMatch.Value.StartsWith("ControlID_", StringComparison.Ordinal))
    {
        long controlValue = 0;

        // Obtain the numeric value of the Top attribute.
        Match topAttributeMatch = Regex.Match(theMatch.Value, "Top=([-]*\\d*)");
        if (topAttributeMatch.Success)
        {
            if (topAttributeMatch.Groups[1].Value.Trim().Equals(""))
            {
                // If blank, set to zero.
                return (theMatch.Value.Replace(
                        topAttributeMatch.Groups[0].Value.Trim(),
                        "Top=0"));
            }
            else if (topAttributeMatch.Groups[1].Value.Trim().StartsWith("-"
                                        , StringComparison.Ordinal))
            {
                // If only a negative sign (syntax error), set to zero.
                return (theMatch.Value.Replace(
                        topAttributeMatch.Groups[0].Value.Trim(), "Top=0"));
            }
            else
            {
                // We have a valid number.
                // Convert the matched string to a numeric value.
```

```
                controlValue = long.Parse(topAttributeMatch.Groups[1].Value,
                        System.Globalization.NumberStyles.Any);
                // If the Top attribute is out of the specified range,
                // set it to zero.
                if (controlValue < 0 || controlValue > 5000)
                {
                    return (theMatch.Value.Replace(
                            topAttributeMatch.Groups[0].Value.Trim(),
                            "Top=0"));
                }
            }
        }
    }

    return (theMatch.Value);
}
```

The callback method for the Replace method is shown here:

```
public static void ComplexReplace(string matchPattern, string source)
{
    MatchEvaluator replaceCallback = new MatchEvaluator(MatchHandler);
    Regex RE = new Regex(matchPattern, RegexOptions.Multiline);
    string newString = RE.Replace(source, replaceCallback);

    Console.WriteLine($"Replaced String = {newString}");
}
```

To use this callback method with the static Replace method, modify the previous Com
plexReplace method as follows:

```
public void ComplexReplace(string matchPattern, string source)
{
    MatchEvaluator replaceCallback = new MatchEvaluator(MatchHandler);
    string newString = Regex.Replace(source, matchPattern, replaceCallback);
    Console.WriteLine("Replaced String = " + newString);
}
```

where *source* is the original string to run the replace operation against, and *matchPat
tern* is the regular expression pattern to match in the *source* string.

If the ComplexReplace method is called from the following code:

```
public static void TestComplexReplace()
{
    string matchPattern = "(ControlID_.*)";
    string source = @"WindowID=Main
    ControlID_TextBox1 Top=-100 Left=0 Text=BLANK
    ControlID_Label1 Top=9999990 Left=0 Caption=Enter Name Here
    ControlID_Label2 Top= Left=0 Caption=Enter Name Here";

    ComplexReplace(matchPattern, source);
}
```

only the `Top` attributes of the `ControlID_*` lines are changed from their original values to 0.

The result of this replace action will change the `Top` attribute value of a `ControlID_*` line to 0 if it is less than 0 or greater than 5,000. Any other tag that contains a `Top` attribute will remain unchanged. The following three lines of the `source` string will be changed from:

```
ControlID_TextBox1 Top=-100 Left=0 Text=BLANK
ControlID_Label1 Top=9999990 Left=0 Caption=Enter Name Here
ControlID_Label2 Top= Left=0 Caption=Enter Name Here";
```

to:

```
ControlID_TextBox1 Top=0 Left=0 Text=BLANK
ControlID_Label1 Top=0 Left=0 Caption=Enter Name Here
ControlID_Label2 Top=0 Left=0 Caption=Enter Name Here";
```

Discussion

The `MatchEvaluator` delegate, which is automatically invoked when it is supplied as a parameter to the `Regex` class's `Replace` method, allows for custom replacement of each string that conforms to the regular expression pattern.

If the current `Match` object is operating on a `ControlID_*` line with a `Top` attribute that is out of the specified range, the code within the `MatchHandler` callback method returns a new modified string. Otherwise, the currently matched string is returned unchanged. This allows you to override the default `Replace` functionality by modifying only that part of the `source` string that meets certain criteria. The code within this callback method gives you some idea of what you can accomplish using this replacement technique.

To make use of this callback method, you need a way to call it from the `ComplexRe` `place` method. First, a variable of type `System.Text.RegularExpressions.MatchEva` `luator` is created. This variable (`replaceCallback`) is the delegate that is used to call the `MatchHandler` method:

```
MatchEvaluator replaceCallback = new MatchEvaluator(MatchHandler);
```

Finally, the `Replace` method is called with the reference to the `MatchEvaluator` delegate passed in as a parameter:

```
string newString = Regex.Replace(source, matchPattern, replaceCallback);
```

See Also

The ".NET Framework Regular Expressions" topic in the MSDN documentation.

7.4 Implementing a Better Tokenizer

Problem

You need a tokenizer—also referred to as a *lexer*—that can split up a string based on a well-defined set of characters.

Solution

With the Split method of the Regex class, you can create a regular expression to indicate the types of tokens and separators that you are interested in gathering. This technique works especially well with equations, since the tokens of an equation are well defined. For example, the code:

```
using System;
using System.Text.RegularExpressions;

public static string[] Tokenize(string equation)
{
    Regex re = new Regex(@"([\+\-\*\(\)\^\\])");
    return (re.Split(equation));
}
```

will divide up a string according to the regular expression specified in the Regex constructor. In other words, the string passed in to the Tokenize method will be divided up based on the delimiters +, -, *, (,), ^, and \. The following method will call the Tokenize method to tokenize the equation (y - 3)*(3111*x^21 + x + 320):

```
public static void TestTokenize()
{
    foreach(string token in Tokenize("(y - 3)*(3111*x^21 + x + 320)"))
        Console.WriteLine("String token = " + token.Trim());
}
```

which displays the following output:

```
string token =
String token = (
String token = y
String token = -
String token = 3
String token = )
String token = *
String token = (
String token = 3111
String token = *
String token = x
String token = ^
String token = 21
String token = +
```

```
String token = x
String token = +
String token = 320
String token = )
String token =
```

Notice that each individual operator, parenthesis, and number has been broken out into its own separate token.

Discussion

In real-world projects, you do not always have the luxury of being able to control the set of inputs to your code. By making use of regular expressions, you can take the original tokenizer and make it flexible enough to allow it to be applied to many types or styles of input.

The key method used here is the `Split` instance method of the `Regex` class. The return value of this method is a string array with elements that include each individual token of the `source` string—the equation, in this case.

Note that the static `Split` method allows `RegexOptions` enumeration values to be used, while the instance method allows for a starting position to be defined and a maximum number of matches to occur. This may have some bearing on whether you choose the static or instance method.

See Also

The ".NET Framework Regular Expressions" topic in the MSDN documentation.

7.5 Returning the Entire Line in Which a Match Is Found

Problem

You have a string or file that contains multiple lines. When a specific character pattern is found on a line, you want to return the entire line, not just the matched text.

Solution

Use the `StreamReader.ReadLine` method to obtain each line in a file to run a regular expression against, as shown in Example 7-4.

Example 7-4. Returning the entire line in which a match is found

```
public static List<string> GetLines(string source, string pattern, bool isFileName)
{
    List<string> matchedLines = new List<string>();
```

```
// If this is a file, get the entire file's text.
if (isFileName)
{
    using (FileStream FS = new FileStream(source, FileMode.Open,
        FileAccess.Read, FileShare.Read))
    {
        using (StreamReader SR = new StreamReader(FS))
        {
            Regex RE = new Regex(pattern, RegexOptions.Multiline);
            string text = "";
            while (text != null)
            {
                text = SR.ReadLine();
                if (text != null)
                {
                    // Run the regex on each line in the string.
                    if (RE.IsMatch(text))
                    {
                        // Get the line if a match was found.
                        matchedLines.Add(text);
                    }
                }
            }
        }
    }
}
else
{
    // Run the regex once on the entire string.
    Regex RE = new Regex(pattern, RegexOptions.Multiline);
    MatchCollection theMatches = RE.Matches(source);

    // Use these vars to remember the last line added to matchedLines
    // so that we do not add duplicate lines.
    int lastLineStartPos = -1;
    int lastLineEndPos = -1;

    // Get the line for each match.
    foreach (Match m in theMatches)
    {
        int lineStartPos = GetBeginningOfLine(source, m.Index);
        int lineEndPos = GetEndOfLine(source, (m.Index + m.Length - 1));

        // If this is not a duplicate line, add it.
        if (lastLineStartPos != lineStartPos &&
            lastLineEndPos != lineEndPos)
        {
            string line = source.Substring(lineStartPos,
                            lineEndPos - lineStartPos);
            matchedLines.Add(line);

            // Reset line positions.
```

```
                lastLineStartPos = lineStartPos;
                lastLineEndPos = lineEndPos;
            }
        }
    }
    return (matchedLines);
}

public static int GetBeginningOfLine(string text, int startPointOfMatch)
{
        if (startPointOfMatch > 0)
        {
            --startPointOfMatch;
        }

        if (startPointOfMatch >= 0 && startPointOfMatch < text?.Length)
        {
            // Move to the left until the first '\n' char is found.
            for (int index = startPointOfMatch; index >= 0; index--)
            {
                if (text?[index] == '\n')
                {
                    return (index + 1);
                }
            }

            return (0);
        }

        return (startPointOfMatch);
}

public static int GetEndOfLine(string text, int endPointOfMatch)
{
    if (endPointOfMatch >= 0 && endPointOfMatch < text?.Length)
    {
        // Move to the right until the first '\n' char is found.
        for (int index = endPointOfMatch; index < text.Length; index++)
        {
            if (text?[index] == '\n')
            {
                return (index);
            }
        }

        return (text.Length);
    }

    return (endPointOfMatch);
}
```

The following method shows how to call the GetLines method with either a filename or a string:

```
public static void TestGetLine()
{
    // Get each line within the file TestFile.txt as a separate string.
    Console.WriteLine();
    List<string> lines = GetLines(@"C:\TestFile.txt", "Line", true);
    foreach (string s in lines)
        Console.WriteLine($"MatchedLine: {s}");

    // Get the lines matching the text "Line" within the given string.
    Console.WriteLine();
    lines = GetLines("Line1\r\nLine2\r\nLine3\nLine4", "Line", false);
    foreach (string s in lines)
        Console.WriteLine($"MatchedLine: {s}");
}
```

Discussion

The GetLines method accepts three parameters:

source
  The string or filename in which to search for a pattern.

pattern
  The regular expression pattern to apply to the *source* string.

isFileName
  Pass in true if *source* is a filename, or false if *source* is a string.

This method returns a List<string> of strings that contains each line in which the regular expression match was found.

The GetLines method can obtain the lines on which matches occur within a string or a file. When a regular expression is run against a file whose name is passed in to the *source* parameter (when *isFileName* equals true) in the GetLines method, the file is opened and read line by line. The regular expression is run against each line, and if a match is found, that line is stored in the matchedLines List<string>. Using the ReadLine method of the StreamReader object saves you from having to determine where each line starts and ends. Determining where a line starts and ends in a string requires some work, as you will see.

Running the regular expression against a string passed in to the *source* parameter (when *isFileName* equals false) in the GetLines method produces a MatchCollection. Each Match object in this collection is used to obtain the line on which it is located in the *source* string. We obtain the line by starting at the position of the first character of the match in the *source* string and moving one character to the left until either an \n character or the beginning of the *source* string is found (this code is found in the GetBeginningOfLine method). This gives you the beginning of the line, which is placed in the variable LineStartPos. Next, we find the end of the line by starting at the last character of the match in the *source* string and moving to the right until either an \n character or the end of the *source* string is found (this code is found in the GetEndOfLine method). This ending position is placed in the LineEnd Pos variable. All of the text between the LineStartPos and LineEndPos will be the line in which the match is found. Each of these lines is added to the matchedLines List<string> and returned to the caller.

Something interesting you can do with the GetLines method is to pass in the string "\n" in the pattern parameter of this method. This trick will effectively return each line of the string or file as a string in the List<string>. While this will work with strings that already have the CRLF characters embedded in them, it will not work on text returned from a file. The reason is that the ReadLine method in the preceding GetLines method will strip off the CRLF characters. To fix this we can simply add these characters back in, as we are performing the match in the GetLines method:

```
// It is necessary to add CRLF chars
// since Readline() strips off these chars
if (RE.IsMatch(text + Environment.NewLine))
```

Finally, note that if more than one match is found on a line, each matching line will be added to the List<string>.

 Take care when adding line break characters back into the text. If you are using and processing this text exclusively on Windows systems, you won't have any issues. However, if you are using other systems, or a mix of systems, you need to make sure you add the correct line break characters—that is, for UNIX and OS X, use only the Linefeed character (\n).

See Also

The ".NET Framework Regular Expressions," "FileStream Class," and "Stream-Reader Class" topics in the MSDN documentation.

7.6 Finding a Particular Occurrence of a Match

Problem

You need to find a specific occurrence of a match within a string. For example, you want to find the third occurrence of a word or the second occurrence of a Social

Security number. In addition, you may need to find every third occurrence of a word in a string.

Solution

To find a particular occurrence of a match in a string, simply subscript the array returned from `Regex.Matches`:

```
public static Match FindOccurrenceOf(string source, string pattern,
                                     int occurrence)
{
    if (occurrence < 1)
    {
        throw (new ArgumentException("Cannot be less than 1",
                                     nameof(occurrence)));
    }

    // Make occurrence zero-based.
    --occurrence;

    // Run the regex once on the source string.
    Regex RE = new Regex(pattern, RegexOptions.Multiline);
    MatchCollection theMatches = RE.Matches(source);

    if (occurrence >= theMatches.Count)
    {
        return (null);
    }
    else
    {
        return (theMatches[occurrence]);
    }
}
```

To find each particular occurrence of a match in a string, build a `List<Match>` on the fly:

```
public static List<Match> FindEachOccurrenceOf(string source, string pattern,
                                               int occurrence)
{
    if (occurrence < 1)
    {
        throw (new ArgumentException("Cannot be less than 1",
                                     nameof(occurrence)));
    }

    List<Match> occurrences = new List<Match>();

    // Run the regex once on the source string.
    Regex RE = new Regex(pattern, RegexOptions.Multiline);
    MatchCollection theMatches = RE.Matches(source);
```

```
        for (int index = (occurrence - 1); index < theMatches.Count;
            index += occurrence)
        {
            occurrences.Add(theMatches[index]);
        }

        return (occurrences);
    }
```

The following method shows how to invoke the two previous methods:

```
public static void TestOccurrencesOf()
{
    Match matchResult = FindOccurrenceOf
                        ("one two three one two three one two three one"
                        + " two three one two three one two three", "two", 2);
    Console.WriteLine($"{matchResult?.ToString()}\t{matchResult?.Index}");

    Console.WriteLine();
    List<Match> results = FindEachOccurrenceOf
                        ("one one two three one two three one "
                        + " two three one two three", "one", 2);
    foreach (Match m in results)
        Console.WriteLine($"{m.ToString()}\t{m.Index}");
}
```

Discussion

This recipe contains two similar but distinct methods. The first method, FindOccur
renceOf, returns a particular occurrence of a regular expression match. The occurrence you want to find is passed in to this method via the occurrence parameter. If
the particular occurrence of the match does not exist—for example, you ask to find
the second occurrence, but only one occurrence exists—a null is returned from this
method. Because of this, you should check that the returned object of this method is
not null before using that object. If the particular occurrence exists, the Match object
that holds the match information for that occurrence is returned.

The second method in this recipe, FindEachOccurrenceOf, works similarly to the Fin
dOccurrenceOf method, except that it continues to find a particular occurrence of a
regular expression match until the end of the string is reached. For example, if you
ask to find the second occurrence, this method would return a List<Match> of zero
or more Match objects. The Match objects would correspond to the second, fourth,
sixth, and eighth occurrences of a match and so on until the end of the string is
reached.

See Also

The ".NET Framework Regular Expressions" and "ArrayList Class" topics in the MSDN documentation.

7.7 Using Common Patterns

Problem

You need a quick list from which to choose regular expression patterns that match standard items. These standard items could be a Social Security number, a zip code, a word containing only characters, an alphanumeric word, an email address, a URL, dates, or one of many other possible items used throughout business applications.

These patterns can be useful in making sure that a user has input the correct data and that it is well formed. These patterns can also be used as an extra security measure to keep hackers from attempting to break your code by entering strange or malformed input (e.g., SQL injection or cross-site-scripting attacks). Note that these regular expressions are not a silver bullet that will stop all attacks on your system; rather, they are an added layer of defense.

Solution

- Match only alphanumeric characters along with the characters -, +, ., and any whitespace:

  ```
  ^([\w\.\+\-]|\s)*$
  ```

 Be careful using the - (hyphen) character within a character class—that is, a regular expression enclosed within [and]. That character is also used to specify a range of characters, as in a-z for "a through z inclusive." If you want to use a literal - character, either escape it with \ or put it at the end of the expression, as shown in the next examples.

- Match only alphanumeric characters along with the characters -, +, ., and any whitespace, with the stipulation that there is at least one of these characters and no more than 10 of these characters:

  ```
  ^([\w\.\+\-]|\s){1,10}$
  ```

- Match a person's name, up to 55 characters:

  `^[a-zA-Z'\'\-\s]{1,55}$`

- Match a positive or negative integer:

  `^(\+|\-)?\d+$`

- Match a positive or negative floating-point number only; this pattern does not match integers:

  `^(\+|\-)?(\d*\.\d+)$`

  Match a floating-point or integer number that can have a positive or negative value:

  `^(\+|\-)?(\d*\.)?\d+$`

- Match a date in the form ##/##/####, where the day and month can be a one- or two-digit value and the year can only be a four-digit value:

  `^\d{1,2}\/\d{1,2}\/\d{4}$`

- Verify if the input is a Social Security number of the form ###-##-####:

  `^\d{3}-\d{2}-\d{4}$`

- Match an IPv4 address:

  `^([0-2]?[0-9]?[0-9]\.){3}[0-2]?[0-9]?[0-9]$`

- Verify that an email address is in the form *name@address* where *address* is not an IP address:

  `^[A-Za-z0-9_\-\.]+@(([A-Za-z0-9\-])+\.)+([A-Za-z\-])+$`

- Verify that an email address is in the form *name@address* where *address* is an IP address:

  `^[A-Za-z0-9_\-\.]+@([0-2]?[0-9]?[0-9]\.){3}[0-2]?[0-9]?[0-9]$`

- Match or verify a URL that uses either the HTTP, HTTPS, or FTP protocol. Note that this regular expression will not match relative URLs:

  `^(http|https|ftp)\://[a-zA-Z0-9\-\.]+\.[a-zA-Z]{2,3}(:[a-zA-Z0-9]*)?/?`
  `([a-zA-Z0-9\-\._\?\,\'/\\\+&%\$#\=~])*$`

- Match only a dollar amount with the optional $ and + or - preceding characters (note that any number of decimal places may be added):

  `^\$?[+-]?[\d,]*(\.\d*)?$`

  This is similar to the previous regular expression, except that no more than two decimal places are allowed:

  `^\$?[+-]?[\d,]*\.?\d{0,2}$`

- Match a credit card number to be entered as four sets of four digits separated with a space, -, or no character at all:

    ```
    ^((\d{4}[- ]?){3}\d{4})$
    ```

- Match a zip code to be entered as five digits with an optional four-digit extension:

    ```
    ^\d{5}(-\d{4})?$
    ```

- Match a North American phone number with an optional area code and an optional - character to be used in the phone number and no extension:

    ```
    ^(\(?[0-9]{3}\)?)?\-?[0-9]{3}\-?[0-9]{4}$
    ```

- Match a phone number similar to the previous regular expression but allow an optional five-digit extension prefixed with either ext or extension:

    ```
    ^(\(?[0-9]{3}\)?)?\-?[0-9]{3}\-?[0-9]{4}(\s*ext(ension)?[0-9]{5})?$
    ```

- Match a full path beginning with the drive letter and optionally match a filename with a three-character extension (note that no .. characters signifying to move up the directory hierarchy are allowed, nor is a directory name with a . followed by an extension):

    ```
    ^[a-zA-Z]:[\\/]([_a-zA-Z0-9]+[\\/]?)*([_a-zA-Z0-9]+\.[_a-zA-Z0-9]{0,3})?$
    ```

- Verify if the input password string matches some specific rules for entering a password (i.e., the password is between 6 and 25 characters in length and contains alphanumeric characters):

    ```
    ^(?=.*\d)(?=.*[a-z])(?=.*[A-Z]).{6,25}$
    ```

- Determine if any malicious characters were input by the user. Note that this regular expression will not prevent all malicious input, and it also prevents some valid input, such as last names that contain a single quote:

    ```
    ^([^\)\(\<\>\"\'\%\&\+\;][(-{2})])*$
    ```

- Extract a tag from an XHTML, HTML, or XML string. This regular expression will return the beginning tag and ending tag, including any attributes of the tag.

    Note that you will need to replace *TAGNAME* with the real tag name you want to search for:

    ```
    <TAGNAME.*?>(.*?)</TAGNAME>
    ```

- Extract a comment line from code. The following regular expression extracts HTML comments from a web page. This can be useful in determining if any HTML comments that are leaking sensitive information need to be removed from your code base before it goes into production:

    ```
    <!--.*?-->
    ```

- Match a C# single-line comment:

    ```
    //.*$
    ```

- Match a C# multiline comment:

```
/\*.*?\*/
```

 While the four aforementioned regular expressions are great for finding tags and comments, they are not foolproof. To accurately find all tags and comments, you need to use a full parser for the language you are targeting.

Discussion

Regular expressions are effective at finding specific information, and they have a wide range of uses. Many applications use them to locate specific information within a larger range of text, as well as to filter out bad input. The filtering action is very useful in tightening the security of an application and preventing an attacker from attempting to use carefully formed input to gain access to a machine on the Internet or a local network. By using a regular expression to allow only good input to be passed to the application, you can reduce the likelihood of many types of attacks, such as SQL injection or cross-site scripting.

The regular expressions presented in this recipe provide only a small cross-section of what you can accomplish with them. You can easily modify these expressions to suit your needs. Take, for example, the following expression, which allows only between 1 and 10 alphanumeric characters, along with a few symbols, as input:

```
^([\w\.\+\-]|\s){1,10}$
```

By changing the {1,10} part of the regular expression to {0,200}, you can make this expression match a blank entry or an entry of the specified symbols up to and including 200 characters.

Note the use of the ^ character at the beginning of the expression and the $ character at the end of the expression. These characters start the match at the beginning of the text and match all the way to the end of the text. Adding these characters forces the regular expression to match the entire string or none of it. By removing these characters, you can search for specific text within a larger block of text. For example, the following regular expression matches only a string containing nothing but a US zip code (there can be no leading or trailing spaces):

```
^\d{5}(-\d{4})?$
```

This version matches only a zip code with leading or trailing spaces (notice the addition of the \s* to the beginning and ending of the expression):

```
^\s*\d{5}(-\d{4})?\s*$
```

However, this modified expression matches a zip code found anywhere within a string (including a string containing just a zip code):

```
\d{5}(-\d{4})?
```

Use the regular expressions in this recipe and modify them to suit your needs.

See Also

Introducing Regular Expressions by Michael Fitzgerald and *Regular Expressions Cookbook* by Jan Goyvaerts and Steven Levithan (both O'Reilly).

CHAPTER 8

Filesystem I/O

8.0 Introduction

This chapter deals with a number of filesystem-related subjects, such as directory- or folder-based programming tasks. Some of the more advanced topics in filesystem I/O (input/output) are also touched on, such as:

- Locking subsections of a file
- Monitoring for certain filesystem actions
- Version information in files
- File compression

Various file and directory I/O techniques are used throughout the recipes to show you how to perform tasks such as creating, opening, deleting, reading, and writing with files and directories. This is fundamental knowledge that will help you understand the file I/O recipes and how to modify them for your purposes.

A number of the recipes have been updated to use the `async` and `await` operators to help alleviate the latency you'd typically encounter when dealing with the filesystem or network when performing file I/O. Using `async` and `await` improves your code's overall responsiveness by allowing the I/O operations to occur but not to block the calling thread as they normally would until they've completed.

Unless otherwise specified, you need the following `using` statements in any program that uses snippets or methods from this chapter:

```
using System;
using System.IO;
```

8.1 Searching for Directories or Files Using Wildcards

Problem

You are attempting to find one or more specific files or directories that may or may not exist within the current filesystem. You might need to use wildcard characters in order to widen the search—for example, searching for all usermode dump files in a filesystem. These files have a *.dmp* extension.

Solution

There are several methods of obtaining this information. The first three methods return a string array containing the full path of each item. The next three methods return an object that encapsulates a directory, a file, or both.

The static `GetFileSystemEntries` method on the `Directory` class returns a string array containing the names of all files and directories within a single directory, for example:

```
public static void DisplayFilesAndSubDirectories(string path)
{
    if (string.IsNullOrWhiteSpace(path))
        throw new ArgumentNullException(nameof(path));

    string[] items = Directory.GetFileSystemEntries(path);
    Array.ForEach(items, item =>
    {
        Console.WriteLine(item);
    });
}
```

The static `GetDirectories` method on the `Directory` class returns a string array containing the names of all directories within a single directory. The following method, `DisplayDirs`, shows how you might use it:

```
public static void DisplaySubDirectories(string path)
{
    if (string.IsNullOrWhiteSpace(path))
        throw new ArgumentNullException(nameof(path));

    string[] items = Directory.GetDirectories(path);
    Array.ForEach(items, item =>
    {
        Console.WriteLine(item);
    });
}
```

The static `GetFiles` method on the `Directory` class returns a string array containing the names of all files within a single directory. The following method is very similar to DisplayDirs but calls `Directory.GetFiles` instead of `Directory.GetDirecto` ries:

```
public static void DisplayFiles(string path)
{
    if (string.IsNullOrWhiteSpace(path))
        throw new ArgumentNullException(nameof(path));

    string[] items = Directory.GetFiles(path);
    Array.ForEach(items, item =>
    {
        Console.WriteLine(item);
    });
}
```

These next two methods return an object instead of simply a string. The `GetFileSys temInfos` method of the `DirectoryInfo` object returns a strongly typed array of `File SystemInfo` objects (that is, of `DirectoryInfo` and `FileInfo` objects) representing the directories and files within a single directory. The following example calls the `Get FileSystemInfos` method to retrieve an array of `FileSystemInfo` objects representing all the items in a particular directory and then lists a string of display information for `FileSystemInfo` to the console window. The display information is created by the extension method `ToDisplayString` on `FileSystemInfo`:

```
public static void DisplayDirectoryContents(string path)
{
    if (string.IsNullOrWhiteSpace(path))
        throw new ArgumentNullException(nameof(path));

    DirectoryInfo mainDir = new DirectoryInfo(path);
    var fileSystemDisplayInfos =
        (from fsi in mainDir.GetFileSystemInfos()
        where fsi is FileSystemInfo || fsi is DirectoryInfo
        select fsi.ToDisplayString()).ToArray();

    Array.ForEach(fileSystemDisplayInfos, s =>
    {
        Console.WriteLine(s);
    });
}

public static string ToDisplayString(this FileSystemInfo fileSystemInfo)
{
    string type = fileSystemInfo.GetType().ToString();
    if (fileSystemInfo is DirectoryInfo)
        type = "DIRECTORY";
    else if (fileSystemInfo is FileInfo)
        type = "FILE";
    return $"{type}: {fileSystemInfo.Name}";
}
```

The output for this code is shown here:

```
DIRECTORY: MyNestedTempDir
DIRECTORY: MyNestedTempDirPattern
FILE: MyTempFile.PDB
FILE: MyTempFile.TXT
```

The GetDirectories instance method of the DirectoryInfo object returns an array of DirectoryInfo objects representing only subdirectories in a single directory. For example, the following code calls the GetDirectories method to retrieve an array of DirectoryInfo objects and then displays the Name property of each object to the console window:

```
public static void DisplayDirectoriesFromInfo(string path)
{
    if (string.IsNullOrWhiteSpace(path))
        throw new ArgumentNullException(nameof(path));

    DirectoryInfo mainDir = new DirectoryInfo(path);
    DirectoryInfo[] items = mainDir.GetDirectories();
    Array.ForEach(items, item =>
    {
        Console.WriteLine($"DIRECTORY: {item.Name}");
    });
}
```

The GetFiles instance method of the DirectoryInfo object returns an array of FileInfo objects representing only the files in a single directory. For example, the following code calls the GetFiles method to retrieve an array of FileInfo objects, and then it displays the Name property of each object to the console window:

```
public static void DisplayFilesFromInfo(string path)
{
    if (string.IsNullOrWhiteSpace(path))
        throw new ArgumentNullException(nameof(path));

    DirectoryInfo mainDir = new DirectoryInfo(path);
    FileInfo[] items = mainDir.GetFiles();
    Array.ForEach(items, item =>
    {
        Console.WriteLine($"FILE: {item.Name}");
    });
}
```

The static GetFileSystemEntries method on the Directory class returns all files and directories in a single directory that match pattern:

```
public static void DisplayFilesWithPattern(string path, string pattern)
{
    if (string.IsNullOrWhiteSpace(path))
        throw new ArgumentNullException(nameof(path));
    if (string.IsNullOrWhiteSpace(pattern))
```

```
        throw new ArgumentNullException(nameof(pattern));

    string[] items = Directory.GetFileSystemEntries(path, pattern);
    Array.ForEach(items, item =>
    {
        Console.WriteLine(item);
    });
}
```

The static `GetDirectories` method on the `Directory` class returns only those directories in a single directory that match `pattern`:

```
public static void DisplayDirectoriesWithPattern(string path, string pattern)
{
    if (string.IsNullOrWhiteSpace(path))
        throw new ArgumentNullException(nameof(path));
    if (string.IsNullOrWhiteSpace(pattern))
        throw new ArgumentNullException(nameof(pattern));

    string[] items = Directory.GetDirectories(path, pattern);
    Array.ForEach(items, item =>
    {
        Console.WriteLine(item);
    });
}
```

The static `GetFiles` method on the `Directory` class returns only those files in a single
directory that match `pattern`:

```
public static void DisplayFilesWithGetFiles(string path, string pattern)
{
    if (string.IsNullOrWhiteSpace(path))
        throw new ArgumentNullException(nameof(path));
    if (string.IsNullOrWhiteSpace(pattern))
        throw new ArgumentNullException(nameof(pattern));

    string[] items = Directory.GetFiles(path, pattern);
    Array.ForEach(items, item =>
    {
        Console.WriteLine(item);
    });
}
```

These next three methods return an object instead of simply a string. The first
instance method is `GetFileSystemInfos`, which returns both directories and files in a
single directory that match `pattern`:

```
public static void DisplayDirectoryContentsWithPattern(string path,
    string pattern)
{
    if (string.IsNullOrWhiteSpace(path))
        throw new ArgumentNullException(nameof(path));
    if (string.IsNullOrWhiteSpace(pattern))
```

```
    throw new ArgumentNullException(nameof(pattern));

DirectoryInfo mainDir = new DirectoryInfo(path);
var fileSystemDisplayInfos =
    (from fsi in mainDir.GetFileSystemInfos(pattern)
    where fsi is FileSystemInfo || fsi is DirectoryInfo
    select fsi.ToDisplayString()).ToArray();

Array.ForEach(fileSystemDisplayInfos, s =>
{
    Console.WriteLine(s);
});
}
```

The GetDirectories instance method returns only directories (contained in the DirectoryInfo object) in a single directory that match pattern:

```
public static void DisplayDirectoriesWithPatternFromInfo(string path,
    string pattern)
{
    if (string.IsNullOrWhiteSpace(path))
        throw new ArgumentNullException(nameof(path));
    if (string.IsNullOrWhiteSpace(pattern))
        throw new ArgumentNullException(nameof(pattern));

    DirectoryInfo mainDir = new DirectoryInfo(path);
    DirectoryInfo[] items = mainDir.GetDirectories(pattern);
    Array.ForEach(items, item =>
    {
        Console.WriteLine($"DIRECTORY: {item.Name}");
    });
}
```

The GetFiles instance method returns only file information (contained in the FileInfo object) in a single directory that matches pattern:

```
public static void DisplayFilesWithInstanceGetFiles(string path, string pattern)
{
    if (string.IsNullOrWhiteSpace(path))
        throw new ArgumentNullException(nameof(path));
    if (string.IsNullOrWhiteSpace(pattern))
        throw new ArgumentNullException(nameof(pattern));

    DirectoryInfo mainDir = new DirectoryInfo(path);
    FileInfo[] items = mainDir.GetFiles(pattern);
    Array.ForEach(items, item =>
    {
        Console.WriteLine($"FILE: {item.Name}");
    });
}
```

Discussion

If you need just an array of strings containing paths to both directories and files, you can use the static method `Directory.GetFileSystemEntries`. The string array returned does not include any information about whether an individual element is a directory or a file. Each string element contains the entire path to either a directory or file contained within the specified path.

To quickly and easily distinguish between directories and files, use the `Directory.GetDirectories` and `Directory.GetFiles` static methods. These methods return arrays of directory names and filenames. These methods return an array of string objects. Each element contains the full path to the directory or file.

Returning a string is fine if you do not need any other information about the directory or file returned or if you are going to need more information for only one of the files returned. It is more efficient to use the static methods to get the list of filenames and just retrieve the `FileInfo` for the ones you need than to have all of the `FileInfo`s constructed for the directory, as the instance methods will do. If you need to access attributes, lengths, or times on every one of the files, you should consider using the instance methods that retrieve the `FileInfo` details.

The instance method `GetFileSystemInfos` returns an array of strongly typed `FileSystemInfo` objects. (The `FileSystemInfo` object is the base class to the `DirectoryInfo` and `FileInfo` objects.) Therefore, you can test whether the returned type is a `DirectoryInfo` or `FileInfo` object using the `is` or `as` keyword. Once you know what subclass the object really is, you can cast the object to that type and begin using it.

To get only `DirectoryInfo` objects, use the overloaded `GetDirectories` instance method. To get only `FileInfo` objects, use the overloaded `GetFiles` instance method. These methods return an array of `DirectoryInfo` and `FileInfo` objects, respectively, each element of which encapsulates a directory or file.

There are certain behaviors to be aware of for the patterns you can provide when filtering the results from `GetFiles` or `GetFileSystemInfos`:

- The pattern cannot contain any of the `InvalidPathChars` and cannot use the "go back up in the folder structure one level" symbol (`..`).

- The order in which the items in the array are returned is not guaranteed, but you can use `Sort` or order the results in a query.

- When an extension is exactly three characters, the behavior is different in that the pattern will match on any files with those first three characters in the extension.

- `*.htm` returns files having an extension of *.htm*, *.html*, *.htma*, and so on.

- When an extension has fewer than or more than three characters, the pattern will perform exact matching.

- `*.cs` returns only files having an extension of *.cs*.

See Also

The "DirectoryInfo Class," "FileInfo Class," and "FileSystemInfo Class" topics in the MSDN documentation.

8.2 Obtaining the Directory Tree

Problem

You need to get a directory tree, potentially including filenames, extending from any point in the directory hierarchy. In addition, each directory or file returned must be in the form of an object encapsulating that item. This will allow you to perform operations on the returned objects, such as deleting the file, renaming the file, or examining/changing its attributes. Finally, you potentially need the ability to search for a specific subset of these items based on a pattern, such as finding only files with the *.pdb* extension.

Solution

By calling the `GetFileSystemInfos` instance method, you can retrieve all of the files and directories down the directory hierarchy from any starting point as an enumerable list:

```
public static IEnumerable<FileSystemInfo> GetAllFilesAndDirectories(string dir)
{
    if (string.IsNullOrWhiteSpace(dir))
        throw new ArgumentNullException(nameof(dir));

    DirectoryInfo dirInfo = new DirectoryInfo(dir);
    Stack<FileSystemInfo> stack = new Stack<FileSystemInfo>();

    stack.Push(dirInfo);
    while (dirInfo != null || stack.Count > 0)
    {
        FileSystemInfo fileSystemInfo = stack.Pop();
        DirectoryInfo subDirectoryInfo = fileSystemInfo as DirectoryInfo;
        if (subDirectoryInfo != null)
        {
            yield return subDirectoryInfo;
            foreach (FileSystemInfo fsi in subDirectoryInfo.GetFileSystemInfos())
                stack.Push(fsi);
            dirInfo = subDirectoryInfo;
```

```
        }
        else
        {
            yield return fileSystemInfo;
            dirInfo = null;
        }
    }
}
```

To display the results of the file and directory retrieval, use the following query:

```
public static void DisplayAllFilesAndDirectories(string dir)
{
    if (string.IsNullOrWhiteSpace(dir))
        throw new ArgumentNullException(nameof(dir));

    var strings = (from fileSystemInfo in GetAllFilesAndDirectories(dir)
                    select fileSystemInfo.ToDisplayString()).ToArray();

    Array.ForEach(strings, s => { Console.WriteLine(s); });
}
```

Since the results are queryable, you don't have to retrieve information about *all* files and directories. The following query uses a case-insensitive comparison to obtain a listing of all files with the extension of *.pdb* that reside in directories that contain *Chapter 1*:

```
public static void DisplayAllFilesWithExtension(string dir, string extension)
{
    if (string.IsNullOrWhiteSpace(dir))
        throw new ArgumentNullException(nameof(dir));
    if (string.IsNullOrWhiteSpace(extension))
        throw new ArgumentNullException(nameof(extension));

    var strings = (from fileSystemInfo in GetAllFilesAndDirectories(dir)
                    where fileSystemInfo is FileInfo &&
                        fileSystemInfo.FullName.Contains("Chapter 1") &&
                        (string.Compare(fileSystemInfo.Extension, extension,
                            StringComparison.OrdinalIgnoreCase) == 0)
                    select fileSystemInfo.ToDisplayString()).ToArray();

    Array.ForEach(strings, s => { Console.WriteLine(s); });
}
```

Discussion

To obtain a tree representation of a directory and the files it contains, you could use recursive iterators in a method like this:

```
public static IEnumerable<FileSystemInfo> GetAllFilesAndDirectoriesWithRecursion(
    string dir)
{
    if (string.IsNullOrWhiteSpace(dir))
```

```
                throw new ArgumentNullException(nameof(dir));

        DirectoryInfo dirInfo = new DirectoryInfo(dir);
        FileSystemInfo[] fileSystemInfos = dirInfo.GetFileSystemInfos();
        foreach (FileSystemInfo fileSystemInfo in fileSystemInfos)
        {
            yield return fileSystemInfo;
            if (fileSystemInfo is DirectoryInfo)
            {
                foreach (FileSystemInfo fsi in
    GetAllFilesAndDirectoriesWithRecursion(fileSystemInfo.FullName))
                    yield return fsi;
            }
        }
    }

    public static void DisplayAllFilesAndDirectoriesWithRecursion(string dir)
    {
        if (string.IsNullOrWhiteSpace(dir))
            throw new ArgumentNullException(nameof(dir));

        var strings = (from fileSystemInfo in
                        GetAllFilesAndDirectoriesWithRecursion(dir)
                        select fileSystemInfo.ToDisplayString()).ToArray();

        Array.ForEach(strings, s => { Console.WriteLine(s); });
    }
```

The main difference between this and the Solution code is that this uses *recursive iterators*, and the Solution uses *iterative iterators* and an explicit stack.

 You would not want to use the recursive iterator method, as the performance is in fact O($n * d$), where n is the number of FileSystemInfos and d is the depth of the directory hierarchy—which is typically log n. See the demonstration code.

You can check the performance with the following code if the Solution methods are renamed to DisplayAllFilesAndDirectoriesWithoutRecursion and DisplayAllFilesWithExtensionWithoutRecursion, respectively:

```
string dir = Environment.GetFolderPath(Environment.SpecialFolder.ProgramFiles);

// list all of the files without recursion
Stopwatch watch1 = Stopwatch.StartNew();
DisplayAllFilesAndDirectoriesWithoutRecursion(tempDir1);
watch1.Stop();
Console.WriteLine("*************************");

// list all of the files without using recursion
Stopwatch watch2 = Stopwatch.StartNew();
```

```
    DisplayAllFilesAndDirectoriesWithoutRecursion(tempDir1);
    watch2.Stop();
    Console.WriteLine("**************************");
    Console.WriteLine(
        $"Non-Recursive method time elapsed {watch1.Elapsed.ToString()}");
    Console.WriteLine($"Recursive method time elapsed {watch2.Elapsed.ToString()}");
```

Here is the code without recursion methods:

```
public static void DisplayAllFilesAndDirectoriesWithoutRecursion(string dir)
{
    var strings = from fileSystemInfo in
                    GetAllFilesAndDirectoriesWithoutRecursion(dir)
                  select fileSystemInfo.ToDisplayString();

    foreach (string s in strings)
        Console.WriteLine(s);
}

public static void DisplayAllFilesWithExtensionWithoutRecursion(string dir,
    string extension)
{
    var strings = from fileSystemInfo in
                    GetAllFilesAndDirectoriesWithoutRecursion(dir)
                  where fileSystemInfo is FileInfo &&
                        fileSystemInfo.FullName.Contains("Chapter 1") &&
                        (string.Compare(fileSystemInfo.Extension, extension,
                                        StringComparison.OrdinalIgnoreCase) == 0)
                  select fileSystemInfo.ToDisplayString();

    foreach (string s in strings)
        Console.WriteLine(s);
}

public static IEnumerable<FileSystemInfo>
    GetAllFilesAndDirectoriesWithoutRecursion(
    string dir)
{
    DirectoryInfo dirInfo = new DirectoryInfo(dir);
    Stack<FileSystemInfo> stack = new Stack<FileSystemInfo>();

    stack.Push(dirInfo);
    while (dirInfo != null || stack.Count > 0)
    {
        FileSystemInfo fileSystemInfo = stack.Pop();
        DirectoryInfo subDirectoryInfo = fileSystemInfo as DirectoryInfo;
        if (subDirectoryInfo != null)
        {
            yield return subDirectoryInfo;
            foreach (FileSystemInfo fsi in subDirectoryInfo.GetFileSystemInfos())
                stack.Push(fsi);
            dirInfo = subDirectoryInfo;
        }
```

```
        else
        {
            yield return fileSystemInfo;
            dirInfo = null;
        }
    }
}
```

See Also

The "DirectoryInfo Class," "FileInfo Class," and "FileSystemInfo Class" topics in the MSDN documentation.

8.3 Parsing a Path

Problem

You need to separate the constituent parts of a path and place them into separate variables.

Solution

Use the static methods of the Path class:

```
public static void DisplayPathParts(string path)
{
    if (string.IsNullOrWhiteSpace(path))
        throw new ArgumentNullException(nameof(path));

    string root = Path.GetPathRoot(path);
    string dirName = Path.GetDirectoryName(path);
    string fullFileName = Path.GetFileName(path);
    string fileExt = Path.GetExtension(path);
    string fileNameWithoutExt = Path.GetFileNameWithoutExtension(path);
    StringBuilder format = new StringBuilder();
    format.Append($"ParsePath of {path} breaks up into the following pieces:" +
        $"{Environment.NewLine}");
    format.Append($"\tRoot: {root}{Environment.NewLine}");
    format.Append($"\tDirectory Name: {dirName}{Environment.NewLine}");
    format.Append($"\tFull File Name: {fullFileName}{Environment.NewLine}");
    format.Append($"\tFile Extension: {fileExt}{Environment.NewLine}");
    format.Append($"\tFile Name Without Extension: {fileNameWithoutExt}" +
        $"{Environment.NewLine}");
    Console.WriteLine(format.ToString());
}
```

If the string C:\test\tempfile.txt is passed to this method, the output looks like this:

```
ParsePath of C:\test\tempfile.txt breaks up into the following pieces:
        Root: C:\
        Directory Name: C:\test
        Full File Name: tempfile.txt
        File Extension: .txt
        File Name Without Extension: tempfile
```

Discussion

The `Path` class contains methods that can be used to parse a given path. Using these classes is much easier and less error-prone than writing path- and filename-parsing code. If these classes are not used, you could also introduce security holes into your application if the information gathered from manual parsing routines is used in security decisions for your application. There are five main methods used to parse a path: `GetPathRoot`, `GetDirectoryName`, `GetFileName`, `GetExtension`, and `GetFileNameWithoutExtension`. Each has a single parameter, `path`, which represents the path to be parsed:

GetPathRoot
>   This method returns the root directory of the path. If no root is provided in the path, such as when a relative path is used, this method returns an empty string, not `null`.

GetDirectoryName
>   This method returns the complete path for the directory containing the file.

GetFileName
>   This method returns the filename, including the file extension. If no filename is provided in the path, this method returns an empty string, not `null`.

GetExtension
>   This method returns the file's extension. If no extension is provided for the file or no file exists in the path, this method returns an empty string, not `null`.

GetFileNameWithoutExtension
>   This method returns the root filename without the file extension.

Be aware that these methods do not actually determine whether the drives, directories, or even files exist on the system that runs these methods. These methods are string parsers, and if you pass one of them a string in some strange format (such as \\ZY:\foo), it will try to do what it can with it anyway:

```
ParsePath of \\ZY:\foo breaks up into the following pieces:
        Root: \\ZY:\foo
        Directory Name:
        Full File Name: foo
        File Extension:
        File Name Without Extension: foo
```

These methods will, however, throw an exception if illegal characters are found in the path.

To determine whether files or directories exist, use the static `Directory.Exists` or `File.Exists` method.

See Also

The "Path Class" topic in the MSDN documentation.

8.4 Launching and Interacting with Console Utilities

Problem

You have an application that you need to automate and that takes input only from the standard input stream. You need to drive this application via the commands it will take over the standard input stream.

Solution

Say you need to drive the *cmd.exe* application to display the current time with the `TIME /T` command (you could just run this command from the command line, but this way we can demonstrate an alternative method to drive an application that responds to standard input). The way to do this is to launch a process that is looking for input on the standard input stream. This is accomplished via the `Process` class `StartInfo` property, which is an instance of a `ProcessStartInfo` class. `StartInfo` has fields that control many details of the environment in which the new process will execute, and the `Process.Start` method will launch the new process with those options.

First, make sure that the `StartInfo.RedirectStandardInput` property is set to `true`. This setting notifies the process that it should read from standard input. Then, set the `StartInfo.UseShellExecute` property to `false`, because if you were to let the shell launch the process for you, it would prevent you from redirecting standard input.

Once this is done, launch the process and write to its standard input stream as shown in Example 8-1.

Example 8-1. RunProcessToReadStdIn method

```
public static void RunProcessToReadStandardInput()
{
    Process application = new Process();
    // Run the command shell.
    application.StartInfo.FileName = @"cmd.exe";
```

```
    // Turn on command extensions for cmd.exe.
    application.StartInfo.Arguments = "/E:ON";

    application.StartInfo.RedirectStandardInput = true;

    application.StartInfo.UseShellExecute = false;

    application.Start();

    StreamWriter input = application.StandardInput;
    // Run the command to display the time.
    input.WriteLine("TIME /T");

    // Stop the application we launched.
    input.WriteLine("exit");
}
```

Discussion

Redirecting the input stream for a process allows you to programmatically interact with certain applications and utilities that you would otherwise not be able to automate without additional tools. Once the input has been redirected, you can write into the standard input stream of the process by reading the `Process.StandardInput` property, which returns a `StreamWriter`. Once you have that, you can send things to the process via `WriteLine` calls, as shown earlier.

To use `StandardInput`, you have to specify `true` for the `StartInfo` property's `RedirectStandardInput` property. Otherwise, reading the `StandardInput` property throws an exception.

When `UseShellExecute` is `false`, you can use `Process` only to create executable processes. Normally you can use the `Process` class to perform operations on the file, such as printing a Microsoft Word document. Another difference when `UseShellExecute` is set to `false` is that the working directory is not used to find the executable, so you must be mindful to pass a full path or have the executable on your PATH environment variable.

See Also

The "Process Class," "ProcessStartInfo Class," "RedirectStandardInput Property," and "UseShellExecute Property" topics in the MSDN documentation.

8.5 Locking Subsections of a File

Problem

You need to read or write data from or to a section of a file, and you want to make sure that no other processes or threads can access, modify, or delete the file until you have finished with it.

Solution

To lock out other processes from accessing your file while you are using it, you use the `Lock` method of the `FileStream` class. The following code creates a file from the `fileName` parameter and writes two lines to it. The entire file is then locked via the `Lock` method. While the file is locked, the code goes off and does some other processing; when this code returns, the file is closed and thereby unlocked:

```
public static async Task CreateLockedFileAsync(string fileName)
{
    if (string.IsNullOrWhiteSpace(fileName))
        throw new ArgumentNullException(nameof(fileName));

    FileStream fileStream = null;
    try
    {
        fileStream = new FileStream(fileName,
                FileMode.Create,
                FileAccess.ReadWrite,
                FileShare.ReadWrite, 4096, useAsync: true);

        using (StreamWriter writer = new StreamWriter(fileStream))
        {
            await writer.WriteLineAsync("The First Line");
            await writer.WriteLineAsync("The Second Line");
            await writer.FlushAsync();

            try
            {
                // Lock all of the file.
                fileStream.Lock(0, fileStream.Length);

                // Do some lengthy processing here...
                Thread.Sleep(1000);
            }
            finally
            {
                // Make sure we unlock the file.
                // If a process terminates with part of a file locked or closes
                // a file that has outstanding locks, the behavior is undefined
                // which is MS speak for bad things....
```

```
                fileStream.Unlock(0, fileStream.Length);
            }

            await writer.WriteLineAsync("The Third Line");
            fileStream = null;
        }
    }
    finally
    {
        if (fileStream != null)
            fileStream.Dispose();
    }
}
```

 Note that in the CreateLockedFileAsync method we are using the async and await operators. The async operator allows you to indicate that a method is eligible for suspension at certain points, and the await operator designates those suspension points in your code —which means that the compiler knows that the async method can't continue past that point until the awaited asynchronous process is complete. While it waits, the caller gets control back. This helps your program in that the thread for the caller is not blocked and can perform other work, but the method will still act as if it was called synchronously.

Discussion

If a file is opened within your application and the FileShare parameter of the File
Stream.Open call is set to FileShare.ReadWrite or FileShare.Write, other code in
your application can view or alter the contents of the file while you are using it. To
handle file access with more granularity, use the Lock method of the FileStream
object to prevent other code from overwriting all or a portion of your file. Once you
are done with the locked portion of your file, you can call the Unlock method on the
FileStream object to allow other code in your application to write data to that por‐
tion of the file.

To lock an entire file, use the following syntax:

```
fileStream.Lock(0, fileStream.Length);
```

To lock a portion of a file, use the following syntax:

```
fileStream.Lock(4, fileStream.Length - 4);
```

This line of code locks the entire file except for the first four characters. Note that you
can lock an entire file and still open it multiple times, as well as write to it.

If another thread is accessing this file, you might see an IOException thrown during the call to one of the WriteAsync, FlushAsync, or Close methods. For example, the following code is prone to such an exception:

```
public static async Task CreateLockedFileWithExceptionAsync(string fileName)
{

    FileStream fileStream = null;
    try
    {
        fileStream = new FileStream(fileName,
                FileMode.Create,
                FileAccess.ReadWrite,
                FileShare.ReadWrite, 4096, useAsync: true);
        using (StreamWriter streamWriter = new StreamWriter(fileStream))
        {
            await streamWriter.WriteLineAsync("The First Line");
            await streamWriter.WriteLineAsync("The Second Line");
            await streamWriter.FlushAsync();

            // Lock all of the file.
            fileStream.Lock(0, fileStream.Length);

            FileStream writeFileStream = null;
            try
            {
                writeFileStream = new FileStream(fileName,
                                        FileMode.Open,
                                        FileAccess.Write,
                                        FileShare.ReadWrite, 4096,
                                        useAsync: true);
                using (StreamWriter streamWriter2 =
                    new StreamWriter(writeFileStream))
                {
                    await streamWriter2.WriteAsync("foo ");
                    try
                    {
                        streamWriter2.Close(); // --> Exception occurs here!
                    }
                    catch
                    {
                        Console.WriteLine(
                        "The streamWriter2.Close call generated an exception.");
                    }
                    streamWriter.WriteLine("The Third Line");
                }
                writeFileStream = null;
            }
            finally
            {
                if (writeFileStream != null)
                    writeFileStream.Dispose();
```

```
                }
            }
            fileStream = null;
        }
        finally
        {
            if (fileStream != null)
                fileStream.Dispose();
        }
    }
```

This code produces the following output:

```
The streamWriter2.Close call generated an exception.
```

Even though `streamWriter2`, the second `StreamWriter` object, writes to a locked file, it is only when the `streamWriter2.Close` method is executed that the `IOException` is thrown.

If the code for this recipe were rewritten as follows:

```
public static async Task CreateLockedFileWithUnlockAsync(string fileName)
{
    FileStream fileStream = null;
    try
    {
        fileStream = new FileStream(fileName,
                                    FileMode.Create,
                                    FileAccess.ReadWrite,
                                    FileShare.ReadWrite, 4096, useAsync: true);
        using (StreamWriter streamWriter = new StreamWriter(fileStream))
        {
            await streamWriter.WriteLineAsync("The First Line");
            await streamWriter.WriteLineAsync("The Second Line");
            await streamWriter.FlushAsync();

            // Lock all of the file.
            fileStream.Lock(0, fileStream.Length);

            // Try to access the locked file...
            FileStream writeFileStream = null;
            try
            {
                writeFileStream = new FileStream(fileName,
                                    FileMode.Open,
                                    FileAccess.Write,
                                    FileShare.ReadWrite, 4096,
                                    useAsync: true);
                using (StreamWriter streamWriter2 =
                    new StreamWriter(writeFileStream))
                {
                    await streamWriter2.WriteAsync("foo");
                    fileStream.Unlock(0, fileStream.Length);
```

```
                    await streamWriter2.FlushAsync();
                }
                writeFileStream = null;
            }
            finally
            {
                if (writeFileStream != null)
                    writeFileStream.Dispose();
            }
        }
        fileStream = null;
    }
    finally
    {
        if (fileStream != null)
            fileStream.Dispose();
    }
}
```

no exception is thrown. This is because the code unlocked the `FileStream` object that initially locked the entire file. This action also freed all of the locks on the file that this `FileStream` object was holding onto. In the example, the `streamWriter2.WriteA sync("Foo")` method had written Foo to the stream's buffer but had not flushed it, so the string Foo was still waiting to be flushed and written to the actual file. Keep this situation in mind when interleaving the opening, locking, and closing of streams. Sometimes mistakes in code are not immediately found during code reviews, unit testing, or formal quality assurance, and this can lead to some bugs that are more difficult to track down, so tread carefully when using file locking.

See Also

The "StreamWriter Class," "FileStream Class," and "Asynchronous Programming with Async and Await" topics in the MSDN documentation.

8.6 Waiting for an Action to Occur in the Filesystem

Problem

You need to be notified when a particular event occurs in the filesystem, such as the renaming of a file or directory, the increasing or decreasing of the size of a file, the deletion of a file or directory, the creation of a file or directory, or even the changing of a file's or directory's attribute(s). However, this notification must occur synchronously. In other words, the application cannot continue unless a specific action occurs to a file or directory.

Solution

The `WaitForChanged` method of the `FileSystemWatcher` class can be called to wait synchronously for an event notification. This is illustrated by the `WaitForZipCrea tion` method shown in Example 8-2, which waits for an action—more specifically, the creation of the *Backup.zip* file somewhere on the *C:* drive—to be performed before proceeding to the next line of code, which is the `WriteLine` statement. Finally, we spin off a task to do the actual work of creating the file. By doing this as a `Task`, we allow the processing to occur on a separate thread when one becomes available and the `FileSystemWatcher` to detect the file creation.

Example 8-2. WaitForZipCreation method

```
public static void WaitForZipCreation(string path, string fileName)
{
    if (string.IsNullOrWhiteSpace(path))
        throw new ArgumentNullException(nameof(path));
    if (string.IsNullOrWhiteSpace(fileName))
        throw new ArgumentNullException(nameof(fileName));

    FileSystemWatcher fsw = null;
    try
    {
        fsw = new FileSystemWatcher();
        string [] data = new string[] {path,fileName};
        fsw.Path = path;
        fsw.Filter = fileName;
        fsw.NotifyFilter = NotifyFilters.LastAccess | NotifyFilters.LastWrite
            | NotifyFilters.FileName | NotifyFilters.DirectoryName;

        // Run the code to generate the file we are looking for
        // Normally you wouldn't do this as another source is creating
        // this file
        Task work = Task.Run(() =>
        {
            try
            {
                // wait a sec...
                Thread.Sleep(1000);
                // create a file in the temp directory
                if (data.Length == 2)
                {
                    string dataPath = data[0];
                    string dataFile = path + data[1];
                    Console.WriteLine($"Creating {dataFile} in task...");
                    FileStream fileStream = File.Create(dataFile);
                    fileStream.Close();
                }
            }
            catch (Exception e)
```

```
        {
            Console.WriteLine(e.ToString());
        }
    });

    // Don't await the work task finish, as we detect that
    // through the FileSystemWatcher
    WaitForChangedResult result =
        fsw.WaitForChanged(WatcherChangeTypes.Created);
    Console.WriteLine($"{result.Name} created at {path}.");
}
catch(Exception e)
{
    Console.WriteLine(e.ToString());
}
finally
{
    // clean it up
    File.Delete(fileName);
    fsw?.Dispose();
}
}
```

Discussion

The `WaitForChanged` method returns a `WaitForChangedResult` structure that contains the properties listed in Table 8-1.

Table 8-1. WaitForChangedResult properties

Property	Description
Change Type	Lists the type of change that occurred. This change is returned as a `WatcherChangeTypes` enumeration. The values of this enumeration can possibly be ORed together.
Name	Holds the name of the file or directory that was changed. If the file or directory was renamed, this property returns the changed name. Its value is set to `null` if the operation method call times out.
OldName	The original name of the modified file or directory. If this file or directory was not renamed, this property will return the same value as the `Name` property. Its value is set to `null` if the operation method call times out.
TimedOut	Holds a Boolean indicating whether the `WaitForChanged` method timed out (`true`) or not (`false`).

The way we are currently making the `WaitForChanged` call could possibly block indefinitely. To prevent the code from hanging forever on the `WaitForChanged` call, you can specify a timeout value of three seconds as follows:

```
WaitForChangedResult result =
        fsw.WaitForChanged(WatcherChangeTypes.Created, 3000);
```

The `NotifyFilters` enumeration allows you to specify the types of files or folders to watch for, as shown in Table 8-2.

Table 8-2. NotifyFilters enumeration

Enumeration value	Definition
FileName	Name of the file
DirectoryName	Name of the directory
Attributes	The file or folder attributes
Size	The file or folder size
LastWrite	The date the file or folder last had anything written to it
LastAccess	The date the file or folder was last opened
CreationTime	The time the file or folder was created
Security	The security settings of the file or folder

See Also

The "FileSystemWatcher Class," "NotifyFilters Enumeration," and "WaitForChange-dResult Structure" topics in the MSDN documentation.

8.7 Comparing Version Information of Two Executable Modules

Problem

You need to programmatically compare the version information of two executable modules. An executable module is a file that contains executable code, such as an *.exe* or *.dll* file. The ability to compare the version information of two executable modules can be very useful to an application in situations such as:

- Trying to determine if it has all of the "right" pieces present to execute.
- Deciding on an assembly to dynamically load through reflection.
- Looking for the newest version of a file or *.dll* from many files spread out in the local filesystem or on a network.

Solution

Use the `CompareFileVersions` method to compare executable module version information. This method accepts two filenames, including their paths, as parameters. The version information of each module is retrieved and compared. This file returns a `FileComparison` enumeration, defined as follows:

```
public enum FileComparison
{
    Error = 0,
```

```
            Newer = 1,
            Older = 2,
            Same = 3
    }
```

The code for the `CompareFileVersions` method is shown in Example 8-3.

Example 8-3. CompareFileVersions method

```
private static FileComparison ComparePart(int p1, int p2) =>
    p1 > p2 ? FileComparison.Newer :
        (p1 < p2 ? FileComparison.Older : FileComparison.Same);

public static FileComparison CompareFileVersions(string file1, string file2)
{
    if (string.IsNullOrWhiteSpace(file1))
        throw new ArgumentNullException(nameof(file1));
    if (string.IsNullOrWhiteSpace(file2))
        throw new ArgumentNullException(nameof(file2));

    FileComparison retValue = FileComparison.Error;
    // get the version information
    FileVersionInfo file1Version = FileVersionInfo.GetVersionInfo(file1);
    FileVersionInfo file2Version = FileVersionInfo.GetVersionInfo(file2);

    retValue = ComparePart(file1Version.FileMajorPart,
        file2Version.FileMajorPart);
    if (retValue != FileComparison.Same)
    {
        retValue = ComparePart(file1Version.FileMinorPart, file2Version.FileMinorPart);
        if (retValue != FileComparison.Same)
        {
            retValue = ComparePart(file1Version.FileBuildPart,
                        file2Version.FileBuildPart);
            if (retValue != FileComparison.Same)
                retValue = ComparePart(file1Version.FilePrivatePart,
                        file2Version.FilePrivatePart);
        }
    }
    return retValue;
}
```

Discussion

Not all executable modules have version information. If you load a module with no version information using the `FileVersionInfo` class, you will not provoke an exception, nor will you get `null` back for the object reference. Instead, you will get a valid `FileVersionInfo` object with all data members in their initial state, which is `null` for .NET objects.

Assemblies actually have two sets of version information: the version information available in the assembly manifest and the PE (portable executable) file version information. FileVersionInfo reads the assembly manifest version information.

The first action this method takes is to determine whether the two files passed in to the file1 and file2 parameters actually exist. If so, the static GetVersionInfo method of the FileVersionInfo class is called to get version information for the two files.

The CompareFileVersions method attempts to compare each portion of the file's version number using the following properties of the FileVersionInfo object returned by GetVersionInfo:

FileMajorPart
> The first two bytes of the version number.

FileMinorPart
> The second two bytes of the version number.

FileBuildPart
> The third two bytes of the version number.

FilePrivatePart
> The final two bytes of the version number.

The full version number is composed of these four parts, making up an 8-byte number representing the file's version number.

The CompareFileVersions method first compares the FileMajorPart version information of the two files. If these are equal, the FileMinorPart version information of the two files is compared. This continues through the FileBuildPart and finally the FilePrivatePart version information values. If all four parts are equal, the files are considered to have the same version number. If either file is found to have a higher number than the other file, it is considered to be the latest version.

See Also

The "FileVersionInfo Class" topic in the MSDN documentation.

8.8 Querying Information for All Drives on a System

Problem

Your application needs to know if a drive (HDD, CD drive, DVD drive, BluRay drive, etc.) is available and ready to be written to and/or read from and if you have enough available free space on the drive.

Solution

Use the various properties in the `DriveInfo` class as shown here:

```
public static void DisplayAllDriveInfo()
{
    DriveInfo[] drives = DriveInfo.GetDrives();
    Array.ForEach(drives, drive =>
    {
        if (drive.IsReady)
        {
            Console.WriteLine($"Drive {drive.Name} is ready.");
            Console.WriteLine($"AvailableFreeSpace: {drive.AvailableFreeSpace}");
            Console.WriteLine($"DriveFormat: {drive.DriveFormat}");
            Console.WriteLine($"DriveType: {drive.DriveType}");
            Console.WriteLine($"Name: {drive.Name}");
            Console.WriteLine("RootDirectory.FullName: " +
                $"{drive.RootDirectory.FullName}");
            Console.WriteLine($"TotalFreeSpace: {drive.TotalFreeSpace}");
            Console.WriteLine($"TotalSize: {drive.TotalSize}");
            Console.WriteLine($"VolumeLabel: {drive.VolumeLabel}");
        }
        else
        {
            Console.WriteLine($"Drive {drive.Name} is not ready.");
        }
        Console.WriteLine();
    });
}
```

This code will display the results in the following format. Because each system is different, the results will vary:

```
Drive C:\ is ready.
AvailableFreeSpace: 143210795008
DriveFormat: NTFS
DriveType: Fixed
Name: C:\
RootDirectory.FullName: C:\
TotalFreeSpace: 143210795008
TotalSize: 159989886976
VolumeLabel: Vol1

Drive D:\ is ready.
AvailableFreeSpace: 0
DriveFormat: UDF
DriveType: CDRom
Name: D:\
RootDirectory.FullName: D:\
TotalFreeSpace: 0
TotalSize: 3305965568
VolumeLabel: Vol2
```

```
Drive E:\ is ready.
AvailableFreeSpace: 4649025536
DriveFormat: UDF
DriveType: CDRom
Name: E:\
RootDirectory.FullName: E:\
TotalFreeSpace: 4649025536
TotalSize: 4691197952
VolumeLabel: Vol3

Drive F:\ is not ready
```

Of particular interest are the IsReady and AvailableFreeSpace properties. The IsReady property determines if the drive is ready to be queried, written to, or read from but is not terribly reliable, as this state could quickly change. When using IsReady, be sure to account for the case where the drive becomes not ready as well. The AvailableFreeSpace property returns the free space on that drive in bytes.

Discussion

The DriveInfo class from the .NET Framework allows you to easily query information on one particular drive or on all drives in the system. To query the information from a single drive, use the code in Example 8-4.

Example 8-4. Getting information from a specific drive

```
DriveInfo drive = new DriveInfo("D");
if (drive.IsReady)
    Console.WriteLine($"The space available on the D:\\ drive: " +
            $"{drive.AvailableFreeSpace}");
else
    Console.WriteLine("Drive D:\\ is not ready.");
```

Notice that only the drive letter is passed in to the DriveInfo constructor. The drive letter can be either uppercase or lowercase—it does not matter. The next thing you will notice with the code in the Solution to this recipe is that the IsReady property is always tested for true before either using the drive or querying its properties. If we did not test this property for true and for some reason the drive was not ready (e.g., a CD was not in the drive at that time), a System.IO.IOException would be returned stating "The device is not ready." The DriveInfo constructor was not used for the Solution to this recipe. Instead, the static GetDrives method of the DriveInfo class was used to return an array of DriveInfo objects. Each DriveInfo object in this array corresponds to one drive on the current system.

The DriveType property of the DriveInfo class returns an enumeration value from the DriveType enumeration. This enumeration value identifies what type of drive the current `DriveInfo` object represents. Table 8-3 identifies the various values of the `DriveType` enumeration.

Table 8-3. DriveType enumeration values

Enum value	Description
CDRom	This can be a CD-ROM, CD writer, DVD-ROM, DVD, or Blu-ray writer drive.
Fixed	This is the fixed drive, such as an HDD. Note that USB HDDs fall into this category.
Network	A network drive.
NoRootDirectory	No root directory was found on this drive.
Ram	A RAM disk.
Removable	A removable storage device.
Unknown	Some other type of drive than those listed here.

In the `DriveInfo` class there are two very similar properties, `AvailableFreeSpace` and `TotalFreeSpace`. Both properties will return the same value in most cases. However, `AvailableFreeSpace` also takes into account any disk-quota information for a particular drive. You can find disk-quota information by right-clicking a drive in Windows Explorer and selecting the Properties pop-up menu item. This displays the Properties page for the drive. Click the Quota tab on the Properties page to view the quota information for the drive. If the Enable Quota Management checkbox is unchecked, then disk-quota management is disabled, and the `AvailableFreeSpace` and `TotalFreeSpace` properties should be equal.

See Also

The "DriveInfo Class" topic in the MSDN documentation.

8.9 Compressing and Decompressing Your Files

Problem

You need a way to compress a file using one of the stream-based classes without being constrained by the 4 GB limit imposed by the framework classes. In addition, you need a way to decompress the file to allow you to read it back in.

Solution

Use the `System.IO.Compression.DeflateStream` or the `System.IO.Compression.GZipStream` classes to read and write compressed data to a file using a "chunking" routine. The `CompressFileAsync`, `DecompressFileAsync`, and `Decompress` methods shown in Example 8-5 demonstrate how to use these classes to compress and decompress files on the fly.

Example 8-5. The CompressFileAsync and DecompressFileAsync methods

```
/// <summary>
/// Compress the source file to the destination file.
/// This is done in 1MB chunks to not overwhelm the memory usage.
/// </summary>
/// <param name="sourceFile">the uncompressed file</param>
/// <param name="destinationFile">the compressed file</param>
/// <param name="compressionType">the type of compression to use</param>
public static async Task CompressFileAsync(string sourceFile,
                             string destinationFile,
                             CompressionType compressionType)
{
    if (string.IsNullOrWhiteSpace(sourceFile))
        throw new ArgumentNullException(nameof(sourceFile));

    if (string.IsNullOrWhiteSpace(destinationFile))
        throw new ArgumentNullException(nameof(destinationFile));

    FileStream streamSource = null;
    FileStream streamDestination = null;
    Stream streamCompressed = null;

    int bufferSize = 4096;
    using (streamSource = new FileStream(sourceFile,
            FileMode.OpenOrCreate, FileAccess.Read, FileShare.None,
            bufferSize, useAsync: true))
    {
        using (streamDestination = new FileStream(destinationFile,
            FileMode.OpenOrCreate, FileAccess.Write, FileShare.None,
            bufferSize, useAsync: true))
        {
            // read 1MB chunks and compress them
            long fileLength = streamSource.Length;

            // write out the fileLength size
            byte[] size = BitConverter.GetBytes(fileLength);
            await streamDestination.WriteAsync(size, 0, size.Length);

            long chunkSize = 1048576; // 1MB
            while (fileLength > 0)
            {
                // read the chunk
                byte[] data = new byte[chunkSize];
                await streamSource.ReadAsync(data, 0, data.Length);

                // compress the chunk
                MemoryStream compressedDataStream =
```

```
                new MemoryStream();

        if (compressionType == CompressionType.Deflate)
            streamCompressed =
                new DeflateStream(compressedDataStream,
                    CompressionMode.Compress);
        else
            streamCompressed =
                new GZipStream(compressedDataStream,
                    CompressionMode.Compress);

        using (streamCompressed)
        {
            // write the chunk in the compressed stream
            await streamCompressed.WriteAsync(data, 0, data.Length);
        }
        // get the bytes for the compressed chunk
        byte[] compressedData =
            compressedDataStream.GetBuffer();

        // write out the chunk size
        size = BitConverter.GetBytes(chunkSize);
        await streamDestination.WriteAsync(size, 0, size.Length);

        // write out the compressed size
        size = BitConverter.GetBytes(compressedData.Length);
        await streamDestination.WriteAsync(size, 0, size.Length);

        // write out the compressed chunk
        await streamDestination.WriteAsync(compressedData, 0,
            compressedData.Length);

        // subtract the chunk size from the file size
        fileLength -= chunkSize;

        // if chunk is less than remaining file use
        // remaining file
        if (fileLength < chunkSize)
            chunkSize = fileLength;
        }
    }
    }
}

/// <summary>
/// This function will decompress the chunked compressed file
/// created by the CompressFile function.
/// </summary>
/// <param name="sourceFile">the compressed file</param>
/// <param name="destinationFile">the destination file</param>
/// <param name="compressionType">the type of compression to use</param>
public static async Task DecompressFileAsync(string sourceFile,
```

```csharp
                            string destinationFile,
                            CompressionType compressionType)
{
    if (string.IsNullOrWhiteSpace(sourceFile))
        throw new ArgumentNullException(nameof(sourceFile));
    if (string.IsNullOrWhiteSpace(destinationFile))
        throw new ArgumentNullException(nameof(destinationFile));

    FileStream streamSource = null;
    FileStream streamDestination = null;
    Stream streamUncompressed = null;

    int bufferSize = 4096;
    using (streamSource = new FileStream(sourceFile,
            FileMode.OpenOrCreate, FileAccess.Read, FileShare.None,
            bufferSize, useAsync: true))
    {
        using (streamDestination = new FileStream(destinationFile,
            FileMode.OpenOrCreate, FileAccess.Write, FileShare.None,
            bufferSize, useAsync: true))
        {
            // read the fileLength size
            // read the chunk size
            byte[] size = new byte[sizeof(long)];
            await streamSource.ReadAsync(size, 0, size.Length);
            // convert the size back to a number
            long fileLength = BitConverter.ToInt64(size, 0);
            long chunkSize = 0;
            int storedSize = 0;
            long workingSet = Process.GetCurrentProcess().WorkingSet64;
            while (fileLength > 0)
            {
                // read the chunk size
                size = new byte[sizeof(long)];
                await streamSource.ReadAsync(size, 0, size.Length);
                // convert the size back to a number
                chunkSize = BitConverter.ToInt64(size, 0);
                if (chunkSize > fileLength ||
                    chunkSize > workingSet)
                    throw new InvalidDataException();

                // read the compressed size
                size = new byte[sizeof(int)];
                await streamSource.ReadAsync(size, 0, size.Length);
                // convert the size back to a number
                storedSize = BitConverter.ToInt32(size, 0);
                if (storedSize > fileLength ||
                    storedSize > workingSet)
                    throw new InvalidDataException();

                if (storedSize > chunkSize)
                    throw new InvalidDataException();
```

```
            byte[] uncompressedData = new byte[chunkSize];
            byte[] compressedData = new byte[storedSize];
            await streamSource.ReadAsync(compressedData, 0,
                compressedData.Length);

            // uncompress the chunk
            MemoryStream uncompressedDataStream =
                new MemoryStream(compressedData);

            if (compressionType == CompressionType.Deflate)
                streamUncompressed =
                    new DeflateStream(uncompressedDataStream,
                        CompressionMode.Decompress);
            else
                streamUncompressed =
                    new GZipStream(uncompressedDataStream,
                        CompressionMode.Decompress);

            using (streamUncompressed)
            {
                // read the chunk in the compressed stream
                await streamUncompressed.ReadAsync(uncompressedData, 0,
                    uncompressedData.Length);
            }

            // write out the uncompressed chunk
            await streamDestination.WriteAsync(uncompressedData, 0,
                uncompressedData.Length);

            // subtract the chunk size from the file size
            fileLength -= chunkSize;

            // if chunk is less than remaining file use remaining file
            if (fileLength < chunkSize)
                chunkSize = fileLength;
        }
    }
}
```

The CompressionType enumeration is defined as follows:

```
public enum CompressionType
{
    Deflate,
    GZip
}
```

Discussion

The CompressFileAsync method accepts a path to the source file to compress, a path to the destination of the compressed file, and a CompressionType enumeration value indicating which type of compression algorithm to use (Deflate or GZip). This method produces a file containing the compressed data.

The `DecompressFileAsync` method accepts a path to the source compressed file to decompress, a path to the destination of the decompressed file, and a `Compression Type` enumeration value indicating which type of decompression algorithm to use (Deflate or GZip).

The `TestCompressNewFile` method shown in Example 8-6 exercises the `CompressFi leAsync` and `DecompressFileAsync` methods defined in the Solution section of this recipe.

Example 8-6. Using the CompressFile and DecompressFile methods

```
public static async void TestCompressNewFileAsync()
{
    byte[] data = new byte[10000000];
    for (int i = 0; i < 10000000; i++)
        data[i] = (byte)i;


    using(FileStream fs =
        new FileStream(@"C:\NewNormalFile.txt",
            FileMode.OpenOrCreate, FileAccess.ReadWrite, FileShare.None,
            4096, useAsync:true))
    {
        await fs.WriteAsync(data, 0, data.Length);
    }

    await CompressFileAsync(@"C:\NewNormalFile.txt", @"C:\NewCompressedFile.txt",
        CompressionType.Deflate);

    await DecompressFileAsync(@"C:\NewCompressedFile.txt",
        @"C:\NewDecompressedFile.txt",
        CompressionType.Deflate);

    await CompressFileAsync(@"C:\NewNormalFile.txt", @"C:\NewGZCompressedFile.txt",
        CompressionType.GZip);

    await DecompressFileAsync(@"C:\NewGZCompressedFile.txt",
        @"C:\NewGZDecompressedFile.txt",
        CompressionType.GZip);

    //Normal file size == 10,000,000 bytes
    //GZipped file size == 84,362
    //Deflated file size == 42,145
    //Pre .NET 4.5 GZipped file size == 155,204
    //Pre .NET 4.5 Deflated file size == 155,168
```

```
            // 36 bytes are related to the GZip CRC
}
```

When this test code is run, we get three files with different sizes. The first file, *New-NormalFile.txt*, is 10,000,000 bytes in size. The *NewCompressedFile.txt* file is 42,145 bytes. The final file, *NewGzCompressedFile.txt*, file is 84,362 bytes. As you can see, there is not much difference between the sizes for the files compressed with the `Defla teStream` class and the `GZipStream` class. The reason for this is that both compression classes use the same compression/decompression algorithm (i.e., the lossless Deflate algorithm as described in the RFC 1951: Deflate 1.3 specification).

In .NET 4.5, the `GZipStream` and `DeflateStream` classes have been updated to use the `zlib library` (*http://www.zlib.net/*) behind the scenes to perform the compression, which has improved the compression ratios. You can see this if you run the older version of the `CompressFile` and `DecompressFile` methods on prior versions of the .NET Framework, as shown in Example 8-7.

Example 8-7. Pre–.NET 4.5 version of the CompressFile and DecompressFile methods

```
/// <summary>
/// Compress the source file to the destination file.
/// This is done in 1MB chunks to not overwhelm the memory usage.
/// </summary>
/// <param name="sourceFile">the uncompressed file</param>
/// <param name="destinationFile">the compressed file</param>
/// <param name="compressionType">the type of compression to use</param>
public static void CompressFile(string sourceFile,
                                string destinationFile,
                                CompressionType compressionType)
{
    if (sourceFile != null)
    {
        FileStream streamSource = null;
        FileStream streamDestination = null;
        Stream streamCompressed = null;

        using (streamSource = File.OpenRead(sourceFile))
        {
            using (streamDestination = File.OpenWrite(destinationFile))
            {
                // read 1MB chunks and compress them
                long fileLength = streamSource.Length;

                // write out the fileLength size
                byte[] size = BitConverter.GetBytes(fileLength);
                streamDestination.Write(size, 0, size.Length);

                long chunkSize = 1048576; // 1MB
                while (fileLength > 0)
```

```
        {
            // read the chunk
            byte[] data = new byte[chunkSize];
            streamSource.Read(data, 0, data.Length);

            // compress the chunk
            MemoryStream compressedDataStream =
                new MemoryStream();

            if (compressionType == CompressionType.Deflate)
                streamCompressed =
                    new DeflateStream(compressedDataStream,
                        CompressionMode.Compress);
            else
                streamCompressed =
                    new GZipStream(compressedDataStream,
                        CompressionMode.Compress);

            using (streamCompressed)
            {
                // write the chunk in the compressed stream
                streamCompressed.Write(data, 0, data.Length);
            }
            // get the bytes for the compressed chunk
            byte[] compressedData =
                compressedDataStream.GetBuffer();

            // write out the chunk size
            size = BitConverter.GetBytes(chunkSize);
            streamDestination.Write(size, 0, size.Length);

            // write out the compressed size
            size = BitConverter.GetBytes(compressedData.Length);
            streamDestination.Write(size, 0, size.Length);

            // write out the compressed chunk
            streamDestination.Write(compressedData, 0,
                compressedData.Length);

            // subtract the chunk size from the file size
            fileLength -= chunkSize;

            // if chunk is less than remaining file use
            // remaining file
            if (fileLength < chunkSize)
                chunkSize = fileLength;
        }
    }
    }
    }
}
}
```

```csharp
/// <summary>
/// This function will decompress the chunked compressed file
/// created by the CompressFile function.
/// </summary>
/// <param name="sourceFile">the compressed file</param>
/// <param name="destinationFile">the destination file</param>
/// <param name="compressionType">the type of compression to use</param>
public static void DecompressFile(string sourceFile,
                                  string destinationFile,
                                  CompressionType compressionType)
{
    FileStream streamSource = null;
    FileStream streamDestination = null;
    Stream streamUncompressed = null;

    using (streamSource = File.OpenRead(sourceFile))
    {
        using (streamDestination = File.OpenWrite(destinationFile))
        {
            // read the fileLength size
            // read the chunk size
            byte[] size = new byte[sizeof(long)];
            streamSource.Read(size, 0, size.Length);
            // convert the size back to a number
            long fileLength = BitConverter.ToInt64(size, 0);
            long chunkSize = 0;
            int storedSize = 0;
            long workingSet = Process.GetCurrentProcess().WorkingSet64;
            while (fileLength > 0)
            {
                // read the chunk size
                size = new byte[sizeof(long)];
                streamSource.Read(size, 0, size.Length);
                // convert the size back to a number
                chunkSize = BitConverter.ToInt64(size, 0);
                if (chunkSize > fileLength ||
                    chunkSize > workingSet)
                    throw new InvalidDataException();

                // read the compressed size
                size = new byte[sizeof(int)];
                streamSource.Read(size, 0, size.Length);
                // convert the size back to a number
                storedSize = BitConverter.ToInt32(size, 0);
                if (storedSize > fileLength ||
                    storedSize > workingSet)
                    throw new InvalidDataException();

                if (storedSize > chunkSize)
                    throw new InvalidDataException();

                byte[] uncompressedData = new byte[chunkSize];
```

```
byte[] compressedData = new byte[storedSize];
streamSource.Read(compressedData, 0,
    compressedData.Length);

// uncompress the chunk
MemoryStream uncompressedDataStream =
    new MemoryStream(compressedData);

if (compressionType == CompressionType.Deflate)
    streamUncompressed =
        new DeflateStream(uncompressedDataStream,
            CompressionMode.Decompress);
else
    streamUncompressed =
        new GZipStream(uncompressedDataStream,
            CompressionMode.Decompress);

using (streamUncompressed)
{
    // read the chunk in the compressed stream
    streamUncompressed.Read(uncompressedData, 0,
        uncompressedData.Length);
}

// write out the uncompressed chunk
streamDestination.Write(uncompressedData, 0,
    uncompressedData.Length);

// subtract the chunk size from the file size
fileLength -= chunkSize;

// if chunk is less than remaining file use remaining file
if (fileLength < chunkSize)
    chunkSize = fileLength;
            }
        }
    }
}
```

You may be wondering why you would pick one class over the other if they use the same algorithm. One good reason is that the GZipStream class adds a CRC (cyclic redundancy check) to the compressed data to determine if it has been corrupted. If the data has been corrupted, an InvalidDataException is thrown with the statement "The CRC in GZip footer does not match the CRC calculated from the decompressed data." By catching this exception, you can determine if your data is corrupted.

In the Decompress method, it's possible for some InvalidDataException instances to be thrown:

```
// read the chunk size
size = new byte[sizeof(long)];
```

```
streamSource.Read(size, 0, size.Length);
// convert the size back to a number
chunkSize = BitConverter.ToInt64(size, 0);
if (chunkSize > fileLength || chunkSize > workingSet)
    throw new InvalidDataException();

// read the compressed size
size = new byte[sizeof(int)];
streamSource.Read(size, 0, size.Length);
// convert the size back to a number
storedSize = BitConverter.ToInt32(size, 0);
if (storedSize > fileLength || storedSize > workingSet)
    throw new InvalidDataException();
if (storedSize > chunkSize)
    throw new InvalidDataException();

byte[] uncompressedData = new byte[chunkSize];
byte[] compressedData = new byte[storedSize];
```

The code is reading in a buffer that may have been tampered with, so we need to check not only for stability but also for security reasons. Since `Decompress` will actually allocate memory based on the numbers derived from the buffer, it needs to be careful about what those numbers turn out to be, and we don't want to unwittingly bring in other code that has been injected into the stream either. The very basic checks being done here are to ensure that:

- The size of the chunk is not bigger than the file length.
- The size of the chunk is not bigger than the current program working set.
- The size of the compressed chunk is not bigger than the file length.
- The size of the compressed chunk is not bigger than the current program working set.
- The size of the compressed chunk is not bigger than the actual chunk size.

See Also

The "DeflateStream Class" and "GZipStream" topics in the MSDN documentation.

CHAPTER 9

Networking and Web

9.0 Introduction

Connectivity is more important than ever in solutions, and the .NET Framework provides a number of ways to help you support that need. .NET provides many lower-level classes to help make network programming easier than many environments that preceded it. There is a great deal of functionality to assist you with tasks such as:

- Building network-aware applications
- Downloading files via FTP
- Sending and receiving HTTP requests
- Getting a higher degree of control using TCP/IP and sockets directly

In the areas in which Microsoft has not provided managed classes to access networking functionality (such as some of the methods exposed by the `WinInet` API for Internet connection settings), there is always P/Invoke, so you can code to the Win32 API, as we'll explore in this chapter. With all of the functionality at your disposal in the `System.Net` namespaces, you can also write network utilities very quickly.

In addition to the lower-level networking support, .NET embraces the World Wide Web and has incorporated support for the Web into every nook and cranny of what most .NET developers encounter when building their solutions today. Web services (both REST and SOAP based) are in heavy use, and ASP.NET is one of the main players in the web application space. Given the general need to work with HTML and TCP/IP name resolution, and because uniform resource indicators (URIs) and uniform resource locators (URLs) are being used for more and more purposes, developers need tools to help them concentrate on building the best web interactive applications possible. This chapter is dedicated to taking care of some of the grunge that comes along with programming when the Web is involved. It is not a Web Services or ASP.NET tutorial but rather covers some functionality that developers can use in ASP.NET applications and services and other C#-based applications that interact with networks and the Web.

9.1 Handling Web Server Errors

Problem

You have obtained a response from a web server, and you want to make sure that there were no errors in processing the initial request, such as failing to connect, being redirected, timing out, or failing to validate a certificate. You want to avoid checking for all of the different response codes available.

Solution

Check the `StatusCode` property of the `HttpWebResponse` class to determine what category of status this `StatusCode` falls into and return an enumeration value (`Response Categories`) representing the category. This technique allows you to use a broader approach to dealing with response codes:

```
public static ResponseCategories CategorizeResponse(HttpWebResponse httpResponse)
{
    // Just in case there are more success codes defined in the future
    // by HttpStatusCode, we will check here for the "success" ranges
    // instead of using the HttpStatusCode enum, as it overloads some
    // values
    int statusCode = (int)httpResponse.StatusCode;
    if ((statusCode >= 100) && (statusCode <= 199))
    {
        return ResponseCategories.Informational;
    }
    else if ((statusCode >= 200) && (statusCode <= 299))
    {
        return ResponseCategories.Success;
    }
    else if ((statusCode >= 300) && (statusCode <= 399))
    {
        return ResponseCategories.Redirected;
    }
    else if ((statusCode >= 400) && (statusCode <= 499))
    {
        return ResponseCategories.ClientError;
    }
    else if ((statusCode >= 500) && (statusCode <= 599))
    {
        return ResponseCategories.ServerError;
    }
```

```
        return ResponseCategories.Unknown;
    }
```

The `ResponseCategories` enumeration is defined like this:

```
public enum ResponseCategories
{
    Unknown,        // unknown code  ( < 100 or > 599)
    Informational,  // informational codes (100 <= 199)
    Success,        // success codes (200 <= 299)
    Redirected,     // redirection code (300 <= 399)
    ClientError,    // client error code (400 <= 499)
    ServerError     // server error code (500 <= 599)
}
```

Discussion

There are five different categories of status codes on an HTTP response, as shown in Table 9-1.

Table 9-1. Categories of HTTP response status codes

Category	Available range	HttpStatusCode defined range
Informational	100–199	100–101
Successful	200–299	200–206
Redirection	300–399	300–307
Client Error	400–499	400–426
Server Error	500–599	500–505

Each of the status codes defined by Microsoft in the .NET Framework is assigned an enumeration value in the `HttpStatusCode` enumeration. These status codes reflect what can happen when a request is submitted. The web server is free to return a status code in the available range, even if it is not currently defined for most commercial web servers. The defined status codes are listed in RFC 2616—Section 10 for HTTP/1.1.

You are trying to figure out the broad category of the status of the request. You achieve this by inspecting the `HttpResponse.StatusCode` property, comparing it to the defined status code ranges for HTTP, and returning the appropriate `ResponseCatego ries` value.

When dealing with `HttpStatusCode`, you will notice that there are certain `HttpSta tusCode` flags that map to the same status code value. An example of this is `HttpSta tusCode.Ambiguous` and `HttpStatusCode.MultipleChoices`, which both map to HTTP status code 300. If you try to use both of these in a switch statement on the

`HttpStatusCode`, you will get the following error because the C# compiler cannot tell the difference:

```
error CS0152: The label 'case 300:' already occurs in this switch statement.
```

See Also

HTTP: The Definitive Guide (O'Reilly); the "HttpStatusCode Enumeration" topic in the MSDN documentation; and HTTP/1.1 RFC 2616—Section 10 Status Codes (*http://bit.ly/stat-codes*).

9.2 Communicating with a Web Server

Problem

You want to send a request to a web server in the form of a `GET` or `POST` request. After you send the request to a web server, you want to get the results of that request (the response) from the web server.

Solution

Use the `HttpWebRequest` class in conjunction with the `WebRequest` class to create and send a request to a server.

Take the `Uri` (universal resource identifier; defined in RFC 3986) of the resource, the method to use in the request (`GET` or `POST`), and the data to send (only for `POST` requests), and use this information to create an `HttpWebRequest`, as shown in Example 9-1.

Example 9-1. Communicating with a web server

```
using System.Net;
using System.IO;
using System.Text;

// GET overload
public static HttpWebRequest GenerateHttpWebRequest(Uri uri)
{
    // create the initial request
    HttpWebRequest httpRequest = (HttpWebRequest)WebRequest.Create(uri);
    // return the request
    return httpRequest;
}

// POST overload
public static HttpWebRequest GenerateHttpWebRequest(Uri uri,
    string postData,
```

```
        string contentType)
{
    // create the initial request
    HttpWebRequest httpRequest = GenerateHttpWebRequest(uri);

    // Get the bytes for the request, should be pre-escaped
    byte[] bytes = Encoding.UTF8.GetBytes(postData);

    // Set the content type of the data being posted.
    httpRequest.ContentType = contentType;
        //"application/x-www-form-urlencoded"; for forms
        //"application/json" for json data
        //"application/xml" for xml data

    // Set the content length of the string being posted.
    httpRequest.ContentLength = postData.Length;

    // Get the request stream and write the post data in
    using (Stream requestStream = httpRequest.GetRequestStream())
    {
        requestStream.Write(bytes, 0, bytes.Length);
    }
    // return the request
    return httpRequest;
}
```

Once you have an HttpWebRequest, you send the request and get the response using the GetResponse method. It takes the newly created HttpWebRequest as input and returns an HttpWebResponse. The following example performs a GET for the *index.aspx* page from the *http://localhost/mysite* website:

```
HttpWebRequest request =
    GenerateHttpWebRequest(new Uri("http://localhost/mysite/index.aspx"));

using(HttpWebResponse response = (HttpWebResponse) request.GetResponse())
{
    // This next line uses CategorizeResponse from Recipe 9.1.
    if(CategorizeResponse(response)==ResponseCategories.Success)
    {
        Console.WriteLine("Request succeeded");
    }
}
```

You generate the HttpWebRequest, send it and get the HttpWebResponse, then check for success using the CategorizeResponse method from Recipe 9.1.

Discussion

The `WebRequest` and `WebResponse` classes encapsulate all of the functionality to perform basic web communications. `HttpWebRequest` and `HttpWebResponse` are derived from these classes and provide the HTTP-specific support.

At the most fundamental level, to perform an HTTP-based web transaction, you use the `Create` method on the `WebRequest` class to get a `WebRequest` that can be cast to an `HttpWebRequest` (so long as the scheme is `http://` or `https://`). This `HttpWebRequest` is then submitted to the web server in question when the `GetResponse` method is called, and it returns an `HttpWebResponse` that can then be inspected for the response data.

See Also

The "WebRequest Class," "WebResponse Class," "HttpWebRequest Class," and "HttpWebResponse Class" topics in the MSDN documentation, and the Universal Resource Identifier RFC (*http://bit.ly/1KvPJT1*).

9.3 Going Through a Proxy

Problem

Many companies have a proxy server (sometimes called a *web proxy*) that allows employees to access the Internet, while preventing outsiders from accessing the company's internal network. The problem is that to create an application that accesses the Internet from within your company, you must first connect to your proxy and then send information through it, rather than directly out to an Internet web server.

Solution

To get an `HttpWebRequest` successfully through a specific proxy server, you need to set up a `WebProxy` object with the settings to validate your specific request to a given proxy. Since this function is generic for any request, you can create the `AddProxyInfo ToRequest` method:

```
public static HttpWebRequest AddProxyInfoToRequest(HttpWebRequest httpRequest,
    Uri proxyUri,
    string proxyId,
    string proxyPassword,
    string proxyDomain)
{
    if (httpRequest == null)
        throw new ArgumentNullException(nameof(httpRequest));

    // create the proxy object
```

```
    WebProxy proxyInfo = new WebProxy();
    // add the address of the proxy server to use
    proxyInfo.Address = proxyUri;
    // tell it to bypass the proxy server for local addresses
    proxyInfo.BypassProxyOnLocal = true;
    // add any credential information to present to the proxy server
    proxyInfo.Credentials = new NetworkCredential(proxyId,
        proxyPassword,
        proxyDomain);
    // assign the proxy information to the request
    httpRequest.Proxy = proxyInfo;

    // return the request
    return httpRequest;
}
```

If all requests are going to go through the same proxy, in the 1.x versions of the Framework you used the static `Select` method on the `GlobalProxySelection` class to set up the proxy settings for all `WebRequests`. In versions after 1.x, the `WebRequest.DefaultWebProxy` property should be used:

```
// Set it up to go through the same proxy for all requests to this Uri
Uri proxyURI = new Uri("http://webproxy:80");

// in 1.1 you used to do this:
//GlobalProxySelection.Select = new WebProxy(proxyURI);

// Now in 2.0 and above you do this:
WebRequest.DefaultWebProxy = new WebProxy(proxyURI);
```

Discussion

`AddProxyInfoToRequest` takes the URI of the proxy and creates a `Uri` object, which is used to construct the `WebProxy` object. The `WebProxy` object is set to bypass the proxy for local addresses and then the credential information is used to create a `NetworkCredential` object. The `NetworkCredential` object represents the authentication information necessary for the request to succeed at this proxy and is assigned to the `WebProxy.Credentials` property. Once the `WebProxy` object is completed, it is assigned to the `Proxy` property of the `HttpWebRequest`, and the request is ready to be submitted.

To get the proxy settings for the current user from Internet Explorer, you can use the `System.Net.WebRequest.GetSystemWebProxy` method and then assign the returned `IWebProxy` to either the proxy on the `HttpWebRequest` or the `DefaultWebProxy` property on the `WebRequest`:

```
WebRequest.DefaultWebProxy = WebRequest.GetSystemWebProxy();
```

See Also

The "WebProxy Class," "NetworkCredential Class," and "HttpWebRequest Class" topics in the MSDN documentation.

9.4 Obtaining the HTML from a URL

Problem

You need to get the HTML returned from a web server in order to examine it for items of interest. For example, you could examine the returned HTML for links to other pages or for headlines from a news site.

Solution

You can use the methods for web communication that were set up in Recipes 9.1 and 9.2 to make the HTTP request and verify the response; then, you can get at the HTML via the `ResponseStream` property of the `HttpWebResponse` object:

```
public static async Task<string> GetHtmlFromUrlAsync(Uri url)
{
    string html = string.Empty;
    HttpWebRequest request = GenerateHttpWebRequest(url);
    using(HttpWebResponse response =
        (HttpWebResponse) await request.GetResponseAsync())
    {
        if (CategorizeResponse(response) == ResponseCategories.Success)
        {
            // get the response stream.
            Stream responseStream = response.GetResponseStream();
            // use a stream reader that understands UTF8
            using(StreamReader reader =
                new StreamReader(responseStream, Encoding.UTF8))
            {
                html = reader.ReadToEnd();
            }
        }
    }
    return html;
}
```

Discussion

The `GetHtmlFromUrlAsync` method gets a web page using the `GenerateHttpWebRe` `quest` and `GetResponse` methods, verifies the response using the `CategorizeRes` `ponse` method, and then, once it has a valid response, starts looking for the HTML that was returned.

The `GetResponseStream` method on the `HttpWebResponse` provides access to the body of the message that was returned in a `System.IO.Stream` object. To read the data, you instantiate a `StreamReader` with the response stream and the `UTF8` property of the `Encoding` class to allow for the UTF8-encoded text data to be read correctly from the stream. Then call the `StreamReader`'s `ReadToEnd` method, which puts all of the content in the string variable called `html`, and return it.

See Also

The "HttpWebResponse.GetResponseStream Method," "Stream Class," and "String-Builder Class" topics in the MSDN documentation.

9.5 Using the Web Browser Control

Problem

You need to display HTML-based content in a WinForms-based application.

Solution

Use the `System.Windows.Forms.WebBrowser` class to embed web browser functionality into your application. The Cheapo-Browser seen in Figure 9-1 shows some of the capabilities of this control.

While this is a not a production quality user interface (it is called Cheapo-Browser for a reason!) it can be used to select a web address, display the content, navigate forward and backward, cancel the request, go to the home page, add HTML directly to the control, print the HTML or save it, and finally, enable or disable the context menu inside of the browser window. The `WebBrowser` control is capable of much more, but this recipe is meant to give you a taste of what is possible. It would be well worth exploring its capabilities further to see what other needs it might fill.

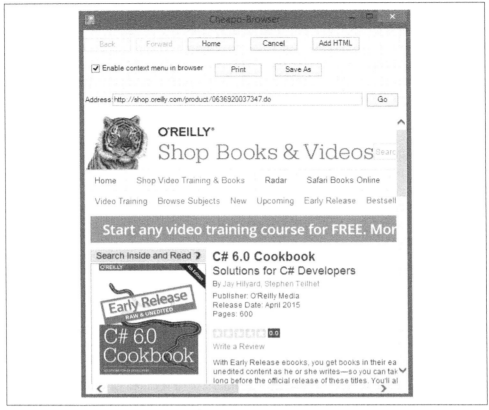

Figure 9-1. The web browser control

When you add your HTML (<h1>Hey you added some HTML!</h1>), it is displayed as shown in Figure 9-2.

The code to accomplish this is rather simple:

```
this._webBrowser.Document.Body.InnerHtml = "<h1>Hey you added some HTML!</h1>";
```

The navigation to a web page is equally trivial:

```
Uri uri = new Uri(this._txtAddress.Text);
this._webBrowser.Navigate(uri);
```

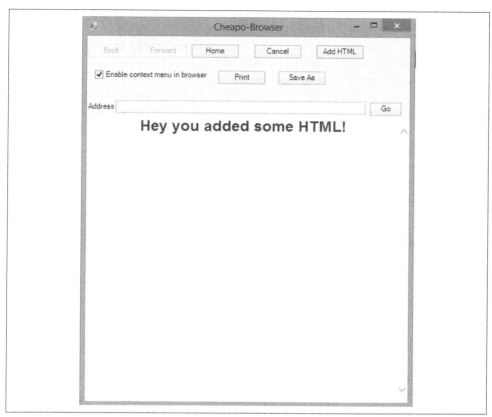

Figure 9-2. Adding HTML to the Cheapo-Browser

The nice thing about the way that navigation is handled is that you can subscribe to the Navigated event so that you are notified when the navigation has completed. This allows code to spin this off in a thread and then come back to it once it is fully loaded. The event provides a WebBrowserNavigatedEventArgs class that has a Url property to tell the URL of the document that has been navigated to:

```
private void _webBrowser_Navigated(object sender, WebBrowserNavigatedEventArgs e)
{
    // Update with where we ended up in case of redirection
    // from the original Uri.
    this._txtAddress.Text = e.Url.ToString();
    this._btnBack.Enabled = this._webBrowser.CanGoBack;
    this._btnForward.Enabled = this._webBrowser.CanGoForward;
}
```

Discussion

Way back in the 1.x versions of the .NET Framework, embedding a web browser in your WinForms application was much more difficult and error-prone. Now there is a .NET-based web browser control to handle the hard stuff. You no longer have to struggle with some of the COM interop issues that could arise while you're trying to hook up to browser events. This is a good opportunity to blur the line between your desktop and web applications even further and use the power of a rich client combined with web flexibility.

See Also

The "WebBrowser Class" topic in the MSDN documentation.

9.6 Prebuilding an ASP.NET Website Programmatically

Problem

You want to prebuild your website to avoid compilation delays and to avoid the hosting scenario in which source code needs to be on the server.

Solution

Use the `ClientBuildManager` to prebuild your website into an assembly. To prebuild the website, you must specify:

- The virtual directory for the web application
- The physical path to the web application directory
- The location where you want to build the web application
- Flags that help control the compilation

To prebuild the web application in the sample code for the book, first retrieve the directory where the web application is located, and then provide a virtual directory name and a location for the web application to build to:

```
string cscbWebPath = GetWebAppPath();

if(cscbWebPath.Length > 0)
{
    string appVirtualDir = @"CSCBWeb";
    string appPhysicalSourceDir = cscbWebPath;

    // Make the target an adjacent directory as it cannot be in the same tree
    // or the build manager screams...
```

```
string appPhysicalTargetDir =
    Path.GetDirectoryName(cscbWebPath) + @"\ BuildCSCB";
```

Next, set up the flags for the compile using the `PrecompilationFlags` enumeration. The `PrecompilationFlags` values are listed in Table 9-2.

Table 9-2. PrecompilationFlags enumeration values

Flag value	Purpose
AllowPartiallyTrus tedCallers	Add the APTC attribute to the built assembly.
Clean	Remove any existing compiled image.
CodeAnalysis	Build for code analysis.
Default	Use the default compile options.
DelaySign	DelaySign the assembly.
FixedNames	Assembly generated with fixed names for pages. No batch compilation is performed, just individual compilation.
ForceDebug	Ensure that the assembly is compiled for debugging.
OverwriteTarget	The target assembly should be overwritten if it exists.
Updateable	Ensure the assembly is updateable.

To build a debug image and make sure it is created successfully if the compilation is good, use the `ForceDebug` and `OverwriteTarget` flags:

```
PrecompilationFlags flags = PrecompilationFlags.ForceDebug |
                        PrecompilationFlags.OverwriteTarget;
```

The `PrecompilationFlags` are then stored in a new instance of the `ClientBuildMana gerParameter` class, and the `ClientBuildManager` is created with the parameters that have been set up for it. To accomplish the prebuild, you call the `PrecompileApplica tion` method. Notice that there is an instance of a class called `MyClientBuildManager Callback` that is passed to the `PrecompileApplication` method:

```
ClientBuildManagerParameter cbmp = new ClientBuildManagerParameter();
cbmp.PrecompilationFlags = flags;

ClientBuildManager cbm =
    new ClientBuildManager(appVirtualDir,
                           appPhysicalSourceDir,
                           appPhysicalTargetDir,
                           cbmp);
MyClientBuildManagerCallback myCallback = new MyClientBuildManagerCallback();
cbm.PrecompileApplication(myCallback);
}
```

The `MyClientBuildManagerCallback` class is derived from the `ClientBuildManager Callback` class and allows the code to receive notifications during the compilation of the web application. The `ClientBuildManagerCallback` methods have `LinkDemands` on them, which require that the callback methods also have them. Compiler errors, parsing errors, and progress notifications are all available. In the `MyClientBuildMana gerCallback` class, they are all implemented to write to the debug stream and the console:

```
public class MyClientBuildManagerCallback : ClientBuildManagerCallback
{
    public MyClientBuildManagerCallback()
        : base()
    {
    }

    [PermissionSet(SecurityAction.Demand, Unrestricted = true)]
    public override void ReportCompilerError(CompilerError error)
    {
        string msg = $"Report Compiler Error: {error.ToString()}";
        Debug.WriteLine(msg);
        Console.WriteLine(msg);
    }

    [PermissionSet(SecurityAction.Demand, Unrestricted = true)]
    public override void ReportParseError(ParserError error)
    {
        string msg = $"Report Parse Error: {error.ToString()}";
        Debug.WriteLine(msg);
        Console.WriteLine(msg);
    }

    [PermissionSet(SecurityAction.Demand, Unrestricted = true)]
    public override void ReportProgress(string message)
    {
        string msg = $"Report Progress: {message}";
        Debug.WriteLine(msg);
        Console.WriteLine(msg);
    }
}
```

The output from a successful compilation of the CSCB website looks like this:

```
Report Progress: Building directory '/CSCBWeb/Properties'.
Report Progress: Building directory '/CSCBWeb'.
```

Discussion

`ClientBuildManager` is actually a thin wrapper around the `BuildManager` class, `BuildManager` classwhich does most of the heavy lifting of the compilation. `Client BuildManager` makes it more straightforward to ensure that all the important parts of the web application are addressed, while `BuildManager` gives a bit more fine-grained control. The `ClientBuildManager` also allows for subscribing to `appdomain` notification events such as start, shutdown, and unload, allowing for error handling in the event that the `appdomain` is going away during a prebuild.

To prebuild applications in ASP.NET without resorting to the `ClientBuildManager`, you can post an HTTP request to the website in the format *http://server/webapp/precompile.axd*. The *precompile.axd* "document" triggers an ASP.NET `HttpHandler` for this that will prebuild the website for you. This is handled by the *aspnet_compiler.exe* module, which essentially wraps the `ClientBuildManager` functionality.

See Also

The "ClientBuildManager," "ClientBuildManagerParameters," "BuildManager," and "ASP.NET Web Site Precompilation" topics in the MSDN documentation.

9.7 Escaping and Unescaping Data for the Web

Problem

You need to transform data for use in web operations from escaped to unescaped format or vice versa for proper transmission. This escaping and unescaping should follow the format outlined in RFC 2396—Uniform Resource Identifiers (URI): Generic Syntax.

Solution

Use the `Uri` class static methods for escaping and unescaping data and `Uri`s.

To escape data, use the static `Uri.EscapeDataString` method, as shown here:

```
string data = "<H1>My html</H1>";
Console.WriteLine($"Original Data: {data}");
Console.WriteLine();

string escapedData = Uri.EscapeDataString(data);
Console.WriteLine($"Escaped Data: {escapedData}");
Console.WriteLine();

// Output from above code is
// Original Data: <H1>My html</H1>
//
// Escaped Data: %3CH1%3EMy%20html%3C%2FH1%3E
```

To unescape the data, use the static `Uri.UnescapeDataString` method:

```
string unescapedData = Uri.UnescapeDataString(escapedData);
Console.WriteLine($"Unescaped Data: {unescapedData}");
Console.WriteLine();

// Output from above code is
```

```
//
// Unescaped Data: <H1>My html</H1>
```

To escape a `Uri`, use the static `Uri.EscapeUriString` method:

```
string uriString = "http://user:password@localhost:8080/www.abc.com/" +
    "home page.htm?item=1233;html=<h1>Heading</h1>#stuff";
Console.WriteLine($"Original Uri string: {uriString}");
Console.WriteLine();

string escapedUriString = Uri.EscapeUriString(uriString);
Console.WriteLine($"Escaped Uri string: {escapedUriString}");
Console.WriteLine();

// Output from above code is
//
// Original Uri string: http://user:password@localhost:8080/www.abc.com/home
// page.htm?item=1233;html=<h1>Heading</h1>#stuff
//
// Escaped Uri string: http://user:password@localhost:8080/www.abc.com/home
// %20page.htm?item=1233;html=%3Ch1%3EHeading%3C/h1%3E#stuff
```

In case you are wondering why escaping a `Uri` has its own method (`EscapeUri String`), take a look at what the escaped `Uri` looks like if you use `Uri.EscapeData String` and `Uri.UnescapeDataString` on it:

```
// Why not just use EscapeDataString to escape a Uri?  It's not picky enough...
string escapedUriData = Uri.EscapeDataString(uriString);
Console.WriteLine($"Escaped Uri data: {escapedUriData}");
Console.WriteLine();

Console.WriteLine(Uri.UnescapeDataString(escapedUriString));

// Output from above code is
//
// Escaped Uri data: http%3A%2F%2Fuser%3Apassword%40localhost%3A8080%2Fwww.abc.
// com%2Fhome%20page.htm%3Fitem%3D1233%3Bhtml%3D%3Ch1%3EHeading%3C%2Fh1%3E%23
// stuff

// http://user:password@localhost:8080/www.abc.com/home page.htm?item=1233;html
// =<h1>Heading</h1>#stuff
```

Notice that the :, /, :, @, and ? characters get escaped when they shouldn't, which is why you use the `EscapeUriString` method for `Uri`s.

Discussion

`EscapeUriString` assumes that there are no escape sequences already present in the string being escaped. The escaping follows the convention set down in RFC 2396 for converting all reserved characters and characters with a value greater than 128 to their hexadecimal format.

In Section 2.2 of RFC 2396, it states that the reserved characters are:

;|/| ? |:| @ | & | = | + | $ | ,

The `EscapeUriString` method is useful when you are creating a `System.Uri` object to ensure that the `Uri` is escaped correctly.

See Also

The "EscapeUriString Method," "EscapeUriData Method," and "Unescape-DataString Method" topics in the MSDN documentation.

9.8 Checking Out a Web Server's Custom Error Pages

Problem

You have an application that needs to know what custom error pages are set up for the various HTTP error return codes on a given IIS server.

Solution

Use the `System.DirectoryServices.DirectoryEntry` class to talk to the Internet Information Server (IIS) metabase to find out which custom error pages are set up. The metabase holds the configuration information for the web server. `DirectoryEntry` uses the Active Directory IIS service provider to communicate with the metabase by specifying the "IIS" scheme in the constructor for the `DirectoryEntry`:

```
// This is a case-sensitive entry in the metabase
// You'd think it was misspelled but you would be mistaken...
const string WebServerSchema = "IIsWebServer";

// set up to talk to the local IIS server
string server = "localhost";

// Create a dictionary entry for the IIS server with a fake
// user and password.  Credentials would have to be provided
// if you are running as a regular user
using (DirectoryEntry w3svc =
    new DirectoryEntry($"IIS://{server}/w3svc",
            "Domain/UserCode", "Password"))
{
```

Once the connection is established, the web server schema entry is specified to show where the IIS settings are kept (`IIsWebServer`). The `DirectoryEntry` has a property that allows access to its children (`Children`), and the `SchemaClassName` is checked for each entry to see if it is in the web server settings section. Once the web server settings are found, the web root node is located, and from there, the `HttpErrors` property is retrieved. `HttpErrors` is a comma-delimited string that indicates the HTTP error code, the HTTP suberror code, the message type, and the path to the HTML file to serve when this error occurs. To accomplish this, just write a LINQ query to get all of the `HttpErrors`, as shown in Example 9-2. Once the `HttpErrors` are retrieved, use the `Split` method to break this into a string array that allows the code to access the individual values and write them out. The code for carrying out these operations is shown in Example 9-2.

Example 9-2. Finding custom error pages

```
// Use a regular query expression to
// select the http errors for all websites on the machine
var httpErrors = from site in w3svc?.Children.OfType<DirectoryEntry>()
                 where site.SchemaClassName == WebServerSchema
                 from siteDir in site.Children.OfType<DirectoryEntry>()
                 where siteDir.Name == "ROOT"
                 from httpError in siteDir.Properties["HttpErrors"].OfType<string>()
                 select httpError;

// use eager evaluation to convert this to the array
// so that we don't requery on each iteration.  We would miss
// updates to the metabase that occur during execution, but
// that is a small price to pay vs. the requery cost.
// This will force the evaluation of the query now once.
string[] errors = httpErrors.ToArray();
foreach (var httpError in errors)
{
    //400,*,FILE,C:\WINDOWS\help\iisHelp\common\400.htm
    string[] errorParts = httpError.ToString().Split(',');
    Console.WriteLine("Error Mapping Entry:");
    Console.WriteLine($"\tHTTP error code: {errorParts[0]}");
    Console.WriteLine($"\tHTTP sub-error code: {errorParts[1]}");
    Console.WriteLine($"\tMessage Type: {errorParts[2]}");
    Console.WriteLine($"\tPath to error HTML file: {errorParts[3]}");
}
```

We could, of course, have done this without using LINQ to query the metabase, which would have looked like Example 9-3.

Example 9-3. Finding custom error pages without LINQ

```
foreach (DirectoryEntry site in w3svc?.Children)
{
    if (site != null)
    {
        using (site)
        {
            // check all web servers on this box
            if (site.SchemaClassName == WebServerSchema)
            {
```

```csharp
// get the metabase entry for this server
string metabaseDir = $"/w3svc/{site.Name}/ROOT";

if (site.Children != null)
{
    // find the ROOT directory for each server
    foreach (DirectoryEntry root in site.Children)
    {
        using (root)
        {
            // did we find the root dir for this site?
            if (root?.Name.Equals("ROOT",
                StringComparison.OrdinalIgnoreCase) ?? false)
            {
                // get the HttpErrors
                if (root?.Properties.Contains("HttpErrors") == true)
                {
                    // write them out
                    PropertyValueCollection httpErrors =
                        root?.Properties["HttpErrors"];
                    for (int i = 0; i < httpErrors?.Count; i++)
                    {
                        //400,*,FILE,
                        //C:\WINDOWS\help\iisHelp\common\400.htm
                        string[] errorParts =
                            httpErrors?[i].ToString().Split(',');
                        Console.WriteLine("Error Mapping Entry:");
                        Console.WriteLine($"\tHTTP error code:" +
                            $"{errorParts[0]}");
                        Console.WriteLine($"\tHTTP sub-error code:" +
                            $"{errorParts[1]}");
                        Console.WriteLine($"\tMessage Type: " +
                            $"{errorParts[2]}");
                        Console.WriteLine(
                            $"\tPath to error HTML file:
                            {errorParts[3]}");
                    }
                }
            }
        }
    }
}
```

At this point, an application could cache these settings for mapping its own error results, or it could dynamically modify the error pages to provide customized content. The takeaway here is that the settings information for the web server is readily available to all applications with a bit of coding.

Discussion

`System.DirectoryServices.DirectoryEntry` is usually used for Active Directory programming, but it is able to use any of the providers that are available for Active Directory as well. This approach allows code to examine the IIS metabase for both the older-style IIS 5.x metabases as well as the newer IIS metabases that ship with Windows Server.

In Example 9-2, where LINQ was used to query the metabase, a number of interesting things are occurring. The query is walking the metabase hierarchy to retrieve the `HttpErrors`, but note that the `DirectoryEntry.Children` property is a `DirectoryEntries` collection class. `DirectoryEntries` does support `IEnumerable`, but it does not support `IEnumerable<T>`, which LINQ uses to do its work. See Recipe 4.10 for more of an explanation about this. The `OfType<DirectoryEntry>` extension method returns the strongly typed `IEnumerable<DirectoryEntry>` from the `IEnumerable` interface supported by `DirectoryEntries`. This is done to find the website and the root directory, after which `OfType<string>` is used to get an enumerable list of strings with the `HttpErrors` in it:

```
var httpErrors = from site in w3svc?.Children.OfType<DirectoryEntry>()
                 where site.SchemaClassName == WebServerSchema
                 from siteDir in site.Children.OfType<DirectoryEntry>()
                 where siteDir.Name == "ROOT"
                 from httpError in
                     siteDir.Properties["HttpErrors"].OfType<string>()
                 select httpError;
```

We've written this query using the usual query expression syntax, but we could also have built it using what is known as *explicit dot notation* syntax, which would look like this:

```
var httpErrors = w3svc?.Children.OfType<DirectoryEntry>()
                 .Where(site => site.SchemaClassName == WebServerSchema)
                 .SelectMany(siteDir =>
                     siteDir.Children.OfType<DirectoryEntry>())
                 .Where(siteDir => siteDir.Name == "ROOT")
                 .SelectMany<DirectoryEntry, string>(siteDir =>
                 siteDir.Properties["HttpErrors"].OfType<string>());
```

Explicit dot notation syntax is simply calling the extension methods that LINQ is built upon directly from the collection type or interface that has been extended. These extension methods are defined in the `System.Core` assembly on the static `Enumerable` class in the `System.Linq` namespace and are the foundation upon which the query expression syntax is built. Query expression syntax tells the C# compiler to use these extension methods to perform the query requested.

The use of `SelectMany` is implied in the normal query syntax through the use of multiple `from` statements. `SelectMany` allows the query to collapse the results into a single

---

set so that we have `IEnumerable<string>` as the `httpErrors` result; if `Select` were used, it would be `IEnumerable<IEnumerable<string>>`, which would be a set of string collections instead of one contiguous collection.

To build the query in the first place, you might find it easier to start out with separate smaller queries and then combine them. When using the explicit dot notation syntax, you can easily recombine the subqueries, as shown here:

```
// Break up the query using Explicit dot notation into getting the site,
// then the http error property values.

var sites = w3svc?.Children.OfType<DirectoryEntry>()
            .Where(child => child.SchemaClassName == WebServerSchema)
            .SelectMany(child => child.Children.OfType<DirectoryEntry>());

var httpErrors = sites
                .Where(site => site.Name == "ROOT")
                .SelectMany<DirectoryEntry,string>(site =>
                    site.Properties["HttpErrors"].OfType<string>());

// Combine the query using Explicit dot notation.
var combinedHttpErrors = w3svc?.Children.OfType<DirectoryEntry>()
                        .Where(site => site.SchemaClassName == WebServerSchema)
                        .SelectMany(siteDir =>
                            siteDir.Children.OfType<DirectoryEntry>())
                        .Where(siteDir => siteDir.Name == "ROOT")
                        .SelectMany<DirectoryEntry, string>(siteDir =>
                            siteDir.Properties["HttpErrors"].OfType<string>());
```

See Also

The "SelectMany<TSource, TResult> method," "OfType<TResult> method," "HttpErrors [IIS]," "IIS Metabase Properties," and "DirectoryEntry Class" topics in the MSDN documentation.

9.9 Writing a TCP Server

Problem

You need to create a server that listens on a port for incoming requests from a TCP client in either a secured or unsecured fashion. These client requests can then be processed at the server, and any responses can be sent back to the client. Recipe 9.10 shows how to write a TCP client to interact with this server.

Solution

Use the `MyTcpServer` class created here to listen on a TCP-based endpoint for requests arriving on a given port:

```
class MyTcpServer
{
    #region Private Members
    private TcpListener _listener;
    private IPAddress _address;
    private int _port;
    private bool _listening;
    private string _sslServerName;
    private object _syncRoot = new object();
    #endregion

    #region CTORs

    public MyTcpServer(IPAddress address, int port, string sslServerName = null)
    {
        _port = port;
        _address = address;
        _sslServerName = sslServerName;
    }
    #endregion // CTORs
```

The TCPServer class has four properties:

- Address, an IPAddress
- Port, an int
- Listening, a bool
- SSLServerName, a string

These return the current address and port on which the server is listening, the listening state, and the name of the SSL (Secure Sockets Layer) server that the TcpServer is listening as:

```
#region Properties
public IPAddress Address { get; }

public int Port { get; }

public bool Listening { get; private set; }

public string SSLServerName { get; }
#endregion
```

The ListenAsync method tells the MyTcpServer class to start listening on the specified address and port combination. You create and start a TcpListener, and then run a Task to call its AcceptTcpClientAsync method to wait for a client request to arrive. Once the client connects, the ProcessClientAsync method is run to service the client interaction.

The listener shuts down after serving the client:

```csharp
#region Public Methods
public async Task ListenAsync(CancellationToken cancellationToken =
default(CancellationToken))
{
    cancellationToken.ThrowIfCancellationRequested();
    try
    {
        lock (_syncRoot)
        {
            _listener = new TcpListener(Address, Port);

            // fire up the server
            _listener.Start();

            // set listening bit
            Listening = true;
        }

        // Enter the listening loop.
        do
        {
            Console.Write("Looking for someone to talk to... ");
            // Wait for connection
            try
            {
                cancellationToken.ThrowIfCancellationRequested();
                await Task.Run(async () =>
                {
                    TcpClient newClient =
                        await _listener.AcceptTcpClientAsync();
                    Console.WriteLine("Connected to new client");
                    await ProcessClientAsync(newClient, cancellationToken);
                },cancellationToken);
            }
            catch (OperationCanceledException)
            {
                // the user cancelled
                Listening = false;
            }
        }
        while (Listening);
    }
    catch (SocketException se)
    {
        Console.WriteLine($"SocketException: {se}");
    }
    finally
    {
        // shut it down
        StopListening();
    }
}
```

The StopListening method is called to stop the TCPServer from listening for requests:

```
public void StopListening()
{
    if (Listening)
    {
        lock (_syncRoot)
        {
            // set listening bit
            Listening = false;
            try
            {
                // shut it down if it is listening
                if (_listener.Server.IsBound)
                    _listener.Stop();
            }
            catch (ObjectDisposedException)
            {
                // if we try to stop listening while waiting
                // for a connection in AcceptTcpClientAsync (since it blocks)
                // it will throw an ObjectDisposedException here
                // Since we know in this case we are shutting down anyway
                // just note that we cancelled
                Console.WriteLine("Cancelled the listener");
            }
        }
    }
}
#endregion
```

The ProcessClientAsync method shown in Example 9-4 executes to serve a connected client. It determines if the server name for an SSL connection has been set and if so, creates an SslStream using TcpClient.GetStream and using the configured server name to get the server certificate. It then authenticates using the Authentica teAsServer method. If SSL is not being used, ProcessClientAsync gets the Network Stream from the client using the TcpClient.GetStream method and then reads the whole request. After sending back a response, it shuts down the client connection.

Example 9-4. ProcessClientAsync method

```
#region Private Methods
private async Task ProcessClientAsync(TcpClient client,
    CancellationToken cancellationToken = default(CancellationToken))
{
    cancellationToken.ThrowIfCancellationRequested();
    try
    {
        // Buffer for reading data
        byte[] bytes = new byte[1024];
```

```
StringBuilder clientData = new StringBuilder();

Stream stream = null;
if (!string.IsNullOrWhiteSpace(SSLServerName))
{
    Console.WriteLine($"Talking to client over SSL using {SSLServerName}");
    SslStream sslStream = new SslStream(client.GetStream());
    sslStream.AuthenticateAsServer(GetServerCert(SSLServerName), false,
        SslProtocols.Default, true);
    stream = sslStream;
}
else
{
    Console.WriteLine("Talking to client over regular HTTP");
    stream = client.GetStream();
}
// get the stream to talk to the client over
using (stream)
{
    // set initial read timeout to 1 minute to allow for connection
    stream.ReadTimeout = 60000;
    // Loop to receive all the data sent by the client.
    int bytesRead = 0;
    do
    {
        // THIS SEEMS LIKE A BUG, but it apparently isn't...
        // When we use Read, the first time it works fine, and then on the
        // second read when there is no data the IOException is thrown for
        // the timeout resulting from the 1 second timeout set on the
        // NetworkStream. If we use ReadAsync, it just hangs forever when
        // there is no data on the second read. This is because timeouts
        // are ignored on the Socket class when Async is used.
        try
        {
            // We use Read here and not ReadAsync as if you call ReadAsync
            // it will not timeout as you might expect (see note above)
            bytesRead = stream.Read(bytes, 0, bytes.Length);
            if (bytesRead > 0)
            {
                // Translate data bytes to an ASCII string and append
                clientData.Append(
                    Encoding.ASCII.GetString(bytes, 0, bytesRead));
                // decrease read timeout to 1/2 second now that data is
                // coming in.
                stream.ReadTimeout = 500;
            }
        }
        catch (IOException ioe)
        {
            // read timed out, all data has been retrieved
            Trace.WriteLine($"Read timed out: {ioe}");
            bytesRead = 0;
```

```
            }
        }
        while (bytesRead > 0);

        Console.WriteLine($"Client says: {clientData}");

        // Thank them for their input
        bytes = Encoding.ASCII.GetBytes("Thanks call again!");

        // Send back a response.
        await stream.WriteAsync(bytes, 0, bytes.Length, cancellationToken);
    }
}
finally
{
    // stop talking to client
    client?.Close();
}
}
```

Finally, the `GetServerCert` method retrieves the `X509Certificate` when the `TcpServer` is set up to use SSL. This expects that the certificate is accessible in the Personal certificate store on the local machine. If it is a self-signed certificate, then the certificate will need to be available in the Trusted Root certificate store as well:

```
private static X509Certificate GetServerCert(string subjectName)
{
    using (X509Store store =
        new X509Store(StoreName.My, StoreLocation.LocalMachine))
    {
        store.Open(OpenFlags.ReadOnly);
        X509CertificateCollection certificate =
            store.Certificates.Find(X509FindType.FindBySubjectName,
                subjectName, true);

        if (certificate.Count > 0)
            return (certificate[0]);
        else
            return (null);
    }
}
```

Here's an example of a simple server that listens for clients until the Escape key is pressed:

```
class Program
{
    private static MyTcpServer _server;
    private static CancellationTokenSource _cts;

    static void Main()
```

```
{
    _cts = new CancellationTokenSource();
    try
    {
        // We don't await this call as we want to continue so
        // that the Console UI can process keystrokes
        RunServer(_cts.Token);
    }
    catch(Exception ex)
    {
        Console.WriteLine(ex.ToString());
    }
    string msg = "Press Esc to stop the server...";
    Console.WriteLine(msg);
    ConsoleKeyInfo cki;
    while (true)
    {
        cki = Console.ReadKey();
        if (cki.Key == ConsoleKey.Escape)
        {
            _cts.Cancel();
            _server.StopListening();
            break; // allow exit
        }
    }
    Console.WriteLine("");
    Console.WriteLine("All done listening");
}

private static async Task RunServer(CancellationToken cancellationToken)
{
    try
    {
        await Task.Run(async() =>
        {
            cancellationToken.ThrowIfCancellationRequested();
            _server = new MyTcpServer(IPAddress.Loopback, 55555);
            await _server.ListenAsync(cancellationToken);
        }, cancellationToken);
    }
    catch (OperationCanceledException)
    {
        Console.WriteLine("Cancelled.");
    }
}
}
```

When talking to the MyTcpClient class in Recipe 9.10, the server gives output like this:

```
Press Esc to stop the server...
Looking for someone to talk to... Connected to new client
Client says: Just wanted to say hi
```

```
Looking for someone to talk to... Connected to new client
Client says: Just wanted to say hi again
Looking for someone to talk to... Connected to new client
Client says: Are you ignoring me?
Looking for someone to talk to... Connected to new client
Client says: I'll not be ignored! (round 0)
Looking for someone to talk to... Connected to new client
Client says: I'll not be ignored! (round 1)
Looking for someone to talk to... Connected to new client
Client says: I'll not be ignored! (round 2)
Looking for someone to talk to... Connected to new client
Client says: I'll not be ignored! (round 3)
Looking for someone to talk to... Connected to new client
Client says: I'll not be ignored! (round 4)
Looking for someone to talk to... Connected to new client
Client says: I'll not be ignored! (round 5)
Looking for someone to talk to... Connected to new client
Client says: I'll not be ignored! (round 6)
Looking for someone to talk to... Connected to new client
Client says: I'll not be ignored! (round 7)
Looking for someone to talk to... Connected to new client
Client says: I'll not be ignored! (round 8)
Looking for someone to talk to... Connected to new client
Client says: I'll not be ignored! (round 9)
Looking for someone to talk to... Connected to new client
Client says: I'll not be ignored! (round 10)
    [more output follows...]
```

Discussion

The Transmission Control Protocol (TCP) is the protocol used by the majority of traffic on the Internet today. TCP is responsible for the correct delivery of data packets from one endpoint to another. It uses the Internet Protocol (IP) to make the delivery. IP handles getting the packets from node to node; TCP detects when packets are not correct, are missing, or are sent out of order, and it arranges for missing or damaged packets to be resent. The TCPServer class is a basic server mechanism for dealing with requests that come from clients over TCP.

MyTcpServer takes the IP address and port passed in the constructor method and creates a TcpListener on that IPAddress and port. Once created, the TcpListener.Start method is called to start up the server. The AcceptTcpClientAsync method is called to listen for requests from TCP-based clients and is awaited for a connection from a client. Once the client connects, the ProcessClientAsync method is executed. In this method, the server reads request data from the client and returns a brief acknowledgment. The server disconnects from the client via TcpClient.Close. The server stops listening when the StopListening method is called, which takes the server offline by calling TcpListener.Stop.

To support secured requests, you can set the SSLServerName in the TcpServer constructor, which identifies the certificate to use for authentication.

The program running the server would then supply this name in the constructor like this:

```
_server = new MyTcpServer(IPAddress.Loopback, 55555, "CSharpCookBook.net");
```

In the ListenAsync method, we used the lock statement:

```
public async Task ListenAsync(CancellationToken cancellationToken =
    default(CancellationToken))
{
    cancellationToken.ThrowIfCancellationRequested();
    try
    {
        lock (_syncRoot)
        {
            _listener = new TcpListener(Address, Port);

            // fire up the server
            _listener.Start();

            // set listening bit
            Listening = true;
        }
```

 MSDN defines lock as follows: "The lock keyword marks a statement block as a critical section by obtaining the mutual-exclusion lock for a given object, executing a statement, and then releasing the lock." While this is true, you can more simply think "no other thread will run in the section of code inside the brackets for the lock statement until the first thread is finished." Those of you who like to push the envelope might think, "Hey, I could use async and await inside the lock statement and then it would yield to the next thread, right?" Yes, technically you could, but you shouldn't, as that is almost certainly going to cause deadlocks in your application. The code you await could be taking out locks itself and causing the deadlocking. The code inside the lock could also then resume on another thread (since when you await, it doesn't usually resume on the same thread), so you would be unlocking from a different thread than you established the lock on. This is a "Very Bad Thing," so please don't do it.

See Also

The "IPAddress Class," "TcpListener Class," "SslStream Class," "lock statement," and "TcpClient Class" topics in the MSDN documentation.

9.10 Writing a TCP Client

Problem

You want to interact with a TCP-based server in a secured or unsecured fashion.

Solution

Use the `MyTcpClient` class shown in Example 9-5 to connect to and converse with a TCP-based server by passing the address, port, and SSL server name (if authenticated) of the server to talk to, using the `System.Net.TcpClient` class. This example will talk to the server from Recipe 9.9.

Example 9-5. MyTcpClient class

```
class MyTcpClient : IDisposable
{
    private TcpClient _client;
    private IPEndPoint _endPoint;
    private bool _disposed;

    #region Properties
    public IPAddress Address { get; }

    public int Port { get; }

    public string SSLServerName { get; }

    #endregion

    public MyTcpClient(IPAddress address, int port, string sslServerName = null)
    {
        Address = address;
        Port = port;
        _endPoint = new IPEndPoint(Address, Port);
        SSLServerName = sslServerName;
    }

    public async Task ConnectToServerAsync(string msg)
    {
        try
        {
            _client = new TcpClient();
            await _client.ConnectAsync(_endPoint.Address,_endPoint.Port);

            Stream stream = null;
            if (!string.IsNullOrWhiteSpace(SSLServerName))
            {
                SslStream sslStream =
```

```csharp
                new SslStream(_client.GetStream(), false,
                    new RemoteCertificateValidationCallback(
                        CertificateValidationCallback));
            sslStream.AuthenticateAsClient(SSLServerName);
            DisplaySSLInformation(SSLServerName, sslStream, true);
            stream = sslStream;
        }
        else
        {
            stream = _client.GetStream();
        }
        using (stream)
        {
            // Get the bytes to send for the message
            byte[] bytes = Encoding.ASCII.GetBytes(msg);

            // send message
            Console.WriteLine($"Sending message to server: {msg}");
            await stream?.WriteAsync(bytes, 0, bytes.Length);

            // Get the response
            // Buffer to store the response bytes.
            bytes = new byte[1024];

            // Display the response
            int bytesRead = await stream?.ReadAsync(bytes, 0, bytes.Length);
            string serverResponse =
                Encoding.ASCII.GetString(bytes, 0, bytesRead);
            Console.WriteLine($"Server said: {serverResponse}");
        }
    }
    catch (SocketException se)
    {
        Console.WriteLine($"There was an error talking to the server: {se}");
    }
    finally
    {
        Dispose();
    }
}

#region IDisposable Members

public void Dispose()
{
    Dispose(true);
    GC.SuppressFinalize(this);
}

private void Dispose(bool disposing)
{
    if (!_disposed)
```

```csharp
        {
            if (disposing)
            {
                _client?.Close();
            }
            _disposed = true;
        }
    }

    #endregion

    private bool CertificateValidationCallback(object sender,
            X509Certificate certificate,
            X509Chain chain,
            SslPolicyErrors sslPolicyErrors)
    {
        if (sslPolicyErrors == SslPolicyErrors.None)
        {
            return true;
        }
        else
        {
            if (sslPolicyErrors == SslPolicyErrors.RemoteCertificateChainErrors)
            {
                Console.WriteLine("The X509Chain.ChainStatus returned an array of " +
                    "X509ChainStatus objects containing error information.");
            }
            else if (sslPolicyErrors ==
                SslPolicyErrors.RemoteCertificateNameMismatch)
            {
                Console.WriteLine(
                    "There was a mismatch of the name on a certificate.");
            }
            else if (sslPolicyErrors ==
                SslPolicyErrors.RemoteCertificateNotAvailable)
            {
                Console.WriteLine("No certificate was available.");
            }
            else
            {
                Console.WriteLine("SSL Certificate Validation Error!");
            }

            Console.WriteLine("");
            Console.WriteLine("SSL Certificate Validation Error!");
            Console.WriteLine(sslPolicyErrors.ToString());

            return false;
        }
    }

    private static void DisplaySSLInformation(string serverName,
```

```
        SslStream sslStream, bool verbose)
    {
        DisplayCertInformation(sslStream.RemoteCertificate, verbose);

        Console.WriteLine("");
        Console.WriteLine($"SSL Connect Report for : {serverName}");
        Console.WriteLine("");
        Console.WriteLine(
            $"Is Authenticated:            {sslStream.IsAuthenticated}");
        Console.WriteLine($"Is Encrypted:                {sslStream.IsEncrypted}");
        Console.WriteLine($"Is Signed:                   {sslStream.IsSigned}");
        Console.WriteLine($"Is Mutually Authenticated:   " +
            $"{sslStream.IsMutuallyAuthenticated}");
        Console.WriteLine("");
        Console.WriteLine($"Hash Algorithm:              {sslStream.HashAlgorithm}");
        Console.WriteLine($"Hash Strength:               {sslStream.HashStrength}");
        Console.WriteLine(
            $"Cipher Algorithm:          {sslStream.CipherAlgorithm}");
        Console.WriteLine(
            $"Cipher Strength:           {sslStream.CipherStrength}");
        Console.WriteLine("");
        Console.WriteLine($"Key Exchange Algorithm:      " +
            $"{sslStream.KeyExchangeAlgorithm}");
        Console.WriteLine($"Key Exchange Strength:       " +
            $"{sslStream.KeyExchangeStrength}");
        Console.WriteLine("");
        Console.WriteLine(4"SSL Protocol:                {sslStream.SslProtocol}");
    }

    private static void DisplayCertInformation(X509Certificate remoteCertificate,
        bool verbose)
    {
        Console.WriteLine("");
        Console.WriteLine("Certficate Information for:");
        Console.WriteLine($"{remoteCertificate.Subject}");
        Console.WriteLine("");
        Console.WriteLine("Valid From:");
        Console.WriteLine($"{remoteCertificate.GetEffectiveDateString()}");
        Console.WriteLine("Valid To:");
        Console.WriteLine($"{remoteCertificate.GetExpirationDateString()}");
        Console.WriteLine("Certificate Format:");
        Console.WriteLine($"{remoteCertificate.GetFormat()}");
        Console.WriteLine("");
        Console.WriteLine("Issuer Name:");
        Console.WriteLine($"{remoteCertificate.Issuer}");

        if (verbose)
        {
            Console.WriteLine("Serial Number:");
            Console.WriteLine($"{remoteCertificate.GetSerialNumberString()}");
            Console.WriteLine("Hash:");
            Console.WriteLine($"{remoteCertificate.GetCertHashString()}");
```

```
            Console.WriteLine("Key Algorithm:");
            Console.WriteLine($"{remoteCertificate.GetKeyAlgorithm()}");
            Console.WriteLine("Key Algorithm Parameters:");
            Console.WriteLine(
                $"{remoteCertificate.GetKeyAlgorithmParametersString()}");
            Console.WriteLine("Public Key:");
            Console.WriteLine($"{remoteCertificate.GetPublicKeyString()}");
        }
    }
}
```

To use the `MyTcpClient` in a program, you can simply create an instance of it and call `ConnectToServerAsync` to send a request. In the `TalkToServerAsync` method, you first make three calls to the server to test the basic mechanism and `await` the results from the `MakeClientCallToServer` method. Next, you enter a loop to really pound on it and spawn a number of `Task` requests that each `await` the `MakeClientCallTo Server` method. This verifies that the server's mechanism for handling multiple requests is sound:

```
static void Main()
{
    Task serverChat = TalkToServerAsync();
    serverChat.Wait();
    Console.WriteLine(@"Press the ENTER key to continue...");
    Console.Read();
}

private static async Task MakeClientCallToServerAsync(string msg)
{
    MyTcpClient client = new MyTcpClient(IPAddress.Loopback, 55555);
    // Uncomment to use SSL to talk to the server
    //MyTcpClient client = new MyTcpClient(IPAddress.Loopback, 55555,
    //    "CSharpCookBook.net");
    await client.ConnectToServerAsync(msg);
}

private static async Task TalkToServerAsync()
{
    await MakeClientCallToServerAsync("Just wanted to say hi");
    await MakeClientCallToServerAsync("Just wanted to say hi again");
    await MakeClientCallToServerAsync("Are you ignoring me?");

    // now send a bunch of messages...
    string msg;
    for (int i = 0; i < 100; i++)
    {
        msg = $"I'll not be ignored! (round {i})";
        RunClientCallAsTask(msg);
    }
}
```

```
private static void RunClientCallAsTask(string msg)
{
    Task work = Task.Run(async () =>
    {
        await MakeClientCallToServerAsync(msg);
    });
}
```

The output on the client side for this exchange of messages is:

```
Sending message to server: Just wanted to say hi
Server said: Thanks call again!
Sending message to server: Just wanted to say hi again
Server said: Thanks call again!
Sending message to server: Are you ignoring me?
Server said: Thanks call again!
Press the ENTER key to continue...
Sending message to server: I'll not be ignored! (round 1)
Sending message to server: I'll not be ignored! (round 0)
Sending message to server: I'll not be ignored! (round 2)
Sending message to server: I'll not be ignored! (round 3)
Sending message to server: I'll not be ignored! (round 4)
Sending message to server: I'll not be ignored! (round 6)
Sending message to server: I'll not be ignored! (round 5)
Sending message to server: I'll not be ignored! (round 7)
Sending message to server: I'll not be ignored! (round 9)
Sending message to server: I'll not be ignored! (round 10)

[once all requests are set up as tasks you see the responses...]

Server said: Thanks call again!
Server said: Thanks call again!
Server said: Thanks call again!
Server said: Thanks call again!
Server said: Thanks call again!
Server said: Thanks call again!
Server said: Thanks call again!
Server said: Thanks call again!
Server said: Thanks call again!
Server said: Thanks call again!
Server said: Thanks call again!
```

Discussion

MyTcpClient.ConnectToServerAsync is designed to send one message, get the response, display it as a string, and then close the connection. To accomplish this, it creates a System.Net.TcpClient and connects to the server by calling the TcpClient.ConnectAsync method. ConnectAsync targets the server using an IPEnd Point built from the address and port that you passed to the MyTcpClient constructor.

MyTcpClient.ConnectToServerAsync then gets the bytes for the string using the Encoding.ASCII.GetBytes method. Once it has the bytes to send, it gets either the NetworkStream or the SslStream from the underlying System.Net.TcpClient by calling its GetStream method and then sends the message using the TcpClient.Write Async method.

To receive the response from the server, MyTcpClient.ConnectToServerAsync calls the blocking TcpClient.ReadAsync method. Once ReadAsync is awaited and returns, the bytes are decoded to get the string that contains the response from the server. The connections are then closed and the client ends.

To support secured requests, you can set the SSLServerName in the TcpClient constructor, which identifies the certificate to use for authentication.

The program running the client would then supply this name in the constructor like this:

```
MyTcpClient client =
    new MyTcpClient(IPAddress.Loopback, 55555, "CSharpCookBook.net");
```

When using a secured connection, we use the DisplaySSLInformation and Display CertInformation methods of MyTcpClient to display all of the details of the connection as they pertain to the certificate and security status:

```
Certficate Information for:
CN=CSharpCookBook.net

Valid From:
12/27/2014 7:29:31 PM
Valid To:
12/31/2039 6:59:59 PM
Certificate Format:
X509

Issuer Name:
CN=CSharpCookBook.net
Serial Number:
0F0E1C4148C6A09C42EDEDAFCD2E83E2
Hash:
664E30B62C4FB9DBEE0C29F27A15E5EDE2C46187
Key Algorithm:
1.2.840.113549.1.1.1
Key Algorithm Parameters:
0500
Public Key:
3082020A0282020100EAB6004CD3F2F5214773E8FE4FA40FE610F1C27E888276E81EBBB86020B904
3B136CF02197C928ED0BCA8339A31334059C2744A8BB617849BBC98C8B242FC360C88BF62E2C491B
1A6F951DDB65E0036D8839AC6695B26CD3E50DD749A5610C8564CF99EE79FED272D04A3100B51A4A
4BAE076BB8129E39B382ED1FDB8382A2D3C057D7F46072DDDE0654083E1F2CB4E25685B5EE4B4F25
F3D2561B61869D9C39B9FB389E6A06D9DEFA6693D94C6A1F2CA34462B3D9C68CF91A179B0957050E
```

A9A30D508C067C216CAD59CA9E846B0EBA02472333BBF2462415B13567EBF6930FC1000EECC3EA70
9867B8BD6869BF828B8EBA5BA2E4A7660B46B798A8BB8D046FFE1C767F5A77AF1CD6E83F9E013AB1
748264F89617D9C106813F554B8AF4184AC58B55A1A58ABAA2F171CDBFF6923C27FE801FEE5D3664
87F54FAD184B0FCBB874532EC8E6B3BAA322F05DB6AD99E5982B98AD43C0E9BB2356270DB07BA5E5
AAE2F0B66E630A6A0435FDFC61DB46B0FF348AF5D2285C74A35E8AAFC86F45C0E674C2D9FE98B6C1
17208668CF4B03DD77948AE45AE84D33178C3042B1155E58D3B49492697D5CA4CF4AB24549E4A240
CCEB6CF61CEF6F33F412A91BC32803136A6481B6B246FEA5A3943EEB7FDA5E54CC561DE737BBB380
BC2B467F1A5B8CA1BDFC66B6B4E60DCCC7C3912449D0BF8B9878D22C04A36A09898D2AAED0CE32DB
770203010001

```
SSL Connect Report for : CSharpCookBook.net

Is Authenticated:          True
Is Encrypted:              True
Is Signed:                 True
Is Mutually Authenticated: False

Hash Algorithm:            Sha1
Hash Strength:             160
Cipher Algorithm:          Aes256
Cipher Strength:           256

Key Exchange Algorithm:    44550
Key Exchange Strength:     256

SSL Protocol:              Tls
Sending message to server: I'll not be ignored! (round 95)
Server said: Thanks call again!
```

In the Solution, we added the IDisposable interface implementation to the MyTcp
Client class as follows:

```csharp
#region IDisposable Members

public void Dispose()
{
    Dispose(true);
    GC.SuppressFinalize(this);
}

private void Dispose(bool disposing)
{
    if (!_disposed)
    {
        if (disposing)
        {
            _client?.Close();
        }
        _disposed = true;
    }
}

#endregion
```

We did this to handle the closing of the private `TcpClient` instance variable `_client` correctly, as it provides its own `Close` method so that it can perform some logging and clean up its resources. `SuppressFinalize` is called in the `Dispose` method to inform the garbage collector that the object has already been cleaned up fully.

See Also

The "TcpClient Class," "SslStream Class," "NetworkStream Class," "IDisposable Interface," and "Encoding.ASCII Property" topics in the MSDN documentation.

9.11 Simulating Form Execution

Problem

You need to send a collection of name/value pairs to simulate a form being executed on a browser to a location identified by a URL.

Solution

Use the `System.Net.WebClient` class to send a set of name/value pairs to the web server using the `UploadValues` method. This class enables you to masquerade as the browser executing a form by setting up the name/value pairs with the input data. The input field ID is the name, and the value to use in the field is the value:

```
// In order to use this, you need to run the CSCBWeb project first.
Uri uri = new Uri("http://localhost:4088/WebForm1.aspx");
WebClient client = new WebClient();

// Create a series of name/value pairs to send
// Add necessary parameter/value pairs to the name/value container.
NameValueCollection collection = new NameValueCollection()
    { {"Item", "WebParts"},
        {"Identity", "foo@bar.com"},
        {"Quantity", "5"} };

Console.WriteLine(
    $"Uploading name/value pairs to URI {uri.AbsoluteUri} ...");

// Upload the NameValueCollection.
byte[] responseArray =
    await client.UploadValuesTaskAsync(uri, "POST", collection);

// Decode and display the response.
Console.WriteLine(
    $"\nResponse received was {Encoding.UTF8.GetString(responseArray)}");
```

The *WebForm1.aspx* page, which receives and processes this data, looks like this:

```
<%@ Page Language="C#" AutoEventWireup="true" CodeFile="WebForm1.aspx.cs"
    Inherits="WebForm1" %>

<!DOCTYPE html PUBLIC "-//W3C//DTD XHTML 1.0 Transitional//EN"
"http://www.w3.org/TR/xhtml1/DTD/xhtml1-transitional.dtd">

<html xmlns="http://www.w3.org/1999/xhtml">
<head runat="server">
    <title>Untitled Page</title>
</head>
<body>
    <form id="form1" runat="server">
    <div>


        <asp:Table ID="Table1" runat="server" Height="139px" Width="361px">
            <asp:TableRow runat="server">
                <asp:TableCell runat="server"><asp:Label ID="Label1"
                runat="server"
Text="Identity"></asp:Label></asp:TableCell>
                <asp:TableCell runat="server"><asp:TextBox ID="Identity"
runat="server"/></asp:TableCell>
            </asp:TableRow>
            <asp:TableRow runat="server">
                <asp:TableCell runat="server"><asp:Label ID="Label2"
                runat="server"
Text="Item"></asp:Label></asp:TableCell>
                <asp:TableCell runat="server"><asp:TextBox ID="Item"
runat="server"/></asp:TableCell>
            </asp:TableRow>
            <asp:TableRow runat="server">
                <asp:TableCell runat="server"><asp:Label ID="Label3"
                runat="server"
Text="Quantity"></asp:Label></asp:TableCell>
                <asp:TableCell runat="server"><asp:TextBox ID="Quantity"
runat="server"/></asp:TableCell>
            </asp:TableRow>
            <asp:TableRow runat="server">
                <asp:TableCell runat="server"></asp:TableCell>
                <asp:TableCell runat="server"><asp:Button ID="Button1"
                runat="server"
onclick="Button1_Click" Text="Submit" /></asp:TableCell>
            </asp:TableRow>
        </asp:Table>

    </div>
    </form>
</body>
</html>
```

The *WebForm1.aspx.cs* codebehind looks like this:

```
using System;
using System.Web;

public partial class WebForm1 : System.Web.UI.Page
{
    protected void Page_Load(object sender, EventArgs e)
    {
        if(HttpContext.Current.Request.HttpMethod.ToUpper() == "POST")
            WriteOrderResponse();
    }
    protected void Button1_Click(object sender, EventArgs e)
    {
        WriteOrderResponse();
    }

    private void WriteOrderResponse()
    {
        string response = "Thanks for the order!<br/>";
        response += "Identity: " + Request.Form["Identity"] + "<br/>";
        response += "Item: " + Request.Form["Item"] + "<br/>";
        response += "Quantity: " + Request.Form["Quantity"] + "<br/>";
        Response.Write(response);
    }
}
```

The output from the form execution looks like this:

```
Uploading name/value pairs to URI http://localhost:4088/WebForm1.aspx ...

Response received was ?Thanks for the order!<br/>Identity: foo@bar.com<br/>Item:
 WebParts<br/>Quantity: 5<br/>

<!DOCTYPE html PUBLIC "-//W3C//DTD XHTML 1.0 Transitional//EN" "http://www.w3.or
g/TR/xhtml1/DTD/xhtml1-transitional.dtd">

<html xmlns="http://www.w3.org/1999/xhtml">
<head><title>
        Untitled Page
</title></head>
<body>
    <form name="form1" method="post" action="WebForm1.aspx" id="form1">
<input type="hidden" name="__VIEWSTATE" id="__VIEWSTATE" value="/wEPDwULLTE3NDA4
NzI10TJkZHS2esbeFu36oKf1n3XvCfLBFbminq7tuASWazSmVzNV" />

    <div>

                <table id="Table1" border="0" height="139" width="361">
        <tr>
                <td><span id="Label1">Identity</span></td><td><input name="Ident
ity" type="text" id="Identity" /></td>
        </tr><tr>
                <td><span id="Label2">Item</span></td><td><input name="Item" typ
```

```
e="text" id="Item" /></td>
        </tr><tr>
                <td><span id="Label3">Quantity</span></td><td><input name="Quant
ity" type="text" id="Quantity" /></td>
        </tr><tr>
                <td></td><td><input type="submit" name="Button1" value="Submit"
id="Button1" /></td>
        </tr>
</table>

    </div>

<input type="hidden" name="__VIEWSTATEGENERATOR" id="__VIEWSTATEGENERATOR" value
="B6E7D48B" />
<input type="hidden" name="__EVENTVALIDATION" id="__EVENTVALIDATION" value="/wEd
AAWO/dj0xplxW6YoKRXH5OHbmz/pl7ppA227nN6820C6Sskwyhj63BXMkV5ahbRAQpWWUallXbdbKxLN
IxdB86x+zfg78Z8BXhXifTCAVkevd657ebmKYjtae5uEq9PVWd0RhH/uhX8f6dI/Hiyy1p14" /></fo
rm>

<!-- Visual Studio Browser Link -->
<script type="application/json" id="__browserLink_initializationData">
    {"appName":"Unknown","requestId":"c7ee16b51c9b4bccae0c3c79a9fba779"}
</script>
<script type="text/javascript" src="http://localhost:2976/eef9532a4f984be0b28884
3bb4cee559/browserLink" async="async"></script>
<!-- End Browser Link -->

</body>
</html>
```

Discussion

The WebClient class makes it easy to upload form data to a web server in the common format of a set of name/value pairs. You can see this technique in the call to UploadValuesTaskAsync that takes a URI (*http://localhost:4088/WebForm1.aspx*), the HTTP method to use (POST), and the NameValueCollection you created (collection).

> Note that the asynchronous version of the UploadValues* methods is called and that the one used (UploadValuesTaskAsync) is the one specific to using with async and await.

You populate the NameValueCollection with the data for each field on the form by calling its Add method, passing the id of the input field as the name and the value to put in the field as the value. In this example, you fill in the Identity field with foo@bar.com, the Item field with WebParts, and the Quantity field with 5. You then print out the resulting response from the POST to the console window.

See Also

The "WebClient Class" topic in the MSDN documentation.

9.12 Transferring Data via HTTP

Problem

You need to download data from or upload data to a location specified by a URL; this data can be either an array of bytes or a file.

Solution

Use the WebClient.UploadDataTaskAsync or WebClient.DownloadDataTaskAsync methods to transfer data using a URL.

To download the data for a web page, do the following:

```
Uri uri = new Uri("http://localhost:4088/DownloadData.aspx");

// make a client
using (WebClient client = new WebClient())
{
    // get the contents of the file
    Console.WriteLine($"Downloading {uri.AbsoluteUri}");
    // download the page and store the bytes
    byte[] bytes;
    try
    {
        // NOTE: There is also a DownloadDataAsync that is used in the older
        // EAP pattern, which we do not use here.
        bytes = await client.DownloadDataTaskAsync(uri);
    }
    catch (WebException we)
    {
        Console.WriteLine(we.ToString());
        return;
    }
    // Write the HTML out
    string page = Encoding.UTF8.GetString(bytes);
    Console.WriteLine(page);

}
```

This will produce the following output:

```
Downloading http://localhost:4088/DownloadData.aspx
?

<!DOCTYPE html PUBLIC "-//W3C//DTD XHTML 1.0 Transitional//EN" "http://www.w3.or
g/TR/xhtml1/DTD/xhtml1-transitional.dtd">

<html xmlns="http://www.w3.org/1999/xhtml">
<head><title>
        Download Data
</title></head>
<body>
    <form name="Form1" method="post" action="DownloadData.aspx" id="Form2">
        <input type="hidden" name="__VIEWSTATE"
value="dDwyMDQwNjUzNDY2Ozs+kS9hguYm9369sybDqmIow0AvxBg=" />
    <span id="Label1" style="Z-INDEX: 101; LEFT: 142px; POSITION: absolute;
TOP: 164px">This is downloaded html!</span>
    </form>

<!-- Visual Studio Browser Link -->
<script type="application/json" id="__browserLink_initializationData">
    {"appName":"Unknown","requestId":"b43b962ff6264058b5dbf17aed23a082"}
</script>
<script type="text/javascript" src="http://localhost:3587/db7b63d3424649c7a10386
29bc71b103/browserLink" async="async"></script>
<!-- End Browser Link -->

</body>
</html>
```

You can also download data to a file using `DownloadFileTaskAsync`:

```csharp
Uri uri = new Uri("http://localhost:4088/DownloadData.aspx");

// make a client
using (WebClient client = new WebClient())
{
    // go get the file
    Console.WriteLine($"Retrieving file from {uri}...{Environment.NewLine}");
    // get file and put it in a temp file
    string tempFile = Path.GetTempFileName();
    try
    {
        // NOTE: There is also a DownloadFileAsync that is used in the older
        // EAP pattern, which we do not use here.
        await client.DownloadFileTaskAsync(uri, tempFile);
    }
    catch (WebException we)
    {
        Console.WriteLine(we.ToString());
        return;
    }
    Console.WriteLine($"Downloaded {uri} to {tempFile}");
}
```

This will produce output similar to the following (temporary file path and name will change):

```
Retrieving file from http://localhost:4088/DownloadData.aspx...

Downloaded http://localhost:4088/DownloadData.aspx to C:\Users\jhilyard\AppData\
Local\Temp\tmpA5D7.tmp
```

To upload a file to a URL, use UploadFileTaskAsync like so:

```
Uri uri = new Uri("http://localhost:4088/UploadData.aspx");
// make a client
using (WebClient client = new WebClient())
{
    Console.WriteLine($"Uploading to {uri.AbsoluteUri}");
    try
    {
        // NOTE: There is also a UploadFileAsync that is used in the older
        // EAP pattern, which we do not use here.
        await client.UploadFileTaskAsync(uri, "SampleClassLibrary.dll");
        Console.WriteLine($"Uploaded successfully to {uri.AbsoluteUri}");
    }
    catch (WebException we)
    {
        Console.WriteLine(we.ToString());
    }
}
```

The code for an ASPX page that could receive this would look as follows:

```
using System;
using System.Web;

public partial class UploadData : System.Web.UI.Page
{
    protected void Page_Load(object sender, EventArgs e)
    {
        foreach (string f in Request.Files.AllKeys)
        {
            HttpPostedFile file = Request.Files[f];
            // need to have write permissions for the directory to write to
            try
            {
                string path = Server.MapPath(".") + @"\" + file.FileName;
                file.SaveAs(path);
                Response.Write("Saved " + path);
            }
            catch (HttpException hex)
            {
                // return error information specific to the save
                Response.Write("Failed to save file with error: " +
                    hex.Message);
            }
```

```
        }
      }
    }
```

 Note that while the preceding ASPX page will receive and store the file, it is a basic sample meant to illustrate uploading with Web Client. When building a page to receive files, make sure you deal with the security aspects of file uploads as specified in the Unrestricted File Upload vulnerability described by OWASP (Open Web Application Security Project) on its website (*https://www.owasp.org/index.php/Unrestricted_File_Upload*).

This will produce the following output:

```
Uploading to http://localhost:4088/UploadData.aspx
Uploaded successfully to http://localhost:4088/UploadData.aspx
```

Discussion

WebClient simplifies downloading of files and bytes in files, as these are common tasks when you are dealing with the Web. The more traditional stream-based method for downloading can also be accessed via the OpenReadTaskAsync method on the Web Client.

See Also

The "WebClient Class" topic in the MSDN documentation and the OWASP website (*https://www.owasp.org*).

9.13 Using Named Pipes to Communicate

Problem

You need a way to use named pipes to communicate with another application across the network.

Solution

Use the NamedPipeClientStream and NamedPipeServerStream in the System.IO.Pipes namespace. You can then create a client and server to work with named pipes.

To use the NamedPipeClientStream class, you need some code like that shown in Example 9-6.

Example 9-6. Using the NamedPipeClientStream class

```
using System;
using System.Text;
using System.IO.Pipes;
using System.Threading.Tasks;

namespace NamedPipes
{
    class NamedPipeClientConsole
    {
        static void Main()
        {
            Task client = RunClient();
            client.Wait();

            Console.WriteLine("Press Enter to exit...");
            Console.ReadLine();
        }

        private static async Task RunClient()
        {
            Console.WriteLine("Initiating client, looking for server...");
            // set up a message to send
            string messageText = "Sample text message!";
            int bytesRead;

            // set up the named pipe client and close it when complete
            using (NamedPipeClientStream clientPipe =
                    new NamedPipeClientStream(".", "mypipe", PipeDirection.InOut,
                    PipeOptions.None))
            {
                // connect to the server stream
                await clientPipe.ConnectAsync();
                // set the read mode to message
                clientPipe.ReadMode = PipeTransmissionMode.Message;

                // write the message ten times
                for (int i = 0; i < 10; i++)
                {
                    Console.WriteLine($"Sending message: {messageText}");
                    byte[] messageBytes = Encoding.Unicode.GetBytes(messageText);
                    // check and write the message
                    if (clientPipe.CanWrite)
                    {
                        await clientPipe.WriteAsync(
                            messageBytes, 0, messageBytes.Length);
                        await clientPipe.FlushAsync();
                        // wait till it is read
                        clientPipe.WaitForPipeDrain();
                    }
```

```
            // set up a buffer for the message bytes
            messageBytes = new byte[256];
            do
            {
                // collect the message bits in the stringbuilder
                StringBuilder message = new StringBuilder();

                // read all of the bits until we have the
                // complete response message
                do
                {
                    // read from the pipe
                    bytesRead =
                        await clientPipe.ReadAsync(
                            messageBytes, 0, messageBytes.Length);
                    // if we got something, add it to the message
                    if (bytesRead > 0)
                    {
                        message.Append(
                            Encoding.Unicode.GetString(messageBytes, 0,
                                bytesRead));
                        Array.Clear(messageBytes, 0, messageBytes.Length);
                    }
                }
                while (!clientPipe.IsMessageComplete);

                // set to zero as we have read the whole message
                bytesRead = 0;
                Console.WriteLine($"    Received message: " +
                    $"{message.ToString()}");
            }
            while (bytesRead != 0);

        }
    }

    }
  }
}
```

Then, to set up a server for the client to talk to, you use the `NamedPipeServerStream` class, as shown in Example 9-7.

Example 9-7. Setting up a server for the client

```
using System;
using System.Text;
using System.IO.Pipes;
using System.Threading.Tasks;

namespace NamedPipes
```

```
{
    class NamedPipeServerConsole
    {
        static void Main()
        {
            Task server = RunServer();
            server.Wait();

            // make our server hang around so you can see the messages sent
            Console.WriteLine("Press Enter to exit...");
            Console.ReadLine();
        }

        private static async Task RunServer()
        {
            Console.WriteLine("Initiating server, waiting for client...");
            // Start up our named pipe in message mode and close the pipe
            // when done.
            using (NamedPipeServerStream serverPipe = new
                    NamedPipeServerStream("mypipe", PipeDirection.InOut, 1,
                    PipeTransmissionMode.Message, PipeOptions.None))
            {
                // wait for a client...
                await serverPipe.WaitForConnectionAsync();

                // process messages until the client goes away
                while (serverPipe.IsConnected)
                {
                    int bytesRead = 0;
                    byte[] messageBytes = new byte[256];
                    // read until we have the message then respond
                    do
                    {
                        // build up the client message
                        StringBuilder message = new StringBuilder();

                        // check that we can read the pipe
                        if (serverPipe.CanRead)
                        {
                            // loop until the entire message is read
                            do
                            {
                                bytesRead =
                                    await serverPipe.ReadAsync(messageBytes, 0,
                                                messageBytes.Length);

                                // got bytes from the stream so add them to the
                                // message
                                if (bytesRead > 0)
                                {
                                    message.Append(
                                        Encoding.Unicode.GetString(messageBytes, 0,
```

```
                                        bytesRead));
                    Array.Clear(messageBytes, 0,
                        messageBytes.Length);
                }
            }
            while (!serverPipe.IsMessageComplete);
        }

        // if we got a message, write it out and respond
        if (message.Length > 0)
        {
            // set to zero as we have read the whole message
            bytesRead = 0;
            Console.WriteLine($"Received message: " +
                $"{message.ToString()}");

            // return the message text we got from the
            // client in reverse
            char[] messageChars =
                message.ToString().Trim().ToCharArray();
            Array.Reverse(messageChars);
            string reversedMessageText = new string(messageChars);

            // show the return message
            Console.WriteLine($"    Returning Message: " +
                $"{{reversedMessageText}}");

            // write the response
            messageBytes = Encoding.Unicode.GetBytes(messageChars);
            if (serverPipe.CanWrite)
            {
                // write the message
                await serverPipe.WriteAsync(messageBytes, 0,
                    messageBytes.Length);
                // flush the buffer
                await serverPipe.FlushAsync();
                // wait till read by client
                serverPipe.WaitForPipeDrain();
            }
        }
    }
    while (bytesRead != 0);
}
}
}
}
```

Discussion

Named pipes are a mechanism to allow interprocess or intermachine communications in Windows. The .NET Framework has provided managed access to named pipes, which makes it much easier to utilize named pipes in managed applications. In many cases, you could use Windows Communication Foundation (WCF) to set up the server and client code and even provide a named pipe binding to accomplish this as well. It depends on what your application requirements call for, as well as at what level of the application stack you want to work. If you have an existing application that sets up a named pipe, why use WCF when you can just connect directly? Using named pipes is like using sockets and keeps your code very close to the pipe. The benefit is that there are fewer code layers to process; the drawback is that you have to do more in terms of message processing.

In the Solution, we created some code to use NamedPipeClientStream and NamedPipe ServerStream. The interaction between these two goes like this:

1. The server process is started; it fires up a NamedPipeServerStream and then calls WaitForConnectionAsync to wait for a client to connect:

```
// Start up our named pipe in message mode and close the pipe
// when done.
using (NamedPipeServerStream serverPipe = new
        NamedPipeServerStream("mypipe", PipeDirection.InOut, 1,
            PipeTransmissionMode.Message, PipeOptions.None))
{
    // wait for a client...
    await serverPipe.WaitForConnectionAsync();
```

2. The client process is created; it fires up a NamedPipeClientStream, calls ConnectAsync, and connects to the server process:

```
// set up the named pipe client and close it when complete
using (NamedPipeClientStream clientPipe =
    new NamedPipeClientStream(".","mypipe",
        PipeDirection.InOut,PipeOptions.None))
{
    // connect to the server stream
    await clientPipe.ConnectAsync();
```

3. The server process sees the connection from the client and then calls IsConnec ted in a loop, looking for messages from the client until the connection is gone:

```
// process messages until the client goes away
while (serverPipe.IsConnected)
{
    // More processing code in here...
}
```

4. The client process then writes a number of messages to the server process using WriteAsync, FlushAsync, and WaitForPipeDrain:

```
string messageText = "Sample text message!";

// write the message ten times
for (int i = 0; i < 10; i++)
{
    Console.WriteLine($"Sending message: {messageText}");
    byte[] messageBytes = Encoding.Unicode.GetBytes(messageText);
    // check and write the message
    if (clientPipe.CanWrite)
    {
        await clientPipe.WriteAsync(
            messageBytes, 0, messageBytes.Length);
        await clientPipe.FlushAsync();
        // wait till it is read
        clientPipe.WaitForPipeDrain();
    }
    // response processing....
}
```

5. When the client process receives the response from the server, it reads the message bytes until complete. If the message sending is complete, the NamedPipe ClientStream goes out of the scope of the using statement and closes (thereby closing the connection on the client side) and then waits to go away when the user presses Enter:

```
// set up a buffer for the message bytes
messageBytes = new byte[256];
do
{
    // collect the message bits in the stringbuilder
    StringBuilder message = new StringBuilder();

    // read all of the bits until we have the
    // complete response message
    do
    {
        // read from the pipe
        bytesRead =
            await clientPipe.ReadAsync(
                messageBytes, 0, messageBytes.Length);
        // if we got something, add it to the message
        if (bytesRead > 0)
        {
            message.Append(
                    Encoding.Unicode.GetString(messageBytes, 0,
                        bytesRead));
            Array.Clear(messageBytes, 0, messageBytes.Length);
```

```
            }
        }
        while (!clientPipe.IsMessageComplete);

        // set to zero as we have read the whole message
        bytesRead = 0;
        Console.WriteLine($"    Received message: {message.ToString()}");
    }
    while (bytesRead != 0);
```

6. The server process notes that the client has closed the pipe connection via the failed IsConnected call in the while loop. The NamedPipeServerStream goes out of the scope of the using statement, which closes the pipe.

The client output looks like this:

```
Initiating client, looking for server...
Sending message: Sample text message!
    Received message: !egassem txet elpmaS
Sending message: Sample text message!
    Received message: !egassem txet elpmaS
Sending message: Sample text message!
    Received message: !egassem txet elpmaS
Sending message: Sample text message!
    Received message: !egassem txet elpmaS
Sending message: Sample text message!
    Received message: !egassem txet elpmaS
Sending message: Sample text message!
    Received message: !egassem txet elpmaS
Sending message: Sample text message!
    Received message: !egassem txet elpmaS
Sending message: Sample text message!
    Received message: !egassem txet elpmaS
Sending message: Sample text message!
    Received message: !egassem txet elpmaS
Sending message: Sample text message!
    Received message: !egassem txet elpmaS
Sending message: Sample text message!
    Received message: !egassem txet elpmaS
Press Enter to exit...
```

The server output looks like this:

```
Initiating server, waiting for client...
Received message: Sample text message!
    Returning Message: !egassem txet elpmaS
Received message: Sample text message!
    Returning Message: !egassem txet elpmaS
Received message: Sample text message!
    Returning Message: !egassem txet elpmaS
Received message: Sample text message!
    Returning Message: !egassem txet elpmaS
Received message: Sample text message!
    Returning Message: !egassem txet elpmaS
```

```
Received message: Sample text message!
    Returning Message: !egassem txet elpmaS
Received message: Sample text message!
    Returning Message: !egassem txet elpmaS
Received message: Sample text message!
    Returning Message: !egassem txet elpmaS
Received message: Sample text message!
    Returning Message: !egassem txet elpmaS
Received message: Sample text message!
    Returning Message: !egassem txet elpmaS
Press Enter to exit...
```

The `PipeOptions` enumeration controls how the pipe operations function. The enumeration values are described in Table 9-3.

Table 9-3. PipeOptions enumeration values

Member name	Description
None	No specific options are specified.
WriteThrough	When writing to the pipe, operations will not return control until the write is accomplished at the server. Without this flag, writes are buffered, and the write returns more quickly.
Asychronous	Enables asynchronous pipe usage (calls return immediately and process in the background).

See Also

The "Named Pipes," "NamedPipeClientStream Class," "NamedPipeServerStream Class," and "System.IO.Pipes Namespace" topics in the MSDN documentation.

9.14 Pinging Programmatically

Problem

You want to check a computer's availability on the network.

Solution

Use the `System.Net.NetworkInformation.Ping` class to determine if a machine is available. In the `TestPing` method, create an instance of the `Ping` class. Send a ping request using the `Send` method. The `SendPingAsync` method is asynchronous and when `awaited` returns a `PingReply` that you can examine for the result of the ping. You can also perform the second ping request asynchronously using the older `SendA sync` method, after hooking up to the `Ping` class for the `PingCompleted` event. The second parameter of the `SendAsync` method holds a user token value that will be returned to the `pinger_PingCompleted` event handler when the ping is complete.

SendPingAsync should be used when async and await are available to you, but if you were doing this on an older framework, SendAsync would be your only async option. The token returned can be used to identify requests between the initiation and completion code:

```
public static async Task TestPing()
{
    System.Net.NetworkInformation.Ping pinger =
        new System.Net.NetworkInformation.Ping();
    PingReply reply = await pinger.SendPingAsync("www.oreilly.com");
    DisplayPingReplyInfo(reply);

    pinger.PingCompleted += pinger_PingCompleted;
    pinger.SendAsync("www.oreilly.com", "oreilly ping");
}
```

The DisplayPingReplyInfo method shows some of the more common pieces of data you want to get from a ping, such as the RoundtripTime and the Status of the reply. These can be accessed from those properties on the PingReply:

```
private static void DisplayPingReplyInfo(PingReply reply)
{
    Console.WriteLine("Results from pinging " + reply.Address);
    Console.WriteLine(
        $"\tFragmentation allowed?: {!reply.Options.DontFragment}");
    Console.WriteLine($"\tTime to live: {reply.Options.Ttl}");
    Console.WriteLine($"\tRoundtrip took: {reply.RoundtripTime}");
    Console.WriteLine($"\tStatus: {reply.Status.ToString()}");
}
```

The event handler for the PingCompleted event is the pinger_PingCompleted method. This event handler follows the usual EventHandler convention of the sender object and event arguments. The argument type for this event is PingCompletedEventArgs. The PingReply can be accessed in the Reply property of the event arguments. If the ping was canceled or an exception was thrown, that information can be accessed via the Cancelled and Error properties. The UserState property on the PingCompletedEventArgs class holds the user token value provided in SendAsync:

```
private static void pinger_PingCompleted(object sender, PingCompletedEventArgs e)
{
    PingReply reply = e.Reply;
    DisplayPingReplyInfo(reply);

    if (e.Cancelled)
        Console.WriteLine($"Ping for {e.UserState.ToString()} was cancelled");
    else
        Console.WriteLine(
            $"Exception thrown during ping: {e.Error?.ToString()}");
}
```

The output from DisplayPingReplyInfo looks like this:

```
Results from pinging 23.3.106.121
        Fragmentation allowed?: True
        Time to live: 60
        Roundtrip took: 13
        Status: Success
```

Discussion

Ping uses an Internet Control Message Protocol (ICMP) echo request message as defined in RFC 792. If a computer is not reached successfully by the ping request, it does not necessarily mean that the computer is unreachable. Many factors can prevent a ping from succeeding aside from the machine being offline. Network topology, firewalls, packet filters, and proxy servers all can interrupt the normal flow of a ping request. By default, Windows Firewall disables ICMP traffic, so if you are having difficulty pinging a machine, check the firewall settings on that machine.

See Also

The "Ping Class," "PingReply Class," and "PingCompleted Event" topics in the MSDN documentation.

9.15 Sending SMTP Mail Using the SMTP Service

Problem

You want to be able to send email via SMTP from your program, but you don't want to learn the SMTP protocol and handcode a class to implement it.

Solution

Use the System.Net.Mail namespace, which contains classes to take care of the harder parts of constructing an SMTP-based email message. The System.Net.Mail.MailMessage class encapsulates constructing an SMTP-based message, and the System.Net.Mail.SmtpClient class provides the sending mechanism for sending the message to an SMTP server. SmtpClient does depend on there being an SMTP server set up somewhere for it to relay messages through. You add attachments by creating instances of System.Net.Mail.Attachment and providing the path to the file as well as the media type:

```
// send a message with attachments
string from = "authors@oreilly.com";
string to = "authors@oreilly.com";
MailMessage attachmentMessage = new MailMessage(from, to);
attachmentMessage.Subject = "Hi there!";
attachmentMessage.Body = "Check out this cool code!";
// many systems filter out HTML mail that is relayed
```

```
attachmentMessage.IsBodyHtml = false;
// set up the attachment
string pathToCode = @"..\..\09_NetworkingAndWeb.cs";
Attachment attachment =
    new Attachment(pathToCode,
        MediaTypeNames.Application.Octet);
attachmentMessage.Attachments.Add(attachment);

// or just send text
MailMessage textMessage = new MailMessage("authors@oreilly.com",
                    "authors@oreilly.com",
                    "Me again",
                    "You need therapy, talking to yourself is one thing but
writing code to send email is a whole other thing...");
```

To send a simple email with no attachments, call the `System.Net.Mail.MailMessage` constructor with just the to address, from address, subject, and body information. This version of the `MailMessage` constructor simply fills in those items, and then you can pass it to `SmtpClient.Send` to send it along:

```
// If you have one, you can bounce this off the local SMTP service.
// The local SMTP service needs to have relaying set up to go through
// a real email server like you used to be able to do in IIS6...
//SmtpClient client = new SmtpClient("localhost");

// Since we live in a more security-conscious time, we would provide the
// correct parameters to connect to the SMTP server with the hostname,
// port, SSL enabled, and your credentials.
// NOTE: If you don't replace the current values you will get a
// XXX exception like this:
// System.Net.Mail.SmtpException: The SMTP host was not found. --->
// System.Net.WebException: The remote name could not be resolved:
// 'YOURSMTPSERVERHERE'
using (SmtpClient client = new SmtpClient("YOURSMTPSERVERHERE", 999))
{
    client.EnableSsl = true;
    client.Credentials = new NetworkCredential("YOURSMTPUSERNAME",
    // "YOURSMTPPASSWORD");
    await client.SendMailAsync(attachmentMessage);
}
```

Discussion

SMTP stands for Simple Mail Transfer Protocol, as defined in RFC 2821. To take advantage of the support for SMTP mail in the .NET Framework using the `System.Net.Mail.SmtpClient` class, you must specify an SMTP server to relay the messages through. In older versions of Windows (pre–Windows 8/Windows Server 2012), the operating system came with an SMTP server that could be installed as part of IIS. In the Solution, the code shows how you could use the `SmtpClient` to take advantage of this feature by specifying `"localhost"` for the server to connect to, which indicates that the local machine is the SMTP relay server. Setting up the SMTP service may not be possible in your network environment, and you may need to use the `SmtpClient` class to set up credentials to connect to the SMTP server on the network directly, as shown in the Solution:

```
using(SmtpClient client = new SmtpClient("YOURSMTPSERVERHERE",999))
{
    client.EnableSsl = true;
    client.Credentials = new NetworkCredential("YOURSMTPUSERNAME",
    // "YOURSMTPPASSWORD");
    await client.SendMailAsync(attachmentMessage);
}
```

The `MediaTypeNames.class` used in the Solution identifies the attachment type. The valid attachment types are listed in Table 9-4.

Table 9-4. MediaTypeNames.Attachment values

Name	Description
Octet	The data is not interpreted as any specific type.
Pdf	The data is in Portable Data Format.
Rtf	The data is in Rich Text Format.
Soap	The data is a SOAP document.
Zip	The data is compressed.

See Also

The "Using SMTP for Outgoing Messages," "SmtpMail Class," "MailMessage Class," and "MailAttachment Class" topics in the MSDN documentation.

9.16 Using Sockets to Scan the Ports on a Machine

Problem

You want to determine the open ports on a machine to see where the security risks are.

Solution

Use the `CheapoPortScanner` class constructed for your use; its code is shown in Example 9-8. `CheapoPortScanner` uses the `Socket` class to attempt to open a socket and connect to an address on a given port. The `ScanAsync` method supports reporting progress via `IProgress<T>` for each port in the range supplied to the `CheapoPortS canner` constructor or in the default range (1 to 65535). By default, `CheapoPortScan ner` will scan the local machine.

Example 9-8. CheapoPortScanner class

```
public class CheapoPortScanner
{
    #region Private consts and members
    private const int PORT_MIN_VALUE = 1;
    private const int PORT_MAX_VALUE = 65535;
    private List<int> _openPorts;
    private List<int> _closedPorts;
    #endregion
```

There are two properties on `CheapoPortScanner` that bear mentioning. The `Open Ports` and `ClosedPorts` properties return a `ReadOnlyCollection` of type `int` that is a list of the port numbers that are open and closed, respectively. Their code is shown in Example 9-9.

Example 9-9. OpenPorts and ClosedPorts properties

```
#region Properties
public ReadOnlyCollection<int> OpenPorts =>
    new ReadOnlyCollection<int>(_openPorts);
public ReadOnlyCollection<int> ClosedPorts =>
    new ReadOnlyCollection<int>(_closedPorts);

public int MinPort { get; } = PORT_MIN_VALUE;
public int MaxPort { get; } = PORT_MAX_VALUE;
public string Host { get; } = "127.0.0.1"; // localhost

#endregion // Properties
#region CTORs & Init code
public CheapoPortScanner()
{
    // defaults are already set for ports and localhost
    SetupLists();
}

public CheapoPortScanner(string host, int minPort, int maxPort)
{
    if (minPort > maxPort)
        throw new ArgumentException("Min port cannot be greater than max port");
    if (minPort < PORT_MIN_VALUE || minPort > PORT_MAX_VALUE)
        throw new ArgumentOutOfRangeException(
            $"Min port cannot be less than {PORT_MIN_VALUE} " +
            $"or greater than {PORT_MAX_VALUE}");
    if (maxPort < PORT_MIN_VALUE || maxPort > PORT_MAX_VALUE)
        throw new ArgumentOutOfRangeException(
            $"Max port cannot be less than {PORT_MIN_VALUE} " +
            $"or greater than {PORT_MAX_VALUE}");

    this.Host = host;
    this.MinPort = minPort;
```

```csharp
        this.MaxPort = maxPort;
        SetupLists();
    }

    private void SetupLists()
    {
        // set up lists with capacity to hold half of range
        // since we can't know how many ports are going to be open
        // so we compromise and allocate enough for half

        // rangeCount is max - min + 1
        int rangeCount = (this.MaxPort - this.MinPort) + 1;
        // if there are an odd number, bump by one to get one extra slot
        if (rangeCount % 2 != 0)
            rangeCount += 1;
        // reserve half the ports in the range for each
        _openPorts = new List<int>(rangeCount / 2);
        _closedPorts = new List<int>(rangeCount / 2);
    }
    #endregion // CTORs & Init code

    #region Progress Result
    public class PortScanResult
    {
        public int PortNum { get; set; }

        public bool IsPortOpen { get; set; }
    }

    #endregion // Progress Result

    #region Private Methods
    private async Task CheckPortAsync(int port, IProgress<PortScanResult> progress)
    {
        if (await IsPortOpenAsync(port))
        {
            // if we got here it is open
            _openPorts.Add(port);

            // notify anyone paying attention
            progress?.Report(
                new PortScanResult() { PortNum = port, IsPortOpen = true });
        }
        else
        {
            // server doesn't have that port open
            _closedPorts.Add(port);
            progress?.Report(
                new PortScanResult() { PortNum = port, IsPortOpen = false });
        }
    }
```

```
private async Task<bool> IsPortOpenAsync(int port)
{
    Socket sock = null;
    try
    {
        // make a TCP based socket
        sock = new Socket(AddressFamily.InterNetwork,
                        SocketType.Stream,
                        ProtocolType.Tcp);
        // connect
        await Task.Run(() => sock.Connect(this.Host, port));
        return true;
    }
    catch (SocketException se)
    {
        if (se.SocketErrorCode == SocketError.ConnectionRefused)
            return false;
        else
        {
            //An error occurred when attempting to access the socket.
            Debug.WriteLine(se.ToString());
            Console.WriteLine(se.ToString());
        }
    }
    finally
    {
        if (sock?.Connected ?? false)
            sock?.Disconnect(false);
        sock?.Close();
    }
    return false;
}
#endregion
```

The trigger method for the CheapoPortScanner is ScanAsync. ScanAsync will check all of the ports in the range specified in the constructor. The LastPortScanSummary method will dump the pertinent information about the last scan to the console output stream:

```
#region Public Methods
public async Task ScanAsync(IProgress<PortScanResult> progress)
{
    for (int port = this.MinPort; port <= this.MaxPort; port++)
        await CheckPortAsync(port, progress);
}

public void LastPortScanSummary()
{
    Console.WriteLine($"Port Scan for host at {this.Host}");
    Console.WriteLine($"\tStarting Port: {this.MinPort}");
    Console.WriteLine($"\tEnding Port: {this.MaxPort}");
    Console.WriteLine($"\tOpen ports: {string.Join(",", _openPorts)}");
```

```
        Console.WriteLine($"\tClosed ports: {string.Join(",", _closedPorts)}");
    }

    #endregion // Public Methods
}
```

The `TestPortScanner` method demonstrates how to use `CheapoPortScanner` by scanning ports 75–85 on the local machine. A `Progress<CheapoPortScanner.PortS canResult>` reporter is created and in the `ProgressChanged` event is subscribed to with an anonymous method to report the progress for the scan. Next, `TestPortScan ner` calls the `ScanAsync` method with the `Progress<T>` we created to get progress reports as the scanner works. Finally, it calls `LastPortScanSummary` to show the full results of the scan, including the closed ports as well as the open ones:

```
public static async Task TestPortScanner()
{
    // do a specific range
    Console.WriteLine("Checking ports 75-85 on localhost...");
    CheapoPortScanner cps =
        new CheapoPortScanner("127.0.0.1", 75, 85);
    var progress = new Progress<CheapoPortScanner.PortScanResult>();
    progress.ProgressChanged += (sender, args) =>
    {
        Console.WriteLine(
            $"Port {args.PortNum} is " +
            $"{args.IsPortOpen ? "open" : "closed"}");
    };
    await cps.ScanAsync(progress);
    cps.LastPortScanSummary();

    // do the local machine, whole port range 1-65535
    //cps = new CheapoPortScanner();
    //await cps.Scan(progress);
    //cps.LastPortScanSummary();
}
```

Here is the output for the port scanner as shown:

```
Checking ports 75-85 on localhost...
Port 75 is closed
Port 76 is closed
Port 77 is closed
Port 78 is closed
Port 79 is closed
Port 80 is open
Port 81 is closed
Port 82 is closed
Port 83 is closed
Port 84 is closed
Port 85 is closed
Port Scan for host at 127.0.0.1
        Starting Port: 75
```

```
Ending Port: 85
Open ports: 80
Closed ports: 75,76,77,78,79,81,82,83,84,85
```

Discussion

Open ports on a machine are significant because they indicate the presence of a program listening on them. Hackers look for "open" ports as ways to enter your systems without permission. `CheapoPortScanner` is an admittedly rudimentary mechanism for checking for open ports, but it demonstrates the principle well enough to provide a good starting point.

 If you run this on a corporate network, you may quickly get a visit from your network administrator, as you may set off alarms in some intrusion-detection systems. Be judicious in your use of this code.

See Also

The "Socket Class" and "Sockets" topics in the MSDN documentation.

9.17 Using the Current Internet Connection Settings

Problem

Your program wants to use the current Internet connection settings without forcing the user to add them to your application manually.

Solution

Read the current Internet connectivity settings with the `InternetSettingsReader` class provided for you in Example 9-10. `InternetSettingsReader` calls some methods of the `WinINet` API via P/Invoke to retrieve current Internet connection information.

P/Invoke (Platform Invoke) is the .NET Framework mechanism for performing native calls into unmanaged (not run in the .NET CLR) code. When you are using P/Invoke, the data being passed between managed and unmanaged code needs to be marshaled across that boundary. *Marshaling* is the process of making the calls between the layers and converting the parameter and return data from managed to unmanaged types and then back again. Typically structures are used to transfer sets of data, as they are value types on the stack and can be used as in/out parameters to transfer the data, whereas classes are reference types that would exist on the heap and typically can only be used as in parameters.

You do the majority of the work in setting up the structures that `WinINet` uses and then marshaling the structure pointers correctly to retrieve the values.

Example 9-10. InternetSettingsReader class

```
public class InternetSettingsReader
{
    #region Private Members
    string _proxyAddr;
    int _proxyPort = -1;
    bool _bypassLocal;
    string _autoConfigAddr;
    List<string> _proxyExceptions;
    PerConnFlags _flags;
    #endregion

    #region CTOR
    public InternetSettingsReader()
    {
    }
    #endregion
```

Each property of `InternetSettingsReader` shown in Example 9-11 calls into the `GetInternetConnectionOption` method, which returns an `InternetConnectionOption`. The `InternetConnectionOption` structure holds all of the pertinent data for the value being returned, and that value is then retrieved based on what type of value was requested by the specific properties.

Example 9-11. InternetSettingsReader properties

```
#region Properties
public string ProxyAddress
{
    get
    {
        InternetConnectionOption ico =
```

```
            GetInternetConnectionOption(
                PerConnOption.INTERNET_PER_CONN_PROXY_SERVER);
        // parse out the addr and port
        string proxyInfo = Marshal.PtrToStringUni(
                                ico.m_Value.m_StringPtr);
        ParseProxyInfo(proxyInfo);
        return _proxyAddr;
    }
}
public int ProxyPort
{
    get
    {
        InternetConnectionOption ico =
            GetInternetConnectionOption(
                PerConnOption.INTERNET_PER_CONN_PROXY_SERVER);
        // parse out the addr and port
        string proxyInfo = Marshal.PtrToStringUni(
                                ico.m_Value.m_StringPtr);
        ParseProxyInfo(proxyInfo);
        return _proxyPort;
    }
}
public bool BypassLocalAddresses
{
    get
    {
        InternetConnectionOption ico =
            GetInternetConnectionOption(
                PerConnOption.INTERNET_PER_CONN_PROXY_BYPASS);
        // bypass is listed as <local> in the exceptions list
        string exceptions =
            Marshal.PtrToStringUni(ico.m_Value.m_StringPtr);

        if (exceptions.IndexOf("<local>") != -1)
            _bypassLocal = true;
        else
            _bypassLocal = false;
        return _bypassLocal;
    }
}
public string AutoConfigurationAddress
{
    get
    {
        InternetConnectionOption ico =
            GetInternetConnectionOption(
                PerConnOption.INTERNET_PER_CONN_AUTOCONFIG_URL);
        // get these straight
        _autoConfigAddr =
            Marshal.PtrToStringUni(ico.m_Value.m_StringPtr);
        if (_autoConfigAddr == null)
```

```
                _autoConfigAddr = "";
            return _autoConfigAddr;
        }
    }
    public IList<string> ProxyExceptions
    {
        get
        {
            InternetConnectionOption ico =
                GetInternetConnectionOption(
                    PerConnOption.INTERNET_PER_CONN_PROXY_BYPASS);
            // exceptions are seperated by semi colon
            string exceptions =
                Marshal.PtrToStringUni(ico.m_Value.m_StringPtr);
            if (!string.IsNullOrEmpty(exceptions))
            {
                _proxyExceptions = new List<string>(exceptions.Split(';'));
            }
            return _proxyExceptions;
        }
    }
    public PerConnFlags ConnectionType
    {
        get
        {
            InternetConnectionOption ico =
                GetInternetConnectionOption(
                    PerConnOption.INTERNET_PER_CONN_FLAGS);
            _flags = (PerConnFlags)ico.m_Value.m_Int;

            return _flags;
        }
    }
}

#endregion

#region Private Methods
private void ParseProxyInfo(string proxyInfo)
{
    if (!string.IsNullOrEmpty(proxyInfo))
    {
        string[] parts = proxyInfo.Split(':');
        if (parts.Length == 2)
        {
            _proxyAddr = parts[0];
            try
            {
                _proxyPort = Convert.ToInt32(parts[1]);
            }
            catch (FormatException)
            {
                // no port
```

```
                _proxyPort = -1;
            }
        }
        else
        {
            _proxyAddr = parts[0];
            _proxyPort = -1;
        }
    }
}
```

The `GetInternetConnectionOption` method shown in Example 9-12 does the heavy lifting as far as communicating with `WinINet`. First, an `InternetPerConnOptionList` is created as well as an `InternetConnectionOption` structure to hold the returned value. The `InternetConnectionOption` structure is then pinned so that the garbage collector does not move the structure in memory, and the `PerConnOption` value is assigned to determine what Internet option to retrieve. `Marshal.SizeOf` is used to determine the size of the two managed structures in unmanaged memory. These values are used to initialize the size values for the structures, which allows the operating system to determine the version of the unmanaged structure it's dealing with.

The `InternetPerConnOptionList` is initialized to hold the option values, and then the `WinINet` function `InternetQueryOption` is called. You fill the `InternetConnectio nOption` type by using the `Marshal.PtrToStructure` method, which maps the data from the unmanaged structure containing the `InternetConnectionOption` data from unmanaged code to the managed object instance, and then the managed version is returned with the value.

Example 9-12. GetInternetConnectionOption method

```
private static InternetConnectionOption GetInternetConnectionOption(
    PerConnOption pco)
{
    //Allocate the list and option.
    InternetPerConnOptionList perConnOptList = new InternetPerConnOptionList();
    InternetConnectionOption ico = new InternetConnectionOption();
    //pin the option structure
    GCHandle gch = GCHandle.Alloc(ico, GCHandleType.Pinned);
    //initialize the option for the data we want
    ico.m_Option = pco;
    //Initialize the option list for the default connection or LAN.
    int listSize = Marshal.SizeOf(perConnOptList);
    perConnOptList.dwSize = listSize;
    perConnOptList.szConnection = IntPtr.Zero;
    perConnOptList.dwOptionCount = 1;
    perConnOptList.dwOptionError = 0;
    // figure out sizes & offsets
    int icoSize = Marshal.SizeOf(ico);
```

```
        // alloc enough memory for the option (native memory not .NET heap)
        perConnOptList.options =
            Marshal.AllocCoTaskMem(icoSize);

        // Make pointer from the structure
        IntPtr optionListPtr = perConnOptList.options;
        Marshal.StructureToPtr(ico, optionListPtr, false);

        //Make the query
        if (NativeMethods.InternetQueryOption(
            IntPtr.Zero,
            75, //(int)InternetOption.INTERNET_OPTION_PER_CONNECTION_OPTION,
            ref perConnOptList,
            ref listSize) == true)
        {
            //retrieve the value
            ico =
                (InternetConnectionOption)Marshal.PtrToStructure(
                                perConnOptList.options,
                                typeof(InternetConnectionOption));
        }
        // free the COM memory
        Marshal.FreeCoTaskMem(perConnOptList.options);
        //unpin the structs
        gch.Free();

        return ico;
    }
    #endregion
}
```

The use of `InternetSettingsReader` is demonstrated in the `GetInternetSettings`
method shown in Example 9-13. The proxy information is retrieved and displayed to
the console here, but could easily be stored in another program for use as proxy
information when connecting. See Recipe 9.3 for details on setting up the proxy
information for a `WebRequest`.

Example 9-13. Using the InternetSettingsReader

```
public static void GetInternetSettings()
{
        Console.WriteLine("");
        Console.WriteLine("Reading current internet connection settings");
        InternetSettingsReader isr = new InternetSettingsReader();
        Console.WriteLine($"Current Proxy Address: {isr.ProxyAddress}");
        Console.WriteLine($"Current Proxy Port: {isr.ProxyPort}");
        Console.WriteLine($"Current ByPass Local Address setting: " +
            $"{{isr.BypassLocalAddresses}");
        Console.WriteLine("Exception addresses for proxy (bypass):");
        string exceptions;
        if (isr.ProxyExceptions?.Count > 0)
```

```
        exceptions = "\t" + (string.Join(",", isr.ProxyExceptions?.ToArray())));
    else
        exceptions = "\tNone";
    Console.WriteLine($"Proxy connection type: {isr.ConnectionType.ToString()}");
    Console.WriteLine("");
}
```

Here is the output for the Solution:

```
Reading current internet connection settings
Current Proxy Address: http=127.0.0.1
Current Proxy Port: -1
Current ByPass Local Address setting: False
Exception addresses for proxy (bypass):
        <-loopback>
Proxy connection type: PROXY_TYPE_DIRECT
```

Discussion

The WinInet Windows Internet (WinInet) API is the unmanaged API for interacting with the FTP, HTTP, and Gopher protocols. This API can be used to fill in where managed code leaves off, such as with the Internet configuration settings shown in the Solution. It can also be used for downloading files, working with cookies, and participating in Gopher sessions. Keep in mind that WinInet is meant to be a client-side API and is not suited for server-side or service applications; issues could arise in your application from improper usage.

There is a huge amount of information available to the C# programmer directly through the BCL (base class library), but at times you still need to roll up your sleeves and talk to the Win32 API. Even in situations in which restricted privileges are the norm, it is not always out of bounds to create a small assembly that needs enhanced access to do P/Invoke. It can have its access locked down so as not to become a risk to the system. We show how you could restrict an assembly like this in Recipe 11.6, and you would need to assert the SecurityPermission with SecurityPermission Flag.UnmanagedCode.

See Also

The "InternetQueryOption Function [WinInet]," "Interoperating with Unmanaged Code," and "Using P/Invoke to Call Unmanaged APIs from Your Managed Classes" topics in the MSDN documentation.

9.18 Transferring Files Using FTP

Problem

You want to programmatically download and upload files using the File Transfer Protocol (FTP).

Solution

Use the `System.Net.FtpWebRequest` class to perform these operations. You create `FtpWebRequests` from the `WebRequest` class's `Create` method by specifying the URI for the FTP download. In the example that follows, the source code from the latest edition of the *C# Cookbook* is the target for the download. A `FileStream` is opened for the target and then is wrapped by a `BinaryWriter`. A `BinaryReader` is created with the response stream from the `FtpWebRequest`. Then, the stream is read, and the target is written until the entire file has been downloaded. This series of operations is demonstrated in Example 9-14 in the `FtpDownloadAsync` method.

Example 9-14. Using the System.Net.FtpWebRequest class

```
public static async Task FtpDownloadAsync(Uri ftpSite, string targetPath)
{
    try
    {
        FtpWebRequest request =
            (FtpWebRequest)WebRequest.Create(
            ftpSite);

        request.Credentials = new NetworkCredential("anonymous",
            "authors@oreilly.com");
        using (FtpWebResponse response =
            (FtpWebResponse)await request.GetResponseAsync())
        {
            Stream data = response.GetResponseStream();
            File.Delete(targetPath);
            Console.WriteLine(
                $"Downloading {ftpSite.AbsoluteUri} to {targetPath}...");

            byte[] byteBuffer = new byte[4096];
            using (FileStream output = new FileStream(targetPath, FileMode.CreateNew,
                FileAccess.ReadWrite,FileShare.ReadWrite, 4096, useAsync: true))
            {
                int bytesRead = 0;
                do
                {
                    bytesRead = await data.ReadAsync(byteBuffer, 0,
                        byteBuffer.Length);
                    if (bytesRead > 0)
```

```
                        await output.WriteAsync(byteBuffer, 0, bytesRead);
                }
                while (bytesRead > 0);
            }
            Console.WriteLine($"Downloaded {ftpSite.AbsoluteUri} to {targetPath}");
        }
    }
    catch (WebException e)
    {
        Console.WriteLine(
            $"Failed to download {ftpSite.AbsoluteUri} to {targetPath}");
        Console.WriteLine(e);
    }
}
```

Here is an example of calling the `FtpDownloadAsync` method:

```
Uri downloadFtpSite =
    new Uri("ftp://ftp.oreilly.com/pub/examples/csharpckbk/CSharpCookbook.zip");
string targetPath = "CSharpCookbook.zip";
await NetworkingAndWeb.FtpDownloadAsync(downloadFtpSite, targetPath);
```

To upload a file, use `FtpWebRequest` to get a stream on the request using `GetRequest Stream` and use it to upload the file. Once the file has been opened and written into the request stream, execute the request by calling `GetResponse` and check the `Status Description` property for the result of the operation. This is demonstrated here in the `FtpUploadAsync` method:

```
public static async Task FtpUploadAsync(Uri ftpSite, string uploadFile)
{
    Console.WriteLine($"Uploading {uploadFile} to {ftpSite.AbsoluteUri}...");
    try
    {
        FileInfo fileInfo = new FileInfo(uploadFile);
        FtpWebRequest request =
            (FtpWebRequest)WebRequest.Create(
            ftpSite);
        request.Method = WebRequestMethods.Ftp.UploadFile;
        //if working with text files and going across operating system platforms,
        //you might want to set this value to false to avoid line ending problems
        request.UseBinary = true;
        request.ContentLength = fileInfo.Length;
        request.Credentials = new NetworkCredential("anonymous",
            "authors@oreilly.com");
        byte[] byteBuffer = new byte[4096];
        using (Stream requestStream = await request.GetRequestStreamAsync())
        {
            using (FileStream fileStream =
                new FileStream(uploadFile, FileMode.Open, FileAccess.Read,
                FileShare.Read, 4096, useAsync: true))
            {
                int bytesRead = 0;
```

```
            do
            {
                bytesRead = await fileStream.ReadAsync(byteBuffer, 0,
                            byteBuffer.Length);
                if (bytesRead > 0)
                    await requestStream.WriteAsync(byteBuffer, 0, bytesRead);
            }
            while (bytesRead > 0);
        }
    }
    using (FtpWebResponse response =
        (FtpWebResponse) await request.GetResponseAsync())
    {
        Console.WriteLine(response.StatusDescription);
    }
    Console.WriteLine($"Uploaded {uploadFile} to {ftpSite.AbsoluteUri}...");
}
catch (WebException e)
{
    Console.WriteLine(
        $"Failed to upload {uploadFile} to {ftpSite.AbsoluteUri}.");
    Console.WriteLine(((FtpWebResponse)e.Response).StatusDescription);
    Console.WriteLine(e);
}
}
```

Here is an example of calling the `FtpUploadAsync` method:

```
string uploadFile = "SampleClassLibrary.dll";
Uri uploadFtpSite =
    new Uri($"ftp://localhost/{uploadFile}");
await NetworkingAndWeb.FtpUploadAsync(uploadFtpSite, uploadFile);
```

Discussion

The File Transfer Protocol is defined in RFC 959 and is one of the main ways files are distributed over the Internet. The port number for FTP is usually 21. Happily, you don't have to really know much about how FTP works in order to use it. This could be useful to your applications in automatic download of information from a dedicated FTP site or in providing automatic update capabilities.

See Also

The "FtpWebRequest Class," "FtpWebResponse Class," "WebRequest Class," and "WebResponse Class" topics in the MSDN documentation.

CHAPTER 10

XML

10.0 Introduction

Extensible Markup Language (XML) is a simple, portable, and flexible way to represent data in a structured format. XML is used in a myriad of ways, from acting as the foundation of web-based messaging protocols such as SOAP to being one of the more popular ways to store configuration data (such as the *web.config*, *machine.config*, or *security.config* files in the .NET Framework). Microsoft recognized the usefulness of XML to developers and has done a nice job of giving you choices concerning the trade-offs involved. Sometimes you want to simply run through an XML document looking for a value in a read-only cursorlike fashion; other times you need to be able to randomly access various pieces of the document; and sometimes, it is handy to be able to query and work with XML declaratively. Microsoft provides classes such as `XmlReader` and `XmlWriter` for lighter access and `XmlDocument` for full Document Object Model (DOM) processing support. To support querying an XML document or constructing XML declaratively, C# provides LINQ to XML (also known as XLINQ) in the form of the `XElement` and `XDocument` classes.

It is likely that you will be dealing with XML in .NET to one degree or another. This chapter explores some of the uses for XML and XML-based technologies, such as XPath and XSLT, as well as showing how these technologies are used by and sometimes replaced by LINQ to XML. It also explores topics such as XML validation and transformation of XML to HTML.

10.1 Reading and Accessing XML Data in Document Order

Problem

You need to read in all the elements of an XML document and obtain information about each element, such as its name and attributes.

Solution

Create an `XmlReader` and use its `Read` method to process the document as shown in Example 10-1.

Example 10-1. Reading an XML document

```
public static void AccessXml()
{
    // New LINQ to XML syntax for constructing XML
    XDocument xDoc = new XDocument(
                    new XDeclaration("1.0", "UTF-8", "yes"),
                    new XComment("My sample XML"),
                    new XProcessingInstruction("myProcessingInstruction",
                        "value"),
                    new XElement("Root",
                        new XElement("Node1",
                            new XAttribute("nodeId", "1"), "FirstNode"),
                        new XElement("Node2",
                            new XAttribute("nodeId", "2"), "SecondNode"),
                        new XElement("Node3",
                            new XAttribute("nodeId", "1"), "ThirdNode")
                    )
                    );

    // write out the XML to the console
    Console.WriteLine(xDoc.ToString());

    // create an XmlReader from the XDocument
    XmlReader reader = xDoc.CreateReader();
    reader.Settings.CheckCharacters = true;
    int level = 0;
    while (reader.Read())
    {
        switch (reader.NodeType)
        {
            case XmlNodeType.CDATA:
                Display(level, $"CDATA: {reader.Value}");
                break;
            case XmlNodeType.Comment:
                Display(level, $"COMMENT: {reader.Value}");
                break;
            case XmlNodeType.DocumentType:
```

```
                Display(level, $"DOCTYPE: {reader.Name}={reader.Value}");
                break;
            case XmlNodeType.Element:
                Display(level, $"ELEMENT: {reader.Name}");
                level++;
                while (reader.MoveToNextAttribute())
                {
                    Display(level, $"ATTRIBUTE: {reader.Name}='{reader.Value}'");
                }
                break;
            case XmlNodeType.EndElement:
                level--;
                break;
            case XmlNodeType.EntityReference:
                Display(level, $"ENTITY: {reader.Name}", reader.Name);
                break;
            case XmlNodeType.ProcessingInstruction:
                Display(level, $"INSTRUCTION: {reader.Name}={reader.Value}");
                break;
            case XmlNodeType.Text:
                Display(level, $"TEXT: {reader.Value}");
                break;
            case XmlNodeType.XmlDeclaration:
                Display(level, $"DECLARATION: {reader.Name}={reader.Value}");
                break;
        }
    }
}

private static void Display(int indentLevel, string format, params object[] args)
{
    for (int i = 0; i < indentLevel; i++)
        Console.Write(" ");
    Console.WriteLine(format, args);
}
```

This code dumps the XML document in a hierarchical format:

```
<!--My sample XML-->
<?myProcessingInstruction value?>
<Root>
  <Node1 nodeId="1">FirstNode</Node1>
  <Node2 nodeId="2">SecondNode</Node2>
  <Node3 nodeId="1">ThirdNode</Node3>
</Root>
COMMENT: My sample XML
INSTRUCTION: myProcessingInstruction=value
ELEMENT: Root
 ELEMENT: Node1
  ATTRIBUTE: nodeId='1'
  TEXT: FirstNode
 ELEMENT: Node2
  ATTRIBUTE: nodeId='2'
```

```
    TEXT: SecondNode
ELEMENT: Node3
 ATTRIBUTE: nodeId='1'
 TEXT: ThirdNode
```

Discussion

Reading existing XML and identifying different node types is one of the fundamental actions that you will need to perform when dealing with XML. The code in the Solution creates an XmlReader from a declaratively constructed XML document and then iterates over the nodes while re-creating the formatted XML for output to the console window.

The Solution shows you how to create an XML document by using an XDocument and composing the XML inline using various XML to LINQ classes, such as XElement, XAttribute, XComment, and so on:

```
XDocument xDoc = new XDocument(
                new XDeclaration("1.0", "UTF-8", "yes"),
                new XComment("My sample XML"),
                new XProcessingInstruction("myProcessingInstruction",
                    "value"),
                new XElement("Root",
                    new XElement("Node1",
                        new XAttribute("nodeId", "1"), "FirstNode"),
                    new XElement("Node2",
                        new XAttribute("nodeId", "2"), "SecondNode"),
                    new XElement("Node3",
                        new XAttribute("nodeId", "1"), "ThirdNode")
                )
              );
```

Once the XDocument has been established, you need to configure the settings for the XmlReader on an XmlReaderSettings object instance via the XmlReader.Settings property. These settings tell the XmlReader to check for any illegal characters in the XML fragment:

```
// create an XmlReader from the XDocument
XmlReader reader = xDoc.CreateReader();
reader.Settings.CheckCharacters = true;
```

The while loop iterates over the XML by reading one node at a time and examining the NodeType property of the reader's current node to determine what type of XML node it is:

```
while (reader.Read())
{
    switch (reader.NodeType)
    {
```

The `NodeType` property is an `XmlNodeType` enumeration value that specifies the types of XML nodes that can be present. The `XmlNodeType` enumeration values are shown in Table 10-1.

Table 10-1. The XmlNodeType enumeration values

Name	Description
`Attribute`	An attribute node of an element.
`CDATA`	A marker for sections of text to escape that would usually be treated as markup.
`Comment`	A comment in the XML: `<!-- my comment -->`
`Document`	The root of the XML document tree.
`DocumentFragment`	A document fragment node.
`DocumentType`	The document type declaration.
`Element`	An element tag: `<myelement>`
`EndElement`	An end element tag: `</myelement>`
`EndEntity`	Returned at the end of an entity after `ResolveEntity` is called.
`Entity`	An entity declaration.
`EntityReference`	A reference to an entity.
`None`	The node returned if `Read` has not yet been called on the `XmlReader`.
`Notation`	A notation in the DTD (document type definition).
`ProcessingInstruction`	The processing instruction: `<?pi myProcessingInstruction?>`
`SignificantWhitespace`	Whitespace when a mixed-content model is used or when whitespace is being preserved.
`Text`	Text content for a node.
`Whitespace`	The whitespace between markup entries.
`XmlDeclaration`	The first node in the document that cannot have children: `<?xml version='1.0'?>`

See Also

The "XmlReader Class," "XmlNodeType Enumeration," and "XDocument Class" topics in the MSDN documentation.

10.2 Querying the Contents of an XML Document

Problem

You have a large and complex XML document, and you need to find various pieces of information, such as all of the contents in a specific element that have a particular attribute setting. You want to query the XML structure without having to iterate through all the nodes in the XML document and search for a particular item by hand.

Solution

Use the new Language Integrated Query (LINQ) to XML API to query the XML document for the items of interest. LINQ allows you to select elements based on element and attribute values, order the results, and return an `IEnumerable`-based collection of the resulting data, as shown in Example 10-2.

Example 10-2. Querying an XML document with LINQ

```
private static XDocument GetAClue() => new XDocument(
                    new XDeclaration("1.0", "UTF-8", "yes"),
                    new XElement("Clue",
                        new XElement("Participant",
                            new XAttribute("type", "Perpetrator"), "Professor Plum"),
                        new XElement("Participant",
                            new XAttribute("type", "Witness"), "Colonel Mustard"),
                        new XElement("Participant",
                            new XAttribute("type", "Witness"), "Mrs. White"),
                        new XElement("Participant",
                            new XAttribute("type", "Witness"), "Mrs. Peacock"),
                        new XElement("Participant",
                            new XAttribute("type", "Witness"), "Mr. Green"),
                        new XElement("Participant",
                            new XAttribute("type", "Witness"), "Miss Scarlet"),
                        new XElement("Participant",
                            new XAttribute("type", "Victim"), "Mr. Boddy")
                    ));
```

Notice the similarity between the structure of the XML and the structure of the code when we use LINQ to construct this XML fragment in the `GetAClue` method:

```
    public static void QueryXml()
    {
        XDocument xDoc = GetAClue();

        // set up the query looking for the married female participants
        // who were witnesses
        var query = from p in xDoc.Root.Elements("Participant")
                    where p.Attribute("type").Value == "Witness" &&
                        p.Value.Contains("Mrs.")
```

```
            orderby p.Value
            select p.Value;

        // write out the nodes found (Mrs. Peacock and Mrs. White in this instance,
        // as it is sorted)
        foreach (string s in query)
        {
            Console.WriteLine(s);
        }
    }
```

This outputs the following for the LINQ to XML example:

```
Mrs. Peacock
Mrs. White
```

To query an XML document without LINQ, you could also use XPath. In .NET, this means using the System.Xml.XPath namespace and classes such as XPathDocument, XPathNavigator, and XPathNodeIterator. LINQ to XML also supports using XPath to identify items in a query through the XElement.XPathSelectElements method.

In the following example, you use these classes to select nodes from an XML document that holds members from the board game *Clue* (or *Cluedo*, as it is known outside North America) and their various roles. You want to be able to select the married female participants who were witnesses to the crime. To do this, pass an XPath expression to query the XML data set, as shown in Example 10-3.

Example 10-3. Querying an XML document with XPath

```
public static void QueryXML()
{
    XDocument xDoc = GetAClue();

    using (StringReader reader = new StringReader(xDoc.ToString()))
    {
        // Instantiate an XPathDocument using the StringReader.
        XPathDocument xpathDoc = new XPathDocument(reader);

        // Get the navigator.
        XPathNavigator xpathNav = xpathDoc.CreateNavigator();

        // Get up the query looking for the married female participants
        // who were witnesses.
        string xpathQuery =
            "/Clue/Participant[attribute::type='Witness'][contains(text(),'Mrs.')]";
        XPathExpression xpathExpr = xpathNav.Compile(xpathQuery);

        // Get the nodeset from the compiled expression.
        XPathNodeIterator xpathIter = xpathNav.Select(xpathExpr);

        // Write out the nodes found (Mrs. White and Mrs.Peacock, in this instance).
```

```
        while (xpathIter.MoveNext())
        {
            Console.WriteLine(xpathIter.Current.Value);
        }
    }
}
```

This outputs the following for the XPath example:

```
Mrs. White
Mrs. Peacock
```

Discussion

Query support is a first-class citizen in C# when you are using LINQ. LINQ to XML brings a more intuitive syntax to writing queries for most developers than XPath and thus is a welcome addition to the language. XPath is a valuable tool to have in your arsenal if you are working with systems that deal with XML extensively, but in many cases, you know what you want to ask for; you just don't know the syntax in XPath. For developers with even minimal SQL experience, querying in C# just got a lot easier:

The XML being worked on in this recipe looks like this:

```
<?xml version='1.0'?>
<Clue>
  <Participant type="Perpetrator">Professor Plum</Participant>
  <Participant type="Witness">Colonel Mustard</Participant>
  <Participant type="Witness">Mrs. White</Participant>
  <Participant type="Witness">Mrs. Peacock</Participant>
  <Participant type="Witness">Mr. Green</Participant>
  <Participant type="Witness">Miss Scarlet</Participant>
  <Participant type="Victim">Mr. Boddy</Participant>
</Clue>
```

This query says, "Select all of the Participant elements where the Participant is a witness and her title is Mrs.":

```
// set up the query looking for the married female participants
// who were witnesses
var query = from p in xDoc.Root.Elements("Participant")
            where p.Attribute("type").Value == "Witness" &&
                p.Value.Contains("Mrs.")
            orderby p.Value
            select p.Value;
```

Contrast this with the same query syntax in XPath:

```
// set up the query looking for the married female participants
// who were witnesses
string xpathQuery =
  "/Clue/Participant[attribute::type='Witness'][contains(text(),'Mrs.')]";
```

Both ways of performing the query have merit, but the issue to consider is how easily the next developer will be able to understand what you have written. It is very easy to break code that is not well understood.

 Generally, more developers understand SQL than XPath, even with all of the web service work today. This may differ from your experience, especially if you do a lot of cross-platform work, but the point is to think of LINQ as not just another syntax, but as a way to make your code more readable by a broader audience of developers. Code is rarely owned by one person, even in the short term, so why not make it easy for those who come after you? After all, you may be on the other side of that coin someday. Let's break down the two queries a bit more.

The LINQ query uses some of the keywords in C#:

- `var` indicates to the compiler to expect an inferred type based on the result set.
- `from`, which is known as the generator, provides a data source for the query to operate on as well as a range variable to allow access to the individual element.
- `where` allows for a Boolean condition to be applied to each element of the data source to determine if it should be included in the result set.
- `orderby` determines the sort order of the result set based on the number of elements and indicators of `ascending` or `descending` per element. Multiple criteria can be specified for multiple levels of sorting.
- `select` indicates the sequence of values that will be returned after all evaluation of conditions. This is also referred to as projection of the values.

This means that our syntax can be boiled down as follows:

- `from p in xDoc.Root.Elements("Participant")` says, "Get all of the `Partici`pants under the root-level node `Clue`."
- `where p.Attribute("type").Value == "Witness"` says, "Select only `Partici`pants with an attribute called `type` with a value of `Witness`."
- `&& p.Value.Contains("Mrs.")` says, "Select only `Participants` with a value that contains `Mrs.`".
- `orderby (string) p.Value` says, "Order the `participants` by name in ascending order."
- `select (string) p.Value` says, "Select the value of the `Participant` elements where all of the previous criteria have been met."

The XPath syntax performs the same function:

- /Clue/Participant says, "Get all of the Participants under the root-level node Clue."
- Participant[attribute::type='Witness'] says, "Select only Participants with an attribute called type with a value of Witness."
- Participant[contains(text(),'Mrs.')] says, "Select only Participants with a value that contains Mrs.".

Put them all together, and you get all of the married female participants who were witnesses in both cases, with the additional twist for LINQ that it sorted the results.

See Also

The "Query Expressions," "XElement Class," and "XPath, reading XML" topics in the MSDN documentation.

10.3 Validating XML

Problem

You are accepting an XML document created by another source, and you want to verify that it conforms to a specific schema. This schema may be in the form of an XML schema (XSD or XML–XDR). Alternatively, you want the flexibility to use a document type definition (DTD) to validate the XML.

Solution

Use the XDocument.Validate method and XmlReader.Settings property to validate XML documents against any descriptor document, such as an XSD, a DTD, or an XDR, as shown in Example 10-4. Validating the XML that you generate from your software as part of your testing will save you from bugs later when you're integrating with other systems (or components of your systems) and is highly encouraged!

Example 10-4. Validating XML

```
public static void ValidateXml()
{
    // open the bookbad.xml file
    XDocument book = XDocument.Load(@"..\..\BookBad.xml");
    // create XSD schema collection with book.xsd
    XmlSchemaSet schemas = new XmlSchemaSet();
    schemas.Add(null,@"..\..\Book.xsd");
    // wire up handler to get any validation errors
```

```csharp
        book.Validate(schemas, settings_ValidationEventHandler);

        // create a reader to roll over the file so validation fires
        XmlReader reader = book.CreateReader();
        // report warnings as well as errors
        reader.Settings.ValidationFlags =
            XmlSchemaValidationFlags.ReportValidationWarnings;
        // use XML Schema
        reader.Settings.ValidationType = ValidationType.Schema;
        // roll over the XML
        while (reader.Read())
        {
            if (reader.NodeType == XmlNodeType.Element)
            {
                Console.Write($"<{reader.Name}");
                while (reader.MoveToNextAttribute())
                {
                    Console.Write($"{reader.Name}='{reader.Value}'");
                }
                Console.Write(">");
            }
            else if (reader.NodeType == XmlNodeType.Text)
            {
                Console.Write(reader.Value);
            }
            else if (reader.NodeType == XmlNodeType.EndElement)
            {
                Console.WriteLine($"</{reader.Name}>");
            }
        }
    }
}

private static void settings_ValidationEventHandler(object sender,
    ValidationEventArgs e)
{
    Console.WriteLine($"Validation Error Message: {e.Message}");
    Console.WriteLine($"Validation Error Severity: {e.Severity}");
    Console.WriteLine($"Validation Error Line Number: {e.Exception?.LineNumber}");
    Console.WriteLine(
        $"Validation Error Line Position: {e.Exception?.LinePosition}");
    Console.WriteLine($"Validation Error Source: {e.Exception?.Source}");
    Console.WriteLine($"Validation Error Source Schema: " +
                    $"{{e.Exception?.SourceSchemaObject}");
    Console.WriteLine($"Validation Error Source Uri: {e.Exception?.SourceUri}");
    Console.WriteLine($"Validation Error thrown from: {e.Exception?.TargetSite}");
    Console.WriteLine($"Validation Error callstack: {e.Exception?.StackTrace}");
}
```

Discussion

The Solution illustrates how to use the XDocument and XmlReader to validate the
book.xml document against a *book.xsd* XSD definition file. DTDs were the original

way to specify the structure of an XML document, but it has become more common to use XSD since it reached W3C Recommendation status in May 2001. XDR was a predecessor of XSD provided by Microsoft, and, while you might encounter it in existing systems, it should not be used for new development.

The first thing to do is create an XmlSchemaSet to hold your XSD file (*book.xsd*) and call the Add method to add the XSD to the XmlSchemaSet. Call the Validate method on the XDocument with the XmlSchemaSet and the handler method for validation events. Now that the validation is mostly set up, we can set a few more items on the XmlReader created from the XDocument. The ValidationFlags property on the XmlReaderSettings allows for signing up for warnings in validation, processing identity constraints during validation, and processing inline schemas, and allows for attributes that may not be defined in the schema:

```
// create XSD schema collection with book.xsd
XmlSchemaSet schemas = new XmlSchemaSet();
schemas.Add(null,@"..\..\Book.xsd");
// wire up handler to get any validation errors
book.Validate(schemas, settings_ValidationEventHandler);

// create a reader to roll over the file so validation fires
XmlReader reader = book.CreateReader();
// report warnings as well as errors
reader.Settings.ValidationFlags =
    XmlSchemaValidationFlags.ReportValidationWarnings;
// use XML Schema
reader.Settings.ValidationType = ValidationType.Schema;
```

 To perform DTD validation, use a DTD and ValidationType.DTD, and to perform XDR validation, use an XDR schema and Valida tionType.XDR.

The settings_ValidationEventHandler function then examines the ValidationE ventArgs object passed when a validation error occurs and writes the pertinent information to the console:

```
private static void settings_ValidationEventHandler(object sender,
    ValidationEventArgs e)
{
    Console.WriteLine($"Validation Error Message: {e.Message}");
    Console.WriteLine($"Validation Error Severity: {e.Severity}");
    Console.WriteLine(
        $"Validation Error Line Number: {e.Exception?.LineNumber}");
    Console.WriteLine(
        $"Validation Error Line Position: {e.Exception?.LinePosition}");
    Console.WriteLine($"Validation Error Source: {e.Exception?.Source}");
    Console.WriteLine($"Validation Error Source Schema: " +
```

```
                    $"{{e.Exception?.SourceSchemaObject}}");
    Console.WriteLine($"Validation Error Source Uri: {e.Exception?.SourceUri}");
    Console.WriteLine(
        $"Validation Error thrown from: {e.Exception?.TargetSite}");
    Console.WriteLine($"Validation Error callstack: {e.Exception?.StackTrace}");
}
```

You then proceed to roll over the XML document and write out the elements and attributes:

```
while (readerOld.Read())
{
    if (readerOld.NodeType == XmlNodeType.Element)
    {
        Console.Write($"<{readerOld.Name}");
        while (reader.MoveToNextAttribute())
        {
            Console.Write($"{readerOld.Name}='{readerOld.Value}'");
        }
        Console.Write(">");
    }
    else if (readerOld.NodeType == XmlNodeType.Text)
    {
        Console.Write(reader.Value);
    }
    else if (readerOld.NodeType == XmlNodeType.EndElement)
    {
        Console.WriteLine($"</{readerOld.Name}>");
    }
}
```

The *BookBad.xml* file contains the following:

```
<?xml version="1.0" encoding="utf-8"?>
<Book xmlns="http://tempuri.org/Book.xsd" name="C# Cookbook">
    <Chapter>File System IO</Chapter>
    <Chapter>Security</Chapter>
    <Chapter>Data Structures and Algorithms</Chapter>
    <Chapter>Reflection</Chapter>
    <Chapter>Threading and Synchronization</Chapter>
    <Chapter>Numbers and Enumerations</Chapter>
    <BadElement>I don't belong here</BadElement>
    <Chapter>Strings and Characters</Chapter>
    <Chapter>Classes And Structures</Chapter>
    <Chapter>Collections</Chapter>
    <Chapter>XML</Chapter>
    <Chapter>Delegates, Events, and Anonymous Methods</Chapter>
    <Chapter>Diagnostics</Chapter>
    <Chapter>Toolbox</Chapter>
    <Chapter>Unsafe Code</Chapter>
    <Chapter>Regular Expressions</Chapter>
    <Chapter>Generics</Chapter>
    <Chapter>Iterators and Partial Types</Chapter>
```

```
        <Chapter>Exception Handling</Chapter>
        <Chapter>Web</Chapter>
        <Chapter>Networking</Chapter>
    </Book>
```

The *book.xsd* file contains the following:

```
<?xml version="1.0" ?>
<xs:schema id="NewDataSet" targetNamespace="http://tempuri.org/Book.xsd"
xmlns:mstns="http://tempuri.org/Book.xsd"
    xmlns="http://tempuri.org/Book.xsd"
    xmlns:xs="http://www.w3.org/2001/XMLSchema"
    xmlns:msdata="urn:schemas-microsoft-com:xml-msdata"
    attributeFormDefault="qualified" elementFormDefault="qualified">
  <xs:element name="Book">
    <xs:complexType>
      <xs:sequence>
        <xs:element name="Chapter" nillable="true"
                    minOccurs="0" maxOccurs="unbounded">
          <xs:complexType>
            <xs:simpleContent
msdata:ColumnName="Chapter_Text" msdata:Ordinal="0">
              <xs:extension base="xs:string">
              </xs:extension>
            </xs:simpleContent>
          </xs:complexType>
        </xs:element>
      </xs:sequence>
      <xs:attribute name="name" form="unqualified" type="xs:string"/>
    </xs:complexType>
  </xs:element>
</xs:schema>
```

When this is run, the following output is generated, showing the validation failure occurring on BadElement:

```
Validation Error Message: The element 'Book' in namespace 'http://tempuri.org/Bo
ok.xsd' has invalid child element 'BadElement' in namespace 'http://tempuri.org/
Book.xsd'. List of possible elements expected: 'Chapter' in namespace 'http://te
mpuri.org/Book.xsd'.
Validation Error Severity: Error
Validation Error Line Number: 0
Validation Error Line Position: 0
Validation Error Source:
Validation Error Source Schema:
Validation Error Source Uri:
Validation Error thrown from:
Validation Error callstack:
<Book xmlns='http://tempuri.org/Book.xsd' name='C# Cookbook'><Chapter>File Syste
m IO</Chapter>
<Chapter>Security</Chapter>
<Chapter>Data Structures and Algorithms</Chapter>
<Chapter>Reflection</Chapter>
```

```
<Chapter>Threading and Synchronization</Chapter>
<Chapter>Numbers and Enumerations</Chapter>
<BadElement>I don't belong here</BadElement>
<Chapter>Strings and Characters</Chapter>
<Chapter>Classes And Structures</Chapter>
<Chapter>Collections</Chapter>
<Chapter>XML</Chapter>
<Chapter>Delegates, Events, and Anonymous Methods</Chapter>
<Chapter>Diagnostics</Chapter>
<Chapter>Toolbox</Chapter>
<Chapter>Unsafe Code</Chapter>
<Chapter>Regular Expressions</Chapter>
<Chapter>Generics</Chapter>
<Chapter>Iterators and Partial Types</Chapter>
<Chapter>Exception Handling</Chapter>
<Chapter>Web</Chapter>
<Chapter>Networking</Chapter>
</Book>
```

See Also

The "XmlReader Class," "XmlSchemaSet Class," "ValidationEventHandler Class," "ValidationType Enumeration," and "XDocument Class" topics in the MSDN documentation.

10.4 Detecting Changes to an XML Document

Problem

You need to inform one or more classes or components that a node in an XML document has been inserted or removed or had its value changed.

Solution

To track changes to an active XML document, subscribe to the events published by the XDocument class. XDocument publishes events for when a node is changing and when it has changed for both the pre- and post-conditions of a node change.

Example 10-5 shows a number of event handlers defined in the same scope as the DetectXMLChanges method, but they could just as easily be callbacks to functions on other classes that are interested in the manipulation of the live XML document.

DetectXMLChanges loads an XML fragment you define in the method; wires up the event handlers for the node events; adds, changes, and removes some nodes to trigger the events; and then writes out the resulting XML.

Example 10-5. Detecting changes to an XML document

```
public static void DetectXmlChanges()
{
    XDocument xDoc = new XDocument(
                        new XDeclaration("1.0", "UTF-8", "yes"),
                        new XComment("My sample XML"),
                        new XProcessingInstruction("myProcessingInstruction",
                            "value"),
                        new XElement("Root",
                            new XElement("Node1",
                                new XAttribute("nodeId", "1"), "FirstNode"),
                            new XElement("Node2",
                                new XAttribute("nodeId", "2"), "SecondNode"),
                            new XElement("Node3",
                                new XAttribute("nodeId", "1"), "ThirdNode"),
                            new XElement("Node4",
                                new XCData(@"<>\&'"))
                        )
                    );
    //Create the event handlers.
    xDoc.Changing += xDoc_Changing;
    xDoc.Changed += xDoc_Changed;
    // Add a new element node.
    XElement element = new XElement("Node5", "Fifth Element");
    xDoc.Root.Add(element);

    // Change the first node
    //doc.DocumentElement.FirstChild.InnerText = "1st Node";
    if(xDoc.Root.FirstNode.NodeType == XmlNodeType.Element)
        ((XElement)xDoc.Root.FirstNode).Value = "1st Node";

    // remove the fourth node
    var query = from e in xDoc.Descendants()
                where e.Name.LocalName == "Node4"
                select e;
    XElement[] elements = query.ToArray<XElement>();
    foreach (XElement xelem in elements)
    {
        xelem.Remove();
    }
    // write out the new xml
    Console.WriteLine();
    Console.WriteLine(xDoc.ToString());
    Console.WriteLine();
}
```

Example 10-6 shows the event handlers from the XDocument, along with one formatting method, WriteElementInfo. This method takes an action string and gets the name and value of the object being manipulated. Both of the event handlers invoke this formatting method, passing the corresponding action string.

Example 10-6. XDocument event handlers and WriteElementInfo method

```
private static void xDoc_Changed(object sender, XObjectChangeEventArgs e)
{
    //Add - An XObject has been or will be added to an XContainer.
    //Name - An XObject has been or will be renamed.
    //Remove - An XObject has been or will be removed from an XContainer.
    //Value - The value of an XObject has been or will be changed. In addition, a
    //change in the serialization of an empty element (either from an empty tag to
    //start/end tag pair or vice versa) raises this event.
    WriteElementInfo("changed", e.ObjectChange, (XObject)sender);
}

private static void xDoc_Changing(object sender, XObjectChangeEventArgs e)
{
    //Add - An XObject has been or will be added to an XContainer.
    //Name - An XObject has been or will be renamed.
    //Remove - An XObject has been or will be removed from an XContainer.
    //Value - The value of an XObject has been or will be changed. In addition, a
    //change in the serialization of an empty element (either from an empty tag to
    //start/end tag pair or vice versa) raises this event.
    WriteElementInfo("changing", e.ObjectChange, (XObject)sender);
}

private static void WriteElementInfo(string action, XObjectChange change,
    XObject xobj)
{
    if (xobj != null)
        Console.WriteLine($"XObject: <{xobj.NodeType.ToString()}> "+
            $"{action} {change} with value {xobj}");
    else
        Console.WriteLine("XObject: <{xobj.NodeType.ToString()}> " +
            $"{action} {change} with null value");
}
```

The `DetectXmlChanges` method results in the following output:

```
XObject: <Element> changing Add with value <Node5>Fifth Element</Node5>
XObject: <Element> changed Add with value <Node5>Fifth Element</Node5>
XObject: <Text> changing Remove with value FirstNode
XObject: <Text> changed Remove with value FirstNode
XObject: <Text> changing Add with value 1st Node
XObject: <Text> changed Add with value 1st Node
XObject: <Element> changing Remove with value <Node4><![CDATA[<>\&']]></Node4>
XObject: <Element> changed Remove with value <Node4><![CDATA[<>\&']]></Node4>

<!--My sample XML-->
<?myProcessingInstruction value?>
<Root>
  <Node1 nodeId="1">1st Node</Node1>
  <Node2 nodeId="2">SecondNode</Node2>
  <Node3 nodeId="1">ThirdNode</Node3>
```

```
    <Node5>Fifth Element</Node5>
  </Root>
```

Discussion

The XDocument class is derived from the XElement class. XDocument can also contain a DTD (XDocumentType), a root element (XDocument.Root), comments (XComment), and processing instructions (XProcessingInstruction). Typically, you would use XElement for constructing most types of XML documents, but if you need to specify any of the preceding items, use XDocument.

See Also

The "XDocument Class" and "XObjectChangeEventHandler delegate" topics in the MSDN documentation.

10.5 Handling Invalid Characters in an XML String

Problem

You are creating an XML string. Before adding a tag containing a text element, you want to check it to determine whether the string contains any of the following invalid characters:

```
<
>
"
'
&
```

If any of these characters are encountered, you want them to be replaced with their escaped form:

```
&lt; (<)
&gt; (>)
&quot; (")
&apos; (')
&amp; (&)
```

Solution

There are different ways to accomplish this, depending on which XML-creation approach you are using. If you are using XElement, either using the XCData object or just adding the text directly as the value of the XElement will take care of the proper escaping. If you are using XmlWriter, the WriteCData, WriteString, WriteAttribute String, WriteValue, and WriteElementString methods take care of this for you. If you are using XmlDocument and XmlElements, the XmlElement.InnerText method will handle these characters.

In the first way to handle invalid characters using XElement, the XCData object will wrap the invalid character text in a CDATA section, as shown in the creation of the InvalidChars1 element in the example that follows. The second way using XElement is to assign the text as the value of the XElement, and that will automatically escape the text for you, as shown in the creation of the InvalidChars2 element:

```
// set up a string with our invalid chars
string invalidChars = @"<>\&'";
XElement element = new XElement("Root",
                        new XElement("InvalidChars1",
                            new XCData(invalidChars)),
                        new XElement("InvalidChars2",invalidChars));
Console.WriteLine($"Generated XElement with Invalid Chars:\r\n{element}");
Console.WriteLine();
```

The output from this is:

```
Generated XElement with Invalid Chars:
<Root>
  <InvalidChars1><![CDATA[<>\&']]></InvalidChars1>
  <InvalidChars2>&lt;&gt;\&amp;'</InvalidChars2>
</Root>
```

In the first way to handle invalid characters using XmlWriter, the WriteCData method will wrap the invalid character text in a CDATA section, as shown in the creation of the InvalidChars1 element in the example that follows. The second way using XmlWriter is to use the WriteElementString method to automatically escape the text for you, as shown in the creation of the InvalidChars2 element:

```
// Set up a string with our invalid chars.
string invalidChars = @"<>\&'";
XmlWriterSettings settings = new XmlWriterSettings();
settings.Indent = true;
using (XmlWriter writer = XmlWriter.Create(Console.Out, settings))
{
    writer.WriteStartElement("Root");
    writer.WriteStartElement("InvalidChars1");
    writer.WriteCData(invalidChars);
    writer.WriteEndElement();
    writer.WriteElementString("InvalidChars2", invalidChars);
    writer.WriteEndElement();
}
```

The output from this is:

```
<?xml version="1.0" encoding="IBM437"?>
<Root>
  <InvalidChars1><![CDATA[<>\&']]></InvalidChars1>
```

```
    <InvalidChars2>&lt;&gt;\&amp;'</InvalidChars2>
</Root>
```

There are two ways you can handle this problem with `XmlDocument` and `XmlElement`. The first way is to surround the text you are adding to the XML element with a CDATA section and add it to the `InnerXML` property of the `XmlElement`:

```
// Set up a string with our invalid chars.
string invalidChars = @"<>\&'";

// create the first invalid character node
XmlElement invalidElement1 = xmlDoc.CreateElement("InvalidChars1");

// wrap the invalid chars in a CDATA section and use the
// InnerXML property to assign the value, as it doesn't
// escape the values, just passes in the text provided
invalidElement1.AppendChild(xmlDoc.CreateCDataSection(invalidChars));
```

The second way is to let the `XmlElement` class escape the data for you, by assigning the text directly to the `InnerText` property like this:

```
// Set up a string with our invalid chars.
string invalidChars = @"<>\&'";
// create the second invalid character node
XmlElement invalidElement2 = xmlDoc.CreateElement("InvalidChars2");

// Add the invalid chars directly using the InnerText
// property to assign the value as it will automatically
// escape the values
invalidElement2.InnerText = invalidChars;

// append the element to the root node
root.AppendChild(invalidElement2);
```

The whole `XmlDocument` is created with these `XmlElements` in this code:

```
public static void HandleInvalidChars()
{
    // set up a string with our invalid chars
    string invalidChars = @"<>\&'";
    XElement element = new XElement("Root",
                        new XElement("InvalidChars1",
                            new XCData(invalidChars)),
                        new XElement("InvalidChars2",invalidChars));
    Console.WriteLine($"Generated XElement with Invalid Chars:\r\n{element}");
    Console.WriteLine();

    XmlWriterSettings settings = new XmlWriterSettings();
    settings.Indent = true;
    using (XmlWriter writer = XmlWriter.Create(Console.Out, settings))
    {
        writer.WriteStartElement("Root");
        writer.WriteStartElement("InvalidChars1");
```

```
            writer.WriteCData(invalidChars);
            writer.WriteEndElement();
            writer.WriteElementString("InvalidChars2", invalidChars);
            writer.WriteEndElement();
    }
    Console.WriteLine();

    XmlDocument xmlDoc = new XmlDocument();
    // create a root node for the document
    XmlElement root = xmlDoc.CreateElement("Root");
    xmlDoc.AppendChild(root);

    // create the first invalid character node
    XmlElement invalidElement1 = xmlDoc.CreateElement("InvalidChars1");
    // wrap the invalid chars in a CDATA section and use the
    // InnerXML property to assign the value as it doesn't
    // escape the values, just passes in the text provided
    invalidElement1.AppendChild(xmlDoc.CreateCDataSection(invalidChars));
    // append the element to the root node
    root.AppendChild(invalidElement1);

    // create the second invalid character node
    XmlElement invalidElement2 = xmlDoc.CreateElement("InvalidChars2");
    // Add the invalid chars directly using the InnerText
    // property to assign the value as it will automatically
    // escape the values
    invalidElement2.InnerText = invalidChars;
    // append the element to the root node
    root.AppendChild(invalidElement2);

    Console.WriteLine($"Generated XML with Invalid Chars:\r\n{xmlDoc.OuterXml}");
    Console.WriteLine();
}
```

The XML created by this procedure (and output to the console) looks like this:

```
Generated XML with Invalid Chars:
<Root><InvalidChars1><![CDATA[<>\&']]></InvalidChars1><InvalidChars2>&lt;&gt;\&a
mp;'</InvalidChars2></Root>
```

Discussion

The CDATA node allows you to represent the items in the text section as character data, not as escaped XML, for ease of entry. Normally, these characters would need to be in their escaped format (e.g., < for <), but the CDATA section allows you to enter them as regular text.

When you use the CDATA tag in conjunction with the InnerXml property of the XmlEle ment class, you can submit characters that would normally need to be escaped first. The XmlElement class also has an InnerText property that will automatically escape any markup found in the string assigned. This allows you to add these characters without having to worry about them.

See Also

The "XElement Class," "XCData Class," "XmlDocument Class," "XmlWriter Class," "XmlElement Class," and "CDATA Sections" topics in the MSDN documentation.

10.6 Transforming XML

Problem

You have a raw XML document that you need to convert into a more readable format. For example, you have personnel data that is stored as an XML document, and you need to display it on a web page or place it in a comma-delimited text file for legacy system integration. Unfortunately, not everyone wants to sort through reams of XML all day; they would rather read the data as a formatted list or within a grid with defined columns and rows. You need a method of transforming the XML data into a more readable form as well as into the comma-delimited format.

Solution

The solution for this problem is to use LINQ to XML to perform a transformation in C#. In the example code, you transform some personnel data from a fictitious business stored in *Personnel.xml*. The data is first transformed into HTML, and then into comma-delimited format:

```
// LINQ way
XElement personnelData = XElement.Load(@"..\..\Personnel.xml");
// Create HTML
XElement personnelHtml =
    new XElement("html",
        new XElement("head"),
        new XElement("body",
            new XAttribute("title","Personnel"),
            new XElement("p",
                new XElement("table",
                    new XAttribute("border","1"),
                    new XElement("thead",
                        new XElement("tr",
                            new XElement("td","Employee Name"),
                            new XElement("td","Employee Title"),
                            new XElement("td","Years with Company"),
                            new XElement("td","Also Known As")
                            )
                        ),
                    new XElement("tbody",
                        from p in personnelData.Elements("Employee")
```

```
                    select new XElement("tr",
                        new XElement("td", p.Attribute("name").Value),
                        new XElement("td", p.Attribute("title").Value),
                        new XElement("td",
                            p.Attribute("companyYears").Value),
                        new XElement("td", p.Attribute("nickname").Value)
                        )
                    )
                )
            )
        )
    );

personnelHtml.Save(@"..\..\Personnel_LINQ.html");

var queryCSV = from p in personnelData.Elements("Employee")
               orderby p.Attribute("name").Value descending
               select p;
StringBuilder sb = new StringBuilder();
foreach(XElement e in queryCSV)
{
    sb.AppendFormat($"{EscapeAttributeForCSV(e, "name")}," +
        $"{EscapeAttributeForCSV(e, "title")}," +
        $"{EscapeAttributeForCSV(e, "companyYears")}," +
        $"{EscapeAttributeForCSV(e, "nickname")}" +
        $"{Environment.NewLine}");
}
using(StreamWriter writer = File.CreateText(@"..\..\Personnel_LINQ.csv"))
{
    writer.Write(sb.ToString());
}
```

The output from the LINQ transformation to CSV is shown here:

```
Rutherford,CEO,27,""BigTime""
Chas,Salesman,3,""Money""
Bob,Customer Service,1,""Happy""
Alice,Manager,12,""Business""
```

The *Personnel.xml* file contains the following items:

```
<?xml version="1.0" encoding="utf-8"?>
<Personnel xmlns:xsi="http://www.w3.org/2001/XMLSchema-instance">
    <Employee name="Bob" title="Customer Service" companyYears="1"
        nickname="&quot;Happy&quot;"/>
    <Employee name="Alice" title="Manager" companyYears="12"
        nickname="&quot;Business&quot;"/>
    <Employee name="Chas" title="Salesman" companyYears="3"
        nickname="&quot;Money&quot;"/>
    <Employee name="Rutherford" title="CEO" companyYears="27"
        nickname="&quot;BigTime&quot;"/>
</Personnel>
```

You might be wondering why the nickname attribute values have extra double quotes in the CSV output. This is to support RFC 4180, "Common Format and MIME Type for CSV Files," which says, "If double-quotes are used to enclose fields, then a double-quote appearing inside a field must be escaped by preceding it with another double quote." We do this with the EscapeAttributeForCSV method:

```
private static string EscapeAttributeForCSV(XElement element,
    string attributeName)
{
    string attributeValue = element.Attribute(attributeName).Value;
    //RFC-4180, paragraph "If double-quotes are used to enclose fields, then a
    //double-quote appearing inside a field must be escaped by preceding it with
    //another double quote."
    return attributeValue.Replace("\"", "\"\"");
}
```

This approach is discussed more in Recipe 10.8.

We can also accomplish this solution using an XSLT stylesheet to transform the XML into another format using the XslCompiledTransform class. First, load the stylesheet for generating HTML output and then perform the transformation to HTML via XSLT using the *PersonnelHTML.xsl* stylesheet. After that, transform the data to comma-delimited format using the *PersonnelCSV.xsl* stylesheet:

```
// Create a resolver with default credentials.
XmlUrlResolver resolver = new XmlUrlResolver();
resolver.Credentials = System.Net.CredentialCache.DefaultCredentials;

// transform the personnel.xml file to html
XslCompiledTransform transform = new XslCompiledTransform();
XsltSettings settings = new XsltSettings();
// disable both of these (the default) for security reasons
settings.EnableDocumentFunction = false;
settings.EnableScript = false;
// load up the stylesheet
transform.Load(@"..\..\PersonnelHTML.xsl",settings,resolver);
// perform the transformation
transform.Transform(@"..\..\Personnel.xml",@"..\..\Personnel.html");
```

The *PersonnelHTML.xsl* stylesheet looks like this:

```
<?xml version="1.0" encoding="UTF-8"?>
<xsl:stylesheet version="1.0" xmlns:xsl="http://www.w3.org/1999/XSL/Transform"
                xmlns:xs="http://www.w3.org/2001/XMLSchema">
  <xsl:template match="/">
    <html>
      <head />
      <body title="Personnel">
        <xsl:for-each select="Personnel">
          <p>
            <xsl:for-each select="Employee">
              <xsl:if test="position()=1">
```

```
<table border="1">
  <thead>
    <tr>
      <td>Employee Name</td>
      <td>Employee Title</td>
      <td>Years with Company</td>
      <td>Also Known As</td>
    </tr>
  </thead>
  <tbody>
    <xsl:for-each select="../Employee">
      <tr>
        <td>
          <xsl:for-each select="@name">
            <xsl:value-of select="." />
          </xsl:for-each>
        </td>
        <td>
          <xsl:for-each select="@title">
            <xsl:value-of select="." />
          </xsl:for-each>
        </td>
        <td>
          <xsl:for-each select="@companyYears">
            <xsl:value-of select="." />
          </xsl:for-each>
        </td>
        <td>
          <xsl:for-each select="@nickname">
            <xsl:value-of select="." />
          </xsl:for-each>
        </td>
      </tr>
    </xsl:for-each>
  </tbody>
</table>
            </xsl:if>
          </xsl:for-each>
        </p>
      </xsl:for-each>
    </body>
  </html>
</xsl:template>
</xsl:stylesheet>
```

To generate the HTML screen in Figure 10-1, use the *PersonnelHTML.xsl* stylesheet and the *Personnel.xml* file.

Employee Name	Employee Title	Years with Company	Also Known As
Bob	Customer Service	1	"Happy"
Alice	Manager	12	"Business"
Chas	Salesman	3	"Money"
Rutherford	CEO	27	"BigTime"

Figure 10-1. Personnel HTML table generated from Personnel.xml

Here is the HTML source for the LINQ transformation:

```
<?xml version="1.0" encoding="utf-8"?>
<html>
  <head />
  <body title="Personnel">
    <p>
      <table border="1">
        <thead>
          <tr>
            <td>Employee Name</td>
            <td>Employee Title</td>
            <td>Years with Company</td>
            <td>Also Known As</td>
          </tr>
        </thead>
        <tbody>
          <tr>
            <td>Bob</td>
            <td>Customer Service</td>
            <td>1</td>
            <td>"Happy"</td>
          </tr>
          <tr>
            <td>Alice</td>
            <td>Manager</td>
            <td>12</td>
            <td>"Business"</td>
          </tr>
          <tr>
            <td>Chas</td>
            <td>Salesman</td>
            <td>3</td>
            <td>"Money"</td>
          </tr>
          <tr>
            <td>Rutherford</td>
            <td>CEO</td>
            <td>27</td>
            <td>"BigTime"</td>
          </tr>
        </tbody>
```

```
        </table>
      </p>
    </body>
  </html>
```

Here is the HTML source for the XSLT transformation:

```
<?xml version="1.0" encoding="utf-8"?>
<html>
  <head />
  <body title="Personnel">
    <table border="1">
      <thead>
        <tr>
          <td>Employee Name</td>
          <td>Employee Title</td>
          <td>Years with Company</td>
        </tr>
      </thead>
      <tbody>
        <tr>
          <td name="Bob" />
          <td title="Customer Service" />
          <td name="Bob" />
        </tr>
        <tr>
          <td name="Alice" />
          <td title="Manager" />
          <td name="Alice" />
        </tr>
        <tr>
          <td name="Chas" />
          <td title="Salesman" />
          <td name="Chas" />
        </tr>
        <tr>
          <td name="Rutherford" />
          <td title="CEO" />
          <td name="Rutherford" />
        </tr>
      </tbody>
    </table>
  </body>
</html>
```

To generate comma-delimited output, use *PersonnelCSV.xsl* and *Personnel.xml*:

```
// transform the personnel.xml file to comma-delimited format

// load up the stylesheet
XslCompiledTransform transformCSV = new XslCompiledTransform();
XsltSettings settingsCSV = new XsltSettings();
// disable both of these (the default) for security reasons
settingsCSV.EnableDocumentFunction = false;
```

```
settingsCSV.EnableScript = false;
transformCSV.Load(@"..\..\PersonnelCSV.xsl", settingsCSV, resolver);

// perform the transformation
XsltArgumentList xslArg = new XsltArgumentList();
CsvExtensionObject xslExt = new CsvExtensionObject();
xslArg.AddExtensionObject("urn:xslext", xslExt);
XPathDocument xPathDoc = new XPathDocument(@"..\..\Personnel.xml");
XmlWriterSettings xmlWriterSettings = new XmlWriterSettings();
xmlWriterSettings.ConformanceLevel = ConformanceLevel.Fragment;
using (XmlWriter writer = XmlWriter.Create(@"..\..\Personnel.csv",
    xmlWriterSettings))
{
    transformCSV.Transform(xPathDoc, xslArg, writer);
}
```

The *PersonnelCSV.xsl* stylesheet is shown here:

```
<?xml version="1.0" encoding="UTF-8"?>
<xsl:stylesheet version="1.0" xmlns:xsl="http://www.w3.org/1999/XSL/Transform"
                xmlns:xs="http://www.w3.org/2001/XMLSchema"
                xmlns:xslext="urn:xslext">
<xsl:output method="text" encoding="UTF-8"/>
    <xsl:template match="/">
        <xsl:for-each select="Personnel">
            <xsl:for-each select="Employee">
                <xsl:for-each select="@name">
                    <xsl:value-of
                        select="xslext:EscapeAttributeForCSV(string(.))" />
                </xsl:for-each>,<xsl:for-each select="@title">
                    <xsl:value-of
                        select="xslext:EscapeAttributeForCSV(string(.))" />
                </xsl:for-each>,<xsl:for-each select="@companyYears">
                    <xsl:value-of
                        select="xslext:EscapeAttributeForCSV(string(.))" />
                </xsl:for-each>,<xsl:for-each select="@nickname">
                    <xsl:value-of
                        select="xslext:EscapeAttributeForCSV(string(.))" />
                </xsl:for-each>
                <xsl:text> &#xd;&#xa;</xsl:text>
            </xsl:for-each>
        </xsl:for-each>
    </xsl:template>
</xsl:stylesheet>
```

The output from the *PersonnelCSV.xsl* stylesheet is shown here:

```
Bob,Customer Service,1,""Happy""
Alice,Manager,12,""Business""
Chas,Salesman,3,""Money""
Rutherford,CEO,27,""BigTime""
```

Once again we do some work to support RFC 4180, "Common Format and MIME Type for CSV Files," with the `EscapeAttributeForCSV` method on the `CsvExtensionObject` that we passed as an `Extension` object to the transform, which is discussed in more detail in Recipe 10.8:

```
public class CsvExtensionObject
{
    public string EscapeAttributeForCSV(string attributeValue) =>
        attributeValue.Replace("\"", "\"\"");
}
```

Discussion

XSLT is a very powerful way to transform XML from one format to another. That being said, the capacity that LINQ brings in C# to perform XML transformations without having to shell out to another parser or process is very compelling. This means that to perform XML transformations in your applications, you no longer have to understand XSLT syntax or maintain application code in both C# and XSLT. This also means that when reviewing code from other team members, you no longer have to go into separate files to understand what the transformation is doing; it's all C# and all right there.

XSLT is by no means dead or inappropriate as a method for transforming XML; it is simply no longer the only realistic alternative for C# developers. XSLT can still be used with all of the existing XML API in .NET and will continue to be feasible for years to come. Our challenge to you is to try implementing a transformation in LINQ that you currently have in XSLT and see for yourself the possibilities with LINQ.

When you are performing transformations using XSLT, there are many overrides for the `XslCompiledTransform.Transform` method. Since `XmlResolver` is an abstract class, you need to use either the `XmlUrlResolver` or the `XmlSecureResolver` or pass null as the `XmlResolver`-typed argument. The `XmlUrlResolver` will resolve URLs to external resources, such as schema files, using the FILE, HTTP, and HTTPS protocols. The `XmlSecureResolver` restricts the resources that you can access by requiring you to pass in evidence, which helps prevent cross-domain redirection in XML.

If you are accepting XML from the Internet, it could easily redirect to a site where malicious XML is waiting to be downloaded and executed if you are not using the `XmlSecureResolver`. If you pass null for the `XmlResolver`, you are saying you do not want to resolve any external resources. Microsoft has declared the null option to be obsolete, and it shouldn't be used anyway because you should always use some type of `XmlResolver`.

XSLT is a very powerful technology that allows you to transform XML into just about any format you can think of, but it can be frustrating at times. The simple need of a carriage return/line feed combination in the XSLT output was such a trial that we were able to find more than 20 different message board requests for help on how to do this! After looking at the W3C spec for XSLT, we found you could do this combination using the `xsl:text` element like this:

```
<xsl:text> &#xd;&#xa;</xsl:text>
```

The  stands for a hexadecimal 13, or a carriage return, and the
 stands for a hexadecimal 10, or a line feed. This is output at the end of each employee's data from the XML.

See Also

The "XslCompiledTransform Class," "XmlResolver Class," "XmlUrlResolver Class," "XmlSecureResolver Class," and "xsl:text" topics in the MSDN documentation.

10.7 Validating Modified XML Documents Without Reloading

Problem

You are using the `XDocument` or the `XmlDocument` to modify an XML document loaded in memory. Once the document has been modified, the modifications need to be verified, and schema defaults need to be enforced.

Solution

Use the `XDocument.Validate` method to perform the validation and apply schema defaults and type information.

Create an `XmlSchemaSet` with the XML Schema document (*book.xsd*) and an `XmlReader` and then load the *book.xml* file using `XDocument.Load`:

```
// Create the schema set
XmlSchemaSet xmlSchemaSet = new XmlSchemaSet();
// add the new schema with the target namespace
// (could add all the schema at once here if there are multiple)
xmlSchemaSet.Add("http://tempuri.org/Book.xsd",
    XmlReader.Create(@"..\..\Book.xsd"));
XDocument book = XDocument.Load(@"..\..\Book.xml");
```

Set up a `ValidationEventHandler` to catch any errors and then call `XDocument.Validate` with the schema set and the event handler to validate *book.xml* against the *book.xsd* schema:

```
ValidationHandler validationHandler = new ValidationHandler();
ValidationEventHandler validationEventHandler =
    validationHandler.HandleValidation;
// validate after load
book.Validate(xmlSchemaSet, validationEventHandler);
```

The ValidationHandler class holds the current validation state in a ValidXml property and the code for the ValidationEventHandler implementation method Handle
Validation:

```
public class ValidationHandler
{
    private object _syncRoot = new object();

    public ValidationHandler()
    {
        lock(_syncRoot)
        {
            // set the initial check for validity to true
            this.ValidXml = true;
        }
    }

    public bool ValidXml { get; private set; }

    public void HandleValidation(object sender, ValidationEventArgs e)
    {
        lock(_syncRoot)
        {
            // we got called so this isn't valid
            ValidXml = false;
            Console.WriteLine($"Validation Error Message: {e.Message}");
            Console.WriteLine($"Validation Error Severity: {e.Severity}");
            Console.WriteLine($"Validation Error Line Number: " +
                            $"{{e.Exception?.LineNumber}");
            Console.WriteLine($"Validation Error Line Position: " +
                            $"{{e.Exception?.LinePosition}");
            Console.WriteLine($"Validation Error Source: {e.Exception?.Source}");
                Console.WriteLine($"Validation Error Source Schema: " +
                    "{e.Exception?.SourceSchemaObject}");
            Console.WriteLine($"Validation Error Source Uri: " +
                            $"{{e.Exception?.SourceUri}");
            Console.WriteLine($"Validation Error thrown from: " +
                            $"{{e.Exception?.TargetSite}");
            Console.WriteLine($"Validation Error callstack: " +
                            $"{{e.Exception?.StackTrace}");
        }
    }
}
```

If you are wondering what the `lock` statement is for in the preceding code sample, check out Recipe 12.2 for a full explanation. The short version is that multiple threads can't run in a `lock` statement.

Add a new element node that is not in the schema into the XDocument and then call `Validate` again with the schema set and event handler to revalidate the changed XDo cument. If the document triggers any validation events, then the `validationHan dler.ValidXml` property is set to `false` in the `ValidationHandler` instance:

```
// add in a new node that is not in the schema
// since we have already validated, no callbacks fire during the add...
book.Root.Add(new XElement("BogusElement","Totally"));
// now we will do validation of the new stuff we added
book.Validate(xmlSchemaSet, validationEventHandler);

if (validationHandler.ValidXml)
    Console.WriteLine("Successfully validated modified LINQ XML");
else
    Console.WriteLine("Modified LINQ XML did not validate successfully");
Console.WriteLine();
```

You could also use the `XmlDocument.Validate` method to perform the validation in a similar fashion to XDocument:

```
string xmlFile = @"..\..\Book.xml";
string xsdFile = @"..\..\Book.xsd";

// Create the schema set
XmlSchemaSet schemaSet = new XmlSchemaSet();
// add the new schema with the target namespace
// (could add all the schema at once here if there are multiple)
schemaSet.Add("http://tempuri.org/Book.xsd", XmlReader.Create(xsdFile));

// load up the xml file
XmlDocument xmlDoc = new XmlDocument();
// add the schema
xmlDoc.Schemas = schemaSet;
```

Load the *book.xml* file into the XmlDocument, set up a `ValidationEventHandler` to catch any errors, and then call `Validate` with the event handler to validate *book.xml* against the *book.xsd* schema:

```
// validate after load
xmlDoc.Load(xmlFile);
ValidationHandler handler = new ValidationHandler();
ValidationEventHandler eventHandler = handler.HandleValidation;
xmlDoc.Validate(eventHandler);
```

Add a new element node that is not in the schema into the XmlDocument and then call `Validate` again with the event handler to revalidate the changed XmlDocument. If the document triggers any validation events, then the `ValidationHandler.ValidXml` property is set to `false`:

```
// add in a new node that is not in the schema
// since we have already validated, no callbacks fire during the add...
XmlNode newNode = xmlDoc.CreateElement("BogusElement");
newNode.InnerText = "Totally";
// add the new element
xmlDoc.DocumentElement.AppendChild(newNode);
// now we will do validation of the new stuff we added
xmlDoc.Validate(eventHandler);

if (handler.ValidXml)
    Console.WriteLine("Successfully validated modified XML");
else
    Console.WriteLine("Modified XML did not validate successfully");
```

Discussion

One advantage to using `XmlDocument` over `XDocument` is that there is an override to the `XmlDocument.Validate` method that allows you to pass a specific `XmlNode` to validate. This fine-grained control is not available on `XDocument`.

```
public void Validate(
    ValidationEventHandler validationEventHandler,
    XmlNode nodeToValidate
);
```

One other approach to this problem is to instantiate an instance of the `XmlNodeReader` with the `XmlDocument` and then create an `XmlReader` with validation settings, as shown in Recipe 10.3. This would allow for continual validation while the reader navigated through the underlying XML.

The output from running the code is listed here:

```
Validation Error Message: The element 'Book' in namespace 'http://tempuri.org/Bo
ok.xsd' has invalid child element 'BogusElement'. List of possible elements expe
cted: 'Chapter' in namespace 'http://tempuri.org/Book.xsd'.
Validation Error Severity: Error
Validation Error Line Number: 0
Validation Error Line Position: 0
Validation Error Source:
Validation Error Source Schema:
Validation Error Source Uri:
Validation Error thrown from:
Validation Error callstack:
Modified LINQ XML did not validate successfully

Validation Error Message: The element 'Book' in namespace 'http://tempuri.org/Bo
ok.xsd' has invalid child element 'BogusElement'. List of possible elements expe
cted: 'Chapter' in namespace 'http://tempuri.org/Book.xsd'.
```

```
Validation Error Severity: Error
Validation Error Line Number: 0
Validation Error Line Position: 0
Validation Error Source:
Validation Error Source Schema:
Validation Error Source Uri: file:///C:/CSCB6/CSharpRecipes/Book.xml
Validation Error thrown from:
Validation Error callstack:
Modified XML did not validate successfully
```

Notice that the `BogusElement` element you added was not part of the schema for the Book element, so you got a validation error along with the information about where the error occurred. Finally, you got a report that the modified XML did not validate correctly.

See Also

Recipe 10.2; the "XDocument Class" and "XmlDocument.Validate" topics in the MSDN documentation.

10.8 Extending Transformations

Problem

You want to perform operations that are outside the scope of the transformation technology to include data in the transformed result.

Solution

If you are using LINQ to XML, you can call out to a function directly when transforming the result set, as shown here by the call to `GetErrata`:

```
XElement publications = XElement.Load(@"..\..\publications.xml");
XElement transformedPublications =
    new XElement("PublishedWorks",
        from b in publications.Elements("Book")
        select new XElement(b.Name,
                    new XAttribute(b.Attribute("name")),
                    from c in b.Elements("Chapter")
                    select new XElement("Chapter", GetErrata(c))));
Console.WriteLine(transformedPublications.ToString());
Console.WriteLine();
```

The `GetErrata` method used in the preceding sample is listed here:

```
private static XElement GetErrata(XElement chapter)
{
    // In here we could go do other lookup calls (XML, database, web service)
    // to get information to add back in to the transformation result
    string errata = $"{chapter.Value} has {chapter.Value.Length} errata";
```

```
        return new XElement("Errata", errata);
    }
```

If you are using XSLT, you can add an extension object to the transformation that can perform the operations necessary based on the node it is passed. You accomplish this by using the XsltArgumentList.AddExtensionObject method. This object you've created (XslExtensionObject) can then be accessed in the XSLT and a method called on it to return the data you want included in the final transformed result:

```
string xmlFile = @"..\..\publications.xml";
string xslt = @"..\..\publications.xsl";

//Create the XslCompiledTransform and load the style sheet.
XslCompiledTransform transform = new XslCompiledTransform();
transform.Load(xslt);
// load the xml
XPathDocument xPathDoc = new XPathDocument(xmlFile);

// make up the args for the stylesheet with the extension object
XsltArgumentList xslArg = new XsltArgumentList();
XslExtensionObject xslExt = new XslExtensionObject();
xslArg.AddExtensionObject("urn:xslext", xslExt);

// send output to the console and do the transformation
using (XmlWriter writer = XmlWriter.Create(Console.Out))
{
    transform.Transform(xPathDoc, xslArg, writer);
}
```

Note that when the extension object is added to the XsltArgumentList, it supplies a namespace of urn:xslext. This namespace is used in the XSLT stylesheet to reference the object. The XSLExtensionObject is defined here:

```
// Our extension object to help with functionality
public class XslExtensionObject
{
    public XPathNodeIterator GetErrata(XPathNodeIterator nodeChapter)
    {
        // In here we could go do other lookup calls (XML, database, web service)
        // to get information to add back in to the transformation result
        nodeChapter.MoveNext();
        string errata = $"<Errata>{nodeChapter.Current.Value} has " +
            $"{nodeChapter.Current.Value.Length} errata</Errata>";
        XmlDocument xDoc = new XmlDocument();
        xDoc.LoadXml(errata);
        XPathNavigator xPathNav = xDoc.CreateNavigator();
        xPathNav.MoveToChild(XPathNodeType.Element);
        XPathNodeIterator iter = xPathNav.Select(".");
        return iter;
    }
}
```

The `GetErrata` method is called during the execution of the XSLT stylesheet to provide data in `XPathNodeIterator` format to the transformation. The `xmlns:xslext` namespace is declared as `urn:xslext`, which matches the namespace value you passed as an argument to the transformation. In the processing of the `Book` template for each `Chapter`, an `xsl:value-of` is called with the `select` criteria containing a call to the `xslext:GetErrata` method. The stylesheet makes the call, as shown here:

```
<xsl:stylesheet version="1.0" xmlns:xsl="http://www.w3.org/1999/XSL/Transform"
    xmlns:xslext="urn:xslext">
    <xsl:template match="/">
        <xsl:element name="PublishedWorks">
            <xsl:apply-templates/>
        </xsl:element>
    </xsl:template>
    <xsl:template match="Book">
        <Book>
            <xsl:attribute name ="name">
                <xsl:value-of select="@name"/>
            </xsl:attribute>
            <xsl:for-each select="Chapter">
                <Chapter>
                    <xsl:value-of select="xslext:GetErrata(/)"/>
                </Chapter>
            </xsl:for-each>
        </Book>
    </xsl:template>
</xsl:stylesheet>
```

The outputs for the two approaches are the same and look like this (partial listing):

```
<PublishedWorks>
  <Book name="Subclassing and Hooking with Visual Basic">
    <Chapter>
      <Errata>Introduction has 12 errata</Errata>
    </Chapter>
    ...
  </Book>
  <Book name="C# Cookbook">
    <Chapter>
      <Errata>Numbers has 7 errata</Errata>
    </Chapter>
    ...
  </Book>
  <Book name="C# Cookbook 2.0">
    <Chapter>
      <Errata>Numbers and Enumerations has 24 errata</Errata>
    </Chapter>
    ...
  </Book>
  <Book name="C# 3.0 Cookbook">
    <Chapter>
      <Errata>Language Integrated Query (LINQ) has 32 errata</Errata>
```

```
        </Chapter>
        ...
      </Book>
      <Book name="C# 6.0 Cookbook">
        <Chapter>
          <Errata>Classes and Generics has 20 errata</Errata>
        </Chapter>
        <Chapter>
          <Errata>Collections, Enumerators, and Iterators has 39 errata</Errata>
        </Chapter>
        <Chapter>
          <Errata>Data Types has 10 errata</Errata>
        </Chapter>
        <Chapter>
          <Errata>LINQ and Lambda Expressions has 27 errata</Errata>
        </Chapter>
        <Chapter>
          <Errata>Debugging and Exception Handling has 32 errata</Errata>
        </Chapter>
        <Chapter>
          <Errata>Reflection and Dynamic Programming has 34 errata</Errata>
        </Chapter>
        <Chapter>
          <Errata>Regular Expressions has 19 errata</Errata>
        </Chapter>
        <Chapter>
          <Errata>Filesystem I/O has 14 errata</Errata>
        </Chapter>
        <Chapter>
          <Errata>Networking and Web has 18 errata</Errata>
        </Chapter>
        <Chapter>
          <Errata>XML has 3 errata</Errata>
        </Chapter>
        <Chapter>
          <Errata>Security has 8 errata</Errata>
        </Chapter>
        <Chapter>
          <Errata>Threading, Synchronization, and Concurrency has 43 errata</Errata>
        </Chapter>
        <Chapter>
          <Errata>Toolbox has 7 errata</Errata>
        </Chapter>
      </Book>
    </PublishedWorks>
```

Discussion

Using LINQ to XML, you can extend your transformation code to include additional logic simply by adding method calls that know how to operate and return XElements. This is simply adding another method call to the query that contributes to the result set, and no additional performance penalty is assessed just by the call. Certainly if the operation is expensive it could slow down the transformation, but this is now easily located when your code is profiled.

The ability to call custom code from inside an XSLT stylesheet is very powerful, but should be used cautiously. Adding code like this into stylesheets usually renders them less useful in other environments. If the stylesheet never has to be used to transform XML in another parser, this can be a good way to offload work that is either difficult or impossible to accomplish in regular XSLT syntax.

The sample data used in the Solution is presented here:

```xml
<?xml version="1.0" encoding="utf-8"?>
<Publications>
  <Book name="Subclassing and Hooking with Visual Basic">
    <Chapter>Introduction</Chapter>
    <Chapter>Windows System-Specific Information</Chapter>
    <Chapter>The Basics of Subclassing and Hooks</Chapter>
    <Chapter>Subclassing and Superclassing</Chapter>
    <Chapter>Subclassing the Windows Common Dialog Boxes</Chapter>
    <Chapter>ActiveX Controls and Subclassing</Chapter>
    <Chapter>Superclassing</Chapter>
    <Chapter>Debugging Techniques for Subclassing</Chapter>
    <Chapter>WH_CALLWNDPROC</Chapter>
    <Chapter>WH_CALLWNDPROCRET</Chapter>
    <Chapter>WH_GETMESSAGE</Chapter>
    <Chapter>WH_KEYBOARD and WH_KEYBOARD_LL</Chapter>
    <Chapter>WH_MOUSE and WH_MOUSE_LL</Chapter>
    <Chapter>WH_FOREGROUNDIDLE</Chapter>
    <Chapter>WH_MSGFILTER</Chapter>
    <Chapter>WH_SYSMSGFILTER</Chapter>
    <Chapter>WH_SHELL</Chapter>
    <Chapter>WH_CBT</Chapter>
    <Chapter>WH_JOURNALRECORD</Chapter>
    <Chapter>WH_JOURNALPLAYBACK</Chapter>
    <Chapter>WH_DEBUG</Chapter>
    <Chapter>Subclassing .NET WinForms</Chapter>
    <Chapter>Implementing Hooks in VB.NET</Chapter>
  </Book>
  <Book name="C# Cookbook">
    <Chapter>Numbers</Chapter>
    <Chapter>Strings and Characters</Chapter>
    <Chapter>Classes And Structures</Chapter>
    <Chapter>Enums</Chapter>
    <Chapter>Exception Handling</Chapter>
    <Chapter>Diagnostics</Chapter>
    <Chapter>Delegates and Events</Chapter>
    <Chapter>Regular Expressions</Chapter>
    <Chapter>Collections</Chapter>
    <Chapter>Data Structures and Algorithms</Chapter>
    <Chapter>File System IO</Chapter>
```

```
    <Chapter>Reflection</Chapter>
    <Chapter>Networking</Chapter>
    <Chapter>Security</Chapter>
    <Chapter>Threading</Chapter>
    <Chapter>Unsafe Code</Chapter>
    <Chapter>XML</Chapter>
  </Book>
  <Book name="C# Cookbook 2.0">
    <Chapter>Numbers and Enumerations</Chapter>
    <Chapter>Strings and Characters</Chapter>
    <Chapter>Classes And Structures</Chapter>
    <Chapter>Generics</Chapter>
    <Chapter>Collections</Chapter>
    <Chapter>Iterators and Partial Types</Chapter>
    <Chapter>Exception Handling</Chapter>
    <Chapter>Diagnostics</Chapter>
    <Chapter>Delegates, Events, and Anonymous Methods</Chapter>
    <Chapter>Regular Expressions</Chapter>
    <Chapter>Data Structures and Algorithms</Chapter>
    <Chapter>File System IO</Chapter>
    <Chapter>Reflection</Chapter>
    <Chapter>Web</Chapter>
    <Chapter>XML</Chapter>
    <Chapter>Networking</Chapter>
    <Chapter>Security</Chapter>
    <Chapter>Threading and Synchronization</Chapter>
    <Chapter>Unsafe Code</Chapter>
    <Chapter>Toolbox</Chapter>
  </Book>
  <Book name="C# 3.0 Cookbook">
    <Chapter>Language Integrated Query (LINQ)</Chapter>
    <Chapter>Strings and Characters</Chapter>
    <Chapter>Classes And Structures</Chapter>
    <Chapter>Generics</Chapter>
    <Chapter>Collections</Chapter>
    <Chapter>Iterators, Partial Types, and Partial Methods </Chapter>
    <Chapter>Exception Handling</Chapter>
    <Chapter>Diagnostics</Chapter>
    <Chapter>Delegates, Events, and Lambda Expressions</Chapter>
    <Chapter>Regular Expressions</Chapter>
    <Chapter>Data Structures and Algorithms</Chapter>
    <Chapter>File System IO</Chapter>
    <Chapter>Reflection</Chapter>
    <Chapter>Web</Chapter>
    <Chapter>XML</Chapter>
    <Chapter>Networking</Chapter>
    <Chapter>Security</Chapter>
    <Chapter>Threading and Synchronization</Chapter>
    <Chapter>Toolbox</Chapter>
    <Chapter>Numbers and Enumerations</Chapter>
  </Book>
  <Book name="C# 6.0 Cookbook">
```

```
        <Chapter>Classes and Generics</Chapter>
        <Chapter>Collections, Enumerators, and Iterators</Chapter>
        <Chapter>Data Types</Chapter>
        <Chapter>LINQ and Lambda Expressions</Chapter>
        <Chapter>Debugging and Exception Handling</Chapter>
        <Chapter>Reflection and Dynamic Programming</Chapter>
        <Chapter>Regular Expressions</Chapter>
        <Chapter>Filesystem I/O</Chapter>
        <Chapter>Networking and Web</Chapter>
        <Chapter>XML</Chapter>
        <Chapter>Security</Chapter>
        <Chapter>Threading, Synchronization, and Concurrency</Chapter>
        <Chapter>Toolbox</Chapter>
    </Book>
</Publications>
```

See Also

The "LINQ, transforming data" and "XsltArgumentList Class" topics in the MSDN documentation.

10.9 Getting Your Schemas in Bulk from Existing XML Files

Problem

You have come on to a new project in which XML was used for data transmission, but the programmers who came before you didn't use an XSD for one reason or another. You need to generate beginning schema files for each of the XML examples.

Solution

Use the `XmlSchemaInference` class to infer schema from the XML samples. The `GenerateSchemasForDirectory` function in Example 10-7 enumerates all of the XML files in a given directory and processes each of them using the `GenerateSchemasForFile` method. `GenerateSchemasForFile` uses the `XmlSchemaInference.InferSchema` method to get the schemas for the given XML file. Once the schemas have been determined, `GenerateSchemasForFile` rolls over the collection and saves out each schema to an XSD file using a `FileStream`.

Example 10-7. Generating an XML schema

```
public static void GenerateSchemasForFile(string file)
{
    // set up a reader for the file
    using (XmlReader reader = XmlReader.Create(file))
    {
        XmlSchemaSet schemaSet = new XmlSchemaSet();
```

```
        XmlSchemaInference schemaInference =
                        new XmlSchemaInference();

        // get the schema
        schemaSet = schemaInference.InferSchema(reader);

        string schemaPath = string.Empty;
        foreach (XmlSchema schema in schemaSet.Schemas())
        {
            // make schema file path and write it out
            schemaPath = $"{Path.GetDirectoryName(file)}\\" +
                            $"{Path.GetFileNameWithoutExtension(file)}.xsd";
            using (FileStream fs =
                new FileStream(schemaPath, FileMode.OpenOrCreate))
            {
                schema.Write(fs);
                fs.Flush();
            }
        }
    }
}

public static void GenerateSchemasForDirectory(string dir)
{
    // make sure the directory exists
    if (Directory.Exists(dir))
    {
        // get the files in the directory
        string[] files = Directory.GetFiles(dir, "*.xml");
        foreach (string file in files)
        {
            GenerateSchemasForFile(file);
        }
    }
}
```

The `GenerateSchemasForDirectory` method can be called like this:

```
// Get the directory two levels up from where we are running.
DirectoryInfo di = new DirectoryInfo(@"..\..");
string dir = di.FullName;
// Generate the schema.
GenerateSchemasForDirectory(dir);
```

Discussion

Having an XSD for the XML files in an application allows for:

- Validation of XML presented to the system
- Documentation of the semantics of the data

- Programmatic discovery of the data structure through XML reading methods

Using the `GenerateSchemasForFile` method can jump-start the process of developing schema for your XML, but each schema should be reviewed by the team member responsible for producing the XML. This will help to ensure that the rules as stated in the schema are correct and also that additional items, such as schema default values and other relationships, are added. Any relationships that were not present in the example XML files would be missed by the schema generator.

See Also

The "XmlSchemaInference Class" and "XML Schemas (XSD) Reference" topics in the MSDN documentation.

10.10 Passing Parameters to Transformations

Problem

You need to transform some data using a mostly common pattern. For the few data items that could change between transformations, you don't want to have a separate mechanism for each variation.

Solution

If you are using LINQ to XML, simply build a method to encapsulate the transformation code and pass parameters to the method just as you normally would for other code:

```
// transform using LINQ instead of XSLT
string storeTitle = "Hero Comics Inventory";
string pageDate = DateTime.Now.ToString("F");
XElement parameterExample = XElement.Load(@"..\..\ParameterExample.xml");
string htmlPath = @"..\..\ParameterExample_LINQ.htm";
TransformWithParameters(storeTitle, pageDate, parameterExample, htmlPath);

// now change the parameters
storeTitle = "Fabulous Adventures Inventory";
pageDate = DateTime.Now.ToString("D");
htmlPath = @"..\..\ParameterExample2_LINQ.htm";
TransformWithParameters(storeTitle, pageDate, parameterExample, htmlPath);
```

The `TransformWithParameters` method looks like this:

```
private static void TransformWithParameters(string storeTitle, string pageDate,
    XElement parameterExample, string htmlPath)
{
    XElement transformedParameterExample =
        new XElement("html",
```

```
        new XElement("head"),
        new XElement("body",
            new XElement("h3", $"Brought to you by {storeTitle} " +
                    $"on {pageDate}{Environment.NewLine}"),
            new XElement("br"),
            new XElement("table",
                new XAttribute("border","2"),
                new XElement("thead",
                    new XElement("tr",
                        new XElement("td",
                            new XElement("b","Heroes")),
                        new XElement("td",
                            new XElement("b","Edition")))),
                new XElement("tbody",
                    from cb in parameterExample.Elements("ComicBook")
                    orderby cb.Attribute("name").Value descending
                    select new XElement("tr",
                            new XElement("td",cb.Attribute("name").Value),
                            new XElement("td",
                                cb.Attribute("edition").Value)))))));
    transformedParameterExample.Save(htmlPath);
}
```

If you are using XSLT to perform transformations, use the `XsltArgumentList` class to pass arguments to the XSLT transformation. This technique allows the program to generate an object (such as a dynamic string) for the stylesheet to access and use while it transforms the given XML file. The `storeTitle` and `pageDate` arguments are passed in to the transformation in the following example. The `storeTitle` is for the title of the comic store, and `pageDate` is the date for which the report is run. You add these using the `AddParam` method of the `XsltArgumentList` object instance `args`:

```
//transform using XSLT and parameters
XsltArgumentList args = new XsltArgumentList();
args.AddParam("storeTitle", "", "Hero Comics Inventory");
args.AddParam("pageDate", "", DateTime.Now.ToString("F"));

// Create a resolver with default credentials.
XmlUrlResolver resolver = new XmlUrlResolver();
resolver.Credentials = System.Net.CredentialCache.DefaultCredentials;
```

The `XsltSettings` class allows for changing the behavior of the transformation. If you use the `XsltSettings.Default` instance, you can do the transformation without allowing scripting or the use of the document XSLT function, as they can be security risks. If the stylesheet is from a trusted source, you can just create an `XsltSettings` object and use it, but it is better to be safe. Further changes to the code could open it up to use with untrusted XSLT stylesheets:

```
XslCompiledTransform transform = new XslCompiledTransform();
// load up the stylesheet
transform.Load(@"..\..\ParameterExample.xslt", XsltSettings.Default,
```

```
        resolver);
    // perform the transformation
    FileStream fs = null;
    using (fs =
        new FileStream(@"..\..\ParameterExample.htm",
                         FileMode.OpenOrCreate, FileAccess.Write))
    {
        transform.Transform(@"..\..\ParameterExample.xml", args, fs);
    }    XslCompiledTransform transform = new XslCompiledTransform();
        // Load up the stylesheet.
        transform.Load(@"..\..\ParameterExample.xslt", XsltSettings.Default,
            resolver);

        // Perform the transformation.
        FileStream fs = null;
        using (fs = new FileStream(@"..\..\ParameterExample.htm",
            FileMode.OpenOrCreate, FileAccess.Write))
        {
            transform.Transform(@"..\..\ParameterExample.xml", args, fs);
        }
```

To show the different parameters in action, now you change storeTitle and page
Date and run the transformation again:

```
    // now change the parameters and reprocess
    args = new XsltArgumentList();
    args.AddParam("storeTitle", "", "Fabulous Adventures Inventory");
    args.AddParam("pageDate", "", DateTime.Now.ToString("D"));
    using (fs = new FileStream(@"..\..\ParameterExample2.htm",
        FileMode.OpenOrCreate, FileAccess.Write))
    {
        transform.Transform(@"..\..\ParameterExample.xml", args, fs);
    }
```

The *ParameterExample.xml* file contains the following:

```
    <?xml version="1.0" encoding="utf-8" ?>
    <?xml-stylesheet href="ParameterExample.xslt" type="text/xsl"?>
    <ParameterExample>
        <ComicBook name="The Amazing Spider-Man" edition="1"/>
        <ComicBook name="The Uncanny X-Men" edition="2"/>
        <ComicBook name="Superman" edition="3"/>
        <ComicBook name="Batman" edition="4"/>
        <ComicBook name="The Fantastic Four" edition="5"/>
    </ParameterExample>
```

The *ParameterExample.xslt* file contains the following:

```
    <?xml version="1.0" encoding="UTF-8" ?>
    <xsl:stylesheet version="1.0" xmlns:xsl="http://www.w3.org/1999/XSL/Transform">
      <xsl:output method="html" indent="yes" />
      <xsl:param name="storeTitle"/>
      <xsl:param name="pageDate"/>
```

```
<xsl:template match="ParameterExample">
  <html>
    <head/>
    <body>
      <h3>
        <xsl:text>Brought to you by </xsl:text>
        <xsl:value-of select="$storeTitle"/>
        <xsl:text> on </xsl:text>
        <xsl:value-of select="$pageDate"/>
        <xsl:text> &#xd;&#xa;</xsl:text>
      </h3>
      <br/>
      <table border="2">
        <thead>
          <tr>
            <td>
              <b>Heroes</b>
            </td>
            <td>
              <b>Edition</b>
            </td>
          </tr>
        </thead>
        <tbody>
          <xsl:apply-templates/>
        </tbody>
      </table>
    </body>
  </html>
</xsl:template>
<xsl:template match="ComicBook">
  <tr>
    <td>
      <xsl:value-of select="@name"/>
    </td>
    <td>
      <xsl:value-of select="@edition"/>
    </td>
  </tr>
</xsl:template>
</xsl:stylesheet>
```

The output from the first transformation using XSLT to *ParameterExample.htm* or using LINQ to *ParameterExample_LINQ.htm* is shown in Figure 10-2.

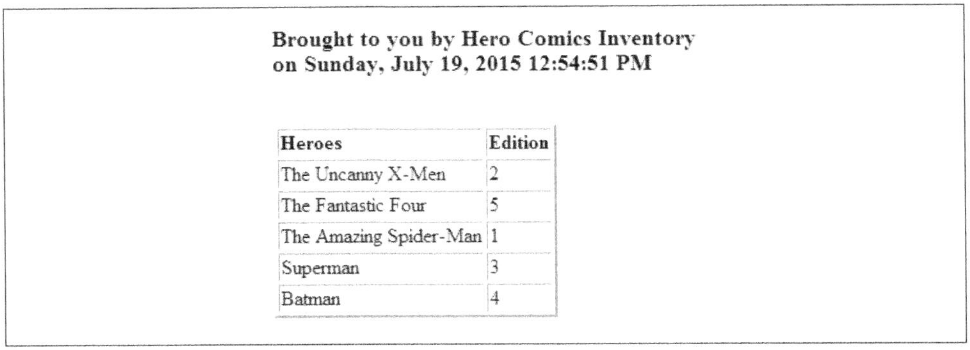
Brought to you by Hero Comics Inventory
on Sunday, July 19, 2015 12:54:51 PM

Heroes	Edition
The Uncanny X-Men	2
The Fantastic Four	5
The Amazing Spider-Man	1
Superman	3
Batman	4

Figure 10-2. Output from the first set of parameters

Output from the second transformation using XSLT to *ParameterExample2.htm* or using LINQ to *ParameterExample2_LINQ.htm* is shown in Figure 10-3.

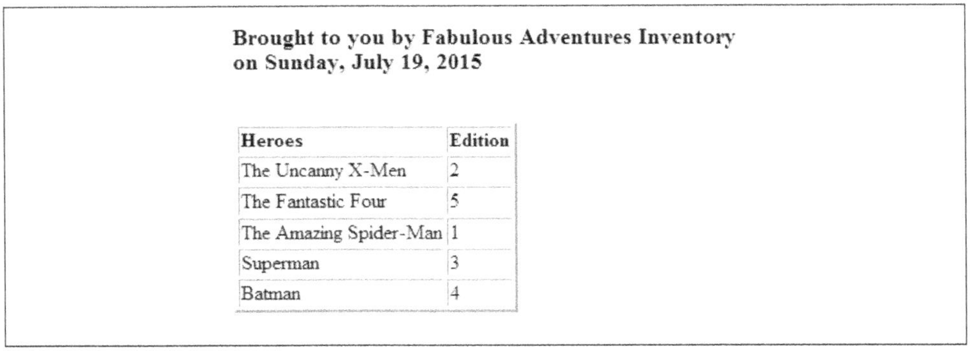
Brought to you by Fabulous Adventures Inventory
on Sunday, July 19, 2015

Heroes	Edition
The Uncanny X-Men	2
The Fantastic Four	5
The Amazing Spider-Man	1
Superman	3
Batman	4

Figure 10-3. Output from the second set of parameters

Discussion

Both approaches allow you to templatize your code and provide parameters to modify the output. With the LINQ to XML method, the code is all in .NET, and .NET analysis tools can be used to measure the impact of the transformation. Using the declarative style of the code conveys the intent more clearly than having to go to the external XSLT file. If you don't know XSLT, you don't have to learn it, as you can do it in code now.

If you already know XSLT, you can continue to leverage it. Being able to pass information to the XSLT stylesheet allows for a much greater degree of flexibility when you are designing reports or user interfaces via XSLT transformations. This capability can help you customize the output based on just about any criteria you can think of, as the data being passed in is totally controlled by your program. Once you get the hang of using parameters with XSLT, a whole new level of customization becomes possible. As an added bonus, it is portable between environments.

See Also

The "LINQ, transforming data," "XsltArgumentList Class," and "XsltSettings Class" topics in the MSDN documentation.

CHAPTER 11

Security

11.0 Introduction

The security of running code in .NET revolves around the concept of Code Access Security (CAS). CAS determines the trustworthiness of an assembly based upon its origin and the characteristics of the assembly itself, such as its hash value. For example, code installed locally on the machine is more trusted than code downloaded from the Internet. The runtime will also validate an assembly's metadata and type safety before that code is allowed to run.

There are many mechanisms that we can use to write secure code and protect data using the .NET Framework. In this chapter, we explore such topics as controlling access to types, encryption/decryption, randomizing numbers for use with encryption, securely storing data, and using programmatic and declarative security.

11.1 Encrypting and Decrypting a String

Problem

You have data in a string that you want to be able to encrypt and decrypt—perhaps a password or software key—which will be stored in some form, such as in a file or the registry. You want to keep this string a secret so that users cannot take this information from you.

Solution

Encrypting the string will help to prevent users from being able to read and decipher the information. The CryptoString class shown in Example 11-1 contains two static methods to encrypt and decrypt a string and two static properties to retrieve the generated key and initialization vector (IV—a random number used as a starting point to encrypt data) after encryption has occurred.

Example 11-1. CryptoString class

```
using System;
using System.Security.Cryptography;

public sealed class CryptoString
{
    private CryptoString() {}

    private static byte[] savedKey = null;
    private static byte[] savedIV = null;

    public static byte[] Key { get; set; }

    public static byte[] IV { get; set; }

    private static void RdGenerateSecretKey(RijndaelManaged rdProvider)
    {
        if (savedKey == null)
        {
            rdProvider.KeySize = 256;
            rdProvider.GenerateKey();
            savedKey = rdProvider.Key;
        }
    }

    private static void RdGenerateSecretInitVector(RijndaelManaged rdProvider)
    {
        if (savedIV == null)
        {
            rdProvider.GenerateIV();
            savedIV = rdProvider.IV;
        }
    }

    public static string Encrypt(string originalStr)
    {
        // Encode data string to be stored in memory.
        byte[] originalStrAsBytes = Encoding.ASCII.GetBytes(originalStr);
        byte[] originalBytes = {};

        // Create MemoryStream to contain output.
        using (MemoryStream memStream = new
                MemoryStream(originalStrAsBytes.Length))
        {
            using (RijndaelManaged rijndael = new RijndaelManaged())
            {
                // Generate and save secret key and init vector.
```

```
            RdGenerateSecretKey(rijndael);
            RdGenerateSecretInitVector(rijndael);

            if (savedKey == null || savedIV == null)
            {
                throw (new NullReferenceException(
                        "savedKey and savedIV must be non-null."));
            }

            // Create encryptor and stream objects.
            using (ICryptoTransform rdTransform =
                    rijndael.CreateEncryptor((byte[])savedKey.
                    Clone(),(byte[])savedIV.Clone()))
            {
                using (CryptoStream cryptoStream = new CryptoStream(memStream,
                    rdTransform, CryptoStreamMode.Write))
                {
                    // Write encrypted data to the MemoryStream.
                    cryptoStream.Write(originalStrAsBytes, 0,
                            originalStrAsBytes.Length);
                    cryptoStream.FlushFinalBlock();
                    originalBytes = memStream.ToArray();
                }
            }
        }

    }
    // Convert encrypted string.
    string encryptedStr = Convert.ToBase64String(originalBytes);
    return (encryptedStr);
}

public static string Decrypt(string encryptedStr)
{
    // Unconvert encrypted string.
    byte[] encryptedStrAsBytes = Convert.FromBase64String(encryptedStr);
    byte[] initialText = new Byte[encryptedStrAsBytes.Length];

    using (RijndaelManaged rijndael = new RijndaelManaged())
    {
        using (MemoryStream memStream = new MemoryStream(encryptedStrAsBytes))
        {
            if (savedKey == null || savedIV == null)
            {
                throw (new NullReferenceException(
                        "savedKey and savedIV must be non-null."));
            }

            // Create decryptor and stream objects.
            using (ICryptoTransform rdTransform =
                    rijndael.CreateDecryptor((byte[])savedKey.Clone(),
                    (byte[])savedIV.Clone()))
```

```
        {
            using (CryptoStream cryptoStream = new CryptoStream(memStream,
                rdTransform, CryptoStreamMode.Read))
            {
                // Read in decrypted string as a byte[].
                cryptoStream.Read(initialText, 0, initialText.Length);
            }
        }
    }
}

    // Convert byte[] to string.
    string decryptedStr = Encoding.ASCII.GetString(initialText);
    return (decryptedStr);
    }
}
```

Discussion

The CryptoString class contains only static members, except for the private instance constructor, which prevents anyone from directly creating an object from this class.

This class uses the *Rijndael algorithm* to encrypt and decrypt a string. This algorithm is found in the System.Security.Cryptography.RijndaelManaged class. This algorithm requires a secret key and an initialization vector; both are byte arrays. You can generate a random secret key by calling the GenerateKey method on the RijndaelManaged class. This method accepts no parameters and returns void. The generated key is placed in the Key property of the RijndaelManaged class. The GenerateIV method generates a random initialization vector and places this vector in the IV property of the RijndaelManaged class.

The byte array values in the Key and IV properties must be stored for later use and not modified. This is due to the nature of private-key encryption classes, such as RijndaelManaged. The Key and IV values must be used by both the encryption and decryption routines to successfully encrypt and decrypt data.

The SavedKey and SavedIV private static fields contain the secret key and initialization vector, respectively. The secret key is used by both the encryption and decryption methods to encrypt and decrypt data. This is why there are public properties for these values, so they can be stored somewhere secure for later use. This means that any strings encrypted by this object must be decrypted by this object. The initialization vector is there to make it much more difficult to deduce the secret key from the encrypted string. The initialization vector does this by making two identical encrypted strings (encrypted with the same key) look very different in their encrypted forms.

Two methods in the `CryptoString` class, `RdGenerateSecretKey` and `RdGenerateSe cretInitVector`, are used to generate a secret key and initialization vector when none exists. The `RdGenerateSecretKey` method generates the secret key, which is placed in the `SavedKey` field. Likewise, the `RdGenerateSecretInitVector` generates the initialization vector, which is placed in the `SavedIV` field. There is only one key and one IV generated for this class. This enables the encryption and decryption routines to have access to the same key and IV information at all times.

The `Encrypt` and `Decrypt` methods of the `CryptoString` class do the actual work of encrypting and decrypting a string. The `Encrypt` method accepts a string that you want to encrypt and returns an encrypted string. The following code calls this method and passes in a string to be encrypted:

```
string encryptedString = CryptoString.Encrypt("MyPassword");
Console.WriteLine($"encryptedString: {encryptedString}");

// Get the key and IV used so you can decrypt it later.
byte [] key = CryptoString.Key;
byte [] IV = CryptoString.IV;
```

Once the string is encrypted, the key and IV are stored for later decryption. This method displays:

```
encryptedString: NmmKqBO4iPT+BDxgLVwzgQ==
```

Note that your output may differ since you will be using a different key and IV value. The following code sets the key and IV used to encrypt the string and then calls the `Decrypt` method to decrypt the previously encrypted string:

```
CryptoString.Key = key;
CryptoString.IV = IV;
string decryptedString = CryptoString.Decrypt(encryptedString);
Console.WriteLine($"decryptedString: {decryptedString}");
```

This method displays:

```
decryptedString: MyPassword
```

There does not seem to be any problem with using escape sequences such as \r, \n, \r\n, or \t in the string to be encrypted. In addition, using a quoted string literal, with or without escaped characters, works without a problem:

```
@"MyPassword"
```

See Also

Recipe 11.2; the "System.Cryptography Namespace," "MemoryStream Class," "ICrypto Transform Interface," and "RijndaelManaged Class" topics in the MSDN documentation.

11.2 Encrypting and Decrypting a File

Problem

You have sensitive information that must be encrypted before it is written to a file that might be stored in a nonsecure area. This information must also be decrypted before it is read back in to the application.

Solution

Use multiple cryptography providers and write the data to a file in encrypted format. This is accomplished in the following class, which has a constructor that expects an instance of the `System.Security.Cryptography.SymmetricAlgorithm` class and a path for the file. The `SymmetricAlgorithm` class is an abstract base class for all cryptographic providers in .NET, so you can be reasonably assured that this class could be extended to cover all of them. This example implements support for TripleDES and Rijndael.

The following namespaces are needed for this solution:

```
using System;
using System.Text;
using System.IO;
using System.Security.Cryptography;
```

The class `SecretFile` (see Example 11-2) can be used for TripleDES as shown:

```
// Use TripleDES.
using (TripleDESCryptoServiceProvider tdes = new
        TripleDESCryptoServiceProvider())
{
    SecretFile secretTDESFile = new SecretFile(tdes,"tdestext.secret");

    string encrypt = "My TDES Secret Data!";
    Console.WriteLine($"Writing secret data: {encrypt}");
    secretTDESFile.SaveSensitiveData(encrypt);

    // Save for storage to read file.
    byte [] key = secretTDESFile.Key;
    byte [] IV = secretTDESFile.IV;

    string decrypt = secretTDESFile.ReadSensitiveData();
    Console.WriteLine($"Read secret data: {decrypt}");
}
```

To use `SecretFile` with Rijndael, just substitute the provider in the constructor like this:

```
// Use Rijndael.
using (RijndaelManaged rdProvider = new RijndaelManaged())
```

```
    {
        SecretFile secretRDFile = new SecretFile(rdProvider,"rdtext.secret");

        string encrypt = "My Rijndael Secret Data!";

        Console.WriteLine($"Writing secret data: {encrypt}");
        secretRDFile.SaveSensitiveData(encrypt);
        // Save for storage to read file.
        byte [] key = secretRDFile.Key;
        byte [] IV = secretRDFile.IV;

        string decrypt = secretRDFile.ReadSensitiveData();
        Console.WriteLine($"Read secret data: {decrypt}");
    }
```

Example 11-2 shows the implementation of SecretFile.

Example 11-2. SecretFile class

```
public class SecretFile
{
    private byte[] savedKey = null;
    private byte[] savedIV = null;
    private SymmetricAlgorithm symmetricAlgorithm;
    string path;

    public byte[] Key { get; set; }

    public byte[] IV { get; set; }

    public SecretFile(SymmetricAlgorithm algorithm, string fileName)
    {
        symmetricalgorithm;
        path = fileName;
    }

    public void SaveSensitiveData(string sensitiveData)
    {
        // Encode data string to be stored in encrypted file.
        byte[] encodedData = Encoding.Unicode.GetBytes(sensitiveData);

        // Create FileStream and crypto service provider objects.
        using (FileStream fileStream = new FileStream(path,
                                        FileMode.Create,
                                        FileAccess.Write))
        {
            // Generate and save secret key and init vector.
            GenerateSecretKey();
            GenerateSecretInitVector();

            // Create crypto transform and stream objects.
            using (ICryptoTransform transform =
```

```
                    symmetricAlgorithm.CreateEncryptor(savedKey,
                            savedIV))
        {
            using (CryptoStream cryptoStream =
                    new CryptoStream(fileStream, transform,
                                    CryptoStreamMode.Write))
            {
                // Write encrypted data to the file.
                cryptoStream.Write(encodedData, 0, encodedData.Length);
            }
        }
    }
}

public string ReadSensitiveData()
{
    string decrypted = "";

    // Create file stream to read encrypted file back.
    using (FileStream fileStream = new FileStream(path,
                                    FileMode.Open,
                                    FileAccess.Read))
    {
        // Print out the contents of the encrypted file.
        using (BinaryReader binReader = new BinaryReader(fileStream))
        {
            Console.WriteLine("---------- Encrypted Data ---------");
            int count = (Convert.ToInt32(binReader.BaseStream.Length));
            byte [] bytes = binReader.ReadBytes(count);
            char [] array = Encoding.Unicode.GetChars(bytes);
            string encdata = new string(array);
            Console.WriteLine(encdata);
            Console.WriteLine($"---------- Encrypted Data ---------
                        {Environment.NewLine}");

            // Reset the file stream.
            fileStream.Seek(0,SeekOrigin.Begin);

            // Create decryptor.
            using (ICryptoTransform transform =
                symmetricAlgorithm.CreateDecryptor(savedKey, savedIV))
            {
                using (CryptoStream cryptoStream = new CryptoStream(fileStream,
                                            transform,
                                            CryptoStreamMode.Read))
                {
                    // Print out the contents of the decrypted file.
                    using (StreamReader srDecrypted =
                            new StreamReader(cryptoStream, new UnicodeEncoding()))
                    {
                        Console.WriteLine("---------- Decrypted Data ---------");
                        decrypted = srDecrypted.ReadToEnd();
```

```
                    Console.WriteLine(decrypted);
                    Console.WriteLine($"---------- Decrypted Data ---------
                                {Environment.NewLine}");
                }
            }
        }
    }
}

    return decrypted;
}

private void GenerateSecretKey()
{
    if (null != (symmetricAlgorithm as TripleDESCryptoServiceProvider))
    {
        TripleDESCryptoServiceProvider tdes;
        tdes = symmetricAlgorithm as TripleDESCryptoServiceProvider;
        tdes.KeySize = 192; // Maximum key size
        tdes.GenerateKey();
        savedKey = tdes.Key;
    }
    else if (null != (symmetricAlgorithm as RijndaelManaged))
    {
        RijndaelManaged rdProvider;
        rdProvider = symmetricAlgorithm as RijndaelManaged;
        rdProvider.KeySize = 256; // Maximum key size
        rdProvider.GenerateKey();
        savedKey = rdProvider.Key;
    }
}

private void GenerateSecretInitVector()
{
    if (null != (symmetricAlgorithm as TripleDESCryptoServiceProvider))
    {
        TripleDESCryptoServiceProvider tdes;
        tdes = symmetricAlgorithm as TripleDESCryptoServiceProvider;
        tdes.GenerateIV();
        savedIV = tdes.IV;
    }
    else if (null != (symmetricAlgorithm as RijndaelManaged))
    {
        RijndaelManaged rdProvider;
        rdProvider = symmetricAlgorithm as RijndaelManaged;
        rdProvider.GenerateIV();
        savedIV = rdProvider.IV;
    }
}
```

If the SaveSensitiveData method is used to save the following text to a file:

```
This is a test
This is sensitive data!
```

the `ReadSensitiveData` method will display the following information from this same file:

```
---------- Encrypted Data --------
??????????????????????????????????????????????
---------- Encrypted Data --------

---------- Decrypted Data ---------
This is a test
This is sensitive data!
---------- Decrypted Data ---------
```

Discussion

Encrypting data is essential to many applications, especially those that store information in easily accessible locations. Once data is encrypted, a decryption scheme is required to restore the data back to an unencrypted form without losing any information.

The encryption schemes used in this recipe are TripleDES and Rijndael. The reasons for using Triple DES are:

- TripleDES employs symmetric encryption, meaning that a single private key is used to encrypt and decrypt data. This process allows much faster encryption and decryption, especially as the streams of data become larger.

- TripleDES encryption is much harder to crack than the older DES encryption and is widely considered to be of high strength.

- If you wish to use another type of encryption, you can easily convert this recipe using any provider derived from the `SymmetricAlgorithm` class.

- TripleDES is widely deployed in the industry today.

The main drawback to TripleDES is that both the sender and receiver must use the same key and initialization vector (IV) in order to encrypt and decrypt the data successfully. If you wish to have an even more secure encryption scheme, use the Rijndael scheme. This type of encryption scheme is highly regarded as a solid encryption scheme, since it is fast and can use larger key sizes than TripleDES. However, it is still a symmetric cryptosystem, which means that it relies on shared secrets. For a cryptosystem that uses shared public keys with private keys that are never shared between parties, use an asymmetric cryptosystem, such as RSA or DSA.

See Also

The "SymmetricAlgorithm Class," "TripleDESCryptoServiceProvider Class," and "RijndaelManaged Class" topics in the MSDN documentation.

11.3 Cleaning Up Cryptography Information

Problem

You will be using the cryptography classes in the FCL to encrypt and/or decrypt data. In doing so, you want to make sure that no data (e.g., seed values or keys) is left in memory for longer than you are using the cryptography classes. An attacker can sometimes find this information in memory and use it to break your encryption or, worse, to break your encryption, modify the data, and then re-encrypt the data, forcing your application to use tainted data rather than valid data.

Solution

To clear out the key and initialization vector (or seed), you need to call the Clear method on whichever SymmetricAlgorithm- or AsymmetricAlgorithm-derived class you are using. Clear reinitializes the Key and IV properties, preventing them from being found in memory. You call it after saving the key and IV so that you can decrypt later. Example 11-3 shows how to encrypt a string and then clean up immediately afterward to provide the smallest window possible for potential attackers.

Example 11-3. Cleaning up cryptography information

```
using System;
using System.Text;
using System.IO;
using System.Security.Cryptography;

public static void CleanUpCrypto()
{
    string originalStr = "SuperSecret information";
    // Encode data string to be stored in memory.
    byte[] originalStrAsBytes = Encoding.ASCII.GetBytes(originalStr);

    // Create MemoryStream to contain output.
    MemoryStream memStream = new MemoryStream(originalStrAsBytes.Length);
    RijndaelManaged rijndael = new RijndaelManaged();

    // Generate secret key and init vector.
    rijndael.KeySize = 256;
    rijndael.GenerateKey();
    rijndael.GenerateIV();
```

```
    // Save the key and IV for later decryption.
    byte [] key = rijndael.Key;
    byte [] IV = rijndael.IV;

    // Create encryptor and stream objects.
    ICryptoTransform transform = rijndael.CreateEncryptor(rijndael.Key,
        rijndael.IV);
    CryptoStream cryptoStream = new CryptoStream(memStream, transform,
        CryptoStreamMode.Write);

    // Write encrypted data to the MemoryStream.
    cryptoStream.Write(originalStrAsBytes, 0, originalStrAsBytes.Length);
    cryptoStream.FlushFinalBlock();

    // Release all resources as soon as we are done with them
    // to prevent retaining any information in memory.
    memStream.Close();
    cryptoStream.Close();
    transform.Dispose();
    // This clear statement regens both the key and the init vector so that
    // what is left in memory is no longer the values you used to encrypt with.
    rijndael.Clear();
}
```

You can also make your life a little easier by taking advantage of the using statement, instead of having to remember to manually call each of the Close methods individually. This code block shows how to use the using statement:

```
public static void CleanUpCryptoWithUsing()
{
    string originalStr = "SuperSecret information";
    // Encode data string to be stored in memory.
    byte[] originalStrAsBytes = Encoding.ASCII.GetBytes(originalStr);
    byte[] originalBytes = { };

    // Create MemoryStream to contain output.
    using (MemoryStream memStream = new MemoryStream(originalStrAsBytes.Length))
    {
        using (RijndaelManaged rijndael = new RijndaelManaged())
        {
            // Generate secret key and init vector.
            rijndael.KeySize = 256;
            rijndael.GenerateKey();
            rijndael.GenerateIV();

            // Save off the key and IV for later decryption.
            byte[] key = rijndael.Key;
            byte[] IV = rijndael.IV;

            // Create encryptor and stream objects.
            using (ICryptoTransform transform =
                    rijndael.CreateEncryptor(rijndael.Key, rijndael.IV))
```

```
        {
            using (CryptoStream cryptoStream = new
                    CryptoStream(memStream, transform,
                      CryptoStreamMode.Write))
            {
                // Write encrypted data to the MemoryStream.
                cryptoStream.Write(originalStrAsBytes, 0,
                        originalStrAsBytes.Length);
                cryptoStream.FlushFinalBlock();
            }
        }
    }
    }
}
```

Discussion

To make sure your data is safe, you need to close the `MemoryStream` and `Crypto Stream` objects as soon as possible, as well as calling `Dispose` on the `ICryptoTrans form` implementation to clear out any resources used in this encryption. The `using` statement makes this process much easier, makes your code easier to read, and leads to fewer programming mistakes.

See Also

The "SymmetricAlgorithm.Clear Method" and "AsymmetricAlgorithm.Clear Method" topics in the MSDN documentation.

11.4 Preventing String Tampering in Transit or at Rest

Problem

You need to send some text across a network to another machine for processing or perhaps place it in a storage medium for later retrieval. You need to verify that this text remains unmodified, untampered with, and uncorrupted.

Solution

Calculate a hash value from the string, digitally sign the hash value, and send both the string and its digital signature to the recipient (a public key will also be provided to the recipient). Once the destination receives this information, it can determine whether the string is the same one that was initially sent by verifying its digital signature, which cannot be forged or manipulated.

Before getting into the details of how this works, first we'll look at the code used to digitally sign some string data and, in turn, verify that this string has not changed using this same digital signature. In Example 11-4, the `AntiTamper` class contains two methods, `SignString` and `VerifySignedString`, which perform each of these duties. The `SignString` method takes a clear text string and generates a digital signature from it. The `VerifySignedString` method is used by the code that receives the string to determine if the string has been modified in any way prior to reception.

Example 11-4. The AntiTamper class

```
public class AntiTamper
{
    static private readonly int RSA_KEY_SIZE = 2048;


    public static byte[] SignString(string clearText, out string rsaPublicKey)
    {
        byte[] signature = null;
        rsaPublicKey = null;

        byte[] encodedClearText = Encoding.Unicode.GetBytes(clearText);

        using (SHA512CryptoServiceProvider sha512 =
                        new SHA512CryptoServiceProvider())
        {
            using (RSACryptoServiceProvider rsa =
                    new RSACryptoServiceProvider(RSA_KEY_SIZE))
            {
                signature = rsa.SignData(encodedClearText, sha512);

                rsaPublicKey = rsa.ToXmlString(false);
            }
        }

        return signature;
    }

    public static bool VerifySignedString(string clearText, byte[] signature,
                                    string rsaPublicKey)
    {
        bool verified = false;
        byte[] encodedClearText = Encoding.Unicode.GetBytes(clearText);

        using (SHA512CryptoServiceProvider sha512 =
                        new SHA512CryptoServiceProvider())
        {
            using (RSACryptoServiceProvider rsa =
                    new RSACryptoServiceProvider(RSA_KEY_SIZE))
            {
                rsa.FromXmlString(rsaPublicKey);

                verified = rsa.VerifyData(encodedClearText, sha512, signature);
```

```
            }
        }

        return verified;
    }
}
```

The `VerifyStringIntegrity` method shows how to use the `AntiTamper` class to sign and verify a string. The `VerifyStringIntegrity` method first calls the `SendData` method. This method encapsulates the code that would exist on the sender's side, but you will need to add code to actually send the complete message to the receiver. Before the message is sent, this method generates a digital signature from the string data that we want to protect from tampering. You generate the digital signature by calling the static `AntiTamper.SignString` method. This method returns a digital signature as a `byte[]` and the RSA public key information through an `out` parameter. The RSA public key information is required by the verification method, `ReceiveData`.

 It is important to understand that the receiver needs three things: the original string data, its digital signature, and the public key. The string data and signature can be sent together in the same message; however, the public key could be sent either along with the message or distributed through a separate channel. This separate channel could be one of several mechanisms: a signed and encrypted email message, a secure FTP server, an X.509 certificate signed by a trusted third-party authority, Simple Public Key Infrastructure (SPKI), or Pretty Good Privacy (PGP) used to sign and encrypt the public key to prove that it originated from the expected party.

Whatever mechanism you use to distribute the public key, it is critical that the recipient trusts that this key is indeed originating from the correct party.

The second method, `ReceiveData`, receives the string data, the generated digital signature, and the RSA public key information, which is used to verify the digital signature against the string data received. This method encapsulates the code that would exist on the receiver's side, but you will need to add code to actually receive the complete message from the sender. If the digital signature indeed proves that the string data has not been tampered with, a `Boolean` value of `true` is returned; otherwise, `false` is returned, indicating that the string data has been modified or tampered with:

```
public static void VerifyStringIntegrity()
{
    string originalString = "This is the string that we'll be testing.";

    // Create a hash value from the original string value we need to protect
    //    and sign the hash value
    string rsaPublicKey;
```

```
        byte[] signature = SendData(originalString, out rsaPublicKey);

        // Uncomment the code below to quickly test handling a tampered string:
        //     originalString += "a";
        // Uncomment the code below to quickly test handling a tampered signature:
        //     signature[1] = 100;

        // Now, verify that the string has not been corrupted, nor tampered with
        if (ReceiveData(originalString, signature, rsaPublicKey))
        {
            Console.WriteLine(
                "The original string was NOT corrupted or tampered with.");
        }
        else
        {
            Console.WriteLine(
                "ALERT:  The original string was corrupted and/or tampered with.");
        }
    }


    private static byte[] SendData(string originalString, out string rsaPublicKey)
    {
        // Digitally sign the string data
        byte[] signature = AntiTamper.SignString(originalString, out rsaPublicKey);

        // Send the data to its destination...

        return signature;
    }

    private static bool ReceiveData(string originalString, byte[] signature,
                                    string rsaPublicKey)
    {
        // Receive the data from the sender...

        // Verify the digital signature
        return (AntiTamper.VerifySignedString(originalString, signature,
            rsaPublicKey));
    }
```

The output of this method is shown here when the string is uncorrupted:

```
The original string was NOT corrupted or tampered with.
```

The output of this method is shown here when the string has been corrupted:

```
ALERT:  The original string was corrupted and/or tampered with.
```

To see this in action, simply uncomment one of the following two commented lines
in the VerifyStringIntegrity method:

```
// Uncomment the code below to quickly test handling a tampered string:
    originalString += "a";
```

or:

```
// Uncomment the code below to quickly test handling a tampered signature:
    signature[1] = 100;
```

Discussion

Hash values are useful in determining if data has been modified or corrupted at rest or in transit. A hash value—or even a checksum, or *cyclic redundancy check* (CRC) value—is first calculated from the data you are trying to protect. This hash value along with the data is then sent to the receiver. The receiver recalculates the hash value based on the data received. If the new hash value matches the hash value received, the data has not changed; otherwise, the data has been modified or corrupted at some point.

 It is critical that both sides agree on a hash algorithm that will be used. Either the SHA-256 or SHA-512 algorithm is a good secure choice as well as an industry standard.

While this hashing technique works well in flagging data that has become corrupted or has been modified accidentally, it cannot protect against an attacker surreptitiously modifying the data in an attempt to gain access to a system or plant false information in an attempt to blackmail or extort. If only a hash value is used to protect the data, an attacker can intercept the data (using a Man-in-the-Middle attack), modify the data, and then regenerate a new hash from the modified data. The old hash value is then replaced with the new one before the data is resent to the intended receiver. The intended receiver is none the wiser that the data has been tampered with; since, from the receiver's point of view, the hash the receiver generates is exactly the same as the one received. To prevent against these types of attacks, a more robust system is needed. This is where digital signatures come into play.

A digital signature is generated through an *asymmetric* public key cryptography algorithm. This means that there are two keys. The first key is a public key that can be distributed to all parties that will receive the signed data. This public key will be used to verify the digital signature of the received data. The second key is a private key that must remain securely in the hands of the party sending the data. The private key is used only to initially sign the data before it is sent to the receiver. The public and private keys work together, one to sign the data and the other to prove not only that the signature is from the intended sender, but also that the data signed with this signature has not been tampered with, modified, or corrupted.

If the private key is stolen, an attacker will be able to digitally sign data as if he were the legitimate sender of the data. Never send the private key to parties other than those required to have it, and never transmit or store it in plain text.

Here is how data is digitally signed by the sender. The `AntiTamper.SignString` method is called, and the data to be signed is passed into the first argument (`clear Text`) and a string variable (`rsaPublicKey`) is passed in as the second argument. The `rsaPublicKey` variable will eventually hold the public key information, which must be used to verify the signature later in the `AntiTamper.VerifySignedString` method:

```
public static byte[] SignString(string clearText, out string rsaPublicKey)
{
    byte[] signature = null;
    rsaPublicKey = null;

    byte[] encodedClearText = Encoding.Unicode.GetBytes(clearText);

    using (SHA512CryptoServiceProvider sha512 =
                        new SHA512CryptoServiceProvider())
    {
        using (RSACryptoServiceProvider rsa =
            new RSACryptoServiceProvider(RSA_KEY_SIZE))
        {
            signature = rsa.SignData(encodedClearText, sha512);

            rsaPublicKey = rsa.ToXmlString(false);
        }
    }

    return signature;
}
```

First the `SignString` method creates a `SHA512CryptoServiceProvider` object that will be used to create a hash that will be digitally signed. Note here that we are creating a SHA-512 hash value for the data that we need to protect. However, we are not actually signing the data we are protecting; rather, we are signing the SHA-512 hash value. This is important because asymmetric cryptography algorithms are inherently slow. If we signed the data we were protecting—and that data could be extremely large (e.g., megabytes or gigbaytes in size)—our signing process would slow down the system. By signing the much smaller hash value (in our case, 512 bytes), we don't have to worry about performance bottlenecks.

Next, an `RSACryptoServiceProvider` object is created that will be used to sign the data. The `RSACryptoServiceProvider.SignData` instance method accepts the clear text data to be signed in the form of a `byte[]` as well as our hashing algorithm

(SHA-512). These are used to generate a hash value, which in turn generates a digital signature. Only the digital signature is returned by this method.

There is one final very important step, which is to capture the public key information generated by this `RSACryptoServiceProvider` object. We do this by calling the `RSA CryptoServiceProvider.ToXmlString` instance method. This method returns the public key information necessary to verify the signature.

 When calling `ToXMLString`, pass in the `Boolean` value of `false` to return only the public key. If you pass in `true`, both the public and private key will be returned. As mentioned before, it is imperative that the private key is protected and not accidentally distributed.

Now all the sender has to do is send the data, the digital signature, and the public key information returned by the `AntiTamper.SignString` method to the intended recipient:

```
private static byte[] SendData(string originalString, out string rsaPublicKey)
{
    // Digitally sign the string data
    byte[] signature = AntiTamper.SignString(originalString, out rsaPublicKey);

    // Send the data and the signature to its destination...

    return signature;
}
```

The recipient then calls the `AntiTamper.VerifySignedString` method, passing in the received data, the digital signature, and the public key information. Note that the `AntiTamper` class will need to be referenced in both the sender's and receiver's code:

```
private static bool ReceiveData(string originalString, byte[] signature,
                                string rsaPublicKey)
{
    // Receive the data and signature from the sender...

    // Verify the digital signature
    return (AntiTamper.VerifySignedString(originalString, signature,
        rsaPublicKey));
}
```

The `VerifySignedString` method must use the same `SHA512CryptoServicePro vider` object that the sender used in the previous `SignString` method; otherwise, the signature will not be verified. An `RSACryptoServiceProvider` object is also created, but before this object is used to verify the signature, the `RSACryptoServicePro vider.FromXmlString` method is called to import the public key information needed to properly verify the signature. Finally, the `RSACryptoServiceProvider.VerifyData` method is called to verify the data along with its signature. This method returns a Boolean `true` if the string data was not tampered with or corrupted, and `false` otherwise:

```
public static bool VerifySignedString(string clearText, byte[] signature,
                                      string rsaPublicKey)
{
    bool verified = false;
    byte[] encodedClearText = Encoding.Unicode.GetBytes(clearText);

    using (SHA512CryptoServiceProvider sha512 =
                    new SHA512CryptoServiceProvider())
    {
        using (RSACryptoServiceProvider rsa =
                new RSACryptoServiceProvider(RSA_KEY_SIZE))
        {
            rsa.FromXmlString(rsaPublicKey);

            verified = rsa.VerifyData(encodedClearText, sha512, signature);
        }
    }

    return verified;
}
```

See Also

The "RSACryptoServiceProvider Class," "SHA512CryptoServiceProvider Class," and "Encoding.Unicode.GetBytes Method" topics in the MSDN documentation. For more on public keys, see the Wikipedia article "Public-key cryptography" (*http://bit.ly/1ixa8xt*).

11.5 Making a Security Assert Safe

Problem

You want to assert that at a particular point in the call stack, a given permission is available for all subsequent calls. However, doing this can easily open a security hole to allow other malicious code to spoof your code or to create a back door into your component. You want to assert a given security permission, but you want to do so in a secure and efficient manner.

Solution

To make this approach secure, you need to call `Demand` on the permissions that the subsequent calls need. This makes sure that code that doesn't have these permissions can't slip by due to the `Assert`. The `Demand` ensures that you have indeed been granted this permission before using the Assert to short-circuit the stackwalk. This is demonstrated by the function CallSecureFunctionSafelyAndEfficiently, which performs a Demand and an Assert before calling SecureFunction, which in turn does a Demand for a ReflectionPermission.

The code listing for CallSecureFunctionSafelyAndEfficiently is shown in Example 11-5.

Example 11-5. CallSecureFunctionSafelyAndEfficiently function

```
public static void CallSecureFunctionSafelyAndEfficiently()
{
    // Set up a permission to be able to access nonpublic members
    // via reflection.
    ReflectionPermission perm =
        new ReflectionPermission(ReflectionPermissionFlag.MemberAccess);

    // Demand the permission set we have compiled before using Assert
    // to make sure we have the right before we Assert it. We do
    // the Demand to ensure that we have checked for this permission
    // before using Assert to short-circuit stackwalking for it, which
    // helps us stay secure, while performing better.
    perm.Demand();

    // Assert this right before calling into the function that
    // would also perform the Demand to short-circuit the stack walk
    // each call would generate. The Assert helps us to optimize
    // our use of SecureFunction.
    perm.Assert();

    // We call the secure function 100 times but only generate
    // the stackwalk from the function to this calling function
    // instead of walking the whole stack 100 times.
    for(int i=0;i<100;i++)
    {
        SecureFunction();
    }
}
```

The code listing for SecureFunction is shown here:

```
    public static void SecureFunction()
    {
        // Set up a permission to be able to access nonpublic members
        // via reflection.
        ReflectionPermission perm =
            new ReflectionPermission(ReflectionPermissionFlag.MemberAccess);

        // Demand the right to do this and cause a stackwalk.
        perm.Demand();
```

```
    // Perform the action here...
}
```

Discussion

In the demonstration function `CallSecureFunctionSafelyAndEfficiently`, the function you are calling (`SecureFunction`) performs a `Demand` on a `ReflectionPermission` to ensure that the code can access nonpublic members of classes via reflection. Normally, this would result in a stackwalk for every call to `SecureFunction`. The `Demand` in `CallSecureFunctionSafelyAndEfficiently` is there only to protect against the usage of the `Assert` in the first place. To make this more efficient, you can use `Assert` to state that all functions issuing `Demand`s that are called from this one do not have to stackwalk any further. The `Assert` says stop checking for this permission in the call stack. In order to do this, you need the permission to call `Assert`.

The problem comes in with this `Assert`, as it opens up a potential luring attack where `SecureFunction` is called via `CallSecureFunctionSafelyAndEfficiently`, which calls `Assert` to stop the `Demand` stackwalks from `SecureFunction`. If unauthorized code without `ReflectionPermission` were able to call `CallSecureFunctionSafelyAndEfficiently`, the `Assert` would prevent the `SecureFunction` `Demand` call from determining that there is some code in the call stack without the proper rights. This is the power of the call stack checking in the CLR when a `Demand` occurs.

To protect against this, you issue a `Demand` for the `ReflectionPermission` needed by `SecureFunction` in `CallSecureFunctionSafelyAndEfficiently` to close this hole before issuing the `Assert`. The combination of this `Demand` and the `Assert` causes you to do one stackwalk instead of the original 100 that would have been caused by the `Demand` in `SecureFunction`.

Security optimization techniques, such as using `Assert` in this case (even though it isn't the primary reason to use `Assert`), can help class library and control developers who are trusted to perform `Assert`s in order to speed the interaction of their code with the CLR; but if used improperly, these techniques can also open up holes in the security picture. This example shows that you can have both performance and security where secure access is concerned.

If you are using `Assert`, be mindful that stackwalk overrides should never be made in a class constructor. Constructors are not guaranteed to have any particular security context, nor are they guaranteed to execute at a specific point in time. Thus, the call stack is not well defined, and `Assert` used in this context can produce unexpected results.

One other thing to remember with `Assert` is that you can have only one active `Assert` in a function at a given time. If you `Assert` the same permission twice, a

`SecurityException` is thrown by the CLR. You must revert the original `Assert` by first using `RevertAssert`. Then, you can declare the second `Assert`.

See Also

The "CodeAccessSecurity.Assert Method," "CodeAccessSecurity.Demand Method," "CodeAccessSecurity.RevertAssert Method," and "Overriding Security Checks" topics in the MSDN documentation.

11.6 Verifying That an Assembly Has Been Granted Specific Permissions

Problem

When your assembly requests optional permissions (such as asking for disk access to enable users to export data to disk as a product feature) using the `SecurityAction.RequestOptional` flag, it might or might not actually obtain those permissions. Regardless, your assembly will still load and execute. You need a way to verify whether your assembly actually obtained those permissions. This can help prevent many security exceptions from being thrown. For example, if you optionally requested read/write permissions on the registry but did not receive them, you could disable the user interface controls that are used to read and store application settings in the registry.

Solution

Check to see if your assembly received the optional permissions using the `PermissionSet.IsSubsetOf` method like this:

```
using System;
using System.Text.RegularExpressions;
using System.Web;
using System.Net;
using System.Security;

Regex regex = new Regex(@"http://www\.oreilly\.com/.*");
WebPermission webConnectPerm = new WebPermission(NetworkAccess. Connect,regex);

PermissionSet pSet = new PermissionSet(PermissionState.None);
pSet.AddPermission(webConnectPerm);
if (pSet.IsSubsetOf(Assembly.GetExecutingAssembly().PermissionSet))
{
    // Connect to the O'Reilly site.
}
```

This code sets up a `Regex` for the O'Reilly website and then uses it to create a `WebPer` `mission` for connecting to that site and all sites containing the string. You then check the `WebPermission` by creating a new `PermissionSet` object with no access to the protected resource (i.e., `PermissionState.None`), adding the `webConnectPerm` permission to this newly created `PermissionSet` object, and finally checking if this new `PermissionSet` object is a subset of the executing assembly's permission set.

Discussion

The `IsSubsetOf` method is a lightweight way of determining whether permission is granted for an assembly without first incurring the full stackwalk that a `Demand` gives you. Note, however, that once you exercise any code that performs a `Demand`, the full stackwalk will then take place.

One reason you might design an assembly to have optional permissions is for deployment in different customer scenarios. In some scenarios (such as desktop applications), it might be acceptable to have an assembly that can perform more robust actions (talk to a database, create network traffic, etc.). In other scenarios, you can defer these actions if the customer does not wish to grant enough permissions for these extra services to function.

See Also

The "WebPermission Class," "SecurityManager Class," and "IsGranted Method" topics in the MSDN documentation.

11.7 Minimizing the Attack Surface of an Assembly

Problem

Someone attacking your assembly will first attempt to find out as many things as possible about your assembly and then use this information in constructing the attack(s). The more surface area you give to attackers, the more they have to work with. You need to minimize what your assembly is allowed to do so that if an attacker is successful in taking it over, the attacker will not have the necessary privileges to do any damage to the system.

Solution

Use the `SecurityAction.RequestRefuse` enumeration member to indicate, at an assembly level, the permissions that you do not wish this assembly to have. This will force the CLR to refuse these permissions to your code and will ensure that, even if another part of the system is compromised, your code cannot be used to perform functions that it does not need the rights to do.

The following example allows the assembly to perform file I/O as part of its minimal permission set but explicitly refuses to allow this assembly to have permissions to skip verification:

```
[assembly: FileIOPermission(SecurityAction.RequestMinimum,Unrestricted=true)]
[assembly: SecurityPermission(SecurityAction.RequestRefuse,
            SkipVerification=false)]
```

Discussion

Once you have determined what permissions your assembly needs as part of your normal security testing, you can use `RequestRefuse` to lock down your code. If this seems extreme, think of scenarios in which your code could be accessing a data store containing sensitive information, such as Social Security numbers or salary information. This proactive step can help you show your customers that you take security seriously and can help defend your interests in case a break-in occurs on a system containing your code.

One serious consideration with this approach is that the use of `RequestRefuse` marks your assembly as partially trusted. This in turn prevents it from calling any strong-named assembly that hasn't been marked with the `AllowPartiallyTrustedCallers` attribute.

See Also

The "Using Libraries from Partially Trusted Code," "SecurityAction Enumeration," and "Global Attributes" topics in the MSDN documentation.

11.8 Obtaining Security and/or Audit Information

Problem

You need to obtain the security rights and/or audit information for a file or registry key.

Solution

When obtaining security and/or audit information for a file, use the static `GetAccess Control` method of the `File` class to obtain a `System.Security.AccessControl.Fil eSecurity` object. Use the `FileSecurity` object to access the security and audit information for the file. These steps are demonstrated in Example 11-6.

Example 11-6. Obtaining security audit information

```csharp
public static void ViewFileRights()
{
    // Get security information from a file.
    string file = @"C:\Windows\win.ini";
    FileSecurity fileSec = File.GetAccessControl(file);
    DisplayFileSecurityInfo(fileSec);
}

public static void DisplayFileSecurityInfo(FileSecurity fileSec)
{
    Console.WriteLine($"GetSecurityDescriptorSddlForm:
            {fileSec.GetSecurityDescriptorSddlForm(AccessControlSections.All)}");

    foreach (FileSystemAccessRule ace in
            fileSec.GetAccessRules(true, true, typeof(NTAccount)))
    {
        Console.WriteLine("\tIdentityReference.Value:
                        {ace.IdentityReference.Value}");
        Console.WriteLine($"\tAccessControlType: {ace.AccessControlType}");
        Console.WriteLine($"\tFileSystemRights: {ace.FileSystemRights}");
        Console.WriteLine($"\tInheritanceFlags: {ace.InheritanceFlags}");
        Console.WriteLine($"\tIsInherited: {ace.IsInherited}");
        Console.WriteLine($"\tPropagationFlags: {ace.PropagationFlags}");

        Console.WriteLine("----------------\r\n\r\n");
    }

    foreach (FileSystemAuditRule ace in
            fileSec.GetAuditRules(true, true, typeof(NTAccount)))
    {
        Console.WriteLine("\tIdentityReference.Value:
                        {ace.IdentityReference.Value}");
        Console.WriteLine($"\tAuditFlags: {ace.AuditFlags}");
        Console.WriteLine($"\tFileSystemRights: {ace.FileSystemRights}");
        Console.WriteLine($"\tInheritanceFlags: {ace.InheritanceFlags}");
        Console.WriteLine($"\tIsInherited: {ace.IsInherited}");
        Console.WriteLine($"\tPropagationFlags: {ace.PropagationFlags}");

        Console.WriteLine("----------------\r\n\r\n");
    }

    Console.WriteLine($"GetGroup(typeof(NTAccount)).Value:
                    {fileSec.GetGroup(typeof(NTAccount)).Value}");
    Console.WriteLine($"GetOwner(typeof(NTAccount)).Value:
                    {fileSec.GetOwner(typeof(NTAccount)).Value}");

    Console.WriteLine("-------------------------------------\r\n\r\n\r\n");
}
```

These methods produce the following output:

```
GetSecurityDescriptorSddlForm:  O:SYG:SYD:AI(A;ID;FA;;;SY)(A;ID;FA;;;BA)
                    (A;ID;0x1200a9;;;BU)(A;ID;0x1200a9;;;AC)
        IdentityReference.Value: NT AUTHORITY\SYSTEM
        AccessControlType: Allow
        FileSystemRights: FullControl
        InheritanceFlags: None
        IsInherited: True
        PropagationFlags: None
----------------


        IdentityReference.Value: BUILTIN\Administrators
        AccessControlType: Allow
        FileSystemRights: FullControl
        InheritanceFlags: None
        IsInherited: True
        PropagationFlags: None
----------------


        IdentityReference.Value: BUILTIN\Users
        AccessControlType: Allow
        FileSystemRights: ReadAndExecute, Synchronize
        InheritanceFlags: None
        IsInherited: True
        PropagationFlags: None
----------------


        IdentityReference.Value:
                    APPLICATION PACKAGE AUTHORITY\ALL APPLICATION PACKAGES
        AccessControlType: Allow
        FileSystemRights: ReadAndExecute, Synchronize
        InheritanceFlags: None
        IsInherited: True
        PropagationFlags: None
----------------


    GetGroup(typeof(NTAccount)).Value: NT AUTHORITY\SYSTEM
    GetOwner(typeof(NTAccount)).Value: NT AUTHORITY\SYSTEM
```

When obtaining security and/or audit information for a registry key, use the `GetAc`
`cessControl` instance method of the `Microsoft.Win32.RegistryKey` class to obtain a
`System.Security.AccessControl.RegistrySecurity` object. Use the `RegistrySe`
`curity` object to access the security and audit information for the registry key. These
steps are demonstrated in Example 11-7.

Example 11-7. Getting security or audit information for a registry key

```csharp
public static void ViewRegKeyRights()
{
    // Get security information from a registry key.
    using (RegistryKey regKey =
        Registry.CurrentUser.OpenSubKey(@"Software\Microsoft\VisualStudio\14.0"))
    {
        RegistrySecurity regSecurity = regKey.GetAccessControl();
        DisplayRegKeySecurityInfo(regSecurity);
    }
}

public static void DisplayRegKeySecurityInfo(RegistrySecurity regSec)
{
    Console.WriteLine($"GetSecurityDescriptorSddlForm:
            {fileSec.GetSecurityDescriptorSddlForm(AccessControlSections.All)}");

    foreach (RegistryAccessRule ace in
            regSec.GetAccessRules(true, true, typeof(NTAccount)))
    {
        Console.WriteLine("\tIdentityReference.Value:
                        {ace.IdentityReference.Value}");
        Console.WriteLine($"\tAccessControlType: {ace.AccessControlType}");
        Console.WriteLine($"\tFileSystemRights: {ace.FileSystemRights}");
        Console.WriteLine($"\tInheritanceFlags: {ace.InheritanceFlags}");
        Console.WriteLine($"\tIsInherited: {ace.IsInherited}");
        Console.WriteLine($"\tPropagationFlags: {ace.PropagationFlags}");

        Console.WriteLine("----------------\r\n\r\n");
    }

    foreach (RegistryAuditRule ace in
            regSec.GetAuditRules(true, true, typeof(NTAccount)))
    {
        Console.WriteLine("\tIdentityReference.Value:
                        {ace.IdentityReference.Value}");
        Console.WriteLine($"\tAuditFlags: {ace.AuditFlags}");
        Console.WriteLine($"\tFileSystemRights: {ace.FileSystemRights}");
        Console.WriteLine($"\tInheritanceFlags: {ace.InheritanceFlags}");
        Console.WriteLine($"\tIsInherited: {ace.IsInherited}");
        Console.WriteLine($"\tPropagationFlags: {ace.PropagationFlags}");

        Console.WriteLine("----------------\r\n\r\n");
    }
    Console.WriteLine($"GetGroup(typeof(NTAccount)).Value:
                    {fileSec.GetGroup(typeof(NTAccount)).Value}");
    Console.WriteLine($"GetOwner(typeof(NTAccount)).Value:
                    {fileSec.GetOwner(typeof(NTAccount)).Value}");

    Console.WriteLine("-------------------------------------\r\n\r\n\r\n");
}
```

These methods produce the following output:

```
GetSecurityDescriptorSddlForm:  O:S-1-5-21-3613598369-3284219489-1294304910-1001G:
        S-1-5-21-3613598369-3284219489-1294304910-1001D:
        (A;OICIID;KA;;;S-1-5-21-3613598369-3284219489-1294304910-1001)
        (A;OICIID;KA;;;SY)(A;OICIID;KA;;;BA)(A;OICIID;KR;;;RC)
    IdentityReference.Value: VM_Win81_VS14\Teilhet
    AccessControlType: Allow
    RegistryRights: FullControl
    InheritanceFlags: ContainerInherit, ObjectInherit
    IsInherited: True
    PropagationFlags: None
-----------------


    IdentityReference.Value: NT AUTHORITY\SYSTEM
    AccessControlType: Allow
    RegistryRights: FullControl
    InheritanceFlags: ContainerInherit, ObjectInherit
    IsInherited: True
    PropagationFlags: None
-----------------


    IdentityReference.Value: BUILTIN\Administrators
    AccessControlType: Allow
    RegistryRights: FullControl
    InheritanceFlags: ContainerInherit, ObjectInherit
    IsInherited: True
    PropagationFlags: None
-----------------


    IdentityReference.Value: NT AUTHORITY\RESTRICTED
    AccessControlType: Allow
    RegistryRights: ReadKey
    InheritanceFlags: ContainerInherit, ObjectInherit
    IsInherited: True
    PropagationFlags: None
-----------------


GetGroup(typeof(NTAccount)).Value: VM_WIN81_VS14\Teilhet
GetOwner(typeof(NTAccount)).Value: VM_WIN81_VS14\Teilhet
```

Discussion

The essential method that is used to obtain the security information for a file or registry key is GetAccessControl. When this method is called on the RegistryKey object, a RegistrySecurity object is returned. However, when this method is called on a File class, a FileSecurity object is returned. The RegistrySecurity and FileSecur ity objects essentially represent a Discretionary Access Control List (DACL), which is what developers writing code in unmanaged languages such as C++ are used to working with.

The `RegistrySecurity` and `FileSecurity` objects each contain a list of security rules that has been applied to the system object that it represents. The `RegistrySecurity` object contains a list of `RegistryAccessRule` objects, and the `FileSecurity` object contains a list of `FileSystemAccessRule` objects. These rule objects are the equivalent of the Access Control Entries (ACE) that make up the list of security rules within a DACL.

System objects other than just the `File` class and `RegistryKey` object allow security privileges to be queried. Table 11-1 lists all the .NET Framework classes that return a security object type and what that type is. In addition, the rule-object type that is contained in the security object is also listed.

Table 11-1. List of all *Security and *AccessRule objects and the types to which they apply

Class	Object returned by the GetAccessControl method	Rule-object type contained within the security object
Directory	DirectorySecurity	FileSystemAccessRule
DirectoryInfo	DirectorySecurity	FileSystemAccessRule
EventWaitHandle	EventWaitHandleSecurity	EventWaitHandleAccessRule
File	FileSecurity	FileSystemAccessRule
FileInfo	FileSecurity	FileSystemAccessRule
FileStream	FileSecurity	FileSystemAccessRule
Mutex	MutexSecurity	MutexAccessRule
RegistryKey	RegistrySecurity	RegistryAccessRule
Semaphore	SemaphoreSecurity	SemaphoreAccessRule

The abstraction of a system object's DACL through the `*Security` objects and the abstraction of a DACL's ACE through the `*AccessRule` objects allows easy access to the security privileges of that system object. In previous versions of the .NET Framework, these DACLs and their ACEs would have been accessible only in unmanaged code. With the .NET 2.0 Framework and later, you now have access to view and program these objects.

See Also

Recipe 11.9; the "System.IO.File.GetAccessControl Method," "System.Security. AccessControl.FileSecurity Class," "Microsoft.Win32.RegistryKey.GetAccessControl Method," and "System.Security.AccessControl.RegistrySecurity Class" topics in the MSDN documentation.

11.9 Granting or Revoking Access to a File or Registry Key

Problem

You need to change the security privileges of either a file or registry key programmatically.

Solution

The code shown in Example 11-8 grants and then revokes the ability to perform write actions on a registry key.

Example 11-8. Granting and revoking the right to perform write actions on a registry key

```
public static void GrantRevokeRegKeyRights()
{
    NTAccount user = new NTAccount(@"WRKSTN\ST");

    using (RegistryKey regKey = Registry.LocalMachine.OpenSubKey(
                        @"SOFTWARE\MyCompany\MyApp"))
    {
        GrantRegKeyRights(regKey, user, RegistryRights.WriteKey,
                    InheritanceFlags.None, PropagationFlags.None,
                    AccessControlType.Allow);

        RevokeRegKeyRights(regKey, user, RegistryRights.WriteKey,
                    InheritanceFlags.None, PropagationFlags.None,
                    AccessControlType.Allow)
    }
}

public static void GrantRegKeyRights(RegistryKey regKey,
                            NTAccount user,
                            RegistryRights rightsFlags,
                            InheritanceFlags inherFlags,
                            PropagationFlags propFlags,
                            AccessControlType actFlags)
{
    RegistrySecurity regSecurity = regKey.GetAccessControl();

    RegistryAccessRule rule = new RegistryAccessRule(user, rightsFlags, inherFlags,
                                            propFlags, actFlags);
    regSecurity.AddAccessRule(rule);
    regKey.SetAccessControl(regSecurity);
}
```

```
public static void RevokeRegKeyRights(RegistryKey regKey,
                                      NTAccount user,
                                      RegistryRights rightsFlags,
                                      InheritanceFlags inherFlags,
                                      PropagationFlags propFlags,
                                      AccessControlType actFlags)
{
    RegistrySecurity regSecurity = regKey.GetAccessControl();

    RegistryAccessRule rule = new RegistryAccessRule(user, rightsFlags, inherFlags,
                                                     propFlags, actFlags);
    regSecurity.RemoveAccessRuleSpecific(rule);

    regKey.SetAccessControl(regSecurity);
}
```

The code shown in Example 11-9 grants and then revokes the ability to delete a file.

Example 11-9. Granting and revoking the right to delete a file

```
public static void GrantRevokeFileRights()
{
    NTAccount user = new NTAccount(@"WRKSTN\ST");

    string file = @"c:\FOO.TXT";
    GrantFileRights(file, user, FileSystemRights.Delete, InheritanceFlags.None,
                    PropagationFlags.None, AccessControlType.Allow);

    RevokeFileRights(file, user, FileSystemRights.Delete, InheritanceFlags.None,
                     PropagationFlags.None, AccessControlType.Allow);
}

public static void GrantFileRights(string file,
                                   NTAccount user,
                                   FileSystemRights rightsFlags,
                                   InheritanceFlags inherFlags,
                                   PropagationFlags propFlags,
                                   AccessControlType actFlags)
{
    FileSecurity fileSecurity = File.GetAccessControl(file);
    FileSystemAccessRule rule = new FileSystem AccessRule(user, rightsFlags,
                                                          inherFlags, propFlags,
                                                          actFlags);
    fileSecurity.AddAccessRule(rule);
    File.SetAccessControl(file, fileSecurity);
}

public static void RevokeFileRights(string file,
                                    NTAccount user,
                                    FileSystemRights rightsFlags,
                                    InheritanceFlags inherFlags,
                                    PropagationFlags propFlags,
```

```
                         AccessControlType actFlags)
{
    FileSecurity fileSecurity = File.GetAccessControl(file);

    FileSystemAccessRule rule = new FileSystemAccessRule(user, rightsFlags,
                                                 inherFlags, propFlags,
                                                 actFlags);
    fileSecurity.RemoveAccessRuleSpecific(rule);
    File.SetAccessControl(file, fileSecurity);
}
```

Discussion

When granting or revoking access rights on a file or registry key, you need two
things. The first is a valid NTAccount object. This object essentially encapsulates a user
or group account, and is required to create either a new RegistryAccessRule or a
new FileSystemAccessRule. The NTAccount identifies the user or group this access
rule will apply to. Note that the string passed in to the NTAccount constructor must be
changed to a valid user or group name that exists on your machine. If you pass in the
name of an existing user or group account that has been disabled, an IdentityNotMap
pedException will be thrown with the message "Some or all identity references could
not be translated."

The second item you need is either a valid RegistryKey object, if you are modifying
security access to a registry key, or a string containing a valid path and filename to an
existing file. These objects will have security permissions either granted to them or
revoked from them.

Once these two items have been obtained, you can use the second item to obtain a
security object, which contains the list of access-rule objects. For example, the following code obtains the security object for the registry key HKEY-LOCAL_MACHINE\SOFT
WARE\MyCompany\MyApp:

```
RegistryKey regKey = Registry.LocalMachine.OpenSubKey(
                         @"SOFTWARE\MyCompany\MyApp");
RegistrySecurity regSecurity = regKey.GetAccessControl();
```

The following code obtains the security object for the *FOO.TXT* file:

```
string file = @"c:\FOO.TXT";
FileSecurity fileSecurity = File.Get AccessControl(file);
```

Now that you have your particular security object, you can create an access-rule
object that will be added to it. To do this, you need to create a new access rule. For a
registry key, you have to create a new RegistryAccessRule object, and for a file, you
have to create a new FileSystemAccessRule object. To add this access rule to the correct security object, you call the SetAccessControl method on the security object.
Note that RegistryAccessRule objects can be added only to RegistrySecurity

objects, and `FileSystemAccessRule` objects can be added only to `FileSecurity` objects.

To remove an access-rule object from a system object, you follow the same set of steps, except that you call the `RemoveAccessRuleSpecific` method instead of `AddAccessRule`. `RemoveAccessRuleSpecific` accepts an access-rule object and attempts to remove the rule that exactly matches this rule object from the security object. As always, you must remember to call the `SetAccessControl` method to apply any changes to the actual system object.

For a list of other classes that allow security permissions to be modified programmatically, see Recipe 11.8.

See Also

Recipe 11.8; the "System.IO.File.GetAccessControl Method," "System.Security.AccessControl.FileSecurity Class," "System.Security.AccessControl.FileSystemAccessRule Class," "Microsoft.Win32.RegistryKey.GetAccessControl Method," "System.Security.AccessControl.RegistrySecurity Class," and "System.Security.AccessControl.RegistryAccessRule Class" topics in the MSDN documentation.

11.10 Protecting String Data with Secure Strings

Problem

You need to store sensitive information, such as a Social Security number, in a string. However, you do not want prying eyes to be able to view this data in memory.

Solution

Use the `SecureString` object.

To copy text from a stream object to a `SecureString` object, use the following method:

```
public static SecureString CreateSecureString(StreamReader secretStream)
{
    SecureString secretStr = new SecureString();
    char buf;
    while (secretStream.Peek() >= 0)
    {
        buf = (char)secretStream.Read();
        secretStr.AppendChar(buf);
    }

    // Make the secretStr object read-only.
    secretStr.MakeReadOnly();
```

```
        return (secretStr);
    }
```

To copy text from a string containing sensitive data, use the following method:

```
    public static SecureString CreateSecureString(string secret)
    {
        SecureString secretStr = new SecureString();
        char[] buf = new char[1];
        foreach (char c in secret)
        {
            secretStr.AppendChar(c);
        }

        // Make the secretStr object read-only
        secretStr.MakeReadOnly();

        return (secretStr);
    }
```

To pull the plain text out of a `SecureString` object, use the following method:

```
    public static void ReadSecureString(SecureString secretStr)
    {
        // In order to read back the string, you need to use some special methods.
        IntPtr secretStrPtr = Marshal.SecureStringToBSTR(secretStr);
        string nonSecureStr = Marshal.PtrToStringBSTR(secretStrPtr);

        // Use the unprotected string.
        Console.WriteLine($"nonSecureStr = {nonSecureStr}");

        Marshal.ZeroFreeBSTR(secretStrPtr);

        if (!secretStr.IsReadOnly())
        {
            secretStr.Clear();
        }
    }
```

Discussion

A `SecureString` object is designed specifically to contain string data that you want to keep secret. Some of the data you may want to store in a `SecureString` object would be a Social Security number, a credit card number, a PIN, a password, an employee ID, or any other type of sensitive information.

This string data is automatically encrypted immediately upon being added to the `SecureString` object, and it is automatically decrypted when the string data is extracted from the `SecureString` object. The encryption is one of the highlights of using this object.

Another feature of a SecureString object is that when the MakeReadOnly method is called, the SecureString becomes immutable. Any attempt to modify the string data within the read-only SecureString object causes an InvalidOperationException to be thrown. Once a SecureString object is made read-only, it cannot go back to a read/write state. However, you need to be careful when calling the Copy method on an existing SecureString object. This method will create a new instance of the Secure String object on which it was called, with a copy of its data. However, this new SecureString object is now readable and writable. You should review your code to determine if this new SecureString object should be made read-only similarly to its original SecureString object.

 The SecureString object can be used only on Windows 2000 (with Service Pack 3 or greater) or later operating system.

In this recipe, you create a SecureString object from data read in from a stream or a simple string. This data could also come from a char* using unsafe code. The Secure String object contains a constructor that accepts a parameter of this type in addition to an integer parameter that takes a length value, which determines the number of characters to pull from the char*.

Getting data out of a SecureString object is not obvious at first glance. There are no methods to return the data contained within a SecureString object. To accomplish this, you must use two static methods on the Marshal class. The first is the Secure StringToBSTR, which accepts your SecureString object and returns an IntPtr. This IntPtr is then passed into the PtrToStringBSTR method, also on the Marshal class. The PtrToStringBSTR method then returns an unsecure String object containing your decrypted string data.

Once you are done using the SecureString object, you should call the static Zero FreeBSTR method on the Marshal class to zero out any memory allocated when extracting the data from the SecureString. As an added safeguard, you should call the Clear method of the SecureString object to zero out the encrypted string from memory. If you have made your SecureString object read-only, you will not be able to call the Clear method to wipe out its data. In this situation, you must either call the Dispose method on the SecureString object (the use of a using block would be preferable here) or rely on the garbage collector to remove the SecureString object and its data from memory.

Notice that when you pull a SecureString object into an unsecure String, its data becomes viewable by an attacker. So it may seem pointless to go through the trouble of using a `SecureString` when you are just going to convert it into an insecure `String`. However, by using a `SecureString`, you narrow the window of opportunity for an attacker to view this data in memory. In addition, some APIs only accept a `SecureString` as a parameter so that you don't have to convert it to an unsecure `String`. The `ProcessStartInfo`, for example, accepts a password in its `Password` property as a `SecureString` object.

 The `SecureString` object is not a silver bullet for securing your data. It is, however, another layer of defense you can add to your application.

See Also

The "Secure String Class" topic in the MSDN documentation.

11.11 Securing Stream Data

Problem

You want to use the TCP server in Recipe 9.9 to communicate with the TCP client in Recipe 9.10. However, you need to encrypt the communication and verify that it has not been tampered with in transit.

Solution

Replace the `NetworkStream` class with the more secure `SslStream` class on both the client and the server. The code for the more secure TCP client, `TCPClient_SSL`, is shown in Example 11-10 (changes are in boldface).

Example 11-10. TCPClient_SSL class

```
class TCPClient_SSL
{
    private TcpClient _client = null;
    private IPAddress _address = IPAddress.Parse("127.0.0.1");
    private int _port = 5;
    private IPEndPoint _endPoint = null;

    public TCPClient_SSL(string address, string port)
    {
        _address = IPAddress.Parse(address);
        _port = Convert.ToInt32(port);
        _endPoint = new IPEndPoint(_address, _port);
    }
```

```
public void ConnectToServer(string msg)
{
    try
    {
        using (client = new TcpClient())
        {
            client.Connect(_endPoint);

            using(SslStreamsslStream = newSslStream(_client.GetStream(), false,
                new RemoteCertificateValidationCallback
                        (CertificateValidationCallback)))
            {
                sslStream.AuthenticateAsClient("MyTestCert2");

                // Get the bytes to send for the message.
                byte[] bytes = Encoding.ASCII.GetBytes(msg);
                // Send message.
                Console.WriteLine($"Sending message to server: { msg}");
                sslStream.Write(bytes, 0, bytes.Length);

                // Get the response.
                // Buffer to store the response bytes.
                bytes = new byte[1024];

                // Display the response.
                int bytesRead = sslStream.Read(bytes, 0, bytes.Length);
                string serverResponse = Encoding.ASCII.GetString(bytes, 0,
                    bytesRead);
                Console.WriteLine($"Server said: { serverResponse}");
            }
        }
    }
    catch (SocketException e)
    {
        Console.WriteLine
                ($"There was an error talking to the server: {e.ToString()}");
    }
}

private bool CertificateValidationCallback(objectsender,
            X509Certificate certificate, X509Chain chain,
            SslPolicyErrors sslPolicyErrors)
{
    if (sslPolicyErrors == SslPolicyErrors.None)
    {
        return true;
    }
    else
    {
        if (sslPolicyErrors == SslPolicyErrors.RemoteCertificateChainErrors)
        {
```

```
                        Console.WriteLine("The X509Chain.ChainStatus returned an array " +
                                "of X509ChainStatus objects containing error information.");
                }
                else if (sslPolicyErrors ==
                            SslPolicyErrors.RemoteCertificateNameMismatch)
                {
                    Console.WriteLine(
                                "There was a mismatch of the name on a certificate.");
                }
                else if (sslPolicyErrors ==
                            SslPolicyErrors.RemoteCertificateNotAvailable)
                {
                    Console.WriteLine("No certificate was available.");
                }
                else
                {
                    Console.WriteLine("SSL Certificate Validation Error!");
                }
            }
            Console.WriteLine(Environment.NewLine +
                            "SSL Certificate Validation Error!");
            Console.WriteLine(sslPolicyErrors.ToString());

            return false;
        }
}
```

The new code for the more secure TCP server, TCPServer_SSL, is shown in
Example 11-11 (changes are in boldface).

Example 11-11. TCPServer_SSL class

```
class TCPServer_SSL
{
    private TcpListener _listener = null;
    private IPAddress _address = IPAddress.Parse("127.0.0.1");
    private int _port = 55555;

    #region CTORs
    public TCPServer_SSL()
    {
    }

    public TCPServer_SSL (string address, string port)
    {
        _port = Convert.ToInt32(port);
        _address = IPAddress.Parse(address);
    }
    #endregion // CTORs

    #region Properties
```

```csharp
public IPAddress Address
{
    get { return _address; }
    set { _address = value; }
}

public int Port
{
    get { return _port; }
    set { _port = value; }
}
#endregion

public void Listen()
{
    try
    {
      _using_(listener = new TcpListener(_address, _port))
        {
            // Fire up the server.
            listener.Start();

            // Enter the listening loop.
            while (true)
            {
                Console.Write("Looking for someone to talk to... ");

                // Wait for connection.
                TcpClient newClient = _listener.AcceptTcpClient();
                Console.WriteLine("Connected to new client");

                // Spin a thread to take care of the client.
                ThreadPool.QueueUserWorkItem(new WaitCallback(ProcessClient),
                                         newClient);
            }
        }
    }
    catch (SocketException e)
    {
        Console.WriteLine($"SocketException: {e}");
    }
    finally
    {
        // Shut it down.
        _listener.Stop();
    }

    Console.WriteLine("Hit any key (where is ANYKEY?) to continue...");
    Console.Read();
}

private void ProcessClient(object client)
```

```
{
    using (TcpClient newClient = (TcpClient)client)
    {
        // Buffer for reading data.
        byte[] bytes = new byte[1024];
        string clientData = null;

        using (Ssl Stream sslStream = new SslStream(newClient.GetStream()))
        {
            sslStream.AuthenticateAsServer(GetServerCert("MyTestCert2"), false,
                                           SslProtocols.Default, true);

            // Loop to receive all the data sent by the client.
            int bytesRead = 0;
            while ((bytesRead = sslStream.Read(bytes, 0, bytes.Length)) != 0)
            {
                // Translate data bytes to an ASCII string.
                clientData = Encoding.ASCII.GetString(bytes, 0, bytesRead);
                Console.WriteLine($"Client says: {clientData}");
                // Thank them for their input.
                bytes = Encoding.ASCII.GetBytes("Thanks call again!");

                // Send back a response.
                ssl Stream.Write(bytes, 0, bytes.Length);
            }
        }
    }
}

private static X509Certificate GetServerCert(string subjectName)
{
    X509Store store = new X509Store(StoreName.My, StoreLocation.LocalMachine);
    store.Open(OpenFlags.ReadOnly);
    X509CertificateCollection certificate =
            store.Certificates.Find(X509FindType.FindBySubjectName,
                                    subjectName, true);
    if (certificate.Count > 0)
        return (certificate[0]);
    else
        return (null);
}
}
```

Discussion

For more information about the inner workings of the TCP server and client and
how to run these applications, see Recipes 9.9 and 9.10. In this recipe, we will cover
only the changes needed to convert the TCP server and client to use the SslStream
object for secure communication.

The SslStream object uses the SSL protocol to provide a secure encrypted channel on which to send data. However, encryption is just one of the security features built into the SslStream object. Another feature of SslStream is that it detects malicious or even accidental modification to the data. Even though the data is encrypted, it may become modified during transit. To determine if this has occurred, the data is signed with a hash before it is sent; when it is received, the data is rehashed and the two hashes are compared. If both hashes are equivalent, the message arrived intact; if the hashes are not equivalent, then somehow the data was modified during transit.

The SslStream object also has the ability to use client and/or server certificates to authenticate the client and/or the server as well as allowing the client to pass a certificate to the server if the client also needs to prove identity to the server. These certificates are used to prove the identity of the issuer. For example, if a client attaches to a server using SSL, the server must provide a certificate to the client to prove that the server is who it says it is. This certificate must be issued by a trusted authority. All trusted certificates are stored on the client in its root certificate store.

To ensure that the TCP server and client can communicate successfully, you need to set up an X.509 certificate that will be used to authenticate the TCP server. To do this, you set up a test certificate using the *makecert.exe* utility. This utility is installed with Visual Studio and must be run from the Admin Visual Studio Command Prompt. The syntax for creating a simple certificate is as follows:

```
makecert -r -pe -n "CN=CSharpCookBook.net" -a sha512 -len 4096
         -cy authority -sv CSCBNet.pvk CSCBNet.cer
```

The options are defined as follows:

-r
   The certificate will be self-signed. Self-signed certificates are often created and signed by the developer of a website to facilitate testing of that site before it is moved into production. Self-signed certificates offer no evidence that the site is legitimate.

-pe
   The certificate's private key will be exportable so that it can be included in the certificate.

-n "CN=CSharpCookBook.net"
   The publisher's certificate name. The name follows the "CN=" text.

-a sha512
   The algorithm used to create the digital signature. sha512 is the strongest available.

-len 4096
   The number of bits in the length of the key.

`-cy authority`
> The type of this certificate. The type can either be end (end entity) or authority (cert authority).

`-sv CSCBNet.pvk`
> The name of the private key file that will be generated for the subject.

The final argument to the *makecert.exe* utility is the output filename, in this case *CSCBNet.cer*. This will generate the certificate in this file in the current working directory on the hard drive. Additionally, a second file is generated called *CSCBNet.pvk*. This is the private key file. Both the private key file and the certificate file need to be converted to a *personal information exchange (.pfx)* file. You accomplish this by running the *Pvk2Pfx.exe* tool from the Admin Visual Studio Command Prompt as follows:

```
pvk2pfx.exe -pvk CSCBNet.pvk -spc CSCBNet.cer -pfx CSCBNet.pfx -po CSCB
```

The options are defined as follows:

`-pvk`
> The name of the private key file.

`-spc`
> The name of the certificate file.

`-pfx`
> The name of the generated personal information exchange file.

`-po`
> The new password for the generated personal information exchange file.

The next step is opening Windows Explorer and right-clicking the *CSCBNet.cer* file. This will display a pop-up menu. Click the Install Certificate menu item, and a wizard will start up, allowing you to import this *.cer* file into the certificate store. The first dialog box of the wizard is shown in Figure 11-1. Click Next.

Figure 11-1. The first step of the Certificate Import wizard

The next step in the wizard allows you to choose the certificate store in which you want to install your certificate. This dialog is shown in Figure 11-2. Keep the defaults and click Next.

The final step in the wizard is shown in Figure 11-3. On this dialog, click Finish.

After you click Finish, you'll see the message box in Figure 11-4, indicating that the import was successful.

Once the certificate file is successfully imported, you need to import the *.pfx* file using the Certificate Import wizard. Right-click the *CSCBNet.pfx* file. A pop-up menu is displayed. Click the Install PFX menu item and the wizard will start. The first dialog box of the wizard is shown in Figure 11-5. Keep the default settings and click Next.

Figure 11-2. Specifying a certificate store in the Certificate Import wizard

The next step in this wizard, shown in Figure 11-6, asks you to choose a *.pfx* file to import. Browse to the file using the Browse button and then click Next.

The next step, shown in Figure 11-7, asks for the password used to create this *.pfx* file. Note that this password was the one we used in the *Pvk2Pfx.exe* command-line tool. The actual password was passed in to this tool through the –po switch. For our example, we use the text CSCB as the password. Type this into the text box on this page of the wizard and click Next.

This next step, shown in Figure 11-8, asks you to choose the certificate store in which to store this *.pfx* information. Keep the defaults and click Next.

Figure 11-3. The last step of the Certificate Import wizard

Figure 11-4. The Certificate Import Successful message

Figure 11-5. Specifying a private key store in the Certificate Import wizard

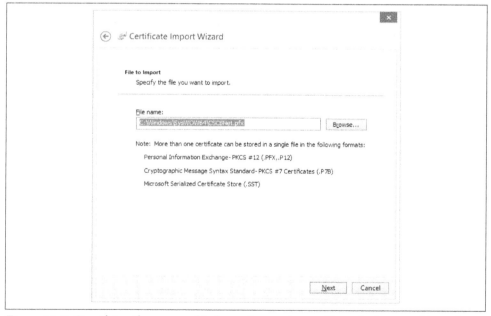

Figure 11-6. Specifying the personal information exchange file to be imported into the certificate store

Figure 11-7. Entering in the password of the personal information exchange file

Figure 11-8. Specifying a certificate store for the personal information exchange file in the Certificate Import wizard

The final step in the wizard, shown in Figure 11-9, simply shows the information you specified on the previous pages of the wizard. Click Finish to complete the import. After you click the Finish button, you'll see the message box in Figure 11-4, indicating that the import was successful.

At this point, you can run the TCP server and client, and they should communicate successfully.

To use the `SslStream` in the TCP server project, you need to create a new `SslStream` object to wrap the `TcpClient` object:

```
SslStream SslStream = new SslStream(newClient.GetStream());
```

Before you can use this new stream object, you must authenticate the server using the following line of code:

```
SslStream.AuthenticateAsServer(GetServerCert("MyTestCert2"),
                    false, SslProtocols.Default, true);
```

Figure 11-9. The personal information exchange File Import Successful message

The `GetServerCert` method finds the server certificate used to authenticate the server. Notice the name passed in to this method; it is the same as the publisher's certificate name switch used with the *makecert.exe* utility (see the `-n` switch). This certificate is returned from the `GetServerCert` method as an `X509Certificate` object. The next argument to the `AuthenticateAsServer` method is `false`, indicating that a client certificate is not required. The `SslProtocols.Default` argument indicates that the authentication mechanism (SSL 2.0, SSL 3.0, TLS 1.0, or PCT 1.0) is chosen based on what is available to the client and server. The final argument indicates that the certificate will be checked to see whether it has been revoked.

To use the `SslStream` in the TCP client project, you create a new `SslStream` object, a bit differently from how it was created in the TCP server project:

```
SslStream SslStream = new SslStream(_client.GetStream(), false,
        new RemoteCertificateValidationCallback(CertificateValidationCallback));
```

This constructor accepts a stream from the `_client` field, a `false` indicating that the stream associated with the `_client` field will be closed when the `Close` method of the `SslStream` object is called, and a delegate that validates the server certificate. The `CertificateValidationCallback` method is called whenever a server certificate needs to be validated. The server certificate is checked, and any errors are passed into this delegate method to allow you to handle them as you wish.

The `AuthenticateAsClient` method is called next to authenticate the server:

```
SslStream.AuthenticateAsClient("MyTestCert2");
```

As you can see, with a little extra work, you can replace the current stream type you are using with the `SslStream` to gain the benefits of the SSL protocol.

See Also

The "SslStream Class" topic in the MSDN documentation.

11.12 Encrypting web.config Information

Problem

You need to encrypt data within a *web.config* file programmatically.

Solution

To encrypt data within a *web.config* file section, use the following method:

```
public static void EncryptWebConfigData(string appPath,
                                    string protectedSection,
                                    string dataProtectionProvider)
{
    System.Configuration.Configuration webConfig =
            WebConfigurationManager.OpenWebConfiguration(appPath);
    ConfigurationSection webConfigSection =
            webConfig.GetSection(protectedSection);

    if (!webConfigSection.SectionInformation.IsProtected)
    {
```

```
            webConfigSection.SectionInformation.ProtectSection(
                                          dataProtectionProvider);
            webConfig.Save();
        }
    }
```

To decrypt data within a *web.config* file section, use the following method:

```
public static void DecryptWebConfigData(string appPath, string protectedSection)
{
    System.Configuration.Configuration webConfig =
            WebConfigurationManager.OpenWebConfiguration(appPath);
    ConfigurationSection webConfigSection =
            webConfig.GetSection(protectedSection);

    if (webConfigSection.Section Information.IsProtected)
    {
        webConfigSection.SectionInformation.UnprotectSection();
        webConfig.Save();
    }
}
```

You will need to add the System.Web and System.Configuration DLLs to your project before this code will compile.

Discussion

To encrypt data, you can call the EncryptWebConfigData method with the following arguments:

```
EncryptWebConfigData("/WebApplication1", "appSettings",
                     "DataProtectionConfigurationProvider");
```

The first argument is the virtual path to the web application, the second argument is the section that you want to encrypt, and the last argument is the data protection provider that you want to use to decrypt the data.

The EncryptWebConfigData method uses the virtual path passed into it to open the *web.config* file. You do this using the OpenWebConfiguration static method of the Web ConfigurationManager class:

```
System.Configuration.Configuration webConfig =
    WebConfigurationManager.OpenWebConfiguration(appPath);
```

This method returns a System.Configuration.Configuration object, which you use to get the section of the *web.config* file that you wish to encrypt. You accomplish this through the GetSection method:

```
ConfigurationSection webConfigSection = webConfig.GetSection(protectedSection);
```

This method returns a ConfigurationSection object that you can use to encrypt the section. This is done through a call to the ProtectSection method:

```
webConfigSection.SectionInformation.ProtectSection(dataProtectionProvider);
```

The dataProtectionProvider argument is a string identifying which data protection provider you want to use to encrypt the section information. The two available providers are DpapiProtectedConfigurationProvider and RsaProtectedConfigurationProvider. The DpapiProtectedConfigurationProvider class makes use of the Data Protection API (DPAPI) to encrypt and decrypt data. The RsaProtectedConfigurationProvider class makes use of the RsaCryptoServiceProvider class in the .NET Framework to encrypt and decrypt data.

The final step to encrypting the section information is to call the Save method of the System.Configuration.Configuration object. This saves the changes to the *web.config* file. If this method is not called, the encrypted data will not be saved.

To decrypt data within a *web.config* file, you can call the DecryptWebConfigData method with the following parameters:

```
DecryptWebConfigData("/WebApplication1", "appSettings");
```

The first argument is the virtual path to the web application; the second argument is the section that you want to encrypt.

The DecryptWebConfigData method operates very similarly to the EncryptWebConfigData method, except that it calls the UnprotectSection method to decrypt the encrypted data in the *web.config* file:

```
webConfigSection.SectionInformation.UnprotectSection();
```

If you encrypt data in the *web.config* file using this technique, the data will automatically be decrypted when the web application accesses the encrypted data in the *web.config* file.

See Also

The "System.Configuration.Configuration Class" topic in the MSDN documentation.

11.13 Obtaining a Safer File Handle

Problem

You want more security when manipulating an unmanaged file handle than a simple IntPtr can provide.

Solution

Use the Microsoft.Win32.SafeHandles.SafeFileHandle object to wrap an existing unmanaged file handle:

```
public static void WriteToFileHandle(IntPtr hFile)
{
    // Wrap our file handle in a safe handle wrapper object.
    using (Microsoft.Win32.SafeHandles.SafeFileHandle safeHFile =
        new Microsoft.Win32.SafeHandles.SafeFileHandle(hFile, true))
    {
        // Open a FileStream object using the passed-in safe file handle.
        using (FileStream fileStream = new FileStream(safeHFile,
                FileAccess.ReadWrite))
        {
            // Flush before we start to clear any pending unmanaged actions.
            fileStream.Flush();

            // Operate on file here.
            string line = "Using a safe file handle object";

            // Write to the file.
            byte[] bytes = Encoding.ASCII.GetBytes(line);
            fileStream.Write(bytes,0,bytes.Length);
        }
    }
    // Note that the hFile handle is invalid at this point.
}
```

The `SafeFileHandle` constructor takes two arguments. The first is an `IntPtr` that contains a handle to an unmanaged resource. The second argument is a Boolean value, where `true` indicates that the handle will always be released during finalization, and `false` indicates that the safeguards that force the handle to be released during finalization are turned off. Unless you have an extremely good reason to turn off these safeguards, it is recommended that you always set this Boolean value to `true`.

Discussion

A `SafeFileHandle` object contains a single handle to an unmanaged file resource. This class has two major benefits over using an `IntPtr` to store a handle—critical finalization and prevention of handle recycling attacks. The `SafeFileHandle` is seen by the garbage collector as a critical finalizer, due to the fact that one of the `SafeFile Handle`'s base classes is `CriticalFinalizerObject`. The garbage collector separates finalizers into two categories: critical and noncritical. The noncritical finalizers are run first, followed by the critical finalizers. If a `FileStream`'s finalizer flushes any data, it can assume that the `SafeFileHandle` object is still valid, because the `SafeFileHan dle` finalizer is guaranteed to run after the `FileStream`'s.

 The `Close` method on the `FileStream` object will also close its underlying `SafeFileHandle` object.

Since the `SafeFileHandle` falls under critical finalization, it means that the underlying unmanaged handle is always released (i.e., the `SafeFileHandle.ReleaseHandle` method is always called), even in situations in which the `AppDomain` is corrupted and/or shutting down or the thread is being aborted. This will prevent resource handle leaks.

The `SafeFileHandle` object also helps to prevent handle recycling attacks. The operating system aggressively tries to recycle handles, so it is possible to close one handle and open another soon afterward and get the same value for the new handle. One way an attacker will take advantage of this is by forcing an accessible handle to close on one thread while it's possibly still being used on another, in the hope that the handle will be recycled quickly and used as a handle to a new resource, perhaps one that the attacker does not have permission to access. If the application still has this original handle and is actively using it, data corruption could be an issue.

Since this class inherits from the `SafeHandleZeroOrMinusOneIsInvalid` class, a handle value of `0` or `-1` is considered an invalid handle.

See Also

The "Microsoft.Win32.SafeHandles.SafeFileHandle Class" topic in the MSDN documentation.

11.14 Storing Passwords

Problem

You need to store passwords for users of your application in a safe and secure manner. However, you do not want to allow anyone with elevated privileges, such as an administrator of the system, to have any way to decrypt the stored passwords. Additionally, if this information is stolen by an attacker, you want to make it as difficult as possible for her to uncover the original passwords.

Solution

Rather than using a two-way encryption algorithm to encrypt the passwords, which can also be used to decrypt the passwords with the right key, we will use a one-way hashing algorithm with a salt value to store the passwords in a more secure manner. Rather than comparing clear-text passwords we will compare hash values, thereby hiding the real password from prying eyes.

This recipe uses methods from Recipe 11.10—most notably the Cre ateSecureString and ReadSecureString methods.

We'll start out by creating the method that accepts a clear-text password and returns both a unique salt value (as an out parameter) and the hashed and salted password (as the return value):

```
const int HASH_ITERATIONS = 43;
const string HASH_ALGORITHM = "SHA-512";
const int SALT_LENGTH = 64;

public static SecureString GeneratePasswordHashAndSalt(SecureString passwd,
                                                       out SecureString salt)
{
    // First generate the unique salt we will use to hash with
    salt = GenerateSalt();

    // Create salted hash
    string hashedPwd = GenerateHash(passwd, salt);

    return CreateSecureString(hashedPwd);
}
```

Next we'll write the method that generates a cryptographically strong random number, which we will use as the salt value:

```
private static SecureString GenerateSalt()
{
    RNGCryptoServiceProvider rng = new RNGCryptoServiceProvider();

    byte[] salt = new byte[SALT_LENGTH];
    rng.GetBytes(salt);

    return CreateSecureString(Convert.ToBase64String(salt));
}
```

And, of course, we'll need a method that accepts both the unhashed password as well as our salt value, created in the previous method GenerateSalt, and then returns the final hashed password/salt combination:

```
private static string GenerateHash(SecureString clearTextData, SecureString salt)
{
    if (salt?.Length > 0)
    {
        // Combine password and salt before hashing
        byte[] clearTextDataArray =
                Encoding.UTF8.GetBytes(ReadSecureString(clearTextData));
        byte[] clearTextSaltArray =
            Convert.FromBase64String(ReadSecureString(salt));
```

```
byte[] clearTextDataSaltArray = new byte[clearTextDataArray.Length +
                                clearTextSaltArray.Length];
Array.Copy(clearTextDataArray, 0, clearTextDataSaltArray,
            0, clearTextDataArray.Length);
Array.Copy(clearTextSaltArray, 0, clearTextDataSaltArray,
            clearTextDataArray.Length, clearTextSaltArray.Length);

// Use a secure hashing algorithm
HashAlgorithm alg = HashAlgorithm.Create(HASH_ALGORITHM);

byte[] hashedPwd = null;

for (int index = 0; index < HASH_ITERATIONS; index++)
{
    if (hashedPwd == null)
    {
        // Initial hash of the cleartext password
        hashedPwd = alg.ComputeHash(clearTextDataSaltArray);
    }
    else
    {
        // Re-hash the hash for added entropy
        hashedPwd = alg.ComputeHash(hashedPwd);
    }
}

return Convert.ToBase64String(hashedPwd);
}
else
{
    throw new ArgumentException(
     $"Salt parameter {nameof(salt)} cannot be empty or null. " +
      "This is a security violation.");
}
}
```

This GenerateHash method simply combines both the password and salt values into a single byte[] and then computes the hash for this combined value. For additional security, the resulting hash value is rehashed many times over. The number of hashing iterations is controlled by the HASH_ITERATIONS constant.

Once this final hashed/salted password value is created, we need to store both this value as well as the unique salt value for this user in a data store. This pseudocode gives you the general idea. You can modify this to work with whatever data store you are using:

```
public static void SaveHashedPassword(string userName, SecureString pwdHash,
                                        SecureString salt)
{
    string base64PwdHash = ReadSecureString(pwdHash);
    string base64Salt = ReadSecureString(salt);
```

```
// Store in DB
// INSERT users ('user', 'pwd', 'salt', ...)
//                (userName, base64PwdHash, base64Salt, ...)}
```

The pwdHash and salt parameters should be fed from the return value and out parameter of the GeneratePasswordHashAndSalt method, respectively.

Now that we can create our hashed/salted password, we need a way to compare what the user enters into the password text box on the login form of his application to the hash that is stored in the data store. The following method will salt and hash the password entered by the user and then compare that value to what is stored in the data store for that same user (i.e., the original hashed/salted password the user created):

```
public static bool ComparePasswords(SecureString storedHashedPwd,
                                    SecureString storedSalt,
                                    SecureString clearTextPwd)
{
    try
    {
        // First hash the clear text pwd using the same technique
        byte[] userEnteredHashedPwd =
                Convert.FromBase64String(GenerateHash(clearTextPwd,
                    storedSalt));

        // Get the stored hashed pwd/salt
        byte[]originalHashedPwd =
                Convert.FromBase64String(ReadSecureString(storedHashedPwd));

        // Now compare the two hashes
        // If true, the user entered password is correct
        if (userEnteredHashedPwd.SequenceEqual(originalHashedPwd))
            return true;
    }
    catch(ArgumentException ae)
    {
        // You should log this error and return false here
        Console.WriteLine(ae.Message);
        return false;
    }

    return false;
}
```

When calling this method, you must retrieve the storedHashedPwd and salt arguments from the data store where they were initially stored. Originally, we had saved these values using the pseudocode in the SaveHashedPassword method. Here is another pseudocode method to retrieve those values:

```
public static void RetrieveHashedPasswordAndSalt(string userName,
                                                 out SecureString
                                                     storedHashedPwd,
```

```
                                          out SecureString storedSalt)
{
    // Get from DB
    // SELECT pwd, salt FROM users WHERE user = ?
    // SetString(userName);

    storedHashedPwd = CreateSecureString(getFromResultSet("pwd"));
    storedSalt = CreateSecureString(getFromResultSet ("salt"));
}
```

Again, you should modify this pseudocode to handle your particular data store.

Discussion

Before getting into the details of how to use this code, let's discuss the constant values used in this code:

```
const int HASH_ITERATIONS = 43;
const string HASH_ALGORITHM = "SHA-512";
const int SALT_LENGTH = 64;
```

First, the HASH_ITERATIONS value simply defines how many times the clear-text password/salt combination will be hashed. In this case the password/salt value is hashed, the resulting hash is again hashed, and so on, for a total of 43 times. If you require more entropy in the hash, you should increase this value; it could easily be increased to 100, 200, 500, or even 1,000. However, keep in mind that it requires processing power to create these hashes, and an attacker (presumably with a bot net) could forcibly cause many hashes to be generated, resulting in a denial of service to your application.

 Displaying a CAPTCHA when prompting a user to register and log in and locking a user out after several unsuccessful login attempts are measures you can use to prevent or deter denial-of-service attacks that are focused on keeping your servers busy generating hash values.

The HASH_ALGORITHM value defines the hashing algorithm to use. It is safe to use either SHA-256 or SHA-512, although SHA-512 is safer to use. Do not use easily broken hashing algorithms, such as MD5 or SHA-1, as they will significantly reduce the amount of time it takes an attacker to crack your hashes. In fact, do not use anything weaker than the SHA-256 algorithm.

Finally, the SALT_LENGTH value is the number of bytes that will make up the salt value. These bytes are generated from a cryptographically strong random-number generator. A salt length of 64 bytes was chosen here, but a smaller or larger size could also be used. We chose 64 because it's the same size as the hashed password/salt, which forces an attacker to determine which one is the salt value and which one is the hashed value before he can use rainbow tables or reverse lookups on the hashes. If you decide to use SHA-256, then you can reduce the SALT_LENGTH to 32 bytes to be equivalent in size to the hash value.

Moving on to implementing this code in your application, there are two places where this code should be used—in the user registration and login forms on your site. First, we'll step through the registration process:

1. The user chooses to register a username and password for this site.

2. The site asks the user to enter in a username and password, which is then passed into the GeneratePasswordHashAndSalt method, producing both a unique salt value and a hashed/salted password for this user.

3. The username entered by the user is verified against the data store to determine if an existing user exists.

4. If no previously entered username exists, the username, hashed/salted password, and unique salt value are stored in the data store.

For this recipe, we assume the use of the System.Windows.Con trols.PasswordBox control on both the registration and login forms. This control can be found in the *PresentationFramework.dll*. This control has a built-in property, SecurePassword, that allows us to retrieve a password already stored in a SecureString object as opposed to a normal String object.

The code will look something like this:

```
public bool Register()
{
    try
    {
        ...

        SecureString salt;
        SecureString pwdHash =
          GeneratePasswordHashAndSalt(myRegPasswordTextBox.SecurePassword,
              out salt);

        // Test to make sure this user is available to be registered
        if (UserDoesNotExist(myRegUserNameTextBox.Text))
        {
            SaveHashedPassword(userName, pwdHash, salt);
            return true;
        }
        else
        {
```

```
                return false;
        }
    }
    catch(Exception e)
    {
        // An error occurred, login failure!
        return false;
    }
}
```

The first method that we call is `GeneratePasswordHashAndSalt`, in order to generate a new unique salt value for this user and to salt and hash the password the user registered with.

 It is important that a unique salt value is generated for each user. Using the same salt for each user is insecure, since it makes it easier for the attacker to uncover all hashed passwords. All the attacker has to do is determine the one salt value and apply it to each hash value that she generates.

The last thing we do in this method is test to make sure that this username does not already exist in the data store. If it does not exist, we continue on to store this username, the hashed/salted password, and the unique salt in the data store using the `SaveHashedPassword` method. Otherwise, the registration process is halted and the user must enter a different username.

This is the process when the user returns to the site and attempts to log in with her credentials:

1. The user enters her username and password.

2. The unique salt value and the originally hashed/salted password for this user is obtained from the data store.

3. The password the user entered into the site (obtained in step #1) and the unique salt value for this user (obtained in step #2) as well as the hashed/salted password (also obtained in step #2) are passed into the `ComparePasswords` method.

4. The `ComparePasswords` method simply salts and hashes the user's password using the original salt value stored for this particular user and then compares that resulting hash to the original hash stored for the user.

5. If the hashes are exactly the same, the user can continue authenticating; otherwise, the user is prevented from authenticating.

The code will look something like this:

```
public bool Login()
{
```

```
        try
        {
            ...

            string userName = myLoginUserNameTextBox.Text;

            SecureString storedHashedPwd;
            SecureString storedSalt;
            RetrieveHashedPasswordAndSalt(userName, out storedHashedPwd,
                out storedSalt);


            if (ComparePasswords(storedHashedPwd, storedSalt,
                            myLoginPwdTextBox.SecurePassword))
            {
                // Password hashes match
                return true;
            }
            else
            {
                // Password hashes do not match, login failure!
                return false;
            }
        }
        catch(Exception e)
        {
            // An error occurred, login failure!
            return false;
        }
    }
```

First, this code uses the username entered by the user to retrieve both the hashed/salted password and the user's unique salt value from the data store using the `Retrie` `veHashedPasswordAndSalt` method. These two values, along with the password entered by the user in the login form, are passed into the `ComparePasswords` method. This method hashes and salts the password that the user entered in the login form using the same salt value returned by the `RetrieveHashedPasswordAndSalt` method. If the hashed/salted password that the user entered in the login form is the same as the hashed/salted password stored in the data store, then the passwords match and the authentication process is allowed to continue. Otherwise, the authentication fails.

See Also

The "System.Windows.Controls.PasswordBox Class," "System.Security.Cryptography.RNGCryptoServiceProvider Class," and "System.Security.SecureString Class" topics in the MSDN documentation.

CHAPTER 12

Threading, Synchronization, and Concurrency

12.0 Introduction

A *thread* represents a single flow of execution logic in a program. Some programs never need more than a single thread to execute efficiently, but many do, and that is what this chapter is about. Threading in .NET allows you to build responsive and efficient applications. Many applications need to perform multiple actions at the same time (such as user interface interaction and data processing), and threading provides the capability to achieve this. Being able to have your application perform multiple tasks is a very liberating and yet complicating factor in your application design. Once you have multiple threads of execution in your application, you need to start thinking about what data in your application needs to be protected from multiple accesses, what data could cause threads to develop an interdependency that could lead to *deadlocking* (Thread A has a resource that Thread B is waiting for, and Thread B has a resource that Thread A is waiting for), and how to store data you want to associate with the individual threads. You will also want to consider *race conditions* when dealing with threads. A race condition occurs when two threads access a shared variable at the same time. Both threads read the variable and get the same value and then race to see which thread can write the value last to the shared variable. The last thread to write to the variable "wins," as it is writing over the value that the first thread wrote. You will explore some of these issues to help you take advantage of this wonderful capability of the .NET Framework. You will also see the areas where you need to be careful and items to keep in mind while designing and creating your multithreaded application.

Synchronization is about coordinating activities between threads or processes while making sure that data being accessed by multiple threads or processes stays valid.

Synchronization allows threads and processes to operate in unison. Understanding the constructs that allow you to have multiple threads executing in your program gives you the power to create more scalable applications that can better utilize available resources.

Concurrency is about various aspects of your program cooperating and working in tandem to achieve goals. When operations are running concurrently in your application, you have multiple actions occurring at the same time. Concurrency is fostered by synchronization of threads.

12.1 Creating Per-Thread Static Fields

Problem

Static fields, by default, are shared between threads within an application domain. You need to allow each thread to have its own nonshared copy of a static field, so that this static field can be updated on a per-thread basis.

Solution

Use `ThreadStaticAttribute` to mark any `static` fields as not shareable between threads:

```
public class Foo
{
    [ThreadStaticAttribute()]
    public static string bar = "Initialized string";
}
```

Discussion

By default, static fields are shared between all threads that access these fields in the same application domain. To see this, you'll create a class with a static field called bar and a static method to access and display the value contained in this field:

```
private class ThreadStaticField
{
    [ThreadStaticAttribute()]
    public static string bar = "Initialized string";

    public static void DisplayStaticFieldValue()
    {
        string msg = $"{Thread.CurrentThread.GetHashCode()}" +
            $"{ contains static field value of: {ThreadStaticField.bar} ";
        Console.WriteLine(msg);
    }
}
```

Next, create a test method that accesses this static field both on the current thread and on a newly spawned thread:

```
private static void TestStaticField()
{
    ThreadStaticField.DisplayStaticFieldValue();

    Thread newStaticFieldThread =
        new Thread(ThreadStaticField.DisplayStaticFieldValue);

    newStaticFieldThread.Start();

    ThreadStaticField.DisplayStaticFieldValue();
}
```

This code displays output that resembles the following:

```
9 contains static field value of: Initialized string
10 contains static field value of: Initialized string
9 contains static field value of: Initialized string
```

In the preceding example, the current thread's hash value is 9, and the new thread's hash value is 10. These values will vary from system to system. Notice that both threads are accessing the same static bar field. Next, add the ThreadStaticAttribute to the static field:

```
private class ThreadStaticField
{
    [ThreadStaticAttribute()]
    public static string bar = "Initialized string";

    public static void DisplayStaticFieldValue()
    {
        string msg = $"{Thread.CurrentThread.GetHashCode()}" +
            $"{ contains static field value of: {ThreadStaticField.bar} ";
        Console.WriteLine(msg);
    }
}
```

Now, output resembling the following is displayed:

```
9 contains static field value of: Initialized string
10 contains static field value of:
9 contains static field value of: Initialized string
```

Notice that the new thread returns a null for the value of the static bar field. This is the expected behavior. The bar field is initialized only in the first thread that accesses it. In all other threads, this field is initialized to null. Therefore, it is imperative that you initialize the bar field in all threads before it is used.

Remember to initialize any static field that is marked with Thread StaticAttribute before it is used in any thread; that is, this field should be initialized in the method passed in to the ThreadStart delegate. You should make sure to not initialize the static field using a field initializer as shown in the prior code, since only one thread gets to see that initial value.

The bar field is initialized to the "Initialized string" string literal before it is used in the first thread that accesses this field. In the previous test code, the bar field was accessed first, and, therefore, it was initialized in the current thread. Suppose you were to remove the first line of the TestStaticField method, as shown here:

```
private static void TestStaticField()
{
    //ThreadStaticField.DisplayStaticFieldValue();

    Thread newStaticFieldThread =
        new Thread(ThreadStaticField.DisplayStaticFieldValue);

    newStaticFieldThread.Start();

    ThreadStaticField.DisplayStaticFieldValue();
}
```

This code now displays similar output to the following:

```
10 contains static field value of: Initialized string
9 contains static field value of:
```

The current thread does not access the bar field first and therefore does not initialize it. However, when the new thread accesses it first, it does initialize it.

Note that adding a static constructor to initialize the static field marked with this attribute will still follow the same behavior. Static constructors are executed only one time per application domain.

See Also

The "ThreadStaticAttribute Attribute" and "Static Modifier (C#)" topics in the MSDN documentation.

12.2 Providing Thread-Safe Access to Class Members

Problem

You need to provide thread-safe access through accessor functions to an internal member variable.

The following `NoSafeMemberAccess` class shows three methods: `ReadNumericField`, `IncrementNumericField`, and `ModifyNumericField`. While all of these methods access the internal `numericField` member, the access is currently not safe for multithreaded access:

```
public static class NoSafeMemberAccess
{
    private static int numericField = 1;

    public static void IncrementNumericField()
    {
        ++numericField;
    }

    public static void ModifyNumericField(int newValue)
    {
        numericField = newValue;
    }

    public static int ReadNumericField() => (numericField);
}
```

Solution

`NoSafeMemberAccess` could be used in a multithreaded application, and therefore it must be made thread-safe. Consider what would occur if multiple threads were calling the `IncrementNumericField` method at the same time. It is possible that two calls could occur to `IncrementNumericField` while the `numericField` is updated only once. To protect against this, you will modify this class by creating an object that you can lock against in critical sections of the code:

```
public static class SaferMemberAccess
{
    private static int numericField = 1;
    private static object syncObj = new object();

    public static void IncrementNumericField()
    {
        lock(syncObj)
        {
            ++numericField;
        }
    }

    public static void ModifyNumericField(int newValue)
    {
        lock (syncObj)
        {
            numericField = newValue;
        }
```

```
        }

        public static int ReadNumericField()
        {
            lock (syncObj)
            {
                return (numericField);
            }
        }
    }
```

Using the `lock` statement on the `syncObj` object lets you synchronize access to the `numericField` member. This now makes all three methods safe for multithreaded access.

Discussion

To mark a block of code as a critical section, you use the `lock` keyword. The `lock` keyword should not be used on a public type or on an instance out of the control of the program, as this can contribute to deadlocks. Examples of this are using the `"this"` pointer, the type object for a class (`typeof(MyClass)`), or a string literal (`"MyLock"`). If you are attempting to protect code in only public static methods, you could also use the `System.Runtime.CompilerServices.MethodImpl` attribute for this purpose with the `MethodImplOption.Synchronized` value:

```
[MethodImpl (MethodImplOptions.Synchronized)]
public static void MySynchronizedMethod()
{
}
```

There is a problem with synchronization using an object such as `syncObj` in the `Safe rMemberAccess` example. If you lock an object or type that can be accessed by other objects within the application, other objects may also attempt to lock this same object.

A *deadlock* is a situation in which two programs or threads of execution that are sharing the same resources are effectively preventing each other from accessing the resources, resulting in both being blocked and stopping execution.

A quick example of a deadlock is:

1. Thread 1 accesses Resource A and grabs a lock on it.

2. Thread 2 accesses Resource B and grabs a lock on it.

3. Thread 1 attempts to grab Resource B but is waiting for Thread 2 to let go.

4. Thread 2 attempts to grab Resource A but is waiting for Thread 1 to let go.

5. At this point the threads are deadlocked.

This will manifest itself in poorly written code that locks itself, such as the following code:

```
public class DeadLock
{
    public void Method1()
    {
        lock(this)
        {
            // Do something.
        }
    }
}
```

When `Method1` is called, it locks the current `deadLock` object. Unfortunately, any object that has access to the `DeadLock` class may also lock it, as shown here:

```
public class AnotherCls
{
    public void DoSomething()
    {
        DeadLock deadLock = new DeadLock();
        lock(deadLock)
        {
            Thread thread = new Thread(deadLock.Method1);
            thread.Start();
            // Do some time-consuming task here.
        }
    }
}
```

The `DoSomething` method obtains a lock on the `deadLock` object and then attempts to call the `Method1` method of the `deadLock` object on another thread, after which a very long task is executed. While the long task is executing, the lock on the deadLock object prevents Method1 from being called on the other thread. Only when this long task ends, and execution exits the critical section of the DoSomething method, will the Method1 method be able to acquire a lock on this object. As you can see, this can become a major headache to track down in a much larger application.

Jeffrey Richter came up with a relatively simple method to remedy this situation, which he details quite clearly in the article "Safe Thread Synchronization" in the January 2003 issue of *MSDN Magazine*. His solution is to create a private field within the class on which to synchronize. Only the object itself can acquire this private field; no outside object or type may acquire it. This solution is also now the recommended practice in the MSDN documentation for the lock keyword. The DeadLock class can be rewritten as follows to fix this problem:

```
public class DeadLock
{
    private object syncObj = new object();

    public void Method1()
    {
        lock(syncObj)
        {
            // Do something.
        }
    }
}
```

Now in the DeadLock class, you are locking on the internal syncObj, while the DoSomething method locks on the DeadLock class instance. This resolves the deadlock condition, but the DoSomething method still should not lock on a public type. Therefore, change the AnotherCls class like so:

```
public class AnotherCls
{
    private object deadLockSyncObj = new object();

    public void DoSomething()
    {
        DeadLock deadLock = new DeadLock();
        lock(deadLockSyncObj)
        {
            Thread thread = new Thread(deadLock.Method1);
            thread.Start();
            // Do some time-consuming task here.
        }
    }
}
```

Now the AnotherCls class has an object of its own to protect access to the DeadLock class instance in DoSomething instead of locking on the public type.

To clean up your code, you should stop locking any objects or types except for the synchronization objects that are private to your type or object, such as the syncObj in the fixed DeadLock class. This recipe makes use of this pattern by creating a static syncObj object within the SaferMemberAccess class. The IncrementNumericField, ModifyNumericField, and ReadNumericField methods use this syncObj to synchronize access to the numericField field. Note that if you do not need a lock while the numericField is being read in the ReadNumericField method, you can remove this lock block and simply return the value contained in the numericField field.

 Minimizing the number of critical sections within your code can significantly improve performance. Use what you need to secure resource access, but no more.

If you require more control over locking and unlocking of critical sections, you might want to try using the overloaded static Monitor.TryEnter methods. These methods allow more flexibility by introducing a timeout value. The lock keyword will attempt to acquire a lock on a critical section indefinitely. However, with the TryEnter method, you can specify a timeout value in milliseconds (as an integer) or as a Time Span structure. The TryEnter methods return true if a lock was acquired and false if it was not. Note that the overload of the TryEnter method that accepts only a single parameter does not block for any amount of time. This method returns immediately, regardless of whether the lock was acquired.

The updated class using the Monitor methods is shown in Example 12-1.

Example 12-1. Using Monitor methods

```
public static class MonitorMethodAccess
{
    private static int numericField = 1;
    private static object syncObj = new object();
    public static object SyncRoot => syncObj;

    public static void IncrementNumericField()
    {
        if (Monitor.TryEnter(syncObj, 250))
        {
            try
            {
                ++numericField;
            }
            finally
            {
                Monitor.Exit(syncObj);
```

```
                }
            }
        }

    public static void ModifyNumericField(int newValue)
    {
        if (Monitor.TryEnter(syncObj, 250))
        {
            try
            {
                numericField = newValue;
            }
            finally
            {
                Monitor.Exit(syncObj);
            }
        }
    }

    public static int ReadNumericField()
    {
        if (Monitor.TryEnter(syncObj, 250))
        {
            try
            {
                return (numericField);
            }
            finally
            {
                Monitor.Exit(syncObj);
            }
        }

        return (-1);
    }
    [MethodImpl (MethodImplOptions.Synchronized)]
    public static void MySynchronizedMethod()
    {
    }
}
```

Note that with the `TryEnter` methods, you should always check to see whether the lock was in fact acquired. If not, your code should wait and try again or return to the caller.

You might think at this point that all of the methods are thread-safe. Individually, they are, but what if you are trying to call them and you expect synchronized access between two of the methods? If `ModifyNumericField` and `ReadNumericField` are used one after the other by Class 1 on Thread 1 at the same time Class 2 is using these methods on Thread 2, locking or `Monitor` calls will not prevent Class 2 from modifying the value before Thread 1 reads it. Here is a series of actions that demonstrates this:

Class 1, Thread 1
    Calls `ModifyNumericField` with `10`

Class 2, Thread 2
    Calls `ModifyNumericField` with `15`

Class 1, Thread 1
    Calls `ReadNumericField` and gets 15, not 10

Class 2, Thread 2
    Calls `ReadNumericField` and gets 15, which it expected

To solve this problem of synchronizing reads and writes, the calling class needs to manage the interaction. The external class can accomplish this by using the `Monitor` class to establish a lock on the exposed synchronization object `SyncRoot` from `Moni torMethodAccess`, as shown here:

```
int num = 0;
if(Monitor.TryEnter(MonitorMethodAccess.SyncRoot,250))
{
    MonitorMethodAccess.ModifyNumericField(10);
    num = MonitorMethodAccess.ReadNumericField();
    Monitor.Exit(MonitorMethodAccess.SyncRoot);
}
Console.WriteLine(num);
```

When you are learning to code for thread-safe access, it is helpful to brush up on deadlock prevention algorithms, such as the Banker's Algorithm by Edsger Dijkstra, and operating system books to help you think your way through the code you are creating and how it will react.

See Also

The "Lock Statement," "Thread Class," and "Monitor Class" topics in the MSDN documentation; the "Safe Thread Synchronization" article in the January 2003 issue of *MSDN Magazine*; the Wikipedia articles "Banker's algorithm" (*http://bit.ly/1LxeiRy*) and "Deadlock Prevention algorithms" (*http://bit.ly/1NNbvnM*).

12.3 Preventing Silent Thread Termination

Problem

An exception thrown in a spawned worker thread will cause this thread to be silently terminated if the exception is unhandled. You need to make sure all exceptions are handled in all threads. If an exception happens in this new thread, you want to handle it and be notified of its occurrence.

Solution

You must add exception handling to the method that you pass to the `ThreadStart` delegate with a `try-catch`, `try-finally`, or `try-catch-finally` block. The code to do this is shown in Example 12-2 in bold.

Example 12-2. Preventing silent thread termination

```
public class MainThread
{
    public void CreateNewThread()
    {
        // Spawn new thread to do concurrent work
        Thread newWorkerThread = new Thread(Worker.DoWork);
        newWorkerThread.Start();
    }
}

public class Worker
{
    // Method called by ThreadStart delegate to do concurrent work
    public static void DoWork ()
    {
        try
        {
            // Do thread work here
            throw new Exception("Boom!");
        }
        catch(Exception e)
        {
            // Handle thread exception here
            Console.WriteLine(e.ToString());
            // Do not rethrow exception
        }
        finally
        {
            // Do thread cleanup here
        }
    }
}
```

Discussion

If an unhandled exception occurs in the main thread of an application, the main thread terminates, along with your entire application. An unhandled exception in a spawned worker thread, however, will terminate only that thread. This will happen without any visible warnings, and your application will continue to run as if nothing happened, or worse, may start to act strangely due to corrupted data or improper execution and interaction of the worker threads.

Simply wrapping an exception handler around the Start method of the Thread class will not catch the exception on the newly created thread. The Start method is called within the context of the current thread, not the newly created thread. It also returns immediately once the thread is launched, so it isn't going to wait around for the thread to finish. Therefore, the exception thrown in the new thread will not be caught since it is not visible to any other threads.

If the exception is rethrown from the catch block, the finally block of this structured exception handler will still execute. However, after the finally block is finished, the rethrown exception is, at that point, rethrown. The rethrown exception cannot be handled and the thread terminates. If there is any code after the finally block, it will not be executed, since an unhandled exception occurred.

 Never rethrow an exception at the highest point in the exception-handling hierarchy within a thread. Since no exception handlers can catch this rethrown exception, it will be considered unhandled, and the thread will terminate after all finally blocks have been executed.

What if you use the ThreadPool and QueueUserWorkItem? This method will still help you because you added the handling code that will execute inside the thread. Just make sure you have the finally block set up so that you can notify yourself of exceptions and clean up any outstanding resources in other threads as shown earlier.

To provide a last-chance exception handler for your WinForms application, you need to hook up to two separate events. The first event is System.AppDomain.CurrentDomain.UnhandledException, which will catch all unhandled exceptions in the current AppDomain on worker threads; it will not catch exceptions that occur on the main UI thread of a WinForms application. See Recipe 5.8 for more information on the System.AppDomain.UnhandledException event. To catch those, you need to hook up to the second event, System.Windows.Forms.Application.ThreadException, which will catch unhandled exceptions in the main UI thread. Also see Recipe 5.7 for more information about the ThreadException event.

See Also

The "Thread Class" and "Exception Class" topics in the MSDN documentation.

12.4 Being Notified of the Completion of an Asynchronous Delegate

Problem

You need a way of receiving notification from an asynchronously invoked delegate that it has finished. This scheme must allow your code to continue processing without having to constantly call `IsCompleted` in a loop or to rely on the `WaitOne` method. Since the asynchronous delegate will return a value, you must be able to pass this return value back to the invoking thread.

Solution

Use the `BeginInvoke` method to start the asynchronous delegate, but use the first parameter to pass a callback delegate to the asynchronous delegate, as shown in Example 12-3.

Example 12-3. Getting notification on completion of an anonymous delegate

```
public class AsyncAction2
{
    public void CallbackAsyncDelegate()
    {
        AsyncCallback callBack = DelegateCallback;

        AsyncInvoke method1 = TestAsyncInvoke.Method1;
        Console.WriteLine(
            $"Calling BeginInvoke on Thread {Thread.CurrentThread.ManagedThreadId}");
        IAsyncResult asyncResult = method1.BeginInvoke(callBack, method1);

        // No need to poll or use the WaitOne method here, so return to the calling
        // method.
        return;
    }

    private static void DelegateCallback(IAsyncResult iresult)
    {
        Console.WriteLine(
            $"Getting callback on Thread {Thread.CurrentThread.ManagedThreadId});
        AsyncResult asyncResult = (AsyncResult)iresult;
        AsyncInvoke method1 = (AsyncInvoke)asyncResult.AsyncDelegate;

        int retVal = method1.EndInvoke(asyncResult);
        Console.WriteLine($"retVal (Callback): {retVal}");
    }
}
```

This callback delegate will call the `DelegateCallback` method on the thread on which the method was invoked when the asynchronous delegate is finished processing. If the thread is currently executing other code, the callback will wait until the thread is free. The thread will continue to exist, as the system knows that a callback is pending, so you do not have to account for the thread not being there when the callback is ready to be invoked.

The following code defines the `AsyncInvoke` delegate and the asynchronously invoked static method `TestAsyncInvoke.Method1`:

```
public delegate int AsyncInvoke2();

public class TestAsyncInvoke2
{
    public static int Method1()
    {
        Console.WriteLine(
            $"Invoked Method1 on Thread {Thread.CurrentThread.ManagedThreadId}");
        return (1);
    }
}
```

To run the asynchronous invocation, create an instance of the `AsyncAction` class and call the `CallbackAsyncDelegate` method like so:

```
AsyncAction2 aa2 = new AsyncAction2();
aa2.CallbackAsyncDelegate();
```

The output for this code is shown next. Note that the thread ID for `Method1` is different:

```
Calling BeginInvoke on Thread 9
Invoked Method1 on Thread 10
Getting callback on Thread 10
retVal (Callback): 1
```

Discussion

The asynchronous delegates in this recipe are created and invoked in the same fashion as the asynchronous delegate in Recipe 12.3. Instead of using the `IsCompleted` property to determine when the asynchronous delegate is finished processing (or using the `WaitOne` method to block for a specified time while the asynchronous delegate continues processing), this recipe uses a callback to indicate to the calling thread that the asynchronous delegate has finished processing and that its return value, `ref` parameter values, and `out` parameter values are available.

Invoking a delegate in this manner is much more flexible and efficient than simply polling the `IsCompleted` property to determine when a delegate finishes processing. When polling this property in a loop, the polling method cannot return and allow the application to continue processing. A callback is also better than using a `WaitOne` method, since the `WaitOne` method will block the calling thread and prevent processing from occurring.

The `CallbackAsyncDelegate` method in this recipe makes use of the first parameter to the `BeginInvoke` method of the asynchronous delegate to pass in another delegate. This contains a callback method to be called when the asynchronous delegate finishes processing. After calling `BeginInvoke`, this method can now return, and the application can continue processing; it does not have to wait in a polling loop or be blocked while the asynchronous delegate is running.

The `AsyncInvoke` delegate that is passed into the first parameter of the `BeginInvoke` method is defined as follows:

```
public delegate void AsyncCallback(IAsyncResult ar)
```

When this delegate is created, as shown here, the callback method passed in, `DelegateCallback`, will be called as soon as the asynchronous delegate completes:

```
AsyncCallback callBack = new AsyncCallback(DelegateCallback);
```

`DelegateCallback` will not run on the same thread as `BeginInvoke` but rather on a `Thread` from the `ThreadPool`. This callback method accepts a parameter of type `IAsyncResult`. You can cast this parameter to an `AsyncResult` object within the method and use it to obtain information about the completed asynchronous delegate, such as its return value, any `ref` parameter values, and any `out` parameter values. If the delegate instance that was used to call `BeginInvoke` is still in scope, you can just pass the `IAsyncResult` to the `EndInvoke` method. In addition, this object can obtain any state information passed into the second parameter of the `BeginInvoke` method. This state information can be any object type.

The `DelegateCallback` method casts the `IAsyncResult` parameter to an `AsyncResult` object and obtains the asynchronous delegate that was originally called. The `EndInvoke` method of this asynchronous delegate is called to process any return value, `ref` parameters, or `out` parameters. If any state object was passed in to the `BeginInvoke` method's second parameter, it can be obtained here through the following line of code:

```
object state = asyncResult.AsyncState;
```

See Also

The "AsyncCallback Delegate" topic in the MSDN documentation.

12.5 Storing Thread-Specific Data Privately

Problem

You want to store thread-specific data discovered at runtime. This data should be accessible only to code running within that thread.

Solution

Use the `AllocateDataSlot`, `AllocateNamedDataSlot`, or `GetNamedDataSlot` method on the `Thread` class to reserve a *thread local storage* (TLS) slot. Using TLS, you can store a large object in a data slot on a thread and use it in many different methods—without having to pass the structure as a parameter.

For this example, a class called `ApplicationData` represents a set of data that can grow to be very large:

```
public class ApplicationData
{
    // Application data is stored here.
}
```

Before you can use this structure, there must be a data slot in TLS to store the class. First, `GetNamedDataSlot` is called to get the `appDataSlot`. Since `appDataSlot` doesn't exist, by default `GetNamedDataSlot` creates it. The following code creates an instance of the `ApplicationData` class and stores it in the data slot named `appDataSlot`:

```
ApplicationData appData = new ApplicationData();
Thread.SetData(Thread.GetNamedDataSlot("appDataSlot"), appData);
```

Whenever you need this class, you can retrieve it with a call to `Thread.GetData`. The following line of code gets the `appData` structure from the data slot named `appDataSlot`:

```
ApplicationData storedAppData = (ApplicationData)Thread.GetData(
    Thread.GetNamedDataSlot("appDataSlot"));
```

At this point, the `storedAppData` structure can be read or modified. After the action has been performed on `storedAppData`, it must be placed back into the data slot named `appDataSlot`:

```
Thread.SetData(Thread.GetNamedDataSlot("appDataSlot"), storedAppData);
```

Once the application is finished using this data, you can release the data slot from memory using the following method call:

```
Thread.FreeNamedDataSlot("appDataSlot");
```

The `HandleClass` class in Example 12-4 shows how TLS can be used to store a structure.

Example 12-4. Using TLS to store a structure

```
public class HandleClass
{
    public static void Run()
    {
        // Create structure instance and store it in the named data slot
        ApplicationData appData = new ApplicationData();
        Thread.SetData(Thread.GetNamedDataSlot("appDataSlot"), appData);

        // Call another method that will use this structure
        HandleClass.MethodB();

        // When done, free this data slot
        Thread.FreeNamedDataSlot("appDataSlot");
    }

    public static void MethodB()
    {
        // Get the instance from the named data slot
        ApplicationData storedAppData = (ApplicationData)Thread.GetData(
            Thread.GetNamedDataSlot("appDataSlot"));

        // Modify the ApplicationData

        // When finished modifying this data, store the changes back into
        // into the named data slot
        Thread.SetData(Thread.GetNamedDataSlot("appDataSlot"),
            storedAppData);

        // Call another method that will use this structure
        HandleClass.MethodC();
    }

    public static void MethodC()
    {
        // Get the instance from the named data slot
        ApplicationData storedAppData =
            (ApplicationData)Thread.GetData(Thread.GetNamedDataSlot("appDataSlot"));

        // Modify the data

        // When finished modifying this data, store the changes back into
        // the named data slot
        Thread.SetData(Thread.GetNamedDataSlot("appDataSlot"), storedAppData);
    }
}
```

Discussion

Thread local storage is a convenient way to store data that is usable across method calls without the user having to pass the structure to the method or even knowing where the structure was actually created.

Data stored in a named TLS data slot is available only to that thread; no other thread can access a named data slot of another thread. The data stored in this data slot is accessible from anywhere within the thread. This setup essentially makes this data global to the thread. You should be aware that TLS slots are a limited resource and can vary based on platform.

To create a named data slot, use the static `Thread.GetNamedDataSlot` method. This method accepts a single parameter, *name*, that defines the name of the data slot. This name should be unique; if a data slot with the same name exists, then the contents of that data slot will be returned, and a new data slot will not be created. This action occurs silently; there is no exception thrown or error code to inform you that you are using a data slot someone else created. To be sure that you are using a unique data slot, use the `Thread.AllocateNamedDataSlot` method. This method throws a `System.ArgumentException` if a data slot already exists with the same name. Otherwise, it operates similarly to the `GetNamedDataSlot` method.

Note that this named data slot is created on every thread in the process, not just the thread that called this method. This fact should not be much more than an inconvenience to you, though, since the data in each data slot can be accessed only by the thread that contains it. In addition, if a data slot with the same name was created on a separate thread and you call `GetNamedDataSlot` on the current thread with this name, none of the data in any data slot on any thread will be destroyed.

`GetNamedDataSlot` returns a `LocalDataStoreSlot` object that is used to access the data slot. Note that you can't create this class using the new keyword; you must create it through one of the `AllocateDataSlot` or `AllocateNamedDataSlot` methods on the `Thread` class.

To store data in this data slot, use the static `Thread.SetData` method. This method takes the object passed in to the *data* parameter and stores it in the data slot defined by the *dataSlot* parameter.

The static `Thread.GetData` method retrieves the object stored in a data slot. This method retrieves a `LocalDataStoreSlot` object that is created through the `Thread.GetNamedDataSlot` method. The `GetData` method then returns the object that was stored in that particular data slot. Note that the object returned might have to be cast to its original type before it can be used.

The static method `Thread.FreeNamedDataSlot` will free the memory associated with a named data slot. This method accepts the name of the data slot as a `string` and, in turn, frees the memory associated with that data slot. Remember that when a data slot is created with `GetNamedDataSlot`, a named data slot is also created on all of the other threads running in that process. This is not really a problem when you're creating data slots with the `GetNamedDataSlot` method because, if a data slot exists with this name, a `LocalDataStoreSlot` object that refers to that data slot is returned, a new data slot is not created, and the original data in that data slot is not destroyed.

This situation becomes more of a problem when you're using the `FreeNamedDataSlot` method. This method will free the memory associated with the data slot name passed in to it for all threads, not just the thread that it was called on. Freeing a data slot before all threads have finished using the data within that data slot can be disastrous to your application.

A way to work around this problem is to not call the `FreeNamedDataSlot` method at all. When a thread terminates, all of its data slots in TLS are freed automatically. The side effect of not calling `FreeNamedDataSlot` is that the slot is taken up until the garbage collector determines that the thread on which the slot was created has finished and the slot can be freed.

If you know the number of TLS slots you need for your code at compile time, consider using the `ThreadStaticAttribute` on a static field of your class to set up TLS-like storage.

See Also

The "Thread Local Storage and Thread Relative Static Fields," "ThreadStaticAttribute Attribute," and "Thread Class" topics in the MSDN documentation.

12.6 Granting Multiple Access to Resources with a Semaphore

Problem

You have a resource you want only a certain number of clients to access at a given time.

Solution

Use a semaphore to enable resource-counted access to the resource. For example, if you have an Xbox One and a copy of *Halo 5* (the resource) and a development staff eager to blow off some steam (the clients), you have to synchronize access to the Xbox One. Since the Xbox One has up to eight controllers, up to eight clients can be playing at any given time. The rules of the house are that when you die, you give up your controller.

To accomplish this, create a class called `Halo5Session` with a `Semaphore` called `_Xbox One` like this:

```
public class Halo5Session
{
    // A semaphore that simulates a limited resource pool.
    private static Semaphore _XboxOne;
```

To get things rolling, you need to call the `Play` method, as shown in Example 12-5, on the `Halo5Session` class.

Example 12-5. Play method

```
public static void Play()
{
    // An XboxOne has 8 controller ports so 8 people can play at a time
    // We use 8 as the max and zero to start with as we want Players
    // to queue up at first until the XboxOne boots and loads the game
    //
    using (_XboxOne = new Semaphore(0, 8, "XboxOne"))
    {
        using (ManualResetEvent GameOver =
            new ManualResetEvent(false))
        {
            //
            // 13 Players log in to play
            //
            List<XboxOnePlayer.PlayerInfo> players =
                new List<XboxOnePlayer.PlayerInfo>() {
                    new XboxOnePlayer.PlayerInfo { Name="Igor",Dead=GameOver},
                    new XboxOnePlayer.PlayerInfo { Name="AxeMan",Dead=GameOver},
                    new XboxOnePlayer.PlayerInfo { Name="Dr. Death",
                        Dead=GameOver},
                    new XboxOnePlayer.PlayerInfo { Name="HaPpyCaMpEr",
                        Dead=GameOver},
                    new XboxOnePlayer.PlayerInfo { Name="Executioner",
                        Dead=GameOver},
                    new XboxOnePlayer.PlayerInfo { Name="FragMan",Dead=GameOver},
                    new XboxOnePlayer.PlayerInfo { Name="Beatdown",
                        Dead=GameOver},
                    new XboxOnePlayer.PlayerInfo { Name="Stoney",Dead=GameOver},
                    new XboxOnePlayer.PlayerInfo { Name="Pwned",Dead=GameOver},
                    new XboxOnePlayer.PlayerInfo { Name="Big Dawg",
                        Dead=GameOver},
                    new XboxOnePlayer.PlayerInfo { Name="Playa",Dead=GameOver},
                    new XboxOnePlayer.PlayerInfo { Name="BOOM",Dead=GameOver},
                    new XboxOnePlayer.PlayerInfo { Name="Mr. Mxylplyx",
                        Dead=GameOver}
```

```
                };

            foreach (XboxOnePlayer.PlayerInfo player in players)
            {
                Thread t = new Thread(XboxOnePlayer.JoinIn);

                // put a name on the thread
                t.Name = player.Name;
                // fire up the player
                t.Start(player);
            }

            // Wait for the XboxOne to spin up and load Halo5 (3 seconds)
            Console.WriteLine("XboxOne initializing...");
            Thread.Sleep(3000);
            Console.WriteLine(
                "Halo 5 loaded & ready, allowing 8 players in now...");

            // The XboxOne has the whole semaphore count.  We call
            // Release(8) to open up 8 slots and
            // allows the waiting players to enter the XboxOne(semaphore)
            // up to eight at a time.
            //
            _XboxOne.Release(8);

            // wait for the game to end...
            GameOver.WaitOne();
        }
    }
}
```

The first thing the Play method does is to create a new semaphore that has a maximum resource count of 8 and a name of _XboxOne. This is the semaphore that will be used by all of the player threads to gain access to the game. A ManualResetEvent called GameOver is created to track when the game has ended.

To simulate the developers, you create a thread for each with its own XboxOne Player.PlayerInfo class instance to contain the player name and a reference to the original GameOver.ManualResetEvent held in the Dead event on the PlayerInfo, which indicates the player has died. To create the thread you use the Parameterized ThreadStart delegate, which takes the method to execute on the new thread in the constructor, but also allows you to pass the data object directly to a new overload of the Thread.Start method.

Once the players are in motion, the Xbox One "initializes" and then calls Release on the semaphore to open eight slots for player threads to grab on to, and then waits until it detects that the game is over from the firing of the Dead event for the player.

The players initialize on separate threads and run the JoinIn method, as shown in Example 12-6. First they open the Xbox One semaphore by name and get the data that was passed to the thread. Once they have the semaphore, they call WaitOne to queue up to play. Once the initial eight slots are opened or another player "dies," then the call to WaitOne unblocks and the player "plays" for a random amount of time and then dies. Once the players are dead, they call Release on the semaphore to indicate their slot is now open. If the semaphore reaches its maximum resource count, the GameOver event is set.

Example 12-6. JoinIn method

```
public class XboxOnePlayer
{
    public class PlayerInfo
    {
        public ManualResetEvent Dead {get; set;}
        public string Name {get; set;}
    }

    // Death Modes for Players
    private static string[] _deaths = new string[7]{"bought the farm",
                        "choked on a rocket",
                        "shot their own foot",
                        "been captured",
                        "fallen to their death",
                        "died of lead poisoning",
                        "failed to dodge a grenade",
                        };

    /// <summary>
    /// Thread function
    /// </summary>
    /// <param name="info">PlayerInfo item</param>
    public static void JoinIn(object info)
    {
        // open up the semaphore by name so we can act on it
        using (Semaphore XboxOne = Semaphore.OpenExisting("XboxOne"))
        {

            // get the data object
            PlayerInfo player = (PlayerInfo)info;

            // Each player notifies the XboxOne they want to play
            Console.WriteLine($"{player.Name} is waiting to play!");

            // they wait on the XboxOne (semaphore) until it lets them
            // have a controller
            XboxOne.WaitOne();

            // The XboxOne has chosen the player! (or the semaphore has
```

```
        // allowed access to the resource...)
        Console.WriteLine($"{player.Name} has been chosen to play. " +
            $"Welcome to your doom {player.Name}. >:)");

        // figure out a random value for how long the player lasts
        System.Random rand = new Random(500);
        int timeTillDeath = rand.Next(100, 1000);

        // simulate the player is busy playing till they die
        Thread.Sleep(timeTillDeath);

        // figure out how they died
        rand = new Random();
        int deathIndex = rand.Next(6);

        // notify of the player's passing
        Console.WriteLine($"{player.Name} has {_deaths[deathIndex]} " +
        "and gives way to another player");

        // if all ports are open, everyone has played and the game is over
        int semaphoreCount = XboxOne.Release();
        if (semaphoreCount == 3)
        {
            Console.WriteLine("Thank you for playing, the game has ended.");
            // set the Dead event for the player
            player.Dead.Set();
        }
    }
  }
 }
}
```

When the Play method is run, output similar to the following is generated:

```
Igor is waiting to play!
AxeMan is waiting to play!
Dr. Death is waiting to play!
HaPpyCaMpEr is waiting to play!
Executioner is waiting to play!
FragMan is waiting to play!
Beatdown is waiting to play!
Stoney is waiting to play!
Pwned is waiting to play!
Big Dawg is waiting to play!
Playa is waiting to play!
XboxOne initializing...
BOOM is waiting to play!
Mr. Mxylplyx is waiting to play!
Halo 5 loaded & ready, allowing 8 players in now...
Stoney has been chosen to play. Welcome to your doom Stoney. >:)
Executioner has been chosen to play. Welcome to your doom Executioner. >:)
Beatdown has been chosen to play. Welcome to your doom Beatdown. >:)
Pwned has been chosen to play. Welcome to your doom Pwned. >:)
```

```
Playa has been chosen to play. Welcome to your doom Playa. >:)
HaPpyCaMpEr has been chosen to play. Welcome to your doom HaPpyCaMpEr. >:)
Big Dawg has been chosen to play. Welcome to your doom Big Dawg. >:)
FragMan has been chosen to play. Welcome to your doom FragMan. >:)
Playa has been captured and gives way to another player
Stoney has been captured and gives way to another player
Pwned has been captured and gives way to another player
Big Dawg has been captured and gives way to another player
Mr. Mxylplyx has been chosen to play. Welcome to your doom Mr. Mxylplyx. >:)
BOOM has been chosen to play. Welcome to your doom BOOM. >:)
FragMan has was captured and gives way to another player
Dr. Death has been chosen to play. Welcome to your doom Dr. Death. >:)
HaPpyCaMpEr has been captured and gives way to another player
Igor has been chosen to play. Welcome to your doom Igor. >:)
Beatdown has been captured and gives way to another player
Executioner has been captured and gives way to another player
AxeMan has been chosen to play. Welcome to your doom AxeMan. >:)
BOOM has died of lead poisoning and gives way to another player
Thank you for playing, the game has ended.
Mr. Mxylplyx has died of lead poisoning and gives way to another player
```

Discussion

Semaphores are used primarily for resource counting and are available cross-process when named (as they are based on the underlying kernel semaphore object). *Cross-process* may not sound too exciting to many .NET developers until they realize that it also means *cross-AppDomain*. Say you are creating additional AppDomains to hold assemblies you are loading dynamically that you don't want to stick around for the whole life of your main AppDomain; the semaphore can help you keep track of how many are loaded at a time. Being able to control access up to a certain number of users can be useful in many scenarios (socket programming, custom thread pools, etc.).

See Also

The "Semaphore," "ManualResetEvent," and "ParameterizedThreadStart" topics in the MSDN documentation.

12.7 Synchronizing Multiple Processes with the Mutex

Problem

You have two processes or AppDomains that are running code with actions that you need to coordinate.

Solution

Use a named `Mutex` as a common signaling mechanism to do the coordination. A named `Mutex` can be accessed from both pieces of code even when running in different processes or `AppDomains`.

One situation in which this can be useful is when you are using shared memory to communicate between processes. The `SharedMemoryManager` class presented in this recipe will show the named `Mutex` in action by setting up a section of shared memory that can be used to pass serializable objects between processes. The "server" process creates a `SharedMemoryManager` instance, which sets up the shared memory and then creates the `Mutex` as the initial owner. The "client" process then also creates a `SharedMemoryManager` instance that finds the shared memory and hooks up to it. Once this connection is established, the "client" process then sets up to receive the serialized objects and waits until one is sent by waiting on the `Mutex` the "server" process created. The "server" process then takes a serializable object, serializes it into the shared memory, and releases the `Mutex`. It then waits on it again so that when the "client" has received the object, it can release the `Mutex` and give control back to the "server." The "client" process that was waiting on the `Mutex` then deserializes the object from the shared memory and releases the `Mutex`.

In the example, you will send the `Contact` structure, which looks like this:

```
[StructLayout(LayoutKind.Sequential)]
[Serializable()]
public struct Contact
{
    public string _name;
    public int _age;
}
```

The "server" process code to send the `Contact` looks like this:

```
// create the initial shared memory manager to get things set up
using(SharedMemoryManager<Contact> sm =
    new SharedMemoryManager<Contact>("Contacts",8092))
{
    // this is the sender process

    // launch the second process to get going
    string processName = Process.GetCurrentProcess().MainModule.FileName;
    int index = processName.IndexOf("vshost");
    if (index != -1)
    {
        string first = processName.Substring(0, index);
        int numChars = processName.Length - (index + 7);
        string second = processName.Substring(index + 7, numChars);

        processName = first + second;
```

```
    }
    Process receiver = Process.Start(
        new ProcessStartInfo(
            processName,
            "Receiver"));

    // give it 5 seconds to spin up
    Thread.Sleep(5000);

    // make up a contact
    Contact man;
    man._age = 23;
    man._name = "Dirk Daring";

    // send it to the other process via shared memory
    sm.SendObject(man);
}
```

The "client" process code to receive the Contact looks like this:

```
// create the initial shared memory manager to get things set up
using(SharedMemoryManager<Contact> sm =
    new SharedMemoryManager<Contact>("Contacts",8092))
{

    // get the contact once it has been sent
    Contact c = (Contact)sm.ReceiveObject();

    // Write it out (or to a database...)
    Console.WriteLine("Contact {0} is {1} years old.",
                      c._name, c._age);

    // show for 5 seconds
    Thread.Sleep(5000);
}
```

The way this usually works is that one process creates a section of shared memory backed by the paging file using the System.IO.MemoryMappedFiles.MemoryMappedFile. You can see in Example 12-7 where the MemoryMappedFile is set up in the constructor code for the SharedMemoryManager and the private SetupSharedMemory method. The constructor takes a name to use as part of the shared memory name and the base size of the shared memory block to allocate. It is the base size because the SharedMemoryManager has to allocate a bit extra for keeping track of the data moving through the buffer.

Example 12-7. Constructor and SetupSharedMemory private method

```
public SharedMemoryManager(string name,int sharedMemoryBaseSize)
{
    // can only be built for serializable objects
    if (!typeof(TransferItemType).IsSerializable)
```

```
        throw new ArgumentException(
            $"Object {typeof(TransferItemType)} is not serializeable.");

    if (string.IsNullOrEmpty(name))
        throw new ArgumentNullException(nameof(name));

    if (sharedMemoryBaseSize <= 0)
        throw new ArgumentOutOfRangeException(nameof(sharedMemoryBaseSize),
            "Shared Memory Base Size must be a value greater than zero");

    // set name of the region
    Name = name;

    // save base size
    SharedMemoryBaseSize = sharedMemoryBaseSize;

    // set up the shared memory region
    MemMappedFile = MemoryMappedFile.CreateOrOpen(Name, MemoryRegionSize);

    // set up the mutex
    MutexForSharedMem = new Mutex(true, MutexName);
}
```

The code to send an object through the shared memory is contained in the SendOb
ject method, as shown in Example 12-8. First, it checks to see if the object being sent
is indeed serializable by checking the IsSerializable property on the type of the
object. If the object is serializable, an integer with the size of the serialized object and
the serialized object content are written out to the shared memory section. Then, the
Mutex is released to indicate that there is an object in the shared memory. It then
waits on the Mutex again to wait until the "client" has received the object.

Example 12-8. SendObject method

```
public void SendObject(TransferItemType transferObject)
{
    // create a memory stream, initialize size
    using (MemoryStream ms = new MemoryStream())
    {
        // get a formatter to serialize with
        BinaryFormatter formatter = new BinaryFormatter();
        try
        {
            // serialize the object to the stream
            formatter.Serialize(ms, transferObject);

            // get the bytes for the serialized object
            byte[] bytes = ms.ToArray();

            // check that this object will fit
            if(bytes.Length + sizeof(Int32)  > MemoryRegionSize)
```

```
        {
            string msg =
                $"{typeof(TransferItemType)} object instance serialized" +
                $"to {bytes.Length} bytes which is too large for the shared " +
                $"memory region";

            throw new ArgumentException(msg, nameof(transferObject));
        }

        // write to the shared memory region
        using (MemoryMappedViewStream stream =
            MemMappedFile.CreateViewStream())
        {
            BinaryWriter writer = new BinaryWriter(stream);
            writer.Write(bytes.Length); // write the size
            writer.Write(bytes); // write the object
        }
    }
    finally
    {
        // signal the other process using the mutex to tell it
        // to do receive processing
        MutexForSharedMem.ReleaseMutex();

        // wait for the other process to signal it has received
        // and we can move on
        MutexForSharedMem.WaitOne();
    }
    }
}
```

The ReceiveObject method shown in Example 12-9 allows the client to wait until there is an object in the shared memory section and then reads the size of the serialized object and deserializes it to a managed object. It then releases the Mutex to let the sender know to continue.

Example 12-9. ReceiveObject method

```
public TransferItemType ReceiveObject()
{
    // wait on the mutex for an object to be queued by the sender
    MutexForSharedMem.WaitOne();

    // get the object from the shared memory
    byte[] serializedObj = null;
    using (MemoryMappedViewStream stream =
        MemMappedFile.CreateViewStream())
    {
        BinaryReader reader = new BinaryReader(stream);
        int objectLength = reader.ReadInt32();
        serializedObj = reader.ReadBytes(objectLength);
```

```
    }

    // set up the memory stream with the object bytes
    using (MemoryStream ms = new MemoryStream(serializedObj))
    {
        // set up a binary formatter
        BinaryFormatter formatter = new BinaryFormatter();

        // get the object to return
        TransferItemType item;
        try
        {
            item = (TransferItemType)formatter.Deserialize(ms);
        }
        finally
        {
            // signal that we received the object using the mutex
            MutexForSharedMem.ReleaseMutex();
        }
        // give them the object
        return item;
    }
}
```

Discussion

A `Mutex` is designed to give mutually exclusive (thus the name) access to a single resource. A `Mutex` can be thought of as a cross-process named `Monitor`, which "enters" the `Mutex` by waiting on it and becoming the owner, then "exits" by releasing the `Mutex` for the next thread that is waiting on it. If a thread that owns a `Mutex` ends, the `Mutex` is released automatically.

 Using a `Mutex` is slower than using a `Monitor`, as a `Monitor` is a purely managed construct, whereas a `Mutex` is based on the `Mutex` kernel object. A `Mutex` cannot be "pulsed" as can a `Monitor`, but it can be used across processes while a `Monitor` cannot. Finally, the `Mutex` is based on `WaitHandle`, so it can be waited on with other objects derived from `WaitHandle`, like `Semaphore` and the event classes.

The `SharedMemoryManager` class is listed in its entirety in Example 12-10.

Example 12-10. SharedMemoryManager classes

```
/// <summary>
/// Class for sending objects through shared memory using a mutex
/// to synchronize access to the shared memory
/// </summary>
```

```csharp
public class SharedMemoryManager<TransferItemType> : IDisposable
{
    #region Private members
    private bool disposed = false;
    #endregion

    #region Construction / Cleanup
    public SharedMemoryManager(string name,int sharedMemoryBaseSize)
    {
        // can only be built for serializable objects
        if (!typeof(TransferItemType).IsSerializable)
            throw new ArgumentException(
                $"Object {typeof(TransferItemType)} is not serializeable.");

        if (string.IsNullOrEmpty(name))
            throw new ArgumentNullException(nameof(name));

        if (sharedMemoryBaseSize <= 0)
            throw new ArgumentOutOfRangeException("sharedMemoryBaseSize",
                "Shared Memory Base Size must be a value greater than zero");

        // set name of the region
        Name = name;

        // save base size
        SharedMemoryBaseSize = sharedMemoryBaseSize;

        // set up the shared memory region
        MemMappedFile = MemoryMappedFile.CreateOrOpen(Name, MemoryRegionSize);

        // set up the mutex
        MutexForSharedMem = new Mutex(true, MutexName);
    }

    ~SharedMemoryManager()
    {
        // make sure we close
        Dispose(false);
    }

    public void Dispose()
    {
        Dispose(true);
        GC.SuppressFinalize(this);
    }

    private void Dispose(bool disposing)
    {
        // Check to see if Dispose has already been called.
        if (!this.disposed)
        {
            CloseSharedMemory();
```

```csharp
        }
        disposed = true;
    }

    private void CloseSharedMemory()
    {
        if(MemMappedFile != null)
            MemMappedFile.Dispose();
    }

    public void Close()
    {
        CloseSharedMemory();
    }
    #endregion

    #region Properties
    /// <summary>
    /// How big of a memory mapped file to have
    /// </summary>
    public int SharedMemoryBaseSize { get; protected set; }

    /// <summary>
    /// The actual size of the memory region to include size of the
    /// object being transferred
    /// </summary>
    private long MemoryRegionSize => (long)(SharedMemoryBaseSize + sizeof(Int32));

    /// <summary>
    /// Name of the shared memory region
    /// </summary>
    private string Name { get; }

    /// <summary>
    /// The name of the mutex protecting the shared region
    /// </summary>
    private string MutexName => $"{typeof(TransferItemType)}mtx{Name}";

    /// <summary>
    /// The mutex protecting the shared region
    /// </summary>
    private Mutex MutexForSharedMem { get; } = null;

    /// <summary>
    /// The MemoryMappedFile used to transfer objects
    /// </summary>
    private MemoryMappedFile MemMappedFile { get; } = null;

    #endregion

    #region Public Methods
    /// <summary>
```

```
/// Send a serializeable object through the shared memory
/// and wait for it to be picked up
/// </summary>
/// <param name="transferObject"> the object to send</param>
public void SendObject(TransferItemType transferObject)
{
    // create a memory stream, initialize size
    using (MemoryStream ms = new MemoryStream())
    {
        // get a formatter to serialize with
        BinaryFormatter formatter = new BinaryFormatter();
        try
        {
            // serialize the object to the stream
            formatter.Serialize(ms, transferObject);

            // get the bytes for the serialized object
            byte[] bytes = ms.ToArray();

            // check that this object will fit
            if(bytes.Length + sizeof(Int32)  > MemoryRegionSize)
            {
                string msg =
                    $"{typeof(TransferItemType)} object instance serialized" +
                    $"to {bytes.Length} bytes which is too large for the " +
                    $"shared memory region";

                throw new ArgumentException(msg, nameof(transferObject));
            }

            // write to the shared memory region
            using (MemoryMappedViewStream stream =
                MemMappedFile.CreateViewStream())
            {
                BinaryWriter writer = new BinaryWriter(stream);
                writer.Write(bytes.Length); // write the size
                writer.Write(bytes); // write the object
            }
        }
        finally
        {
            // signal the other process using the mutex to tell it
            // to do receive processing
            MutexForSharedMem.ReleaseMutex();

            // wait for the other process to signal it has received
            // and we can move on
            MutexForSharedMem.WaitOne();
        }
    }
}
```

```
/// <summary>
/// Wait for an object to hit the shared memory and then deserialize it
/// </summary>
/// <returns>object passed</returns>
public TransferItemType ReceiveObject()
{
    // wait on the mutex for an object to be queued by the sender
    MutexForSharedMem.WaitOne();

    // get the object from the shared memory
    byte[] serializedObj = null;
    using (MemoryMappedViewStream stream =
        MemMappedFile.CreateViewStream())
    {
        BinaryReader reader = new BinaryReader(stream);
        int objectLength = reader.ReadInt32();
        serializedObj = reader.ReadBytes(objectLength);
    }

    // set up the memory stream with the object bytes
    using (MemoryStream ms = new MemoryStream(serializedObj))
    {
        // set up a binary formatter
        BinaryFormatter formatter = new BinaryFormatter();

        // get the object to return
        TransferItemType item;
        try
        {
            item = (TransferItemType)formatter.Deserialize(ms);
        }
        finally
        {
            // signal that we received the object using the mutex
            MutexForSharedMem.ReleaseMutex();
        }
        // give them the object
        return item;
    }
}
#endregion
}
```

See Also

The "MemoryMappedFiles," "MemoryMappedFile Class," "Mutex," and "Mutex Class"
topics in the MSDN documentation.

12.8 Using Events to Make Threads Cooperate

Problem

You have multiple threads that need to be served by a server, but only one can be served at a time.

Solution

Use an `AutoResetEvent` to notify each thread when it is going to be served. For example, a diner has a cook and multiple waitresses. The waitresses can keep bringing in orders, but the cook can serve up only one at a time. You can simulate this with the Cook class shown in Example 12-11.

Example 12-11. Using events to make threads cooperate

```
public class Cook
{
    public string Name { get; set; }

    public static AutoResetEvent OrderReady =
        new AutoResetEvent(false);

    public void CallWaitress()
    {
        // we call Set on the AutoResetEvent and don't have to
        // call Reset like we would with ManualResetEvent to fire it
        // off again. This sets the event that the waitress is waiting for
        // in GetInLine
        // order is ready....
        Console.WriteLine($"{Name} finished order!");
        OrderReady.Set();
    }
}
```

The `Cook` class has an `AutoResetEvent` called `OrderReady` that the cook will use to tell the waiting waitresses that an order is ready. Since there is only one order ready at a time, and this is an equal-opportunity diner, the waitress who has been waiting longest gets her order first. The `AutoResetEvent` allows for just signaling the single thread when you call `Set` on the `OrderReady` event.

The `Waitress` class has the `PlaceOrder` method that is executed by the thread. `Place Order` takes an `object` parameter, which is passed in from the call to `t.Start` in the next code block. The `Start` method uses a `ParameterizedThreadStart` delegate, which takes an `object` parameter. `PlaceOrder` has been set up to be compatible with it. It takes the `AutoResetEvent` passed in and calls `WaitOne` to wait until the order is ready. Once the Cook fires the event enough times that this waitress is at the head of the line, the code finishes:

```
public class Waitress
{
    public static void PlaceOrder(string waitressName, AutoResetEvent orderReady)
    {
        // order is placed....
        Console.WriteLine($"Waitress {waitressName} placed order!");
        // wait for the order...
        orderReady.WaitOne();
        // order is ready....
        Console.WriteLine($"Waitress {waitressName} got order!");
    }
}
```

The code to run the "diner" creates a Cook and spins off the Waitress threads, and then calls all waitresses when their orders are ready by calling Set on the AutoResetE vent:

```
// We have a diner with a cook who can only serve up one meal at a time
Cook Mel = new Cook() { Name = "Mel" };
string[] waitressNames = { "Flo", "Alice", "Vera", "Jolene", "Belle" };

// Have waitresses place orders
foreach (var waitressName in waitressNames)
{
    Task.Run(() =>
        {
            // The Waitress places the order and then waits for the order
            Waitress.PlaceOrder(waitressName, Cook.OrderReady);
        });
}

// Have the cook fill the orders
for (int i = 0; i < waitressNames.Length; i++)
{
    // make the waitresses wait...
    Thread.Sleep(2000);
    // ok, next waitress, pickup!
    Mel.CallWaitress();
}
```

Discussion

There are two types of events, AutoResetEvent and ManualResetEvent. There are two main differences between the events. The first is that AutoResetEvents release only one of the threads that are waiting on the event, while a ManualResetEvent will release all of them when Set is called. The second difference is that when Set is called on an `AutoResetEvent`, it is automatically reset to a nonsignaled state, while the `Man ualResetEvent` is left in a signaled state until the `Reset` method is called.

The output from the sample code looks like this:

```
Waitress Alice placed order!
Waitress Flo placed order!
Waitress Vera placed order!
Waitress Jolene placed order!
Mel finished order!
Waitress Alice got order!
Waitress Belle placed order!
Mel finished order!
Waitress Jolene got order!
Mel finished order!
Waitress Belle got order!
Mel finished order!
Waitress Flo got order!
Mel finished order!
Waitress Vera got order!
```

See Also

The "AutoResetEvent" and "ManualResetEvent" topics in the MSDN documentation and *Programming Applications for Microsoft Windows*, Fourth Edition (Microsoft Press).

12.9 Performing Atomic Operations Among Threads

Problem

You are operating on data from multiple threads and want to ensure that each operation is carried out fully before performing the next operation from a different thread.

Solution

Use the `Interlocked` family of functions to ensure atomic access. `Interlocked` has methods to increment and decrement values, add a specific amount to a given value, exchange an original value for a new value, compare the current value to the original value, and exchange the original value for a new value if it is equal to the current value.

To increment or decrement an integer value, use the `Increment` or `Decrement` methods, respectively:

```
int i = 0;
long l = 0;
Interlocked.Increment(ref i); // i = 1
Interlocked.Decrement(ref i); // i = 0
```

```
Interlocked.Increment(ref l); // l = 1
Interlocked.Decrement(ref i); // l = 0
```

To add a specific amount to a given integer value, use the Add method:

```
Interlocked.Add(ref i, 10); // i = 10;
Interlocked.Add(ref l, 100); // l = 100;
```

To replace an existing value, use the Exchange method:

```
string name = "Mr. Ed";
Interlocked.Exchange(ref name, "Barney");
```

To check if another thread has changed a value out from under the existing code before replacing the existing value, use the CompareExchange method:

```
int i = 0;
double runningTotal = 0.0;
double startingTotal = 0.0;
double calc = 0.0;
for (i = 0; i < 10; i++)
{
    do
    {
        // store of the original total
        startingTotal = runningTotal;
        // do an intense calculation
        calc = runningTotal + i * Math.PI * 2 / Math.PI;
    }
    // check to make sure runningTotal wasn't modified
    // and replace it with calc if not.  If it was,
    // run through the loop until we get it current
    while (startingTotal !=
        Interlocked.CompareExchange(
            ref runningTotal, calc, startingTotal));
}
```

Discussion

In an operating system like Microsoft Windows, with its ability to perform preemptive multitasking, you must give certain considerations to data integrity when working with multiple threads. There are many synchronization primitives to help secure sections of code, as well as signal when data is available to be modified. To this list is added the capability to perform operations that are guaranteed to be atomic in nature.

If there has not been much threading or assembly language in your past, you might wonder what the big deal is and why you need these atomic functions at all. The basic reason is that the line of code written in C# ultimately has to be translated down to a machine instruction, and along the way, the one line of code written in C# can turn into multiple instructions for the machine to execute. If the machine has to execute multiple instructions to perform a task and the operating system allows for preemption, it is possible that these instructions may not be executed as a unit. They could be interrupted by other code that modifies the value being changed by the original line of C# code in the middle of the C# code being executed. As you can imagine, this could lead to some pretty spectacular errors, or it might just round off the lottery number that keeps a certain C# programmer from winning the big one.

Threading is a powerful tool, but like most "power" tools, you have to understand its operation to use it effectively and safely. Threading bugs are notorious for being some of the most difficult to debug, as the runtime behavior is not constant. Trying to reproduce them can be a nightmare and adding logging can change the behavior, or worse, make the issue disappear! Recognizing that working in a multithreaded environment imposes a certain amount of forethought about protecting data access, and understanding when to use the Interlocked class, will go a long way toward preventing long, frustrating evenings with the debugger.

See Also

The "Interlocked" and "Interlocked Class" topics in the MSDN documentation.

12.10 Optimizing Read-Mostly Access

Problem

You are operating on data that is mostly read with occasional updates and want to perform these actions in a thread-safe but efficient manner.

Solution

Use ReaderWriterLockSlim to give multiple-read/single-write access with the capacity to upgrade the lock from read to write. As an example, say a developer is starting a new project. Unfortunately, the project is understaffed, so the developer has to respond to tasks from many other individuals on the team. Each of the other team members will also ask the developer for status updates on their tasks, and some can even change the priority of the tasks the developer is assigned.

The developer is assigned a task via the AddTask method. To protect the Developer Tasks collection we use a write lock on ReaderWriterLockSlim, calling EnterWrite Lock when adding the task to the DeveloperTasks collection and ExitWriteLock when the addition is complete:

```
public void AddTask(DeveloperTask newTask)
{
    try
    {
```

```
Lock.EnterWriteLock();
// if we already have this task (unique by name)
// then just accept the add as sometimes people
// give you the same task more than once :)
var taskQuery = from t in DeveloperTasks
                where t == newTask
                select t;
if (taskQuery.Count<DeveloperTask>() == 0)
{
    Console.WriteLine($"Task {newTask.Name} was added to developer");
    DeveloperTasks.Add(newTask);
}
    }
    finally
    {
        Lock.ExitWriteLock();
    }
}
```

When a project team member needs to know about the status of a task, they call the
IsTaskDone method, which uses a read lock on the ReaderWriterLockSlim by calling
EnterReadLock and ExitReadLock:

```
public bool IsTaskDone(string taskName)
{
    try
    {
        Lock.EnterReadLock();
        var taskQuery = from t in DeveloperTasks
                        where t.Name == taskName
                        select t;
        if (taskQuery.Count<DeveloperTask>() > 0)
        {
            DeveloperTask task = taskQuery.First<DeveloperTask>();
            Console.WriteLine($"Task {task.Name} status was reported.");
            return task.Status;
        }
    }
    finally
    {
        Lock.ExitReadLock();
    }
    return false;
}
```

There are certain managerial members of the team who have the right to increase the
priority of the tasks they assigned to the developer. They accomplish this by calling
the IncreasePriority method on the Developer. IncreasePriority uses an
upgradable lock on ReaderWriterLockSlim by first calling the EnterUpgradeable
Lock method to acquire a read lock, and then, if the task is in the queue, upgrading to
a write lock in order to adjust the priority of the task. Once the priority is adjusted,

the write lock is released, which degrades the lock back to a read lock, and that lock is released through a call to ExitUpgradeableReadLock:

```
public void IncreasePriority(string taskName)
{
    try
    {
        Lock.EnterUpgradeableReadLock();
        var taskQuery = from t in DeveloperTasks
                        where t.Name == taskName
                        select t;
        if(taskQuery.Count<DeveloperTask>()>0)
        {
            DeveloperTask task = taskQuery.First<DeveloperTask>();
            Lock.EnterWriteLock();
            task.Priority++;
            Console.WriteLine($"Task {task.Name}" +
                $" priority was increased to {task.Priority}" +
                " for developer");
            Lock.ExitWriteLock();
        }
    }
    finally
    {
        Lock.ExitUpgradeableReadLock();
    }
}
```

Discussion

The ReaderWriterLockSlim was created to replace the existing ReaderWriterLock for a number of reasons:

- ReaderWriterLock was more than five times slower than using a Monitor.
- Recursion semantics of ReaderWriterLock were not standard and were broken in some thread reentrancy cases.
- The upgrade lock method is nonatomic in ReaderWriterLock.

While the ReaderWriterLockSlim is only about two times slower than the Monitor, it is more flexible and prioritizes writes, so in "few write, many read" scenarios, it is more scalable than the Monitor. There are also methods to determine what type of lock is held as well as how many threads are waiting to acquire it.

By default, lock acquisition recursion is disallowed. If you call EnterReadLock twice, you get a LockRecursionException. You can enable lock recursion by passing a Lock RecusionPolicy.SupportsRecursion enumeration value to the constructor overload of ReaderWriterLockSlim that accepts it. Even though it is possible to enable lock recursion, it is generally discouraged, as it complicates matters and creates issues that are not fun to debug.

 There are some scenarios where the ReaderWriterLockSlim is not appropriate for use, although most of these are not applicable to everyday development:

- Due to the incompatible HostProtection attributes, Reader WriterLockSlim is precluded from use in SQL Server CLR scenarios.

- Because ReaderWriterLockSlim doesn't mark critical regions, hosts that use thread aborts won't know that it will be harmed by them, so issues will arise in the hosted AppDomains.

- ReaderWriterLockSlim cannot handle asynchronous exceptions (thread aborts, out of memory, etc.) and could end up with a corrupt lock state, which could cause deadlocks or other issues.

- ReaderWriterLockSlim has thread affinity, so it usually cannot be used with async and await. For those cases, use Semaphore Slim.WaitAsync instead.

The entire code base for the example is listed here:

```
static Developer s_dev = null;
static bool s_end = false;

/// <summary>
/// </summary>
public static void TestReaderWriterLockSlim()
{
    s_dev = new Developer(15);
    LaunchTeam(s_dev);
    Thread.Sleep(10000);
}

private static void LaunchTeam(Developer dev)
{
    LaunchManager("CTO", dev);
    LaunchManager("Director", dev);
    LaunchManager("Project Manager", dev);
    LaunchDependent("Product Manager", dev);
    LaunchDependent("Test Engineer", dev);
    LaunchDependent("Technical Communications Professional", dev);
    LaunchDependent("Operations Staff", dev);
    LaunchDependent("Support Staff", dev);
}
```

```csharp
public class DeveloperTaskInfo
{
    public string Name { get; set; }
    public Developer Developer { get; set; }
}

private static void LaunchManager(string name, Developer dev)
{
    var dti = new DeveloperTaskInfo() { Name = name, Developer = dev };
    Task manager = Task.Run(() => {
        Console.WriteLine($"Added {dti.Name} to the project...");
        DeveloperTaskManager mgr = new DeveloperTaskManager(dti.Name,
            dti.Developer);
    });
}

private static void LaunchDependent(string name, Developer dev)
{
    var dti = new DeveloperTaskInfo() { Name = name, Developer = dev };
    Task manager = Task.Run(() => {
        Console.WriteLine($"Added {dti.Name} to the project...");
        DeveloperTaskDependent dep =
            new DeveloperTaskDependent(dti.Name, dti.Developer);
    });
}

public class DeveloperTask
{
    public DeveloperTask(string name)
    {
        Name = name;
    }

    public string Name { get; set; }
    public int Priority { get; set; }
    public bool Status { get; set; }

    public override string ToString() => this.Name;

    public override bool Equals(object obj)
    {
        DeveloperTask task = obj as DeveloperTask;
        return this.Name == task?.Name;
    }

    public override int GetHashCode() => this.Name.GetHashCode();
}

public class Developer : IDisposable
{
    /// <summary>
```

```
/// Dictionary for the tasks
/// </summary>
private List<DeveloperTask> DeveloperTasks { get; } =
    new List<DeveloperTask>();
private ReaderWriterLockSlim Lock { get; set; } = new ReaderWriterLockSlim();
private System.Threading.Timer Timer { get; set; }
private int MaxTasks { get; }

public Developer(int maxTasks)
{
    // the maximum number of tasks before the developer quits
    MaxTasks = maxTasks;
    // do some work every 1/4 second
    Timer = new Timer(new TimerCallback(DoWork), null, 1000, 250);
}

~Developer()
{
    Dispose(true);
}

// Execute a task
protected void DoWork(Object stateInfo)
{
    ExecuteTask();
    try
    {
        Lock.EnterWriteLock();
        // if we finished all tasks, go on vacation!
        if (DeveloperTasks.Count == 0)
        {
            s_end = true;
            Console.WriteLine(
                "Developer finished all tasks, go on vacation!");
            return;
        }

        if (!s_end)
        {
            // if we have too many tasks quit
            if (DeveloperTasks.Count > MaxTasks)
            {
                // get the number of unfinished tasks
                var query = from t in DeveloperTasks
                            where t.Status == false
                            select t;
                int unfinishedTaskCount = query.Count<DeveloperTask>();

                s_end = true;
                Console.WriteLine(
                    "Developer has too many tasks, quitting! " +
                    $"{unfinishedTaskCount} tasks left unfinished.");
```

```csharp
            }
        }
        else
            Timer.Dispose();
    }
    finally
    {
        Lock.ExitWriteLock();
    }
}

public void AddTask(DeveloperTask newTask)
{
    try
    {
        Lock.EnterWriteLock();
        // if we already have this task (unique by name)
        // then just accept the add as sometimes people
        // give you the same task more than once :)
        var taskQuery = from t in DeveloperTasks
                        where t == newTask
                        select t;
        if (taskQuery.Count<DeveloperTask>() == 0)
        {
            Console.WriteLine($"Task {newTask.Name} was added to developer");
            DeveloperTasks.Add(newTask);
        }
    }
    finally
    {
        Lock.ExitWriteLock();
    }
}

/// <summary>
/// Increase the priority of the task
/// </summary>
/// <param name="taskName">name of the task</param>
public void IncreasePriority(string taskName)
{
    try
    {
        Lock.EnterUpgradeableReadLock();
        var taskQuery = from t in DeveloperTasks
                        where t.Name == taskName
                        select t;
        if(taskQuery.Count<DeveloperTask>()>0)
        {
            DeveloperTask task = taskQuery.First<DeveloperTask>();
            Lock.EnterWriteLock();
            task.Priority++;
            Console.WriteLine($"Task {task.Name}" +
```

```
                        $" priority was increased to {task.Priority}" +
                        " for developer");
                Lock.ExitWriteLock();
            }
        }
        finally
        {
            Lock.ExitUpgradeableReadLock();
        }
    }

    // <summary>
    // Allows people to check if the task is done
    // </summary>
    // <param name="taskName">name of the task</param>
    // <returns>False if the taks is undone or not in the list,
    // true if done</returns>
    public bool IsTaskDone(string taskName)
    {
        try
        {
            Lock.EnterReadLock();
            var taskQuery = from t in DeveloperTasks
                            where t.Name == taskName
                            select t;
            if (taskQuery.Count<DeveloperTask>() > 0)
            {
                DeveloperTask task = taskQuery.First<DeveloperTask>();
                Console.WriteLine($"Task {task.Name} status was reported.");
                return task.Status;
            }
        }
        finally
        {
            Lock.ExitReadLock();
        }
        return false;
    }

    private void ExecuteTask()
    {
        // look over the tasks and do the highest priority
        var queryResult =   from t in DeveloperTasks
                            where t.Status == false
                            orderby t.Priority
                            select t;
        if (queryResult.Count<DeveloperTask>() > 0)
        {
            // do the task
            DeveloperTask task = queryResult.First<DeveloperTask>();
            task.Status = true;
            task.Priority = -1;
```

```
            Console.WriteLine($"Task {task.Name} executed by developer.");
        }
    }

    #region IDisposable Support
    private bool disposedValue = false; // To detect redundant calls

    protected virtual void Dispose(bool disposing)
    {
        if (!disposedValue)
        {
            if (disposing)
            {
                Lock?.Dispose();
                Lock = null;
                Timer?.Dispose();
                Timer = null;
            }
            disposedValue = true;
        }
    }

    public void Dispose()
    {
        Dispose(true);
    }
    #endregion
}

public class DeveloperTaskManager : DeveloperTaskDependent, IDisposable
{
    private System.Threading.Timer ManagerTimer { get; set; }

    public DeveloperTaskManager(string name, Developer taskExecutor) :
        base(name, taskExecutor)
    {
        // intervene every 2 seconds
        ManagerTimer =
            new Timer(new TimerCallback(Intervene), null, 0, 2000);
    }

    ~DeveloperTaskManager()
    {
        Dispose(true);
    }

    // Intervene in the plan
    protected void Intervene(Object stateInfo)
    {
        ChangePriority();
        // developer ended, kill timer
        if (s_end)
```

```
            {
                ManagerTimer.Dispose();
                TaskExecutor = null;
            }
        }

        public void ChangePriority()
        {
            if (DeveloperTasks.Count > 0)
            {
                int taskIndex = _rnd.Next(0, DeveloperTasks.Count - 1);
                DeveloperTask checkTask = DeveloperTasks[taskIndex];
                // make those developers work faster on some random task!
                if (TaskExecutor != null)
                {
                    TaskExecutor.IncreasePriority(checkTask.Name);
                    Console.WriteLine(
                        $"{Name} intervened and changed priority for task
{checkTask.Name}");
                }
            }
        }

        #region IDisposable Support
        private bool disposedValue = false; // To detect redundant calls

        protected override void Dispose(bool disposing)
        {
            if (!disposedValue)
            {
                if (disposing)
                {
                    ManagerTimer?.Dispose();
                    ManagerTimer = null;
                    base.Dispose(disposing);
                }
                disposedValue = true;
            }
        }

        public new void Dispose()
        {
            Dispose(true);
        }
        #endregion
    }

    public class DeveloperTaskDependent : IDisposable
    {
        protected List<DeveloperTask> DeveloperTasks { get; set; }
            = new List<DeveloperTask>();
        protected Developer TaskExecutor { get; set; }
```

```csharp
    protected Random _rnd = new Random();
    private Timer TaskTimer { get; set; }
    private Timer StatusTimer { get; set; }

    public DeveloperTaskDependent(string name, Developer taskExecutor)
    {
        Name = name;
        TaskExecutor = taskExecutor;
        // add work every 1 second
        TaskTimer = new Timer(new TimerCallback(AddWork), null, 0, 1000);
        // check status every 3 seconds
        StatusTimer = new Timer(new TimerCallback(CheckStatus), null, 0, 3000);
    }


    ~DeveloperTaskDependent()
    {
        Dispose();
    }

    // Add more work to the developer
    protected void AddWork(Object stateInfo)
    {
        SubmitTask();
        // developer ended, kill timer
        if (s_end)
        {
            TaskTimer.Dispose();
            TaskExecutor = null;
        }
    }

    // Check Status of work with the developer
    protected void CheckStatus(Object stateInfo)
    {
        CheckTaskStatus();
        // developer ended, kill timer
        if (s_end)
        {
            StatusTimer.Dispose();
            TaskExecutor = null;
        }
    }

    public string Name { get; set; }

    public void SubmitTask()
    {
        int taskId = _rnd.Next(10000);
        string taskName = $"({taskId} for {Name})";
        DeveloperTask newTask = new DeveloperTask(taskName);
```

```
        if (TaskExecutor != null)
        {
            TaskExecutor.AddTask(newTask);
            DeveloperTasks.Add(newTask);
        }
    }

    public void CheckTaskStatus()
    {
        if (DeveloperTasks.Count > 0)
        {
            int taskIndex = _rnd.Next(0, DeveloperTasks.Count - 1);
            DeveloperTask checkTask = DeveloperTasks[taskIndex];
            if (TaskExecutor != null &&
                TaskExecutor.IsTaskDone(checkTask.Name))
            {
                Console.WriteLine($"Task {checkTask.Name} is done for {Name}");
                // remove it from the todo list
                DeveloperTasks.Remove(checkTask);
            }
        }
    }

    #region IDisposable Support
    private bool disposedValue = false; // To detect redundant calls

    protected virtual void Dispose(bool disposing)
    {
        if (!disposedValue)
        {
            if (disposing)
            {
                TaskTimer?.Dispose();
                TaskTimer = null;
                StatusTimer?.Dispose();
                StatusTimer = null;
            }
            disposedValue = true;
        }
    }

    public void Dispose()
    {
        Dispose(true);
    }
    #endregion
}
```

You can see the series of events in the project in the output. The point at which the developer has had enough is highlighted:

```
Added CTO to the project...
Added Director to the project...
```

```
Added Project Manager to the project...
Added Product Manager to the project...
Added Test Engineer to the project...
Added Technical Communications Professional to the project...
Added Operations Staff to the project...
Added Support Staff to the project...
Task (6267 for CTO) was added to developer
Task (6267 for CTO) status was reported.
Task (6267 for CTO) priority was increased to 1 for developer
CTO intervened and changed priority for task (6267 for CTO)
Task (6267 for Director) was added to developer
Task (6267 for Director) status was reported.
Task (6267 for Director) priority was increased to 1 for developer
Director intervened and changed priority for task (6267 for Director)
Task (6267 for Project Manager) was added to developer
Task (6267 for Project Manager) status was reported.
Task (6267 for Project Manager) priority was increased to 1 for developer
Project Manager intervened and changed priority for task (6267 for Project
Manager)
Task (6267 for Product Manager) was added to developer
Task (6267 for Product Manager) status was reported.
Task (6267 for Technical Communications Professional) was added to developer
Task (6267 for Technical Communications Professional) status was reported.
Task (6267 for Operations Staff) was added to developer
Task (6267 for Operations Staff) status was reported.
Task (6267 for Support Staff) was added to developer
Task (6267 for Support Staff) status was reported.
Task (6267 for Test Engineer) was added to developer
Task (5368 for CTO) was added to developer
Task (5368 for Director) was added to developer
Task (5368 for Project Manager) was added to developer
Task (6153 for Product Manager) was added to developer
Task (913 for Test Engineer) was added to developer
Task (6153 for Technical Communications Professional) was added to developer
Task (6153 for Operations Staff) was added to developer
Task (6153 for Support Staff) was added to developer
Task (6267 for Product Manager) executed by developer.
Task (6267 for Technical Communications Professional) executed by developer.
Task (6267 for Operations Staff) executed by developer.
Task (6267 for Support Staff) executed by developer.
Task (6267 for CTO) priority was increased to 2 for developer
CTO intervened and changed priority for task (6267 for CTO)
Task (6267 for Director) priority was increased to 2 for developer
Director intervened and changed priority for task (6267 for Director)
Task (6267 for Project Manager) priority was increased to 2 for developer
Project Manager intervened and changed priority for task (6267 for Project
Manager)
Task (6267 for Test Engineer) executed by developer.
Task (7167 for CTO) was added to developer
Task (7167 for Director) was added to developer
Task (7167 for Project Manager) was added to developer
Task (5368 for Product Manager) was added to developer
```

Task (6153 for Test Engineer) was added to developer
Task (5368 for Technical Communications Professional) was added to developer
Task (5368 for Operations Staff) was added to developer
Task (5368 for Support Staff) was added to developer
Task (5368 for CTO) executed by developer.
Task (5368 for Director) executed by developer.
Task (5368 for Project Manager) executed by developer.
Task (6267 for CTO) status was reported.
Task (6267 for Director) status was reported.
Task (6267 for Project Manager) status was reported.
Task (913 for Test Engineer) status was reported.
Task (6267 for Technical Communications Professional) status was reported.
Task (6267 for Technical Communications Professional) is done for Technical
Communications Professional
Task (6267 for Product Manager) status was reported.
Task (6267 for Product Manager) is done for Product Manager
Task (6267 for Operations Staff) status was reported.
Task (6267 for Operations Staff) is done for Operations Staff
Task (6267 for Support Staff) status was reported.
Task (6267 for Support Staff) is done for Support Staff
Task (6153 for Product Manager) executed by developer.
Task (2987 for CTO) was added to developer
Task (2987 for Director) was added to developer
Task (2987 for Project Manager) was added to developer
Task (7167 for Product Manager) was added to developer
Task (4126 for Test Engineer) was added to developer
Task (7167 for Technical Communications Professional) was added to developer
Task (7167 for Support Staff) was added to developer
Task (7167 for Operations Staff) was added to developer
Task (913 for Test Engineer) executed by developer.
Task (6153 for Technical Communications Professional) executed by developer.
Developer has too many tasks, quitting! 21 tasks left unfinished.
Task (6153 for Operations Staff) executed by developer.
Task (5368 for CTO) priority was increased to 0 for developer
CTO intervened and changed priority for task (5368 for CTO)
Task (5368 for Director) priority was increased to 0 for developer
Director intervened and changed priority for task (5368 for Director)
Task (5368 for Project Manager) priority was increased to 0 for developer
Project Manager intervened and changed priority for task (5368 for Project
Manager)
Task (6153 for Support Staff) executed by developer.
Task (4906 for Product Manager) was added to developer
Task (7167 for Test Engineer) was added to developer
Task (4906 for Technical Communications Professional) was added to developer
Task (4906 for Operations Staff) was added to developer
Task (4906 for Support Staff) was added to developer
Task (7167 for CTO) executed by developer.
Task (7167 for Director) executed by developer.
Task (7167 for Project Manager) executed by developer.
Task (5368 for Product Manager) executed by developer.
Task (6153 for Test Engineer) executed by developer.
Task (5368 for Technical Communications Professional) executed by developer.

```
Task (5368 for Operations Staff) executed by developer.
Task (5368 for Support Staff) executed by developer.
Task (2987 for CTO) executed by developer.
Task (2987 for Director) executed by developer.
Task (2987 for Project Manager) executed by developer.
Task (7167 for Product Manager) executed by developer.
Task (4126 for Test Engineer) executed by developer.
```

See Also

The "ReaderWriterLockSlim" topic in the MSDN documentation.

12.11 Making Your Database Requests More Scalable

Problem

You want to make your database calls as efficient and scalable as possible from a caller's perspective.

Solution

Use async, await, and the *Async versions of the database calls so that other work can be accomplished with threads in the program while you wait for the database I/O to complete.

 If you aren't familiar with async and await, which were introduced in C# 5.0, see the MSDN topic "Asynchronous Programming with Async and Await" for more details.

If you use SqlConnection and SqlCommand, you would use the SqlConnection.OpenA sync and the SqlCommand.ExecuteReaderAsync method to open and query the database asynchronously:

```
using (SqlConnection conn =
    new SqlConnection(Settings.Default.NorthwindConnectionString))
{
    await conn.OpenAsync();
    SqlCommand cmd = new SqlCommand("SELECT * FROM CUSTOMERS", conn);
    SqlDataReader reader = await cmd.ExecuteReaderAsync();
    while (reader.Read())
    {
        Console.WriteLine($"Customer {reader["ContactName"].ToString()} " +
            $"from {reader["CompanyName"].ToString()}");
    }
}
```

If you use Entity Framework, you can use the `IQueryable<T>.ToListAsync` extension method to open the connection and execute the query asynchronously:

```
using (var efContext = new NorthwindEntities())
{
    var list = await (from cust in efContext.Customers
                select cust).ToListAsync();

    foreach(var cust in list)
    {
        Console.WriteLine($"Customer {cust.ContactName} " +
            $"from {cust.CompanyName}");
    }
}
```

If you wanted to write a new record using `EntityFramework` and then get it back to check it, you would use the `System.Data.Entity.DbContext.SaveChangesAsync` method after adding a new entity to the context. Then you could use the `IQuerya ble<T>.FirstOrDefaultAsync` extension method to retrieve just the first matching item or null:

```
// Make a new customer and save them
Customer c = new Customer();
c.CustomerID = "JENNA";
c.ContactName = "Jenna Roberts";
c.CompanyName = "Flamingo Industries";
efContext.Customers.Add(c);
await efContext.SaveChangesAsync();

var jenna = await efContext.Customers.Where(cu =>
                    cu.ContactName == "Jenna Roberts").FirstOrDefaultAsync();
Console.WriteLine($"New Customer {jenna.ContactName} " +
        $"from {jenna.CompanyName}");
}
```

Discussion

While some of the database technologies have currently implemented `async` support, not all of them are so lucky. LINQ to SQL is still derived from `System.Data.Linq.DataContext`, which does not have `async` support. While you can still use LINQ to SQL for non-`async` operations like so:

```
using (var l2sContext = new NorthwindLinq2SqlDataContext())
{
    var list = (from cust in l2sContext.Customers
                select cust);
    foreach (var cust in list)
    {
        Console.WriteLine($"Customer {cust.ContactName} " +
            $"from {cust.CompanyName}");
    }
}
```

if you tried to use the `async` support as shown here with LINQ to SQL, you will get this error:

```
var list = await (from cust in l2sContext.Customers
                  select cust).ToListAsync();
// Additional information: The source IQueryable doesn't implement
// IDbAsyncEnumerable<NorthwindLinq2Sql.Customer>. Only sources that implement
// IDbAsyncEnumerable can be used for Entity Framework
```

If you want `async` support for your database actions, you need to either use the `System.Data.SqlClient` constructs (like `SqlConnection`, `SqlDataReader`, etc.) or use Entity Framework 6 or above.

See Also

See the "System.Data.SqlClient namespace," "Asynchronous Programming with Async and Await," and "Entity Framework Async Query & Save" topics in the MSDN documentation.

12.12 Running Tasks in Order

Problem

You have primary tasks that need to complete before secondary tasks are executed in your application.

Solution

Use `Task.ContinueWith` to execute a follow-on task once a primary task has been completed.

`ContinueWith` allows you to append a task to be executed asynchronously upon the completion of an original task. This is useful in instances when some of the tasks have an ordering constraint and some do not.

As an example, think about the 4 × 400 meter relay in the Olympics. There are a number of primary tasks (runners who run the first leg of the relay for each country), followed by tasks that depend on the result of the first task (the runners who are running the remaining legs of the relay). None of the dependent tasks can start until the previous task (the passing of the baton) is finished.

To represent each of the runners in the relay, we have a `RelayRunner` class that contains the `Country` the runner is representing, the `Leg` of the race he or she will run, if he or she has the baton currently (`HasBaton`), and how long it took him or her to run the leg of the relay (`LegTime`). Finally, we have a method to make the `RelayRunner` sprint when it is his or her turn (`Sprint`).

```
public class RelayRunner
{
    public string Country { get; set; }
    public int Leg { get; set; }
    public bool HasBaton { get; set; }
    public TimeSpan LegTime { get; set; }
    public int TotalLegs { get; set; }

    public RelayRunner Sprint()
    {
        Console.WriteLine(
            $"{Country} for Leg {Leg} has the baton and is running!");
        Random rnd = new Random();
        int ms = rnd.Next(100, 1000);
        Task.Delay(ms);
        // finished....
        LegTime = new TimeSpan(0,0,0,0,ms);
        if (Leg == TotalLegs)
            Console.WriteLine($"{Country} has finished the race!");
        return this;
    }
}
```

Now that we have runners, we need to set up the countries for them to run for (coun
tries), and some tracking about who is running for each team (teams); who is in the
race in general (runners); and who are the first-leg runners (firstLegRunners):

```
// Relay race in the olympics
string[] countries = { "Russia", "France", "England", "United States",
                        "India", "Germany", "China" };
Task<RelayRunner>[,] teams = new Task<RelayRunner>[countries.Length, 4];
List<Task<RelayRunner>> runners = new List<Task<RelayRunner>>();
List<Task<RelayRunner>> firstLegRunners = new List<Task<RelayRunner>>();
```

We will populate these collections with the runners such that the first-leg runner
from each team has the baton; and if the runner is not the first runner from his or her
team, his or her start is subject to when the prior runner on the team finishes (Contin
ueWith):

```
for (int i = 0; i < countries.Length; i++)
{
    for (int r = 0; r < 4; r++)
    {
        var runner = new RelayRunner()
        {
            Country = countries[i],
            Leg = r+1,
            HasBaton = r == 0 ? true : false,
            TotalLegs = 4
        };

        if (r == 0) // add starting leg for country
```

```
        {
            Func<RelayRunner> funcRunner = runner.Sprint;
            teams[i, r] = new Task<RelayRunner>(funcRunner);
            firstLegRunners.Add(teams[i, r]);
        }
        else // add other legs for country
        {
            teams[i, r] = teams[i, r - 1].ContinueWith((lastRunnerRunning) =>
                {
                    var lastRunner = lastRunnerRunning.Result;
                    // Handoff the baton
                    Console.WriteLine($"{lastRunner.Country} hands off from " +
                        $"{lastRunner.Leg} to {runner.Leg}!");
                    Random rnd = new Random();
                    int fumbleChance = rnd.Next(0, 10);
                    if (fumbleChance > 8)
                    {
                        Console.WriteLine(
                            $"Oh no! {lastRunner.Country} for Leg " +
                            $"{runner.Leg} fumbled the hand off from Leg " +
                            $"{lastRunner.Leg}!");
                        Thread.Sleep(1000);
                        Console.WriteLine($"{lastRunner.Country} for Leg " +
                            $"{runner.Leg}" +
                            " recovered the baton and is running again!");
                    }
                    lastRunner.HasBaton = false;
                    runner.HasBaton = true;
                    return runner.Sprint();
                });
        }
        // add to our list of runners
        runners.Add(teams[i, r]);
    }
}
```

To simulate the starting gun, we will use `Parallel.ForEach` to call `Start` on each of the first-leg-runner tasks. This guarantees a more random start than if we had done a simple `for` loop:

```
//Fire the gun to start the race!
Parallel.ForEach(firstLegRunners, r =>
{
    r.Start();
});
```

Finally, we use the list of all of the `Task<RelayRunner>` tasks and call `Task.WaitAll` in order to wait for the finish of the race:

```
// Wait for everyone to finish
Task.WaitAll(runners.ToArray());
```

Discussion

While running tasks in a certain order goes against parallelism in general—as it would be best for scalability to be able to run a set of tasks independently in any order—the reality is that most tasks do have an order and being able to represent that order in code is useful. `ContinueWith` provides a number of overloads with many parameters to control the action taken after the initial task completes. Table 12-1 lists the types of control structures available as parameters.

Table 12-1. ContinueWith parameters

Value	Description
`Action<Task>`	The action to run when the initial task completes. This will be passed the original task as a reference.
`Func<Task, TRe sult>`	The function to run when the initial task completes. This will be passed the original task as a reference.
`CancellationToken`	The token assigned to the continuation task to allow for cancelling of the continuation.
`TaskScheduler`	The scheduler to use for this task (other than the default if a different scheduling algorithm is necessary based on the tasks).
`Object`	A state object to pass into the continuation.

To display the standings at the end of the race, we used the following code, which groups the runners by team and adds together their times (`LegTime`) with the LINQ `Sum` extension method:

```
Console.WriteLine("\r\nRace standings:");

var standings = from r in runners
                group r by r.Result.Country into countryTeams
                select countryTeams;

string winningCountry = string.Empty;
int bestTime = int.MaxValue;

HashSet<Tuple<int, string>> place = new HashSet<Tuple<int, string>>();
foreach (var team in standings)
{
    var time = team.Sum(r => r.Result.LegTime.Milliseconds);
    if (time < bestTime)
    {
        bestTime = time;
        winningCountry = team.Key;
    }
    place.Add(new Tuple<int, string>(time,
        $"{team.Key} with a time of {time}ms"));
}
int p = 1;
foreach(var item in place.OrderBy(t => t.Item1))
```

```
    {
        Console.WriteLine($"{p}: {item.Item2}");
        p++;
    }
    Console.WriteLine($"\n\nThe winning team is from {winningCountry}");
```

The output from the race will look similar to this:

```
France for Leg 1 has the baton and is running!
United States for Leg 1 has the baton and is running!
Russia for Leg 1 has the baton and is running!
England for Leg 1 has the baton and is running!
France hands off from 1 to 2!
England hands off from 1 to 2!
Russia hands off from 1 to 2!
United States hands off from 1 to 2!
Russia for Leg 2 has the baton and is running!
Oh no! England for Leg 2 fumbled the hand off from Leg 1!
Oh no! France for Leg 2 fumbled the hand off from Leg 1!
United States for Leg 2 has the baton and is running!
Russia hands off from 2 to 3!
United States hands off from 2 to 3!
Russia for Leg 3 has the baton and is running!
Russia hands off from 3 to 4!
United States for Leg 3 has the baton and is running!
Russia for Leg 4 has the baton and is running!
United States hands off from 3 to 4!
United States for Leg 4 has the baton and is running!
United States has finished the race!
Russia has finished the race!
Germany for Leg 1 has the baton and is running!
Germany hands off from 1 to 2!
Germany for Leg 2 has the baton and is running!
Germany hands off from 2 to 3!
Germany for Leg 3 has the baton and is running!
India for Leg 1 has the baton and is running!
India hands off from 1 to 2!
India for Leg 2 has the baton and is running!
Germany hands off from 3 to 4!
Germany for Leg 4 has the baton and is running!
India hands off from 2 to 3!
India for Leg 3 has the baton and is running!
India hands off from 3 to 4!
India for Leg 4 has the baton and is running!
India has finished the race!
China for Leg 1 has the baton and is running!
Germany has finished the race!
China hands off from 1 to 2!
China for Leg 2 has the baton and is running!
China hands off from 2 to 3!
China for Leg 3 has the baton and is running!
China hands off from 3 to 4!
China for Leg 4 has the baton and is running!
```

```
China has finished the race!
France for Leg 2 recovered the baton and is running again!
France for Leg 2 has the baton and is running!
France hands off from 2 to 3!
France for Leg 3 has the baton and is running!
France hands off from 3 to 4!
France for Leg 4 has the baton and is running!
France has finished the race!
England for Leg 2 recovered the baton and is running again!
England for Leg 2 has the baton and is running!
England hands off from 2 to 3!
England for Leg 3 has the baton and is running!
England hands off from 3 to 4!
England for Leg 4 has the baton and is running!
England has finished the race!

Race standings:
1: India with a time of 696ms
2: Germany with a time of 698ms
3: China with a time of 699ms
4: Russia with a time of 1510ms
5: United States with a time of 1540ms
6: France with a time of 2659ms
7: England with a time of 3625ms


The winning team is from India
```

See Also

The "Task.ContinueWith," "Task.WaitAll," and "Parallel.ForEach" topics in the MSDN documentation and *Concurrency in C# Cookbook*, by Stephen Cleary (O'Reilly).

CHAPTER 13

Toolbox

13.0 Introduction

Every programmer has a certain set of routines that he refers back to and uses over and over again. These utility functions are usually bits of code that are not provided by any particular language or framework. This chapter is a compilation of utility routines that we have gathered during our time with C# and the .NET Framework. The types of things we share in this chapter are:

- Power management events
- Determining the path for various locations in the operating system
- Interacting with services
- Inspecting the Global Assembly Cache
- Message queuing

It is a grab bag of code that can help to solve a specific need while you are working on a larger set of functionality in your application.

13.1 Dealing with Operating System Shutdown, Power Management, or User Session Changes

Problem

You want to be notified whenever the operating system or a user has initiated an action that requires your application to shut down or be inactive (user logoff, remote session disconnect, system shutdown, hibernate/restore, etc.). This notification will allow you to have your application respond gracefully to the changes.

Solution

Use the `Microsoft.Win32.SystemEvents` class to get notification of operating system, user session change, and power management events. The `RegisterForSystemEvents` method shown next hooks up the five event handlers necessary to capture these events and should be placed in the initialization section for your code:

```
public static void RegisterForSystemEvents()
{
    // always get the final notification when the event thread is shutting down
    // so we can unregister
    SystemEvents.EventsThreadShutdown +=
        new EventHandler(OnEventsThreadShutdown);
    SystemEvents.PowerModeChanged +=
        new PowerModeChangedEventHandler(OnPowerModeChanged);
    SystemEvents.SessionSwitch +=
        new SessionSwitchEventHandler(OnSessionSwitch);
    SystemEvents.SessionEnding +=
        new SessionEndingEventHandler(OnSessionEnding);
    SystemEvents.SessionEnded +=
        new SessionEndedEventHandler(OnSessionEnded);
}
```

The `EventsThreadShutdown` event notifies you of when the thread that is distributing the events from the `SystemEvents` class is shutting down so that you can unregister the events on the `SystemEvents` class if you have not already done so. The `PowerMode Changed` event triggers when the user suspends or resumes the system from a suspended state. The `SessionSwitch` event is triggered by a change in the logged-on user. The `SessionEnding` event is triggered when the user is trying to log off or shut down the system, and the `SessionEnded` event is triggered when the user is actually logging off or shutting down the system.

You can unregister the events using the `UnregisterFromSystemEvents` method. `UnregisterFromSystemEvents` should be called from the termination code of your Windows Form, user control, or any other class that may come and go, as well as from one other area shown later in the recipe:

```
private static void UnregisterFromSystemEvents()
{
    SystemEvents.EventsThreadShutdown -=
        new EventHandler(OnEventsThreadShutdown);
    SystemEvents.PowerModeChanged -=
        new PowerModeChangedEventHandler(OnPowerModeChanged);
    SystemEvents.SessionSwitch -=
        new SessionSwitchEventHandler(OnSessionSwitch);
    SystemEvents.SessionEnding -=
        new SessionEndingEventHandler(OnSessionEnding);
    SystemEvents.SessionEnded -=
        new SessionEndedEventHandler(OnSessionEnded);
}
```

Since the events exposed by SystemEvents are static, if you are using them in a section of code that could be invoked multiple times (secondary Windows Form, user control, monitoring class, etc.), you *must* unregister your handlers, or you will cause memory leaks in the application.

The SystemEvents handler methods are the individual event handlers for each event that has been subscribed to in RegisterForSystemEvents. The first handler to cover is the OnEventsThreadShutdown handler. It is essential that your handlers are unregistered if this event fires, as the notification thread for the SystemEvents class is going away, and the class may be gone before your application is. If you haven't unregistered before that point, you will cause memory leaks, so add a call to UnregisterFromSystemEvents into this handler as shown here:

```
private static void OnEventsThreadShutdown(object sender, EventArgs e)
{
    Debug.WriteLine(
        "System event thread is shutting down, no more notifications.");

    // Unregister all our events as the notification thread is going away
    UnregisterFromSystemEvents();
}
```

The next handler to explore is the OnPowerModeChanged method. This handler can report the type of power management event through the Mode property of the PowerModeEventChangedArgs parameter. The Mode property has the PowerMode enumeration type and specifies the event type through the enumeration value contained therein:

```
private static void OnPowerModeChanged(object sender,
    PowerModeChangedEventArgs e)
{
    // power mode is changing
    switch (e.Mode)
    {
        case PowerModes.Resume:
            Debug.WriteLine("PowerMode: OS is resuming from suspended state");
            break;
        case PowerModes.StatusChange:
            Debug.WriteLine(
                "PowerMode: There was a change relating to the power" +
                " supply (weak battery, unplug, etc..)");
            break;
        case PowerModes.Suspend:
            Debug.WriteLine("PowerMode: OS is about to be suspended");
            break;
    }
}
```

The next three handlers all deal with operating system session states. They are OnSes
sionSwitch, OnSessionEnding, and OnSessionEnded. Handling all three of these
events covers all of the operating system session state transitions that your application
may need to worry about. In OnSessionEnding, there is a SessionEndingEventArgs
parameter, which has a Cancel member. This Cancel member allows you to request
that the session not end if it is set to false. Code for the three handlers is shown in
Example 13-1.

Example 13-1. OnSessionSwitch, OnSessionEnding, and OnSessionEnded handlers

```
private static void OnSessionSwitch(object sender, SessionSwitchEventArgs e)
{
    // check reason
    switch (e.Reason)
    {
        case SessionSwitchReason.ConsoleConnect:
            Debug.WriteLine("Session connected from the console");
            break;
        case SessionSwitchReason.ConsoleDisconnect:
            Debug.WriteLine("Session disconnected from the console");
            break;
        case SessionSwitchReason.RemoteConnect:
            Debug.WriteLine("Remote session connected");
            break;
        case SessionSwitchReason.RemoteDisconnect:
            Debug.WriteLine("Remote session disconnected");
            break;
        case SessionSwitchReason.SessionLock:
            Debug.WriteLine("Session has been locked");
            break;
        case SessionSwitchReason.SessionLogoff:
            Debug.WriteLine("User was logged off from a session");
            break;
        case SessionSwitchReason.SessionLogon:
            Debug.WriteLine("User has logged on to a session");
            break;
        case SessionSwitchReason.SessionRemoteControl:
            Debug.WriteLine("Session changed to or from remote status");
            break;
        case SessionSwitchReason.SessionUnlock:
            Debug.WriteLine("Session has been unlocked");
            break;
    }
}

private static void OnSessionEnding(object sender, SessionEndingEventArgs e)
{
    // true to cancel the user request to end the session, false otherwise
    e.Cancel = false;
    // check reason
```

```
    switch(e.Reason)
    {
        case SessionEndReasons.Logoff:
            Debug.WriteLine("Session ending as the user is logging off");
            break;
        case SessionEndReasons.SystemShutdown:
            Debug.WriteLine("Session ending as the OS is shutting down");
            break;
    }
}

private static void OnSessionEnded(object sender, SessionEndedEventArgs e)
{
    switch (e.Reason)
    {
        case SessionEndReasons.Logoff:
            Debug.WriteLine("Session ended as the user is logging off");
            break;
        case SessionEndReasons.SystemShutdown:
            Debug.WriteLine("Session ended as the OS is shutting down");
            break;
    }
}
```

Discussion

The .NET Framework provides many opportunities to get feedback from the system when there are changes due to user or system interactions. The SystemEvents class exposes more events than just the ones used in this recipe. For a full listing, see Table 13-1.

Table 13-1. The SystemEvents events

Value	Description
DisplaySettingsChanged	User changed display settings.
DisplaySettingsChanging	Display settings are changing.
EventsThreadShutdown	Thread listening for system events is terminating.
InstalledFontsChanged	User added or removed fonts.
PaletteChanged	User switched to an application with a different palette.
PowerModeChanged	User suspended or resumed the system.
SessionEnded	User shut down the system or logged off.
SessionEnding	User is attempting to shut down the system or log off.
SessionSwitch	The currently logged-in user changed.
TimeChanged	User changed system time.
TimerElapsed	A Windows timer interval expired.
UserPreferenceChanged	User changed a preference in the system.

Value	Description
UserPreferenceChanging	User is trying to change a preference in the system.

 Keep in mind that these are system events. Therefore, the amount of work done in the handlers should be kept to a minimum, so the system can move on to the next task.

The notifications from SystemEvents come on a dedicated thread for raising these events. In a UI application, you will need to get back onto the correct user interface thread before updating a UI with any of this information, using one of the various methods for doing so (Control.BeginInvoke, Control.Invoke, or Background Worker).

Note that .NET Core (the open source version of .NET for cross-platform coding) does not include a Microsoft.Win32.SystemEvents class at the time of this writing, so this recipe will not work on .NET Core (until someone adds it!).

See Also

The "SystemEvents Class," "PowerModeChangedEventArgs Class," "SessionEndedE-ventArgs Class," "SessionEndingEventArgs Class," and "SessionSwitchEventArgs Class" topics in the MSDN documentation.

13.2 Controlling a Service

Problem

You need to programmatically manipulate a service that your application interacts with.

Solution

Use the System.ServiceProcess.ServiceController class to control the service. ServiceController allows you to interact with an existing service and to read and change its properties. In the example, it will be used to manipulate the ASP.NET State Service. The name, the service type, and the display name are easily available from the ServiceName, ServiceType, and DisplayName properties:

```
ServiceController scStateService = new ServiceController("COM+ Event System");
Console.WriteLine($"Service Type: {scStateService.ServiceType.ToString()}");
Console.WriteLine($"Service Name: {scStateService.ServiceName}");
Console.WriteLine($"Display Name: {scStateService.DisplayName}");
```

The `ServiceType` enumeration has a number of values, as shown in Table 13-2.

Table 13-2. The ServiceType enumeration values

Value	Description
`Adapter`	Service that serves a hardware device
`FileSystemDriver`	Driver for the filesystem (kernel level)
`InteractiveProcess`	Service that communicates with the desktop
`KernelDriver`	Low-level hardware device driver
`RecognizerDriver`	Driver for identifying filesystems on startup
`Win32OwnProcess`	Win32 program that runs as a service in its own process
`Win32ShareProcess`	Win32 program that runs as a service in a shared process such as SvcHost

One useful task is to determine a service's dependents. The services that depend on the current service are accessed through the `DependentServices` property, an array of `ServiceController` instances (one for each dependent service):

```
foreach (ServiceController sc in scStateService.DependentServices)
    Console.WriteLine($"{scStateService.DisplayName} is depended on by: " +
                           $" {sc.DisplayName}");
```

By contrast, the `ServicesDependedOn` array contains `ServiceController` instances for each of the services the current service depends on:

```
foreach (ServiceController sc in scStateService.ServicesDependedOn)
    Console.WriteLine(
        $"{scStateService.DisplayName} depends on: {sc.DisplayName}");
```

One of the most important things about services is what state they are in. A service doesn't do much good if it is supposed to be running and it isn't—or worse yet, if it is supposed to be disabled (perhaps as a security risk) and isn't. To find out the current status of the service, check the `Status` property. For this example, the original state of the service will be saved, so it can be restored later in the `originalState` variable:

```
Console.WriteLine($"Status: {scStateService.Status}");
// save original state
ServiceControllerStatus originalState = scStateService.Status;
```

Now that we have set up the proper access, we can start to work with the service methods. If a service is stopped, it can be started with the `Start` method. First, check if the service is stopped, and then, once `Start` has been called on the `ServiceControl ler` instance, call the `WaitForStatus` method to make sure that the service started. `WaitForStatus` can take a timeout value so that the application is not waiting forever for the service to start in the case of a problem:

```
TimeSpan serviceTimeout = TimeSpan.FromSeconds(60);
// if it is stopped, start it
```

```
if (scStateService.Status == ServiceControllerStatus.Stopped)
{
    scStateService.Start();
    // wait up to 60 seconds for start
    scStateService.WaitForStatus(ServiceControllerStatus.Running,
        serviceTimeout);
}
Console.WriteLine($"Status: {scStateService.Status}");
```

Services can also be paused. If the service is paused, the application needs to determine if it can be continued by checking the CanPauseAndContinue property. If so, the Continue method will get the service going again, and the WaitForStatus method should be called to wait until it does:

```
// if it is paused, continue
if (scStateService.Status == ServiceControllerStatus.Paused)
{
    if (scStateService.CanPauseAndContinue)
    {
        scStateService.Continue();
        // wait up to 60 seconds for start
        scStateService.WaitForStatus(ServiceControllerStatus.Running,
            serviceTimeout);
    }
}
Console.WriteLine($"Status: {scStateService.Status}");

// Should be running at this point.
```

To determine if a service can be stopped, you use the CanStop property. If it can be stopped, then stopping it is a matter of calling the Stop method followed by WaitFor Status:

```
// can we stop it?
if (scStateService.CanStop)
{
    scStateService.Stop();
    // wait up to 60 seconds for stop
    scStateService.WaitForStatus(ServiceControllerStatus.Stopped,
        serviceTimeout);
}
Console.WriteLine($"Status: {scStateService.Status}");
```

Even though CanStop could have returned true, if we are not running under an administrative context, we would have gotten this exception when trying to stop the service:

```
A first chance exception of type 'System.InvalidOperationException' occurred in
System.ServiceProcess.dll
Additional information: Cannot open EventSystem service on computer '.'.
```

See the Discussion section for how to set up proper security access for the code.

Now it is time to set the service back to how you found it. The `originalState` variable has the original state, and the `switch` statement holds actions for taking the service from the current stopped state to its original state:

```
// set it back to the original state
switch (originalState)
{
    case ServiceControllerStatus.Stopped:
        if (scStateService.CanStop)
            scStateService.Stop();
        break;
    case ServiceControllerStatus.Running:
        scStateService.Start();
        // wait up to 60 seconds for start
        scStateService.WaitForStatus(ServiceControllerStatus.Running,
            serviceTimeout);
        break;
    case ServiceControllerStatus.Paused:
        // if it was paused and is stopped, need to restart so we can pause
        if (scStateService.Status == ServiceControllerStatus.Stopped)
        {
            scStateService.Start();
            // wait up to 60 seconds for start
            scStateService.WaitForStatus(ServiceControllerStatus.Running,
                serviceTimeout);
        }
        // now pause
        if (scStateService.CanPauseAndContinue)
        {
            scStateService.Pause();
            // wait up to 60 seconds for paused
            scStateService.WaitForStatus(ServiceControllerStatus.Paused,
                serviceTimeout);
        }
        break;
}
```

To be sure that the `Status` property is correct on the service, the application should call `Refresh` to update it before testing the value of the `Status` property. Once the application is done with the service, call the `Close` method:

```
scStateService.Refresh();
Console.WriteLine($"Status: {scStateService.Status.ToString()}");

// close it
scStateService.Close();
```

Discussion

Services run many of the operating system functions today. They usually run under a system account (`LocalSystem`, `NetworkService`, `LocalService`) or a specific user account that has been granted specific permissions and rights. If your application uses a service, this is a good way to determine if everything for the service to run is set up and configured properly before your application attempts to use it. Not all applications depend on services directly. But if your application does, or you have written a service as part of your application, it can be handy to have an easy way to check the status of your service and possibly correct the situation.

When you are manipulating services, the question of access comes into play. While in earlier Microsoft operating systems (pre–Windows 7) you could call the `ServiceCon troller` APIs without any special privileges, with the introduction of User Account Control you now have to be in an administrative context to access methods that affect the service operation. You can still inspect the properties of the service without this level of access, but if you want to Start, Stop, and so on, you need to have elevated privileges.

To accomplish this in code, you would add an *app.manifest* file to your application by right-clicking the project and selecting Add*New Item and selecting the Application Manifest File, as shown in Figure 13-1.

Figure 13-1. The Application Manifest File creation window

In the *asmv1:assembly\trustinfo\security\requestedPrivileges* section of the file the default requested execution level is to run as the person invoking the code:

```
<requestedExecutionLevel level="asInvoker" uiAccess="false" />
```

To allow access to the service methods, we will change this so our code requires an administrative context by setting the `level` attribute to `requireAdministrator`:

```
<!-- Necessary for service interaction in Recipe 13.2 Controlling a Service -->
<requestedExecutionLevel level="requireAdministrator" uiAccess="false"/>
```

This will ensure that when the code is run, it requires the user to have enough rights to perform the actions we are requesting.

See Also

The "ServiceController Class" and "ServiceControllerStatus Enumeration" topics in the MSDN documentation.

13.3 List What Processes an Assembly Is Loaded In

Problem

You want to know what current processes have a given assembly loaded.

Solution

Use the `GetProcessesAssemblyIsLoadedIn` method that we've created for this purpose to return a list of processes that contain a given assembly. `GetProcessesAssemblyIsLoadedIn` takes the filename of the assembly to look for (such as *mscoree.dll*) and then gets a list of the currently running processes on the machine by calling `Process.GetProcesses`. It then searches the processes to see if the assembly is loaded into any of them. When found in a process, that `Process` object is projected into an enumerable set of `Process` objects. The iterator for the set of processes found is returned from the query:

```
public static IEnumerable<Process> GetProcessesAssemblyIsLoadedIn(
    string assemblyFileName)
{
    // System and Idle are not actually processes, so there are no modules
    // associated and we skip them.

    var processes = from process in Process.GetProcesses()
                    where process.ProcessName != "System" &&
                          process.ProcessName != "Idle"
                    from ProcessModule processModule in process.SafeGetModules()
                    where processModule.ModuleName.Equals(assemblyFileName,
                        StringComparison.OrdinalIgnoreCase)
                    select process;
    return processes;
}
```

The `Process.GetSafeModules` extension method gets a list of the modules that the caller is authorized to see for the process. If we just accessed the `Modules` property directly, we would get a series of different access errors depending on the caller's security context:

```csharp
public static ProcessModuleCollection SafeGetModules(this Process process)
{
    List<ProcessModule> listModules = new List<ProcessModule>();
    ProcessModuleCollection modules =
            new ProcessModuleCollection(listModules.ToArray());
    try
    {
        modules = process.Modules;
    }
    catch (InvalidOperationException) { }
    catch (PlatformNotSupportedException) { }
    catch (NotSupportedException) { }
    catch (Win32Exception wex)
    {
        Console.WriteLine($"Couldn't get modules for {process.ProcessName}: " +
                            $"{wex.Message}");
    }
    // return either the modules or an empty collection
    return modules;
}
```

Discussion

In some circumstances, such as when you are uninstalling software or debugging version conflicts, it is beneficial to know if an assembly is loaded into more than one process. By quickly getting a list of the `Process` objects that the assembly is loaded in, you can narrow the scope of your investigation.

The following code uses this routine to look for .NET 4 processes:

```csharp
string searchAssm = "mscoree.dll";
var processes = GetProcessesAssemblyIsLoadedIn(searchAssm);
foreach (Process p in processes)
    Console.WriteLine($"Found {searchAssm} in {p.MainModule.ModuleName}");
```

When you're running the `GetProcessesAssemblyIsLoadedIn` method, the user's security context plays a large role in how much the code can discover. If the caller is a normal Windows user not running in the administrative context (which must be entered into explicitly), you would see a number of processes reported that cannot have their modules examined, as shown in Example 13-2.

Example 13-2. Normal user security context output example

```
Couldn't get modules for dasHost: Access is denied
Couldn't get modules for WUDFHost: Access is denied
```

```
Couldn't get modules for StandardCollector.Service: Access is denied
Couldn't get modules for winlogon: Access is denied
Couldn't get modules for svchost: Access is denied
Couldn't get modules for FcsSas: Access is denied
Couldn't get modules for VBCSCompiler: Access is denied
Couldn't get modules for svchost: Access is denied
Couldn't get modules for coherence: Access is denied
Couldn't get modules for coherence: Access is denied
Couldn't get modules for svchost: Access is denied
Couldn't get modules for MOMService: Access is denied
Couldn't get modules for svchost: Access is denied
Couldn't get modules for csrss: Access is denied
Couldn't get modules for svchost: Access is denied
Couldn't get modules for vmms: Access is denied
Couldn't get modules for dwm: Access is denied
Found mscoree.dll in Microsoft.VsHub.Server.HttpHostx64.exe
Couldn't get modules for wininit: Access is denied
Couldn't get modules for svchost: Access is denied
Couldn't get modules for prl_tools: Access is denied
Couldn't get modules for coherence: Access is denied
Couldn't get modules for MpCmdRun: Access is denied
Couldn't get modules for svchost: Access is denied
Couldn't get modules for svchost: Access is denied
Couldn't get modules for audiodg: Access is denied
Couldn't get modules for mqsvc: Access is denied
Couldn't get modules for WmiApSrv: Access is denied
Couldn't get modules for conhost: Access is denied
Couldn't get modules for sqlwriter: Access is denied
Couldn't get modules for svchost: Access is denied
Couldn't get modules for svchost: Access is denied
Found mscoree.dll in CSharpRecipes.exe
Couldn't get modules for WmiPrvSE: Access is denied
Couldn't get modules for spoolsv: Access is denied
Couldn't get modules for svchost: Access is denied
Couldn't get modules for WmiPrvSE: Access is denied
Couldn't get modules for svchost: Access is denied
Found mscoree.dll in msvsmon.exe
Couldn't get modules for csrss: Access is denied
Couldn't get modules for dllhost: Access is denied
Couldn't get modules for svchost: Access is denied
Couldn't get modules for SearchIndexer: Access is denied
Couldn't get modules for WmiPrvSE: Access is denied
Found mscoree.dll in VBCSCompiler.exe
Couldn't get modules for svchost: Access is denied
Couldn't get modules for OSPPSVC: Access is denied
Couldn't get modules for WmiPrvSE: Access is denied
Couldn't get modules for smss: Access is denied
Couldn't get modules for IpOverUsbSvc: Access is denied
Couldn't get modules for lsass: Access is denied
Couldn't get modules for services: Access is denied
Couldn't get modules for MsMpEng: Access is denied
Couldn't get modules for msdtc: Access is denied
```

```
Couldn't get modules for prl_tools_service: Access is denied
Couldn't get modules for inetinfo: Access is denied
Couldn't get modules for sppsvc: Access is denied
```

When we run the same call to the GetProcessesAssemblyIsLoadedIn method under an administrative context, we get output similar to Example 13-3.

Example 13-3. Administrative user security context output example

```
Found mscoree.dll in VBCSCompiler.exe
Found mscoree.dll in Microsoft.VsHub.Server.HttpHostx64.exe
Found mscoree.dll in msvsmon.exe
Found mscoree.dll in VBCSCompiler.exe
Couldn't get modules for audiodg: Access is denied
Found mscoree.dll in ElevatedPrivilegeActions.vshost.exe
Couldn't get modules for sppsvc: Access is denied
```

Since this is a diagnostic function, you will need FullTrust security access to use this method.

Note that the query skips inspection for the System and Idle processes:

```
var processes = from process in Process.GetProcesses()
                where process.ProcessName != "System" &&
                    process.ProcessName != "Idle"
                from ProcessModule processModule in process.SafeGetModules()
                where processModule.ModuleName.Equals(assemblyFileName,
                    StringComparison.OrdinalIgnoreCase)
                select process;
```

The Modules collection can't be used to examine these two processes, so it throws a Win32Exception. There are two other processes you might see access denied for: audiodg and sppsvc:

- audiodg is a DRM-protected process used to host audio drivers so that they can be run in login sessions isolated from locally logged-in users.
- sppsvc is a Microsoft software protection platform service that can be used to prevent the use of software without a license.

Since both of those services are sensitive in the operating system, you can see why they would not be accessible through Process enumeration.

See Also

The "Process Class," "ProcessModule Class," and "GetProcesses Method" topics in the MSDN documentation.

13.4 Using Message Queues on a Local Workstation

Problem

You need a way to disconnect two components of your application (such as a web service endpoint and the processing logic) such that the first component only has to worry about formatting the instructions. The bulk of the processing can then occur in the second component.

Solution

Use message queues to separate this work, and use the `MQWorker` class shown here in both the first and second components to write and read messages to and from the associated message queue.

 Message queues provide an asynchronous communications protocol between parties, meaning that the sender and receiver of the message do not need to interact with the message queue at the same time. Messages placed onto the queue are stored until the recipient retrieves them. They allow you to ensure messages don't get lost, keep the work segmented, handle inconsistent loads, and scale your application by having multiple workers that can read from a queue.

`MQWorker` uses the local message-queuing services to store and retrieve messages. The queue pathname is supplied in the constructor, and the existence of the queue is checked in the `SetUpQueue` method:

```
class MQWorker : IDisposable
{
    private bool _disposed;
    private string _mqPathName;
    MessageQueue _queue;

    public MQWorker(string queuePathName)
    {
        if (string.IsNullOrEmpty(queuePathName))
            throw new ArgumentNullException(nameof(queuePathName));

        _mqPathName = queuePathName;

        SetUpQueue();
    }
```

`SetUpQueue` creates a message queue of the supplied name using the `MessageQueue` class if none exists. It accounts for the scenario in which the message-queuing services are running on a workstation computer. In that situation, it makes the queue private, as that is the only type of queue allowed on a workstation:

```
private void SetUpQueue()
{
    // See if the queue exists, create it if not
    if (!MessageQueue.Exists(_mqPathName))
    {
        try
        {
            _queue = MessageQueue.Create(_mqPathName);
        }
        catch (MessageQueueException mqex)
        {
            // see if we are running on a workgroup computer
            if (mqex.MessageQueueErrorCode ==
                    MessageQueueErrorCode.UnsupportedOperation)
            {
                string origPath = _mqPathName;
                // must be a private queue in workstation mode
                int index = _mqPathName.ToLowerInvariant().
                                IndexOf("private$",
                                    StringComparison.OrdinalIgnoreCase);
                if (index == -1)
                {
                    // get the first \
                    index = _mqPathName.IndexOf(@"\",
                                StringComparison.OrdinalIgnoreCase);
                    // insert private$\ after server entry
                    _mqPathName = _mqPathName.Insert(index + 1, @"private$\");
                    // try try again
                    try
                    {
                        if (!MessageQueue.Exists(_mqPathName))
                            _queue = MessageQueue.Create(_mqPathName);
                        else
                            _queue = new MessageQueue(_mqPathName);
                    }
                    catch (Exception)
                    {
                        // set original as inner exception
                        throw new Exception(
                            $"Failed to create message queue with {origPath}" +
                            $" or {_mqPathName}", mqex);
                    }
                }
            }
        }
    }
    else
    {
        _queue = new MessageQueue(_mqPathName);
    }
```

```
        }
    }
```

The `SendMessage` method sends a message to the queue to set up in the constructor. The body of the message is supplied in the body parameter, and then an instance of `System.Messaging.Message` is created and populated. The `BinaryMessageFormatter` is used to format the message, as it enables larger volumes of messages to be sent with fewer resources than does the default `XmlMessageFormatter`. To make messages persistent (so that they stick around until they are processed and are not lost if the machine loses power), it sets the `Recoverable` property to `true`. Finally, the `Body` is set, and the message is sent:

```
public void SendMessage(string label, string body)
{
    Message msg = new Message();
    // label our message
    msg.Label = label;
    // override the default XML formatting with binary
    // as it is faster (at the expense of legibility while debugging)
    msg.Formatter = new BinaryMessageFormatter();
    // make this message persist (causes message to be written
    // to disk)
    msg.Recoverable = true;
    msg.Body = body;
    _queue?.Send(msg);
}
```

The `ReadMessage` method reads messages from the queue set up in the constructor by creating a `Message` object and calling its `Receive` method. The message formatter is set to the `BinaryMessageFormatter` for the `Message`, since that is how we write to the queue. Finally, the body of the message is returned from the method:

```
public string ReadMessage()
{
    Message msg = null;
    msg = _queue.Receive();
    msg.Formatter = new BinaryMessageFormatter();
    return (string)msg.Body;
}


#region IDisposable Members

public void Dispose()
{
    Dispose(true);
    GC.SuppressFinalize(this);
}

private void Dispose(bool disposing)
{
```

```
            if (!this._disposed)
            {
                if (disposing)
                    _queue.Dispose();

                _disposed = true;
            }
        }
        #endregion
    }
```

To show how the MQWorker class is used, the following example creates an MQWorker. It then sends a message (a small blob of XML) using SendMessage and retrieves it using ReadMessage:

```
// NOTE: Message Queue services must be set up for this to work.
// This can be added in Add/Remove Windows Components.

using (MQWorker mqw = new MQWorker(@".\MQWorkerQ")) {
    string xml = "<MyXml><InnerXml location=\"inside\"/></MyXml>";
    Console.WriteLine("Sending message to message queue: " + xml);
    mqw.SendMessage("Label for message", xml);
    string retXml = mqw.ReadMessage();
    Console.WriteLine("Read message from message queue: " + retXml);
}
```

Discussion

Message queues are very useful when you are attempting to distribute the processing load for scalability purposes. Without question, using a message queue adds overhead to the processing because the messages must travel through the infrastructure of MSMQ. One benefit, however, is that MSMQ allows your application to spread out across multiple machines, so there can be a net gain in processing. Another advantage is that message queuing supports reliable asynchronous handling of the messages so that the sending side can be confident that the receiving side will get the message without the sender having to wait for confirmation. The message queue services are not installed by default, but can be installed through the Add/Remove Windows Components applet in Control Panel.

Using a message queue to buffer your processing logic from high volumes of requests (such as in the web service scenario presented earlier) can lead to more stability and ultimately produce more throughput for your application by using multiple reader processes on multiple machines.

See Also

The "Message Class" and "MessageQueue Class" topics in the MSDN documentation.

13.5 Capturing Output from the Standard Output Stream

Problem

You want to capture output that is going to the standard output stream from within your C# program.

Solution

Use the `Console.SetOut` method to capture and release the standard output stream. `SetOut` sets the standard output stream to whatever `System.IO.TextWriter`-based stream it is handed. To capture the output to a file, create a `StreamWriter` to write to it, and set that writer using `SetOut`. We use `Path.GetTempFileName` to get a location to write our log to that is accessible by the identity calling the code.

Now when `Console.WriteLine` is called, the output goes to the `StreamWriter`, not to `stdout`, as shown here:

```
try
{
    Console.WriteLine("Stealing standard output!");
    string logfile = Path.GetTempFileName();
    Console.WriteLine($"Logging to: {logfile}");
    using (StreamWriter writer = new StreamWriter(logfile))
    {
        // steal stdout for our own purposes...
        Console.SetOut(writer);

        Console.WriteLine("Writing to the console... NOT!");

        for (int i = 0; i < 10; i++)
            Console.WriteLine(i);
    }
}
catch(IOException e)
{
    Debug.WriteLine(e.ToString());
    return ;
}
```

To restore writing to the standard output stream, create another `StreamWriter`. This time, call the `Console.OpenStandardOutput` method to acquire the standard output stream and use `SetOut` to set it once again. Now calls to `Console.WriteLine` appear on the console again:

```
// Recover the standard output stream so that a
// completion message can be displayed.
StreamWriter standardOutput = new StreamWriter(Console.OpenStandardOutput());
standardOutput.AutoFlush = true;
```

```
Console.SetOut(standardOutput);
Console.WriteLine("Back to standard output!");
```

The console output from this code looks similar to this:

```
Stealing standard output!
Logging to: C:\Users\user\AppData\Local\Temp\tmpFE7C.tmp
Back to standard output!
```

The logfile we created contains the following after the code is executed:

```
Writing to the console... NOT!
0
1
2
3
4
5
6
7
8
9
```

Discussion

Redirecting the standard output stream inside of the program may seem a bit anti-quated. But consider the situation when you're using another class that writes information to this stream. You don't want the output to appear in your application, but you have to use the class. This could also be useful if you create a small launcher application to capture output from a console application or if you are using a third-party assembly that insists on outputting lots of verbose messages that would be confusing to your user.

See Also

The "Console.SetOut Method," "Console.OpenStandardOutput Method," "Path.Get-TempFilePath Method," and "StreamWriter Class" topics in the MSDN documentation.

13.6 Capturing Standard Output for a Process

Problem

You need to be able to capture standard output for a process you are launching.

Solution

Use the `RedirectStandardOutput` property of the `Process.StartInfo` class to capture the output from the process. By redirecting the standard output stream of the process, you read it when the process terminates. UseShellExecute is a property on the ProcessInfo class that tells the runtime whether or not to use the Windows shell to start the process. By default, it is turned on (true) and the shell runs the program, which means that the output cannot be redirected. UseShellExecute needs to be turned off (set to false) so the redirection can occur.

In this example, a Process object for *cmd.exe* is set up with arguments to perform a directory listing, and then the output is redirected. A logfile is created to hold the resulting output, and the Process.Start method is called:

```
Process application = new Process();
// run the command shell
application.StartInfo.FileName = @"cmd.exe";

// get a directory listing from the current directory
application.StartInfo.Arguments = @"/Cdir " + Environment.CurrentDirectory;
Console.WriteLine($"Running cmd.exe with arguments:" +
    $"{application.StartInfo.Arguments}");

// redirect standard output so we can read it
application.StartInfo.RedirectStandardOutput = true;
application.StartInfo.UseShellExecute = false;

// Create a log file to hold the results in the current EXE directory
string logfile = Path.GetTempFileName();
Console.WriteLine($"Logging to: {logfile}");
using (StreamWriter logger = new StreamWriter(logfile))
{
    // start it up
    application.Start();
```

Once the process is started, the StandardOutput stream can be accessed and a reference to it held. Once the application finishes, the code then reads in the information from the output stream that was written while the application ran and writes it to the logfile that was set up previously. Finally, the logfile is closed and then the Process object is closed:

```
    application.WaitForExit();

    string output = application.StandardOutput.ReadToEnd();

    logger.Write(output);
}

// close the process object
application.Close();
```

The temporary logfile we created using Path.GetTempPathFile holds information similar to the following output:

```
Volume in drive C has no label.
Volume Serial Number is DDDD-FFFF

Directory of C:\CS60_Cookbook\CSCB6\CSharpRecipes\bin\Debug

04/11/2015  04:27 PM    <DIR>          .
04/11/2015  04:27 PM    <DIR>          ..
02/05/2015  10:06 PM             724 BigSpenders.xml
02/05/2015  10:05 PM             719 Categories.xml
02/05/2015  04:04 PM          64,566 CSCBCover.bmp
12/31/2014  05:23 PM         489,269 CSharpCookbook.zip
04/11/2015  04:27 PM         495,616 CSharpRecipes.exe
04/11/2015  04:27 PM          31,154 CSharpRecipes.exe.CodeAnalysisLog.xml
02/05/2015  09:53 PM           3,075 CSharpRecipes.exe.config
04/11/2015  04:27 PM               0
CSharpRecipes.exe.lastcodeanalysissucceeded
04/11/2015  04:27 PM         775,680 CSharpRecipes.pdb
02/05/2015  04:04 PM       5,190,856 EntityFramework.dll
02/05/2015  04:04 PM         620,232 EntityFramework.SqlServer.dll
02/05/2015  04:04 PM         154,645 EntityFramework.SqlServer.xml
02/05/2015  04:04 PM       3,645,119 EntityFramework.xml
03/09/2015  02:51 PM           6,569 IngredientList.txt
04/04/2015  09:55 AM         513,536 Newtonsoft.Json.dll
04/04/2015  09:55 AM         494,336 Newtonsoft.Json.xml
03/09/2015  02:51 PM       4,390,912 Northwind.mdf
04/06/2015  04:11 PM          51,712 NorthwindLinq2Sql.dll
04/06/2015  04:11 PM         128,512 NorthwindLinq2Sql.pdb
04/11/2015  01:18 PM         573,440 Northwind_log.ldf
03/09/2015  02:51 PM              80 RecipeChapters.txt
04/06/2015  04:11 PM          16,384 SampleClassLibrary.dll
04/06/2015  04:11 PM           1,283 SampleClassLibrary.dll.CodeAnalysisLog.xml
04/06/2015  04:11 PM               0
SampleClassLibrary.dll.lastcodeanalysissucceeded
04/06/2015  04:11 PM          11,776 SampleClassLibrary.pdb
12/02/2014  03:35 PM             387 SampleClassLibraryTests.xml
04/11/2015  03:48 PM           8,704 SharedCode.dll
04/11/2015  03:48 PM          15,872 SharedCode.pdb
              28 File(s)     17,685,158 bytes
               2 Dir(s)  67,929,718,784 bytes free
```

Discussion

Redirecting standard output can be of great use for tasks like automated build scenarios or test harnesses. While not quite as easy as simply placing > after the command line for a process at the command prompt, this approach is more flexible, as the stream output can be reformatted to XML or HTML for posting to a website. It also provides the opportunity to send the data to multiple locations at once, which the simple command-line redirect function in Windows can't do.

Waiting to read from the stream until the application has finished ensures that there will be no deadlock issues. If the stream is accessed synchronously before this time, then it's possible for the parent to block the child. At a minimum, the child will wait until the parent has finished reading from the stream before it continues writing to it. So, by postponing the read until the end, you save the child some performance degradation at the cost of some additional time at the end.

See Also

The "ProcessStartInfo.RedirectStandardOutput Property" and "ProcessStartInfo.UseShellExecute Property" topics in the MSDN documentation.

13.7 Running Code in Its Own AppDomain

Problem

You want to run code isolated from the main part of your application.

Solution

Create a separate `AppDomain` to run the code using the `AppDomain.CreateDomain` method. `CreateDomain` allows the application to control many aspects of the `AppDomain` being created, like the security environment, `AppDomain` settings, and base paths for the `AppDomain`. To demonstrate this, the following code creates an instance of the `RunMe` class (shown in full later in this recipe) and calls the `PrintCurrentAppDomain` `Name` method. This prints the name of the `AppDomain` where the code is running:

```
AppDomain myOwnAppDomain = AppDomain.CreateDomain("MyOwnAppDomain");
// print out our current AppDomain name
RunMe rm = new RunMe();
rm.PrintCurrentAppDomainName();
```

Now, you create an instance of the `RunMe` class in the `"MyOwnAppDomain"` `AppDomain` by calling `CreateInstance` on the `AppDomain`. We pass `CreateInstance` the module and type information necessary for constructing the type, and it returns an `Objec tHandle`.

We can then retrieve a proxy to the instance running in the `AppDomain` by taking the returned `ObjectHandle` and casting it to a `RunMe` reference using the `Unwrap` method:

```
// Create our RunMe class in the new appdomain
Type adType = typeof(RunMe);
ObjectHandle objHdl =
    myOwnAppDomain.CreateInstance(adType.Module.Assembly.FullName,
        adType.FullName);
// unwrap the reference
RunMe adRunMe = (RunMe)objHdl.Unwrap();
```

The `PrintCurrentAppDomainName` method is called on the `RunMe` instance in the "MyOwnAppDomain" `AppDomain`, and it prints out "Hello from MyOwnAppDomain!". The `AppDomain` is unloaded via `AppDomain.Unload` and the program terminates:

```
// make a call on the toolbox
adRunMe.PrintCurrentAppDomainName();

// now unload the appdomain
AppDomain.Unload(myOwnAppDomain);
```

The `RunMe` class is defined here. It inherits from `MarshalByRefObject`, as that allows you to retrieve the proxy reference when you call `Unwrap` on the `ObjectHandle` and have the calls on the class remoted into the new `AppDomain`. The `PrintCurrentApp-DomainName` method simply accesses the `FriendlyName` property on the current `AppDomain` and prints out the "Hello from {*AppDomain*}!" message:

```
public class RunMe : MarshalByRefObject
{
    public RunMe()
    {
        PrintCurrentAppDomainName();
    }

    public void PrintCurrentAppDomainName()
    {
        string name = AppDomain.CurrentDomain.FriendlyName;
        Console.WriteLine($"Hello from {name}!");
    }
}
```

The output from this example is shown here:

```
Hello from CSharpRecipes.exe!
Hello from CSharpRecipes.exe!
Hello from MyOwnAppDomain!
Hello from MyOwnAppDomain!
```

Discussion

Isolating code in a separate `AppDomain` is overkill for something as trivial as this example, but it demonstrates that code can be executed remotely in an `AppDomain` created by your application. There are six overloads for the `CreateDomain` method, and each adds a bit more complexity to the `AppDomain` creation. In situations in which the isolation or configuration benefits outweigh the complexities of not only setting up a separate `AppDomain` but debugging code in it as well, it is a useful tool. A good real-world example is hosting a separate `AppDomain` to run ASP.NET pages outside of the normal ASP.NET environment (though this is truly a nontrivial usage) or loading third-party code into a secondary `AppDomain` for isolation.

See Also

The "AppDomain Class," "AppDomain.CreateDomain Method," and "ObjectHandle Class" topics in the MSDN documentation.

13.8 Determining the Operating System and Service Pack Version of the Current Operating System

Problem

You want to know the current operating system and service pack.

Solution

Use the `GetOSAndServicePack` method shown in Example 13-4 to get a string representing the current operating system and service pack. `GetOSAndServicePack` uses the `Environment.OSVersion` property to get the version information for the operating system and checks the registry for the "official" name of the OS. The `Operating System` class retrieved from `Environment.OSVersion` has a property for the service pack, called `ServicePack`. These values are all returned as the operating system name, version, and service pack string.

Example 13-4. GetOSAndServicePack method

```
public static string GetOSAndServicePack()
{
    // Get the current OS info
    OperatingSystem os = Environment.OSVersion;
    RegistryKey rk =
        Registry.LocalMachine.OpenSubKey(
            @"SOFTWARE\Microsoft\Windows NT\CurrentVersion");
    string osText = (string)rk?.GetValue("ProductName");
    if (string.IsNullOrWhiteSpace(osText))
        osText = os.VersionString;
    else
        osText = (
            $"{osText} {os.Version.Major}.{os.Version.Minor}.{os.Version.Build}");
    if (!string.IsNullOrWhiteSpace(os.ServicePack))
        osText = $"{osText} {os.ServicePack}";
    return osText;
}
```

Discussion

Enabling your application to know the current operating system and service pack allows you to include that information in debugging reports and in the About box (if you have one) for your application. This simple knowledge, transmitted through your support department, can save you hours in debugging time. It is well worth making this information available so your support department can easily direct your clients to it if they cannot otherwise locate it.

See Also

The "Environment.OSVersion Property" and "OperatingSystem Class" topics in the MSDN documentation.

Index

Symbols

I

ICloneable interface, 32
ICollection objects, 93
IComparable<T> interface, 6, 10
IComparable<T>.CompareTo method, 7
IComparer<T> interface, 10
IComparer<T> method, 8
IDeepCopy<T> interface, 32
IDictionary interface, 246
IDisposable interface, 51
IEnumerable interface, 152, 192
IEnumerable<T> interface, 58, 86, 104, 110, 192
IEnumerator<T> interface, 104
if-then statements, 78
image files, converting, 127
Immutable classes, 117
ImmutableDictionary<TKey,TValue>, 117
imported types, obtaining, 291
IncrementNumericField method, 578
inheritance
    determining characteristics, 298
    enumerations and, 124
initialization vector (IV), 522
InnerException property, 226
INotifyPropertyChanged, 182, 318
INotifyPropertyChanging, 182
Install Certificate menu, 555
instance fields, 31
instance methods. dynamically invoking, 306
interfaces
    advanced searches of, 193
    determining public, 296
    ICloneable, 32
    IComparable<T>, 6, 10
    IComparer<T>, 10
    IDeepCopy<T>, 32
    IDictionary, 246
    IDisposable, 51
    IEnumerable, 152, 192
    IEnumerable<T>, 58, 86, 104, 110, 192
    IEnumerator<T>, 104
    IShallowCopy<T>, 32
    support for nongeneric, 190
    System.Collections.Generic.IEnumera-
        ble<T>, 86
    System.Collections.Generic.IEnumera-
        tor<T>, 86
Interlocked functions, 611
internalList, 102

Internet connection settings, using current, 454
Internet Control Message Protocol (ICMP), 447
Internet Information Server (IIS), 409
Internet Protocol (IP), 420
InternetSettingsReader class, 454
intersect set operation, 154
IntPtr, 564
invalid characters, 482
InvalidCastException, 192
InvalidOperationException, 220
invocation lists, 60
IsDefined method, 138
IShallowCopy<T> interface, 32
IsReady property, 381
IsSubclassOf method, 297
IsSubsetOf method, 536
Items array property, 43
iterative iterators, 364
iterators
    benefits of, 85, 103
    choices available, 112
    dealing with finally Blocks in, 105
    defined, 85
    recursive vs. iterative, 364

J

joining, across data repositories, 168

K

Keys property, 94, 118
keys, sorting in dictionaries, 93
keywords
    checked, 134
    default, 53, 75
    Dynamic, 288
    dynamic, 312
    fixed, 199
    from, 151, 192
    in LINQ, 151
    lock, 580
    new, 76
    orderby, 151, 161
    out, 14
    select, 151
    this, 199
    throw, 225
    var, 151
    where, 52, 151

L

lambda expressions
  defined, 148
  example of, 148
  filtering with, 156
  implementing closures with, 65
  outer variables and, 199
  using, 195
  using different parameter modifies in, 200
Language enumeration, 137
LayoutKind.Explicit layout kind, 3
lazy computation, 85
lexers, 341
line break characters, 346
LINQ (Language Integrated Query)
  benefits of, 147, 194
  bridging disparate data domains with, 168
  data domains encompassed, 148
  finding custom error pages with, 410
  functional extensions for, 164
  keywords in, 151, 473
  LINQ expression, 76
  LINQ queries, 26, 93
  LINQ Select, 118
  LINQ to ADO.NET, 176
  LINQ to Entities, 174
  LINQ to Objects, 47, 86
  LINQ to XML, 174, 465, 468, 470, 486, 498,
    506
  PLINQ (Parallel LINQ), 204
  querying configuration files with, 171
  querying type interface information with,
    193
  set operators in, 155
  speeding operations with parallelism, 204
  tasks handled by, 148
  to SQL, 159, 628
  using without IEnumerable<T> support,
    190
List<T> class, 72, 86, 90
List<T>.Sort method, 6
ListDictionary class, 84
lists
  finding duplicates in, 86
  invocation, 60
  maintaining order of, 90
  nested, 109
  performing multiple operations on, 70
  reversing contents of sorted, 47

  testing elements in, 99
  transforming XML data into, 486
little-endian encoding, 131
local message-queuing services, 649
local variables, accessing, 308
LocalIntranet permission, 287
localization, 161
LocalVariableInfo object, 310
LocalVariables property, 308
lock keyword, 580
Lock method, 370
lock statements, 105, 421

M

MailMessage constructor, 448
MakeBase64EncodedStringForMime method,
  126
makecert.exe utility, 554
Man-in-the-Middle attack, 529
manual locking, avoiding, 114
ManualResetEvent, 610
marshaling, 455
Match instance method, 332
MatchEvaluator delegate, 338
Math.Floor method, 133, 134
Math.Round method, 132, 133, 134
maximum value, 95
MaxValue field, 135
MediaTypeNames.Attachment values, 449
MemberAccess privilege, 287
memberName argument, 295
MemberwiseClone method, 34
memory, shared, 600
message queues, 150, 649
MessageQueue, 151
MethodBody class, 308
MethodInfo.GetBaseDefinition method, 299
methods
  *Async methods, 627
  accessed via reflection, 226
  accessing local variables within, 308
  Add, 91, 97
  AddProxyInfoToRequest, 398
  AllocateDataSlot, 591
  AllocateNamedDataSlot, 591
  AppDomain.CreateDomain, 657
  Application_DispatcherUnhandledExcep-
    tion, 250
  Assembly.GetReferencedAssemblies, 288

About the Authors

Jay Hilyard has been developing applications for the Windows platform for over 20 years and for .NET for more than 15 of those. He has published numerous articles in *MSDN Magazine* and currently works at Newmarket (an Amadeus company) in Portsmouth, NH.

Stephen Teilhet started working with the pre-alpha version of the .NET platform and has been using it ever since. At IBM, he works as the lead security researcher on their static source code security analysis tool, which is used to find vulnerabilities in many different languages including C# and Visual Basic.

Colophon

The animal on the cover of *C# 6.0 Cookbook*, Fourth Edition, is a garter snake (*Thamnophis sirtalis*). Named because their longitudinal stripes resemble those on garters once used to hold up men's socks, garter snakes are easily identified by their distinctive stripes: a narrow stripe down the middle of the back with a broad stripe on each side of it. Color and pattern variations enable them to blend into their native environments, helping them evade predators. They are the most common snake in North America and the only species of snake found in Alaska.

Garter snakes have keeled scales—one or more ridges down the central axis of the scales—giving them a rough texture and lackluster appearance. Adult garter snakes generally range in length between 46 and 130 centimeters (one and a half feet to over four feet). Females are usually larger than males, with shorter tails and a bulge where the body and tail meet.

Female garter sare ovoviviparous, meaning they deliver "live" young that have gestated in soft eggs. Upon delivery, most of the eggs and mucous membranes have broken, which makes their births appear live. Occasionally, a baby will be born still inside its soft shell. A female will usually deliver 10 to 40 babies: the largest recorded number of live babies birthed by a garter snake is 98. Once emerging from their mothers, baby garters are completely independent and must begin fending for themselves. During this time they are most susceptible to predation, and over half of all baby garters die before they are one year old.

Garter snakes are one of the few animals able to eat toads, newts, and other amphibians with strong chemical defenses. Although diets vary depending on their environments, garter snakes mostly eat earthworms and amphibians; however, they occasionally dine on baby birds, fish, and small rodents. Garter snakes have toxic saliva (harmless to humans), which they use to stun or kill their prey before swallowing them whole.

Many of the animals on O'Reilly covers are endangered; all of them are important to the world. To learn more about how you can help, go to *animals.oreilly.com*.

The cover image is from a 19th-century engraving from the Dover Pictorial Archive. The cover fonts are URW Typewriter and Guardian Sans. The text font is Adobe Minion Pro; the heading font is Adobe Myriad Condensed; and the code font is Dalton Maag's Ubuntu Mono.

Get even more for your money.

Join the O'Reilly Community, and register the O'Reilly books you own. It's free, and you'll get:

- $4.99 ebook upgrade offer
- 40% upgrade offer on O'Reilly print books
- Membership discounts on books and events
- Free lifetime updates to ebooks and videos
- Multiple ebook formats, DRM FREE
- Participation in the O'Reilly community
- Newsletters
- Account management
- 100% Satisfaction Guarantee

Signing up is easy:

1. Go to: oreilly.com/go/register
2. Create an O'Reilly login.
3. Provide your address.
4. Register your books.

Note: English-language books only

To order books online:
oreilly.com/store

For questions about products or an order:
orders@oreilly.com

To sign up to get topic-specific email announcements and/or news about upcoming books, conferences, special offers, and new technologies:
elists@oreilly.com

For technical questions about book content:
booktech@oreilly.com

To submit new book proposals to our editors:
proposals@oreilly.com

O'Reilly books are available in multiple DRM-free ebook formats. For more information:
oreilly.com/ebooks

Have it your way.

Lightning Source UK Ltd.
Milton Keynes UK
UKOW07f0012010617
302334UK00005B/8/P